The Challenge of Organizational Change

How Companies Experience It and Leaders Guide It

Rosabeth Moss Kanter
Barry A. Stein
Todd D. Jick

THE FREE PRESS
New York London Toronto Sydney Singapore

FREE PRESS
A Division of Simon & Schuster, Inc.
Rockefeller Center
1230 Avenue of the Americas
New York, NY 10020

Designed by
Manufactured in the United States of America

10 9 8 7 6 5 4 3 2 1

Library of Congress Cataloging-In-Publication Data

The Challenge of organizational change: how companies experience it
and leaders guide it/ [compiled by] Rosabeth Moss Kanter, Barry A.
Stein, Todd D. Jick.
p. cm.
Includes bibliographical references and index.
ISBN 0-7432-5446-5
1. Organizational change. I. Kanter, Rosabeth Moss. II. Stein,
Barry, III. Jick, Todd
HD58.8.C43 1992 92-18386
658.4'06—dc20 CIP

For information regarding the special discounts for bulk purchases, please contact Simon & Schuster Special Sales at 1-800-456-6798 or business@simonandschuster.com

Credits

Grateful acknowledgment is made to the authors and publishers who have granted permission to reprint the following:

Page 69: "Rockport Shoe Company: The Evolution of the Katz Family Business," by James A. Phills, Jr., is reprinted with permission of the author.

Page 80: "Banc One Corporation: Anticipatory Evolution," by Paul S. Myer and Rosabeth Moss Kanter, is reprinted by permission of the authors.

Page 92: "The Sweater Trade, From Hong Kong to New York," by James Lardner, is from "The Sweater Trade, Parts I and II." *The New Yorker*, January 11 and January 18, 1988 issues. Reprinted by permission; © James Lardner. Originally in *The New Yorker*.

Page 108: "Keeping Up with Information: On-Line in the Philippines and London," by John Maxwell Hamilton. *Entangling Alliances* (Arlington, Va.: Seven Locks Press, 1990). Reprinted with permission.

Page 129: "The Rise and Fall of an Entrepreneur," by Thomas R. Ittelson, is reprinted with permission of the author.

Page 145: "Diary of a Middle Manager," by Donna Dubinsky, is reprinted with permission of the author.

Page 151: "Jobs Talks About His Rise and Fall," by Gerald C. Lubenon and Michael Rogers. *Newsweek*, September 30, 1985. Copyright 1985, Newsweek, Inc. All rights reserved. Reprinted by permission of Newsweek, Inc. and Steve Jobs.

Page 154: "John Sculley's Lessons from Inside Apple," by Steven Pearlstein and Lucien Rhodes (originally published as "Corporate Antihero John Sculley"). Reprinted with permission, *Inc.* magazine, October 1987. Copyright © 1987 by Goldhirsh Group Inc., 38 Commercial.

Page 159: "The Big Store: Sears in Maturity." From *The Big Store* by Donald R. Katz. Copyright © 1987 by Donald R. Katz. Used by permission of Viking Penguin, a division of Penguin Books USA Inc.

Page 177: "Power, Greed, and Glory on Wall Street [The Fall of Lehman Brothers]," by Ken Auletta. *The New York Times Magazine*, February 17, 1985. Copyright © 1985 by The New York Times Company. Reprinted by permission.

Page 192: "Champagne Shoot-out in France," by Keith Wheatley. *Sunday Times Magazine,* March 25, 1990. © Times Newspaper Ltd. 1990. Reprinted with permission.

Page 197: "War and Peace: Labor Relations at Two Steelmakers," by Thomas F. O'Boyle and Terence Roth. Reprinted by permission of *The Wall Street Journal*, September 17, 1985. © 1985 Dow Jones & Company, Inc. All Rights Reserved Worldwide.

Page 203: "Class Consciousness Raising," by Stanley W. Angrist, is reprinted with permission of the author.

Page 206: "Weirton to Seek Cuts in Its Work Force," by Pamela Gaynor (originally published as "Weirton Seeks to Cut Its Work Force"). *Pittsburgh Post-Gazette,* October 7, 1987. Reprinted with permission.

Page 254: "Reinventing an Italian Chemical Company: Montedison, 1986." Copyright © 1991 by the President and Fellows of Harvard College. Harvard Business School case 9–392–049. This case was prepared by Joseph L. Bower, Neil Monnery, and William O. Ingle as the basis for class discussion rather than to illustrate either effective or ineffective handling of an administrative situation. Reprinted by permission of the Harvard Business School.

Page 268: "The Human Side of Mergers: The Western–Delta Story," by Cynthia A. Ingols and Paul S. Myers, is reprinted with permission of the authors.

Page 276: Reprinted by permission of *Harvard Business Review*. "The Feudal World of Japanese Manufacturing," by Kuniyasu Sakai (November/December 1990). Copyright © 1990 by the President and Fellows of Harvard College; all rights reserved.

Page 289: Reprinted by permission of *Harvard Business Review*. "The Logic of Global Business: An Interview with ABB's Percy Barnevik," by William Taylor (March/April 1991). Copyright © 1991 by the President and Fellows of Harvard College; all rights reserved.

Page 302: Reprinted by permission of *Harvard Business Review*. "Championing Change: An Interview with Bell Atlantic's CEO Raymond Smith," by Rosabeth Moss Kanter (January/February 1991). Copyright © 1991 by the President and Fellows of Harvard College; all rights reserved.

Page 316: "Driving Quality at Ford," by Gregg Easterbrook (originally published as "Have You Driven a Ford Lately?"). Reprinted with permission from *The Washington Monthly,* October 1986. Copyright by the Washington Monthly Company, 1611 Connecticut Avenue, N.W., Washington, D.C. 20009. (202) 462–0128.

Page 324: Reprinted by permission of *Harvard Business Review*. "The Case of the Downsizing Decision," by Alan S. Train (pseudonym for Barry Stein) (March/April 1991). Copyright © 1991 by the President and Fellows of Harvard College; all rights reserved.

Page 337: "Lucky Stores: Restructuring to Survive the Takeover Threat," by Lisa Richardson and Alistair Williamson, is reprinted with permission of the authors.

Page 349: "Lessons from a Middle Market LBO: The Case of O. M. Scott," by George P. Baker and Karen H. Wruck. *The Journal of Applied Corporate Finance*, vol 4, no. 1 (Spring 1991); reprinted with permission.

Page 398: Excerpts from "Northwest Airlines Confronts Change," by Susan Rosegrant and Todd D. Jick. Harvard Business School case 9–491–036. Copyright © by the President and Fellows of Harvard College.

Page 406: "The Innovator," by Cary Reich. *The New York Times Magazine*, April 21, 1985. Copyright © 1985 by The New York Times Company. Reproduced by permission.

Page 409: "How I Would Turn Around GM," by Ross Perot, is reprinted with permission of the author.

Page 414: "The Painful Reeducation of a Company Man: An Interview with Roger Smith." Reprinted with permission, *Business Monthly* magazine, October 1989. Copyright © 1989 by Goldhirsh Group, Inc., 38 Commercial.

Page 416: "Advice for GM's Bob Stempel," by Paul C. Judge (originally published as "He Didn't Ask, But Here's Some Advice for GM's Bob Stempel"). *The New York Times,* August 5, 1990. Copyright © 1990 by The New York Times Company. Reprinted by permission.

Page 420: Excerpts from "Bob Galvin and Motorola, Inc.," by Todd Jick and Mary Gentile, Harvard Business School case 9–487–062. Copyright © 1987 by the President and Fellows of Harvard College.

Page 432: "The Dilemmas of a Changemaker," by William Shea, is reprinted with permission of *New Management.*

Page 439: Excerpts from "Three in the Middle: The Experience of Making Change at Micro Switch," by Susan Rosegrant and Todd Jick. Harvard Business School case 9–49–022. Copyright © 1990 by the President and Fellows of Harvard College.

Page 450: "Toward a Boundary-less Firm at General Electric," by Mark Potts (originally published as "Seeking a Better Idea: With Cutting Management Tool, GE's Chief Aims to Form a Boundary-less Firm"). © 1990 *The Washington Post.* Reproduced with permission.

Page 456: "British Air's Profitable Private Life," by Steve Lohr. *The New York Times,* May 7, 1989. Copyright © 1989 by The New York Times Company. Reprinted by permission.

Page 463: "IBM's Blue Mood Employees," by Paul B. Carroll. Reprinted by permission of *The Wall Street Journal,* August 8, 1991. © Dow Jones & Company, Inc. All Rights Reserved Worldwide.

Page 467: "Takeover: A Tale of Loss, Change, and Growth," by Dwight Harshbarger. *Academy of Management Executive,* vol. 1, no. 3 (1987). Reprinted with permission of the Academy of Management.

Page 474: "GE Keeps Those Ideas Coming," by Thomas A. Stewart. *Fortune,* August 12, 1991. © 1991 The Time Inc. Magazine Company. All rights reserved.

Page 483: "Downsizing: One Manager's Personal Story," by Amy Levy. Reprinted, by permission of publisher, from *Management Review,* December 1991 © 1991. American Management Association, New York. All rights reserved.

For Matt, Zoe, and those yet to come

Contents

Part III. Change What?

Part V. Action

Acknowledgments

This book grew out of our individual and joint attempts to help current and future managers all over the world improve their management of change.

In 1984, just before joining the Harvard Business School faculty, Rosabeth Moss Kanter designed a course on organizational change at Yale University intended to combine academic change theories with practical, hands-on cases of real managers struggling with change dilemmas. The students were a diverse group, including business students from the School of Management as well as undergraduates and doctoral students in economics and social sciences. Two students, Lisa Richardson and Paul Myers, followed Kanter to the Harvard Business School in 1986. As Research Associates (and, in Myers's case, as doctoral candidate as well), they made many important contributions to this book, including the authorship of some of the change portraits included here.

At the same time, Kanter was collaborating with Barry Stein, a management consultant and consulting firm executive with many years' experience bringing change to European and American organizations, on the development of tools and insights that would guide the dramatic transformations organizations were beginning to experience in the turbulent 1980s, to get ready for the even more competitive 1990s. As the head of Goodmeasure, Inc., Stein had access to the inside story of remarkable organizational changes, working with many of the organizations represented in this book, including Ford, Xerox, IBM, and Security Pacific Bank. Together, Kanter and Stein led numerous hands-on workshops on issues in significant organizational change all over the world, for governments as well as businesses—e.g., for newly privatized Telecom in Australia; British Telecom; Sandoz in Switzerland; Luppo Group in Indonesia and Hong Kong; Procordia in Sweden; local government officials in Holland; and the National Health Service in the United Kingdom; and many other organizations.

Meanwhile, Todd Jick had independently developed a new Harvard Business School course on the management of change. Its emphasis on the action roles in the change process seemed a perfect fit with the other material Kanter and Stein were pulling together with an eye toward creating this book. Jick was invited to join the partnership, contributing an additional perspective and set of materials as well as the experience he was gaining as one of the leaders of General Electric's "Work out," a revolutionary changes process involving the reduction of bureaucracy and the building of a new corporate culture for GE units in many countries.

Jick took principal responsibility for Part IV of the book, on implementation and execution. Kanter and Stein took principal responsibility for Parts I, II, III, and V. Kanter developed Chapters 2 and 6.

This book offers our own analysis and synthesis—a model of organizational change that integrates economic, political, sociological, psychological, and historical insights. It combines this with portraits of organizations as they experience change issues. Chapters 1, 2, 6, 10, and 14 could have been published by themselves as a stand-alone book. In fact, we considered the possibility of putting together just those chapters in a book that would include only the theory, analysis, and lessons for managers. Indeed, those readers interested in our principles and conclusions about change and its management might wish to concentrate on our own long essay chapters. Chapter 1 presents our model, and the structure of the rest of the book reflects that model. The architecture of the book matches the theory.

At the same time, the edited change portraits in other sections of the book give flesh and meaning to the analysis. They offer the chance to supplement learning from theory with learning from experience. As is always the case, theories and models slice reality artificially into chunks for the purpose of examining one issue at a time. But one of our points in our "Big Three Model of Change" is that the rest of organizational life does not remain static while one change issue at a time is addressed. Thus, the change cases in Chapters 3–5, 7–9, and 11–13 portray organizational reality in all of its messiness, chaos, and complexity—while providing a way to deepen one's understanding of what the theory means in practice.

Special thanks are due to Gina Quinn and Susan Rosegrant, Research Associates at the Harvard Business School during the active phase of book-writing. Richard Hackman, Malcolm Salter, Dorothy Leonard-Barton, Chris Argyris, Eleanor Westney, Ron Frank, and Paul Myers were among the colleagues who provided helpful comments and suggestions, though we alone are responsible for the final printed word. The Division of Research of the Harvard Business School deserves special thanks for research support. Free Press President Erwin Glikes and Editor Robert Wallace offered helpful support when it was most needed. Willa Reiser provided her usual excellent facilitation. Magdalene Mallon and the staff at Goodmeasure, Inc. performed their usual miracles behind the scenes. Kevin Kane, the Federal Express agent on the island of Martha's Vineyard, was a useful ally, since summers were the time most writing got done. Family members Matt Stein, Rose Zoltek, and Zoe Jick were truly wonderful throughout.

Boston, Brookline, Cambridge,
and Edgartown, Massachusetts
July 1991

Part I

Orientation

Chapter 1

The "Big Three" Model of Change

The approach of the year 2000, with its millennial label and transformational implications, suggests the possibility of an equally profound change in our economic life and the institutions—primarily business firms—that populate it. In fact, even though the number has a highly spurious precision, its symbolism is appropriate. The world is undergoing many major transitions, some of which involve the meaning of business and the character and shape of the organizations that carry it out.

Most striking is the strong convergence of streams of thought and experience alike coming from academic theorists and practicing managers, from avowed free-market partisans and committed social democrats, from regulators and those regulated, from countries as diverse as Singapore and South Africa, the U.S.A. and the former U.S.S.R., Vietnam and Venezuela. This trend—or more accurately, this tidal wave—is becoming a universal model for organizations, especially large ones.

This model describes more flexible organizations, adaptable to change, with relatively few levels of formal hierarchy and loose boundaries among functions and units, sensitive and responsive to the environment; concerned with stakeholders of all sorts—employees, communities, customers, suppliers, and shareholders. These organizations empower people to take action and be entrepreneurial, reward them for contributions and help them gain in skill and "employability." Overall, these are global organizations characterized by internal and external relationships, including joint ventures, alliances, consortia, and partnerships.

There are, of course, differences in detail. Professional firms, service businesses, and manufacturing organizations do not look identical. Japanese keiretsu are not identical with their American industry and market counterparts. Decentralizing the National Health Service in Britain is not the same task as privatizing British Telecom or breaking up AT&T. Nevertheless, much of this is cosmetic; the management principles, operating values, and critical features defining the day-to-day behavior in those organizations are strikingly similar, and even the differences in detail are disappearing over time as global competition intensifies, confronting firms with a close look at others and forcing the routine and continuing transfer of practices from one to another.

Under these circumstances, the question most appropriate for the 1990s is not *what* the competitive world organization should look like but *how* to become one. Advice on change methodology is itself a flourishing business. Many people tell managers how to achieve competitiveness, though the recipes, the prescriptions, and, above all, the jargon are different. Some offer technologies for implementing a particular concept, such as total quality control. Others tinker with this organizational feature, fix that one, and educate people, the reward being the promised land of organizational transformation.

This sort of "revitalization" is only one route to corporate transformation. There are also "revolutionaries" who are impatient with the slow pace of reformist change or who distrust the managers guiding it. Throw out the whole thing and start over again, they urge. Overthrow management, change control, shuffle the assets, and the organization can be recreated. But these revolutions and battles for control, however effective in one sense, remain costly and unproven in others. In practice, these notions have also led to some prominent media events, such as Italy's Carlo de Benedetti's battle for Société Générale in Belgium, Sir James Goldsmith's takeover of Crown Zellerbach, or KKR's buyout of RJR Nabisco.

Indeed, corporate takeover specialists present themselves as the shock troops of capitalism, preaching the virtues of their approach. T. Boone Pickens, the erstwhile U.S. raider from Mesa Petroleum, became a brief star on the intellectual lecture circuit, founded The Association for Shareholder Rights, and testified before American Congressional committees. Asher Edelman, another American investor, in spare moments between his attacks on undervalued and underprotected companies, taught a class (called "The Art of War") on corporate finance and control at Columbia Business School; he offered to "make it real" for the students by offering an incentive of $100,000 to anyone who identified a suitable candidate, payable if and when he actually took it over. The school asked him to withdraw the incentive. And a third well-known American raider, Carl Icahn, evidently got tired of being seen "only" as a buyer and seller of companies and, upon acquiring TWA, decided to run it personally. (As it turned out, TWA entered bankruptcy in 1992; he might better have stuck with the paper chase.)

There are many views in between the extremes of reform and revolution, of course. And there are times when each is appropriate. But the danger lurking in many discussions of organizational change is that the whole thing starts to sound much simpler than it is. Too much credit is given to leaders when things go well, and too much blame when they go poorly. Yet, despite decades of very good advice to organizations about change, we are struck by how many failures there are and how much can go wrong. Even though both the reformers and the revolutionaries are, in their own ways, utopians, believing in organizational perfectibility, the sad fact is that, almost universally, organizations change as little as they must, rather than as much as they should.

But perfectibility is, in the final analysis, *not* an accurate picture, and not simply because our reach exceeds our grasp. It is impossible because of the very nature of organizations, in which successes in one realm inevitably produce problems in another. Organizations, whatever their specific purposes, are also institutions facilitating the production of dilemmas. And that, ultimately, is the best reason to suppose that there will always be a need for management, if not managers.

Organizations present not just one-time problems to be solved, and their problems are certainly not solved once and for all. Permanent success—a single formula that works forever—is impossible. After every revolution, even the most successful, the revolutionaries have to address continuing internal issues and the new tasks and problems created by the revolution. In short, even revolutionaries have to understand and accept reform. If these tasks are not addressed effectively, they can even destroy the revolution itself and create counterrevolutions.

The recent astonishing transformations which broke up the Soviet Union and its former East European satellites are a striking case in point. Even though we should be extremely cautious about equating countries and whole social systems with organizations, those events suggest an important lesson for organizational change in general. Changes and their effects are distributed throughout organizations. Some of them are visible, some not. Some are captured in the systems and structures of the organization, others in the minds of members, and still others in external adjustments. Some take effect or cause ripples soon, others need to ripen before they can flower. Thus, our ability to recognize changes may be largely limited to the immediately obvious and therefore superficial ones, while ultimately more powerful factors are hidden from our view. As Chapter 2 makes clear, we may be misled by too narrow or short-term perspectives, or by our personal favorite frame of reference, ignoring long-term forces more slowly transforming an organization, and overlooking counterforces and opposing tendencies.

Roadblocks to Progress: The Change Problem

A new ideal of a focused, innovative, and flexible organization is widely accepted around the world, but it is much more difficult to find practical examples of organizations not born that way that have fully transformed themselves to attain this ideal. Is the flexible twenty-first-century organization model wrong? We don't think so. The problem is one of change—getting from here to there. Change is more complex than optimistic managers—or analysts—think. There are several reasons behind the difficulty of finding exemplars that have transformed their organizations to the new model. Each of those reasons tells us something important about change.

First, *it is hard to make changes stick*. Many of the most admired role models for new practices have subsequently stopped them. For example, the exciting and innovative approach taken by Pacific Telesis and the Communications Workers of America (Kanter, 1989) has disappeared, a victim of the departure of its champions (a more or less accidental by-product of other changes) and the subsequent bypassing of the union staff. Another example: People Express Airline, a pioneering attempt to create a fundamentally different organizational form consistent with the best available knowledge about teamwork, collapsed and went out of business, a victim (though some would dispute this) of excessive optimism and an insufficient recognition of the values and benefits of *traditional* bureaucracy. This book is full of examples describing, in all-too-gory detail, the problems of organizational changes launched with the highest of hopes and the best available advice. We see in this more than simply a lack of skill, however.

Some of this may reflect a sociological truism: The originators of innovations are generally not the same as those who take the best advantage of them. What People Express invented but failed to accomplish helped Southwest Airlines build more soundly on Donald Burr's dream. General Motors, which during the late 1960s and early 1970s became famous for some of the most exciting new labor participation ideas (its Tarrytown plant was world-famous), could not sustain its own initiatives and saw them more effectively implemented by Ford, its arch-rival. In one of those wonderful ironies so characteristic of history, Japanese companies seized these innovations to the detriment of their American and European inventors. This truism about organizational innovations applies equally, and more familiarly, to technical innovations. The mouse, the idea of the graphic interface, and even the PC itself were invented by people at Xerox's Palo Alto Research Center. All were commercialized by other firms.

Second, *there are clear limitations to managerial action in making change.* One can wonder if deliberate change in complex organizations is possible at all or whether instead the enormous forces in their environments do not simply swamp any attempt to control them. As Chapter 2 will describe, a line of argument and evidence has been marshaled over the last fifteen years or so that sees in the rise and fall of firms the simple and inexorable play of evolutionary dynamics. From this point of view, managers have at best a secondary role in organizational change, being able merely to carry out the business equivalent of the familiar "You can't fire me; I quit."

There is often an extraordinary disconnection between our theories of change, at least as commonly understood and practiced by managers, and the realities of organizations actually undergoing change. Chapter 10 argues that the eminently sensible advice that constitutes conventional wisdom about managing change often does not work.

There are fundamental limits to the potential for action as a deliberate attempt to change organizations. Not everyone is the chief executive. More than that, even CEOs have to recognize severe constraints on their capacity to make the difference they wish. In general, organizational change cannot be ordered to happen. Conflicts of interest are becoming more and more apparent, and important. In addition to shareholders, other stakeholders with an interest in the organization (e.g., customers, suppliers, employees, or community leaders) are becoming more central, and their legal and operational influence is growing. As one consequence, both the capacity of managers to act and the wisdom of their doing so without consulting others are being reduced. And this issue is particularly important when undertaking major changes, with outcomes that may include power redistribution, possible layoffs, plant closings, and shifts in the very concept of the firm itself.

Large structural changes, such as mergers, acquisitions, restructurings, and takeovers, fail operationally unless they are accompanied by much more involving and fundamentally different grassroots efforts. Indeed, grassroots innovation—often referred to as bottom-up change—is often preferred to large-scale top-down change as a source of enduring results (Kanter, 1983).

Third, *attempts to carry out programmatic continuing change through isolated single efforts are likely to fail because of the effects of system context.* Organizations *are* systems, which means that anything more than trivial and surface changes needs to be seen as rooted in myriad features, and ultimately is an expression of the organization's character. Trying to change one component or one subsystem, then, may be akin to the old story of the primitive who acquired a radiator for his hut, kicking it to get heat, which he understood worked elsewhere.

Some—perhaps many—of these so-called "new" practices worked because they "grew up" in the organization, sharing a common development environment, or because the conditions at the time were favorable, whether recognized or not. There are many examples. Banc One, one of the most consistently profitable and effective banks in the United States (see Chapter 3), has prospered by creating an innovative organization designed to respond directly to its times and needs. Or take Digital Equipment. Kenneth Olsen, its founder and still its CEO, has presided over a justifiably celebrated global computer firm, in part by the use of structures and processes that, though apparently innovative (and certainly different, at least as compared to more traditional competitors such as IBM), was able to build on the attitudes and expectations held by its employees.

Fourth, *the need for change may make it harder to change.* Few maxims are more established than "Necessity is the mother of invention," and it is true, as much research has established, that adversity, which often produces a sense of necessity, does promote innovation. However, it is also true that scarce resources offer a much less hospitable climate for their utilization than abundance. Adversity, in short, may generate lots of ideas, but their realization is much less likely.

In business, this translates into the principle that crisis and decline are less likely to enable revitalization, though that is when the need is great, than are growth and success. One change dilemma, then, is that *the ability of organizations to change significantly appears when the inclination to change is least.* This also suggests that the manager has two very different tasks, which require very different strategies—solving problems (the task of restoration) and realizing positive visions (the task of transformation).

Finally, *some of those best at new practices in one realm may show limitations in others.* Often, the very same leaders who are able to launch one kind of new practice have tragic flaws that reduce their effectiveness in other important areas. How important is that? It depends, as we shall see. For example during the 1980s, American Airlines, under Robert C. Crandall, was a remarkably effective organization, avoiding most of the traps in which its competitors were caught. It kept prices *and* market share up, and put in place a whole series of innovations, for example, in labor relations—the two-tier wage system; in marketing—the frequent flyer program; and with suppliers—the Sabre reservation system.

But American's very innovations, and the style of leadership this required, also created potential problems. For example, the two-tier wage scale for pilots led the lower-tier people to seek parity with their top-tier colleagues, thus putting upward cost pressures on the airline. And this, of course, contributed to strained labor relations, when American's pilot union renegotiated its contract. Because of its success, the frequent flyer program created unexpected costs when travelers cashed in. Similarly, the airline's strong leadership, which enabled it to move fast and effectively, now faces the need to decentralize and add flexibility, as size, geographical scope, and global competition increase.

The role models of transformation—such firms as Xerox, Ford, or Motorola in the United States, or SAS, ICI, and British Air in Europe—demonstrate that it is a long, slow process requiring constancy of leadership attention and commitment, and that the results are not permanent. They also demonstrate that there are no guarantees, since competition may do better in the interim, for reasons that may transcend any simple explanation. For one thing, macroeconomic, political, and environmental variables matter. Capital markets, currency rates, political shifts, tax policy, resource markets, and technology shape organizational fates as much as managerial actions.

A parable about change illustrates one of the problems in understanding it. The nineteenth-century British writer Charles Lamb wrote a wonderful essay in which he imagined how humanity's discovery of cooking came about. Millions of years ago, Lamb supposed, people lived in large extended families, with domestic animals, in crude houses built of wood and thatch, and open to the elements. One day, with everyone gone, a house caught fire by accident, but the only casualty was a neighborhood pig. When the residents returned, all that was left was a plume of smoke, a pile of ashes, and a wonderful smell. Eventually, some of the people poked in the ashes and burned their fingers touching the carcass of the still hot, incinerated pig. When they put the burned fingers into their mouths to cool off the burn, a delicious taste appeared. They had, says Lamb, discovered cooking. Thereafter, when the people of the village wanted to celebrate, they picked out a house, put a pig inside it, and burned the house down!

We suggest a moral to this tale: *If you don't understand why the pig gets cooked, you are going to waste an awful lot of houses.*

This is a very good lesson for managers in general, especially in connection with change. In the absence of a powerful and convincing theory, managers will use whatever tactics are familiar rather than move to something new, which, absent such a theory, may well produce more and newer problems than the traditional approach. Better the devil we know. . .

Today, in light of the challenge of change all around us, the need for a comprehensive understanding of organizational change is clear.

What Is Change?

Language is full of ambiguity; it is at once a source of strength and a source of weakness. Certain words and phrases, however, create special problems. Though they sound specific and are generally treated as if everyone used them identically, they often generate more heat than light. This exactly describes the common experience of people discussing "organizational change."

For centuries philosophers have struggled with definitions of "change," though obviously not in connection with business organizations. For example, there can be few managers today who haven't somewhere been exposed to Heraclitus's famous dictum; "Nothing endures but change." But Heraclitus was emphatically *not* thinking of deliberate—that is, what we would call *intentional*—change, but rather of the change that is a consequence of the inherent potential for development associated with every entity. And that sort of change is closer to what the psychologist Abraham Maslow called "self-actualization."

To the ancient Greeks, in fact, the idea of deliberate and transforming change—tampering with the basic character of things—was, if not actually blasphemy, a sure path to disaster; it is fundamental to their great tragic dramas. In modern Western culture, "change" is a more malleable notion, a means to bend fate to one's own ends, although it is far from clear that this is possible. The Greeks may yet have a point in calling attention to the idea that neither people nor organizations are completely malleable, and we thus need to understand the limits of adaptability. Some things may be achievable, given a starting point; others may not.

The conventional modern idea of change typically assumes that it involves movement between some discrete and rather fixed "states," so that organizational change is a matter of being in State 1 at Time 1 and State 2 at Time 2. Kurt Lewin, a pioneer in the systematic study of planned change (as it became known) in the mid-1940s, developed a now-classic model of change used even by those who never read—or heard of—Lewin. This, of course, makes no difference. The economist John Maynard Keynes once noted: "Practical men, who believe themselves to be quite exempt from any intellectual influence, are usually the slaves of some . . . academic scribbler of a few years back" (Keynes, 1936).

Lewin's model was a simple one, with organizational change involving three stages; unfreezing, changing, and refreezing (Jones, 1968). This quaintly linear and static conception—the organization as ice cube—is so wildly inappropriate that it is difficult to see why it has not only survived but prospered, except for one thing. It offers managers a very straightforward way of planning their actions, by simplifying an extraordinarily complex process into a child's formula. Over the course of this book, we hope readers will develop their own much richer and more powerful understanding of organizational change.

Suffice it to say here, first, that organizations are never frozen, much less refrozen, but are fluid entities with many "personalities." Second, to the extent that there are stages, they overlap and interpenetrate one another in important ways.

Instead, it is more appropriate to view organizational motion as ubiquitous and multidirectional. (See Eccles and Nohria, 1992.) Deliberate change is a matter of grabbing hold of some aspect of the motion and steering it in a particular direction that will be perceived by key players as a new method of operating or as a reason to reorient one's relationship and responsibility to the organization itself, while creating conditions that facilitate and assist that reorientation.

Change involves two very different phenomena. First, it is to some degree in the eyes of the beholder. "Paradigm" theory, as outlined by Thomas Kuhn in his influential book *The Structure of Scientific Revolutions* (Kuhn, 1962), holds that an accumulation of little-noted, stepwise quantitative increments or small-c "change" (one more of something, then still one more) can suddenly be perceived as a qualitative shift or capital-C "Change," as though entering an entirely new state, with phenomena subsequently reinterpreted in terms of this new paradigm. Something similar occurs in the strategic change process in organizations (Kanter, 1983): the announcement of "change" is sometimes merely the decision to identify as mainstream a kind of activity that had existed on the organizational periphery all along. Moreover, the point of view of those who think they are creating change as an intentional process will be different from those who are on the receiving end of changes, and historians might reach still another conclusion. Political interests also come into play in the identification and labeling of change. We should always ask who has a stake in declaring something to be "new and different."

Second, organizational change has an empirical side; it is not entirely perceptual. An organization—any organization—is defined in its operations by the presence of a set of characteristics associated with enduring patterns of behavior, both of the organization as an entity and of people involved in it. If this were not true, if we could not find patterns, we could not really speak of "an" organization at all. Instead, like the title character in the Argentinian writer Jorge Luis Borges's story "Funes, the Memorious," who is plagued by the inability to see categories or patterns, we would have to regard it as an entirely different object at every moment. This would destroy the fundamental value of any organization, which lies in its capacity to accumulate momentum and exhibit reasonable consistency both over time and with respect to the behavior of its individual members.

This consistent patterned behavior of an organization's members over time constitutes one of its very distinctive and most important features, which we can call its *character*. This meaning of character needs to be sharply distinguished from the sort that overly anthropomorphizes organizations, for example by declaring that organizations can have a "heart" or a "soul."

It has long been recognized that organizations have great power to shape behavior, not so much by *forcing* it as by *encouraging* it. Organizations always make some things easier and some things harder, thus making the former more likely and the latter less likely. This is the work not simply of "culture"—something in people's heads—but rather of the formal aspects of the organization, such as its distribution of roles and responsibilities, people's authority to commit resources, existing budget procedures, the physical or geographical arrangement of its space and facilities, differences in information access and availability, and reward and recognition systems. This sort of "character" is rooted in the organization's structure, systems, and culture—elements that embody the momentum of the organization by "acting on" its members, thereby enabling the organization to maintain a recognizable presence over time.

These are also the same elements that are critical to any enduring change. Changes in character shift the behavior of the whole organization, to one degree or another. Where there is not a change in character, change is cosmetic, temporary, and uncertain in its effects—it is small-c "change," so to speak. Transformation—capital-C "Change"—requires a modification in patterned behavior and therefore is reflected in and rooted in a change in character. An understanding of organizational character and its sources, and of how to modify it, is required for effecting deliberate change. This is precisely why people at all levels, including chief executives, can enunciate new directions yet fail ultimately to make the difference they intend. Organizations cannot simply be "ordered" to change.

What is important about organizations is therefore not the occasional or idiosyncratic event or output, but the patterns that are manifested in those outcomes. Organizationally speaking, anything that is unique is not worth much attention, because it is not *organizational* behavior. Since by definition it is not going to recur, managers should not waste their time worrying about it, analyzing it, or setting up ways to prevent its future occurrence. What *is* important is anything that suggests the presence of a pattern of behavior or that could become one. The managerial imperative is very clear. Treat everything as a symptom, seek the underlying pattern, and either reinforce or reduce it. If there is no underlying pattern and no evidence that one is developing, it is not *organizationally* important.

What then *is* organizationally important is simply those things that are more or less likely *as a routine matter*. It is just this capacity of an organization to change the probability of events that gives organizations their power. That capacity, however, is not definitive. Rather, it acts through a bias or a tilt, pressures that can be resisted or overcome in any given case, but that over time and after enough choices are likely to result in a systematic shift away from intended outcomes.

The Importance of Motion: An Action View of Organizations

Our view, then, like that of Heraclitus, stresses continuous flow. Organizations, as we see them, are bundles of activity with common elements that allow activities and people to be grouped and treated as an entity. As activities shift, as new or different units or people are included in activity clusters, what is identified as "the organization" also shifts.

Organizations are always in motion. There is some central thrust or directional tendency—"keeping the herd roughly moving West," as Tom Peters once put it—that results from a combination of the trajectory of past events, pushes arising from the environment, and pulls arising from the strategies embraced by the organization's dominant coalition, all within the context of the organization's character. Of course, the activity clusters (task units, divisions, projects, interest groups, alliances, etc.) themselves are also in motion, and their movements at any time may or may not be in step with each other or with the overall direction.

This framework creates situations similar to the "agency" problem in economics (Pratt and Zeckhauser, 1985)—the problem that occurs when "principals" who own an asset must delegate responsibility for it to "agents" whose stake, interests, and understanding are different. But this framework goes far beyond agency theory in identifying a *coordination* problem and an *implementation* problem as well as a *delegation* problem. These are necessary additions, because organizations consist of *multiple* stakeholders conducting multiple but overlapping activities, and because even coordinated actions do not automatically produce intended results.

This view of organizations is well suited to the demands of the 1990s. Global economic competition coupled with continuous technological change is hastening the evolution of an organizational model that defines the boundaries of organizations as fluid and permeable. It recognizes that influence over organizational acts comes from many sources and directions, and through many pathways, rather than "down" a "chain of command." It understands the limits of authoritative intentions in the face of an organization's tendency to continue on preexisting paths. Organizational names, legal ownership, and charts with formal reporting relationships thus do not entirely or usefully define the ways action occurs—or the way change occurs. Intentional "strategic" acts said to represent *the* organization are only one form of action. There are multiple strategists, and organizational purpose is itself problematic and debatable.

Thus, organizational action in the new model needs to be viewed in terms of *clusters of activity sets* whose membership, composition, ownership, and goals are constantly changing, and in which *projects* rather than *positions* are central. In such an image of an organization, the bonds between actors are more meaningful and ongoing than those of single market transactions but less rigid and immutable than those of positions in authority structures. Action possibilities are neither as fully open as in a market transaction nor as fully constrained and circumscribed as in the classic theory of bureaucracy.

Furthermore, there is great variety in the relationships of individuals to these organizational activity sets. While some people's roles are defined primarily by positions in a hierarchy of authority (e.g., "employees" carrying out predefined tasks through specified procedures), others are defined by the ability to mobilize resources and develop commitment to new tasks (e.g., "corporate entrepreneurs" on the payroll as employees but also receiving additional social, psychic, and/or economic inducements for initiative). Others are defined by market exchanges without the organizational membership bond (e.g., subcontractors and contingent workers). And still others are defined by their dual positions in several hierarchies (e.g., as a contributor to company X in a joint venture or alliance while still "employed by company Y).

More critically, many of these activity sets are themselves only minimally "institutionalized." They do not exist or persist irrespective of the people occupying them. While the named entity under whose auspices activities occur (e.g., Ford Motor Company) may have an existence independent of persons, the limited-purpose associations (project teams) within it may come and go with the initiative and enthusiasm of particular people. For social scientists, this more fluid view of organizations suggests that perhaps network theory or social movement theory is more relevant to the emerging economic world than is bureaucratic theory. At the same time, this also suggests the possibility of formalizing some of these nonhierarchical mechanisms, in their form if not in their details of composition, as "parallel organizations" (Stein and Kanter, 1980).

Viewing an organization as a coalition of interests and a network of activities within a momentum-bearing structure has two implications that are essential for the perspective used in this book. First, change of one sort or another is always occurring, though it may not always be guided by organizational leaders nor be consistent with the purposes of the principal stakeholders. Second, managers concerned with *controlling* events or *guiding* change must be aware of both the nature of the networks within and around the organization (so they are able to form or work through coalitions of interests in order to induce multiple activities and interests to coalesce) and the sources and effects of the organization's momentum.

In this sense, "stability" in an organization is an idealization rather than a reality, an epiphenomenon or a quasi-equilibrium. "Stability" is just motion that is so smooth and involves so little conflict or challenge that it appears on the surface that nothing is moving. Or, to use more technical language, "stability" is better thought of as *unified motion stemming from a coalescence of interests and activities in an environment of adequate relative consistency and certainty.*

Apparent "stability" occurs when resources are abundant and easily obtained; competitors are few and competition is geographically confined by protected markets; technologies are standard and understood; individual and group ambition is constrained (people accept what they have); disasters or system failures are few or are accepted fatalistically; commitments are clear and acceptable to stakeholders; and interests are adequately aligned. General Motors in the United States in the 1950s and 1960s enjoyed this kind of "stability"; so did the telecommunications monopolies in most major countries through the 1970s.

Depart from any of these conditions, as in the globalizing economy of the 1980s, and suddenly the motion is apparent, with change taking center stage. Depart from all of them at once, as seems to be the case in the 1990s, and *responding to change, harnessing change, and creating change become the major management challenges.*

Consider the situation facing most organizations and their leaders today: Resources are scarcer and are obtained with more difficulty. New technologies arise frequently. Individual and group ambition is given free rein, in ever more countries. Crises are common but assumed to be solvable if only managers are good enough. Commitments—of customers, employees, or other stakeholders—are fragile or short-lived because of numerous choices and alternatives. And interests shift and diverge frequently.

How can so much motion be conceptualized and understood, so that leaders can manage it?

The "Big Three" Model: Three Kinds of Motion, Three Forms of Change, Three Roles in the Change Process

To put all this in perspective, it is helpful to focus on three interconnected aspects of organizations: the forces, both external and internal, that set events in motion; the major kinds of change that correspond to each of the external and internal change pressures; and the principal tasks involved in managing the change process.

1. The three kinds of movement:
   - The motion of the organization as a whole as it relates to motion in its *environment*—change that is *macroevolutionary,* historical, and typically related to clusters or whole industries.
   - The motion of the parts of the organization in relation to one another as the organization grows, ages, and progresses through its

life cycle—change that is *micro-evolutionary,* developmental, and typically related to its size or shape, resulting in coordination issues.
- The jockeying for power and struggle for control among individuals and groups with a stake in the organization to make decisions or enjoy benefits as an expression of their own interests—change that focuses on *political dimensions* and involves *revolutionary* activity.

These three kinds of movement help distinguish three basic forms of change, at roughly corresponding levels of analysis.

2. The three forms of change:
   - *Identity* changes in the relationships between the organization as an entity and its environment: the assets it owns and the markets it approaches, the niches it occupies, the relationships it has to its customers and to the organizations that fund it, supply it, and confer legitimacy on it. These changes are related to macro-evolutionary forces, to the motion in the environment and the organization's own capacity to endure over time as a factor in that environment.

     As environmental movement presents pressures and opportunities for change, organizations can subtly change their identities by reformulating their relationships to their environments: changing the businesses in which they operate, the products they offer to the market, the investors who supply capital, and so forth. The most extreme version of identity change is when an organization *becomes something entirely different* (in its businesses, products, ownership, etc.) in order to allow a portion—the asset base, the products, some know-how, the employment base, even a tax carryover—to endure.
   - *Coordination* changes, which involve the internal array of parts—activity sets—constituting the organization. These kinds of changes often (though not exclusively) relate to micro-evolutionary dynamics, to the problems of shape and structure that emerge as organizations grow and age.

     Of course, the effectiveness of an organization at relating to its environment—serving markets, securing resources—also triggers questions of size and shape. But whatever the source of the problem, the need to change the organization's internal configuration, rather than simply to let it evolve, may ultimately result in deliberate *reshaping or revitalizing.*
   - Changes in *control* that stress the political dimension, who is in the dominant coalition, or which interests or set of interests predominates, who owns and governs the organization. This leads to *makeover through takeover* or other changes triggered by shifts in ownership or governance. Such changes deal with "revolution" and are often dramatically revolutionary in their impact on many aspects of the organization.

The three kinds of movement also correspond roughly to three action roles in the change process, the phases in any particular change sequence, and to traditional organizational levels.

3. The three action roles in the change process:
   - Concern for the connection between the organization and its environment, and for the organization's overall direction in light of macro-evolutionary forces, is the province of *change strategists.* The change strategy role often, though not always, occurs at the beginning of a change sequence, and it is usually, though not always, the responsibility of top leaders.
   - Responsibility for the microdynamics of development of the change effort itself, and therefore of its internal organizational structure and coordination as the organization itself moves through its life cycle, lies in the hands of *change implementors.* The implementation role is often associated with "middles"—for example, the middle of a change sequence or the middle levels of the organization. Change implementation, as we are using the concept here, involves project management and execution rather than conception.

     Of course, strategists can also be implementors; and in the course of implementation, middle managers can find themselves considering macro forces and developing grand strategies or reshaping existing strategies because of the realities of execution. Organizational action is also often smoother and more effective when strategists and implementors overlap, so that the distinctions are less marked. Still, this conceptual distinction points to the difference in perspective and responsibilities that follows from leaders wearing their strategy or implementation hats.
   - Generally, toward the end of a change sequence (at least as the "end" is officially conceived), and sometimes at the "bottom" of the organization, are the *change recipients,* those who are strongly affected by the change and its implementation, but without much opportunity to influence those effects. The reactions of change recipients reflect the political and control dimensions of organizations—who benefits, which interests are served.

     A good deal of the tension that invariably arises in major organizational change programs is the direct result of the disjunction between those directing and implementing change—both of whom are sufficiently involved to have at least a degree of control over the change—and those who are powerless, the passive recipients, as it were.

     For more effective change efforts, it usually makes sense to include recipients among the implementors and strategists. But again, we want to point to the inherent difference in perspective involved in being at the receiving end of change. Much resistance to change occurs because recipients bring their own interests, goals, and group memberships to the change table. In some cases, often as a result of their perceived powerlessness, recipients form their own formal associations (e.g., unions) to attempt unilaterally to increase their own power in the responding role.

This model is spelled out in detail throughout the book. Each element is examined in conceptual terms and through illustrations drawn from a wide range of companies, industries, and countries, to provide concrete examples of the change dynamics and change dilemmas involved. Our model illuminates the key areas that must be understood in order to master change. It also makes clear why there are so many possibilities for failure at making change. The three kinds of motion might be leading in very different directions. The three action roles not only involve different responsibilities; they also reflect different perspectives and interests that can interfere in any one group's ability to realize its intentions perfectly.

The perspective in this book stresses many of the changes *happening to* organizations and their members; yet it also helps us understand both the opportunities and the difficulties surrounding *planned* or *intentional* change.

Looking Backward or Looking Forward?: Multiple Possibilities and the Opportunities for Managers

This book integrates a wide range of ideas derived from social science theories and our own extensive observations of companies around the world. It looks at change from the perspective of individuals as well as that of organizational systems. By considering the interplay between environment and actor from many angles, we hope to illuminate the opportunities for change mastery—where some control can be exercised, and where it cannot; what forces must be harnessed, and the ease or difficulty of doing so.

By definition, the events and situations described in the readings have already happened. There is an air of inevitability about such descriptions. As readers, we view them in "20-20 hindsight," and the lessons about what leaders *ought* to have done seem clear. We can identify patterns and develop theories.

However, although understanding the past is all well and good for academics and analysts, practicing managers have a different need: to gauge and affect the future. The task of management consists in taking action with reasonable assurance that desired consequences will stem from those actions. Management amounts to placing bets; it involves the investment of time, energy, and resources in actions assumed to be reasonably suitable to achieving hoped-for results.

From this perspective, the world looks much less inevitable. Managers spend considerable sums on analyses designed to project, predict, forecast, and model all known variables and complex relationships in the quest for underlying inevitabilities of markets or other trends. But the increased motion of today's activated environment makes analyses of this kind more and more suspect except in narrow, constrained domains.

But managers act anyway, even in the absence of perfect knowledge. Without knowing what *must* be, as we look backward from history, they consider what *can* or *might* be. Managers see *multiple possibilities* rather than a single inevitable ending.

Our colleague Richard Hackman has pointed to this tension between forward-looks and backward-looks in academic views of organizations. Theorists proposed the concept of "equifinality" to argue that organizations are systems with a purpose, tending to develop in inevitable ways. But this is a conclusion reached from examining *endings* rather than *beginnings.* Watching a situation unfold as it is happening, instead of after the fact, makes it clear that it is much harder to predict specific events, that surprises or deviations from expected patterns are common. Situations contain multiple possibilities for action.

Multiple possibility theory is in fact particularly well suited to a view of organizations as activity clusters in constant motion, guided by managers trying to steer. Of course, from a historian's perspective, viewed from far away and over a long period of time, coherence and identity may be more apparent than constant motion. But from the point of view of the actors confronting the situation, the choices are far less clear, the options less structured, the results inevitably more mixed, and the rationales highly arguable.

A reasonable, though slightly cynical, view of the world says: "If life give you lemons, learn to like lemonade." Similarly, if organizational life involves continuous flow, then go with that flow. Understanding all the forces and variables involved in organizational change can help managers place their bets in a world of complex motion and multiple possibilities. Ultimately, despite the limits upon what people can control, it is still up to people to act, and in acting they do more than predict the future, they invent it.

In this book, we hope to help make action more effective. We try to capture the complexity of change and make the challenges and dilemmas comprehensible, so their effects can be better understood. We identify the "disconnects" between theory and practice; the critical points at which a manager's compass goes haywire, and why. We counter utopian views that organizations can be "made perfect." But we also show how dealing with reality can help managers understand opportunities as well as limits. We help them see better how they can do what they can even when they cannot control everything.

We attempt here to add a rich historical and political dimension to the more usual managerial, economic, and behavioral views of organizations, and to further the understanding of the link between micro and macro considerations—how the intentions of actors relate to the macro-derived possibilities for effective action.

References

Eccles, Robert G., and Nitin Nohria. 1992. *Beyond the Hype: An Action Framework.* Boston: HBS Press.

Jones, Garth N. 1968. *Planned Organizational Change.* London: Routledge & Kegan Paul.

Kanter, Rosabeth Moss. 1983. *The Change Masters: Innovation and Entrepreneurship in the American Corporation.* New York: Simon & Schuster.

———. 1989. *When Giants Learn to Dance: Mastering the Challenges of Strategy, Management, and Careers in the 1990s.* New York: Simon & Schuster.

Keynes, John Maynard. 1936. *The General Theory of Employment, Interest and Money.* New York: Harcourt Brace.

Kuhn, Thomas S. 1962. *The Structure of Scientific Revolutions.* Chicago: University of Chicago Press.

Pratt, John, and Richard Zeckhauser. 1985. *Principals and Agents: The Structure of Business.* Boston: HBS Press.

Stein, Barry A., and Rosabeth Moss Kanter. 1980. "Building the parallel organization: Toward mechanisms for permanent quality of work life." *Journal of Applied Behavioral Science.* Vol. 16 (Summer), pp. 371–88.

Part II

Change When?

Chapter 2

Organizations and Environments in Motion: The Nature and Scope of Change Pressures

Conventional wisdom says nothing is wrong with us. We rank first in the industry. The analysts love us. The board loves me. We are called "one of the few remaining American institutions."

And yet I have a disturbing sense that we have to make ourselves over. Competitors are moving in from entirely different industries, not only with variations on our existing products, but more and more with entirely different solutions that threaten our markets. I often feel like the CEO of a department store facing mass merchandisers, or a courier company fighting a fax machine. I see digital electronics transforming everything.

I've asked some of our staff to think about even selling off everything, starting from scratch; we'd keep our name—for now sacred, "an institution." I told them to think of Coca-Cola announcing the elimination of its old formula. What would be left of S. S. Kresge if it didn't transform itself into K-Mart?

But if we change, we will almost certainly upset the financial community and the trade press and our employees.

The problem may seem small now, but I fear that when it grows it will quickly become a crisis. . .

—Composite CEO thoughts voiced by Theodore Levitt, "The Case of the Migrating Markets," *Harvard Business Review*, July–August 1990.

"All is flux," wrote Heraclitus, likening history to the flow of a river. "The only constant is change," today's management philosophers say. But change is not always planned, and it is not always desired. Ongoing, ever present forces can induce organizational change regardless of the strategies and intentions of the leaders or "official" keepers of direction-setting, organization-shaping control.

Three clusters of forces create motion in and around organizations—motion that triggers change. First is the relationship between organizations and their environments. The second is organic, "growth" through the life cycle. The third is political, the constant struggle for power. All three occur, in a sense, "outside" of strategic intention or official organizational goals. They pose unintended, unofficial, unwanted, or underground pressures on organizations to change form or direction. They represent, in varying degrees, "inevitable" forces that keep the organization constantly in motion and require a response if the organization is going to be able to do what its shapers and stakeholders desire. The three clusters of forces are also likely to accumulate over time, and such unattended accumulation of change pressures can often result in an abrupt crisis or a radical wrenching change.

Thus, while organization players are trying to act, trying to realize their intentions, the organization is a moving target. It is blown about by environmental winds; it grows and ages and adapts to new leaders as people pass on; and it is shaped by internal power struggles. Sometimes these forces are long-term, gentle, slow, and controllable; at other times, they cause acute crises.

This chapter explores the forces themselves. We shall examine the pressures they put on organizations to change in particular directions, and the perils encountered if change is fumbled. But while we stress the "emergent" dimension of change—outside of official intentions, "external" to official plans—we shall also question whether change must inevitably "happen to" organizations (the passive, pessimistic models of long-term evolution) or whether it can be controlled by decision-makers (the activist, optimistic models of strategy making).

We shall see what kinds of circumstances and what kinds of changes are best illuminated by an examination of each force, and the theories, concepts and models that have been developed to describe it. For example, in life cycle models organizational change occurs in predictable and relatively discrete stages or phases (generally birth, maturity, and decline); furthermore, structures and practices from the founding period and early stages provide a foundation for later stages. This perspective can be contrasted with evolutionary models, in which organizational death is not preordained, and organizations reform and renew themselves to fit the environment. Those that fail to do so decline and die. The focus of evolutionary models is not on aging but on evolutionary forces outside the organization that necessitate change and the intra-organizational dynamics that facilitate or inhibit it. Finally, political models add still a third perspective on an organization: as a battleground for multiple stakeholders, who are each trying to shape the organization's activities in ways that will further their own interests. Change in the political view is the result of such struggles for power.

Environmental Forces: Adaptation and Choice

The first set of forces in emergent change derives from how an organization relates to its environment—the ties it forms with other organizations and its location in a population of other organizations competing for the same scarce or munificent resources, with varying degrees of certainty or uncertainty about how best to compete. Understanding this change dynamic requires a longer historical view of the fate of organizations over time, asking: What accounts for long-term changes in individual organizations and in the population of organizations in an industry?

In numerous industries, from automobile manufacturing to broadcasting, there is a pattern to the history of organizations and their environments.

Technology opens opportunities to conduct formerly fragmented (localized and small-scale) activities efficiently on a larger scale—e.g., from occasional custom crafting to full-scale production; and a new industry is born. At first, only a few entrepreneurs see the potential, but soon many organizations try to gain a foothold. Out of the ensuing competition among organizations and approaches, a few dominant players emerge as winners. An "organization set" soon surrounds the survivors. A network of suppliers grows up to service them, a set of customers comes to depend on their products, and activist groups arise to prod them to serve ends other than sheer profit. "Industry standards" are defined. Some of these are formal and official, backed by contracts, laws, and regulations; some are informal understandings or tacit assumptions about appropriate ways to do business.

The dominant players, and a sprinkling of weaker ones that hang on because they enjoy enough support from some stakeholder groups to continue a marginal existence, compete among themselves for relative position—who is number one, two, and three on any given issue in any given year. Unless the positions are hardened, they are likely to do rather similar things, surviving to compete and exchange places—e.g., last year's number three moving up to number one this year. The "environment" within which this stabilized competition occurs is bounded at first, often geographically, even though customers may be farflung—e.g., the auto industry in the United States through the 1960s, the wine industry in France, the beer industry in Sweden, the garment industry in Hong Kong.

At this point, established players can afford to look inward rather than outward and to concentrate on protecting advantages rather than innovating. After the initial shakeout and industry stabilization, change is often largely incremental, consisting of add-ons to existing offerings by established players.

Then the environment itself shifts. New technology opens still other possibilities and challenges the dominant modes of production or distribution. The relevant arena for competition widens, as players from other places migrate toward each other's resources, as Japanese auto companies did in entering North American and European markets. Challenger groups succeed in gaining political support for changes in laws and regulations, changing the terms of competition, as MCI did in challenging AT&T's monopoly of the U.S. long distance telephone market, forcing the breakup of one of the world's largest companies. Political shifts,such as the move toward a united Europe in 1992, the return of Hong Kong to China in 1997, or the return of the former Soviet bloc nations to independent states with free market economies seeking ties with the West, enlarge the boundaries for competition. Innovators from outside the industry invade, with new approaches that win support.

At this point the "environment" is turbulent, as a new struggle for dominance ensues. The struggle provokes established players to fight to protect the advantages gained from supportive laws, regulations, and stakeholders. But if established organizations cannot erect barriers to entry, then the competition provokes them to rewrite their contracts, restructure their assets, and innovate. Meanwhile, the innovators who caused the turbulence continue to make changes themselves, because they have fewer traditions or long-established interests to protect.

Survival of the fittest has become a tautology that tells us little about the mastery of change. Who are the "fit"? Are they *efficient,* best suited to adapt to external conditions, as determined by "the environment's" invisible judges that select the winners? Are they *lucky* rather than efficient,surviving by chance more than by smart moves? Are they simply *similar* to other organizations, surviving because they reflect a dominant social paradigm? Or are they *innovators* that reshape the environment rather than merely respond to it?

We explore each of these four possibilities in turn, seeking insights into the ways environmental forces shape the pressures and possibilities for change. Three theories should be kept in mind while exploring the four possibilities for how environmental forces push organizations to change. The first, by analogy to biological processes, emphasizes the external determination of the fate of organizations (the *natural selection* model of evolutionary theory). A second focuses on the bargaining for resources and power relationships that organizations employ as they try to manage their environment (called the *resource dependence* perspective). Both approaches share a view that organizational success and survival depend on the "fit" with the external environment, particularly on the ability to secure scarce resources, but they differ on the role played by active management of the environment. A third model, labeled *institutional* theory, holds that organizations seek legitimacy in a social context; they persist or change in order to fit prevailing social norms and expectations.

Survival of the Adapted: How Natural Selection Works

One macro-evolutionary view, known in sociological lingo as "population ecology," sees organizations as buffeted about by forces in the environment, lucky if they manage to get into a favorable position, fated to die if they do not (Hannan, 1977; Hannan and Freeman, 1989). Population ecology draws analogies to the biological evolution of species in exploring how populations of organizations are transformed by environmental changes (Aldrich and Pfeffer, 1976; Hannan and Freeman, 1989). The organizational form that is most effective in getting the resources it needs from its immediate environment and most efficient at using them will prevail within any resource pool, the argument runs. There are niches with varying degrees of crowding; the more crowding, the more competition, and the greater the likelihood that some organizations will die.

Overall, in this view, change for a particular organization occurs through an evolutionary process involving random mutation, environmental selection of those forms fit to survive, and retention or reinforcement of the selected pattern. This model looks at the composition of whole populations of organizations as the unit of analysis. Those better suited to their environment survive, and while the "unfit" die, new organizations are created embodying new forms. The organizations that survive are stable until the next random mutation or shift in niche width sets a change cycle in motion. The volatility resulting from selective retention and creation at the organizational level of analysis creates change at the population level, which then molds, alters, and constrains organization-level change.

Population ecologists have attempted to describe the characteristics of organizations that make it easier or harder to adapt to changing environments. One set of studies, for example, compared generalist and specialist restaurants to see when each kind of firm fared better (Hannan and Freeman, 1984). Specialists (e.g., ethnic or specialty restaurants), engaged in limited activities, did not accumulate slack or idle capacity, and performed efficiently. Generalists (e.g., restaurants with a broad menu) engaged in multiple activities, accumulated slack and idle capacity, and at any time performed less efficiently than specialists. But generalists were more likely to survive in environments that changed in sudden, major ways (rather than constantly and incrementally) or in which diverse activities were complementary rather than conflicting.

Unfortunately, population ecology does not account for change in environments themselves, because "environment" is used in such a nonspecific way, embodying everything from industry to geographic territory. And the theory neglects the role of inter-organizational ties, which we consider vital in understanding organizational change. But clearly, some geographic environments are more "fertile" than others and therefore spawn more organizations. The existence of startups then changes the conditions for current organizations by the technology they produce, and their geographic proximity encourages still other organizations to form to service them (e.g., the network of suppliers and consultants serving the high-technology community in California's Silicon Valley or the small manufacturers serving the apparel industry in northern Italy). Industry environments can also be more or less fertile in providing a context in which new ideas can grow. Customer organizations that use the output of a particular population of organizations can be more or less demanding of change. Resource availability and resource needs shape change.

Survival of the Lucky: Experiment and Chance

In natural selection theories luck or chance plays a more important role than strategic choice—a useful reminder that not every success is the result of planning or active will. The wealthy oil magnate J. Paul Getty supported this notion in revealing his three secrets for success: Get up early, work hard, and find oil. In a similar vein, the successful publisher Malcolm Forbes, Jr., said that his success was due to "choosing the right grandparents." One organizational theorist observed that "the survival of some organizations for great lengths of time is largely a matter of luck . . . such longevity comes about through the workings of chance." Skills play a minor role in corporate survival, in this view. Attempts to create change are doomed to failure, luck theories argue, because "organizations by and large are not capable of more than marginal changes while the environment is so volatile that marginal changes are frequently insufficient to assure survival" (Kaufman, 1985).

Thus, in this view, the only hope for organizational transformation is starting fresh—new organizations replacing old ones, or new organizational units acting autonomously. There is evidence to support the argument that innovation comes from outside an industry, from upstarts or invaders—what has been called "innovation by invasion" (Schon, 1967). Upstarts often change an industry—e.g., major changes in American retailing were brought by Wal-Mart, The Limited, Nordstrom, and Benetton (not by Sears, Penney, or K Mart), and a revolution in telecommunications was triggered by such small upstarts as Wireless and Cable in Britain and MCI in the United States, leading to the privatization of British Telecom and the breakup of AT&T. Just as the entry of new organizations changes the environment for the existing population, effective internal change seems to come from outside. A Strategic Planning Institute study found that in rapidly changing situations (rapid expansion or contraction), business units with managers who came in from outside outperformed those with managers promoted from within; the former exceeded profit goals by 10 percent, while the latter failed to meet them by an average of 15 percent.

Careful examination of some organizational successes shows that luck or chance indeed plays a role in success in an unplanned trial-and-error process—what macro-evolutionary theory might call "variation" (random mutation) and "selection" (the environment rewarding the experiment). Consider the way Honda motorcycles took over and transformed the U.S. market in the 1960s. "Strategy" models stress Honda's deliberate policies of using its dominant market position in Japan to force entry into the U.S. market, which it then developed region by region, expanding that market by redefining a leisure class segment attracted to lightweight motorcycles, and exploiting its comparative advantage via aggressive pricing and advertising. But interviews with key players paint a different picture, in which luck (plus the failure of an initial big-bike strategy) figured prominently (Pascale, 1984).

Honda first moved to the United States with only a modest sales effort because of stringent monetary controls by the Japanese government as well as fears of an unfriendly reception. The operation was begun in Los Angeles because of its large Japanese population. The local Honda managers were so poorly informed that they didn't know the U.S. market was seasonal, and they came at the end of the 1959 season. By April 1960, reports that machines were suffering from oil leaks and clutch failure abounded. The U.S. group was barely hanging on. Honda U.S.A.'s strategy was to push its large machines. While the large machines were shipped to dealers, the Honda crew used the lightweight models personally for errands around Los Angeles. The small machines attracted attention wherever they were driven. Yet even when a Sears buyer called to inquire about them, Honda U.S.A. still didn't diverge from its big-bike strategy. A problem with the larger machines finally prompted them reluctantly to let the smaller motorcycles go to the retailers who wanted them—which turned out to be sporting goods stores. Even though this brought sales momentum, the Honda crew was slow to budge from its emphasis on large machines. As Richard Pascale (1984) observed: "History has it that Honda 'redefined' the U.S. motorcycle industry. In the view of American Honda's start-up team, this was an innovation they backed into—and reluctantly."

Survival of the Similar: The Social Environment

Natural selection models tend to assume that the organizations that survive are the most efficient and effective—in "resource dependency" theory, that they are the best at bargaining for limited resources. Recently another perspective has arisen to challenge both assumptions. Institutional models look at social and political forces surrounding organizations, maintaining that organizations must fit social expectations and values. If they do, they are more likely to survive than if they do not, regardless of efficiency.

Therefore, organizations strive to maintain legitimacy by conforming to institutionalized *beliefs* about how they ought to be constructed. Over time, the organizations that survive tend to look alike not because that is the form best adapted to the economic environment, but because of the transmission and acceptance of values. Thus, rationally "efficient" organizations could fail to gain legitimacy and perish, while inefficient forms may become institutionalized (layered with meaning and thereby established). Fads and fashions are important forces for organizational change in this view; gradually organizations are forced to imitate the practices on which legitimacy has been conferred. This creates structural similarity or "isomorphism."

Pressures for "isomorphism"—for organizations to adopt comparable structures—come from several sources. First, organizations emulate each other because similarity eases interorganizational interaction. Those with central positions in resource allocation networks will be emulated either because it is a condition forced upon an organization or a strategy chosen to increase access. For example, a study of long-lived nineteenth-century American utopian communities showed that the countercultural communal form was maintained as long as the communities could be isolated; once they needed to sell their goods to the outside world, they changed to take on more and more of the appearance of the organizations with which they dealt (Kanter, 1972).

Second, organizations need legitimacy to show that the organization is behaving "appropriately," especially when it is difficult to measure output more directly. School systems, for example, may prove that they are worthy of support by showing that they do what other schools do (Meyer and Rowan, 1977).

Third, when there is uncertainty about success factors, organizations actively seek to emulate role models perceived to be successful, aided by experts and educators that promulgate popular models. To stem its loss of market share to the Japanese, for example, Xerox adopted a policy of "benchmarking"—looking for the companies with the best practices in every aspect of the business and then ensuring that Xerox's practices met or exceeded that standard. By 1992 benchmarking was a centerpiece of total quality management (TQM) programs in Europe and North America; one corporate giant even had a Vice President of Benchmarking, and the American Productivity and Quality Center in Houston had a benchmarking information clearinghouse.

Regardless of technical considerations of efficiency, then, organizations adopt new structures and practices because they are socially sanctioned as the "right ones" and transmitted via experts and educators. Whether we see this as "change for the sake of change" or what an organization must do because of environmental pressures, a process of emulation guides the change. This process might include:

- Imposition of a new practice by a more powerful authority
- Deliberate imitation of another organization's practice, because it is used by another organization perceived as successful
- Authorization of a new practice by powerful professional or certifying organizations
- Inducement to use the practice by other organizations that cannot impose it but offer incentives, such as funding (DiMaggio and Powell, 1983; Scott, 1987)

Change via imitation can trigger still other changes. The process is not static. For example, Japanese organizations borrowed and adapted Western forms in the nineteenth century, after sending teams to visit France, Britain, and the United States to study such organizations as the police and the post office. Imitation can give rise to innovation—often unconsciously (Westney, 1987). The early Japanese postal system was modeled on the British system, but Japan lacked the railways and transport companies that provided the British infrastructure, so the Japanese turned to traditional guilds of runners as carriers for their first postal routes.

Emulation is thus an imperfect process. Perfect information is never available even when practices are observed at first hand. Alternative implicit models (countering the model imitated) carried by an organization's workforce exert an influence (Westney, 1987). There are also deliberate departures from the model, such as (1) selective emulation of only those features that will help the new organization gain legitimacy or avoid shortcomings of the template; and (2) departures that occur as the model is adapted to a setting that lacks some of the organizations that support it in its original setting. Relationship networks—the organization's customers, suppliers, employees, and public supporters—push or prevent change.

Survival of the Savvy: The Role of Choice

How much and when must an organization helplessly change to "fit" its environment, and when can it make the environment "fit" it?

Clearly, "environments" are not hard and fast, no matter how constrained they might seem. It is striking how often innovators from outside the small group of industry giants succeed at imagining the unimaginable, at doing what conventional wisdom said could never be done.

The broadcasting industry in the United States, for example, was dominated by three major networks through the early 1980s (CBS, NBC, and ABC)—until cable and satellite broadcasting became feasible on a large scale. Then Ted Turner's Turner Broadcasting System created CNN (Cable News Network), which became a world force by distributing live programming around the world, not only taking market share from the three dominant networks but also entering attractive new markets in other countries. In 1990 NBC News announced plans to launch a twenty-four-hour news service similar to CNN's Headline News.

Meanwhile, Turner, not standing still, was moving in a number of other directions, including offering cable news broadcasts to schools. In the same year Turner Broadcasting began to offer satellite-delivered news and information programming at supermarket checkout counters. But while Turner went around the major U.S. networks by developing cable broadcasts, another innovator was at work. An Australian, Rupert Murdoch, challenged the three networks head-on with the development of a fourth network, Fox Broadcasting. Clever alliances with regulators helped Fox at every turn. In mid-1990 Fox won permission from the Federal Communications Commission to offer added programming without having to adhere to network TV rules affecting rerun sales.

Some innovations that the established networks had the potential to develop also came from outside. For example, MTV, a network bringing music records to video, was invented not by CBS (which at the time was the world's largest broadcaster and owned the world's largest record company) but by an independent group. MTV also underscored the broadening geographic scope of industries, for it aimed to deliver its product worldwide right from the start and geared programming to that end, rather than simply sell reruns of U.S. programs.

Shifting industry conditions, technological advances, and political events around the world have caused so much change pressure on organizations in the last decades that it is hard to imagine a time when organizations were considered closed systems and studied only in terms of their internal structures and operations. Yet appreciation of the "environment" of organizations as an essential ingredient in understanding their shape and form, their successes and failures, did not become part of the lore of Western management until the late 1960s and 1970s. Businesses practiced "competitive strategy" long before the term became widely used in the early 1980s, and legions of consultants learned to identify ways to gain advantage in particular industries under particular conditions. Finally it became clear to scholars and analysts, as it was becoming clear to leaders and managers, that organizational success depended on a variety of forces outside of the direct control of the organization.

Multiple Environments: Does It Help to Diversify?

"Natural selection" and even "resource dependency" best describe the world of small organizations. Small and less powerful organizations are indeed buffeted by the winds of fortune. The situation is quite different, however, for organizations that become large and powerful. They can sometimes use their power to force other organizations in their environment to meet their terms. Furthermore, there are clear limitations to biological analogies applied to organizations, especially larger ones. Organizations can cut off parts, combine with others, or live in several environments—and this is indeed part of their survival strategy, one way they cushion themselves against being forced to change because of macro-evolutionary processes.

Economic theories of market power emphasize collusive or general market power. If an organization exists in many environments and engages in many activities, it can dominate its environment rather than be dominated by it. Diversification into several fields is thus a choice made by some organizations, supposedly in the interests of "survival of the fittest." "Diversification" was routinely advised by experts in the 1970s. It was said to reduce uncertainty about the firm's viability and ultimate survival and weaken the power of any one set of customers, suppliers, and labor unions (Donaldson and Lorsch, 1983).

But recent research showed that this strategy can be risky, particularly in volatile environments, and it does not necessarily aid survival or insulate an organization from dependence on the environment. A series of studies by Cynthia Montgomery and colleagues found that highly diversified firms had lower market shares in their respective markets than less diversified firms, and when they diversified, they did not enter the most profitable markets. Perhaps they did gain economies of scope from diversifying—but that was more likely to come from engaging in related activities. One study of the ownership in 1982 of 434 large acquisitions made by publicly traded U.S. firms between 1967 and 1969 found that the majority were still held by acquiring firms, though unrelated acquisitions resold at a moderately higher rate (Montgomery and Wilson, 1986). Another study found that unrelated acquisitions were sold at much higher rates than related ones (Porter, 1987). And related acquisitions had greater total dollar gains than unrelated acquisitions (Singh and Montgomery, 1987). On the flip side, firms that divested tended to be weak performers when compared with their industry counterparts, whether divesting for strategic, tactical, or crisis (distress) reasons. Tactical or distress divesters did so as a direct means to improve financial standing, whereas strategic divesters used it as an occasion to reassess firm strategy—which often leads to the stock market's positive reevaluation. Divestment was a last-resort option.

In short, the evidence was accumulating that organizations gain staying power from relatedness, not from diversification—from strength in a particular area and environment, not from hedging their bets by participating in many fields. By the 1990s, "focus" had replaced "diversification" as the advice experts gave to businesses. "Focus" was fashionable as well as economically rational.

Even with focus, organizations participate in diverse environments simply by virtue of their geographic extent (operations in more than one region or country) and internal differentiation of functions (staff that belong to varied professional communities), whether they are in a single industry or many industries. The more complex the organization, the larger the number of contexts in which it operates simultaneously, because of the many networks in which parts of the organization participate. The finance department may in effect operate in a different environment from the research and development group, because they each have different external, interorganizational ties and varying information or resource needs. Certainly in a multinational company the French division may face a very different local environment from the Korean, or the Canadian from the Pakistani. And product or market diversity multiplies the number of environments.

These multiple environments exacerbate the forces for change by pulling the organization in many directions. *Which* environment should it "fit"? Or which environment should it favor, to maximize success prospects? To which standards, from which network, should it conform? Multinational corporations, for example, must not only reconcile the benefits of local tailoring with those of global standardization in products and in strategies but must also face the organizational dilemma of choosing between local or standardized organizational patterns. Within each country are pulls toward similarity in organizational structures and processes regardless of the preference of the distant parent corporation from some other part of the world, induced by the interorganizational linkages sustained by each subunit. Thus, there are contradictory sets of pulls: those from the parent-dominated multinational organization, and those from local organizational fields (Westney, 1988; Bartlett and Ghoshal, 1989). A change pressure, then, from a local environment may reverberate throughout the organization. Organizations may not be able to mount sufficient defenses to protect themselves against all the emergent changes forced upon them from their many environments.

In general, macro-evolutionary change derives from the sweeping forces of history and the shifting populations of organizations and activities that put pressure on any one organization to adapt or innovate. This force for change is largely external; it comes from how *other* organizations behave. But there are also forces for change that come from within, deriving from the very nature of organizations.

Life Cycles, "Growth," and Organic Change Pressures

The Banc One case illuminates the connection between external and internal change.

The successful innovation and steady profitability of Banc One Corporation, especially during almost two decades of turbulence in the financial services industry in the United States, is enviable. Its success can be attributed to its anticipation of environmental shifts, making changes to carve out and protect a valuable niche, transforming itself in the process. Its external success created internal growth management dilemmas. Over a thirty-year period, Banc One changed from an obscure local branch banking system in Columbus, Ohio, and its rural surroundings, heavily reliant on manual technologies, to a technology and product pioneer with a sophisticated network of major banks in five Midwestern states and Texas, with an organization honored for its excellent financial performance and technology leadership.

Banc One's bold moves would lead an observer to think that its leaders had a crystal ball telling them how the environment would change. Consider these examples. Years before American banking regulations changed to allow nonbanks to offer comparable financial products, John Fisher, Banc One's marketing guru, testified before Congress carrying a bogus issue of the *Wall Street Journal* he had had made up with the prescient headline, "Sears Enters Financial Services." The original Columbus bank changed its name to "Banc One" and registered that name in every state in America well before interstate banking was permitted. The company saw the potential of computers to transform banking and invested heavily in state-of-the-art data processing systems. It experimented with automatic teller machines well before others did. And Banc One created partnerships with other firms outside of banking to provide new financial products at a time when banks still operated as isolated, independent local entities. Thus, when environmental forces led to consolidation through takeovers of smaller entities by larger ones, Banc One was ready to be the swallower rather than the swallowee.

But mastering macro-forces was not the only emergent change challenge Banc One faced during this period. Each stage in its growth brought new questions and new pressures to change the organization itself. Some of the changes Banc One was forced to make dealt not with the external environment but with its internal one. Certainly each foray into a new activity raised questions about what to preserve and what to change, in terms of people, operating practices, organizational structure, overall culture, and values. As the banking environment changed, the population of banks changed, and the species, as represented by survivors like Banc One, mutated and evolved—macro-evolutionary change.

At the same time, growth dynamics also forced another kind of evolution—micro-evolutionary change—involving the life cycle of the bank as an organism in its own right. Banc One was getting older. It was getting larger. What are the implications of this kind of emergent change? What forces for change are set in motion simply by the "growth" of organizations?

For Banc One, organizational aging led to succession questions, as the people who had created the new Banc One identity let go of the reins of power; this inevitable change of leadership produced other changes in strategy and direction. Few organizations are able so to institutionalize their practices that they can avoid change when people pass on and are replaced by others. The addition of new people and new banking units also led to unforeseen internal pressures that had little to do with how Banc One dealt with the marketplace.

Questions of corporate culture arose as "newcomers" became a larger and larger part of Banc One; would "we" (the core bank) become more like "them"? How should this kind of growth be handled? Banc One had to focus on values, defining both a culture that could be transmitted to newcomers and a method for doing so, leading to structural innovations like a corporate education center, Banc One College.

Then the organization attained a size that forced structural changes, because it became impossible for all the banks to report directly to top management. A state holding company structure was developed, with a state president located between local presidents and top leaders. Size produced organizational complexity, and the complexity forced managerial changes that brought their own new dilemmas—more steps in the decision-making process, more loops in the communication chain. Aging led to other questions, as once-state-of-the-art infrastructure began to rust and crumble, leading to questions of whether to fix it or to invest in new systems.

Banc One *sought* to grow in size, scope, and geographic extent, as part of its strategy. But even organizations that would like to remain stable find that change is forced upon them by their own aging process. Life does not stand still. There is momentum within organizations as they get older and grow larger, and as the people within them pass on.

Growing in Age and Size: Models of Life Cycle Change from Entrepreneurial Startup to Mature Organization

The concept of "growth" is often used to refer to changes in both age and size. Of course, at startup small size and youth are often correlated, but each has slightly different effects on the life of an organization. Organizational *age* involves accumulated experience—how much needs to be invented versus how much is "given" by tradition and therefore often done unthinkingly whether it fits the situation or not. *Size* involves how much a given structure can handle, and thus changes in size force the organization to cope with a new set of circumstances. Furthermore, it is also important to distinguish size and *complexity*—sometimes correlated, sometimes not; an organization can get bigger up to a point without getting more complex. Complexity forces change more powerfully if it adds nonidentical units, such as a new kind of department. And complexity through variety can come without much change in size. A fourth set of pressures derives from the *rate* of growth—how fast the organization gets larger and more complex. Rapid growth causes acute change problems and management dilemmas.

Organizational life cycle change pressures are clearest at the beginning, as new organizations add people and units. Many companies, when young and small, have a simple structure and operate by informal hands-on control, with the founders occupying multiple roles and making decisions themselves. If the organization grows, it needs to divide into functions involving the addition of department managers, to whom responsibility is delegated. As it develops competence, it can create new products or services; variety in products can lead to a multidivisional structure. The history of many industrial firms shows this pattern. In essence, the trajectory of "growth" involves increasing complexity, requiring changes in structure and process—such as more delegation, formalization of rules and procedures, and eventually mechanisms for integration across different businesses or areas of activity.

One often-cited model posits five typical evolutionary phases as organizations develop from entrepreneurial startups to mature organizations, each terminated by a "revolution," a crisis involving leadership and control (Greiner, 1972). Phase one is called *creativity;* the organization is small, informal, and entrepreneurial. In phase two, *direction,* supervisors appear. *Delegation,* phase three, establishes indirect control through management layers, rules, and procedures. Phase four, *coordination,* involves a formal balance between centralized and decentralized activities. Finally, *collaboration* is based on teams and informal structures with sophisticated and interpersonally skillful members in a highly supportive context.

Thus, as the organization grows—the "evolutionary" process—the system is strained. Perhaps the founding entrepreneur cannot handle administration, or standardizing operations to permit delegation produces too many rules and too little innovation. Such strains can lead to the "revolutionary" process of replacing leaders or changing the system.

Until recently, most theorists considered such transitions to be inevitable, especially in high-growth industries. But the experience of People Express Airlines in getting *big fast* challenges the conventional wisdom. In just two years, between its founding in April 1981 and June 1983, People Express became one of the largest airlines in the world. In the process, it experienced the external shocks and internal challenges that would prompt most organizations to reorganize. But Richard Hackman, a researcher who was also an insider as a People Express consultant, could find no "organizational transition" of the conventional sort. He noted, "Whenever times have been especially tough . . . the response has been the same: a rededication to the growth of the airline, greater efforts to sharpen and teach the precepts, and an increased commitment to the people of the airline" (Hackman, 1984).

Although some structural changes occurred at People Express, the organization and execution of work remained intact, and alternating cycles of evolution and revolution never happened. Nevertheless, stock market performance, operational performance as measured by load and cost, and employee attitudes were all strong. Hackman wondered if People Express had transcended conventional organizational development cycles—or if it had simply put off the inevitable and would eventually pay a high price for having deferred change for so long.

But with the hindsight of a few years later, perhaps life cycle theory has been vindicated after all, at least in identifying the common difficulties of a new organization making it over the hurdles on the way to becoming established. People Express was taken over by Texas Air Corporation in 1987 and disappeared. For People Express, there was no evolution and revolution—but also no survival.

Change Pressures for Young Organizations: Liabilities of Newness

The two most striking facts about new organizations are their high rates of formation, especially in countries with favorable climates for entrepreneurship, and their almost equally high rates of dissolution.

Startups face "liabilities of newness," which pressure them to grow and change, or die (Stinchcombe, 1965). There is a consistent finding that organizations are most likely to disintegrate in the first few years of existence (Aldrich and Auster, 1986). This phenomenon varies by industry. In manufacturing there is a steeper and faster decline in death rates if a company weathers its first few years than in service industries. Because services are labor-intensive rather than capital-intensive, marginal operations can hang on as long as their founders and employees choose to work. But mere survival in the short run does not necessarily produce the market penetration or market share that creates survival in the long run.

There is also evidence that smaller new firms dissolve at a higher rate than larger new firms, perhaps because they were too small to marshal the resources and managerial competence necessary to weather the early growth phase successfully. One study examined 1,903 new firms and then revisited 742 of them a year later (Cooper, Woo, and Dunkelberg, 1989). The larger startups were able to assemble more substantial resources from the beginning. Larger-company founders had more education, more management experience, and goals that were more managerial in nature; they brought in partners and relied more on external investors and professional advisers. After the first year, neither larger nor smaller companies were particularly troubled on the average, and there was considerable flux within firms in both groups. But though the surviving smaller firms had fewer administrative problems than the larger ones—which were growing through adding branches and locations—many more of the smaller firms had died even after this short time.

Small size creates problems almost regardless of age. The highest company dissolution rates have been found among organizations with fewer than twenty-one employees regardless of age; the rate of death of such small firms was higher than the rate for newly created organizations in any size category (Aldrich and Auster, 1986). Smaller organizations face liabilities that are exacerbated if they remain small. They can have trouble raising capital, bear a disproportionate share of the burden of regulation without being able to afford specialist staffs to deal with it, and be less attractive to employees because of limited training and careers. Of course, some of these liabilities can be balanced by advantages—exciting jobs, more challenge, and more chance to share in the financial returns—but even these advantages are often based on the assumption of eventual growth in size. Few people with the entrepreneurial spirit who desire challenging work form very small companies with the expectation that they will remain small forever. Professional organizations, such as law or consulting firms, are an exception, as are "life-style" businesses designed just to support the entrepreneur and his or her family.

New organizations, even larger ones, have a number of barriers to overcome, in both their external environments and their internal operations. Each barrier constitutes a force for change—adaptation, innovation, or disintegration. Foremost among these are barriers to entry into the marketplace; they must compete with existing products with brand recognition and market access. There are the costs of acquiring technology or lining up suppliers or distributors, who might already be committed to serving existing players; the networks and track records of established organizations give them an advantage. Licensing and regulation might be costly and can favor existing firms. Competitors can engage in shady dealings to keep new firms out.

A Japanese executive cataloged the extra hurdles faced by newer, smaller companies: difficulties in recruiting high-level professional managers because of the problems small, margin-squeezed companies have meeting high salary requirements; lack of formal management skills; lack of resources for developing new technologies; disadvantages in negotiating with much larger companies to which small ones are often subcontractors, especially in Japan;

and higher costs of capital because bank loans for small businesses might be at high individual rates, not business rates (Tajika, 1991). The president of a German midsize equipment manufacturer similarly observed that smaller companies in Germany lack the safety net of government protection afforded to large companies, because their large employment base gives them political clout. He also pointed to disadvantages small companies face in international negotiations, including anonymity outside of its country and industry, which could make it harder to attract venture partners. And, he said, "We don't get red-carpet treatment at hotels and airports" (Heintz, 1991).

Furthermore, institutions that confer legitimacy—from government agencies to the press to informal public opinion—can resent the threat to tradition posed by upstarts or might not understand the new organization, especially if it is not only new but *different* as well. The limited experience of new entrants can cause fumbles. Then there are the internal liabilities: the need for creation and clarification of roles and structures consistent with external constraints, and the problem of attracting qualified employees to an uncertain venture without established career paths (Aldrich and Auster, 1986).

Each of these barriers can be overcome, and the external environment can itself shift to favor entrepreneurs and upstarts over established organizations. Witness the venture capital boom in the United States beginning in 1978, when deregulation of major industries made room for startups, the growth of entrepreneurial education programs and magazines to spread experience quickly, and the glorification of entrepreneurs as cultural heroes. This favorable institutional environment makes it easier to get capital, customers, and legitimacy. But still, the need to face and resolve each startup handicap pushes newer organizations to change regardless of the strategic intent of their founders.

Hence, there is a growth imperative for new ventures; it is especially important to gain market share quickly to attract resources and legitimacy. But getting big enough fast enough creates a series of management dilemmas.

Hypergrowth

Extremely rapid growth strains the capacity of an organization and creates a set of common problems. These problems have become well known in the high-technology world of the computer industry. Technological possibilities (starting with the development of the microprocessor in the early 1970s), capital availability, and hungry markets led to a large number of startups growing very rapidly and, in some cases, out of control. Both Osborne and Apple were hypergrowth computer companies founded in California's Silicon Valley in the late 1970s, and both encountered a set of cycles that can destroy the very basis for early success. Apple overcame these to grow and prosper as a world leader in personal computers, but Osborne failed and died after only two years of rapid growth. The cycles can be fatal unless the organization changes significantly.

1. *The early success trap.* Early success is the trigger for hypergrowth, and it certainly provides a morale boost. The morale boost quickly leads to an assumption of the infallibility of leaders, which sets two other forces in motion. First, there is a suspension of criticism, which results in a failure to question and critique decisions and a rejection of performance feedback from the outside world—a "we know better than the market" attitude. Second, the assumption of infallibility can lead the company to go "up a notch" in terms of strategy, as Apple did in naming IBM in TV commercials around 1984. It takes on more formidable competitors and neglects the niche that provided the initial foothold. This results in marketplace competition with powerful competitors that can beat it—thereby undermining the early success.

2. *Volume pressure.* A number of factors push companies with an early success to seek high volume quickly, as Osborne Computer did. These include a low-price strategy, a need to support the learning curve by increasing scale, and an order avalanche caused by market demand. But pressure to produce-and-ship in large volume quickly leads to a neglect of quality. When quality declines, returns of defective products increase, which results in a high cost of correction—thereby producing even more pressures for high volume to spread costs over more units. Neglecting quality also leads to continual tinkering to improve it, which creates instability in the produce model, which means that the company cannot gain efficiencies in production at this scale—thereby reinforcing volume pressures to get still greater scale.

3. *The need for capital.* Rapid growth consumes a great deal of capital. The need for capital often has two consequences. It often creates a premature pressure to go public, which was certainly one of the reasons Osborne failed. Public offerings divert management energy and attention away from the product and the market. Lack of attention can lead to product/market problems, which can create dissatisfied customers and bad press with other capital sources, which exacerbates the need for capital. Then, internally, the need for capital pushes the company toward immediate sales, which can lead to premature product announcements or introductions. This happened with Apple as well as software firms like Lotus and Ashton-Tate. If carelessly thought-through product introductions fail, capital needs again go up. If they are successful, the second product may cannibalize the company's first. In either case, the need for capital because of growth causes hasty decisions with unintended consequences.

4. *The hiring of professional managers.* Birth of the new organization by committed amateurs means that jobs outgrow the first staff hired, which tends to lead to the hiring of professional managers. This very solution, however, can create two kinds of problems. Because the professionals need to be oriented, decision-making may take longer, and the amateurs are often tempted to take back control (therefore bearing all the costs but getting none of the benefits of the professionals). The professionals also want to introduce their professional management tools, which appear to the original employees like bureaucratic constraints—thereby undermining morale and commitment.

5. *The need for passionate commitment.* The uncertainty surrounding the organization, coupled with its founding by committed amateurs, tends to result in a preference for "vision" and passionate commitment. This means a fast-growth company is likely to attract egomaniacs. Indeed, the management sage Peter Drucker once observed that the successful entrepreneur is a "monomaniac with a passion." Egomaniacs, however, are unwilling to relinquish control, which can result in a failure of teamwork and an undermining of the company's ability to coordinate across areas to produce results in a timely and cost-effective fashion.

6. *Innovation dilemmas.* The need for innovation in order to keep products current is coupled with an inability to forecast market demand or production time (because of the lack of an experience base when pursuing innovation). This, in turn, results in slipped schedules—as well as customer discontent.

Hypergrowth puts an organization on a collision course, where it is all too easy to crash. Osborne Computer faced these problems at startup, when the liabilities of newness were too great to overcome. There were competitors in the marketplace already serving customer needs; suppliers were not dependent on Osborne's success for their own; and investors had alternatives from its beginning (Osborne and Dvorak, 1984). Apple, on the other hand, had advantages that offset the liabilities of newness: position as the innovator and market leader for its unique product, a slightly longer period in which to establish problem-solving mechanisms, a coalition of initial investors that included professional managers on the Board of Directors committed to the success of the company. But still, Apple's struggles to cope with the life cycle problems of its early, entrepreneurial period led to a political battle for control (the third change force, to be discussed later in this chapter). John Sculley, a professional manager, ousted cofounder Steven Jobs (Sculley, 1987; Morritz, 1984; Kanter, 1989).

The traps and tragedies of hypergrowth illuminate in heightened form some change dilemmas faced by all organizations that increase their size quickly. Established companies that grow suddenly through acquisition may face many of the same problems. The acquiring company managers feel like conquering heroes and are tempted into the same kind of arrogance as the entrepreneurs who start a wildly successful firm. In order to pay the costs of the acquisitions or to service the debt, they push for volume, inducing the same kind of sloppiness apparent at Osborne; and their needs for capital may distract the attention of top management away from fixing operating problems. The bankruptcy of several major retail chains in the United States or the financial distress of Hooker in Australia illustrates these dynamics.

Rapid growth poses a particularly difficult challenge of change. The entrepreneurial energy responsible for the company's early success can also get in the way of solving the problems of coordination, routinization, and control at the larger size. Leaders must retain the elements of the original model that are responsible for the organization's success and simultaneously make changes that accommodate its larger size, complexity, and rate of growth. The founder and chairman of Nichols Institute, a California-based medical testing company that doubled in size and added new kinds of business between 1988 and 1990, decided that further growth would necessitate the addition of professional managers, the development of managerial talent from within, constant review of the organization structure, the development of a clear transition process to integrate acquisitions, and a pause in the growth strategy whenever the organization itself threatened to get out of control.

Can Growth Be Managed?

One question plaguing managers and management researchers alike is whether the spirit and zest of the early, entrepreneurial stage can be retained as organizations make the transition away from being new, young, or small. The answers from history and theory have been pessimistic.

Max Weber, for example, the great German social theorist, proposed that the entrepreneurial or "charismatic" phase of an organization's history was inherently unstable. Soon, he inferred from his reading of history, the functions of the charismatic founder must be divided among two kinds of leaders, an administrator and an "agitator"—or, in our terms, a visionary. Eventually the rationality and systems of the administrator would prevail, with the regularity and predictability of bureaucracy driving out the innovative spirit of the founding era. Some organizations attempt to overcome this inevitability of bureaucracy through the "routinization of charisma" in rituals, ceremonies, or myths that imbue every succeeding leader with some of the mystique of the founder (Kanter, 1972), but this seems to be only a way of postponing the inevitable triumph of administrative systems.

Not only will bureaucracy prevail, other lines of theory predict, but as the organization grows and ages, it becomes riddled with splits that threaten commitment to the overarching founding vision. The differentiation of functions and lines of business brought about by growth in size creates diverging interests and perspectives, which make it harder and harder to act with a common purpose. One result is "suboptimization," the tendency for each subunit to commit to differing sets of goals and standards, which become more important to them than the goals and objectives of the whole organization. Indeed, human territoriality—the tendency to identify with one's own local group—or a belief in the value of "competition" can lead some organizations to engage in internal conflicts and rivalries that deflect attention from achieving the larger purposes of the whole (Kanter, 1989, Chapter 3).

Furthermore, both aging and enlarging present another inevitable dynamic: the addition of new people, either as replacements for those who leave or as additions to accommodate growth. Pessimists hold that the integration of newcomers has to dilute the organization's original spirit and purpose, unless the organization can become a "total institution" which attempts a thorough job of remaking newcomers in the old mold. Of course, newcomers are a potential source of enrichment via new intelligence brought from the outside (recent training or experience in another organization) or through innovations that they intentionally or unwittingly spawn. But they are also a potential threat to established activities because of their inexperience, their ignorance of traditions and routines, and their lack of relationships. Deciding how to treat newcomers is a major issue as organizations grow. Should the organization try to suppress their potential deviance through thorough education and control, or should it use newcomers to acquire a new perspective? Either way, the organization must accommodate. Regardless of the official choice, growth issues produce forces for change.

The contrast between Hewlett-Packard and Wang Laboratories, two similar high-tech companies, is instructive in this regard. H-P mastered growth dilemmas; Wang fumbled them (Kanter, Kellner-Rogers, and Bowersox, 1982).

Hewlett-Packard was founded before World War II as a manufacturer of electronic test equipment; it had a major growth spurt in the 1960s due to wide product diversification. With rapid growth came decentralization of operations along product lines, internationally. Each product division was designed to operate like a separate business with its own family of products, R&D facilities, manufacturing facilities, and marketing and administrative staffs—an approach that helped H-P grow to 40,000 employees and 4,000 product lines by the early 1980s. H-P wanted to grow in order to maintain its technological leadership and attract the best people, but it also wanted to "stay small" and avoid having more than 2,000 staff in one site—a desire shared by employees who were convinced that more people than this "dehumanized" the workplace. In the early 1980s, the company accommodated these seemingly contradictory goals by growing through the splitting off of new divisions instead of by letting existing ones get bigger.

The split was a carefully conceived and well-executed process, consistent with H-P philosophies. For almost two years, in anticipation of a split, internal organizational changes were initiated. Preparing for a split involved four steps:

1. *Staffing up.* The company would promote from within, train more supervisors and managers, and get them involved in coaching and training production employees. The company usually ran lean in management but deliberately violated this principle near the time of the split.
2. *Diversifying within the division.* H-P would create functional teams organized around particular product lines, and would give each its own identity as well as management. Production was divided into product A assembly, product B assembly, product A test, product B test, etc., and teams organized around individual products performed all steps in the process. The research labs were similarly split by product.
3. *Coordinating cross-functionally.* H-P would increase communication between research, engineering, and manufacturing for particular products, assigning dedicated personnel. It would also create inter-

functional project teams for new products, including marketing and manufacturing as well as engineering.

4. *Splitting*. Finally, H-P would move an intact set of product lines and people to a new plant.

In contrast, Wang Laboratories had no articulated strategy for growth even in 1981, well before the weaknesses in their product/market strategies appeared and the company incurred heavy losses. Founded in 1955 by a Chinese immigrant in Boston, Wang began in electronic testing and measurement but moved into the design and manufacture of electronic calculating machines. Growth was slow and steady until about 1970, when the advent of a new application of old technology caused a rapid increase in sales and profits. By 1982 there were more than 10,000 employees, all located primarily in one region, and the family was still the primary owner and source of top management. Wang had an informal atmosphere that felt vibrant and exciting, with changes taking place daily. A research team observed whole office layouts changing in the course of a week as people dismantled and erected walls like bees building hives, a process that made "growth" visible.

The implicit strategy was short-term and informal: stretch people to meet ever expanding job requirements, expand assignments, and subdivide jobs when people got overloaded. The personalized control of the founding family was maintained while functions were differentiated and product lines grew; the result was conflict and competition across functions. Long-service managers sought to retain as large a territory as possible and a privileged relationship with the chairman in the face of the introduction of outsiders and new management layers. Other area heads tried to enlarge their share of still-ambiguous arenas. Functions and divisions, especially newer ones, tended to operate as separate entities with their own principles and reward systems.

In contrast to Hewlett-Packard's orderly process for accommodating growth, Wang's approach was haphazard and divisive. By 1990 Hewlett-Packard had made a series of smart strategic moves, emerging as a sound survivor in a tough industry, while Wang was in deep crisis. Hewlett-Packard had the luxury that success brings of making further changes in its structure, reconsolidating to improve interdivisional coordination; Wang was scaling down its business and its aspirations under new, nonfamily management.

Maturity: Is Decline Inevitable?

The "last" life cycle stage is maturity, which often presages decline because the organization fails to adapt to changing external conditions. But is this inevitable? Must organizations get "senile"? At least two consequences of growth undermine an organization's capacity to change. First, organizational growth tends to induce greater needs for coordination. A frequent response is the proliferation of administrative functions, which often raises costs and lowers profitability. The ratio of administrative activities to direct production often increases as organizations get larger and older. One imperative for major corporations today is to eliminate such overhead without losing the ability to coordinate diverse activities (Kanter, 1989). Mature organizations have also had time to accumulate interests that benefit from preservation of the status quo. Key constituents often seek to preserve an established balance of claims on future revenue streams. They are aided in this quest by formal planning processes that seek to gain strong unified commitment. To question the existing direction is to undermine the collective commitment (Donaldson, 1990). This helps bolster the argument that only an outsider (as in a takeover attempt) can make or trigger fundamental change. Indeed, a recent study found that a new CEO or a new executive team is associated with subsequent performance improvements for organizations in turbulent environments (Virany, Tushman, and Romanelli, 1992).

There are constraints on top management's freedom to set strategic direction in the mature firm, which interfere with the organization's ability to change (Donaldson and Lorsch, 1983). To protect its competitive position, the enterprise must continue the rate of growth and investment dictated by its industry; there are capital market limits on the ability to retain earnings or use debt; and the need to attract people under a promotion-based reward system means the company must offer career opportunities and therefore expand. The company's belief in its distinctive competence also becomes entrenched, almost ritualistic and unexamined.

Liabilities of newness are more than matched by liabilities of age and size (Aldrich and Auster, 1986), though organizations that get old and large often have deep pockets and other weapons of the dominant with which to fight for survival. One of the problems of age is the dilemma of success. An organization can come to be too good at what it does to permit major innovation. The same capabilities—accumulated habits, skills, knowledge, technical systems, and values—that helped an organization succeed in the past can turn into "core rigidities"—deeply embedded knowledge sets that inhibit innovation (Leonard-Barton, 1992).

Age produces both internal and external handicaps regarding the ability to change, a kind of organizational hardening of the arteries. For example, there are pressures toward internal consistency as the basis for coordination and control, which stifles innovation. There can be a hardening of vested interests and an unwillingness to accept change that threatens them. People might start to think so much alike that they cannot even see alternatives. Conformity grows because established companies tend to recruit those who are compatible, to socialize them, and then to formalize or standardize jobs. At the same time, interorganizational commitments—the guarantee to continue past practices—can produce inertia; suppliers want reliable orders, and customers want a predictable flow of goods. Institutional forces also militate against change—for example, protection by government or by laws and support by elites. Then, as a further irony, if by some miracle the organization does succeed in transforming itself, it could experience the liabilities of newness all over again.

Large and old organizations try to capture benefits of young and small ones by allying with them or emulating them (Aldrich and Auster, 1986). They might establish innovation or new venture units that experiment outside the firm's current strategic realm. But, as numerous examples show, the ability of big and old organizations to revitalize through relationships with young and small ones is limited. The problems when General Motors acquired Electronic Data Systems (reflected in a widely publicized conflict between GM's chief executive Roger Smith and EDS founder H. Ross Perot) were a vivid illustration. And new venture units have proved to be an unstable form, with little impact on an established company (Kanter, 1989, Chapter 8; Kanter *et al.*, 1990, 1992; Kanter and Richardson, 1991). Well-publicized new venture units such as Eastman Kodak and Alcan enjoyed only a brief existence as separate divisions; the mainstream companies housing them still faced renewal challenges in their core businesses.

Ironically, then, the aging of an organization as it proceeds through its life cycle both *causes* change, in early phases, and then ultimately helps to *retard* change. However, the life cycle image takes us only so far, because organizational death is not inevitable. Renewal is possible, though major transformation often amounts to a makeover that leaves little of the original organization in place. Transformation will be explored in Chapter 3 of this book. But the lesson of this exploration of micro-evolutionary change is that leaders cannot afford to ignore the change pressures stemming from life cycle phases.

Political Conflicts and Economic Interests: The Struggle for Control

An organization is not a monolith; it consists of many sets of actors with divergent interests, preferences, and criteria for organizational goals and performance. There are many stakeholders with an interest in the output and benefits, both "inside" and "outside" the organization. Therefore "politics"—the interplay of interests—is a third force for emergent change.

Differences in values and interests among constituencies make it difficult for rational bureaucratic criteria that meet tests of universality and objectivity to prevail in the decision-making process. Political maneuvering is common, although it often occurs unobtrusively and in secret, via selective use of objective criteria, use of legitimate decision processes, and in secret or backstage (Pfeffer, 1977). Power, in turn, is a function of formal authority, resources controlled, or contingencies managed. It consists of lines of supply for resources, for information, and for support, which are in turn a function of location in the organization and network membership (Kanter, 1983).

Thus, politics is the jockeying for position that goes on as groups of individuals advance their own interests and make their own claim on the organization's resources. Such jockeying for position can result in revolutionary shifts in control, which may result in reallocation of resources or changes of organizational direction. The "official" leaders of the organization with the organization-shaping power are challenged in that power by a variety of latent and activated stakeholders, from unions to stockholders. These stakeholders can be viewed as adversaries by the current leaders of an organization, or they can be co-opted (included in the leadership coalition) and treated as potential allies. NCR, the global computer company, identifies five major stakeholders (shareowners, employees, customers, suppliers, and communities), and declares its intention to "create value" for all of them—thereby attempting to avoid power struggles.

Coalitions and Dominant Coalitions

Political models of organizations describe them variously as networks of restricted access where limited exchange opportunities and power imbalances are common; tools for multiple stakeholders, where interest groups bargain and clash; or settings where informal, parochial, and divisive behavior stimulates organizational change. The "official" direction of the organization is thus set by a "dominant coalition" in which power is temporarily concentrated (Thompson, 1967), but the alliance is a dynamic one, subject to perturbation and change. In this view, power is not determined solely by formal position but by agreements struck among stakeholders as interest groups. Indeed, organizations vary in the degree to which those with administrative responsibility in the official hierarchy hold actual power to make things happen. Even in the most bureaucratic organizations, in which officeholders do hold a monopoly of power, there is an undercurrent of bargaining, jockeying for position, and alliance formation that creates potential for change regardless of the organization's official strategy and stated direction.

Though the dominant coalition takes shape because its collective interest is relatively enduring, challenges to its preeminence and new claims to membership are ever present. Thus the political struggle is constant; issues can arise and disappear, challenges to power can succeed, and new groups can achieve prominence. At the same time, the desire of a dominant coalition to maintain its power may cause change or resistance to change in ways that do not benefit the organization as a whole. In traditional companies, the overriding goal of top management has generally been organizational survival, with self-sufficiency a close second. In one study, top executives gave priority to their company's ability to survive on the firm's own resources, if necessary, and their strategies reflected that priority: a balanced funds flow to avoid capital market interference; diversified product lines to free themselves from the competitive imperative of any single product market; internal labor markets to insulate themselves from volatile, mobile external markets (Donaldson and Lorsch, 1983). What self-sufficiency really means is *maintenance of power*.

Many things can upset the balance of power and change the composition of the dominant coalition. External events cause power shifts. For example, the election of Franklin D. Roosevelt led to labor law reform in the United States, which made unions a force in company decisions. Or events activate external constituencies—for example, the rise of conscientious institutional investors and pressure on American companies to divest holdings in South Africa. Or power-holders may exceed their mandate by violating standards—such as a Japanese financial executive causing public embarrassment for the company—thereby leaving a power vacuum. Or a changeover of leaders leaves a temporary opening for others to press their claims.

The politics of coalition formation are more salient when the underlying premises of the organization are unstable, as in a rapidly changing environment, uncertain markets, or the rewriting of rules of the game.

> A manager may well feel quite uncertain about what in fact is going on, and which individuals or groups will support his continued efforts to lead. . . . The identification and mobilization of potentially salient constituencies into a coalition that provides a stable base from which to launch a successful effort in the marketplace must be a dominant strategic focus. [Bower and Weinberg, 1988]

But the choice of coalition members brings biases, which create later problems. For example, when Frank Lorenzo acquired Continental Airlines and tried to revitalize it through bankruptcy, he chose as the key decision-making group not career airline employees or labor representatives but lawyers, former government officials, and financial specialists, all with considerable experience at dealing with government, the courts, and the entrepreneurial financial community. It is not surprising that its group would choose bankruptcy as a means to create change and undo previous commitments. One result was continuing labor strife, which took years to resolve—in part because labor was *not* represented in the dominant coalition.

In successful organizations, the size and shape of the dominant coalition can be a function of organizational imperatives and environmental contingencies, not just of a powerful chief executive's preferences. Leaders might have to co-opt into the coalition representatives of major interest groups; even though co-optation is considered a power move, it also broadens the decision-making body. This very process of including more voices in decisions is itself a force for further change. Summarizing a large number of studies, David Summers (1983) offered these propositions about dominant coalitions:

> The greater the sources of uncertainty for an organization, the larger the size of the dominant coalition and the more heterogeneous its composition. Those responsible for protecting the core technology when it is threatened and those in a position to obtain resources for an organization when resources are scarce will participate in the dominant coalition. For example, the likelihood of a boundary spanner joining the

> dominant coalition will increase considerably when the position allows exclusive access to and control over scarce resources.
>
> The concentration of resources within an organization will tend to reduce the size of the dominant coalition and make it more homogeneous.

Macro-evolutionary forces thus contribute to political dynamics. Environmental shifts change critical contingencies for the organization, such as the competitiveness of the core technology or the availability of resources to pursue goals. Similarly, life cycle forces create shifting political dynamics. As an organization grows, needs and goals change, and so do the groups wielding power. For example, in their early years many hospitals were dominated first by prominent figures in the community, then by physicians, and ultimately by administrators (Perrow, 1961). In the early phase of the life cycle, the dominant coalition tends to include those capable of securing the capital and legitimization necessary for the organization to establish itself; during the growth phase, technical and administrative skills are important; administrators grow even more prominent as organizations age.

POWER AND PRESERVATION PRESSURES

Political dynamics are forces for change, but they also produce inertia, especially for older organizations. For example, political factors can explain why some organizations seem to survive without high performance, becoming in effect "permanently failing organizations" (Meyer and Zucker, 1989). Consider this criticism of corporate inertia:

> Some corporations have a capacity for enduring (and rationalizing) persistently inferior financial performance over extended periods of time (a decade or more) before being provoked into a radical restructuring process. . . . Internal financial disciplines (and perhaps external as well) appear incapable of denying resources to a failing strategy until a genuine operational alternative is presented by those in control. [Donaldson, 1990]

Why don't organizations change when their performance declines? Among the explanations are exit barriers (to new ones); expectations of high future returns, making it worth continuing despite current poor performance; or noneconomic value assigned to the organization—as in family firms for which the survival of the organization has meaning beyond economic ends. Indeed, persistence and performance sometimes have different causes, and the interests of stakeholders may diverge, resulting in political actions to maintain organizations with only limited economic viability (Meyer and Zucker, 1989).

Thus, the motivation to maintain organizations may be much greater among *dependent* actors, who need the organization for an end other than wealth creation, than among owners or suppliers of capital, who value only economic performance. This motivation to preserve the organization can, in turn, serve to entrench current leaders, as stakeholders agree to support management in order to keep their jobs or their customers. As a consequence, management might make strategic choices designed not to produce high performance but to limit or offset the power of still other stakeholders. After observing the behavior of top management in many prominent companies, Gordon Donaldson, an expert on corporate finance—prone by discipline to believe in rationality—commented about the prevalence of irrational behavior serving political ends:

> The implementation of dominant strategic direction involves a complex structure of formal and informal contracts which act to perpetuate the strategy and which the initiating corporate leadership then find difficult or impossible to breach. It is unusual for the incumbent management to initiate major restructuring of its own strategic plans in the absence of a serious and visible threat to the long-term continuity of the corporate entity or of its leadership. When it occurs, the initial challenge is more likely to come from within the established corporate power structure than from the outside. Primary resistance to change comes from the constituencies who have the most to lose from a renegotiation of the claims structure and from the management whose power base depends on its ability to preserve the loyalty and commitment of the existing constituent groups. [Donaldson, 1990]

The ascendancy of various groups to power can make organizational leadership look like pendulum swings between dominant emphases. For example, when a marketing-oriented company led by people who focus solely on marketing begins to flounder, new players may come to power to reassert financial control, resulting in a control-oriented regime, which then tightens operations too much, leading to backlash, rebellion, and the rise of another marketing-oriented regime that will "restore" some of the emphasis of the past. Shifts in membership in organizational power elites can also reflect the impact of government action—changing laws and regulation (Fligstein, 1990).

Political factors often lurk behind strategic decisions—which faction, representing which interests, is "in" or "out of" the dominant coalition affects the company's direction. The Xerox story is instructive. Most people do not associate Xerox with the invention of the personal computer. Yet in 1973 Xerox scientists designed the Alto, the world's first personal computer; by 1976, they had completed a system of personal computing hardware and software not matched in the marketplace until eight years later. Notwithstanding the stated intentions of the Xerox chairman, who had given the scientists their mandate, company management chose not to commercialize the Alto, backing instead a more elaborate office system in which they lagged behind IBM and eventually Apple, though the scientists and their backers did not give up without a fight.

Was this neglect simply a matter of a misplaced bet? Analysts attributed it to power shifts within Xerox—the ascendancy of executives with financial backgrounds, numbers-oriented and nontechnical (Smith and Alexander,

1988). The dominance of financial interests in the leadership coalition reflected Xerox's state in the mid-1970s: a one-product virtual-monopoly bloated and complacent after more than a decade of unprecedented prosperity, yet facing competition and loss of market share for the first time with people at the helm who did not understand the particular technology and markets involved.

Power struggles, therefore, shape an organization's direction in profound ways. The costs are measured not just in time and effort but in strategic mistakes. The benefits come when political conflict allows more voices to be heard and innovation to appear.

Origins and Forms of Political Action

When do power dynamics move from underground ripples to visible revolts? When do organizations get embroiled in overt power struggles? There are several structural sources of political conflict. Stakeholder interests can diverge, thus producing tension and conflict. Winner-take-all situations with scarce resources and the potential to win or lose big create divisive competitions. Lack of a shared commitment due to weak leadership, absence of values, organizational heterogeneity, or sudden environmental shifts also sets the stage for political battles. And poor performance, which produces both a crisis of faith in current leaders and scarcity of resources, provoking the desire to seize one's share, makes an organization vulnerable to power plays.

Political struggles occur between groups as well as among individuals. Political movements within organizations arise at different levels, and their tactics and effects depend on the organizational location of the parties. Sociologists have identified three types (Zald and Berger, 1978).

First, the *coup d'état* is an infiltration of a small but critical group from within to depose existing leaders and install successors. This coup may reflect the personal ambition of individuals or the struggle of a coalition that has a new view of what the strategy should be. *Bureaucratic insurgency* involves a kind of innovation that defies authority—alterations of organizational processes or procedures at middle levels of the organization, though these changes have been explicitly denied by legitimate authorities. Even the most change-resistant organizations are fortunate to have such "innovation against the grain" as a source of improvement (Kanter, 1983). *Mass movements* are familiar in the form of unions; they are organizations of subordinates who press goals of their own, from expressing grievance to seizing power. Politics go underground in large corporate bureaucracies. There is a "push to conspiracy in corporate hierarchical forms" because of a concentration of power and authority; the limited influence of most participants over succession, policy-making, and work conditions; and the high costs of dissent.

People can marshal support for their power struggles through the use of both internal and external coalitions. But every political maneuver involves a concession. When Eastern Airlines was threatened by a machinists' union strike in early 1989, for example, management tried to enlist the pilots' union as an ally. But in creating this coalition for power purposes, management would also have to agree to changes benefiting the pilots. Soon the coalition fell apart.

The recent history of CBS News, once America's most successful broadcast news unit, illustrates politics out of control (Boyer, 1988), creating the opening for an entrepreneur to take over the company. Weakened by years of internal battles, CBS became vulnerable to a shrewd maneuver by Lawrence Tisch. There had been factions within the news organization for years with conflicting views, and the division as a whole was continually fighting with the rest of the company. In 1986 Tisch bought CBS stock and joined its board as a "white knight" protecting the company against Ted Turner's attempted takeover. Tisch was seen as a "folk hero" by the CBS News staff and as a friend by many of its powerful figures, such as Mike Wallace. The head of the news division openly blasted then-CEO Thomas Wyman; Wyman's response hardened Tisch's contempt. Wyman, concerned that Tisch was getting CBS at a bargain price in the wake of the Turner crisis, went to Coca-Cola to solicit an offer.

Meanwhile there was public turmoil at CBS News: Bill Moyers resigned (he made the cover of *Newsweek,* under the heading "Civil War at CBS"), and Dan Rather signed off his broadcasts with "courage." A rump meeting of the board without Tisch and Wyman was held the night before a regular board meeting and essentially decided everything: Coca-Cola was turned down, Wyman was out, and Tisch was made acting CEO. The head of the news division was fired, and the division celebrated.

Tisch then took power and used it. He cut, fired, and divested. A committee to find a new president led to open campaigning by candidates, especially one who cultivated Tisch while ignoring the fact that the staff actively disliked him. There were operations reviews, headcount reductions, and even drastically reduced United Way contributions.

> Suddenly CBS was a different company, and inside CBS the dreamy aura that had surrounded the return of Paley and the rise of Tisch quickly began to fade. People began to mull aloud some hard facts about Tisch's ascent, the most eye-opening being that he had taken over the company. True, it wasn't technically a takeover in the eyes of the regulatory agencies because Tisch hadn't gone beyond the 25% level in his acquisition of CBS stock. . . . He had indeed, as Wyman had warned, taken over the company at bargain-basement prices—twenty-three dollars a share less than Marvin Davis had offered, and forty-three dollars a share less than the Cole proposal. . . . [And] it began to dawn on people that Larry Tisch was doing precisely those things that had caused so much panic over the Turner takeover attempt—namely, dismantling the company. [Boyer, 1988, p. 322]

The news division that had celebrated Tisch's arrival was stunned when it was told to cut its budget by $50 million. An inevitable wave of firings soon followed, including twenty-year veterans like Ike Pappas, who discovered he was fired just before he was to be honored by his church. CBS News star Andy Rooney said at the time: "This guy Tisch put money in this company, but I put my life into the company, and so did Ike Pappas, and so did a lot of other people. I own that company, Tisch does not own that company, that's the way I feel. It's Ike's company more than it is Tisch's company" (Boyer, 1988, p. 328). Dan Rather tried taking the fight public (in a *New York Times* column); Walter Cronkite tried to have another rump session of the board called—but to no avail. Eventually Tisch's appointee as CBS News president tried to use cutbacks to temper Rather's power. Throughout this period, CBS News's ratings were declining.

The struggle among stakeholders was demoralizing and costly. Politics diverted attention and resources from production.

Before uncritically adopting a political perspective, however, let us remember that political models of organizations are very cynical. They deal with personal ambition or the desire of groups to protect and advance their own. They view people as promoting only their own interests instead of acting responsibly as agents of the organization. Indeed, agency theory in economics has arisen to account for the problems that emerge between "principals" (those who "own" the organization in a legal sense) and the "agents" on whom they rely to carry out their intentions (Pratt and Zeckhauser, 1985). Lawrence Tisch would undoubtedly argue that his actions were for the good of CBS as a whole, bringing necessary change resisted by entrenched interests.

The "Upside" of Politics: Conflict as a Positive Factor in Change

Conventional management wisdom held the very idea of "power and politics" in disrepute. Politics was considered a disruptive force, interfering with the organization's ability to pursue its objectives (meaning, of course, the objectives of the current dominant coalition). But recently, examination of organizations that have successfully adapted to new conditions has given credit to one kind of politics: *constructive conflict*.

Successful companies, the argument goes, are always a little off balance. Leaders deliberately provoke *dis*equilibrium to challenge people to argue for new ideas and new possibilities. Resources are not permanently assigned to one group or another; each must bargain for them in a marketplace of ideas. Innovative companies often encourage multiple experiments and open arguments (Kanter, 1983). Ford and Honda are two of the companies said to be characterized by continual, productive conflict (Pascale, 1990)—mostly between departments and divisions, but also to some extent between the organization and such key stakeholders as suppliers or labor. People are struggling not for political position (such as occurs in CEO succession battles) but for commitments to innovation.

Innovation is itself an intensely political process. New ideas always cut across the grain of established interests, and thus they always involve a portion of conflict—conflict over alternative uses for resources, conflict between the proponents of change and the advocates of no change—which inevitably also advances the interests of one group over another. A large part of the job of corporate entrepreneurs who produce innovations is to lobby for support for the power to make the changes the innovation requires. Organizations with higher rates of innovation make it easier for people to challenge the established allocation of resources and divert them or attract them to their causes (Kanter, 1983). Thus, political debate is tacitly encouraged in such organizations, as long as it serves to create positive action—not blockage—and potential improvements in the organization's offerings or functioning. While politics for the sole sake of personal gain is discouraged, competition in ideas is supported.

Several factors are necessary to make this sort of political process a constructive rather than a destructive force. The "interests" at play in this kind of power struggle are defined by ephemeral task identification, not by permanent group affiliation. The benefits received by the "winners" are not significantly greater than those the "losers" will get from continuing organizational membership, and today's losers may have the chance to join the winning team tomorrow. There is an assumption of shared values overall, with conflicts reflecting differences over tactics, not ultimate ends.

But even so, the politics involved in arguments over innovation—in essence, over the direction of change—have been known to split organizations at their core every bit as badly as political battles between labor and management have hurt some traditional manufacturing companies. In one computer company, political factions formed around commitments to a particular technology, with each interest group struggling for a larger share of the resources to pursue a technological path. The groups used classic political techniques: lobbying for support with the board of directors, threatening disruptive actions, sabotaging the other group's experts, and sending spies into the other camp. Ultimately a number of key staff left the company, taking knowledge of their technology to a competitor.

Leaders must walk a fine line, then, in ensuring that political dynamics are above-ground and constructive. They must ensure that the clash of ideas does not result in the formation of hard-and-fast groupings unable to identify with a larger shared vision. Some Japanese companies are known for their skill at this kind of constructive politics. Canon in Japan was revitalized through an innovation that resulted from deliberately created internal turbulence. Its successful development of a personal copier stemmed from constructive conflict between task forces producing new concepts and established divisions wedded to the status quo (Nonaka and Yamanouchi, 1989).

Overall, then, political struggles seem most destructive when only personal ambitions or narrow interests are involved, when the battle is over the reins of power or the size of one's slice of the pie, and there is no productive purpose—new initiative, positive innovation—to be served. But conflict, if it produces new ideas and new possibilities, can be a force for positive change.

Integrating the Forces

The three macro-forces interact in various ways, as we have already seen. An organization's position in its environment, combined with its life cycle stage, tends to set the framework for politics and enables certain kinds of leaders to gain power. The type of leader and the interests he or she represents then account for choices about perceiving and adapting to environmental forces. And as environments change, leaders are replaced.

For example, at birth organizations tend to favor "dreamers," particularly when they are innovating in new niches. As the niche gets more crowded, however, and as the organization grows in size and complexity, dreamers tend to give way to "organizers." Sometimes the replacement occurs after political actions such as *coups d'état,* like the boardroom coup in which Steve Jobs, the cofounder of Apple Computer, was deposed by John Sculley, an organizer. At the same time, the desire for power on the part of leaders often creates a growth imperative, a fervor to build an empire. Incentives might reward this concern for power by pegging pay to the size of a staff or the magnitude of assets under control, as in a prominent corporate compensation system used by U.S. and British companies; such incentives value position over organizational performance and may thus contribute to stagnation and decline.

The history of change in older industries such as railroads, steel, or chemicals reflects just this interplay of life cycle effects (organizational aging) bringing inertia and conservatism; power dynamics (the struggle between management and labor over shares of the spoils) deflecting attention from product innovation and quality; and environmental shifts (new technology, niche size widening to include foreign competitors, and suppliers and customers changing their own strategies) eventually producing industry upheaval, crisis, and consolidation.

Such an interplay of macro-dynamics forms a "creative cycle of business revitalization" (Fruhan, 1987, 1985). First, as a single-product business matures, it might raise pay, giving up profitability to the workforce (labor and/or management) over time as a result of political bargaining. This occurs in part because its leaders assume that everyone else will meet prevailing wage standards—an isomorphism assumption compatible with institutional theory. Then, because of environmental dynamism, a new player enters the business at some point, often from outside the current organizational field, with a lower cost structure. In most cases, the new entrant will be a winner, because the old competitor cannot be competitive even by imitating the newcomer with a replication strategy, because of internal politics and the reluctance of vested interests to give up territory and because of other organizational rigidities in the established player caused by age itself. Labor sometimes fights an existing competitor harder than a new entrant if there is a history of conflict, and closing costs on existing facilities can outweigh the tax benefits of a writeoff of old assets to an existing competitor. Finally, in response to declining profitability, the old player diversifies, as U.S. Steel did, and threatens to shed the old business, which is either fixed or divested. Such a cycle led U.S. Steel to exit from much of its steel-making, becoming USX.

Thus, new organizations enter, and old ones either die off or change form dramatically. The result is a new industry environment, with a different set of players, new interorganizational networks, and different balances of power inside the organizations.

Mastering Emergent Change: Lessons for Leaders

Detailing the three sources of emergent change helps leaders view the larger context in which they are trying to carry out their strategic intentions. Leaders must manage *context* as well as *content*. Even while leaders are formulating tangible goals, forces in the environment are pushing an organization to change, sometimes in unwanted or contradictory directions. And life cycle and political dynamics within the organization are creating still other problems to solve. Leaders must scan the environment, monitor emergent change, and check the appropriateness of actions against the actions of all those groups inside and outside the organization—stakeholders, sources of legitimacy, interest groups, organizations in their network—that represent forces for change through their own motion, or roadblocks to it.

Organizations are human creations, human instruments designed to realize specific purposes through coordination of the combined efforts of many people. "Will" and "intention" are thus central to the idea of organizations. But while official, legally recognized decision-makers try to direct the affairs of an organization so that it will realize its purposes, events and activities far outside the control or even the knowledge of leaders may cause chaos. The story of change must begin with an understanding of major forces propelling and compelling organizational change.

As the twentieth century draws to a close, the macro-forces that provoke evolutionary change are more challenging for leaders and, ***ultimately, are more important factors in the success of their organizations, than the guidance of specific projects that often goes under the banner of "managing change."***

All forces are in motion simultaneously, and they reinforce one another. As technology permits faster travel and communication, and as many countries redefine their borders and their economic relationships, the "environment" for organizations is activated. Industry categories are being redefined, resource flows are being redirected, new networks of companies are being created, and environmental interest groups are more vocally pressing their demands. A more activated environment exaggerates life cycle phenomena.

More organizations can form, and for those that "catch on" trajectories of growth are faster than in more quiescent environments, as we have seen in the computer industry. At the same time, the worldwide competition for resources exacerbates the failings of mature organizations in mature or consolidated industries, making it harder for noncompetitive organizations to survive. Finally, organizational life easily becomes more politicized, as order and consensus decline. Power struggles may become more visible if not more common, as personal ambition soars all over the world, as the rise and fall of organizational fortunes make control struggles more common, and as interest groups press their claims.

Organizational life is shaped by sweeping historical forces with a momentum of their own. Only if these forces are well understood can organizations and their leaders master emergent change. Inertia and resistance to change come not only from within an organization—from prior investments and sunk costs, the conservatism of people or the desire to protect one's turf—but from without, from environments that reinforce familiar patterns. Leaders must monitor and scan the environment to seize opportunities for change while recognizing that vested interests inside and outside may want to prevent change or use it to their advantage.

The first requirement for mastering the macro-forces is awareness of the change dynamics themselves. While making specific, ongoing operational decisions, leaders can also prepare the organization for the consequences of emergent change. By anticipating the trajectory of change, they can make early investments in preparedness—for example:

Environmental Shifts

- Looking at new players in the industry as well as established competitors
- Scanning the world for substitutes or replacements for the products or services they provide
- Watching the actions of critics, challengers, and interest groups to identify emergent needs, gaps, and weaknesses
- Identifying clearly the strengths (core skills or competences) of the organization and investing to maintain them

Organizational Growth

- Building the infrastructure for size changes while still small
- Hedging on fixed capacity compared with variable or flexible capacity, in anticipation of declines

Power and Politics

- Revisiting organizational purpose to reaffirm the consensus under which the dominant coalition governs
- Making provision for leadership succession
- Reexamining distribution of the benefits of organizational membership to ensure they are perceived as fair and adequate
- Including representatives of emergent interests in the leadership coalition

Mastery of emergent change involves preemptive strikes as well as passive anticipation. Leaders can attempt to influence the larger system in which they operate in order to gain a favorable position for their organizations in bargaining for resources or legitimacy. Some organizations seem to "outwit" fate by innovating in ways that change the terms of competition while seeking rules that favor themselves (as American Airlines did with both its computerized reservation system and the world's first frequent flyer program, and as it attempted to do in lobbying the U.S. government for high industry wage and work standards). Some use their capacity to enter another industry, thus enlarging the arena in which they compete, and ensuring that they will survive in some form even if their parent industry shakes down (as Benetton did by entering financial services or AT&T did by converting its telephone credit card to an all-purpose charge card). Still others create networks that generate pooled advantages in controlling more resources (like the Japanese ***keiretsu*** described in Chapter 7), and as many European airlines are attempting to do by forming alliances to position themselves as powerful players when economic unity becomes a reality). In short, it is important to "manage" the larger system, the larger network of which the organization is a part, through innovations in products, markets, and relationships.

Emergent change calls for strong leaders who can accumulate and exert power—thus mastering the political process in order to master the other forces for change. Political factors are prominent sources of organizational inertia, preventing organizations from responding to emergent change until it is too late. Other organizations can prevent one's own from changing because of their own vested interests in the status quo; the chairman of Monsanto has blamed lawyers and regulators for high product liability costs and the fear of litigation that discourages investment in new product innovation, for example. Suppliers or customers, who have made their own commitments based on expectations of continuity, can exit when faced with abrupt change. Vested interests inside, eager to protect their territory, can similarly prevent change. And when the consensus that permits the dominant coalition to govern is a fragile one, leaders can be reluctant to raise the specter of change lest the delicate leadership balance fall apart.

An activated environment ought to favor the survival of organizations that define their purpose and distribute their benefits broadly and inclusively, so as to create a consensus that minimizes disruptive politics. It ought to favor organizations that are superior at a desirable specific skill of value to other organizations, and that form coalitions in order to gain power beyond what they wield as independent entities. It ought to favor organizations that can shift relationships or commitments easily as conditions change, and thus control their growth by favoring partnerships over adding to their own "fixed" base. It ought to favor organizations that use partnerships to ensure joint planning with suppliers or customers, so that the "environment" is prepared for change.

This concept of the flexible organization—variously called self-designing, self-renewing, post-entrepreneurial, an adhocracy, or a meta-corporation—will be tested under fire in the challenging times ahead. The lesson of decades of experience in the industrial era is that the companies that endured, such as DuPont in the United States, ICI in Great Britain, or Siemens in Germany, were "first movers" in their industries (the first to exploit the potential of an innovation on a large scale). They also invested in managerial competence, which enabled them to adapt to growth and to changing times (Chandler, 1990).

The larger lesson of this chapter, however, deals not with preparedness but with potency. The study of history, which presents us with long-term patterns and underlying dynamics in sharp relief, makes it easier to judge success and failure—brilliant moves to cope and adapt or wrong-headed persistence and untimely change. As observers, we can perceive and appreciate the macro-forces better than those people living in the middle of history. The ultimate lesson for leaders, therefore, is a dose of appropriate humility. Leaders are not helpless in the face of the forces for change—but they are not all-powerful either.

References

Aldrich, Howard E. and Ellen R. Auster. 1986. "Even dwarfs started small: Liabilities of age and size and their strategic implications." *Research in Organizational Behavior.* Vol. 8, pp. 165–98.

Aldrich, Howard E., and Jeffrey Pfeffer. 1976. "Environments of organizations." *Annual Review of Sociology.* Vol. 2, pp. 79–105.

Bartlett, Christopher, and Sumantra Ghoshal. 1989. *Managing Across Borders: The Transnational Solution.* Boston: HBS Press.

Bower, Joseph L., and Martha W. Weinberg. 1988. "Statecraft, strategy, and corporate leadership." *California Management Review.* Vol. 30 (Winter), pp. 39–56.

Boyer, Peter J. 1988. *Who Killed CBS? The Undoing of America's Number One News Network.* New York: Random House.

Chandler, Alfred. 1990."The enduring logic of industrial success." *Harvard Business Review.* Vol. 68 (March-April), pp. 130–40.

Cooper, A. C.; C. Y. Woo; and W. C. Dunkelberg. 1989. "Entrepreneurship and the initial size of firms." *Journal of Business Venturing.* Vol. 4 (September), pp. 317–32.

DiMaggio, Paul J., and Walter W. Powell. 1983. "The iron cage revisited: Institutional isomorphism and collective rationalism in organizational fields." *American Sociological Review.* Vol. 48 (April), pp. 147–60.

Donaldson, Gordon. 1990. "Voluntary restructuring: The case of General Mills." *Journal of Financial Economics.* Vol. 27, pp. 117–41.

Donaldson, Gordon, and Jay Lorsch. 1983. *Decision Making at the Top.* New York: Basic Books.

Fligstein, Neil. 1990. *The Transformation of Corporate Control.* Cambridge, MA: Harvard University Press.

Freeman, John, and Michael T. Hannan. 1983. "Niche width and the dynamics of organizational populations." *American Journal of Sociology*. Vol. 88, pp. 1116–45.

Freeman, John; Glen R. Carroll; and Michael T. Hannan. 1983. "The liability of newness: Age dependence in organizational death rates." *American Sociological Review*. Vol. 48 (October), pp. 692–710.

Fruhan, William E., Jr. 1987. "Manage the value gap." Working paper, Harvard Business School.

———. 1985. "Management, labor, and the golden goose." *Harvard Business Review*. Vol. 63 (September–October), pp. 131–41.

Greiner, Larry E. 1972. "Evolution and revolution as organizations grow." *Harvard Business Review*. Vol. 50 (July–August), pp. 37–46.

Hackman, J. Richard. 1984. "The transition that hasn't happened." In J. R. Kimberly and R. E. Quinn (eds.), *Managing Organizational Transitions*. Homewood, IL: Irwin, pp. 29–59.

Hambrick, Donald C. 1981. "Environment, strategy, and power within top management teams." *Administrative Science Quarterly*. Vol. 26, pp. 253–76.

Hannan, Michael. 1977. "The population ecology of organizations." *American Journal of Sociology*. Vol. 82 (March), pp. 929–64.

Hannan, Michael, and John Freeman. 1989. *Organizational Ecology*. Cambridge, MA: Harvard University Press.

———. 1984. "Structural inertia and organizational change." *American Sociological Review*. Vol. 49 (April), pp. 149–64.

Heintz, Peter. 1991. "Small firms keep fit." In "Hidden Champions," *World Link*. Vol. 6 (November–December), pp. 43–57.

Kanter, Rosabeth Moss. 1983. *The Change Masters: Innovation and Entrepreneurship in the American Corporation*. New York: Simon & Schuster.

———. 1972. *Commitment and Community*. Cambridge, MA: Harvard University Press.

———. 1989. *When Giants Learn to Dance: Mastering the Challenges of Strategy, Managements, Careers in the 1990s*. New York: Simon & Schuster.

Kanter, Rosabeth Moss; Myron Kellner-Rogers; and Janis Bowersox. 1982. "Organizational and management dilemmas in successful, growing, high technology companies." In *Managing Growth: A Resource Kit*. Cambridge, MA: Goodmeasure, Inc.

Kanter, Rosabeth Moss; Jeffrey North; Ann Bernstein; and Alistair Williamson. 1990. "Engines of progress: Designing and running entrepreneurial vehicles in established companies—Analog Devices Enterprises, 1980–1988." *Journal of Business Venturing*. Vol. 5 (November), pp. 415–27.

Kanter, Rosabeth Moss; Gina Quinn; and Jeffrey North. 1992. "Engines of progress V: NEES Energy Inc., 1984–1990." *Journal of Business Venturing*. Vol. 7 (January), pp. 73–89.

Kanter, Rosabeth Moss, and Lisa Richardson. 1991. "Engines of progress IV: The Enter-Prize Program at Ohio Bell, 1985–1990." *Journal of Business Venturing*. Vol. 6 (May), pp. 209–29.

Kaufman, Herbert. 1985. *Time, Chance, and Organization*. Chatham, NJ: Chatham House.

Leonard-Barton, Dorothy. 1992. "Core capabilities and core rigidities: A paradox in managing new product development." *Strategic Management Journal*. Vol. 13 (Summer).

Meyer, John, and Brian Rowen. 1977. "Institutionalized organizations: Formal organization as myth and ceremony." *American Journal of Sociology*. Vol. 83, pp. 340–63.

Meyer, Marshall W., and Lynn G. Zucker. 1989. *Permanently Failing Organizations*. Newbury Park, CA: Sage.

Miles, Robert H. 1980. *Macro Organizational Behavior*. Santa Monica, CA: Goodyear.

Montgomery, Cynthia A. 1985. "Product-market diversification and market power." *Academy of Management Journal*. Vol. 28, pp. 789–98.

Montgomery, Cynthia A., and Ann R. Thomas. 1988. "Divestment: Motives and gains." *Strategic Management Journal*. Vol. 9, pp. 93–97.

Montgomery, Cynthia A., and Vicki A. Wilson. 1986. "Mergers that last: A predictable pattern?" *Strategic Management Journal*. Vol. 7, pp. 91–96.

Morritz, Michael. 1984. *The Little Kingdom: The Private Story of Apple Computer*. New York: Morrow.

Nonaka, Ikujiro, and Teruo Yamanouchi. 1989. "Managing innovation as a self-renewing process." *Journal of Business Venturing*. Vol. 14, pp. 199–316.

Oliver, Christine. 1988. "The collective strategy framework: An application to competing predictions of isomorphism." *Administrative Science Quarterly*. Vol. 33, pp. 543–61.

Osborne, Adam, and John Dvorak. 1984. *Hypergrowth: The Rise and Fall of Osborne Computer Corporation*. Berkeley, CA: Idthekkethan Publishing.

Pascale, Richard T. 1984. "Perspectives on strategy: The real story behind Honda's success." *California Management Review*. Vol. 26 (Spring), pp. 47–72.

———. 1990. *Managing on the Edge*. New York: Simon & Schuster.

Perrow, Charles. 1961. "The analysis of goals in complex organizations." *American Sociological Review*. Vol. 26, pp. 854–65.

Pfeffer, Jeffrey. 1977. "Power and resource allocation in organizations." In B. M. Staw and G. R. Salancik (eds.), *New Directions in Organizational Behavior*. Chicago: St. Clair Press, pp. 235–66.

Porter, Michael. 1987. "From competitive advantage to corporate strategy." *Harvard Business Review*. Vol. 65 (May–June), pp. 45–59.

Pratt, John W., and Richard Zeckhauser (eds.). 1985. *Principals and Agents: The Structure of Business*. Boston: Harvard Business School Press.

Schon, Donald. 1967. *Technology and Change*. New York: Delacorte.

Scott, W. Richard. 1987. "The adolescence of institutional theory." *Administrative Science Quarterly*. Vol. 32, pp. 493–511.

Sculley, John. 1987. *Odyssey: Pepsi to Apple*. New York: Harper & Row.

Singh, Harbir, and Cynthia A. Montgomery. 1987. "Corporate acquisition strategies and economic performance." *Strategic Management Journal*. Vol. 8, pp. 377–86.

Smith, Douglas K., and Robert C. Alexander. 1988. *Fumbling the Future: How Xerox Invented, Then Ignored the First Personal Computer*. New York: Morrow.

Stevenson, Howard, and Susan Harmeling. 1988. "The need for a more 'chaotic' theory of management." Working paper, Harvard Business School.

Stinchcombe, Arthur. 1965. "Organizations and social structure." *Handbook of Organizations*. Chicago: Rand McNally, pp. 142–93.

Summers, David V. 1983. "Predicting the shape of dominant coalitions." Working paper, Yale University Department of Sociology.

Tajika, Koji. 1991. "Much depends on the CEO." In "Hidden Champions," *World Link.* Vol. 6 (November–December), pp. 43–57.

Thompson, James D. 1967. *Organizations in Action.* New York: McGraw-Hill.

Van de Ven, Andrew. 1986. "Central problems in the management of innovation." *Management Science.* Vol. 32, pp. 590–607.

Virany, Beverly; Michael Tushman; and Elaine Romanelli. 1992. "Executive succession and organization outcomes in turbulent environments: An organization learning approach." *Organization Science.* Vol. 3 (February), pp. 72–91.

Westney, D. Eleanor. 1987. *Imitation and Innovation: The Transfer of Western Organizational Patterns to Meiji Japan.* Cambridge, MA: Harvard University Press.

———. 1988. "Isomorphism, institutionalization, and the multinational enterprise." Paper presented at the Academy of International Business Annual Meetings, San Diego.

———. Forthcoming. "Internal and external linkages in the MNC: The case of R&D subsidiaries in Japan." In C. Bartlett, Y. Doz, and G. Hedlund (eds.), *Managing The Multinational.* London: Croom Helm.

Zald, Mayer N., and Michael A. Berger. 1978. "Social movements in organizations: Coup d'état, insurgency, and mass movements." *American Journal of Sociology.* Vol. 83, pp. 823–61.

Chapter 3

Fitting or Creating the Environment: "Macro-Evolutionary" Change

Introductory Notes

This chapter offers portraits of organizations from many parts of the world, as they wrestle with and adapt to the forces generated by their different and changing environments.

The first two, "Rockport Shoe Company" and "Banc One Corporation," illustrate through concrete examples very different ways of responding to dramatic changes in their respective lines of business. The case of Rockport illuminates the changes wrought by macro-forces in what once was one of the premier industries of America and, within that, of New England, through the experience of the three generations of its owning family. Banc One, a leading representative of an industry that is feeling some equivalent pressures from environmental change a generation later, shows one very successful way of turning those pressures to its own advantage. Next, "The Sweater Trade" is a vivid example of a successful and innovative adaptation of the traditional apparel industry to the current international environment to which it must respond. The fourth portrait, "Keeping Up with Information: On Line in the Philippines and London," treats technological adaptation, featuring an organization that has carried the process of internationalization—even statelessness—to a perhaps inevitable extreme, in an industry that has existed at all only for the last twenty or so years.

Taken together, these portraits illustrate some of the range and variety of environmental challenges facing business organizations and four very different methods of accommodating competitive pressures. These include: absorption into a larger and more powerful company in the case of Rockport Shoes; nearly flawless execution of a long-range strategy to build a firm fit for the (expected) world to come, for Banc One; creation of a strong branded product company (Liz Claiborne) through effective international alliances, a minimal corporate structure, and the least possible fixed asset base; and finally, a firm (Saztec) that so successfully used the essence of its core technology (information processing) that it can hardly be said to have roots at all, and may thus be close to the perfectly mobile form that some have proposed will be necessary in the future.

"Rockport Shoe Company: The Evolution of the Katz Family Business" tells the story of Samuel Katz, who in 1930, after working for another company, "went out on his own" in the traditional American way. With little capital, he started by subcontracting everything, worked hard, succeeded well enough to buy a factory, then a second, and by 1938 employed more than seven hundred people—a success by any standard. World War II was kind to the business, as it was to many, but 1945 was the high-water mark for Samuel Katz. His son Saul, again in the traditional American way for the second generation, went to college and then graduate school, taking over the company in 1945. It was his ill fortune to preside over the failure of his father's company; by 1970 he declared bankruptcy, left the business to creditors, and started over, in Brazil. This time he was more fortunate. His company eventually became Rockport, one of the great success stories of the 1980s.

The early part of this history reflects population ecology and the hand of the market (in this case, a fairly visible hand) at their clearest—and most applicable. Such theories of "random mutation" and "natural selection," with their emphasis on luck rather than leadership and happenstance rather than strategic decision, apply best to small organizations in industries crowded with them. They lose explanatory power in light of the actions of those that become large and powerful to control their environments.

The numerous crises and failures in Katz shoe businesses before Rockport evolved out of them represented *responses* to environmental pressures. Until World War II, the American shoe industry was prosperous. The war, one of the pivotal events of a century with more than its share of historic events, set forces in motion that ultimately transformed—indeed are still transforming—the global environment. As the tide ran out, so did the Katz family business.

But then, in a fortunate strategic act that reshaped an industry, Ralph Katz (the founder's grandson) and Rockport invented the walking shoe market. Ralph Katz took over his father's second business, turning it into a highly visible and profitable success, reaching revenues of more than $300 million in 1986 and still growing. He did this not by *responding* to the environment but by *reshaping* it. "Natural selection" models lose significance when strategic choices transform the environment. Innovators gain market strength from their ability to shape environments.

The evolutionary saga was not over with the stunning success of Rockport. The American shoe industry underwent a renaissance in the 1980s with the deliberate development of the athletic shoe market, and Rockport was an important part of that development. But unlike the fragmented industry with many small companies that Saul Katz had known, the new industry was dominated by a few marketing giants such as Nike and Reebok. In that environment, it was difficult for even a $300-million company to survive as an independent family business; more capital and more marketing clout were required. In 1987 Rockport was sold to Reebok. This move effectively ended the Katz family business, but the cluster of activities that Rockport comprised continued under the Reebok umbrella.

The Rockport history can be read in terms of many of the theories of macro-evolutionary change presented in the first part of Chapter 2, but some apply better than others, and they tend to address different organizational states. When organizations are small and the environment is crowded with them, success and survival do seem to be a matter of luck, of "random mutation" in the form of a good idea or fortunate timing in adapting to large, seemingly uncontrollable forces—and with the "lucky" seen as the ones "fit" to survive. Innovation driven by entrepreneurship and leadership, however, makes some organizations stand out from the crowd, transforming the industry environment in their own terms. And ultimately, as an industry begins to mature, dominant organizations begin to swallow others to increase their own dominance; the dynamics of strategic choice and organizational power take precedence over luck or chance.

This portrait is subtitled "The Evolution of the Katz Family Business," but it could have been titled "The Evolution of the Katz Family Business*es*" or perhaps even "The Rise and Fall of the Katz Family Businesses." There was not one business, but several, with only the slenderest of threads connecting them. They were in the same industry, with the same U.S. Standard Industrial Code (SIC) category number, but in fact though the name was the same, the industry was not. The technology and manufacturing were altogether different; Samuel Katz would have had great difficulty understanding his grandson's business, though he would surely have appreciated his acumen. And finally, the company is dead. The Katz family profited, Reebok may have profited, but it is not obvious that other stakeholders did—employees and their families, suppliers, customers, communities, and consumers.

What, ultimately, were the options open to any of the Katzes, as they dealt with their company? In principle, of course, they were unlimited. As owners, any one of them could have sold his share of the company. As individuals, they could have gone into another business, taken a job, or retired. As family members, they could have brought in other family members or friends, or set up family trusts. As executives, they could have shifted toward more professional management, themselves serving perhaps in a less central role. Ralph, at least, who saw the company as a sort of extended family, could have recapitalized along the lines of an employee stock ownership plan (ESOP) or some other American device for giving employees equity in the firm. But he did not.

None of these options was exercised. At virtually every point, the Katzes elected to stay in the business, to run it themselves, and to make it succeed. Even Ralph's decision to sell to Reebok was occasioned by the felt need to raise more money, either by selling the whole or by going public, with the latter choice uncertain, costly, and with the potential to leave Ralph with a very different kind of company to run.

Executives facing potential change, whether driven by need or by opportunity, almost always have a more expansive set of possibilities than they consider seriously. The question about what *can* be done by someone in a particular situation is therefore larger than the question they are probably actually addressing, with limited, traditional, expected, and role-related constraints. In some respects, the entrepreneur, innovator, or change agent is simply someone who is prepared to take seriously a possibility that others regard as foolish, dangerous, or wrong. Even in highly turbulent times, more actions, and more effective ones, can be taken than people actually do take in practice. Change is limited by choice, not chance.

The other three portraits in this chapter illustrate these same themes in a variety of other contexts and circumstances. Banc One, headquartered in Columbus, Ohio, is by some standards the top performing bank in the United States, and by any measure among the top handful. At the end of 1990 its total market valuation, as expressed in the price of its common stock, exceeded that of Citicorp, the biggest U.S. bank. Banc One succeeded brilliantly in an industry littered with the skeletons of failed banks, many of which started out bigger, better financed and positioned, and more prestigious.

The Banc One case shows some of the steps taken by its top executives to transform a somewhat ho-hum Midwestern local bank into a banking powerhouse and one of the very few examples of what the bank of the future might actually look like. Several things stand out in this account:

1. John G. McCoy, CEO from 1958 to 1984, was clearly convinced that there *were* major prospects for his bank, and that he and it could do more than simply survive as just another local bank. What McCoy did, others could have done; little if anything about what was then called City National Bank of Columbus made it likelier than others to succeed.
2. He backed that conviction with action, with money, with commitment, and, above all else, with unwavering consistency.
3. He had a definite sense of the direction the banking industry would be forced to go, and he was willing to invest in that belief.
4. He and his team recognized the importance of thinking through the total implications of the bank's vision and the operational characteristics it would require.
5. They were content to move slowly, especially at first, trying out their ideas and gaining experience in the acquisition of other banks.

In addition, the portrait describes many of the operational decisions made by John G. McCoy, his successor, John B. McCoy, and the team, and the mechanisms that were put in place to help convert aspirations to reality. Many actions had important consequences for shaping and refining the character of Banc One, including the decision to shape an explicit corporate culture to enable integration of acquisitions without forcing traumatic change in the core. The decision to purchase the MCorp. banks in 1989 was a "bet-the-company" decision that the Banc One System could encompass further variety successfully.

The third and fourth portraits deal with the impact of the macro-forces of globalization and information technology on organizations. They show some very innovative ways of responding to environmental contingencies. They show that the "environment" consists of numerous other organizations with which ties must be developed. And in both cases, success hinges less on effective operation of a classical closed-system, tightly-bounded, and isolated organization than on flexible, collaborative organizations able to make global relationships.

For Liz Claiborne, Inc., a designer, producer, and distributor of fashionable clothing, the changing business environment simply mirrors what has always been the hallmark of the fashion business: the bewildering, rapid, and sudden shifts from "what's hot" to "what's not." The portrait shows the interplay between internal operations and the changing external environment of tariffs, competition, technology, and trade.

In operations, we watch Jack Listanowsky, Liz Claiborne's senior vice president in charge of Knitwear Manufacturing, as he goes about his job. Even his title is interesting, since Liz Claiborne does no manufacturing whatever—this is in fact one of the secrets of being fast and flexible. Owning things is inherently inflexible, and thus, in a sense, "unfashionable." Instead, the company develops close working relationships with manufacturers in more than a dozen countries.

The relationships among these other firms are not very competitive. On the contrary, we see Listanowsky and principals of one of their suppliers, in Hong Kong, discussing how to involve a third company, in Shanghai, in some of the production requirements. Moreover, they do not act at the traditional arm's length; rather, they appear to be close colleagues and collaborators. They speak a special language, honed by much time together; they know of each other's families and histories; they share common standards and concerns—they worry, for example, about how to modify costly and unhelpful trade and tariff arrangements.

This is not the traditional American model of suppliers attempting to hang onto the business of their customer, with the customer systematically playing one supplier off against another, keeping them off balance and seeking the lowest possible price, or else. Finding firms or people appropriate for the relationships we see in this portrait is not easy; developing them so they work effectively is time-consuming and difficult for both; replacing them would be extremely costly. Both parties have a major stake in making it work, which requires recognizing what in politics would be called the "legitimate interests" of each.

Change, to Jack Listanowsky, is a matter of the continual balance of those interests, the day-to-day adjustment of the fit between the organization's parts, and the addition of new firms as his business expands. The other part of Liz Claiborne's interest in change is occasioned by the continually redefined global structure of tariffs and the international trade in fibers, fabrics, and finished clothing, all treated differently across borders. In this industry more than in many others, there is a long tradition of import–export, trade, and technology problems, and there are well-established industry mechanisms for helping address them. The textile industry in the United States actually began with a man named Slater, who came to America about 1790 with the plans for a proprietary British textile machine in his head.

Two final points bear mentioning. First, the issue for Liz Claiborne, as for many organizations, will come when times are tight and the company has to reduce production, or purchases. It is much easier to adjust and to be accommodating when the pie is growing than when it is not. But the relationships being built can help even under those circumstances, and so they remain good business and a core requirement of flexibility, down as well as up. Second, Liz Claiborne is clearly identified and has identified itself as an American company, even though virtually all of its products are made elsewhere. Nationality, perhaps, is more than anything else a matter of personal sensibility and identity. Listanowsky is proud to be an American, though he spends more time in other countries. He is scornful of most American clothing because of its poor quality, yet he is hurt when he sees a "Made in America" label on inferior goods. He is, perhaps, an example of a new-style businessman, changing but not changed.

In Saztec International, the company featured in "Keeping Up with Information," the globalization process goes to its present extreme. Because of information technology, Saztec's physical location is almost trivial, people and skills are increasingly fungible, and flexibility is total. At the same time, competition is keen, since barriers to entry are small—most of what it takes to be successful is salesmanship and a willingness to take a chance on delivering. By its nature, Saztec's product (data entry services) is a commodity, difficult to differentiate; thus Saztec is forced to search for lower cost and fastest response. In the process, it offers the poorest countries, as defined by their standard of living and wage scale, a way of participating in the highest-technology sector, a curious result and itself a driver of change. Indeed, organizational flexibility increases worker vulnerability, which could provoke political action to protect jobs. Not all change is positive.

The great historian Charles Beard was asked at the very end of a long life if he could summarize what he had learned from his lifelong study of history. He answered with four epigrams. One was this. "The bee fertilizes the flower it robs." Perhaps that is a principal lesson of these portraits of macro-evolutionary change. As organizations adapt to change, their leaders make choices that shift the environment for still other organizations—provoking more adaptation and more innovation.

Rockport Shoe Company

The Evolution of the Katz Family Business

James A. Phills, Jr.

Headquartered in Marlboro, Massachusetts, the Rockport Company designs, oversees the manufacture, and markets a range of casual, dress, and fitness walking shoes. In 1986 Rockport employed just under 400 people and generated $96 million in sales.

Rockport's co-founder, Bruce Katz, is the third generation of his family to run a shoe company. His company is also a third-generation organization. Symbolic of this continuity is the company's headquarters, which are located in a renovated 19th century shoe factory once operated by the firm Bruce Katz's grandfather founded in 1928, Hubbard Shoe Company. Between the heyday of Hubbard, a star in its industry, and the current phenomenal success of Rockport, the Katz family business has changed its form, its manufacturing processes, its product line, its customers, and even its name. Through these mutations it has managed to survive in a domestic industry which has virtually disappeared as a result of foreign competition. Essentially a marketing and R&D firm with its own brand name, the Rockport of the 1980's looks very different from the way it did in the 1970's, and even more different from the firm Bruce Katz's grandfather, Samuel J. Katz, ran from the 1930's to 1950's, and his father, Saul Katz, ran (with his brothers) in the 1950's and 1960's.

The Early Years, 1928–1945: The Rise of Hubbard Shoes

In 1928 Samuel Katz accepted a position managing one of a group of factories for a New England shoe company. After two years of successful performance, he became frustrated by the refusal of the company to provide the rewards it had promised. As the country plunged into the great depression, he decided to go out on his own. The elder Katz began by buying materials and subcontracting the manufacturing to local factories. His customers were wholesalers, fast-growing mail order companies, and chain stores.

Katz quickly discovered that, when the subcontractors had their own orders, his product was rarely delivered on time. Deciding that he needed to have better control over the quality and delivery of his product, he purchased the first Hubbard shoe factory in Rochester, New Hampshire.

As his business grew, Katz expanded Hubbard's original product line and, in 1933, he purchased a second factory in East Rochester, New Hampshire. Expansion continued through the thirties and when his eldest son, Saul, graduated from the University of Pennsylvania's Wharton School of Business in 1938, Hubbard was experiencing growing pains. The two factories employed over 700 workers and had a maturing product line.

Despite the company's clear need for his abilities, Saul was reluctant to enter the business. In the end, the second generation Katz agreed to do it—"for a while."

The Decline of Hubbard: 1945–70

The war years had been kind to the Katz family company. Hubbard had produced a number of products for the military, including army and navy shoes, specialized winter ski boots, and parachutes for fragmentation bombs. Saul Katz commented, "During the war it was easy to sell shoes, if you could make them. There was demand and we certainly weren't importing them at that point." After the war, however, all this slowly began to change. Two trends in particular were to have a negative impact on small to medium-size firms like Hubbard.

First, the shoe industry had traditionally been extremely competitive because of its relatively low barriers to entry.

In the decade that followed the war, the larger producers began to move toward forward vertical integration by acquiring retail outlets. Certain retail groups also integrated backward into manufacturing. In addition, many chain stores with their own brands gained control over the retail distribution channels by establishing a strong presence in the growing number of shopping malls which sprang up as large segments of the population migrated from the cities to the suburbs. These changes made it more difficult for smaller independents like Hubbard to distribute their output and also increased the volatility of demand for this output.

The second industry trend that affected Hubbard was the increasing volume of imported shoes. Between 1955 and 1962 the value of imports rose from $11 to $60 million. Although in absolute terms this level of penetration was just becoming significant, many in the industry were alarmed by an import growth rate that was considerably greater than that of the market. Now at the helm of Hubbard, Saul Katz was deeply involved in monitoring the impact of foreign-produced shoes on the industry.

As the sixties progressed, the flood of imports took its toll, and domestic manufacturers began to fail. From 1962 to 1973 the value of imports grew at compound annual rate of nearly 30%. Overall U.S. employment in footwear manufacturing declined from 219,400 in 1954 to 167,800 in 1972.

It was in this environmental context that Saul Katz struggled to keep the family business alive. The product line of Hubbard's second factory in East Rochester was especially vulnerable to imports and began to falter. About the same time a division of the A. S. Beck corporation in Marlboro, Massachusetts, the Diamond Shoe factory, came up for sale as that company dealt with the deteriorating industry context by divesting various parts of its business. Seeing that Diamond had a better-quality product and an attractive customer base, Katz decided to acquire the Marlboro factory, close down the East Rochester facility, and try to combine the two operations to create a viable business.

Perhaps the plan might have worked, but the move was executed too slowly when difficult decisions about what to do with employees and inventory were postponed. The final move came too late. With cash already drained by the East Rochester operation, the acquisition of the plant in Marlboro had saddled the company with a large amount of debt.

From the time of its acquisition, the Marlboro factory was hindered by lack of professional management. Focused on keeping the original Rochester plant running profitably, Katz was not in sufficiently close touch with Marlboro.

The red ink flowed deeply at Marlboro, and eventually the entire company was forced into bankruptcy. Saul Katz managed to get Hubbard out of bankruptcy in a month and set the business at least back on its knees (though not its feet). However, the Massachusetts plant remained unable to meet even the minimal performance targets necessary to fulfill the requirements of Hubbard's creditors. A short while later Saul Katz closed the factory.

In the meantime, Rochester was suffering its own ills. Within six months of the Marlboro closing, the New Hampshire factory was forced to cut back production from four stories to one. When the liquidation of equipment at Marlboro failed to generate sufficient funds, even that lone story had to be shut down for four weeks until additional financing was arranged. The company was short on cash and frequently uncertain if it would be able to meet the payroll. The intake and disbursement of funds were controlled by the security financing company, and there was virtually no operating flexibility. Despite the apparently inevitable, Saul Katz thought they could make it. "I didn't want to just let the family business go." Not only was his family's company at stake, but his own savings—virtually everything he had worked for since joining the company in 1938—would be forfeit because of the personal endorsements.

Eventually a stressed and exhausted Katz decided he would no longer run the business in its impaired state. One afternoon in 1970 he called in the creditors and said:

> Marlboro is gone. We are down to one story in this factory. We have just gone four weeks without work. The cash is down. All of you are secured. We need additional capital. If you want to provide it, fine. If not, please let me know by the end of the afternoon and it is all yours. But I will not live this way any longer. Either put in more money or take your vested interest.

Two hours later the creditors came back, thanked Katz for his efforts, and wished him luck. They would liquidate the company. The next day Saul Katz boarded a plane for Brazil and began to build another business.

The Second Katz Family Business 1970–1976: Highland Import Company

During the final year at Marlboro, one of the managers Katz had brought in to help turn the factory around had begun talking about Brazil. Apparently the manager had had some interaction with the business community there, and he suggested that Saul Katz consider producing some shoes in Brazil. Katz wasn't interested.

Later, after a second business associate suggested he think about doing some portion of his manufacturing in Brazil, Saul Katz went back to the manager of the Marlboro factory and asked him how they might explore this possibility. A week later he [the manager] introduced Katz to a representative of the American–Brazilian Chamber of Commerce, who was interested in setting up a major importing program of shoes made in Brazil. After a trip to Brazil, an arrangement was made whereby Hubbard would develop and oversee the production of a specific shoe, in Brazil, made for one of its branded customers.

Gradually, as Hubbard sank deeper into financial difficulty, the import part of the business became considerably more profitable than the manufacturing operation. Consequently, as Hubbard continued to struggle, the import activities were spun off and set up as a separate entity—Highland Import Company.

The new firm had problems in the early days. Communication was poor, and the quality of the product was sometimes unacceptable. Fortunately, the company's inspectors in Brazil made certain that only shoes meeting its standards were shipped to customers. When the product did not meet Highland's standards, it insisted the Brazilian factories accept responsibility (including financial) for them.

This arrangement resulted in a strong feeling of product ownership by the manufacturers and a sense of partnership between them and Highland, which prevented many of the reliability problems that had plagued other American firms attempting to import shoes from overseas.

One of Highland's earliest customers was a Greenwich Village sandalmaker and branded distributor named Bort Carleton. Saul Katz showed them a product he had brought back from Brazil, which was somewhat similar to a popular Western-style boot except that it was constructed out of a very unusual and rugged type of leather. Bort Carleton liked the product and agreed to buy it.

Somewhat later Bort came to Highland with another product idea based on the successful Walter Dyer moccasins, handmade in a small shop in Rockport, Massachusetts, from a very unusual imported leather. After talking with Bort Carleton, Saul Katz went to a factory in Brazil known for handsewing, showed them a sample of an unusual type of leather from which he wanted the shoes made, and arranged a supplier for the new material. When the question arose of what to call it, Saul Katz thought for a moment and decided on the name "Rockport." Months later, when the moccasins were delivered, they were identified as "Rockport Shoes"—but only on the order form and not on the product or packaging. The use of Rockport as a brand name would be the brainchild of Saul Katz's young son, Bruce.

The Rockport Shoe Company 1971–1976: The Beginning of a Third-Generation Katz Business

While Saul Katz was busy working with his factories in South America, Bruce was driving around California in a Volkswagen bus, surfing, "meeting people," and doing a variety of odd jobs to meet his minimal financial needs.

One day in 1971, when he was about to run out of money, Bruce returned to Boston to look for more work that might provide him with the funds he needed to build a boat, which he planned to sail around the world. He arrived to find his father running his small import business out of a back room in the building that had once been Hubbard's Marlboro manufacturing facility, which was now an outlet store for another shoe company. The office was equipped with some old filing cabinets, a phone, and a telex machine and was accessible only through a fire door in the back of the shoe store. Years later, Bruce Katz said, "Every day my father had to walk past all the old shoes, the mistakes and overstocked items that put him out of business. I can't imagine it. It must have been sickening. The guy had a tremendous spirit to do it."

For his own part, Bruce had long ago decided that he wanted nothing to do with the footwear business. Thus it was with the same trepidation his father had felt about entering the business in 1938 that Bruce Katz decided to try and make the extra money selling the 3,000 pairs of surplus boots that his father had been left with when Bort Carleton canceled an order. Bruce comforted himself with the assurance that he would sell the boots only until he had enough money to finance his boat.

Every Monday, Bruce Katz set off in his Volkswagen bus to visit leather shops in the region and to see what he could sell. He returned to Boston Tuesday night and loaded his bus with the boots. Wednesday and Thursday he delivered merchandise to his customers, and collected in cash.

After 13 weeks in business, Bruce decided he had saved enough money, so he set off for California again. Shortly thereafter, he accidentally came upon a legendary car that Bruce had "heard about, but never seen in the flesh." It was a 4-year-old black Mercedes Benz sedan with a 6.3-liter engine, one of the fastest production cars of its time, and sported a price tag of $14,000.

Bruce Katz found himself thinking about his experience selling boots back in Massachusetts. He decided that with a car "that fast and comfortable" he could probably make the $14,000 in about 14 weeks by expanding the territory to which he had been limited by his Volkswagen bus. He made the deal, headed east in the Mercedes, and two weeks later was back in Massachusetts selling his father's surplus shoes and boots. This time his business strategy was more sophisticated. Realizing he could make more money by selling five days a week, he hired someone else to do the deliveries. Gradually, as his sales grew, Bruce developed new designs for his own products, for which branded and private label customers would place large orders (100,000 or more pairs). In addition, the consumers seemed to love his shoes; Bruce describes them laughingly as "Indian hippie moccasins with lug soles." Speeding up and down the East Coast, he could sell upward of 500 pairs a week. With virtually no overhead, except gas for his black Mercedes, and gross margins of $3 per pair, Bruce Katz began to make a substantial amount of money. As his venture grew, he decided to become more involved in the industry. He went to his first shoe show in Houston, where he saw a pair of shoes that were imitations of the moccasins he had been selling. When he asked the dealer what they were, he received the reply, "Oh these are kind of Rockport-type shoes." Bruce Katz was stunned to hear the name of the leather out of which they made their leather moccasins.

When he returned to Boston he began to consider seriously the potential of his products. When he noticed people wearing the shoes on the street, he sometimes stopped them to ask where they had purchased the shoes and what they thought of them. Invariably, the people had no idea what they were wearing, but seemed to like them. Some commented, "I wanted to tell my friend how to get a pair, but I didn't know what to tell him because they don't have a name or anything." In fact, though the shoes were called "Rockport" on his father's order forms, they were sold in a plain white box. Bruce recalled the first of what would be many fortunate marketing innovations: "I put a name [Rockport] on the box. What a great marketing move," he says laughingly. The first product to bear officially the Rockport brand name was the "Country Walker," introduced in 1973. About the same time, Bruce Katz expanded his sales force, hiring salesmen to supplement his personal efforts and marketing shoes even on the West Coast.

By 1973 Bruce's income was equal to that of his father's small operation at Highland. This seemed absurd to Bruce, and one day he walked in to his father's office and proposed that they work together:

> You've got all these headaches—Kinney drops you and Thom McAn picks you up. Montgomery Ward wants you and then they don't. It's the same as when you had your own factory. If we had our own business with 1,000 accounts of independent retailers there is no way we could wake up one morning with only 200 left. And besides, I can make as much money selling as you do in your business.

Saul Katz was at first unimpressed by his son's arguments.

> That's all right, Bruce. You are solving a problem for me, and if you're making more money that is OK. But this business [Highland] is doing well. It is nice and small, four or five people, and that's fine for me. I've had all the big business I want.

Bruce persisted, emphasizing the high profit margins in his business. His father continued to resist, pointing out that along with the attractive margins came a whole series of activities in which he had no interest. Marketing, selling, collecting, and getting the inventory to turn were at the top of his list. Eventually the younger Katz's enthusiasm prevailed, and his father agreed to give up his private-label customers and become partners with him. (It helped that Saul Katz was getting increased pressure from some of his customers to be allowed to buy the Rockport styles, which were exclusively Bruce's). However, when Saul Katz gave in, he set a number of conditions for his son:

> If you want to be responsible for those things [marketing, selling, etc.] and you think you're smart enough to tell me what kind of shoes you want to represent, and I agree with you on the shoes, then I will get them made. We'll try it—in a small way—and see just how good you really are.

The two agreed to be equal partners, got a $650,000 line of credit from the Worcester County Bank, replacing that from the Bank of Brazil, and began to design shoes in earnest.

To this point the Rockport story is a tale of three generations of entrepreneurs, using their accumulated learning and expertise to ensure the survival, in one form or another, of a family business. However, as the family business entered the second half of the seventies, something changed, and the Katz business began to transform itself from just another shoe company buffeted by the macro-economic forces of a fiercely competitive industry into a vibrant organization with a national presence, above-average profitability, and the power to influence the environment itself. In 1977 the company had sales of $3.6 million. Over the next ten years the company, slowly but steadily, developed and expanded a revolutionary new product line, by 1987 producing almost $146 million in sales. To achieve this growth, Rockport depended on innovation, not only in its products but also in marketing, manufacturing, and management.

In 1976 Rockport began a conscious strategy to build a strong branded business in the casual segment of the shoes market through intensive product development and aggressive marketing.

Often Bruce would return from trips with seemingly impossible product ideas. But as an "inveterate tinkerer," Katz clung to these ideas until he and his father found a way to make them a reality—often by developing new materials or components not being used in conventional shoemaking. Gradually Rockport's competitive advantage became, in Bruce Katz's words, "producing new and innovative products that no one else had dreamed of, or dared to make."

The company's focus on the casual shoe market was determined partly by its early history, but also partly by the Katzes' belief that there was an opportunity for a firm that could offer Americans alternatives to their common choices for casual footwear—basic canvas sneakers or worn-out dress shoes.

While success bred a host of "me too" products, and this increased competition, a more serious concern to the company became apparent during the middle 1970's: the "fitness" boom and the related explosion of the running shoe business. Even for consumers who didn't run or jog, running shoes began to replace casual shoes as the most common form of leisure-time footwear. Constructed of lighter materials, running shoes weighed much less than Rockport's traditional constructions, in addition to becoming status symbols. Bruce Katz realized that Rockport's success required that the company's casual shoes compete with running shoes in comfort and lightness. He and his father set about engineering such a shoe.

It took two and a half years, was called the RocSport, and was perhaps the first real "high-technology shoe." Its success led the company, from this point forward, to design shoes that were technically sophisticated—in part for their consumer utility and in part to help prevent other companies from copying them.

Spurred on by this experience, the company sought other applications of technology. The increasing presence of personal computers encouraged it to apply information technology to the task of managing and forecasting its inventory. Over the next few years Rockport developed one of the most sophisticated merchandising forecasting systems in the industry, making major investments in both software and hardware. Bruce Katz noted the historical contrast with the days when the building had been Hubbard's factory: "What had once been a building abuzz with the sounds of cutting and stitching shoes became an information factory . . . with operators whose machines were computers instead of sewing machines."

In 1980 the company's growth fell off, and Bruce Katz decided that to support continued demand based on the unique walking characteristics of its shoes, Rockport needed to take a different marketing approach. Katz decided there was an opportunity to create a small niche with great potential—walking shoes. He speculated that walking would, or at least could, emerge as an attractive alternative to running, aerobics, and other demanding athletic activities. It was clear, however, that that would take some nudging and, as a first step, in 1982 he changed the company's pricing structure to permit its marketing budget to be increased from 1–2% to 5–6% of sales.

With the assistance of a Boston-based marketing firm, Rockport began spending heavily to promote walking as a form of exercise. In 1984, for example, it co-sponsored an 11,600-mile trek across the United States by the health and fitness guru Robert Sweetgall. Dubbed "Walk for the Health of It," the event garnered much media attention as Sweetgall stopped to lecture to audiences along the way.

With Rockport's support, he also periodically flew to the University of Massachusetts Medical School's Center for Health Fitness and Human Performance for testing. Ultimately this research, on the physiological effects of fitness walking, resulted in the book *Fitness Walking,* by Sweetgall and the UMass Researchers. In addition, Rockport funded a short documentary entitled *Walk America!,* featuring clips from the cross-country walk, which was distributed to walking clubs and cable television stations around the country.

As a result of these and many other innovative marketing activities, a large number of consumers have come to associate walking shoes with the name "Rockport." It may even be that the company has contributed to the enormous growth in popularity of the activity itself.

Although it is difficult to assess the exact magnitude of the impact of this innovative marketing program on broader market trends and consumer preferences, one thing is clear: The Rockport Company has not been a passive player, and the firm's sales growth speaks for itself. From a base of $7.1 million in 1980, revenues rose at a compound annual growth rate of 54% reaching $96 million in 1986.

Rockport's emphasis on innovation and customer service inevitably made it heavily dependent on the creativity and initiative of its employees. Bruce Katz characterized the company's family spirit and relaxed entrepreneurial climate as key factors in its success. Because of his travels in California, Katz was familiar with the lifestyle and work attitudes of companies such as Apple and Esprit, and consciously tried to create a similar climate at Rockport. Largely as a result of its reputation and rapid growth, the company became known as one of the most challenging and exciting places to work in the industry. Rockport was able to attract many talented employees because of its practice of giving younger and often less experienced people more responsibility in an environment of inventiveness and risk-taking, balanced by a strong system of plans and budgets. As with many successful small firms, Rockport's rapid growth eventually strained its informal and open culture, with the necessary high level and quality of communication, in particular, becoming difficult to maintain.

In 1985, in response to these problems, "Camp Rockport" was started. The company rented a Newport, Rhode Island, mansion and asked each of its 250 employees to participate in a three-day retreat. There, amid Louis XV surroundings, they discussed ways to improve their work, provided input directly to senior executives, and improved their own understanding of the overall business. This annual event helped to reinforce the company's open, participative, and closely knit culture, while also generating a variety of concrete solutions to pressing operational and organizational problems.

On Wednesday, September 17, 1986, Rockport announced that it would be acquired by Reebok International for $118.5 million in cash. The company, in need of additional capital to fund its rapid growth, had been preparing to go public for a number of months. After considering the two alternatives, Bruce Katz had decided to accept the Reebok offer. Reebok was then the second largest athletic shoe firm in the U.S. (Nike was first) with 1985 sales of $307 million. Rockport was to continue to operate autonomously, with Bruce Katz staying as president and with provisions to retain other key members of Rockport's management structure, including Saul Katz. Industry analysts viewed the move favorably, citing proximity among athletic, walking, and casual shoe segments, and potential synergies between Reebok and Rockport.

By the summer of 1987, however, Bruce Katz retired to a newly purchased beachfront condominium in Los Angeles, officially a consultant to his old company. Stanley Kravetz, a new president appointed by Paul Fireman, Reebok's CEO, was guiding the firm through a period of accelerating growth by both acquisition and internal growth. Clearly, Reebok hopes Rockport's tradition of growth through innovation would continue. In Kravetz's own words:

> Our plans for Rockport include maximizing our present opportunities and expanding product lines. . . . Our ultimate goal is to treat our dealers and the consumer fairly by continually producing a good product at a good value. We are in the midst of very healthy growth and our task is to manage that growth with the great pool of resources which have helped us thus far—our people.

Banc One Corporation

Anticipatory Evolution

Paul S. Myers and Rosabeth Moss Kanter

John B. McCoy rose from his desk on the 16th floor of Banc One's Columbus headquarters while the video crew gathered its equipment. He had just finished taping this quarter's "Chairman's Corner" section of the company news video program. Weeks earlier, on June 29, 1989, Banc One, the largest bank holding company in Ohio and one of the U.S. banking industry's top financial performers, announced that it had beaten five other bidders to purchase 20 of MCorp's failed Texas banks. McCoy had just told employees in his taped message, "Banking is people. The uncertainty is over for the people of MCorp. The great spirit of Banc One will make a difference—we will win back customers and make it work. Our goal is to be the biggest and best bank in the state!"

McCoy knew it would be a challenge to transfer Banc One's remarkable success to its largest acquisition, especially at a time when Banc One itself was undergoing major change. With few exceptions, for two decades the company had grown by acquiring small- to medium-size Midwestern banks with good performance records in nondilutive, friendly deals. The Texas banks' assets were equal to one-half those of Banc One, it was located in the South, and it was insolvent. Banc One's past success in integrating newly acquired banks derived from its abilities to nurture an "uncommon partnership" with the new bank (called an "affiliate") and to induce better performance from its managers. The "uncommon partnership" balanced autonomous banking decisions based on knowledge of the community at the local level with a strong set of corporate values and operating principles. . . .

Banc One: Superregional Super Bank

In March, 1989, before the MCorp purchase, Banc One had 56 affiliate banks with 566 offices, 5 nonbank affiliates (i.e., subsidiaries of Banc One), 18,000 employees, and $23.7 billion in assets. Net income had increased at a compound annual growth rate of 18.39% since 1978.

In 1988 Banc One was the most profitable bank holding company as measured by return on average assets among the country's fifty largest banks. Earnings per share and stock price had risen steadily over the past decade.

Banc One was primarily a retail bank which focused on offering loans and other financial services to individual consumers and to small- and medium-size "middle market" firms. Its branches operated as "stores" concentrating on product sales to meet income targets. . . .

The company sought the high-margin business in the retail and middle market loans, industry diversity, and balanced growth. In 1987 the corporation's net interest margin of 5.8% compared to a U.S. regional bank average of 4.41%. Banc One ranked among the 10 largest U.S. banks in both credit card and student lending.

In the corporate segment, Banc One confined its commercial lending to middle market customers largely in the communities in which its affiliate banks operated. Banc One's significant nonbank activities included trust, leasing, and mortgage operations and extensive data processing.

Overall, Banc One's goal was to deliver superior customer service while obtaining high financial returns. Member banks prided themselves on treating customers as individuals rather than mere account numbers. One affiliate president noted, "From the customers' point of view, if you're not delivering that quality personal service they're not going to stay with you." Banc One believed that its customers saw it as an innovative, fast-paced company always on the leading edge of new products and that customers thus expected to receive from Banc One banks the best products and prices. Advertising emphasized service delivery and specific product offerings equally. Banc One invested steadily in technology R&D to develop new retail products, to improve its competitive lead time, to lower costs, and to generate fee income by providing services to other financial institutions. It used a complex and detailed central financial control system for business planning and performance measurement.

History of Innovations

Banc One could trace its heritage back 121 years to when it started in Columbus, Ohio, as City National Bank. Its modern history began when John G. McCoy assumed the presidency upon his father's death in 1958. McCoy made two fundamental decisions: (1) to run "a Tiffany bank rather than a Woolworth's," and (2) to achieve that goal, "to hire the best people and then delegate; there wasn't any use of putting you in if you were the finest in the world, and then telling you how to do it." For the second decision his father offered no model; he had made every decision in the bank himself.

John G.'s guiding principle was "to provide financial services to people," who John G. believed choose a bank "because of one word: convenience." To help implement that principle in his first year, he hired John Fisher, a young radio ad man, as head of a newly created advertising department. John G. commissioned him to "find out what the customer wants" and forbade him to learn how to open an account or make a loan. Soon in charge of marketing and public relations, Fisher created a new image for CNB with slogans like "the loaningest bank in town"; "the best all around bank all around town"; and "the good neighborhood bank," featured on a prize-winning billboard ad in 1961. In less than a decade, deposits grew from $140 million to more than $400 million.

Fisher's creative vision went beyond ad pitches. Some industry observers credited him with revolutionizing banking by coupling technology with marketing. At John G.'s insistence, since the early 1960s the company had set aside approximately 3% of earnings each year for R&D in hopes of identifying ways that technology could improve efficiency and customer service. The company's innovations included introducing the forerunner of the automated teller machine (ATM) in 1969 and in 1972 becoming the first U.S. bank to install ATMs in every branch office. Not all of its innovations took hold. It pioneered efforts, though unsuccessfully, to build a point-of-sale credit card network in 1977 and introduce at-home banking in 1979.

CNB became the first bank to offer credit cards outside of California by introducing the City National BankAmericard (now VISA) in 1966. This innovation not only provided the bank with profits and industry visibility, but it also helped start the charge card revolution which changed Americans' spending practices. The company gained additional national exposure in 1976 when Merrill Lynch picked it as the processing arm of its new Cash Management Account (CMA) venture. The CMA accounts permitted customers to use funds from their brokerage accounts via a debit card or checks provided by the bank. This pathbreaking alliance helped foment the burgeoning revolution in the U.S. financial services industry.

Driven by the success of its credit cards and its partnership with Merrill Lynch, in the 1970s the company expanded its operations by selling its credit- and debit-card processing expertise to other banks, credit unions, thrifts, finance companies, and brokers. By 1989 Banc One was regarded as a data processing powerhouse. It handled its own 3.2 million cards, over 3.5 million cards for third parties (e.g., credit unions), and supplied the check clearing and back office operations for many other banks and financial service firms. In 1989, Banc One's Future Systems Group unveiled Phase I of a new system developed in partnership with Electronic Data Systems (EDS) and Norwest, a Minneapolis bank holding company, to attempt to meet the banking industry's data processing needs for the next 20 years.

At the retail level, Banc One experimented with store concept and design. In Kingsdale, Ohio, the company introduced a full service banking facility called a "Financial Marketplace" with supermarket hours—open 72 hours a week including Sunday afternoons. The state-of-the-art merchandising system comprised boutiques offering home financing, travel services, trust services, business loan operations, a realtor, and investment services. Colorful neon lights identified each separate service area. Interactive (touch-screen) video displays answered customer questions, and drive-in windows made for quick and easy personal service. Four companies leased boutique space: Banc One Investment Services, Banc One Travel, Nationwide Insurance Corp., and HER realtors. Leasing offered Banc One the advantage of learning how to sell products which banks by law could not provide while creating awareness of its own investment and travel subsidiaries. It also directly challenged companies like Sears and American Express, which offered a portfolio of financial services. The success of the Kingsdale store led to a second "supermarket," and both were performing well beyond expectations by 1989.

To ensure continuing innovation, Banc One established a "Greenhouse Group" under John Fisher's leadership in June 1989, to create and nurture new ideas outside of the mainstream of the organization. Initial projects included a toll-free, 24-hour-a-day telephone service; interaffiliate check cashing and deposit service; and a home banking service.

Growth Through Acquisitions

Limited in growth by Ohio law to one-county branching, City National Bank merged in 1968 with a smaller bank, Farmers Savings and Trust ($55.2 million in deposits) to form a bank holding company, the First Banc Group (FBG). Another Ohio law prohibiting nonbank institutions from including the designation "Bank" in their names dictated the new spelling, "Banc." FBG began acquiring small banks around Ohio. Between 1968 and 1980 it bought 22 banks, each under $100 million in assets.

A decade old in 1977 and still growing rapidly, First Banc Group had 16 members and $1.95 billion in aggregate assets. With FBG's next decade in mind, John G. and his colleagues—including FBG's new president (and John G.'s son) John B. McCoy—began to consider the implications of federal limits on the company's growth. With the entire banking industry in upheaval as it faced challenges from other financial institutions, McCoy and others expected revisions in the law against interstate banking. Anticipating that event, FBG sought a new name unique in the country. At John Fisher's suggestion, they selected "Banc One" and registered the name in every state. The name change took place in October 1979. Thereafter, the holding company would be known as *Banc* One, and each bank as *Bank* One, followed by its location. Thus City National Bank became Bank One of Columbus.

Between 1980 and 1983 Banc One began to purchase midsize banks in major markets. Previous acquisitions were in rural and semiurban county seat–type markets. In short order, Banc One bought banks in Cleveland, Akron, Youngstown, and, in June 1983, the $1.6 billion Winters National Bank of Dayton. Winters held assets about one-third the size of those of Banc One.

In 1984 John G. McCoy retired, and his son John B. became CEO in addition to his duties as president; in 1987 John B. became chairman and gave up the presidency. In the meantime, changes in state banking laws that allowed bank holding companies to bank in other states spurred a third phase of Banc One's acquisitions toward purchases of larger banks. Looking first to Indiana, Banc One made a purchase about every two weeks in the fall and winter of 1985 and gained six banks. After months of courtship, Banc One announced in May 1986 that it would purchase American Fletcher Bank of Indianapolis. Banc One increased its assets by more than a third overnight, because American Fletcher held $4.5 billion in assets and was the second largest bank in Indiana. This move gave Banc One the largest market share in the state. Shortly after this, Banc One made acquisitions in Kentucky, Michigan, and Wisconsin.

Nonbank acquisitions, including a mortgage company and travel agencies, complemented Banc One's operations. Four specialty leasing companies (e.g., for photocopiers, telephone switchboards) balanced its retail strategy at the small end of the market. Nonbank holdings accounted for just 7% of earnings, not including the card processing business, which was considered part of the banking operation. This nonbank area, though, was seen as having the most growth potential, perhaps outpacing the rest of the business by 25%–50%.

Integration of New Affiliates

Banc One sought successful banks run by managers with proven track records. CEO John B. McCoy commented in 1986 that "the success [of our acquisitions] will be achieved through basically two things: a local management team that knows the market and a similarity between the two organizations' [Banc One's and the acquisition's] products and services." Of the deals that never went through, 80% failed because of Banc One's lack of confidence in a potential acquisition's current management. With rare exceptions, current officers remained in place after a Banc One acquisition. . . .

Assessment of people was central to acquisition decisions. For example, in the spring of 1989 during the due diligence period in Texas, a team of 20 Banc One analysts and executives from affiliate banks studied MCorp's operations. McCoy recalled:

> Our accounting guy said, "The controls aren't good, but I'm impressed by the people." Then the next guy said something similar. So we went back to focus on the people: why they're here, who the boss is, why they haven't left. When we got comfortable with the people, we went ahead.

McCoy expected the incumbent bank managers to operate the new affiliate profitably and soundly. Banc One put significant pressure on new affiliates to attain higher earnings. It asked each to take a look at its costs, to improve its proficiency in technology, to expand its loan-making capability, and to professionalize its banking workplace. Banc One had an exceptional track record of improving the performance of its new affiliates. The average acquisition increased its return on assets 66%. . . .

To spur performance improvements Banc One assigned a "mentor bank" of comparable asset size to share information and expertise with the new bank and to help it build competence in Banc One's products, systems, and operating procedures. Typically, the mentor bank president and various staff members spent at first two or three days each month visiting the new affiliate. New member banks also sent their personnel to the mentor affiliate, and to other banks, to learn about such functions as data processing and financial controls. . . .

Early in the assimilation of new affiliates, Banc One imposed its powerful financial control system, the Management Information Control System (MICS), as an additional tool to help the banks set and meet performance targets. The MICS tracked all balance sheet and income statement data as well as productivity and loan quality ratios. Affiliates received an inch-thick monthly computer report that included detailed performance results. In the words of one financial officer, "MICS helps an affiliate understand itself better. It tells you where you've been, who you are, and where you want to go." . . .

Despite facing the often frustrating human dilemmas of organizational change, Banc One for the most part smoothly integrated its new acquisitions. Many affiliates gave credit for this success to one element of their new Banc One relationship: the "uncommon partnership."

The Uncommon Partnership

The First Bank Group had adopted "the uncommon partnership" as its slogan, and it became the hallmark of Banc One's relationship with its affiliate banks. McCoy's principle was, "If it involves people, we do it at the local level; if it involves paper, we centralize it." Affiliate autonomy encompassed local lending decisions, pricing based on local market conditions, personnel policies and compensation, and responses to community needs. Such autonomy was "uncommon" in banking. Most holding companies and franchisers imposed a standardized set of rules and practices on their affiliates.

The "uncommon partnership" philosophy was a strong selling point. In one case Banc One's offer to acquire a bank was $6 per share less than a competitor's, but target company directors felt that Banc One's uncommon partnership would provide more long-term value to shareholders so they accepted the lower offer. Treasurer George Meiling explained:

> In the ideal M&A discussion, we don't even talk dollars or price until about the third meeting. We want to get all the social issues and have them understand how it is going to operate. We tell them not to listen to Columbus because we are trying to sell them on the deal. We give them our phone book and have them pick a president of an affiliate they want to talk to. And a lot of banks do it. Our best salespeople are really our presidents.

Banc One tried to bring a number of benefits to newly affiliated banks. While responsibility for traditional banking activities remained with the affiliates, the corporate office in Columbus provided (for a fee) central services including legal, new product development, and marketing. Affiliation also allowed banks to offer a broad range of products not usually offered by small independent banks, such as leasing and commercial lending. The Banc One name itself had great value in attracting customers, since the company's reputation for quality service had brought it national recognition. Affiliates gained leverage from the operational and financial resources of a much larger bank. Banc One shared its enormous product R&D

experience with affiliates. Affiliates could obtain data that helped them predict which products would be most successful in their local markets. . . .

Work Environment

Along with the uncommon partnership, other aspects of Banc One's work environment had always been determined at the top of the company in Columbus and then diffused throughout the various affiliates. Since the Columbus bank accounted for 50% of total company revenue before the 1983 Winters acquisition in Dayton, the operating practices of that bank easily influenced those of the smaller affiliates. But when Dayton became 25% of the company, and Columbus shrank to 30%, John Fisher, now senior vice president, saw the need for some unifying devices. Coincidentally, John B. McCoy had just become CEO. Fisher sensed that McCoy was searching for a platform to call his own, a way to make a distinctive mark on the company that would separate him from his father. He presented to McCoy a "white paper" in October 1984 that proposed quality as that platform. . . .

To address this concern, Fisher proposed a plan that included establishing a corporate positioning theme, creating a training program for executives, and expanding intracorporate communications through a variety of vehicles.

McCoy acted on Fisher's suggestions. In 1985 Banc One selected as its positioning theme the phrase "Nine Thousand People Who Care," a statement of a goal as much as a common identity. All employees were invited to Columbus to celebrate the announcement of the new slogan at a major rally televised on closed circuit around the state for employees who could not attend. By early 1989, after several acquisitions, the slogan stood at "Eighteen Thousand People Who Care."

The company song captured this theme. McCoy remembered once attending an IBM function with Fisher and hearing its company song. "I said, 'We'd never sing a song in our company.' John Fisher said, 'We will, and I'll have tears in your eyes.' A year later, we had a song." Banc One's broadcast advertising included the song, and employees sang it at various celebrations and company events. . . .

One of the most prominent and successful vehicles for transmitting Banc One's values and operating standards was Bank One College. The college was an internal training program originally designed to give senior managers experience working together and to be a catalyst for collaboration and idea exchange among affiliates. The college took participants from their geographically dispersed locations and immersed them in two weeks of intense day and evening experiences. Top executives, including McCoy and Fisher, presented the corporation's operating philosophy and plans. Other classes and presentations honed the managers' problem-solving skills. The college used role-playing and "Outward Bound"–type team-building activities to develop trust, sharing, unity, and cooperation.

College director Beth Luchsinger commented, "Our challenge is to continue fostering innovation while sustaining growth. We use the college as a vehicle to achieve that." While the college's emphasis was always on sharing information and promoting learning between affiliates, conversations with McCoy before each session produced an agenda of specific discussion themes based on current Banc One issues. . . .

One important by-product of the college was the expanded network of relationships formed by the participants. Annual reunions of all the graduates helped maintain these ties. Most who had attended the college praised this consequence of their experience. "It was a fantastic experience," extolled one college alum. "I have 24 great friends now that I'm in touch with all the time. I go to reunions, and the network of relationships just grows and grows, which means more and more information is available. You can't get too much information in this business—it just changes too quickly."

Information-sharing and idea-exchange were central to Banc One's operating philosophy. Management stressed face-to-face meetings, preferring personal interactions to electronic communications. One Banc One executive, who had spent most of his career with IBM, remarked, "The informality of the organization is unique in banks. I was surprised by the willingness to question procedures. That shows a commitment by the organization to encourage people to think and express their ideas." . . .

Many affiliate officers reported calling their peers to inquire about how another achieved a particularly good performance or solved a problem. Karen Horn, CEO of Bank One, Cleveland, a highly experienced bank executive who came to Banc One from the presidency of the Federal Reserve Bank of Cleveland, saw value in this peer exchange:

> When we are dealing with an issue, there are 59 other folks out there that are vaguely in the same business we are that might have good ideas about it. There are also some people in Columbus who might have good ideas about it, and they may be more or less forceful, depending on the situation, in trying to get their ideas implemented. The openness and interchange between the affiliates is one of the enormous strengths of Banc One.

The corporatewide quality program was another unifying force. Bill Bennett, chairman of Bank One, Dayton, had developed a formal quality program in response to lapses in quality caused by merging data systems shortly after its acquisition. His hands-on approach included walking around the various banks' facilities, monitoring quality, and encouraging employees to focus on improving customer service. The success of the program in Dayton led to a systemwide participative quality program under John Fisher's leadership. Included were competitive rankings of affiliates' performance on quality ratings and annual Chairman's Awards for quality leaders. In 1988 some 488 quality teams were addressing issues ranging from the process of sending out a customer statement to the design of a proposed new account.

Awards were abundant. The Chairman's Award was given annually at the Corporate Quality Awards banquet. "We Care" awards were presented regularly to employees to recognize individual or group contributions to superior customer service. . . .

Other celebrations regularly took place. One particularly enthusiastic event welcomed the new Wisconsin affiliates in 1988. June 13 was declared "Name Change Day," the day when the acquired banks would be called Bank One. The day began with a pancake breakfast served by top executives to all Wisconsin employees. Each employee received a Bank One bag filled with "welcome aboard" gifts, including a T-shirt, cap, and balloons. CEO McCoy and other officials spoke at a rally later in the morning. The employee band played the "Bank One" song and, reading off mimeographed pages, everyone sang along and was officially initiated onto the Banc One team.

One of the more controversial aspects of Banc One's culture was its Code of Ethics. Banc One defined ethics as its accountability and responsibility to its depositors and shareholders. When a new bank joined Banc One, each of its employees received a copy of the Code of Ethics that she/he must sign attesting knowledge of and agreement with its contents. The code provided guidelines for behavior regarding conflict of interest, personal conduct, and financial affairs. These latter personal issues raised concerns about violations of privacy and discomfort at the corporation's seeming imposition of a strict morality. . . .

The code also had strict disclosure requirements for officers and directors regarding personal financial obligations. . . .

Some affiliates believed that such disclosure went beyond what an employer was entitled to know. This component of the code was optional for the individual banks.

Leadership

McCoy described his role and activities this way:

Besides chief personnel officer, my other job is Goodwill Ambassador. There are times I feel I'm running for office. On the first day in Texas I tried to walk around as many floors as I could, let people see who we are. We had dinners for all the officers; I talked about our philosophy.

Most press accounts as well as investment analyst reports described Banc One as a superior company with talented and dynamic managers. McCoy personally selected people for the top corporate slots including the state holding company presidents, though he discussed candidates with his key managers individually. Each holding company chose its local bank presidents and officers, though there had not been too many selection decisions due to the usual retention of existing management after acquisitions. . . . McCoy set a high common standard for managerial performance.

Affiliate officers were evaluated on budgeted versus actual earnings (adjusted for events outside of affiliate control) and on ROA. Their bonuses varied as a percentage of total compensation, but were between 10% and 50%. Several senior managers acknowledged that while the monetary bonus played a distinct motivational role, it was not the most important factor. According to one affiliate president, friendly competition among the affiliates was the greatest incentive. . . .

Banc One held onto its best managers. One officer reported that while many of his peers frequently received calls from executive search firms, none had been stolen away by other companies. Low turnover meant high retention of experience and knowledge and maintenance of the extensive networks of relationships among the various affiliates. But high standards also meant that jobs were not sinecures.

Organizational Dilemmas of Growth

In 1987, in response to the complexities of multistate and nonbanking operations, Banc One organized its affiliates into a state holding company structure, with corporate headquarters and staff offices in Columbus. In January 1989 Banc One Ohio had 26 affiliates, including banks in Ohio, Michigan, and Kentucky; Banc One Indiana, 11 affiliates; and Banc One Wisconsin, 19 affiliates. The state holding company structure allowed for future growth, since it could be duplicated as new states were added; it encouraged development of local management talent; and it helped successfully integrate new affiliates.

Sandwiched between the centralized and decentralized features of the Banc One system were some "centralized shared responsibilities": those activities with which central subsidiaries or offices assisted the local banks and holding companies by providing expertise, policy guidelines, and resources for particular products and services. For example, the corporate marketing department assisted affiliates in product development and promotion, and Banc One Services Corporation supplied the data processing/item processing services for all units. In addition, Banc One corporate offices in Columbus in conjunction with the state holding companies and affiliates performed financial analyses and forecasting. Mortgages, investment banking, insurance, and leasing were all shared with central nonbank subsidiaries. To add structure and some direction to these "centralized, shared responsibilities," Banc One created the Services Corporation in January 1988 to handle operations functions for all of the affiliate banks. These functions included data and credit card processing as well as software and system development to support new products. A year later, in a move that further centralized some operations, the Services Corporation was restructured into five major groups to separate the data processing for information services from that for financial services. . . .

The Future Challenge

In February 1989 *Financial World* magazine named Banc One one of 30 great companies for the 1990s, calling it "the cream of a pack of excellent super-regionals" and noting its "highly innovative products and services" and its skill at "digesting new technology and smaller banks." Despite such accolades, concern at the company over limited future growth of its existing customer base and pressure to maintain its record of superior financial performance had led to conservative actions, such as selling credit card receivables to investors and limiting consumer credit lines, and had intensified Banc One's willingness to make a major acquisition.

Banc One named its Chairman McCoy as chairman of Banc One Texas. Thomas Hoaglin, chairman and CEO of Bank One, Dayton, was named president and CEO of the new Texas entity. Under Hoaglin's leadership, Dayton was Banc One's top financial performer in 1988, and the bank won a special quality service award that year. While Banc One also planned to name several more senior executives, McCoy told the *Wall Street Journal,* "We found what appeared to us to be good management at the grassroots level, and that's one of the main things that kept our interest in the organization. . . . Believe me, those of us from Columbus don't know much about Texas, so we're going to rely on Texans to run our Texas bank."

The Sweater Trade, From Hong Kong to New York

James Lardner

. . . Jack Listanowsky had his back to the water and his head buried in the *International Herald Tribune* when I found him in the Harbourside one morning in June of 1986. Listanowsky was on his hundredth trip to Hong Kong, give or take a few trips, and the view had lost its novelty for him. Besides, the newspaper was full of disturbing stories—about labor unrest in the Philippines, a riot in a Thai beach resort, and American charges of corruption against the new government of Panama, among other things. Listanowsky is the senior vice-president in charge of knitwear manufacturing for Liz Claiborne, the fashion company. Claiborne buys knitwear not only in Hong Kong and the United States but also in the Philippines, Thailand, Panama, and eleven other countries. To Claiborne, and to Listanowsky, anything that upsets the peace in such places—or the maintenance of a friendly attitude toward American interests—is a threat.

His mission this time out was to negotiate prices and delivery dates for the knitwear part of Liz Claiborne's Spring One season for 1987. While he was at it, he would monitor progress on the Holiday and Pre-Spring seasons and begin to talk about the shape of Spring Two. (At the time of my visit, there were six seasons in a Claiborne year—Pre-Spring, Spring One, Spring Two, Fall One, Fall Two, and Holiday.) I was in Hong Kong to learn a little about the global clothing business, at Listanowsky's side.

Shortly after I sat down at his table, we were joined by Chris Chan,

Claiborne's chief knitwear operative in Hong Kong. For want of family funds, Chan terminated his education at seventeen and went to work in a knitwear factory, where his father was an assistant manager. . . .

"Manila went on strike yesterday," he announced in the act of seating himself.

"General?" Listanowsky asked.

"Just Vincent's factory," Chan said.

"We have a lot of goods we need right away," Listanowsky said. "Do Kenneth and Jeffrey know?"

"I think they know.". . .

He was talking about Vincent Fang, who ran Fantastic as well as the struck factory in Manila. The Fang family, Listanowsky had told me, also owned clothing factories in Thailand, Malaysia, Ireland, and Panama.

Michael Greenberg joined us a few moments later. Greenberg had just been hired by Claiborne as director of knitwear production and planning for sportswear. He had left his former employ on Friday, had got on a plane to Hong Kong on Sunday, had arrived late Monday night, and was to spend today—Tuesday—learning how Listanowsky, and Claiborne, did things. . . .

In Listanowsky's five years with Claiborne, knitwear had grown from ten to thirty-seven per cent of the company's business, and his trips to the Far East had increased proportionately. Of late, he had been spending nearly half his time away from the New York office, so he had pushed for the right to hire some help.

After driving from the hotel to the New Territories, we spent about ten minutes on local streets before we came to a nine-story building of sooty grayish-brown brick, which a sign identified as Fang Brothers Textiles, Ltd.

We entered a set of offices whose bright décor—white walls, venetian blinds, cabinetry, and plants, all bathed in fluorescent light—reminded me of the Liz Claiborne offices in New York, where I had first met Listanowsky, a few weeks earlier. He seemed nearly as much at home here as there. Without waiting for anyone to acknowledge our arrival, he strode down a hallway and into a conference room, in which we found a young, stylishly dressed Chinese woman preparing for our arrival. Her name was Belinda Chan, and Listanowsky introduced her as "my counterpart at Fang Brothers." Moments later, her boss, Jeffrey Fang, appeared. He seemed absurdly young, in a tanned, thin, smooth-skinned, laid-back sort of way. At Fang Brothers Textiles, Ltd., the torch had clearly been passed to a new generation.

Listanowsky introduced Greenberg to Fang, who asked when Greenberg had gone to work for Claiborne, and shook his head in amazement at the answer.

"At Liz Claiborne, you get hired, you get a boarding pass," Listanowsky said.

Fang, like Listanowsky, had brought a pair of newcomers to the meeting: Chris Ma, who was in charge of yarn and design development, and Damien Chan, who was Belinda's assistant. (None of the Chans in the room were related to each other.) The group settled around a long table, with Fang at one end, the Fang Brothers delegation to his left, and the Claiborne delegation to his right. In front of each participant was a loose-leaf binder containing sketches and specifications for the knitwear part of the Spring One season. Fang and Belinda Chan also had calculators at the ready.

"Why don't I go through the styles?" Listanowsky suggested. "Chris can give the total projections, and I'll give Jeff the target, and we'll go from there." This seemed acceptable to everyone. "O.K., we're in the Fiesta group, in Ready To Wear. The cardigan—total pieces, Chris?"

"Twenty-nine thousand nine hundred," Chris Chan said, not missing a beat. . . .

For the next hour or so, Listanowsky and Chris Chan went line by line, group by group, and item by item through the Spring One season, while Belinda Chan and her assistant displayed the prototypes of the garments. Liz Claiborne has seven lines: Ready To Wear, Lizwear, Liz Sport, Liz Kids', Claiborne (the men's line, a recent addition), Dresses, and Petites. Within each line, for each season, the clothes fall into groups defined by the use of common yarns and colors. . . .

The "target" that Listanowsky spoke of was the retail price. For imported clothing, there is usually a ratio of five or six to one between the retail price and the manufacturer's price; the precise figure depends largely on tariff levels, which vary according to the type of garment. Thus, Listanowsky might say, "We'd like to be eighty on this one," which meant "We want to sell this item for eighty dollars." And Jeffrey Fang would understand that he was being asked to deliver the item for sixteen dollars or thereabouts.

For the most part, during the meeting, Fang merely nodded and scribbled a few things down or punched a few numbers through his calculator. Every once in a while, he asked for a clarification; for example, he wanted to know if a certain cardigan was "three thirty-five or three forty-five"—numbers that referred to a Byzantine classification system with which the United States Customs Service enforces quotas on clothing imports. . . .

From Ready to Wear, Listanowsky moved on to Lizwear—which, he announced with obvious pride, included one sweater that "we're going to do nearly a hundred thousand units on, and it's a long time since we did a hundred thousand units of something."

Normally, I learned, Claiborne bases the quantity of its production runs on the number of garments it expects to sell in the two-month period that each season, typically, stays in the stores. Most items are sellouts, and sometimes they sell out very quickly, but there is no provision for increasing output in response to demand; nor is a garment ever repeated in a subsequent season, although its success might inspire something similar.

"The total is seventy-nine thousand seven hundred for Missy and fifteen thousand six hundred and seventy for Petite," Chris Chan said.

"The target is forty-two," Listanowsky said.

"And for this one I have a request," Chris went on. "If at all possible, I would like to do the Petite in Shanghai, because I owe them two thousand dozen already."

"Be my guest," Fang said.

"We're trying to develop a supplier in Shanghai, and Jeffrey is helping us," Listanowsky explained to Greenberg and me. "The best way to make sure everything is done properly there is to manage it all from here. You give it to them as a package.". . .

"So the Petite goes to Shanghai, right?" Fang said. "Do they take care of the yarn, or do we dye the yarn for them?"

"We dye the yarn—this season," Chris replied. "I already have some lab dips from them, and I'm going to look at their dyeing factory sometime in July. But right now I don't want to take the risk."

Now, at last, they began to talk money—the money that Claiborne would pay to Fang Brothers. But their differences, if there were any, were all but invisible to an outsider; indeed, from the conversation it was not always easy to tell the buyers from the sellers. Occasionally, Listanowsky tried to nudge the cost of a garment down by saying something like "I'm doing a real push to be under fifty," and Fang and Belinda Chan would hold a whispered consultation in Cantonese and come up with a number. At one point, Fang volunteered that a fifty-two-dollar retail price on a striped sleeveless cotton sweater was "crazy," and it turned out that he meant crazy high rather than, as I had assumed, crazy low. Listanowsky nodded. "I think forty-eight would be terrific," he said.

"I think even forty-eight is high," Fang said.

"Do you really?" Listanowsky asked. "Where would you go—forty-five?"

"Forty-five," Fang said.

The discussion was interrupted by the appearance in the doorway of a man wearing an elegantly pressed white shirt and a tie—the latter a rarity in Hong Kong in the summer months. He was Kenneth Fang, at forty-eight the oldest of the brothers, and after greeting Listanowsky and Greenberg he invited me to accompany him to his office. There I asked him about the origins of the family business, and got, in reply, a short history of the clothing-and-textile industry in Hong Kong. In the late nineteen-forties, Kenneth told me, the prospect of revolution, and then the revolution itself, drove two million people from China to Hong Kong, a city, until then, of six hundred thousand. Most of the newcomers were poor and unskilled, but a few, like Kenneth and Jeffrey's father, S. C. Fang, had run spinning or weaving factories in Shanghai. With its population suddenly quintupled, and with the traditional foundation of its economy—trade with China—undermined by the Cold War and the Korean War, Hong Kong needed a new source of revenue. Then, as now, textiles and clothing were an ideal starter industry—one in which capital and technology counted for less than a work force ready to do almost any job at any pay.

S. C. Fang sent his children—four sons and two daughters—to college in the United States, and in the mid-nineteen-sixties the sons began coming back to Hong Kong. (His daughters remained in the States, where one became a dentist and the other a pharmacist.) Kenneth returned in 1964. It was he who guided the family into the knitwear business, which in those days meant gloves, T-shirts, and two basic types of sweater—pullover and cardigan.

"The Hong Kong garment industry was developed in the middle sixties," Kenneth said. "At that time, the only thing Hong Kong could sell was price. We could make jeans that sold for four ninety-nine and T-shirts that sold for three ninety-nine. But the system forced us to upgrade ourselves."

Hong Kong's success in the textile field had already alarmed manufacturers in Europe and the United States, and, at their urging, the Western governments had set up a system of import quotas. The quotas were calculated in terms of quantity rather than value, on the theory that such an arrangement would be easier to enforce and would better reflect the harm to employers and employees in the importing countries—where costs, after all, were much higher. But that decision, Kenneth explained, had an unforeseen effect: it encouraged the Hong Kong manufacturers to move from textiles to clothing and then from simple to fancy clothing, in order to generate more income and employment per square yard. "Ten years ago, Fang Brothers' customers were K mart and Montgomery Ward," he said. "Today, we are making Liz Claiborne dresses, Liz Claiborne sweaters—everything as complicated as possible. This is the ironic effect. You force us to be a first-class, quality maker. You force the Hong Kong industry to move ahead."

One area in which Hong Kong moved ahead was sweaters, notwithstanding a climate that precluded a home market for any but the thinnest of them. Knitwear was a cottage industry at first, with women in tiny apartments knitting panels on so-called hand-knitting machines, which are about the size of an ironing board and are powered by the operator's arm working a lever. Knitters, or the subcontractors who employed them, delivered the finished panels to factories—typically, a floor or part of a floor of a multi-tenanted commercial building—for assembly. As knitwear fashions proliferated, however, the cottage-industry system became impractical. The hand-knitting machine could not shift over from fine-gauge to heavy-gauge yarn or from a jersey stitch to a cable. To handle changes of that order, the knitter had to have access to more than one machine or to a machine that was too sophisticated and expensive to be entrusted to a worker at home. By the early seventies, many of the knitting subcontractors were opening factories in government-owned "industrial estates" and putting all their workers and equipment under one roof. Some sweater-makers—the Fangs among them—decided to go a step further and, dispensing with the subcontractors, do the knitting and the assembling in one place. By all accounts, the Hong Kong clothing industry had emerged smartly from these transitions. At the time of my visit, Hong Kong, with a population of five and a half million, was exporting nearly as much clothing as China, with a population of a billion. Clothing and textiles accounted for forty per cent of Hong Kong's exports and forty-two per cent of its manufacturing employment, and many of the ruling families of the industry had, like the Fangs, begun opening up satellite factories overseas.

Chan spent most of his lunchtime poring over the day's telexes from New York—a hundred pages or so—while Listanowsky talked about Fang Brothers. "We must have gone through—I don't know—thirty or forty costs this morning," he said. "Maybe ten million dollars' worth of merchandise. With some people, we'd spend all day talking about one garment. With Jeffrey, there's a tremendous trust, because of the number of years that we've been doing business. We spend more time talking about maintaining market share and trying to work tight on a product than we do on 'I need another dime or quarter.' We both explain what our needs are, and then we sharpen our pencils and try to see how we can achieve the best end result. If I could work like this everywhere, I wouldn't take aspirin."

I asked if there had been more haggling over price in earlier years. "When I first started going to the Orient, I was much more cautious in my negotiating," he said. "After I shook hands with somebody, I wanted to count the number of fingers I had left. As the years passed and I was doing business with people for back-to-back seasons, relationships started to come into play. Today, it's more of an educational process we're going through with our suppliers. We suggest what we would like to retail something for—the profit margin we'd like—and then we try to form a median point of view that will allow both companies to make a reasonable profit, as opposed to one side getting the better of the deal.'' This kind of easy accommodation was facilitated, Listanowsky said, by Claiborne's willingness to let him make decisions on the spot. Other buyers were forever telling factory people, "I'll have to check with New York on that," but Art Ortenberg, Listanowsky's boss (and Liz Claiborne's husband), never put him in that position. "That's one of the things I admire about Art,'' Listanowsky said. "He gives people full latitude." The same kind of latitude applied to expenses, he said. "Everyone flies business class at Liz Claiborne, and no one says you can't have a harbor-view room at the Regent.''

Later, in the Mercedes heading back to Kowloon, Listanowsky elaborated on the dangers of growing too fast. Liz Claiborne, he said, could do what other companies were doing—scour the world for new countries that wanted to get into the clothing business and had yet to face import quotas. "But if we do that I'm afraid what happened to Izod will happen to us," he said.

I asked him what had happened to Izod.

"Some people would give you a different answer, but I think the business just got away from them,'' Listanowsky said. "It's not that Izod went out of fashion. There was nothing wrong with their fashion. Izod started making goods in a whole lot of factories that they didn't know, and the stuff started coming back to them looking like shit. That's what worries me. I mean, these numbers are really mind-boggling. We probably did eighteen million dollars' worth of business today—wholesale. Maybe nine hundred thousand units. Which is truly amazing, because many companies in the industry close sales for an entire year on less than that."

"A lot less," Greenberg interjected.

"Sometimes I lose sight of how fast we've been growing," Listanowsky said. "Last year at this time, we were operating as a five-hundred-and-fifty-million-dollar company. The year prior to that, we were a three-hundred-fifty-million-dollar company. Now it's eight hundred million, and next year maybe a billion." He paused, and added, "Of course, it's a pleasant problem. It's a problem a lot of people wish they had."

No conversation about the clothing business in Hong Kong gets very far before the subject of quotas comes up—and, once up, it tends to stay up. At the time of my visit, Hong Kong had separate quota agreements with Austria, Canada, Finland, Sweden, the European Economic Community, and the United States—each agreement covering a wide assortment of textile and apparel products. Quota considerations affected every decision that manufacturers and buyers were called on to make. But with the new round of negotiations under way that June in Honolulu between Hong Kong and the

United States, the quota system had become an issue as well as a fact of life.

"You have a situation in which one side—Hong Kong—is trying to stick to the rules that both sides have agreed to, and the country on the other side is under heavy pressure to break those rules," Lawrence Mills, the director-general of the Federation of Hong Kong Industries, told me. "The Multifibre Arrangement"—this was an international agreement, generally referred to as the M.F.A., that established ground rules for textile and apparel quotas—"was designed to deal with a particular economic problem said to exist as far as textiles and apparel are concerned: a problem of sudden and extraordinary economic dislocation. Unfortunately, over the years it has been used as a political instrument rather than an economic one, and we've had to more or less succumb to the pressures that weigh on American Administrations."

At the end of the Second World War, when the victorious powers were exchanging ideas for the future, one idea that met with a lot of favor was to break down barriers to trade. A number of economists had fingered protectionism as a cause of the Great Depression, and, with the war's end, there was fear that the world economy would pick up where it had left off in the nineteen-thirties. To fend off that possibility—and in the reigning spirit of internationalism—representatives of twenty-three nations met in Geneva in October, 1947, and signed the General Agreement on Tariffs and Trade, or GATT, which required tariffs and customs regulations to be applied uniformly; the signatories also declared their intention to press on toward the goal of truly free trade.

The next twenty years were a time of falling tariffs and rapid growth for most of the industrialized world—a confluence of trends hailed by the economics profession as proof that politicians ought to make a practice of doing what economists tell them. But politicians cannot always do what economists tell them.

In the late nineteen-fifties, British and American textile and apparel manufacturers found themselves threatened by new competition, from Hong Kong and Japan, respectively—competition that took the form of cotton cloth, yarn, and a modest quantity of scarves, blouses, sweaters, brassieres, and other simple items of apparel. Long before American automobile, steel, and appliance companies were complaining about cheap Japanese imports, textile and apparel interests were sounding that alarm and calling for measures to avert the "collapse" of their industries.

The most that the Eisenhower Administration would do to appease the textile interests was pressure the Japanese into signing a "voluntary" quota agreement on cotton and cotton products. (Japan did not resist very strenuously, since its economic planners already believed that the future lay with more sophisticated and lucrative industries.) One political party's reluctance, however, was another party's opportunity. By 1960, the textile and apparel manufacturers were criticizing Japan for failing to abide by its agreement, and were pleading for similar protection against other countries' exports. John F. Kennedy, in his Presidential campaign, promised "a comprehensive, industry-wide remedy" and, once in office, quickly organized another trade conference in Geneva; it drafted an agreement known as the Short Term Arrangement, which authorized quotas on cotton textiles and apparel as a way to avoid job losses and "market disruption." The participating countries were to establish the quotas on a bilateral basis, but an importing country had the right to initiate action if market disruption occurred and an exporting country refused to cooperate.

Hong Kong has had to contend with textile quotas since 1959, when Britain first imposed them. When the United States stepped into the act, in 1961, American officials emphasized the temporary nature of their policy: it was to be a brief detour on the road to freer trade. But the Short Term Arrangement was followed by a Long Term Arrangement, which, though initially intended to last five years, wound up, with renewals, lasting twelve; and in 1974 the Long Term Arrangement was succeeded by the Multifibre Arrangement, which covered wool and man-made fibres as well as cotton. The M.F.A. itself was twelve years old at the time of my visit to Hong Kong, and representatives of the signatory nations—now fifty-four in all—were about to assemble in Geneva to try to extend it yet again.

Everybody in the industry seemed to have a story or two to tell about the workings of the quota system. "We make for one of our clients a packable nylon waterproof anorak—a jacket—which goes in a little drawstring pouch," Alex Blum, an American who has been doing business in Hong Kong since 1961, told me. "The United States Customs now insists that that pouch come in under the handbag quota. The pouch costs us thirty cents to make, but because of this ruling it has to have its own label inside—with country of origin, fibre, and care instructions—and a great deal of additional paperwork."

In the early nineteen-eighties, some companies began making jackets with zip-on sleeves. "The only reason for this was quota," an import-export lawyer explained to me. "That way, the garments could be called vests instead of outerwear, and vests fall into what's called the basket category—'other garments.' Quota on jackets was tight at the time, and there were no quotas on vests or sleeves. So people were bringing in vests with half-zippers on the armholes and separately shipping the sleeves with the other half of the zippers, and the stores would zip the sleeves and the vests together, or the customer would do it. This was actually an important fashion item while it lasted, and it lasted until Customs broadened the definition of outerwear to include vests with attachments for sleeves. Then some people said, 'O.K., let's take the zippers off and just leave the armholes open, and the sleeves can be sewn on after they get to the United States.' That worked for a while, until Customs said, 'No, we aren't going to treat as a vest anything that in its imported condition is not commercially viable as a vest. We don't think it's a finished vest; we think it's an unfinished jacket.' So then the importers actually went to the trouble of putting a commercial finish on the armholes, and, after the vests got into the country, removing the finish and adding the sleeves. Well, Customs finally put an end to *that* one by saying, 'If you bring in a part of a jacket, we're going to make you use jacket quota, and that means if you bring in two sleeves we want *two* jackets' worth of quota.' A lot of things you see in the stores are being generated by quota requirements rather than by some designer's great idea. U.S. Customs is the designer, you might say."

The system was quite mad, according to practically all the people who explained it to me. But many of them added that the Hong Kong manufacturers had a knack for turning adversity to advantage. In September of 1984, I learned, the United States government unilaterally reinterpreted the so-called country-of-origin rule for knitwear. Until then, all the importing countries had treated the assembly of a garment—the most complex and labor-intensive phase of production—as the factor that determined its country of origin for quota purposes, and, with that understood, many Hong Kong knitwear companies had moved some or all of their knitting operations to China, to take advantage of lower labor costs. The new ruling threatened to turn a lot of Hong Kong sweaters into Chinese sweaters, thereby barring their import into the United States, since China, as a relatively new participant in the market, had only a small fraction of Hong Kong's quota rights.

William Dorward recounted the country-of-origin controversy for me in highly undiplomatic terms. "There are between twenty-four and thirty manufacturing processes in the production of a sweater," he said. "One of these processes involves the knitting of pieces, of which, generally, five go into the finished sweater. Now, some rather simplistic individual or body—which has probably never been nearer to a knitting factory than the second floor of Bloomingdale's—blindly assumed that the only manufacturing element of any significance was the knitting of the panels. It's an understandable mistake, for anyone who doesn't know the industry. In fact, the knitting is one of the simpler parts of the manufacturing process—and a part that accounts for a small fraction of the cost of production, because it's automatic. If you were to go to one of these factories in China, you'd see dozens of girls standing there pushing levers. That's how difficult it is. However, we live in a world of perceptions, and the perception in the United States was that, somehow or other, those no-good foreigners were being devious again, and exploiting slave labor to produce unreasonably competitive garments in order to disrupt the American industry. It was a unilateral and substantial change in the rules in the middle of the game, and it really threw the industry here into turmoil. Our manufacturers had to start knitting these garments themselves in Hong Kong instead of in China—and because they couldn't find enough workers in Hong Kong to do that kind of job they had to buy an enormous amount of new, computerized knitting machinery. One stroke of Commissioner Von Raab's pen"—William Von Raab is the United States Commissioner of Customs—"forced the industry in Hong Kong to spend hundreds of millions of dollars."

The new country-of-origin rule was a response to pressure from the American knitwear industry, which presumably hoped to weaken the Hong Kong competition. The effect, however, was evidently just the opposite—to make the Hong Kong industry, with its ultra-modern equipment more competitive than ever. . . .

Ricke Knitting Mills, on Flushing Avenue in the Maspeth section of Queens, is a one-story red brick structure that was built in 1955 and looks its age. . . . The office was out of a simpler time in the garment industry, when the families that ran knitwear factories didn't have to worry about competition from farther away than across town. . . . Richard, Joseph, and Bruce Goldman . . . have been running the place since their father, Milton, retired a few years ago. . . .

"Everything I'm wearing is American-made," Richard Goldman announced. "These sneakers cost ninety dollars. Made in America! The jeans are Levi Strauss. Made in America! The socks are made in America. This T-shirt, believe it or not." He tugged at it. "Made in America! . . . We will not buy foreign cars. We will not allow foreign cars in our parking lot. We have two accounts with buyers who drive Audis, and they have to park on the street. I know it sounds stupid, but it's something. America can't support the whole world anymore. We have to let them make it on their own, and Japan is the prime example. I watched a show on Channel 13 about how the Japanese treat American goods.". . .

Later, I asked him about the German and Japanese knitting machines I had seen in back. "If I could buy an American knitting machine, I would," he said. "Even if they were inferior, I'd buy them, and make them better, because if I don't have confidence in what American workers can do, why am I making anything? Why don't I sell insurance for a living?"

Joseph Goldman came into the office while Richard was talking. "The government put the American-made knitting machine out of business," he said. He explained that the last major domestic manufacturer of sweater-knitting machinery, Wildman-Jacquard, abandoned the market after being sold by its parent company, North American Rockwell—an event precipitated by what Joseph Goldman understood to be a pointless antitrust action by the Justice Department. Without Rockwell's backing, he said, Wildman-Jacquard was unable to modernize. . . .

I asked him how his company had been affected by imported sweaters, which, according to some estimates, commanded more than half the American retail market. In Richard Goldman's mind, the import statistics came with names attached—the names of Ricke Knitting Mills' ex-customers. "We used to do a tremendous, tremendous business with Rosanna," he recalled. "They went overseas a hundred per cent. And Christian Dior, they went overseas—that hurt badly."

"Penrose," Joseph Goldman interjected. "My father had that account forever."

"We grew up with Penrose," Richard said.

I repeated an observation I had heard from several fashion-company executives: that American knitwear factories didn't have the patience to deal with small or complicated orders and took a grudging attitude toward the job of making samples. "A lot of mills are run by older men, and they don't want to make samples," Richard said. "We *do* make them, and we make them fast. Liz Claiborne, for instance, needs at least three samples of each garment. It used to be that a mill could pick and choose the garments it wanted to make. My father had a group of core people he could depend on. In January or February, his accounts would call him into the city, and they'd sit down and plan their orders for the whole year. We can't operate like that anymore. If a customer says 'Jump,' we say 'How high?' "

"Liz Claiborne makes goods all over the world. Calvin Klein, London Fog—they're the same way. We've demonstrated to them that we're willing to drop whatever we're doing to satisfy them, as long as they give us the same lead time they do overseas. In the last eighteen months, we've spent a million dollars on electronic knitting machines. It was an all-or-nothing gamble. We have big notes to pay. Things are very, very tight. But we can cover every base now. We might not have tremendous volume, but we have triple-lock machines in four-cut, five-cut, six-cut, seven-cut, eight-cut, and ten-cut. Also, we're a cab ride away from the garment district. The buyers and designers can be here in fifteen minutes."

"A lot of the mills are run by older people who really don't have the vision," Joseph Goldman said. "They're so set in their ways—"

"Right," Richard broke in. "My father used to work on the old flat machines and circular machines, and as we started to become more and more electronic he stopped going into the knitting department. Even though the stitch configurations were the same and the basics of knitting were the same, the programming was so alien to him that he gave up on it. A lot of the older millowners are trying to upgrade their machinery, but they're not upgrading their thinking to go along with it. Running a knitting machine is not only running it for the orders. The beauty of having the computer controls is that we can interrupt an order, make some samples, get back into production, and satisfy two people at the same time. Liz Claiborne—last week, *we* called *them,* and told them to come out and we'd make samples. If I'm not making samples, I'm losing money in future business. We're trying to learn to take some of the things that overseas has been doing and do them here, and one of those things is being able to turn out samples fast."

I asked Richard how he thought his sweaters compared in quality with those from the Far East.

"People will tell you the quality is better overseas—that's nonsense," he said. "They buy machines from the same people we do. Knitting is knitting, whether we do it or they do it or Joe Schmo does it—whether it's done in Taiwan or on Mars. There's only four different things you can do: you can knit, you can tuck, you can miss, you can transfer. That's it."

"The difference is the fact that they pay their people nothing," Joseph said.

"Right. While we might have to pay seven and eight dollars an hour, they're paying maybe twenty-two cents an hour. People talk about quality. I can show you sweaters made in Korea with holes big enough to stick your fist in, and I can show you sweaters made in the United States with holes big enough to stick your fist in. You get what you pay for. My sweaters sell for fifty, sixty, seventy dollars. We make good department-store, specialty-store, middle-of-the-road, upstairs-type merchandise, and we make it well. We know that."

A non-union shop, Ricke Knitting Mills had a hundred and ten employees at the time of my visit, and most of them were women who lived in the neighborhood and walked to work. Unlike many garment manufacturers in the Orient, who favor the piecework system, the Goldmans pay a straight hourly wage. "I consider our workers to be exceptionally good quality," Richard said. "They've been working for us for a long time. We're in a good neighborhood. All right, so we don't do calisthenics in the morning. I know how upset these people get if something is wrong and we bring it back to show them. Some of these women cry! They don't want to make bad goods.

Nothing manufactured is perfect, but we try. I don't see how anybody can survive in this industry over the next ten years if it keeps going the way it's going.

"We've invested all this money in our business, and I'm not looking for aid," Richard went on. "All I'm looking for is a fair market share. The government talks a lot about fair trade. What's fair about it? I can't pay twenty-two cents an hour. We have these industries. They employ people. They require some degree of governmental—I don't want to call it protection, but let's say *care.* We need a little care. In the over-all scheme of things, do you think anybody cares about my hundred and ten employees? No! And these are not people who can be retrained. Buyers call me up and say, 'Can you make this? Can you make that?' I give them a price and they say, 'But I can make it overseas for this much less.' What am I supposed to do? It's not *my* fault. I didn't invent the minimum wage. We've got to pay *x* number of dollars an hour—and we're entitled to make a living also, my brothers and I. We're never going to be millionaires. We're going to make a nice living, provided we can compete. We're not operating this business for our health. We're doing it to make a profit—to buy more machinery and to perpetuate the business. We don't want to see it go down the tubes in a couple of years. Joey's got children, I've got children, my brother Bruce hopefully is going to have kids someday. We'd like to be able to pass it on to them. Whether they want it or not is up to them, but it would be nice to be able to say, 'We've got a business that's seventy years old.' How many people can say that?"

While I was hanging out at Ricke Knitting Mills, I encountered a number of regular visitors—such as Robert Lineburg, a vice-president of Commonwealth Yarn Sales, Inc. Lineburg told me that he had been in plenty of knitting mills in his time, and he offered to explain why Ricke had survived and so many others hadn't.

"The sweater-knit industry evolved because of immigrants who settled this section of the country and invested their blood, sweat, and tears to build a business," he said. "But the next generation decided they wanted their children to go into something maybe one step above—medicine, law, finance. That's been the general trend—into the service-related industries and out of manufacturing. So the older mill-owners today don't have a next generation to hand the mill down to. In order to survive in the knitwear industry, you must be innovative. In order to be innovative, you have to reinvest your profits in new equipment. Some of these older owners will say, 'Look, I've done well over the years. I'm successful. I'm ready to retire. Why should I invest a million dollars of my profits in the business when there's nobody to give it to?' You walk into many knitting firms and look at the equipment they have, and it's thirty years old.

This mill is different. You wouldn't recognize it as the one you walked into five or ten years ago. Their equipment today is totally changed, and they're doing ten different styles at once." . . .

One afternoon a few months later, I accompanied Jack Listanowsky, the man in charge of knitwear production for Liz Claiborne, on a visit to Macy's. The corner of Thirty-fifth Street and Seventh Avenue was teeming with reminders of unemployment, homelessness, and other forms of distress. As soon as we had passed through the revolving door and into Macy's proper, however, the demographics improved noticeably, and so did the mood.

We rode the escalator to the third floor and plunged into a jungle of women's wear—dresses, pants, blouses, sweaters, suits, T-shirts, and sweatshirts, subdivided into designer fiefdoms bearing such names as Calvin Klein, Ellen Tracy, Adrienne Vittadini, and Perry Ellis. A time traveller from the nineteenth century would be as startled by all this frockery, I suspect, as by television sets, vacuum cleaners, air-conditioners, or any of the more celebrated blessings of modern free enterprise.

Sleek sculptured felines stood guard at the gates of some departments; in others, customers could watch fashion shows on television monitors suspended overhead; mannequins were everywhere—mannequins that ran the gamut of hair colors and skin tones, although their body language and facial expressions fell into a narrower range, roughly between supercilious and contemptuous. Striding down the aisle from the east building to the west, Listanowsky told me that he was just back from Peru, where he had been smoothing out some problems with a Brazilian-owned factory that was starting to manufacture for Claiborne; tomorrow morning, he added, he would be off to the Bahamas, where he intended to give up smoking and get back into running—a project to which he had allotted six days. (He had been hoping for two weeks off, but had decided to cut the trip short in order to be back in New York by the time Art Ortenberg returned from *his* vacation.)

From afar, the Liz Claiborne department was all oranges, reds, and yellows, and brightly lit and bustling. Macy's was doing a brisk business for a workday, and a disproportionate number of customers seemed to have wound up in Liz Claiborne's corner.

He about-faced to examine a group of coordinates made of a sweatshirt-like fabric that goes by the name Toughknit. They had come from Fantastic, one of the Fang brothers' factories in Hong Kong, and I remembered that there had been some scheduling problems involving these garments. I asked how the problems had been worked out.

"From a retail point of view, these should have been here two or three weeks sooner," Listanowsky said. "But I'm amazed that they got here at all. The top is out of Hong Kong, the skirt was made in Thailand"—he was checking labels as he spoke—"the dress is from Thailand, the pants are from the Philippines, and then you have a cardigan from Panama. There are five pieces—maybe two hundred thousand units. And there go two more out the door."

Looking where he was pointing, I saw a young woman approach the cash register carrying an orange bottom and a yellow top.

"And there goes some of our Taiwan product," Listanowsky said, indicating a cotton dress with a floral pattern, which another customer was preparing to pay for. Still another customer walked off with a Toughknit and, en route to the cash register, paused to check out a different rack. Listanowsky beamed. "I love to see people holding the garments they're going to buy as they go to look for more," he said.

Clutching a sweatshirt by its shoulder, Listanowsky called my attention to the seam—to its absolute evenness. "This is one of Vincent Fang's" he said. Vincent's product always says 'Buy me! Buy me!' " He sidled across the aisle. "This was made in Brazil," he said, "and I remember this garment very, very well. It's O.K.—it's commercially acceptable. But if I had my druthers I would have been more insistent with the factory about the workmanship. The seam wavers a little bit—it's not clean."

I took this opportunity to ask Listanowsky about his often expressed desire to produce more knitwear in the United States.

"That's something I'm making a big push on," he said. "We're constantly looking for new domestic sources we can develop."

Did that mean that the small proportion of American-made knitwear in the Liz Claiborne line was increasing?

Listanowsky looked uncomfortable. "It might not necessarily work that way," he said." Let's say our domestic production increases fifteen per cent and our over-all production increases forty per cent; then the proportion will decline, and people will say we're doing less domestically, even though we're really doing more."

His assessments of the clothing on the racks became sterner when we drifted away from the Claiborne department to check out the competition. "This is the same price as one by Liz Claiborne—forty-four dollars," he said, running his fingers over a blue top that, as he pointed out, wasn't very different from an item in the Claiborne Toughknit collection. "They're both cotton. But this is a lighter-weight interlock, and they didn't bother with the cover-stitching. To me, also, the ribbing and the body don't match. They're different shades of blue. As a merchandiser, I would be embarrassed to sell this garment. And then I look at where it's made, and that embarrasses me, too—as a person—because it says 'Made in the U.S.A.' "

Keeping Up with the Information

On-line in the Philippines and London

John Maxwell Hamilton

Every workday morning at 7:30 Marian Tabjan (pronounced *tabban'*), a fresh-faced woman in her late 20s, begins her long, familiar journey to a job the world has only begun to understand.

Outside her parents' simple plywood-walled home, which like others in the government housing project in the northern Manila municipality of Malabon has electricity but no telephone, she hails one of the many motorized tricycles that cruise the neighborhood. It taxis her five minutes to within a short uphill walk of a jeepney pickup point. Jeepneys, a distinctive Philippine cultural institution, come in gaudy combinations of bright colors, are decorated with streamers and silver horses mounted on the hood, and have names like "Holy Mary," "Milwaukee," and "Mobile Lounge." Though viewed by foreign visitors as chaos-on-wheels, these vehicles with deep fronts and two rows of benches facing each other in the back are efficient small buses that ply routes throughout the city. The 5- to 10-minute jeepney ride Marian takes drops her within walking distance of a train station. The LRT (Light Rail Transport), as it is called, whisks her through the old part of Manila to the Makati commercial center on the south side of the city. She exits at Sen. Gil J. Puyat Avenue and squeezes on a double-decker bus that lumbers up the street. After 10 minutes she climbs off the bus and darts through the heavy traffic to the other side of the broad thoroughfare. Entering one of the simple steel and glass buildings that have become the dominant modern architectural style throughout the world, Marian walks to the back of the lobby, ascends a flight of dingy stairs to the second floor, and goes through the doors of Saztec Philippines. She freshens up, chats with her colleagues for a few minutes, and is at her desk by 9 A.M., poised to communicate instantly with the world.

Saztec Philippines, one member of the Saztec family of information facilities spread around the world, does data entry. In the lingo of modern communications, that means its data entry operators sit at electronic terminals, converting information printed on paper into computer files. On a given day Filipinos employed by Saztec can be found "keying" American patient records for hospitals in Pomona, Calif., or Greensboro, N.C.; consumer credit reports on British citizens; names and addresses of Stride Rite shoe clients in the United States; switching networks for the Mountain Bell and Pacific Bell telephone systems; articles in *Playboy* and the *Christian Science Monitor;* U.S. presidential speeches; French novels; European patent records; and the Helsinki, Finland, National Library book catalogue.

Saztec is one component of a technological revolution that is reshaping our lives as profoundly as the industrial revolution in the 19th century reshaped the lives of our forebears. Weighing little and operating at speeds that have no meaningful relationship to old-fashioned mail delivery, computers and other modern technology create global interdependencies unimagined only a generation ago, when the experts thought that each country would never need more than one computer.

Global industries spawned by this technology create brand-new services that have become indispensable virtually overnight. As the provider of one of the first services to go abroad, data entry companies like Saztec have helped rewrite the theories of Adam Smith and Karl Marx, who thought that only manufactured goods were economically important and that services must remain as local as a haircut and shoeshine.

Communication networks using high-speed facsimile machines, computer terminals, and satellites and transoceanic fiber optic cables knit together far-flung operations. It is now possible, indeed imperative, for traditional manufacturing companies to function as if borders did not exist at all. Rather than worry about how far corporate headquarters are from manufacturing facilities, executives search for countries that have workers who will toil for low wages or that possess a promising market for sales.

This revolution has also created noneconomic global interdependencies, such as the one that shocked Swedes when it came to light: the Malmö, Sweden, fire department reached its database of street routes by contacting a General Electric computer in Cleveland, Ohio.

The manufacture of computer hardware, software, telecommunications gear, and other information technologies is the largest industry in the United States and "will be the largest industry worldwide by the mid-1990s," says Michael Tyler, a telecommunications consultant with Booz-Allen and Hamilton. But the meaning, if not the magnitude, of this revolution is less clear. As with any sweeping change, new concerns have surfaced. Some are as fundamental as fashioning standards for telephone plugs and dial tones so they will work in all countries. Some are as profound as whether information technology will let developing countries surge ahead or will push them further behind—and what it will mean for the United States and other industrialized countries.

So quickly is change coming that the most basic implication of this revolution—global interdependence—is hard to see.

"What are you doing here?" a worker in Saztec's London office asked when I visited.

"Researching interdependence."

"What," she said with dead seriousness, "does that have to do with us?"

How Alan Fraser Founded Saztec

Alan Fraser seems physically larger than he really is. Six feet or so in height, he is lean and muscled. His sandy hair is cut close, military style, accentuating his jug ears, angular features, and large toothy smile. In keeping with the common impression of New Zealanders, he is outgoing and frank. It is not hard to imagine prospective clients succumbing to his sales pitches or to understand why someone with his command presence preferred to start his own company in 1972 rather than work in someone else's.

"While shaving one morning," he recalls of his first business venture, "I thought what is the simplest thing to sell, and I saw the cap." The cap belonged to his aerosol shaving cream can. He figured he could redesign it with distinct new selling points. It would be a quarter of an inch higher, making the product stand taller on the store shelf; it would have serrated edges, making it easier to take off; it would have the customer's logo imprinted on the top; and it would have a pinhole in the middle so that "unsightly" moisture on the can nozzle would evaporate. Enthused by the idea, he wasted little time looking for a company name. He opened a magazine at random and, finding a story about Aztec Indians, called the company Aztec. Today he admits that the selling points for Aztec caps, especially the pinhole, might not have made much difference to consumers. But the pitch worked well enough with a shaving cream manufacturer, who placed large orders with him. In a year Fraser had enough capital to go into a business with a real future—data entry.

Data entry appealed to Fraser both because it built on his IBM experience without requiring extraordinary technical expertise and because he saw a market. Data entry was changing from the primitive method of punching holes in paper cards to electronic computerization. Businesses were learning the value of managing information, and they wanted help. Although some giant companies like General Motors might have had enough work to keep in-house data entry operators busy every day, many smaller companies then, as now, did not; and those that did have a steady volume of work often preferred not to be distracted by maintaining an operation whose task was peripheral to their central job. IBM stopped selling data entry services for just that reason: it wanted to concentrate on selling equipment.

From the very first, Fraser planned an international operation that would provide high-quality work at a low cost. He targeted the Australian market and set up a small office in Sydney. He planned to subcontract the data entry work in Singapore, where wage levels were about one-half those in Australia. With the help of a silent partner, who continued to work at IBM, Fraser registered the company in Singapore, although not as Aztec. Because another Singapore company had already taken that name, he put an "S" for Singapore on the front of Aztec, making it Saztec.

Fraser's approach to building Saztec was to make bold promises and then find ways of delivering. He got his first contract by challenging a Sydney customer, Computer Accounting Services, to give him a small job as a trial. If he couldn't deliver a high-quality product at the low price he quoted, and do it in four days, he would forgo payment. The problem was that Fraser had not yet tested any data entry facilities in Singapore himself.

Fraser jumped on an airplane and, shortly after landing in Singapore, located a local car dealer with a computer to do the work. But when the data were entered, Fraser discovered many errors, and although the car dealer was willing to do the job again, he did not have time until the next week. Fraser, who was staying in a cheap Singapore hotel to conserve his dwindling resources, desperately looked for another company that could do data entry. Recalling that *Reader's Digest* had such work done in the Philippines, he found Pacific Data in Manila and called the general manager, a Chinese Filipino named Emmanuel B. Cu. The gist of Fraser's call was: This is Saztec; we're doing a test to see how fast you can turn around a data entry job; meet me at the Manila airport tomorrow and I'll give you the data; you must send it to Sydney within 24 hours by plane. (Fraser could not afford to stay overnight in Manila.) Cu agreed to do the job and met Fraser at the airport. Pacific Data delivered on the day promised. "That," Fraser says, "was the start of Saztec."

Within three years, Fraser's daring strategy had created a client base of one-half million Australian dollars annually (about U.S. $600,000 at the time). Saztec gave most of its data conversion jobs to Pacific Data, though some were sent to Singapore to spread what was becoming a large work load.

Fraser experimented with other aspects of the computer business, always with the same bravura. When he wanted to sell Hitachi's up-scale hand calculator in Australia, the Japanese company balked. They had never heard of Saztec. Fraser convinced them to test Saztec by giving him 2,000 computers. In just a couple of days he was back in Japan to announce that he had sold the whole lot, a feat he accomplished by offering the calculators at cost to a discount house.

Saztec's progress since its founding by Alan Fraser in 1972 has not been uniformly up. Data entry, Fraser says, "is a barometer of the global economy." Companies experiencing financial difficulties do not commission big jobs converting data on paper into computerized databases, which can be expensive. When the world economy slumped in the early 1980s, Fraser "thought God might be sending him a message to go teach Bible classes in the islands." Business was so slow he had to let 300 Filipino employees go, reducing the Saztec Philippines staff to six. But within a month of the layoffs, he was hiring again, and within half a year, he was at full capacity. In mid-1989 the facility had 1,000 employees. Each year since 1982, when business rebounded, Fraser has seen at least 100 percent return on equity, he says. In 1989 Saztec Philippines grossed $3.1 million.

Saztec's U.S. operation . . . became Saztec International, under chief executive officer (CEO) Tom Reed. In 1985 it opened a European sales office in London and, two years later, a data entry facility on the western coast of Scotland. It also set up a small sales office in Toronto, Canada. It acquired Presstext News Service, a Washington, D.C., database, which it later sold. Additionally, it has absorbed two companies with which it had worked closely: a data processing and software development company called LMI in Dayton, Ohio, and a data entry facility, Information Control Inc., in an industrial park outside Kansas City, Mo. The latter has a division that sells used computer software.

In 1986 Saztec International made a public stock offering on the over-the-counter market. The stock had a large run-up in value in the first months, something that often happens with new issues. The high expectations, however, quickly collapsed. The company experienced a $1 million loss the first year after going public, which Reed attributes to investments needed for long-term growth. When the stock market tumbled in October 1987, the stock dropped from $7 a share to $1. But in 1989 Saztec International posted a profit of $1 million, sales were double those of the previous year, and the stock was on the rebound. . . .

Flexibility, Speed, and the Global Work Force

The fastest-growing category of jobs in the United States is computer programmers and systems analysts. Businesses that once paid little attention to information management have found they cannot afford to neglect the subject today. "We are keying stuff no one ever dreamed of keying a few years ago: newspaper articles and *Playboy,* or how to grow roses in California," Fraser says. "The reason this has happened is that the cost of storing data is so low and access is so fast. The time will come in the near future when every book is stored on a computer . . . and we will read books on computers. We have the technology. It is possible."

Saztec specializes in library catalogues, hospital patient records, legal documents, and telephone line records. "The most technically interesting job," Fraser says, "is the line record for telephone companies so they can track errors in the system. We get information on lines down to a point that a computer can identify a break at a house on the corner of such-and-such a street and [warn] that the repairman should watch out for the dog. This is one of the most sophisticated examples of a database."

The number of commercial databases for sale has expanded as the use of computers has become more widespread. The 1979–80 edition of the *Directory of Online Databases* listed 400 databases and 59 online services worldwide. The 1987 *Directory* identified 3,487 databases and 547 online services. Subjects include Physician Data Query, which contains cancer treatment measures, and *Zeitscbriftenkatalog der Bayeriscben Staatsbibliotbek Muencben,* which "contains citations to the periodical holdings of the Bavarian State Library." Presstext, which Saztec owned for a time, puts official White House and State Department statements into a computer database. The White House is a subscriber.

Thanks to the database boom, membership in the Information Industry Association more than tripled between 1983 and 1989 to 800. The Washington, D.C.-based organization represents companies that create information products, as Saztec does, and sell them, as many of Saztec's clients do. "We get two or three new members a week," said David Y. Peyton, IIA's director of government relations in 1988. "It is all we can do to remember the new names. Most of them are small companies."

If industrial growth is not diminishing, neither is one other aspect of the information revolution—the global flexibility it engenders. In the days since Fraser undertook his first data entry job, businesses of all kinds have become more adept at using information to knit together workers from vastly different locations and cultures. . . .

Todd Stein is a programmer in Saztec's most sophisticated and free-wheeling facility, located in an industrial park of one-story brick buildings about 10 miles outside Dayton, Ohio. Like many Americans of his generation, Stein has found computers a liberating obsession. He gave up full-time college study to become one of the first three employees hired by LMI, which was formed in 1981 by two Dayton-area men, Dan Leggett and Kent Meyer, and merged with Saztec in 1987. An amiable football player–sized man in his mid-20s, Stein works on computers during the day and then stays to play games on them in the evening.

In keeping with Leggett's and Meyer's relaxed management style and the rapid growth of the company, the offices are spread haphazardly in four bays. A brick props open one door; tables are not in rows; and space is so scarce that private offices also serve as hallways between rooms. Stein and the 20-odd other employees work in blue jeans and sport shirts and take breaks to play a quick game of basketball in the court behind the building. Stein attends college in the evenings, except in the summer, when he enjoys being outdoors. During those months, he often works through his lunch hour and goes home early.

The work environment is not as casual at other Saztec work sites. In the Philippines and Scotland, where large staffs do basic coding jobs, regular work hours are essential to ensure efficient use of equipment and to monitor output. Rather than dress in sports attire, as Stein does, Filipinos wear blue uniforms. This reduces the amount of money they must spend on clothes for work. Chris Dowd, an Australian who is managing director of the Scotland facility, smiles as he tells of the Scotswoman who was uncomfortable with breaks from tradition, such as calling him by his first name. She preferred he wore a suit to work.

Even so, the Saztec watchword is flexibility, not rigidity. When Saztec CEO Tom Reed complains about "having flexibility, but it is not as great as we would like," he is really talking about how much freedom he has come to expect. As the integration of vastly different work forces in Scotland, the Philippines, and the United States shows, Saztec believes in a world liberated from traditional constraints of time and space.

With a telephone call to Madras, India, almost as easy as a call next door, distance is becoming a meaningless concept. Whereas people were once satisfied to send memoranda through interoffice mail, they have begun to use facsimile transmission—fax—over telephone lines, even if the recipient is only one floor away. The need for fast turnaround and low transport costs traditionally dictated putting production facilities close to the customer. But information products do not travel like steel bars or bags of grain. Magnetic computer tapes holding information copied from tons of paper can be slipped into an envelope and tossed on a jet plane.

Distance and time are also of decreasing importance in constructing data entry facilities. A steel company has to think carefully about setting up a mill in another country. It takes three to six years to build a plant and to train its work force; then, once the mill is constructed, the decision to move is costly. But silicon chips and other computer components used in data entry are lightweight, small, and relatively cheap. Between 1972 and 1981, the number of transistors and other components that could be put on a silicon chip doubled annually. Thus, data entry facilities can be started quickly—as Saztec proved shortly after opening its London office in 1985, when it heard that the British Library had decided to computerize its General Catalogue.

When Saztec first heard of the plan to computerize the catalogue, the British Library had already decided to award the lucrative contract to a U.S. company that planned to do the work in New York City. To get the contract open to competitive bidding, Saztec launched a major lobbying campaign. Among the main lobbying points was that Saztec hoped to open a facility in Ardrossan, on the west coast of Scotland, which would give jobs to British subjects, not foreigners. Ardrossan was chosen because a defunct U.S.-owned facility in the vicinity had earlier computerized the Library of Congress card catalogue. Saztec expected to find a potential pool of trained workers in an area that suffered from high unemployment.

With the help of people like David Lambie, a Member of Parliament who represented the Cunningham South electorate that includes Ardrossan, the contract was eventually opened to competitive bidding. In January 1987, Saztec won the 4-year, £1.8 million job and acquired the rights to market the resulting computerized index worldwide for 10 years. Saztec's use of British labor also made the company eligible for British government cash grants.

A month after winning the contract, Saztec Scotland began work in earnest in a two-story red brick building that stands only 75 yards from the gray Irish Sea. It proved difficult to recruit people who had worked in the earlier facility, as many had taken other jobs. Nevertheless, Saztec hired and trained about 100 people in six months. By early 1988 the facility was profitable. Despite the enormous task of devising methods of keying languages as difficult as Greek and Cyrillic on English-language keyboards, the Scottish work force turned out computerized data ahead of the British Library schedule. Yet even this was considered frustratingly slow by Saztec, which in late 1987 briefly considered doing the work elsewhere.

Technological advances have not made proximity entirely irrelevant. The Dayton facility has five full-time data entry operators who do small jobs. Almost daily a local "fulfillment company" sends a cab driver named Rocky to Saztec with coupons received from sales promotions promising calendars and other gifts. Saztec operators key master mailing lists from the coupons. The jobs are not big enough to justify sending them to Manila.

Some complex keying tasks require close contact with the clients to check specifications or questionable data; others require turnaround in one day. Work of this nature is important enough for Saztec to have a facility with 180 full-time data entry operators in Kansas City, Mo. Other data entry companies have a much bigger U.S. presence. In 1988, Appalachian Computer Services had more than 1,400 data entry operators in six plants in rural Kentucky, Illinois, and California.

Nevertheless, the trend is increasingly to go offshore, where wage rates are lower than in the United States, to such places as the Dominican Republic, Mexico, Haiti, Grenada, Barbados, Martinique, St. Kitts, Jamaica, India, Sri Lanka, China, Taiwan, South Korea, and the Philippines.

"There are [offshore information] capabilities out there people just don't realize," says W. Patrick Griffith, who was president of AMR Caribbean Data Services in 1988, before he became vice president of AMR Information Services. "That's why I am so enthusiastic." CDS was established in 1983 when AMR, its parent company and also owner of American Airlines, decided to move its data entry facility for airline tickets from Tulsa, Okla., to Bridgetown, Barbados. In addition to processing an estimated 70 million tickets each year, CDS began to sell its services to other companies. In 1987 it opened a second facility in the Dominican Republic, which had 650 operators in mid-1989 and is expected to grow to 900 in the near future. CDS executives talk about opening a third facility at another site in the Caribbean.

The incentive, Griffith says, is that all kinds of work can be done offshore as a result of improved communications. In one of its biggest jobs, acquired in 1988, CDS keys medical claims for a large Manhattan insurance carrier. The documents arrive by plane; after the information is encoded, it is transmitted back to New York via satellite and leased communication lines, thus shortening the turnaround time. The client can also beam information, such as computer formats, directly to the Dominican Republic facility.

In 1988 Griffith expected that his work force would soon do medical transcription using this two-way electronic communications capability. U.S. physicians would dictate remarks about patients into a microphone; the comments would then be transmitted to Barbados, where they would be typed and beamed back to the United States. The whole process, Griffith said, could be done in four to six hours.

Although by 1989 that job was still on the shelf, as one executive put it, the idea of receiving documents electronically, rather than on paper, was very much alive. The company was vying for a new insurance contract in which claims information would be transmitted to the Caribbean over satellites. "Pure data entry has changed drastically in the last three years because of changes in technology, and it will change just as dramatically in the next three years," says Gary Barras, CDS's vice president for finance, who already regards the sending of information on paper as passé. "A couple of years from now we will be able to offer a product we haven't even conceived now."

Griffith's emphasis on doing more than just keying data offshore is typical of the trend in information industries. Conrad Lealand of Saztec describes his own company as the Rolls Royce of data entry companies. He means that Saztec provides high quality and can, in addition to data entry, do programming and other services needed to actually use the data. Equidata, a Manila-based operation owned by an American, recently started data entry operations with plans to provide data processing services as well. Equidata owner and president James Conway can use processing technology to analyze the Malaysian Yellow Pages, for which he already does data entry, and identify which parts of Kuala Lumpur show the greatest potential for the sale of Yellow Pages ads later. And Augusto C. Lagman, a Filipino entrepreneur, has a financial interest in about 20 computer-related companies in the Philippines, including one that does data entry and another called Systems Resources Inc., which produces customized software. One of SRI's biggest jobs, Lagman says, was a $2 million contract to produce an air base inventory management system for Boeing Services International and to train Americans in its use.

The path a job can travel to take advantage of special skills and technology in one place and cheap labor in another is as complex as the circuit diagram of a computer. Take, for example, the various stops required for the job of cataloguing part of the Helsinki Library: The library card catalogue was microfilmed in Helsinki. Reading from the microfilm, data entry operators in Manila keyed an abbreviated database that listed all book headings. This computerized list went by plane to Sydney, Australia, where a specialized company put it into a computer format compatible with a database in Toronto, Canada. Once this was done, the Toronto database supplied full citations for many standard book titles and thus reduced the amount of information that had to be keyed by hand. Saztec's Dayton processing facility converted the Toronto entries into the proper Finland catalogue classification system and sent them on to Saztec's London office for checking. Filipino workers keyed full citations for the books not in the Toronto database. Saztec's Ardrossan facility did the final editing and quality control on the Manila entries. The Helsinki Library integrated the two sets of entries.

At times it seems as if Saztec is perversely testing the limits of information to unite its work force. In 1988 Saztec moved its headquarters from Los Angeles to Kansas City, Mo., where its large U.S. data entry operation is located. But many executives did not uproot themselves. Kent Meyer, who handles sales and for a time was in charge of all operations, including the Saztec Scotland facility, resisted moving from his home in Dayton. His wife liked Dayton, where she grew up. "We can be anywhere in the United States as long as we have telephone service and Federal Express," Meyer says of the irrelevance of location. Two employees who provide technical support for projects and work on company research and development live in Eugene, Ore. In addition to its full-time data entry operators in Kansas City, Saztec employs about 80 Kansas Citians who work part time on personal computers in their homes.

The ability to use information to manage a company applies not only to information industry companies like Saztec. The quick, cheap transmission of information has made traditional heavy industry light on its feet.

For all the "buy America" talk in the car industry, for instance, truly American-made automobiles are fast becoming as much a myth as the American family farmer. By 1981, Ford Motor Company produced more than one-half of its cars outside the United States and Canada. The Ford Escort, assembled in England and Germany, may use wheel nuts from the United States, defroster grills from Italy, starters from Japan, exhaust flanges from Norway, and tires from Austria. Ford manages its parts procurement system with one of the largest private communication networks in the world.

"With modern transport and communications," a 1987 World Bank report noted, "it probably is no more difficult for today's merchants to organize a putting-out [cottage industry–type] system between New York and Hongkong, or between Tokyo and Seoul, than it was for the early English merchants to organize their putting-out system between London and the surrounding villages." According to Booz-Allen and Hamilton, Inc., the number of leased international telephone lines, the backbone of private communication networks, is expected to grow from 17,000 in 1988 to 34,000 in 1995.

Dallas-based Texas Instruments is a prime example of a company that has created its own dedicated communications system. One-half of its 50 facilities are in Attleboro, Mass.; Johnson City, Tenn.; and other U.S. cities. The other half are located in such spots as Nice, France; Miho, Japan; Buenos Aires, Argentina; Elizabeth, Australia; and Baguio, a city high in the Philippine mountains, where workers cut microchips and configure them for use in computers. The facilities can beam messages to each other via channels leased on eight satellites. As of April 1988, Texas Instruments had 43,500 computer terminals for its 77,000 employees. Dallas can send messages giving

Baguio microchip design specifications; Baguio can order raw materials for production.

With this network, many design and engineering jobs can be done far from the home office. In 1986, Texas Instruments opened a facility in Bangalore, India, where Indian specialists create software used in designing semiconductors. One hundred percent of the designs are exported via satellite. Access to cheap labor was not the chief reason for opening the plant, says Bob Bledsoe, market communications manager for Texas Instruments' data processing group. India has become a leading world software production center, thanks largely to its sizable, well-educated work force. The plant enabled the company to establish a presence in a potentially good, long-term market without raising Indian concerns about being overwhelmed by foreigners.

IBM, which has long had a sales operation in Manila, started buying computer chips in the Philippines in 1985. Worldwide computer networks permit staff to locate needed parts or to send a message to a colleague in any of 55 countries, telling of travel plans and proposing they have lunch when he arrives. When a Filipino salesperson makes a sale, he can connect his computer terminal to a system in Toronto that will "display" model sales contracts; IBM's 80-person repair staff in Manila can diagnose computer problems by connecting their computers to IBM computers in Tokyo, Japan; Tampa, Fla.; or Boulder, Colo.

Global banking, one of the chief economic integrators in the world, also relies on such information networks. The *Economist* estimates that telecommunications accounts for as much as 10 percent of commercial banks' operating costs. Although only a tiny percentage of the 50 million people who live in the Philippines use the automatic bank tellers in Manila and carry Diners Club credit cards, the country's banking system is hooked into the Society of Worldwide Interbank Financial Telecommunications, a global network for transferring money that began operation in 1977. In the mid-1980s, SWIFT handled about one million messages daily between member banks in more than 50 countries.

Improved communications has helped companies create and maintain joint ventures and partnerships such as Fraser's with Saztec International. The SGV Group, a Filipino multinational that calls itself "the largest professional services firm in Asia," formed a joint venture with the large U.S.-based firm of Arthur Anderson in the mid-1980s. Working on 55 IBM computers in blue cubicles, SGV employees write sophisticated software programs. These programs are transmitted to an Arthur Anderson terminal in Chicago, which relays them via telephone lines to clients. In one of its first jobs, SGV converted an Atlanta, Ga., hospital management system—which included everything from billing to patient records—so that it could be used on a more powerful computer system.

Saztec, Texas Instruments, IBM, SGV, and companies like them are breaking down virtually the last bastion of "domestic" economic activity: services. The United States has bowed to the inevitable consequences of global financial markets and agreed that local banks can offer foreign currency accounts. A Danish company has office cleaning operations in 15 countries; its U.S. subsidiary employs 16,000 people. Telemarketing—for instance, selling magazine subscriptions by telephone—is cheaper than the door-to-door selling techniques made famous by the Fuller Brush Company. With declining costs of telecommunication, the day is not far off when English-speaking work forces in tropical Caribbean climes will sell storm windows to Bostonians.

Increased global manufacturing and trade in goods and services mean countries are linked in ways they never were before. Interdependence, however, is not a precise equation, both sides equal in every way. Todd Stein in Dayton and Marian Tabjan in Manila, both valued employees, worry about keeping their jobs in the changing world economy. But Stein's opportunities outside Saztec far exceed Tabjan's, who is reminded daily of the vulnerabilities workers in developing countries face.

Company Flexibility, Worker Vulnerability

Marian Tabjan's personal history is marked, above all, by hard work, a family trait. The eldest of six children, she was born in 1959 in Tondo, one of the poorer sections of Manila. Her parents moved to the Malabon government housing project, situated on reclaimed land, in 1985. Two married brothers were given the Tondo home for their families. For 32 years Mr. Tabjan worked as a mechanic on government tugboats dredging Manila Bay. After retiring, he did what many Filipinos do these days: he took his services overseas to work for a German company dredging the Tigris River in Baghdad, Iraq. He returned after about a year and a half when the Iran–Iraq war broke out. The family jokes that he is now the janitor and principal of the small preschool run by Marian's mother. Named affectionately after Marian, the 40-desk Marian Learning Center fills what otherwise would be the Tabjans' living room. Tuition is 40 pesos, or about $2 a month. After teaching two hours in the school each morning, Mrs. Tabjan commutes to Tondo, where she teaches at a government-run kindergarten from 11 to 1 and then teaches grade six for adults from 6 to 9 in the evening.

After high school, Marian worked while attending college. Her first job was with the Coconut Planters Bank, where she typed information about the replanting program onto primitive data punch cards. After five months she went to the Philippine Coconut Authority. To her disappointment, she was not trained as a programmer as promised; not having a college degree, she was instead assigned clerical work. When a keypunch operator left to have a baby, however, Marian filled in for her. She worked hard to improve her typing skills and kept the job. The next year, 1980, she went to Saztec as a data entry encoder on the night shift. At Saztec she completed her college degree in industrial engineering, rose to become a line supervisor over seven other men and women, and later moved to the statistical department. By 1988 Fraser spotted her as someone to be groomed for more responsibility. He moved her to the quality control department to broaden her experience and then to a supervisory role in the department that sets specifications for work before it is coded and keyed.

"No one knows how many data entry companies there are in Manila," says Eduardo Bagtas, who manages the Saztec finance department. "They are like mushrooms." Most people in the industry guess there are 35 or 40 companies, some with just a few computer terminals. Emmanuel Cu, one of Fraser's partners and now head of the Philippine Association of Data Entry Corporations, formed in 1987, estimates that the number has doubled in the last two years. He has also seen many data entry companies fail during the 20 years he has been in the business.

Saztec's offices are unadorned but clean and air-conditioned. On both the first and second floors of the building, data entry operators sit at 11 rows of tables, eight operators to a row. The humming and beeping of their computer terminals collectively give out the sound of an orchestra tuning up. Statisticians, accountants, engineers, and coders, who prepare documents for the typists, are located in smaller rooms.

Base wages for data entry operators are about one-third those of keyers in the Kansas City facility (who earn $5.00 to $6.50 an hour) and about one-half those paid to Androssan workers. But these wages are attractive for a country with an annual per capita GNP of less than $600. Data entry operators with four years' experience average $2,650, not counting overtime. (The basic workweek is 35 hours, Monday through Friday.) Marian, who has advanced steadily, earns over $4,000 a year.

Comparisons between Saztec and other data entry companies in the Philippines are difficult. Companies do not like to give out salary data for fear of losing a competitive edge, and in any case, actual wages depend on complex systems of bonuses for high-speed, accurate work. Workers at Saztec talk about some firms providing unpleasant employment and paying less than the minimum wage. The data entry facilities that let me visit provided comfortable working conditions and paid the legal minimums at the least. But their wages and benefits were substantially lower than Saztec's.

Saztec provides free medical and dental care in a building behind the office, and it gives employees hospitalization coverage for a small fee. It also gives employees material and money to have their uniforms made, and it has set up a commissary where workers can buy food at cost. Thirty staff members are deaf. Fraser provides slightly over $2 a day to employees who are sent home when work slows down temporarily. After three and a half years on the job, employees receive $25 worth of company stock and the right to buy as much more as they want. As an added bonus, 2.5 percent of the company's before-tax profit goes to a Christmas party and summer outing for staff, the former usually at one of Manila's five-star hotels. "If we don't have a benefit," says Fraser, "it's because we haven't thought of it."

The concept at Saztec, says Erlinda Lorenzo, the administration manager, is that "seniority doesn't count for much. Performance counts." Two-thirds of the staff are women, and women have come to dominate senior positions. Lorenzo started as a clerk. The production manager is Theresa U. Joson, who earns over $12,500 a year.

Fraser, the only non-Filipino working in the facility, thinks of himself as making a contribution to the Philippines. "We are in pioneering days. That is why I love it here." He is scrupulous about running an honest company. In 1986 Saztec was listed as the 1,473d largest company in the country in gross revenue but 38th in return on equity, a factor that reflects the tendency of some companies to understate earnings to avoid taxes. Ed Bagtas, head of Saztec's finance department, says Fraser once wrote a letter to the government asking why he hadn't been taxed more.

To some people Fraser comes across as too confident, too self-righteous. He is capable of defending a decision with utter conviction one day and changing his mind the next—again with total assurance. Not surprisingly, employees are often intimidated by him. But if his level of conviction is extraordinary, he is not alone in his enthusiasm for pioneering in the Philippines. Others, such as James Conway of Equidata, which is just down the street from Saztec, also talk about making a contribution to the country.

Even so, Saztec and its competitors are businesses and, as such, are out to make a profit. Keying is a tedious and carefully monitored job. Using computers, Saztec management can precisely measure a worker's number of keystrokes and accuracy of performance, information that is used to weed out inefficient employees as well as to reward good ones. Fraser sets other tough standards and swiftly fires people who violate rules. New employees cannot become full-fledged staff members with all the benefits unless they have worked one year without being tardy more than one hour. When I first spoke to him in early 1988, the staff numbered well under 500, only about 60 percent of whom were "regular" employees. Each month Saztec workers are rated on a one-to-five scale, a technique Fraser says he drew from his military experience.

Despite the extraordinary benefits Saztec offers, employees feel frustrated. To some degree this is natural in any company. The options for Philippine workers, however, are far narrower than those for their U.S. counterparts. As Saztec CEO Tom Reed notes, turnover among data entry operators in the United States is very high; they can find other, more interesting jobs. That is not the case in the Philippines. Interesting work is scarce.

Many data entry jobs are monotonous, requiring dexterity but not imagination. With the exception of those who repair computers, few employees at Saztec work in a field for which they were educated. They were trained as dentists, teachers, architects, accountants, mathematicians, nurses, and engineers—people for whom there are no jobs, or at least no jobs that pay close to wages at Saztec. One data entry operator, who has a degree in business administration, told me she would take a cut in pay to get experience in her field, if she could. She can't, however, because she must take care of her family. Others have had small businesses that failed. Two-thirds of the Saztec staff are under 30, eager to start ambitious careers. But as Marian Tabjan puts it in her straightforward way, "It's hard to find a job based on your degree."

The contrast with Todd Stein in Dayton is poignant. He could have moved to a better-paying job with a bigger computer-related company long ago, his supervisor told me. Instead, Stein stays at his $34,000-a-year Saztec job because of the opportunities it affords him to take on more responsibility. In 1988, for instance, he supervised sophisticated final mainframe computer programs performed on data that were keyed in the Philippines.

Joblessness is hard to measure in developing countries, but about 40 percent of the work force is generally thought to be under- and unemployed in the Philippines. When Eduardo Bagtas advertises for an accountant to work in the Saztec finance office, he gets 100 applications. The biggest reason data entry operators leave Saztec is to marry or to emigrate to another country where wage levels are higher. In 1988 Fraser estimated his turnover to be about 1 to 2 percent a year. For data entry companies in which pay is not so good, the rate is higher.

The frustration is made all the more intense by workers' fear that instead of moving ahead, they may lose the jobs they have. In the data entry business, as Emmanuel Cu describes the uneven flow of contracts, "it is typhoon or drought." When Saztec hit a dry spell in

November and December of 1987, workers were sent home for a few days. Some have thought about unionizing as a way of protecting themselves, but most seem to recognize they have little to gain in benefits and much to lose. A militant left-wing union made life difficult for the Mattel toy company's manufacturing operations, which employed 3,400 Filipinos. Says one Saztec employee ruefully, "The owners left with their money."

Chapter 4

Growing and Aging: "Micro-Evolutionary" Change

Introductory Notes

This chapter presents the dilemmas of growth through the stories of three organizations at very different times in the organizational life cycle; Metallon, in its planning stage and at birth; Apple Computer during its adolescent "hypergrowth"; and Sears Roebuck as it passes beyond the peak of an astonishing history.

Tom Ittelson's portrait of his own startup, "The Rise and Fall of an Entrepreneur," describes graphically the ups and downs, euphoric highs and despairing lows of people attempting to "birth" a baby company. The situation here is in most ways exactly the opposite of that in a mature organization. There are too many options; nothing is foreclosed, nothing is impossible, and the new baby can be deliberately shaped to meet almost any standard, any dream. If such famous American entrepreneurs as Ken Olsen, Ross Perot, and Steve Jobs did it, so can we.

But reality eventually intrudes into everything. Every decision made by Tom and his founding colleagues eased some steps and constrained others. As Metallon took shape and investors were found to put up the necessary capital, momentum was generated. Control was shared and eventually given up, the need to ensure returns to the venture capitalists drove decisions and constrained choice in ways that were not by any means predicted—perhaps not even predictable. And like many startups, Metallon's founders and first executives often made decisions in the order in which they arose, rather than in the order that would have been most helpful. This process, which might be called "management by squeaky wheel," had its own inevitabilities.

The three pieces about Apple offer a more complex portrait of a complex company. Donna Dubinsky, in "Diary of a Middle Manager," shows the inner workings of the company during its glory days; then founder Steve Jobs speaks in "Jobs Talks About His Rise and Fall," and his successor weighs in, in "John Sculley's Lessons from Within Apple." These offer contrasting views of the best way to manage hypergrowth.

As at Metallon, we see the interplay between the organization as it actually existed and the choices facing people in various positions. Middle managers such as Donna Dubinsky were totally caught up in change, because it was their constant companion. Very properly, they tried to drop occasional organizational anchors to pin things down—"At least we know what's going to happen there!"—recognizing the critical importance of routinizing things. At the same time, they confronted daily tasks that required decisions and action. Their choices shaped the organization in ways that were certainly not intended, but that produced their own reality.

John Sculley stood at a much higher level, *assuming* that his own decisions and actions would be translated neatly into a well-oiled machine, and that his task was to ensure that Apple's strategic orientation would fit its aspirations and capacities. Strikingly, he continued to refer to his experience at Pepsico, which could hardly have been less relevant, as he repeatedly discovered. Jobs, on the other hand, was clearly dismayed by the loss of his own involvement with the fun of developing new products, as he had long ago turned the management of the company over to others. Indeed, the problem of construing stock ownership as a base for organizational control—a problem considered in Chapters 6 and 9—is very clear here.

In the portrait of Sears in "The Big Store: Sears in Maturity," the "colossus of American retailing" is staggering to recover from a situation totally foreign to its people, managers and workers alike. Which is the case? Can it be saved, and what would that mean? Is Sears doomed to continue to slide downhill, as vastly smaller upstarts outmarket, outsell, and outperform it? Is it a dinosaur, or does it simply need executives of the character of founder Julius Rosenwald himself or the legendary General Robert E. Wood, who ran it in the 1930s?

Whatever the answer, we—and Sears executives—should recognize a truly horrifying possibility. The very size, reach, and entrenched history and tradition of Sears—the factors that were responsible for its enormous momentum and market power—are now among its worst enemies. Once an organization's forward momentum is lost, regaining or redirecting it is not only expensive but, much more important, time-consuming as well. It is possible in these circumstances that the very best strategy, brilliantly executed, will require many years to reach fruition. Meanwhile, losses mount, people become dispirited and leave, its equities fall, and its death truly does become certain.

Under those circumstances, what looks like the working out of a life cycle sequence may be instead the consequence either of poor decisions made years earlier or, a related point, of environmental contingencies that occurred but were not necessarily to be expected. In these circumstances, it is *not* the case that nothing can be done; however, it is the case that too little *will* be done, at least at the time when it should be done to make enough of a difference. Katz's story shows clearly just how easily that can happen.

A simple set of propositions may explain Sears's fall, and that of many other firms, small as well as large.

- Conditions of economic success lead managers to believe that more of the same behavior will result in continuing success.

- Systems and procedures are put in place, and routines are established, to ensure continuation of those "successful" practices.
- Many of the investments and commitments made require time for their completion, and cannot be quickly dropped, thus contributing to the momentum long before they produce results.
- When, for whatever reason, performance falters and the competition gains ground, a gap begins to open between revenues and expenses.
- At the beginning, people are very reluctant to take irrevocable actions—to shut things down, reduce salaries, lay people off, shut down half-completed projects, and write off sunk costs.
- However, for similar reasons, it is equally difficult to make new investments and change directions.
- A cycle of failure is thus put in motion, in which firms attempt to catch up with or even reverse falling returns by reducing expenses and eliminating investment.
- Meanwhile, the organizational rigidities maintaining the inappropriate practices continue to affect behavior, even as people's personal commitment declines.
- Failure becomes inevitable.

This sequence becomes likelier as firms get larger, develop a self-image to protect, have a history of success and prosperity, are internally largely closed systems, and are not faced with a clear crisis or sudden contingency. Sears has—or at least, had—options. Managers simply failed to recognize them until it was too late.

As we showed in Chapter 2, the analogy between living beings and organizations, despite being irresistibly seductive, also has significant limits. Moreover, it can lead to wholly misleading conclusions. Chief among these is the illusion of inevitability—the idea that the different stages must arise and, indeed, come in sequence. The seasons of an organization's life are not, unlike those of human beings, immutable. Although in a very real sense every organization necessarily reflects its past, this is a long way from the idea of a genetic blueprint embedded and embodied in every aspect of the organization.

For people within organizations, the right model is critical, because the range of choices available, both in reality and in perception, obviously depends on their assumptions. If leaders believe that maturity leads to senility and death, the only real option is either to delay this transition somehow, milking value from the organization as long as possible (thus creating the famous "cash cow"), or to commit organizational suicide. (In the language of this book, that might include changes of identity as well as dissolution.) If, on the other hand, maturity is really a label applied to a commonly observed cluster of loosely associated characteristics, there are many more options.

What is illustrated well by these three sets of portraits is the importance of history. No matter which stage of the life cycle we look at, actions taken deliberately and with a full range of choices collude to limit further choices, to make likelier a certain path of development. That is not necessarily inherent in the nature of organization; after all, organizations are devices to routinize, to repeat, action. And it reflects an ancient principal. The consequences of our acts go well beyond our intentions and result eventually in a web of confining circumstances. It is not an inevitable life cycle *per se* that is at work, with a relatively fixed sequence of stages, but rather the building of a sort of machine that expresses the consequences of its design, even though unwitting, in everything it does after its shape is constructed. That is why the startup organization, for all the "liabilities of newness" described in Chapter 2, has more freedom in the eyes of its people than the mature organization constrained by the weight of its own habits and experience.

Do managers have choices? Of course. Are they likely to see them? Not always. The problem is precisely to maintain the recognition of a wide range of options, within an organizational structure that enables them to be pursued legitimately and realistically.

The Rise and Fall of an Entrepreneur

Thomas R. Ittelson

Attleboro, Massachusetts, August 1983

We were plotting. Our plans could make us millionaires. We were going to start a company.

David Sigman, Rick Capp, and I sat around the long table in David's dining room. David's wife, Cathy, had set out a dinner for us and we were attacking it while we waited for John Pereira to arrive.

"Where the hell is John?" I asked. "Is he always late for meetings?" They should know, having worked with him for 10 years. I'd known him for only a month.

"Maybe Barbara wouldn't let him out of the house. She can be tough," David remarked.

David, short and affable, with a well-chosen wardrobe and a gift for small talk, knew John's wife well. About the same age and both from large families, she and he had grown up across the street from each other in Norton. "Or maybe John decided to take that job with Leach & Garner." David went on, "Maybe he's going to leave us at the church door."

That was also a fear of mine—that our partnership would fall apart before it even had a chance to form.

David Sigman, Rick Capp, and John Pereira were longtime employees of Technical Materials, Incorporated (TMI), a Lincoln, Rhode Island, manufacturer of specialty materials for the electronics industry. TMI had developed the market for its specific type of product and was now the leading supplier in the world.

David and John had already decided to leave their present jobs with TMI. Either they were going to start a company together, or they were going to go to different firms in the industry.

Leaving TMI would be a major move for all of them. Upon graduating from high school, David had become the first hourly employee at TMI, at a time when sales were almost nothing. John had been with the company since his teens, almost as long as David. TMI was Rick's first job after graduating from college, over 10 years ago. Now TMI employed several hundred people and would soon reach $50 million in sales, growing at a healthy rate of 20 to 30 percent annually.

During my intended partners' time, TMI had grown from an entrepreneurial start-up into a large and successful firm. So successful that in 1982 TMI's two founders, Paul Aicher and Bob Russell—father figures to my partners—sold out to a New York Stock Exchange company, Brush-Wellman of Cleveland. Aicher and Russell each walked away with $25 million in cash from the sale.

David, Rick, and John thought they could get rich too. Their idea was to spin off from TMI and form another company to compete. David and John had been toying with the idea of going out on their own for over a year. Several ineffectual attempts had taken them down a peg, and they had hired me to advise them. I was a management consultant living and working in Cambridge when David and John approached me. . . . I was prepared to advise David, John, and Rick, but with one essential condition: I'd be CEO of the enterprise-to-be. If they agreed, then I would spearhead the task of raising enough venture capital to get us going. All this was to be the topic of tonight's meeting.

"John's here," Cathy said, looking out the window and seeing a light brown Buick pull into the driveway.

"I'm sorry, I had to drop Tracy off at dance practice," John apologized. Slight and wiry with long arms and big hands and a full black beard, he was endearingly sweet and gentle around his son and daughter. I'd liked him from the first.

John's participation was essential to our scheme. He was tops in the industry, one of a kind. Only John could operate the machines that would make our products.

Boston, June 1984

If you fancy yourself an entrepreneur, nothing is as exhilarating as starting a new company. In eight months of money raising, a total of 29 venture-capital firms reviewed our business plan—and 28 of them rejected it. But we needed only one to say yes, and we got it!

Then, in Foley, Hoag & Eliot's posh offices at One Post Office Square in Boston, a relative stranger handed me a check for $1 million and wished us good luck.

I had first met our well-wisher, venture capitalist Jack Carter, three months before. Reportedly the model for the comic-strip hero Steve Canyon, at age 70 the former test pilot showed remarkable faith in his own future—venture investments take years to pay off. Jack was white-haired, with a sailor's tan. He had the look of confidence a man acquires when he feels he has done well in life. . . .

A seasoned hand at venturing, Jack had come out of retirement when the venture-capital market heated up in the early eighties. Years before he had founded the Charles River partnership, an early and successful local venture-capital outfit. After retiring from Charles River at 65, he'd gotten bored. So, when money raising became possible again, he'd started his own new operation.

In 1982, with two partners, Walt Levison and Cliff Smith, Jack formed the Aegis Fund. Aegis's $15-million "start-up" capital pool came from pension funds and university endowments. Clients like Hewlett-Packard, Timkin, Allstate Insurance, and Stanford, Case Western Reserve, and Washington universities, and 15 or so others had all invested in Aegis. Even the Mellon Family Investment Company participated. We were getting a chunk of this money.

The closing documents for our deal were more than two inches thick. I congratulated myself for having read every word. David, Rick, John, and I sat at a long table signing papers and passing them on. That June day in 1984, when Jack handed me Aegis's check, Metallon Engineered Materials Corporation was born. We were a venture-capital-financed, high-tech, start-up company producing specialty materials for the electronics industry.

And I was CEO and on top of the world. . . .

Boston, Spring 1984

"Founders seldom stay together." Dick Testa stated this as a fact, trying to give me good advice. "And you probably won't part friends. Hopefully the business will survive and perhaps prosper. That's the way it happens. Plan on it."

He should know. Testa is the senior founding partner at Testa, Hurwitz & Thibeault, a Boston law firm grown prosperous through its work with venture capitalists and entrepreneurs. As a young man, Dick Testa lawyered the deal that started Digital Equipment. The rest is history.

I did not want to believe his warning—that all partnerships run a serious risk of breaking up—at least not in our case. But I know now that if partnership bonds are weak or flawed, they will break under strain. And since something always goes seriously wrong during start-up, a weak partnership will almost always be torn apart.

John, David, Rick, and I were partners by circumstance. Drawn together because each could contribute to a common goal, we would remain partners only so long as we continued to share those common objectives and that common dependency. . . .

Cambridge, Fall 1983

"What'll we call the business?" was a basic—and not trivial—question. We needed a name that would attract the attention of venture capitalists, a name we could rally around, one that would make us feel good about our enterprise.

Specialty clad metals, our product, are combinations of copper alloy, gold, and solder fused under pressure and then sold in strip form. The copper is used for conductivity and strength; the gold, for chemical resistance; the tin-lead, to improve soldering characteristics. Ultimately, our high-tech composites would become parts in electric connectors, switches, and semiconductors manufactured by AT&T, Motorola, Delco, AMP, and a lot of smaller guys in the field.

"'Metallon'—it means metal in ancient Greek," said my old friend and classics scholar.

And "Metallon" could make a really nice logo, I thought while designing it in my head. The *O* would be like a roller, crushing the tails of the two *Ls* into a strip of metal. . . .

It took me a month to write our business plan, and another to refine it. The plan discussed the market for our products, described our technology, showed how we planned to compete, and documented our expected financial return.

For several weeks I was in and out of Baker Library, at Harvard Business School, and the Barker Engineering Library, at MIT, researching the dynamics of our business and the advantages of our technology. My research showed the market skyrocketing—a growth of more than 35 percent that year. Our product was hot!

Metallon's business plan had all the right elements, all the things that venture capitalists want to see: a well-rounded and complete management team, an exciting and practical technology, rapidly growing sales, what seemed to be a ludicrously large financial return, and so forth. It was an easy-to-read 20 pages, not too slick but still sophisticated, not too detailed but not simplistic. . . .

The generic venture-capitalist rejection goes like this: ". . . sorry, but your plan does not meet our investment criteria at this time." And it was easy to get discouraged after 10 or so venture capitalists told me, "We just can't take the time to understand your business," or "We only invest in biotech—why don't you invent a gene machine?" After all, I was a biochemist by education.

To stay sane, I began playing the Hurray, Another Rejection! game. I promised myself not to quit until 30 venture capitalists had turned us down. When each new rejection came, I'd put a big gold star on the rejection chart on my office wall. Then I'd hold a short rejection party with anyone around: my partners, my wife, my dogs, whoever. Then I'd go right out and talk to another venture-capitalist, getting ever closer to my goal of 30 rejections, when I could stop this nonsense.

I searched each rejection for information that would make our plan more acceptable to the next person who saw it. I would let venture capitalists tell me what they wanted to see.

"That's just too little money for what you're trying to do." So I changed the plan and asked for $1 million instead of our original $750,000.

"We won't invest in anything that can't generate sales of at least $25 to $30 million." So I raised our projected fifth-year revenues to $25 million, up from our original $10 million.

At first this process bothered me. But I soon learned that venture capitalists always discount projections anyway.

"We just assume that your start-up will take longer, cost more money, and result in less of a payoff than you say," Cliff Smith, an Aegis Fund partner, would later tell me. I had to show them our most optimistic, best-cast numbers. Venture capitalists expect no less. I would overstate, they would understate, and it was to be hoped that together we would reach something close to reality.

Cambridge and Boston, Spring 1984

"What you've got here is good!" Rolf Stutz exclaimed as he reviewed Metallon's business plan. "You should be able to get this thing financed."

Stutz should know, I thought. My old Millipore colleague had just founded his own medical instrumentation company with venture-capital financing.

"Do you know John Butz?" Rolf asked. "I'll give him a call and introduce you. He's a CPA friend of mine with contacts in the Boston accounting community. He's just completed some sort of venture deal himself—in Switzerland, I think." I set up a meeting with John Butz.

"I really like what you've outlined in your plan. It's just a matter of beating the bushes until you find a venture capitalist who thinks the same," Butz said after several meetings at my office reviewing our projections.

"Let me introduce you to a sharp partner at Arthur Anderson [one of the "big eight" accounting firms downtown]. We'll see if he has any ideas."

And the "sharp partner" did have an idea. With a glint in his eye, Wayne Mackie said, "I might have the right people for you. I don't know them myself, but the partner across the hall is on their account. Let me show the plan to him, and I'll get back to you."

Mackie called me a week later with encouragement. "The Aegis Fund got your business plan and I think they're interested," Wayne said, sounding pleased with himself. "You should call Jack Carter. He is one of the general partners. Aegis is a brand new fund. That's why you never heard of them. Good luck!"

That's how Jack and I were first connected.

Cambridge and Attleboro, Spring 1984

By early spring of 1984 I was getting tired. We had gone through my target of 30 venture capitalists with no firm commitment yet. However, both Jack Carter of Aegis and Midland Capital, a New York City venture fund, were showing signs of real interest in Metallon.

I'd been meeting with my partners every week and we had all been giving presentations to interested investors. But the money-raising roller-coaster ride had been going on for eight months—longer than anyone had expected—and the troops down in Rhode Island were getting restless.

John threatened again and again to take a job with a fat salary at the Leach & Garner Company. David began making noises about moving to Long Island to join a very small company in the field. Rick's wife, Debbie, was still pressing for the family to return to Illinois, where Rick could work for his father. I was going broke. I was turning away business to spend all my time on Metallon.

We were getting close—I knew it, they knew it. But until we had check in hand, the whole deal could collapse. I was afraid my work would go for nothing.

Boston, June 1984

I didn't know why, but all our important negotiations with venture capitalists were conducted at fancy restaurants over meals. I don't like to negotiate when I am eating. Food is too important to spoil over business. You can't drink and eat spicy food when you are asking a stranger for a million dollars.

But in May 1984, to my relief, we were talking real money, and eating well—Anthony's Pier 4, Harbor Terrace at the Marriott Long Wharf, Julien at the Hotel Meridien. And our conversations were different: the venture capitalists and I had reversed roles. They had begun courting me.

"We work closely with the companies we invest in—help them grow. We're not just in it for the money, we want you guys to succeed."

I didn't really believe that. Money *is* their motivation.

I played one investor off another, and after a series of meetings struck a fair deal with Jack Carter. Personally, we all liked him the best. "Let me write you a letter of intent," Jack said after we had worked out most of the elements of our deal.

I realized at that moment that Jack actually *was* going to finance Metallon! I tried to stay calm and cool and suppress my glee, but I felt a broad grin come over my face. . . .

Now it all went quickly. In the space of several weeks the lawyers had finished their work—to the tune of about $15,000 in legal fees—and the deal was done.

Following the old venturing rule of Half for the money and half for the talent, we got half the company and Aegis got half the company. Going over the legal documents with David, John, and Rick, I had to defend the deal I'd struck with Jack. "That's too much, we'll lose control," my partners lamented.

"If we really want total control, we should put up the million bucks ourselves!" I snapped.

"We don't want to run your business—that's too much work," the venture capitalist had assured us. "We just want a profit from it."

In fact, Jack Carter did deserve a level of control for taking the biggest risk. He could lose a lot of money on this deal. All we risked were minor career setbacks and bruised egos.

"Congratulations, you've just accomplished the easiest task, now you have to run the company!" was Carter's parting wisdom the day he handed over our million-dollar check. . . .

Boston and Providence, July 1984

In the space of a week my partners quit their jobs at TMI: we incorporated in Delaware (where everybody does), issued stock to the four founders and to Aegis, and finally found a banker who understood what we were trying to do and wanted to be a part of it.

Our crusty old-line "Boston banker," Steve Schlegel, was a 26-year-old loan officer in the High Technology Group of Bank of Boston, BOB for short. Jack had introduced me to some higher-ups at BOB, and I had filtered along to Steve. Everything bad I had ever said about bankers, I now took back. Steve really did help Metallon get started. He understood our business and lent us money—three-quarters of a million dollars—to finance our equipment.

Our business plan had gotten us venture capital and bank financing, but the plan was not detailed enough to get us actually started. We put together a step-by-step schedule. I went searching for a plant site, and my partners started buying machines.

None of us had done anything like this before. Naïvely, we were pushing to be in production in six months, an impossible goal that we actually almost met.

Massachusetts/Rhode Island Border Towns, August 1984

"It will need some renovation, but it's solidly built," was the real estate agent's pitch.

He was showing me the Ames Shovel complex in Easton. In this very building the Ames company had made the shovels that George Washington's army used to dig camp at Valley Forge. Thick granite-block walls, wood-beamed roofs—the sense of history was beautiful, but high-tech electronics materials could not be made there.

After about 20 more false starts, I found an empty shell of a building of just the right size in Pawtucket. It had a dirt floor, no walls, no water, and no power, but it did have a landlord who might finance the necessary improvements.

"I feel like a venture capitalist myself," said young Jack Marshall, president of the Marshall Group of construction and property management companies in Rumford, Rhode Island, after we talked him into approving the $200,000 expense. But he was happy to get the place rented. During October 1984, while construction work was still being completed, we moved in. . . .

Pawtucket, Rhode Island, Fall 1984

By September 1984 we had searched unsuccessfully for several months for a suitable main bonding mill.

What's a bonding mill? Think of it as the wringers in an old-fashioned washing machine—only 200 times bigger and 1,000 times heavier. The right mill was critical for us. It would be the keystone of our manufacturing process. We'd been badgering used-equipment dealers looking for the right mill. We'd even contacted dealers in England and France.

"It's in a thousand little pieces!" I yelled at John and Rick as they described the mill they wanted to buy. They had just come back from Buffalo where they'd inspected the packaged parts of a disassembled mill.

"No, it's not," countered John. "It's in 5 big pieces and 995 little ones."

"We're buying a jewel or a pile of scrap," both of them admitted, "and we won't know for sure until it's put back together and we plug it in."

Humor was masking the tension we all felt. It was a make-or-break decision. Our biggest single expenditure, the mill would cost $90,000, plus $6,000 to move it to Pawtucket, plus all the refurbishing costs. We had to do it right.

We nicknamed it Monster Mill. We didn't want such a large one, but it was all we could find when we went shopping. We were trying to save money and time by getting as much used equipment as possible. Monster Mill bought new would have cost five times as much and taken 12 to 18 months to build. We didn't have the extra money or time.

If you drive a Chevrolet that is over five years old, our mill helped make your radiator. It came from the Harrison Radiator division of General Motors in Buffalo. Built in 1936, the mill weighed 35 tons and required three semitrailers with special overweight permits for delivery. We had to build a new door to get it into the building.

By the time we were done refurbishing Monster Mill in January 1985, it had cost us a quarter of a million dollars. But it *was* a jewel of a mill.

"The most capable in the industry," said John. He should know.

Pawtucket, Winter 1984–85

By now we were paying salaries, taxes, rent, electricity bills, telephone bills, and so forth, a total of more than $60,000 a month. A lot of money going out, and nothing coming in. We had quite a network—bankers, accountants, and lawyers in two states; machinery dealers; material suppliers; more phone companies than anyone needs—a raft of people who were looking to profit from our venture. Eleven employees were on the payroll. Our start-up money was filtering through the community in wages, services, and material purchases.

Less than a year before, Metallon had been only a dream. Now

Mayor Henry Kinch of Pawtucket was asking me over to City Hall. I was invited to dinner with Alden Anderson, president of the Rhode Island Hospital Trust, our Providence bank. I enjoyed it.

We all put 70-hour weeks into the business. When I wasn't traveling, visiting customers and suppliers, I'd arrive at the plant before 8 A.M. and leave around 8 P.M. I'd spend five or six hours on business either at the office or at home on Saturday and Sunday too. John would sometimes even sleep at the plant, baby-sitting one of our machines. . . .

The only problem with this level of work is what it does to your mind and your body. In my experience, the mind goes before the body. Suddenly, you are faced with a situation that requires clear thinking, and all you have up top is fuzz. An advantage of having partners is that seldom do all of you fuzz out at the same time. Thus somebody is around who can still think straight.

Pawtucket, Spring 1985

"The only thing you really need to be in business is a customer." John Kimball, a Millipore consultant and former vice chairman of the board of Baxter Travenol Corporation, had impressed that axiom on me early in my business career.

As we approached summer 1985, a year after start-up, our business plan and all our forecasts showed that we should be making some significant sales.

We had printed up promotional literature, done some advertising and direct mail, and set up a sales organization, and were calling on customers. After all the frantic activity of building a plant in record time, we could now actually produce a high-quality product—only to discover, to our amazement, that no one wanted to buy it in anything close to satisfactory quantities! Purchasing agents and design engineers would see us, and they were polite. But they just weren't buying right now, or their inventories were overstocked, or they were undergoing a design review: any number of reasons.

We were caught by surprise in the midst of what was to be one of the steepest and longest cyclical electronic-materials recessions ever. We'd been fooled because industry production was still strong; we hadn't realized that new orders were drying up. We'd been busy getting the plant going and had just recently started selling aggressively.

Later, when actual industrywide figures were published in *Electronic Business,* a leading trade magazine, we would learn that shipments of our type of products decreased in 1985 to a level 40 percent below the prior year. Brush-Wellman's 1985 annual report would announce that TMI's sales were off a staggering 42 percent.

TMI would lay off one-third of its work force, and another competitor, Handy & Harmon, would do the same. Engelhard even got out of the business altogether, so dramatically had the recession hurt its sales. Laid-off workers would stream into our lobby to fill out employment applications.

Our business plan had forecast 20 percent industrywide growth. In reality, our market had been cut in half! It's hard enough to start a business in a growing market; in a contracting market, it's next to impossible.

While the four of us did not really understand the external causes for some time, we did know that things were not going well for our little company. We sat and talked about the situation, and argued. The most bitter disagreements were between David, the partner responsible for sales, and me.

"You should be much more aggressive in contacting customers. You're afraid to visit new people and you're being obstinate," I fumed. I hoped our problems were his fault. If necessary I could step into sales. I would just need an extra 50 hours a week.

"No," he countered, "people who should be good prospects just aren't buying. I don't know what more to do. You don't know anything about the market," he lashed out. "And anyway, I don't like you!"

Our other partners would chime right in, getting into the spirit of the discussion. "If you would just get me the process sheets on time, I'd be able to meet the production schedule," John told Rick.

"If I didn't have so many quality retests on your shoddy samples, I'd have the time. Why don't you make the product right in the first place?" Rick fired back.

We saw our company slipping away from us. The vision was terrifying.

A short time later, a friendly venture capitalist tried to reassure me, "You just started a good business at a bad time." He could philosophize. I was close to panic.

Pawtucket, Summer 1985

A start-up company is like a hot-air balloon, with money being the hot air that keeps you up. Jack Carter had given us enough of that hot air to begin Metallon's journey. We would have to start generating our own cash if we were not to crash to earth. The amount of money a start-up company uses each month is called the "burn rate" in venture terminology. We were burning from $60,000 to $80,000 a month, with no end in sight.

By the middle of 1985, collapse of the business was a grim possibility. I knew we had to have more money to survive.

"We can help you if you need capital; we have the contacts and experience," was what Jack had said when he was courting us a year before.

But he'd meant "happy money," to help us expand because things were going so well. What Metallon needed now was "sad money," just to keep us afloat. And that type of money was in very short supply. After all, with the current market conditions, Jack and other venture capitalists had lots of other little companies to feed, all as hungry as we were.

I gave my partners financial statements every month and did not try to hide our financial position from them. But they were focusing all their efforts on making the plant run. For them, money was just supposed to be there when needed. In the past—to start the business—I had gotten it for them. They expected me to do the same now. . . .

At staff meetings, John would often lash out in frustration at David for not selling enough, at me for not making David sell enough, and at Rick for being so slow. Yelling at one another can be healthy, I told myself. At least we were still talking.

John tried to resign twice in the second half of 1985. Why did he want to give up? As long as Metallon had a penny in the bank, we could still reach our goal. John's desire to leave did not seem rational to me. I talked him out of it both times. I didn't tell Jack about John's threats; my job was to manage the situation. . . .

I was desperately trying to be rational and productive but felt panic building. I knew a CEO could not panic and keep his job. My form of panic is to alternate between activity and paralysis, like an off-on switch. Of the two types of behavior, desperate activity is perhaps the more destructive: trying to do everything that needs to be done at once and demanding the same from everyone else.

Looking back, I think we did amazingly well. Times were tough. We *were* learning, getting better at running our little company. I never lost hope and never really thought we would not make it. There was no alternative to a positive attitude. Under pressure, you begin to realize that when there is too little time or money to do things absolutely right, you must often settle for what is only adequate. Big companies may have the luxury of "striving for excellence." Small entrepreneurial companies sweat for survival.

Pawtucket, Fall 1985

"So what are you going to do about it?" our venture capitalist shouted. Jack Carter was being truculent.

He'd even brought along a new Aegis partner, Steve Roth, to reinforce his "statement of concern." I knew we had a problem. His yelling did not help solve it. He was just taking out his frustrations on me—understandably, since I had talked him into investing in Metallon. Things were not going well with his investment.

And while Jack sensed our problems, I felt that he wasn't spending much time helping us. Aegis was starting another pool of money, Aegis II, and Jack seemed to have fund-raising problems of his own.

Since we had a sales problem, I hired a salesman.

"You should meet Tim," Dale Richards had said to me several months earlier. Tim is Dale's son. "He's got the entrepreneurial bug, and he's a dynamite salesman. A chip off the old block," Dale continued, "and he's a biologist too, like you."

When I met Tim Richards, I liked him immediately. I guess he liked me too. He took the job. Tim had been working for a number of years in sales and market development with Locktite, an adhesives company. He was about the same age I was when I left Millipore. And I saw in him some of the frustrations I had felt back then. He had all the markings of an entrepreneur.

Tim seemed eager to take the risk of working for a struggling young company—to move his wife, Patty, and baby daughter, Jenna, halfway across the country from Chicago and then learn a new field. In fact, he liked the idea; it would be a challenge.

Tim was aboard late in the fall of 1985 in time to man our booth at the Connector Symposium trade show, in Philadelphia. The show was dead—a waste of our limited promotion money. We saw all our competitors but few customers. With the market reaching bottom, no one was buying.

Pawtucket, Fall 1985

We needed enough money to keep our cash balance close to positive while we were "riding out the current market slump." The downturn could not go on forever, and we were selling as hard as we could, especially now that Tim had joined us. Only two more things could be done: lower expenses, and try to raise more capital. I insisted that we four partners go on half pay, and I began to write another business plan.

Running out of cash is not an uncommon problem for entrepreneurial companies. Fund-raising can become a continuous process. So I had maintained contact with some of the more promising potential sources of capital from our last fund-raising efforts a year and a half before. But I discovered that this time around we were much less pretty—sullied by the marketplace. However, we still had suitors.

"We like what you've done so far," Dick Oster, president of Cookson America, said to me in the fall of 1985 as we sat around the enormous conference table in the boardroom of his Providence headquarters. "The market recession is not your fault, and we can help with selling anyway. We'll buy you out, give you guys fat contracts and all the money you'll need. But how are you going to get rid of your venture capitalist?"

This bargain was the best I could get from one of my old industrial contacts. Because I felt Jack was our partner too, and could get no positive reaction from him, I refused to continue these discussions.

NGK Insulators, Dale's contact from Japan, had approached us a year before about licensing our technology. They had even translated our original business plan. I'd stayed in touch, pursuing them aggressively with proper gifts and much courtesy, including a trip to Tokyo that we could not afford. But cross-Pacific negotiations proved agonizingly slow—too slow to save me.

"There is nothing wrong with this business that a little cash won't solve," said Bob Ames, retired executive vice president of Textron in Providence. I knew Bob well enough to ask him for advice.

After all, he said, it was a basically sound business, we had an attractive and well-equipped plant, we knew the technology, and we had started to launch our product into a difficult marketplace. We were "just not launching it fast enough," Bob said. An understatement, I thought!

Boston, Fall 1985

I was beginning to assess my predicament. If the ship is sinking, you throw the least essential weight overboard. If I was having trouble finding more money for the business, what did my partners need me for?

"When it comes to a crunch," said Jim Morgan, "place the entrepreneur first, then the company, and investors third. Ride out the storm with the people you picked. Bet on them in the first place and stay the course. That's just the way General Doriot [the revered grandfather of the venture-capital industry] taught me and it works for us." Morgan is a respected and accomplished venture capitalist and partner in Morgan-Holland Ventures, in Boston. But then he warned, "Other venture capitalists I know do it just the reverse, with people flying everywhere. We don't think that method's right, or really as profitable, in the long run."

In my mind (and I felt in Jack's, too) anything that went wrong with Metallon was in some way my fault. Along with my other problems, I was feeling guilty.

Pawtucket and Boston, January 1986

On Monday morning, January 6, 1986, I arrived at the plant late after driving down from Cambridge. Waiting for me was a big registered-mail package filled with drawings and specifications from the largest purchaser of specialty clad metals in the country—the colossal AT&T. For six fruitless months I had been trying to get Metallon approved as a supplier there. Dale Richards and I had even flown down to Guilford Center, North Carolina, to plead our case with AT&T's corporate purchasing department. Now we could start the approval process.

Then Jack Carter called. He was calm and pleasant but insisted he had to see me right away. I remember thinking that good news usually does not come this way. Handing our precious package to David, I left the plant and drove to Carter's office, in Boston.

I went up Route 95, and then over to the Southeast Expressway. It was midmorning by now, so traffic was not a problem. I parked at the Aquarium garage and walked to the Aegis office in a converted loft down on Milk Street, right by Quincy Market.

The small red-brick building had a pub on the first floor. Mechanically I climbed the steps past the lawyers' offices on the second floor to Aegis's, on the third. We met in the conference room. It was more private than Jack's floor-to-ceiling glassed-in office.

Unbeknownst to me, Jack had met with David, Rick, and John on Sunday, the night before. They'd driven up to Jack's house, in Lincoln. John had instigated the meeting. He'd again threatened to resign. Jack must have seen his million dollars slipping away.

"Hello, Jack. How are you today?" was the most inventive opening I could think of at the time.

Looking calm as he always did, Jack began, "Tom, this is an unpleasant task for me. . . ."

As CEO I was responsible for everything—a genius in success, a scapegoat in failure. I walked the plank—fired by the venture capitalist who had originally backed us and who controlled our stock.

"What happened?" I pleaded, dazed.

There was no discussion. He was resolute. He just wanted to get this unpleasantness over with. Dale Richards would become interim president of Metallon.

"Have you read my employment contract recently?" I asked, now emotionally drained but with a little bit of rebellion still in me.

I knew it didn't matter. If Metallon's only source of funds wanted me out, then I was out. It proved for me again the golden rule: He who has the gold makes the rules.

Cambridge, Spring 1986

The *Wall Street Journal* announced this February, in an article about the electronics industry, that "sales should start rising soon; the industry is showing signs of rebounding."

I'm glad the market's turning around, and I wish my former partners well. Why not? I still own some stock.

I was fired six days after my fortieth birthday. Two weeks later, my wife announced to my surprise that she was pregnant with our first child. Alice was born in May.

Baby, of course, needs a new pair of shoes. I've set up a small consulting business in Cambridge, The Mercury Group, to work with entrepreneurs.

Hypergrowth and Transition at Apple Computer

Diary of a Middle Manager

Donna Dubinsky

When I joined Apple in 1981, we were operating (late 1984) at an annualized rate of $200 million in sales. Two years later, we hit the $1 billion run rate, and we currently are operating at near the $2 billion mark. This rate of growth is unprecedented in American business history and has propelled Apple to the Fortune 500 list within a meager six years of inception. . . .

How can an organization survive such hyper growth? Luck, of course, plays a role. But while luck can help you get started, other explanations are needed for how, on a day-to-day basis, the tasks get done, how the products get designed, built, introduced, shipped, and invoiced. . . .

Shortly after I joined the company, a team of upper level managers created the "Apple Values," an articulated set of corporate values. The values included an emphasis on empathy for the customer, high quality, taking risks, and having fun. New employees were introduced to these values during their orientation, and exposure to them was frequent. . . .

These values set a common goal, a direction in which all employees could move and feel relatively confident that upper management would agree. Middle managers made decisions based on what was right, right being defined in the context of these corporate values. Although such values easily can be dismissed as insincere, they do serve to guide decision making when little time is available to seek the advice or support of upper level management. . . .

Formal communications were an anathema, regular staff meetings nearly impossible. The lack of more formal channels, however, did not preclude communication. In fact, in order to survive hyper growth, near hyper communication was necessary. The key to good communication in this environment was informal, but constant, communication. It was unending streams of phone calls, of casual conversations in hallways, of short term task groups and of one-minute "reality checks" with the boss. It was essential that the core groups of people were physically close to each other because if the informal communication channel was hindered, information was choked off and critical events did not happen. The use of cubicles rather than closed offices also facilitated the informal communications. An associate often would overhear a conversation, pop up over the cubicle, and contribute to the problem under discussion. . . .

Traditionally, the word bureaucracy carries with it negative connotations: excessive paperwork, red tape, delays. Frequently ignored, however, are its positive aspects, i.e., an established, referenceable method for getting repetitive tasks done. A secondary benefit is the ability to guard against incompetence or outright wrongdoing. . . .

Apple's growth and rapid change did not permit the establishment of such a bureaucracy. In a bureaucratic vacuum, informal bondings played a significant role in getting tasks accomplished. In any decision, the right approvals may not have been in place because the approval process itself may not have been defined. Without clear approval authority levels, as a middle manager, I made decisions based on trusting an associate. . . .

For example, if a product manager who I felt was trustworthy submitted a new product to ship, I was confident that he or she had properly approved the price, or checked with the legal department, or notified the sales force. A reliance on trust, however, can create a terrible stress on the organization. If I had been unsure of the competence of this manager, the system could come to a grinding halt while I backtracked to check that all of the appropriate issues were resolved. . . .

In entrepreneurial companies, it is taken for granted that risks are encouraged in research and development, in product design, and in marketing strategy. But at Apple, a more fundamental kind of risk was essential: organizational risk. As a middle manager, I often was put in the position of making decisions beyond my authority, or at least within the gray area of unstated authority levels. In a more seasoned company, making that decision on my own could cause serious organizational repercussions. At Apple, the middle manager had to presume his bosses' agreement, and was comfortable that he was allowed to make mistakes.

My overwhelming impression of Apple during hyper growth was

the constant influx of new people. The new employees were everywhere: in high level jobs, in lower level jobs, working above, below, or next to the people you already knew. At Apple, during nearly any point during 1981 through mid-1983, approximately 20% of the people had been there less than six months.

The most serious result of this continual flow of people was retraining. Just when one product manager, for example, learned how to introduce a new product, he would switch jobs and a new, uninitiated product manager would take his place. Apple seemed to have a frenetic desire to reorganize. One middle manager in the service department used to walk through the halls and, with no provocation, yell "reorganize!!" just as he might yell "fire!!" and you expected to see everyone jump from their cubicles, change places with their neighbors, and sit back down to work again. The marketing department went through so many reorganizations that they would joke, "If your boss calls, be sure to get his name."

With such a rapidly changing business environment, these changes sometimes were intended to meet a business need, but more often reflected a communication need. How do you get people to talk to each other? The simplest solution was to change their reporting relationships.

Reorganization was such a continual process at Apple that we never printed organization charts. Adapting to the continued organizational churn required great flexibility and willingness to work with these new people. At Apple, the new people were not new for long. No apprenticeship period was required by management or peers . . . there simply wasn't time.

The birth of Apple marked the birth of an entire industry. The pioneers were young, creative, quick, and unfettered by notions of what the industry ought to be. Consequently, Apple could not draw from a cadre of middle managers at other, similar companies. There were none. So Apple hired people with relevant, though not strictly comparable, experience. Software product marketing managers previously were software writers, dealer program development specialists previously had worked in a dealership, and sales managers had sold mainframe computers.

The result was a group of middle management Do-ers instead of middle management Managers. With an average age in the late 20's, the middle management group had very limited experience with basic management skills; few tracked the progress of their subordinates, fewer trained them.

Over time, this trend seemed to change, and more seasoned managers from related industries appeared. Now you might see a software marketing manager who had previously been a manager in a book publisher, or a dealer development manager who had managed the dealer channel for a hi-fi manufacturer, or sales managers who had been managers, not salesmen, for DEC, or Prime.

One of the Apple values involves having fun, enjoying your work. Because the breakneck pace of hyper growth could be anything but enjoyable, Apple took care to put the fun back in the job. Nearly every accomplishment deserved a celebration, even those of questionable merit.

The esprit de corps was furthered by such motivators as company-wide goals. In my first year, we set a goal of a $100 million sales quarter. If we met the goal, we each would earn an extra week of vacation. Moreover, if we met the sales goal with a certain profit margin, Apple would pay for each of us to take that vacation in Hawaii. (We met the sales, but not the profit, goal.)

Although we focused on group spirit, individual recognition also was a key element in the puzzle. Performance was rewarded generously with bonuses and/or stock options. In addition to monetary reward, recognition was important. The Vice President of Sales created an Apple Hero award, similar in looks to an Olympic medallion on a ribbon, that was bestowed upon those who had completed an enormous or very difficult project. The Apple Fellow designation was granted to those engineers who had clearly made major breakthroughs in product development.

Along with having fun, Apple encouraged a heavy sense of pride in the company and our products. The "loan-to-own" program allows every employee to receive a computer for free. The philosophy, authored by Steve Jobs, is that "we wouldn't sell you anything we wouldn't want ourselves!"

The Apple logo provided a rallying point for corporate pride, and at times it seemed we were more in the t-shirt, clock, calendar, and button business than in the computer business. But each of these "gimmicks" furthered the identification and dedication of the employees, not to mention our growing band of loyal customers.

From the field organization standpoint, the only way to cope with hyper growth was to decentralize. The Cupertino offices could not and did not dictate much about the day-to-day activities. Decentralization caused problems, such as inconsistent data bases, but the trade-off between decentralization and consistency favored the former. Most importantly, by not requiring the field to receive instructions on everything from Cupertino, we gave them room to get the job done.

I might also mention what was not done: analytical overkill. One incident stands out; my boss needed to request funds from the president to build a warehouse in Boston. He showed me his notes; he merely was going to tell the president the amount of the yearly lease cost. As a newly minted MBA, the idea of approaching the president without a full blown, discounted cash flow analysis was beyond belief, so I offered to prepare one, an offer instantly accepted. After several hours of work, I produced a VisiCalc model that seemed adequate under the circumstances. When my boss returned from the meeting, he told me that the president had glanced for several minutes at my neatly laid-out analysis, looked up and asked one question, "What is the yearly lease cost?". After hearing the response he said, "OK. Let's do it." No time for analysis . . . (late 1985).

Editors' Note

Hypergrowth cannot continue indefinitely without severe stress on the organization, and a need to reevaluate previously successful management philosophies. In 1984, Apple's sales jumped 54% to $1.5 billion, with a 26% increase in 1985 to $1.9 billion.

But the cracks were beginning to show. Apple's leadership in the market was being challenged, and big business acceptance of the new Macintosh line of products was slow.

The first event that had required a change in management style was the introduction of the Lisa computer in 1983, which required an organization that could produce multiple products, targeted to multiple markets, sold through multiple channels of distribution. In a single product, single market, single channel environment, unilateral decisions could be made because, although others might disagree, they were not necessarily dramatically impacted. The new complexity required more structure because many decisions did affect other organizations. If the price decreased on the Lisa, for example, the effect on the Apple III must be considered. If the education market required a color display monitor, we could not force them to purchase the non-color configuration offered to retail dealers.

In addition, competitive pressure was increasing dramatically. IBM had introduced its personal computer in 1981, and its enormous impact in the business market, Apple's target market with the Lisa computer, threatened to limit Apple to the smaller education and home markets.

The company needed to change from being a product driven to a market driven company in order to successfully expand into new markets. Gradually structure became essential. Approval processes needed definition, communications needed to be formalized, and training and disciplined management became critical.

The key to Apple's future success would be to retain those elements of its philosophy that could endure—the values, the esprit de corps, and the pride—while adjusting those that could choke growth. In 1985, the crisis reached its peak as the two warring product divisions created a divisiveness that threatened the entire company. John Sculley's massive reorganization in the summer of 1985, with its subsequent downscaling of the organization, was a heart wrenching event for those of us who had totally dedicated ourselves to building a great company. Yet, had we not taken this bold move, and then started the painful process of creating essential infrastructure, Apple may not have emerged with the strong foundation needed to continue its growth.

Inevitably some of the early spirit suffered as the company struggled to redefine its management practices. But, with its achievement of having become one of the world's major computer vendors, it is clear that Apple moved effectively from hyper growth to a more rational growth, and has taken on its next stage of challenges.

Jobs Talks About His Rise and Fall

Gerald C. Lubenon and Michael Rogers

Well, Apple was about as pure of a Silicon Valley company as you could imagine. We started in a garage. Woz (co-founder Stephen Wozniak) and I both grew up in Silicon Valley. Our role model was Hewlett-Packard [the electronics company]. And so I guess that's what we went into it thinking. Hewlett-Packard, you know, Jobs and Wozniak. And, as you recall, it was a very small company for a long time. But the industry started to grow very rapidly in the 1979–80 time frame. The Macintosh team was what is commonly known now as intrapreneurship—only a few years before the term was coined—a group of people going in essence back to the garage, but in a large company. But again, that was a core team of 50 people. So that attracted a lot of people that really did want to work at a small company, in a way. . . .

You look back at the personal-computer industry, IBM and DEC and Hewlett-Packard weren't the people that invented the personal computer. It took a bunch of rambunctious upstarts, working with very little resources but a certain amount of vision and commitment, to do it. And Apple has clearly now joined that status and the ranks of those other companies. It probably is true that the people who have been able to come up with the innovations in many industries are maybe not the people that either are best skilled at, or, frankly, enjoy running a large enterprise where they lose contact with the day-to-day workings of that innovative process. Dr. Land at Polaroid, he's a perfect example.

I personally, man, I want to build things. I'm 30. I'm not ready to be an industry pundit. I think what I'm best at is creating sort of new innovative products. That's what I enjoy doing. I enjoy, and I'm best working with, a small team of talented people. That's what I did with the Apple II, and that's what I did with the Macintosh. . . .

I don't think that my role in life is to run big organizations and do incremental improvements. Well, you know, I think that John felt that after the reorganization, it was important for me to not be at Apple for him to accomplish what he wanted to accomplish. . . .

The hardest, one of the five most difficult days was that day John said at the analysts meeting about there not being a role for me in the future, and he said it again in another analysts meeting a week later. He didn't say it to me directly, he said it to the press. You've probably had somebody punch you in the stomach and it knocks the wind out of you and you can't breathe. If you relax you'll start breathing again. That's how I felt all summer long. The thing I had to do was try to relax. It was hard. . . .

I, you know, I respect his right to make that decision. . . .

In my wildest imagination, I couldn't have come up with such a wild ending to all of this. I had hoped that my life would take on the quality of an interesting tapestry where I would have weaved in and out of Apple: I would have been there a period of time, and maybe I would have gone off and done something else to contribute, but connected with Apple, and then maybe come back and stay for a lengthy time period and then go off and do something else. But it's just not going to work out that way. . . . I helped shepherd Apple from a garage to a billion-and-a-half-dollar company. I'm probably not the best person in the world to shepherd it to a five- or ten-billion-dollar company, which I think is probably its destiny. And so I haven't got any sort of odd chip on my shoulder about proving anything to myself or anybody else. And remember, though the outside world looks at success from a numerical point of view, my yardstick might be quite different than that. My yardstick may be how every computer that's designed from here on out will have to be at least as good as a Macintosh. . . .

If I had felt that I was the person to run Apple in 1983, then I would have thrown my own name into the hat for the job, which I did not. So it was a conscious decision on my part to find John Sculley.

I think, more important, than who it was, it was which philosophy and perspective. . . .

You know, my philosophy is—it's always been very simple. . . . My philosophy is that everything starts with a great product. So, you know, I obviously believed in listening to customers, but customers can't tell you about the next breakthrough that's going to happen next year that's going to change the whole industry. So you have to listen very carefully. But then you have to go and sort of stow away—you have to go hide away with people that really understand the technology, but also really care about the customers, and dream up this next breakthrough. And that's my perspective, that everything starts with a great product. And that has its flaws. I have certainly been accused of not listening to the customers enough. And I think there is probably a certain amount of that that's valid. . . .

To me, Apple exists in the spirit of the people that work there, and the sort of philosophies and purpose by which they go about their business. So if Apple just becomes a place where computers are a commodity item and where the romance is gone, and where people forget that computers are the most incredible invention that man has ever invented, then I'll feel I have lost Apple. But if I'm a million miles away and all those people still feel those things and they're still working to make the next great personal computer, then I will feel that my genes are still in there.

John Sculley's Lessons from Inside Apple

Steven Pearlstein and Lucien Rhodes

When I arrived, one of the original founders, Mike Markkula, was filling in as CEO, and he was making most of the business decisions. Steve was leading what was then a small project of fewer than 100 people—the Mac—without any profit-and-loss responsibility. And he was only one of several of the company's resident technologists.

After I came, I kept handing Steve more and more authority. By the time of the final blowup, he was in a significant operating role, with more than 1,000 people reporting to him. He was the company's public spokesman and its undisputed resident technologist. I was supposed to be the CEO. Yet I was sandwiched between a visionary chairman above me and an operating executive below me overseeing the most critical parts of the company. And they were one and the same person! It created a nearly impossible situation. . . .

Steve was founder, chairman, and largest shareholder of Apple, and at the time was in charge of building one of the most exciting products in the company—the Mac. And he was only 28 years old. So I felt from the very beginning that it would be naïve to assume that he wasn't going to want to run his own company at some point. I viewed my role when I came in really as a coach to a brilliant young founder, someone who would help him develop the skills he was going to need maybe five or six years later. Even though I held the title of CEO, I knew it was a shared leadership title with the founder. . . .

The overriding consideration in my mind when I came to Apple was that I genuinely liked Steve and was impressed with his ideas and his company. I felt that he was doing things that were going to change the world, in much the same way that Henry Ford and Thomas Edison had done, and I was inspired and excited about the chance to work with him. I knew there were high risks involved, but I was prepared to accept them—both because of the strength of our friendship and because of my willingness to step aside as soon as he and the board felt he was ready to take over the running of the company. But that was wrong. In hindsight, I can't imagine the circumstances under which it could have worked. . . .

Because successful entrepreneurs are almost always convinced of their own invincibility, while successful leaders of high-growth companies have got to admit their vulnerabilities. And that's the catch-22. In my experience, the hardest part of dealing with entrepreneurs is getting them to recognize their own weaknesses. . . .

The Macintosh was as much a personification of Steve Jobs as it was of Apple. It represented a very focused vision of how Steve saw the world. And just as Henry Ford felt when he created the Model T, that he was creating more than simply a product, Steve felt that with the Macintosh he would change the way people would view the computer. He didn't see the need for anyone to be able to modify the machine—you could order it in any color, just as long as it was black, to use the Ford analogy. And what it meant was that, as Apple began to compete in a marketplace where there were lots of alternative products from competitors that offered a wide range of openness, the Macintosh became more and more isolated, because it still focused on the internal vision of the founder rather than on the needs of the customers. And it was becoming clear that our customers wanted more computing power, more memory, more disk capacity, and they wanted more flexibility in terms of connecting the Macintosh to other computers. . . .

When I started at Apple, my theory was to price our computers at a premium and plow some of that back into advertising in order to build market share, which is what you do at a company like Pepsi. Because we were growing so fast, I was able to raise our ad budget from $12 million to $100 million in that first year. But we didn't worry about increasing the R&D budget because we were already spending $40 million a year, and I thought that was plenty. In fact, robbing research to pay for advertising turned out to be a big, big mistake. Here we were, a new-products company in a new-products industry, and we could only turn out a new product every year or two—and then only by burning out our people. . . .

In the case of Apple, my understanding of the business fundamentally changed. . . .

What I soon realized was that the business market was a better one for us than the home market, because in a business market we had a chance of getting the high gross margins that would pay for R&D. That business market was considered very, very high-risk waters for Apple, because up to that point we had not done it successfully. But on the other hand, it was an even higher risk to keep going after the consumer market. . . .

One reason was that the so-called home market proved to be a figment of everyone's imagination. People weren't about to buy a $2,000 computer to play a video game, balance a checkbook, or file recipes. People might use computers at home—for school, if they were kids, or for business, if they were adults. But these were "power uses" that required a different kind of marketing from the standard consumer item. . . .

You have to remember that Apple had become an extraordinarily successful company by going against the conventional wisdom—that it was successful just because it had followed its own instincts rather than listening to the market. That product-driven strategy worked well as long as there wasn't much competition and Apple was, in effect, creating the industry. But once customers began to have real choices, it became very difficult for the people at Apple, because they had created such a success at the beginning by simply driving for the best possible products, by pushing the technology. Now, they were discovering that those things weren't as significant. And it really took a crisis for that point to come home. . . .

The entire personal-computer industry was going into a recession during 1985. We found ourselves with a huge amount of inventory and gross margins that were being badly squeezed. And suddenly, the entire focus of the organization went from "How fast can we build them?" to "How quickly can we bring down inventories and control expenses?" The whole orientation of management shifted in a matter of months. . . .

In this particular crisis at Apple, I had to move quickly to get control of the entire company. At the time, the company was organized along product lines, with the Mac division and the Apple II division acting almost as separate companies, responsible for their own research, development, manufacturing, sales. It wasn't working. So I reorganized the company along functional lines because I had learned at Pepsi that it was at least one good way of giving me immediate control over a very serious situation. . . .

What I had to do was convince people that we were in a crisis, and that we weren't going to get out of it unless we pulled together. There were some decisions that were going to have to be made quickly from the top—and those were the relatively easy ones for someone coming from a big corporation: cutting expenses, putting controls in place. The thing that was going to be more difficult was finding a new direction for the company that people at Apple would continue to feel excited about. How were we going to hold onto the roots of Apple? And there were no shortcuts to that. It couldn't come from a business plan. It had to come, really, from the soul of the company. . . .

In the traditional second-wave corporation stability is a characteristic that people most admire, and so the way information and ideas move through the organization is highly structured. The CEO is essentially at the end of a process of elimination designed to create consensus. But in a third-wave company like Apple, in a fast-growth industry, stability is really a sign of vulnerability. Third-wave companies have to be built around flexibility, and dissent is something that has to be cultivated, not stifled. That means that there is nothing more important than good internal communications. . . .

All companies, even second-wave companies, have informal networks. In a third-wave company, I think it's a matter of legitimizing the network—and empowering it—rather than formalizing it. And what that really requires is a different attitude on the part of the CEO about what the job is about. You can no longer delegate human resources to the personnel department. The CEO has really got to find a way to climb down off his perch and wander around inside the bowels of his organization, whether it's a small company or a large one, and figure out how to glean from it the ideas and creativity that can make the company better. You've got to be resourceful about it, you've got to be able to break into the internal processes of the organization. In small companies, this comes more naturally. But as companies get larger, what happens is that CEOs think they have to remove themselves from these things, and that's trouble. . . .

We did have some cultural issues that were difficult for us to deal with. We've already talked about one—the open Mac. When I first asked how our customers would communicate with other computers, somebody threw a floppy disk at me and said, "This. It's all we'll ever need." And they believed it! Well, we know today that, by the end of this decade, probably 85% of the personal computers that are out there are going to be, in some way, connected to other computers. So the original vision of one person, one computer that was so much part of the Apple culture had to be refined a bit: one person, one computer, but a computer connected to the rest of the world. . . .

I had never viewed Steve as a hero. I thought of him as a protégé, as a friend, but I never understood what a genuine folk hero he was. In the business world I came from, there weren't any folk heroes. There were Henry Ford and Tom Watson Sr., I suppose, but these weren't people who were on the scene. But now, here I was, in a world suddenly surrounded by living, breathing folk heroes, and I was not prepared for it. . . . I had never had more fun in dealing with anybody in my whole life than I did in dealing with Steve Jobs. I do think that an excessive emphasis on heroes can get out of hand. Large organizations cannot run without a very high degree of process and teamwork. . . . But I made sure we didn't purge the symbols. They are all over here—the library, the museum. I've never avoided questions about Steve; I didn't pretend he no longer existed, because that would have been naïve. I was trying to help preserve a company's roots that were almost inseparable between the founder and the company. . . .

I think a better way for corporations to think about carrying the past into the future lies in the idea of genetic change. We know that in the human body, our cells change completely every seven years, and yet the same genetic code is present throughout our life, expressing itself differently in different organisms.

The Big Store

Sears in Maturity

Donald R. Katz

For all of a century Sears, Roebuck has resided within history's most advanced society of producers and consumers as a central warehouse for the culture. Each year, the current sum of American invention was collected and distributed as material portions of a national dream. Americans rocked in Sears cradles, played with Sears toys, wore the company's plain clothing, lined their homes with its ponderous furniture, learned to enjoy something called leisure by virtue of its time-saving machines, and were eventually buried in its coffins and remembered to eternity by offerings from its special tombstone catalog. Time and again surveys confirmed that Sears was the most trusted economic institution in the country. Even as it grew to become one of the seven or eight largest corporations in the world, Sears continued to command the sort of fealty normally reserved for nations and churches. It was a private enterprise ennobled and made powerful by its perceived dedication to a public purpose.

By 1972, as the Sears Tower began to rise high above Chicago, it seemed that a great number of the institutions and ideals that meant something in America had been severely injured. Patriotism, the military, organized religion, big business—all of them seemed to have been taken down a notch. But Sears remained unhumbled. The Tower rose up into the firmament like a great bar graph, a lasting monument to the invincibility and boundlessness and extreme profitability of a company that now accounted for fully 1 percent of the Gross National Product. Two of every three Americans shopped at

Sears within any three months of 1972, and more than half the households in the country contained a Sears credit card. One-third of the families in America—some twenty-five million of them—owed the company an average of $256 for past purchases. There were now almost nine hundred big Sears retail stores, over twenty-six hundred smaller retail and catalog outlets, and well over one hundred warehouses, catalog plants, and other distribution facilities. A single share of original Sears, Roebuck stock was now worth over $20,000, and because of a generous, half-century-old profit-sharing plan, individuals who worked among the half-million employees of the corporation as secretaries and elevator operators were able to retire with stock valued at upward of $500,000.

But then, quite suddenly, Sears began to fall apart. Within five years the seemingly invulnerable company would appear so badly injured and so lacking in direction that it verged on paralysis. Corporate profits from retailing had either stagnated or declined each year since 1972. Interest expenses had fully doubled because of the monetary inflation since 1972, and the general cost of running the massive business had plainly run out of control. The Sears stock price, adjusted for an intervening split, had collapsed from a 1972 high of $61 per share to $24—and it was headed much lower. A spate of lawsuits, government investigations, and adverse publicity had shaken the company. Once-loyal customers had begun to stay away from Sears stores and to avoid the company's venerable catalog in such numbers that it appeared the American middle class, which Sears had decorated and lent physical definition over the years, had given up on the floundering company altogether.

Nobody at Sears was able to fathom what had happened, and nobody had any idea what to do. Nothing decided or decreed at the top of the empire of stores inspired direction or even activity at the bottom. For the first time in modern memory there were layoffs at Sears, and the élan that had characterized life inside the company since World War II had turned into despair and fear. An organization that only five years earlier had seemed utterly unstoppable was now a crippled leviathan, and by 1977 many of those who depended upon Sears, who studied it or loved it, had come to believe that if something was not done very quickly, the company was doomed. . . .

Moments after he finally announced the name of his successor, Ed Telling walked in on Arthur Wood, the chairman of the board of Sears, Roebuck as he faced the man who would lead the great company into its second century. The legendary chairman's desk, as always, was empty of work. There were no contracts visible, no mantles or crowns or bottles of champagne to be seen, nothing to mark the passage of power but the grip of their right hands.

The younger man said, "Thank you, sir."

The chairman turned away and looked down at the haze covering Lake Michigan, then turned back with a quick nod.

The heir to the chairmanship noticed me standing in the doorway. "Come pick me up tomorrow after lunch," he said. "We'll go out to the West Side and look for ghosts."

Lunch comes early at Sears, so it was just noon when we drove out from under the tallest building in the world and headed five miles west, toward the old Headquarters, a red brick complex so wide and long that the author of the early catalogs claimed it was "The Largest Commercial Building in the World." Seven thousand men came to the forty-acre tract of heartland prairie during the mild winter of 1905, and in just nine months of twenty-four-hour labor, they threw up the company's "great works," a place where for several generations goods representing the sum of American invention and know-how were collected and meted out as spare parts for the way people lived.

For sixty-seven years the old West Side plant served as the plexus of the world's greatest mail-order empire, and then the world's largest network of stores. Since the Headquarters was moved downtown, most of the old plant has remained abandoned. The company still maintains the ornamental gardens across the street from the entrance, just as the French attend to their memory of an old order at the gardens of Versailles.

As we pulled up to the old administration building and climbed out into the August heat, the next leader of the company waved his cigar toward a group of workmen at the edge of the complex who were dismantling Sears, Roebuck's first retail store. "That's where I first saw Santa Claus," he said. Then he looked back through the heat at the gray Sears Tower, the vertical company town where robots deliver the mail.

"O.K.," he said after a moment, turning back to the older buildings, "let's go inside." . . . Before 1972, it was a rare member of the middle or upper ranks of the company who had ever worked anywhere else as an adult. The goods-buying side of Sears, headquartered in Chicago, was fragmented into forty-nine quite discrete businesses possessed of a nearly complete operational autonomy and an umbilical relationship to many thousands of companies that produced the more than two hundred thousand different things Sears sold. The selling side was subdivided into five similarly independent "territories," each of them more populous and lucrative than all but a few American corporations. There was also the subsidiary Allstate Insurance Company, as well as a foreign corporation that ran stores throughout South and Central America, and another company that developed and managed huge shopping centers.

Sears had become an enclosed, private civilization, a place with a "corporate culture" that was so old and densely coded that, by the time the term was conjured up by students of modern management, the Sears culture was already calcifying and drawing violently inward upon itself. The men who rose up and tried to change Sears were not necessarily the ones who would have risen to the top of a large enterprise during better times. The executives who were ready to do whatever they thought necessary to redirect the empire included the most gifted, opinionated, aggressive, driven, unusual, mysterious, and in a few cases plainly the craziest inhabitants of the corporate society. As they were swept up by events, they began to act not like the characters in business journals and management primers, but like the characters in novels and plays, full of will and urgency.

By the time it was over, they had changed the way every single inhabitant of the company lived and viewed the world, and they'd changed just as profoundly the way the outside world viewed Sears. When the dust settled, one era of business and businessmen was gone and another had arrived. The great American corporation of the past, which began one hundred years ago with an orphaned box of pocket watches and a kid with a brilliant scheme, had become a variegated, futuristic corporation. Many observers of the events at Sears during the reign of Ed Telling call what happened then a "corporate turnaround," but those who lived through the firestorm know it was nothing if not a revolution.

When the tendentious reference to radical change first came up during our discussions, the chairman of the board began to tap his huge farm-boy fingertips on his empty desk top; he jingled his pocketful of keys with his other hand and tapped both of his size-thirteen shoes on the floor. But, then, he always did that when someone was in the room.

"Sorta wish there's another word but revolution," the chairman said in his strained, almost sweet voice. "But I s'pose so. S'pose that's just what it was." . . .

John Lowe, the King of the West, boarded his company jet and flew up over the Rocky Mountains toward the far edge of his portion of the empire. The de Havilland required just two hours to travel from Los Angeles to the little airstrip ten miles east of Pueblo, Colorado . . . it was Tuesday, the first day of November in 1977. . . . Lowe climbed out and turned his gaunt, no-nonsense face into the sun. He searched the horizon for around ten minutes before he spotted the Falcon bearing Ed Telling and Art Wood coming in from the east. . . .

John Lowe would never forget how uncomfortable the elegant chairman looked as the three of them entered the small executive terminal. . . . And he never forgot that it was Arthur Wood who spoke first.

"John," he said. "I've decided that Ed will succeed me as chairman of the board. I'm going to recommend him at the board meeting next week."

Lowe offered Telling congratulations without disappointment. The Californian had been mentioned as a contender for the chairmanship along with Telling and several others earlier in 1977, but he would be content to continue to rule his fifth of the company from Los Angeles.

Then Ed Telling began to speak in that strained, almost feminine voice that startles those who've taken in the size of the man. He said, "We have to make a change on the Coast, John."

"What do you mean by that?" Lowe said, training his darkest stare back at Telling.

"You've lost credibility with your people, so we have to make a change."

"What do you perceive that I've done to lose my credibility, Ed?"

"It's not what I perceive," Telling said, as Arthur Wood shifted and rocked all over his bright-green chair. "It's what the whole organization perceives."

Lowe thought, "That's a spongy goddamned answer . . . goddamned spongy." But he didn't say it out loud.

All three of the men sitting in the Flower Executive Terminal that day knew that a Sears territorial officer had been questioned rarely in the past—let alone reproached—and they had each been schooled for all of their adult lives in the ways of the incontestable system of local rule at Sears. The tradition was thought to be inviolable.

Lost credibility with his people! His numbers might have slumped a bit the last few quarters, but John Lowe *was* the West. He owned California, Oregon, Washington, Arizona, Utah, Nevada, Idaho, Alaska, and Hawaii, and operated them for Sears from *his* headquarters, which he'd designed and built with his own capital dollars. He was godfather to several of the children of his senior managers and he'd ushered at their weddings. The idea of tearing John Lowe from atop his great pyramid of authority was an affront to everything Sears, Roebuck had meant for half a century; it was inimical to everything the General had intended for Sears, a blow to that special promise of individual autonomy that made Sears different from all the other big companies—and it was exactly what Ed Telling meant to do. But firing a strong and notably independent territorial officer like John Lowe outright could be too much for the organization to bear, so Telling's strategy called for Lowe to resign.

"In light of your long service, John," Telling continued, "we're going to offer you the chance to run the Midwestern Territory."

Lowe knew instantly what Telling wanted. Telling expected his sense of pride to cause him to quit rather than be torn from the power base he'd spent decades constructing in the West. There was nothing in the world John Lowe wanted more than to do the honorable thing. He wanted to stare into Telling's eyes and damn his treacherous violation of the system left in their trust. He wanted to inform Telling of just what he could do with his offer and the entire Midwestern Territory too. But Lowe couldn't quit his job.

Because he once believed that nothing would ever change for mighty Sears, John Lowe was a million dollars underwater that fall. He'd borrowed so heavily to purchase Sears stock that the stunning drop in the value of those shares recently had taken him well beyond the point where he could repay the loans by selling the stock. All of those forty years of fervent labor in fee to Mother Sears had suddenly winnowed down to a single moment on a God-forsaken stretch of high desert, and he was helpless.

"Fine," Lowe managed. "I'll take it." . . .

To outside observers of Sears, to the business press, and even to the Wall Street analysts who watched Sears for a living, the announcement of John Lowe's move to the Midwestern Territory at the press conference in Chicago the next week seemed an innocuous lateral adjustment, or possibly a promotion. The Midwest, after all, had been a powerhouse territory for Sears for many years, and it was still responsible for a larger volume of gross sales than the West. Those not of the company couldn't begin to understand the internal violence of the act. Only members of the private society inside Sears realized that the Far Western Territory was known as John Lowe's "separate kingdom." As the news sped between departments, headquarters, and stores along the company grapevine, only the inhabitants of Sears understood that Ed Telling had killed a king.

The idea of Sears began in 1886, at a terminal alongside a railway track in the middle of nowhere, when a twenty-three-year-old man came upon a means of selling gold-filled pocket watches to rural folks who previously marked their lives by the movement of the sun. By the time Richard Warren Sears moved his budding business from Minnesota to Chicago and teamed up with a quiet watchmaker named Alvah Curtis Roebuck, it was clear that the kid was possessed of a peculiar strain of genius that rendered him capable of convincing otherwise skeptical individuals to buy things they'd never even heard of from a man in Chicago, Illinois, whom they'd never even seen. Richard Sears was so adept at describing the shape of a young nation's material dreams that it was said a few years later that he could sell a breath of air. . . .

By the mid-1950s, during the "management administration" in Washington of Dwight Eisenhower, Sears was widely thought to contain an elite corps made up of the best managers in the world. "One of the most alert management groups in the country," wrote

William Whyte in his classic study, *The Organization Man*. "There is no better illustration of what a business is and what managing it means," wrote Peter Drucker at the beginning of *The Practice of Management*. . . .

The company was able to grow so quickly, and with such incomparable élan, in part because of its unusual structure of corporate governance. As early as 1918, Julius Rosenwald declared that the company had "applied the principles of democracy to a commercial enterprise." . . .

"We have deliberately tried to treat you as free, independent merchants and men," General Robert Wood, Rosenwald's successor, told some former soldiers a few years later. "We have endeavored in a chain-store system to have a cooperative democracy." Under the headline "Goal for Worker: Democracy," the *Chicago Tribune* quoted one of the General's chief lieutenants and polemicists on the urgency of Wood's concept of corporate order in September 1949: "The enemies of democracy in business enterprise are the same as the enemies of democracy in government. . . . They include centralization of administration, an excessive growth of authority, growing dependence upon formal systems, bureaucracy, and mechanistic or technical solutions to human problems." The people of Sears grew to hate centralized business systems just as they hated the centralized orders they'd defeated in Europe.

The formal decentralization of authority at Sears had begun with the creation of the Pacific Coast Territory in 1940. After the war the job was finished when four more regional administrations were set up. The headquarters of the five territories would reside in Los Angeles, Dallas, Atlanta, Chicago, and Philadelphia. Thus Robert E. Wood "widened Sears, Roebuck's frontiers and spread autonomy to the outposts," as *Fortune* magazine put it in a lengthy study of the "art of industrial management." The decentralized structure of Sears, Roebuck became a model of progressive corporate management, and the General became an American business hero with his face on the cover of *Time* magazine. . . .

To its employees, Sears was unlike other big businesses in that it was a place where country boys and infantrymen could speak their minds and still roam free. The loyalty Sears commanded from its people was the envy of other corporations. The young John Lowe was offered a $25,000-a-year job running a major store for the May Company at a time when he was making only $7,000 a year as a minor functionary at Sears. He turned it down.

Why would anyone want to leave Sears? The stores coursed with business, and the catalog that Franklin Delano Roosevelt once suggested should be air-dropped all over the Soviet Union as a testament to capitalism's rewards was still by far the dominant means of buying goods at home. Their sellers were *the* sellers in the business, their buyers were nonpareil, and everyone was free.

Many employees believed the myth that nobody ever left Sears, whereas in fact a huge number of young people filtered through the company ranks. The ones who stayed were true believers. They were soldiers of Sears, and the wind always seemed at their backs. The roads they traveled all seemed to be bordered by schools, post offices, churches, and Sears stores. . . .

A firm policy of promotion from within, and the best profit-sharing and benefit program in the country, so completely enclosed the human ring of the company that by 1954 hardly any of the huge number of people working for Sears had ever worked anywhere else. . . . By the mid-1960s, Sears, Roebuck was a superpower, as invincible a business as the nation it served. Articles about Sears referred to the company as the "colossus of American retailing" or the "monster of the Midway." Journalists invariably digressed in order to express Sears' sales as a percentage of the Gross National Product. One in five Americans shopped the company with regularity, and the internal populace was fast approaching three hundred thousand residents, many more than lived in ancient Athens during the Golden Age.

"Sears is the paragon of retailers," proclaimed a *Fortune* cover story in 1964, and in a reference to the five awesomely powerful territories it said, "It is number one in the U.S., and also number 2, 3, 4, and 5." It was just that big. *Fortune* noted that the company's sales volume was bigger than that of the entire tobacco or furniture industry. Alone Sears dwarfed the American entertainment and lodging industries. . . .

A nationwide free market existed inside Sears. The buyers, most of whom were based at the old West Side plant in Chicago, purchased goods from some twenty thousand loyal manufacturers. They bought things without checks or control from above. But they then had to turn around and "sell" the goods to the store runners out in the Field, where items were rejected, bought, displayed, and even priced according to the desires of the local merchants. Favors, advantages, good dinners, good whiskey, bad jokes, compliments, hot company gossip, political favors, and even—due to Sears' singular system of informal accounting—great piles of money were traded in the internal marketplace. A buyer slipping some money to a store or group manager for a big ad in the local paper was considered an example of good politics instead of bad business. Meanwhile, the territorial officers actually bought goods for their stores privately from local sources. "Buying off the reservation," as it was known, was in direct contravention of corporate policy, but it still occurred. The term "decentralization" now described the raw power that rested in each individual store, each administrative "group" of retail stores, and especially in the almighty territories of the Field, and any effort emanating from company Headquarters ("Headquarters" or "Parent"—the terms were interchangeable, though the latter was spoken with an ironic, rather derisive inflection in the Field) in Chicago that was designed to tell the soldiers of the Field what to do was resisted as a foreign invasion. Al Davies, the ruler of the Southwest Territory (a former Texas A&M boxer who refused to hire an executive not big enough to "whup" him because, he said, "A small man puts forth the wrong side of his nature"), referred to the merest suggestion of control from the "so-called" Parent—"Parent" housed the buying organization but mainly referred to the corporate staff—as "superimposure," a crime Davies associated with mortal sin.

Sears was so completely dominated by the five separate pyramids of authority by the 1960s that Professor Alfred Chandler stated, in his landmark study of corporate structure at the time, that the territories had gained "complete charge of operations." Homage had to be paid to the sanctity and sovereignty of the Field at all times. A 1967 Harvard Business School case study contains a quote from a senior executive at Headquarters who caught himself in the mere suggestion that the stores sold what the Sears buyers bought: "You should not, however, allow this willingness to follow Parent recommendations [in the Field] mislead you. The important thing about autonomy is that it exists—as a right!" A Parent telephone directory of the time contained a bright-yellow page that described the territorial overlords: "For all practical purposes he's 'president' of the territory. . . . A territory v.p. is a man with really sweeping authority. His word is law."

In the spirit of decentralization, each vice-president in charge of one of the five sovereign territories developed his own administrative procedures. Each had authority to design and "drop" his own new stores. They could take out bank loans at will. They protected the right of local store managers to price the goods and select the things they wanted to carry from the warehouses. They could structure a staff around themselves in whatever way they liked, and even after the territories each employed over fifty thousand people, the territory kings preferred to dole out raises and bonuses personally to even the most junior executives. . . .

In 1962 the General sent one of his favorites, Arthur Wood, the son of a personal friend, out from Parent to be schooled in the ways of the Field. Art was to serve temporarily as chief officer of the Far West. He'd run a store in Waukegan, Illinois, for a while, but he needed more seasoning. Even in the separate kingdom of the Far Western Territory, the Field men accepted that the General could do whatever he liked.

Just after the end of the war, the General had declared publicly that Arthur Wood and one other of his favorite Tall Men would eventually run Sears. When Arthur Wood was just a young lawyer at Headquarters, the General would embarrass him by saying, "Young Artie Wood is one of our bright young men and he's going to run this company some day." But even the General acknowledged that the system of local sovereignty had grown so powerful that no man could serve as chairman of Sears without having run one of the territories. So, after serving as a Sears lawyer, the corporate secretary, and then the controller, Arthur Wood was sent out to the separate kingdom to be schooled. An old-style merchant out west named Don Craib was convinced to postpone his retirement to keep Wood out of trouble. The big group managers like John Lowe, then head of the powerhouse Los Angeles stores, tended to take their day-to-day administrative problems to Craib, while Arthur Wood distinguished himself at the Los Angeles Chamber of Commerce, the Music Center, and the new visitors' bureau. It was said that if you called Arthur Wood with a question on a Tuesday you could expect to hear back from him a week from the following Monday.

The late General would have been pleased by the article in *Business Week* that attended the announcement of Arthur Wood's ascension to the chairmanship toward the end of 1972. The article called Wood "a sophisticated urbane intellectual with impeccable social credentials" and went on to proclaim that "his appointment reflected the changing nature of retailing and the necessity for having more than a buyer and seller of goods at the top." . . . Since Art Wood wasn't a merchant, a president for Sears was chosen from among the five territorial officers to serve under him, to be a merchant for him as old Don Craib had been when Wood was out in the Far West being groomed. It just so happened that in 1972 the five kings of the territories included two incredibly nice men. Nobody knew for sure how it happened, but Dean Swift, who ran the South, and Cul Kennedy, of the Midwest, were two of the nicest guys around. Swift was chosen as president. But when Arthur Wood declared that the territorial officers would henceforth report to good old Dean instead of to the chairman, the Field took offense. John Lowe of the West and Ed Telling of the East led the delegation of territorial vice-presidents who approached Wood after the announcement to demand a meeting to which Swift would not be invited. The new chairman agreed to exclude Swift, and at the private meeting the next morning, Lowe reminded the new chairman of just what had made the company strong. Lowe and Telling contended that the territorial officers must have direct access to the chairman. Wood countered by saying that running the largest merchandise company in the world and the fifth-largest insurance company as well, plus dealing with shareholders and government regulators, was too much for one man. The boys, Wood declared, would just have to learn to deal with Dean.

So the boys went back to their palatial headquarters and began to figure out how to get around good old Dean. . . . Meanwhile, the Sears Tower, the stock price, the price/earnings ratio, the profit margins, and the size of the work force all began to top out.

"Being the largest retailer in the world," former chairman Gordon Metcalf had told *Time* magazine, "we thought we should have the largest headquarters in the world." The plan was to rent out the upper floors of the Tower until Sears employees occupied all 110 floors at the end of the century. But as the Parent employees ate their lunches in the ornamental gardens on the West Side, and watched the Tower rise higher over the lake to the east, some of them began, for the first time in their working lives, to feel something akin to doubt. Inside the company, the Tower was named for the vainglorious executive who ordered its construction. It was called "Gordon Metcalf's last erection."

Almost all of the hundreds and thousands of citizens of Sears had grown up and worked in a world of consistent, record-breaking financial success. The vocabulary of decline—talk of "red" profit, "flat growth," or the wonderfully oxymoronic "negative growth"—sounded to the Sears ear like a foreign language. No one was left who remembered the dark hours of 1921, when Julius Rosenwald had bailed out the teetering company with his own money. For most of them, life had been a childhood, the war, and then Sears. Just one battle after another, and all of them won.

Somehow the incredible pride Sears people always talked about had become pridefulness by the early 1970s; the great march of the providers for the American masses had become a strut. By the time the Tower was finished, America seemed to have stepped away from Sears, Roebuck during the few years it took to build the monolith.

There just weren't that many people left in the country who hadn't already acquired their first electric refrigerator, washing machine, freezer, color television, or expanse of wall-to-wall carpeting from Sears. A phenomenon called "market saturation" was occurring in some of the product categories Sears dominated. People were only buying new big items to replace old ones.

And though most people at Sears refused to accept it, there were competitors now. No other company could presume to go head to head with mighty Sears—Montgomery Ward and J. C. Penney lagged so far behind the giant as to be inconsequential—but there were different kinds of threats. The huge regional malls Sears anchored were becoming the scene of the revenge of the small shops. Many decades after Sears raided the Main Street shops and local general stores with a new way of selling, little shops now lined the contrived Main Streets of the malls, swiping customers who previously would have gone directly to Sears.

At the other end of the market were large companies dedicated to selling goods that were even less expensive than the bargains at Sears. The local store runners from Kresge were traditional objects of condescension among the Sears Field people, because they would never fork out for the annual Community Chest drives. Kresge was considered a poor citizen as well as a doomed store, but a fellow named Harry Cunningham had an idea of turning the Kresge stores into emporia designed to house only bargains secured by his opportunistic buyers. Cunningham franchised out half of the old Kresge stores and filled the rest with good deals. Kresge changed its name to K mart, and from the early 1960s the new stores loomed as an obvious threat that Sears chose to ignore.

An agenda cast in the old spirit still called for new stores everywhere and all the time. During the 1960s, the company research department began to point out to senior managers that many of the new stores Sears continued to drop across America were not making good returns. But the leadership had been taught only how to grow, not how to change.

The real volume of retail sales in the United States began to decline during the spring of 1973, just before the quadrupling of the world's oil prices during the Northern winter of that year. The company economist at Sears was warned by a senior officer, toward the end of 1973, that if he disseminated his official forecast of an abrupt and deep recession during 1974, he'd be fired.

Sears, Roebuck was blindsided but good in 1974, and the company took the hit like the tired old veteran it had become. Other national retailers recovered much more quickly from the business slump. Profits at Sears dropped off by $170 million. Sales projections had indicated a 15-percent rise over 1973, and the company didn't even hit 7 percent.

Much more damaging was Arthur Wood's acquiescence to layoffs in response to the slump. Arbitrary staffing cuts that ranged from 1 percent to 10 percent were carried out, many of them up and down the just-completed Tower. As lifelong Sears employees carried their belongings out of the aspiring new Headquarters, it was noted, and passed along the grapevine out to the territories, that the departing members of the family had run into workmen carrying in hundreds of thousands of dollars' worth of house plants to decorate the 110-story testimonial to a company that never failed.

Sears had been warned by the government in the summer of 1973 that it was being watched closely because the corporation was suspected of discriminating against its minority and female employees. The Sears way of allowing well over a thousand people spread all over the country to hire people as they each saw fit—a practice once heralded widely as a brilliant organizational experiment—appeared increasingly anachronistic instead of progressive as public scrutiny of such uncontrolled methods increased. A few months later, the Federal Trade Commission filed a complaint alleging that Sears salesmen in the Field practiced "bait-and-switch" tactics. Bait-and-switch is a venerable maneuver by which a customer arrives in a store in search of an advertised bargain, only to find that only higher-priced items are available. Aside from the adverse publicity, the bait-and-switch and discrimination raps were particularly disturbing to Arthur Wood and some of the other officers, because they all knew the charges were true. They also knew that, despite government threats, they could do little to stop the practices. So much power had been ceded downward from level to level, from territory to group to store, that no officer in Chicago or even the territory kings could make local store managers do much of anything at all. The General could have cut through the localist prerogatives, but the General was dead.

The company was much more than "flat," a word the Searsmen had learned to pronounce by the mid-1970s; it was beginning to writhe in agony. "We know what's going on here," Arthur Wood insisted defensively to *Business Week* but what the kindly gentleman knew was that the sudden economic reversals were straining the delicate tendrils that held Sears, Roebuck together. Two utterly conflicting large-scale institutions within Sears had apparently coalesced around separate histories and ways of life, and now they were moving apart.

On one side were the sellers, the loyal Sears soldiers of the Field, whose ranks now numbered 407,958 workers divided among the five territories. On the other side were the buyers and the corporate staffs. The regulars of the Parent buying and administrative forces included 9,253 strategically situated employees operating out of the monolith in Chicago. Each side had its own leaders, laws, language, and long lists of epigrams and declarations from the General that were regarded as holy writ. Each camp was subdivided into powerful smaller cultures.

Nothing seemed to move easily from top to bottom through the decentralized units anymore, and nothing seemed to move from one side of the map of Sears to another without a fight. Pent-up dissatisfaction with a remote and aging officer corps had been surfacing among younger executives in both Field and Parent camps since the recessional downturn. The place looked to many of the younger men—and they were men, not women, in the middle and upper echelons of the company, just as the government contended—to be run by councils of elders, like some latter-day Indian tribe living in the footsteps of the past.

Arthur Wood may not have been a powerful general executive, and he may not have had an ounce of the thick blood of a merchant in his veins, but he was a student of history and a man with an eye for cultural nuance. The company was such that a chairman couldn't see very deeply into the awesome machinery below him, but as Wood considered the portions of Sears he could see at the beginning of 1975, he perceived the makings of a humiliating business failure and possibly a civil war that could destroy the company.

It was then that Arthur Wood decided to break profoundly with the tradition he'd been elevated to serve!

It was this desire to rescue Sears from its doldrums that prompted Wood and his successors to branch out into financial services. Sears purchased the stock brokerage house Dean Witter Reynolds, the real estate concern Coldwell Banker, started an international import–export business, and launched the Discover bank card, in an attempt to produce "a financial services juggernaut." Sears found, however, that financial services cannot be sold as easily as dry goods. With the Discover card, Sears entered an industry in which it had no established infrastructure, and which was dominated by two very powerful competitors, Visa and Mastercard. Sears has failed miserably in its attempt to become a financial giant, and Allstate Insurance, the original member of the "juggernaut," is the only one which is profitable.

Chapter 5

Power and Politics: "Revolutionary Change"

Introductory Notes

In Chapter 2 the phrase "revolutionary change" was defined as a change associated with major shifts in the internal power structure of the organization—in the "dominant coalition." But it also has another and rather different meaning: that the change is so great that it must be considered a fresh start rather than an extension of what preceded it, and as a corollary that the change occurred suddenly, appearing to arise without any warning, in contrast with more "evolutionary" change. The first sort of revolutionary change implies a literal revolt or at least open warfare, whereas the second could occur without anything of the sort.

In a very real sense a political revolution, whether in organizations or societies, is invariably the result of a very powerful evolutionary process. Nature in general and human life in particular are full of phenomena that appear revolutionary (if not miraculous)—that is, both unexpected and unrelated—yet when understood are recognized as flowing naturally from their preceding conditions. We take most of them for granted; consider lightning, the flowering of the cactus, or ice. The same is true of organizational revolutions. It becomes critical, however, to recognize how revolts evolve, what portends their eruption, and thus, what to do to modify the outcomes.

The first portrait, "Power, Greed and Glory on Wall Street: The Fall of Lehman Brothers," illustrates these points brilliantly. The bare facts are, on the surface, baffling.

Peter G. Peterson was a celebrated and widely admired executive with a brilliant track record of achievement. For five years, he had been CEO of Lehman Brothers Kuhn Loeb, one of the world's premier investment banks, leading it to record profits. For the good of the firm and to better balance his own interests, Peterson asks Lewis Glucksman, a long-standing member of the firm, to become co-CEO. Eight weeks later, to Peterson's complete surprise, and evidently on the basis of entirely personal motivations, Glucksman insists on Peterson's immediate resignation. Thirteen days later, Peterson in fact does resign and Glucksman becomes CEO. Ten months after that, the firm's 134-year history of tradition, prestige, and financial success comes to an end; it is sold to Shearson/American Express.

How can this happen? What accounts for such a bizarre sequence of events? More to the point, is this inevitable? Is this perhaps driven by some external crisis, with Peterson and Glucksman merely the instruments of fate? Or are there, perhaps, forces already in motion within the firm, forces that could with more foresight have been turned aside or countered? And perhaps there is a question even more critical; does this series of events constitute a failure, as it appears, or instead a success?

Several things are clear. The revolution itself clearly has roots within the organization, roots that derive in part from Peterson's rather antiseptic style of management and his lukewarm relationships with his partners, and in part from Glucksman's anger, accumulated over years of experience, at being perceived as inferior and treated in his view as a second-class citizen. But much also derives from the firm's character, which appears more as a temporary association of powerful individuals than a collective instrument to which people are strongly committed.

The moment was critical. At other times, in other circumstances, the same initiating action might not have had the same result. Glucksman might not have felt so keenly his "mistreatment." Or, if he had, Peterson might have been more inclined to resist. Or other partners, or directors, most of whom were passive, might have felt strongly enough to have intervened. Importantly, the organization lacked mechanisms that adequately engaged people; in that sense, it was already weak. Peterson's own attachment was limited, and the very success over which he presided may have simply made it easier for people to separate themselves economically and psychologically from the organization.

Did Lewis Glucksman's actions kill Lehman Brothers Kuhn Loeb? Only in the sense of being a proximate cause. The fact that the firm was sold soon afterward itself suggests people's willingness to end it, with these executive events certainly dispiriting in the extreme. The personal feud strained an already weakened organization, thus reducing people's commitment, thus weakening the organization. The offer from Shearson must have appeared to the partners a heaven-sent opportunity to help Lehman and themselves exit gracefully from an increasingly uncomfortable and perhaps even untenable situation.

There were many possibilities for preventive action all along the line, but the company's very success—a run of five very good years—would have made it very difficult for anyone to have suggested that the firm was in trouble. This is the sense in which organizations create conditions and develop momentum that tends both to prevent recognition of underlying problems and make less likely any action to address them. Under these circumstances, inevitability is not quite the right word, though one can easily understand that it might appear so.

The second portrait, "Champagne Shoot-out in France," is interesting for three reasons. First, the open warfare that exists between M. Racamier, the original CEO of LVMH, and M. Arnault, the challenger, has quite literally been brought about by the former's own actions (though he obviously did not expect it). Second, the whole sequence of events was probably motivated by the least constructive motivation possible, control for the sake of control. Third, the contest exists only at the highest executive levels of the company and probably has little or no operating effect.

This is very much a tempest if not exactly in a teapot, then certainly on the surface. Over and over again, when owners attempt simply to protect their position rather than to mind their business—literally—problems are created that may have little to do with the actual operation and health of the organization. Ownership and control derived purely from legal and financial considerations will always be weak supports without the operational "control" that comes from an effective organization full of committed and empowered people.

Our third portrait, Weirton Steel, illustrates a very different sort of revolution, a revolutionary restructuring with the support, at least in the legal sense, of past management and the firm's shareholders. In this case, the word "revolutionary" suggests a dramatic and extremely marked change, but one carried out by design. The firm, in serious and rapidly worsening financial straits, is turned over to an ESOP—Employee Stock Ownership Plan—a trust in which all employees are shareholders. Although there are now many ESOPs in American firms, very few have become primary vehicles for majority ownership, especially when the firm is large.

Weirton's employees thus have a direct hand in selecting their executives—indeed, en masse they control it. This leads to a paradoxical situation in which people's bosses are in a certain real sense subordinate to those they supposedly manage. As the various portions of the case indicate, Weirton has become profitable, in marked contrast to roughly comparable firms such as Pittsburgh–Wheeling Steel, and has been paying dividends to its owners, the firm's workforce.

However, after a successful round of change, tensions arise and very divisive issues begin to surface. For example, capital improvements were needed, but their cost would reduce dividends at least for a while. And around this decision, other possibilities were floated; possibilities that would perhaps reduce the power of the ESOP, add other "conventional" stockholders, or restructure voting rights. Thus, what began as a revolution may foster still another one, and even more, one that might return the firm to something more like it was before the revolution.

What lessons might be drawn from these stories? What, if anything, can or should executives do to prepare themselves better for these situations? Or is this sort of change an effective and desirable approach under some circumstances. When, for example, should one deliberately foment a revolution? And, of course, the classic question is: *cui bono?* Who benefits from a revolution (and who loses)? Here are a few possible answers.

- It is always appropriate to be more humble than you feel. You are certainly less powerful than you think, and probably less central as well.
- The higher in the organizational hierarchy, the truer this is, and the more important it is to remember it.
- Be extremely alert for advance signals of emerging issues. Construct your own organizational DEW (Distant Early Warning) Line and pay attention to it.
- Build strong relationships with a variety of constituencies and work hard to maintain them. As a corollary, don't expect people always to support you—but keep up the relationship even, perhaps especially, in adverse circumstances.
- Recognize that change takes a long time, at least in the sense that organizations have enormous momentum, and that actions may need to be taken long before the need is "obvious." Great managers must occasionally make unpopular decisions.
- Most of this will be more true as the organization becomes larger, more diversified, and more dispersed geographically.
- Finally, strive to help your organization create and produce products and services that require collective effort and widespread contributions, especially in professional or service firms where people can meet customers' needs individually. But the lesson holds for all kinds of organizations. Interest groups make negative power moves when constructive channels are closed.
- Treat conflict not as a threat to entrenched interests but as a chance to clear the air, as a prod to innovation.

Power, Greed, and Glory on Wall Street

Ken Auletta

For years the resentment had been building. And now, at lunch, it began to erupt. Lewis Glucksman, the co-chief executive officer of Lehman Brothers Kuhn Loeb, a short, rumpled man with the face of a Russian general, who was disparaged by Wall Street blue bloods as a lowly "trader," Lew Glucksman would leave the lunch table determined to remove Peter G. Peterson, his imperious co-C.E.O. at the venerable investment banking house, from his job.

The luncheon took place on July 12, 1983, and the fallout from the explosion it triggered carried the story from the business pages to the front pages.

Thirteen days later, Peterson, a celebrated success story—president of Bell & Howell at the age of 34, Secretary of Commerce under President Nixon and the man who had helped rescue Lehman from collapse in 1973—would be forced out of the firm he had helped steer to five consecutive record profit years.

Ten months later, Wall Street's oldest continuing investment banking partnership, a firm that had survived for 134 years, would fail to survive the reign of Lewis L. Glucksman and would be sold to Shearson/American Express, one of the great whales that now dominate Wall Street. . . .

This is a modern melodrama, the tale of an irreconcilable conflict between two men, a story of cowardice and intrigue, of greed for money and power and glory. In its broader implications, the fall of Lehman provides a window on the forces that are reshaping Wall Street and capitalism.

When Glucksman challenged Peterson, Lehman Brothers was more profitable than it had been at any point in its long history, averaging $15 million a month in pre-tax and pre-bonus profits over the preceding 12 months. With capital of almost $250 million, the firm ranked as one of Wall Street's largest investment banking houses, behind such names as Salomon Brothers; Goldman, Sachs; First Boston; and Morgan Stanley. Unlike dozens of old-line firms that had already succumbed to the pressures of consolidation that had been reshaping Wall Street—W.E. Hutton; Loeb Rhoades; Hayden Stone; Hornblower & Weeks; White, Weld; Kuhn Loeb, for example—Lehman had rebounded strongly from its difficulties of the early 1970's. Business was booming—partners were, by most standards, rich, and some senior partners were making almost $2 million a year in salary, bonus, and dividends from their Lehman stock.

And yet, such is the volatility of Wall Street today that, in a matter of months, Lehman was hemorrhaging, losing money and partners. That selling the firm seemed to be the only way to save it raises questions not only about the leadership of the new management team but also about whether private investment partnerships are destined to become dinosaurs.

Business will go on, of course. . . .

What is lost is a connection to the past that stretched back 134 years and, like the persistence of daylight baseball at Wrigley Field in Chicago, rooted people to a set of shared traditions, a common memory.

The story begins in July of 1983. John B. Carter, president and chief executive officer of the Equitable Life Assurance Society of the United States, the nation's third-largest life insurer, invited Pete Peterson, chairman and co-chief executive of Lehman Brothers, to lunch in a private room at Equitable's corporate headquarters. . . .

Peterson, who just eight weeks earlier had elevated Lew Glucksman to the status of co-C.E.O., suggested Lew be invited as well. Peterson enjoyed taking credit for what he thought was the transformation of Glucksman. After almost 21 years at Lehman, Glucksman, a volcanic yet successful securities trader for the firm, had become a calmer executive; Peterson congratulated himself for the fact that Lew had shed about 70 pounds and rehabilitated a wardrobe once dominated by light suits and wide ties. Besides, Peterson needed him. For three years, Glucksman had managed the day-to-day business of the firm; all of the departments reported to him, and his knowledge of Lehman's affairs was vast. Peterson was hoping eventually to interest Equitable in a joint venture of some kind, and Glucksman's expertise might be needed.

Glucksman and Peterson arrived separately, exchanged perfunctory greetings and then mingled with the other seven guests at opposite ends of the room. It wasn't until they were ready to sit down that Glucksman began to seethe. Peterson had been seated next to Carter at the head of the table, while Glucksman was far down the side of the long table, the equivalent, to him, of being seated in the bleachers.

Then came "the speech," as Glucksman derisively called a Peterson presentation. . . . Glucksman's pale blue eyes narrowed as Peterson talked about the menace of burgeoning Federal deficits, about how Americans, unlike the Japanese, consumed too much and saved too little. He had heard "the speech" so often he could recite it. Noisily, Glucksman fidgeted with the silverware and banged his chair against the table. Peterson, aware of the din from Glucksman's end of the room, attempted from time to time to include his partner in the conversation. Glucksman would respond, according to others present, with his own mini-filibusters.

"John Carter and I both remarked after the luncheon that Lew strove to have the concluding comment on every subject," says Equitable's executive vice president, Robert M. Hendrickson. "It seemed apparent there was a fair amount of tension between Glucksman and Peterson." . . .

In part, the animosity between Peterson and Glucksman flowed from the antagonism that had grown up at Lehman and all over Wall Street between "bankers" and "traders."

Essentially, a trader buys or sells securities—bonds, stocks, options, financial futures, commercial paper, certificates of deposit, Treasury bills, Eurobonds—either for clients (collecting a fee), or gambling directly with the firm's own money. The trader must make quick, firm decisions, often by consulting a jumble of numbers on a cathode-ray tube during and after hurried phone calls.

Bankers, on the other hand, usually have a longer horizon, serving as financial consultants to corporations and earning fees on the putting together of new issues and mergers, and providing advisory services.

Ten or 20 years ago, sales and trading activities were subordinate to banking, offering supplemental services to banking clients; in recent years, as interest rates have fluctuated wildly and new financial products have blossomed, sales and trading have become a profit center, accounting for hefty portions of the revenues of most major investment banking firms. . . .

But the war of stereotypes between bankers and traders persists—"like cowmen and farmers in the West," observes Andrew G.C. Sage 2d, Lehman's most senior partner in terms of service. . . . This polarization was particularly acrimonious at the House of Lehman, where—unlike Goldman, Sachs or Salomon Brothers—there was no history of significant trading prior to Glucksman's arrival in the 1960's.

Until 1980, when Peterson moved the Lehman main offices from the firm's Italian Renaissance-style building at 1 William Street to more corporate-style quarters at 55 Water Street, the trading operation was not even in the same building as banking. Peterson says that when he suggested consolidating Lehman's headquarters in a single location, the banking department resisted. "The toughest decision I had to make was the move to Water Street," he recalls. "The investment banker hated it. They didn't want anything to do with that group. They found them a lower form of species. They were the elite. Those guys over there were referred to as 'animals,' as 'crude,' as 'short term.'"

It gnawed at Lew Glucksman that traders were, he thought, still treated so shabbily. Trading activity, on The Street and at Lehman, was up. Commercial paper and equities—trading and sales functions that he had built almost singlehandedly at Lehman—were up. The banking division's share of Lehman's profits was declining, generating, in 1983, less than a third of the firm's profits. And yet—bankers still held 60 percent of Lehman stock, still permitted nonbanking departments only 35 of the firm's 77 partners. And bankers still had their own man, Pete Peterson, on top. . . .

Now that trading was achieving its day in the sun, Glucksman feared that Peterson was angling to sell the firm (for a substantial premium) within a few years. He believed that Peterson was "greedy," and, because partners were required to begin selling back their stock when they reached 60, he worried that the chairman, then 57, had a secret plan to sell the firm before his 60th birthday. Glucksman, also 57, picked up hints to this effect, but never anything concrete. . . .

Peterson derived his strength from his contacts, his considerable intelligence, and the aggressive preparation he did before meeting a prospective client, which could be dazzling. His skill at bringing in new business staggered even his detractors. . . . But the attention Peterson could lavish on clients was rarely turned toward his partners, much less to those who worked in the trenches.

One of Peterson's Lehman admirers, partner Stephen W. Bershad, says: "He would set his mind on something and see nothing else. He would walk down the hall with a stack of letters, read the mail, write replies and just throw them over his shoulder, assuming someone would be there to pick them up."

He would call partners at all hours, summon them to ride uptown in his chauffered Oldsmobile, and then ignore them as he talked on the telephone or scanned a memorandum. Many partners thought him self-centered, haughty, unfeeling, uncaring.

Glucksman found other things annoying. "Over the last five years, Peterson didn't play an active role in the management of the business," he says. "I brought him up to date. We played a charade with him"—pretending he was in charge. It galled Glucksman that Peterson got all the credit for Lehman successes. "I got sick and tired of Pete always saying the same thing," says Glucksman. "Pete was a guy totally obsessed with the world hearing the name Pete Peterson."

To Glucksman, the way he was treated at lunch at Equitable was the final indignity. He returned to Lehman Brothers that afternoon in a rage. One of those he turned to was partner James S. Boshart 3d, then 38, a 6-foot 5-inch former basketball star at Wake Forest University whom Glucksman had recruited 13 years earlier, partly to improve the Lehman basketball team. Boshart's role at the firm had expanded from clerk in the money market division to chief administrative officer of Lehman. In his various jobs at the firm, Boshart worked directly with Lew Glucksman.

. . . Boshart recalls what Glucksman said to him after the Equitable lunch: "He described the meeting and said he really felt he hadn't been viewed with respect commensurate to his role in the organization."

Glucksman was even more blunt with fellow board member Robert Rubin, his closest friend at Lehman since both had become partners in 1967, and the man he called "my *consigliere*."

Rubin recalls Glucksman saying of Peterson: "I couldn't believe his performance. I'm going to talk to Pete. This can't go on. Something's got to change."

Glucksman Lays Claim to the Helm

The phone in Peterson's office began ringing early the next morning. "Has Mr. Peterson come in yet?" Glucksman asked Melba Duncan, Peterson's principal secretary.

She explained that Peterson was attending a breakfast meeting outside the office. When Peterson arrived around 10 A.M., Miss Duncan told him of Glucksman's calls. Peterson jotted a few notes on a yellow legal pad and walked down the two flights to see Glucksman.

"I just thought it would be one of our weekly meetings," says Peterson. Quickly, he noticed that Lew "seemed a bit tense, as if he were psyching himself up." Peterson put down his pad and, like a doctor talking to a patient, peered at his co-C.E.O. Both men agree on the exchange that followed.

"What do you want out of life, Lew?" asked Peterson.

"I've been giving a lot of thought to my life," answered Glucksman. "You know how important boats and cruising on ships are to me. Kind of in the same way I have satisfaction when I'm in charge of a boat, I'd like to do the same thing at Lehman Brothers."

Peterson was astonished. He remembered how happy and honored Glucksman had said he was when Peterson had volunteered to make him co-C.E.O. eight weeks earlier. He could not imagine that Lew Glucksman, a trader, an inside man who displayed little fondness for the client side of the business, who was hardly known to the outside world, would think he could run Lehman Brothers.

Peterson is a man of many talents, but few associates would say that sensitivity to people is among them. He was unaware that many of his partners, including some he felt close to, while respecting him, did not like him; they had tired of his one-sided conversations. Nor had it occurred to Peterson that Glucksman felt demeaned by him and longed to run Lehman himself.

"This is my whole life," said Glucksman. "I really don't have alternatives. It seems to me that with all of your talents and associations, you have options. You've talked of other things you can do. Are you at the point in your life where you're ready to do other stuff?"

"Lew," said Peterson, "let me see if I understand what you're saying. Are you saying you want to run the business alone?"

"Well, there are things I want to do differently," said Glucksman. "It's time to heal the wounds at Lehman Brothers."

"What wounds? Heal wounds with whom, Lew?"

"You've had this problem with Bob Rubin."

"Yes, I've had problems with Bob Rubin."

Robert S. Rubin had joined Lehman in 1958, after Yale, an M.B.A. from the Harvard Graduate School of Business Administration and service in the Army. As a member of the banking department, Rubin had been singled out as a comer early on, a man who might one day preside over Lehman. Rubin had been on the Lehman board since 1972 and served as co-chairman of the pricing committee, which determined the firm's position in pricing securities before they were sold; he also served on the important commitments committee, which decided on the clients Lehman would do business with. But Bob Rubin's star had faded.

He and Peterson were not on good terms, and it was no coincidence that Rubin had been shunted aside as head of the banking division in 1977, or that his office was on the 41st floor, next to the trading department. His responsibilities, apart from shepherding the RCA account, were vague. The only person reporting to him was his secretary. . . .

"Who else?" asked Peterson.

"Bill Morris," replied Glucksman.

"Yes," responded Peterson, who removed William C. Morris as head of the investment banking division in 1982. He reminded Glucksman that Glucksman had agreed that should be done. . . .

"Who else?" asked Peterson.

"Eric Gleacher."

"Yes," said Peterson. Eric J. Gleacher was a talented mergers and acquisitions partner, but he didn't think Gleacher, who had run the department before Peterson removed him, had the management interest or people skills to run M.& A. "Who else?"

"Henry Breck."

"Yes," said Peterson, who remarked that the head of the Lehman Management Company, Lehman's investment management subsidiary, was "not a guy who builds managers and thinks about marketing."

"Those are only four people out of 77 partners that there have been some problems with," said Peterson. "That's not a great piece of news that I have problems with those four partners."

"I think I can heal the wounds," said Glucksman.

"You mean you think I can't heal them."

"That's right."

"What do you want, Lew?"

"I'm talking about running the business *now*, Pete."

"What do you mean *now*?"

"September 30," said Glucksman, picking the last day of their fiscal year, a day just over two months off. "I don't want to wait the three years for you to retire, because I know now that I'm fresh and eager to do the job. Who knows how I'll feel in three years." Glucksman says he then pressed Peterson for a timetable when he might leave.

Peterson was dumbfounded. He wondered whether Lew had quietly polled the 10 other members of the board and lined up votes. Peterson had assumed that his success at Lehman, his access to corporate boardrooms, would assure him support from Lehman's board of directors in any showdown. But as his mind raced over the names, he was uncertain. He had not said more than a perfunctory hello to some of them for months.

Peterson was not an impulsive man. He liked to sift options. He knew that on his 60th birthday, just three years hence, he would be required to begin cashing in his stock. But, though he had written a memorandum to Rubin and Glucksman on Nov. 26, 1980, which spoke of "my own transition plans" and mentioned his interest in participating in a handful of investments with venture capitalist Eli Jacobs, a friend and business associate over the years, Peterson had no thoughts of leaving so soon.

"Obviously, Lew, you and I have to have many more discussions on this. I want to be sure I understand your problem."

The meeting lasted five hours and ended inconclusively. The two men agreed to talk some more. In the meantime, they would call upon retired partner George W. Ball, who was Under Secretary of State in the Kennedy and Johnson Administrations, whom each respected, to act as a kind of mediator.

Peterson says he was not alarmed. He thought of Lew as a tempestuous person, capable of irrational behavior. He looked on the session, he recalls, as "a first discussion." He thought Glucksman might cool off and retreat.

Glucksman did not retreat. He was a gambler, a trader, used to making instant, firm decisions. After the meeting, he hurried to Bob Rubin's office down the hall and told him and Boshart what happened.

Glucksman said he was quite explicit with Peterson and wanted him out now. He was surprisingly confident Peterson would leave, sensing he did not have the stomach for a fight. Glucksman admits he calculated that Peterson would not want to get into a messy public brawl that could hurt Lehman and tarnish Peterson's public image. Even if Peterson prevailed, he would have to assume that Glucksman would not only move to another firm but also leave Peterson once again to manage Lehman on a day-to-day basis, something Peterson recoiled from.

Glucksman smelled weakness. He had sized up this transaction, and he told Rubin and Boshart he believed that with a generous golden handshake, Peterson would leave. . . .

A Brief Sharing of Power

Peterson began toying with the idea of elevating Glucksman to co-C.E.O. as early as 1981. By that time, all of the divisions at Lehman were reporting to Glucksman, and Peterson was thinking about the eventual succession. In the short run, he told associates he wanted "to build up Lew." In the long term, he had his eye on three younger prospects who were developing broad familiarity with all aspects of the business, and he hoped one of them might one day manage the firm.

The immediate plan began to unfold in early 1983, when Peterson quietly polled a handful of board members about the idea of elevating Glucksman to co-C.E.O. Clearly, Peterson was feeling pressure to assuage Glucksman; he received signals through intermediaries that Lew "wanted more recognition." Glucksman had always made it clear that he wanted managerial freedom to make decisions, which Peterson tried to honor. Peterson knew he needed Glucksman to manage the firm; he believed Glucksman needed him to police costs and to set the strategic framework for growth. Glucksman and Peterson conducted much of their business through others, almost as if they were deeply uncomfortable or apprehensive when together.

In one of their regular meetings in the spring of 1983, Peterson asked Jim Boshart, "Is Lew happy?" Boshart remembers responding that Lew had some frustrations, particularly that he did not receive public credit for actually managing the day-to-day affairs of the firm.

Peterson then said, "The right thing is to make Lew co-C.E.O. My ego can handle it. In every sense we'll be co-C.E.O." . . .

Peterson drafted a memo setting out the division of responsibilities. The memo stipulated that Peterson would—in addition to "continuing to work with investment banking clients"—"focus more time on a number of future initiatives," such as business strategy and development and "expanded special investment activity." Glucksman would, it said, exercise "principal day-to-day responsibility for our various divisions and departments." Together, the memo said, somewhat vaguely, Peterson and Glucksman would "continue to share in basic organizational and strategic decisions" as co-chief executive officers. The chairman felt satisfied, felt he had behaved magnanimously, thinking first of the long-range interests of Lehman.

Glucksman acted pleased, effusively praising Peterson, but says he felt no gratitude. Peterson thought he was being generous; Glucksman saw the move as noblesse oblige. "I was very unenthusiastic about this co-C.E.O. thing," Glucksman says today.

"It was a slap in the face. Another example of Pete's unwillingness to let go when his interests were outside the business." What he really wanted, Glucksman now says, was for Peterson to announce plans to step down eventually, as he thought Peterson planned to do when he wrote the memo in 1980 alerting Rubin and Glucksman of his thoughts about a "transition" at Lehman.

The co-C.E.O. announcement was made on May 16, 1983. After reviewing Lehman's impressive growth, the two-page Peterson memorandum to all Lehman employees concluded: "I doubt that this move will in fact result in Lew and I working more closely together in the future than we have in the past, for that would hardly be possible."

The board and most of the partners were pleased. No matter how crude some partners thought Lew was, he was a proven money maker. Even board member Peter J. Solomon, who made no secret of his dislike for Glucksman, was satisfied. "It was O.K. with me," he says. "I thought everything was terrific. We were in the middle of a bull market. I was banging out deals."

Glucksman Flexes His Muscles

Glucksman began to nibble at Peterson's authority. Instead of consulting the chairman on personnel decisions, Peterson says, Glucksman began to act unilaterally.

Not long after his appointment, Glucksman transferred Edmund A. Hajim, chairman and C.E.O. of the Lehman Management Company (Lemco), to the banking department. When Hajim went to Peterson to protest, the chairman says he was stunned. . . . Though Glucksman himself had recruited Hajim from E.F. Hutton, Glucksman now told Hajim he wanted firmer management of Lemco.

Glucksman insists that Peterson's account is "Untrue. The facts are that we discussed the need to replace Hajim because we felt the business should grow more slowly."

Equally disturbing to Peterson was Glucksman's decision to replace Hajim with investment banker Henry R. Breck, whose management skills were untested. "This was the first indication I had that he was not following our written agreement of May 16, in which all significant organizational changes were to be reviewed in advance," says Peterson.

Despite the chairman's expressions of concern, Glucksman's decision prevailed. Peterson's allies were distraught; they felt he had rolled over and sacrificed Hajim.

The ascendancy of Glucksman frightened many bankers, yet interviews with present and former partners suggest that few saw Peterson as their champion. As the 10th anniversary of his reign at Lehman neared, Peterson had worn thin his welcome. . . . The words that kept coming up when they described Peterson were: "condescending," "self-centered," "vain," "uncaring."

According to board member William E. Welsh, a cheerful man who was popular among most of his partners, "Pete was very standoffish. He was interested in himself. If you met him, you'd witness a monologue." In the end, Peterson was thought to be close to only a handful of partners." . . .

Peterson was largely unaware of these undercurrents. As the chairman of a firm, he felt it was up to him to make painful personnel choices—when bonuses and shares were distributed in September; when promotions were granted—and that to maintain the appearance of fairness he had to keep his distance. . . . Peterson says: "I wasn't running for office. I had a partner. Lew wanted to run operations. I didn't think he would appreciate it if I was in touch with people." . . .

The Decisive Days of July

In their five-hour meeting on July 13, 1983—the day after the Equitable lunch—Glucksman had informed Peterson that he wanted a divorce, and he was willing to pay alimony to get it.

George Ball agreed to enter the picture as a mediator on Thursday,

July 14. He met with Glucksman and Rubin the next day and recalls listening to a Glucksman diatribe against Peterson. "It wasn't very coherent," Ball says. "He was angry. He was jealous. I sat there in a state of considerable surprise because he seemed so incoherent. I could only think of Macbeth's line: 'O, full of scorpions is my mind.' "

Ball came away from this first encounter persuaded that it was no longer possible for the two men to work as a team. Ball also doubted that Peterson could win a board showdown, and felt that even if he managed to, victory would not be worth the price.

Ball reached that conclusion, in part, because Glucksman had suggested in their first meeting that he had secretly polled the board. "It was repeated two or three times that 'We've got the votes. The board is totally on our side,' " recalls Ball.

Glucksman denies implying that he had polled the board; he admits to saying something that could have left that impression: "I think I may have said the following—and I'd say it again—'You put it to a vote, and it's a laydown.' Ball analyzed it and came to the same conclusion."

Peterson made the fateful decision over that weekend. He worried that a fight would tear Lehman apart: If he won, he would again be consumed with day-to-day management of Lehman, and he would probably lose the valuable services of Glucksman; if he lost, he would be humiliated and partners, if forced to choose sides, might suffer retribution. "It's a battle I couldn't afford to win," Peterson told friends. . . .

During almost two weeks of negotiations, Peterson and Glucksman did not confer. All the negotiations for Peterson were handled by Ball and Janklow; for Glucksman, by Rubin, Boshart, and Edwin B. Mishkin of Cleary, Gottlieb, Steen & Hamilton, one of the two principal law firms that regularly represented Lehman. Aside from Glucksman and Peterson, the only partners aware of the secret negotiations were Rubin and Boshart. . . .

On Monday, July 25, a one-sentence memo was delivered to each Lehman board member announcing "a special meeting of the board" to be held the next day at 2 P.M.

When the board gathered in the oak-paneled board room—a replica of the original one at 1 William Street, with Italianate brass chandeliers and Fortuny curtains—Peterson and Glucksman, both glum, took their places at the head of the long table, flanked by nine other directors. . . .

Referring to hand-written notes and sipping an iced tea, Peterson made the following announcement: "Thirteen days ago Lew said he wanted to run this business, and he wanted to run it soon—by September 30. Lew told me this firm has been his whole life, and he didn't have a lot of options. He felt I did." They had quickly agreed,

Peterson said, "to bring in a trusted third party, and that was George Ball, who is outside now." Members of the board say they were stunned.

"My plan had been to remain as co-C.E.O. for two to three years and turn it over to Lew at the end of that time," Peterson continued. With George Ball as an intermediary, several options were discussed. "The theme of all of my options was a gradual transition." The chairman said he had even offered to step aside as co-C.E.O. in May 1984. That was not satisfactory to Lew.

Peterson explained his choices: "I could talk to a number of you and get your reaction. I could see if there were other alternatives. There was no way I could visualize this process without leaks, without divisiveness, without damaging this firm, without recreating the very problems we had done so much to overcome.

"As for Lew, no one on Wall Street knows as much about so many aspects of this business—not just trading, not just money markets—but pricing and distribution and many broad aspects of finance." He is "a rare talent. I have concluded that he is far more indispensable than many of us, and more indispensable than I am."

"As for myself, Lew said I had more options than he did. He's probably right."

Peterson said that he would remain at Lehman until the first of the year and help in any way he could; after Jan. 2, he said, he would be starting a venture capital firm with his friend Eli Jacobs. Then he added: "What I want out of life is to see the firm flourish. And I want my reputation, to the maximum extent possible, protected."

Peterson stood up to leave, saying there were "some retirement arrangements for me," and that Bob Rubin would explain them. If there were any questions, George Ball was outside and could answer them.

Peterson and Glucksman turned to step outside, and as they did the heavy silence was punctured by the booming voice of Peter Solomon, who was seated directly to Peterson's left. "Have you resigned, and are asking us to vote? Or is this an issue open to discussion?"

"I have resigned," said Peterson.

Solomon did not like that answer. . . .

Solomon had joined Lehman in 1963 and risen to partner in 1971. In 1978, he left to become Deputy Mayor of Economic Policy and Development for New York. In 1980, he joined the Carter Administration as counselor to the Treasury Department, rejoining Lehman in 1981.

Solomon glanced around the table, hoping for some support. Most of his partners kept their heads bowed. He said he was outraged that Glucksman and Peterson would take such a momentous step without discussing it with their partners. What right did Glucksman have to decide alone how much of the partners' money to give Peterson? Solomon waited for someone else to speak up. No one did.

Bob Rubin admits he loathed Solomon, thought he was vain and a loudmouth, and he was delighted to see Solomon isolated on the board once again. Rubin could barely suppress a smile as he rose to discuss the proposed terms of Peterson's severance. . . .

"You guys are nuts to allow this to happen!" shouted Peter Solomon. "We represent an investment of $40 million, which dwarfs the investment of Peterson and Glucksman. We are allowing them to harm our investment." Again, Solomon looked about for support.

Silence.

"Come on, guys. That's our money!"

Silence.

Then, like clerks inspecting the details of a legal document, the board members began to quibble about Peterson's severance agreement. For two and a half hours, they reviewed the details of the agreement and debated the draft press release. Finally, they made just one amendment—they asked Peterson to sign a clause, saying he would not, over the next five and a half years, join one of Lehman's five principal competitors: Goldman, Sachs; Salomon Brothers; Morgan Stanley; Merrill Lynch, and First Boston. He agreed. . . .

Solomon again seized the floor. If the board wouldn't discuss larger governance issues (What is a partnership? Who has the ability to make decisions for partners? Why weren't they consulted?), and if they wouldn't discuss money, then he was determined to frustrate the decision by focusing on the draft press release. He demanded that George Ball come in and answer his questions. The draft press release, Solomon said, was so frank in revealing what really happened between Glucksman and Peterson that it would harm Lehman.

Ball reassured him and the board that based on his and Peterson's extensive experience with the press, such candor would invite a one-day story. With nothing hidden, there would be nothing to unearth, and the story would die.

The board acquiesced in the press release without altering a comma. Peterson and Glucksman had correctly anticipated that the board would not resist decisions they made in the board's name; now they returned together to the board room. Glucksman did not make a lengthy presentation, or a particularly emotional one. Speaking quickly, he thanked Peterson for his statesmanship, his good wishes and decade of service to Lehman. Glucksman made but one promise to his partners: In the future, he said, there would be "more participation in the management of Lehman."

The meeting broke three hours after it had begun, and everyone rushed to attend a partners' meeting at 5 P.M. in the auditorium on the 42d floor. Full partnership gatherings were held irregularly, but there was usually one in the fall, and most of the 77 partners were puzzled as to why they had been summoned at this time. Peterson and Glucksman sat alone at a table in the front of the auditorium. Then Peterson rose to speak.

More briefly than at the board meeting, he announced that he was leaving. He explained why, and said an announcement was being delivered to the media at that moment. He thanked the partners and wished them well.

When he finished, Lew Glucksman stood up, turned to Peterson, and uttered words that would haunt many partners for months to come: "Would you now leave and let me be with my partners." (Glucksman remembers dismissing Peterson, but adds: "If I did summarily dismiss him it was in bad taste and inadvertent.") Very little else of what Glucksman said in his brief remarks is remembered.

The partners were even more stunned than the board had been. When the meeting broke, they wandered out of the auditorium singly and then gravitated, like wounded birds, to the offices of colleagues. At a moment when the firm had just concluded the most successful nine-month period in its history, how could this happen? What would this mean for the firm? What would this mean for them?

. . . At the time, most partners put on a public face, professing pleasure that the firm was not put through a protracted succession struggle; they hailed Pete Peterson as a statesman and clapped Lew Glucksman on the back.

But with the passage of time, many partners and board members came to be outraged at what they saw as Glucksman's lust for power, his unwillingness to consult the board on an issue vital to the health of the partnership. Some of Peterson's supporters say the chairman's behavior was "cowardly" because he was unwilling to risk losing.

"Peterson is not without fault; he left as chairman under his own will," observes his friend Enrico Braggiotti of B.C.I. "He could have fought. When Ball told me the story of Glucksman before it was announced, I told him to fight, with the support of B.C.I. He had not the courage to fight. Pete had a very good golden shake of the hand, which I complained about. If Pete had not all this money, perhaps he would have fought."

However, the entire transaction had been rubber-stamped. Board members tend to defend their passivity by stating that they were merely complying with Peterson's wishes, affirming a fait accompli."

. . . Those partners who criticize the board say that board members were preoccupied with their bonuses and their shares, which were decided every September. "Because compensation at the firm has always been set by the top two executives," explains one partner, "a guy can throw you a tip of a half million dollars! The chief executive is the ayatollah."

The board was focused on the riches the firm was gushing and the fears of Glucksman harbored by some members, not on whether the coup made sense for the firm, not on the violations of the consensual traditions of a partnership, not on whether Glucksman possessed the qualities to lead Lehman or whether it was time for Peterson to move on. This was just another transaction. . . .

"We were making money. All the people cared about was their money. Greed," . . . said one embarrassed former partner.

Champagne Shoot-out in France

Keith Wheatley

Ordinary people own bags and suitcases. Luggage is what affluent travellers have. Luggage matches. Inject tradition, chic, fine craftsmanship and astronomical prices into this equation and one has Louis Vuitton, an absurdly profitable French company based around that which can be carried in one hand.

It fits delightfully with Hennessy Cognac (founded 1765) and Moët & Chandon champagne (since 1743) into the LVMH conglomerate. However, this group is no collection of aproned craftsmen and earthy *vignerons*. With a capitalisation of £6 billion it is the largest public company in France. And since 1988 it has been tearing itself apart in a public feud. Not since the *affaire* of the "Giscard diamonds" has the public's appetite for financial scandal been so well catered for.

It is a peculiarly French story, worthy of the court of Louis XV. A tale of hopes betrayed and ungrateful protégés; courageous nobles and upstart princes. Even perfidious Albion makes an appearance. Above all, for many Frenchmen, it crystallises what the country was and what it may yet become. Behind it all is the implacable backdrop of the great merchant families, perhaps wondering if professional managers really care so much for the accumulated wealth of 10 generations?

Bernard Arnault and Henri Racamier are the two principal antagonists. Arnault is 41, built like a delicate marionette with eyebrows by Denis Healey, and a hugely ambitious financier invited into the firm by a rueful Racamier, 78. To the Paris press they are, invariably, the Young Wolf and the Old Lion. Since the demise of Maurice Chevalier, the mantle of the Anglo-Saxons' favourite Frenchman would fit perfectly on the elegant and beautifully mannered Racamier.

Between the two, but definitely in the Arnault camp, sits Anthony Tennant, chairman of the Guinness group. In a saga where stereotypes of age and race are being firmly adhered to, insiders at LVMH say that Tennant has tried to antagonize no one by playing the "affable British fool abroad." The 24 per cent stake Guinness holds in the luxury goods group contributes nearly a sixth of the British company's profits.

More importantly, in the long run, the synergy between the two companies gives them pole position in every important world drinks market. At the time of half-yearly results, just before Christmas, Bernard Arnault commented: "Our co-operation with Guinness is splendid because we have the number one champagne (Moët), the number one cognac (Hennessy), the number one whiskey (Johnny Walker) and the number one gin (Gordons) in the world. So we offer an exceptional array of goods to distributors—and that is the whole reason for our agreement."

Through a company spokesman Tennant has dismissed the continual lawsuits and internecine conflict between Racamier and Arnault as "a minor annoyance," pointing out that net profits continued to grow at around 60 per cent in the first nine months of 1989 on a turnover of 22.5 per cent. Other observers take leave to doubt whether any commercial group can survive such internal savagery untouched. On a more philosophical—yet crucial—level, Racamier himself poses the question of whether the customer seeking luxury, exclusiveness, and *élan* wishes to shop from such corporate brawlers using mass-market language.

Even before the arrival of the aggressive Bernard Arnault, the aesthetic Racamier was prone to doubt the 1987 "marriage" of his beloved Louis Vuitton to the Moët/Hennessy axis. While Moët executives were proud to see their product used like a fire-extinguisher at every Formula One race, Louis Vuitton was planning to sponsor a string quartet performance using four priceless Stradivarius instruments. "Champagne can be found on the shelves of every corner supermarket," Racamier observed at the time. "Our leather goods require exclusive distribution."

Certainly distribution was exclusive, verging on eccentric, when Racamier took over the Louis Vuitton reins in 1977. Paris and Nice were the only retail locations, with huge queues forming outside each at Christmas and holiday times. Now there are five shops in Tokyo alone, with another 15 in the rest of Japan, which is the biggest single market. Worldwide there are 135 Vuitton shops.

Empress Eugénie, wife of Napoleon III, was the unwitting progenitor of the company. She engaged one Louis Vuitton as the royal *layetier* or clothes packer. In the era when a monarch would endure a bumpy coach journey of 1,000 miles across Europe, a servant who could pack clothes in a trunk so that they would not crease was a treasure. Louis Vuitton was the best, and in 1854 he used his imperial prestige to open a trunk-making business.

Gradually the firm expanded into handbags, attaché cases, and valises, all made in the distinctive "Monogram" canvas by craftsmen who are, even now, allowed two hours to shape a simple bag handle. Clients as diverse as Emperor Hirohito and Douglas Fairbanks lent the luggage a cachet which no mere marketing strategy could produce. Nevertheless, Vuitton were not so shy of an eye-catching gimmick that they would decline to make travelling theologian Pierre Teilhard de Chardin a cabin trunk with a fold-out altar.

Racamier married into Vuitton rather than being born to the bag trade. His wife is the great-granddaughter of the entrepreneur *layetier*. Yet for most of his working life Racamier had no contact with the sleepy business, preferring to concentrate on the highly profitable steel trading company that he had founded in the reconstruction boom of the postwar period. Racamier's in-laws begged him to take over Louis Vuitton when he left his own company, aged 65.

"This is my little retirement hobby," he once said to me as we watched an America's Cup yacht race that the company was sponsoring. He was, of course, joking since Racamier still travels an average of 100 days a year on business and during the 1987 America's Cup was known to fly down to Australia for a weekend dinner party if courtesy required it. Apart from yachting, one of his private passions, Racamier can publicly indulge other pleasures: he had the company sponsor grand opera in Milan and major art exhibitions in New York.

Despite the corporate statistics of 135 stores, 2,500 employees, and a turnover close to £750 million, Racamier understands intuitively that the empire he has built relies on an intimacy and exclusivity of image. Of major British companies probably only Jaguar has shared the gift of mass-producing a product that has a patina of craftsmanship and individuality. Every Jaguar owner believes he is buying a Rolls-Royce.

Bernard Arnault may not have been born into this *milieu* but he certainly realises its commercial value. Son of a wealthy Lille family, he was in the U.S.A. attempting to break into real estate development when he made his debut in luxury goods. In 1984 the French government was desperate for someone to take over the bankrupt Boussac textile and retail empire. At Boussac's core was the prestigious Dior fashion house.

Hearing about the opportunity, Arnault lobbied, cajoled and manipulated the government into allowing his £10 million-a-year family firm to reverse into a company 20 times its size. The young Turk, at this time only 35, was ferocious in his slash-and-burn progress through Boussac. Factories were closed and even Dior's star designer Marc Bohan was given his cards.

Insiders say that Arnault suppressed any sensitivity he might have had in his pursuit of total corporate power. Intriguingly, he was a gifted musician when he was younger but discarded his ambitions to be a concert pianist. He has told friends that he was talented but didn't have the "supergift" to be world class. Only the highest level of achievement interested him.

However, it was Racamier who invited the wolf to guard the chicken coop when he suggested that Arnault take a minor stake in LVMH. It was a mistake the genteel *boulevardier* had made once before just a few years earlier when he cemented the alliance with Alain Chevalier, the professional manager who had become head of Moët-Hennessy. In many respects Racamier and Chevalier had identical career stories. The aristocratic family which controlled Moët & Chandon invited Chevalier to expand and diversify its empire just over 20 years ago. He brought in the Hennessy brandy clan with the logic of a joint-distribution arrangement and the seeds of a new giant were sown.

Yet as the rest of the world, and in particular international stockbrokers, woke up to the intrinsic value of worldwide luxury brands, it became apparent that Moët-Hennessy was vulnerable. The two families controlled less than a quarter of the stock. Mysterious names and unknown nominees began to appear on the MH share register, and Chevalier, prompted by the nervous aristocrats, began a search for a "white knight" whom the families could do business with.

Naturally his glance fell on Racamier. A get-to-know-you dinner was arranged at Maxim's. Most of the guests were called Moët, Chandon, Hennessy, or Vuitton. However, within months of the 1987 merger Racamier and Chevalier had become bitter enemies. Trivial events like the printing of company stationery with Racamier's name above Chevalier's caused a quarrel that reverberated across Paris. Around the dinner tables of the 16th *arrondissement* hostesses would adjust guest lists to accommodate the squabbles at LVMH.

Chevalier's supporters said that Racamier was too high and mighty. "He never knew how to conduct himself as part of a group in which someone else was chairman," said Frédéric Chandon de Briailles, chairman of the LVMH advisory board. From Racamier's viewpoint the company was in danger of going down a mass-market route to the beat of a vulgarian drum.

Simultaneously the risk of a hostile bid increased, despite the merger of the two companies. Anthony Tennant was a close friend of Chevalier, and Guinness was invited to take a 3.5 per cent stake in LVMH, which quickly became 20 per cent. For Racamier, already isolated from the corporate action, it was an unmistakable sign that his "merger of equals" was about to become dominated by bottles and booze. His quest for an ally of his own led him to Arnault. "We had identical visions," Racamier confidently announced at the time. His suggestion was that Arnault should bid for 25 per cent of LVMH. Allied with the Vuitton family holding, this would give the two groups control of the whole company. However, Arnault's advisers were specific in their warnings and suggested that he still bought in but aligned himself with the Chevalier/Guinness axis. In July 1988 Arnault formed a joint venture with Guinness called Jacques Rober. Controlled 55 per cent by the Frenchman, this vehicle holds just under half the LVMH stock.

Millions were spent in frantic months of share-buying, dawn raids, and wooing of elderly stockholders. Led by Racamier, the Vuitton family struggled to achieve a 33 per cent shareholding which would make them a "blocking minority." Arnault, spending $600m in just three days, was too strong for them. In February 1989 Chevalier became a casualty when Arnault manoeuvred him out of the company (though Chevalier resurfaced in February this year as the new head of the Balmain perfume and fashion house). Since then there has been almost continuous litigation between the two parties. Various issues of shares, bonds, and warrants have been queried on both sides.

Last November a spokesman for Racamier predicted, with prescient accuracy, that "this will all get very dirty." Since then there have been claims from the Arnault camp that certain Far East subsidiaries of Vuitton have been involved in financial irregularities. Racamier, with characteristic disdain, spent Christmas in the Caribbean sailing on the new yacht he has recently had built.

At 78 the old *gentilhomme* knows that time is not on his side. He must both make peace and find a suitable successor to lead Louis Vuitton. Racamier's track record on the latter task must worry him. Yet he has the energy of a 40-year-old—which was shown in his £53-million takeover of Lanvin, the perfume and fashion chain, last month—plus the experience of an octagenarian, a formidable combination in any business. His support from the Vuitton family appears total.

Guinness is sitting on a £500m paper profit on the LVMH shares, and the joint distribution agreements are too valuable for either side to disturb. Anthony Tennant can quite happily afford to play the "affable fool" until the cows come home.

Meanwhile it looks as if the future belongs to Arnault. His style and techniques would be recognisably successful in any free-market economy, and the shareholders support him. The only question mark is the historical poser of whether it would have been good business to give control of Ferrari to Henry Ford.

War and Peace

Labor Relations at Two Steelmakers

Thomas F. O'Boyle and Terence Roth

STEUBENVILLE, Ohio—Several thousand striking steelworkers gathered here outside the idle Wheeling-Pittsburgh Steel Corp. plant earlier this month to symbolically lynch company Chairman Dennis J. Carney.

As the executive's straw effigy swung from a lamppost, the noisy throng chanted, "Carney must go!" When the figure was lowered, employees burned it while local television cameras filmed the spectacle. One burly steelworker then drove a wooden stake into the scorched form.

Directly across the Ohio River, in Weirton, W.Va., about 2,500 employees of another steel company gathered a few weeks earlier for a ceremony of their own. It was Weirton Steel Corp.'s 40th annual company picnic. Robert L. Loughhead, the affable chairman of the employee-owned company, mingled with the crowd, swigged a few beers, and presented service awards to inductees of Weirton Steel's "25-Year Club."

These incidents tell a tale of two steelmakers whose labor relations—and fortunes in general—are going in opposite directions. Their situations illustrate how, even in the most troubled of basic industries, cooperative labor-management practices can salvage one company while confrontational tactics promise to help sink another.

Weirton has used the most open communications system in Big Steel to break down the old "us vs. them" antagonisms and build a more constructive relationship between labor and management.

"You don't develop the nation's most profitable steelmaker by waving a magic wand," says John Simmons, the president of Participation Associates, a management consulting firm. "You do it by using the very best management techniques."

Wheeling-Pittsburgh, meanwhile, has chosen a combative approach dictated by Mr. Carney, the chief executive. The result: the first strike against a major steel producer since 1959. This approach, once standard in the industry, could conceivably end up destroying the company. Even before the strike began, Wheeling-Pittsburgh obtained bankruptcy-law protection after the United Steelworkers vetoed a debt-restructuring plan.

Many people in the industry believe that Wheeling-Pittsburgh has already sustained irreparable damage, whether or not the strike, now in its ninth week, ends soon. "I don't know how anyone could bring it together as a functioning company after this," asserts John H. Kirkwood, a consultant whose clients include Weirton Steel and who used to be the labor-relations chief at Jones & Laughlin Steel Corp.

Whatever the outcome, Wheeling-Pittsburgh's struggle has enormous implications for the battered U.S. steel industry. Already competitors have seen their order books rise as the company's customers seek alternative suppliers. Moreover, if Wheeling-Pittsburgh won lower wages, then its settlement would be a target for other steelmakers as they negotiate new labor contracts next year. Such a pattern might require further pay cuts at Weirton, whose workers agreed to reduce wages and benefits 20%—and freeze them at that lower level for six years—as a condition of their employee buyout in January 1984.

Today No. 9-ranked Weirton is among the nation's most profitable steelmakers. Last year, it earned $61 million on sales of $1 billion. On almost the same volume, No. 7-ranked Wheeling-Pittsburgh lost $59 million.

Weirton's better situation largely reflects its more cooperative relationship between labor and management. Yet only 3½ years ago, Weirton workers envied the relative security that their Wheeling-Pittsburgh neighbors seemed to enjoy: In March 1982, Weirton's then parent, National Steel Corp., said it planned to abandon the division, and both the mill and the town seemed destined for economic ruin.

"We had a gun to our heads," says Michael Gibson, a Weirton mill worker, recalling the buy-or-die threat that galvanized his 7,800 fellow employees and the community. "We had to buy the mill. It was either that or nothing," he explains. Mr. Gibson got his job back after nearly two years on furlough when employees purchased Weirton. He still has his job today while his brother, Patrick, walks the picket line at Wheeling-Pittsburgh. Michael joins the line on his days off.

Weirton has long held, even in its darkest days, several advantages over Wheeling-Pittsburgh. For one thing, Weirton's production and finishing are more efficient because they are concentrated in one location rather than being dispersed among nine sites in Ohio, Pennsylvania, and West Virginia, as is the case with Wheeling-Pittsburgh. And Weirton's average ton of steel sells for nearly $75 more than its cross-river rival's—a difference of 17%—reflecting the higher prices Weirton can command for its more sophisticated steels.

Despite enormous modernization outlays in recent years, Wheeling-Pittsburgh still lacks first-rate finishing facilities. As a result, "a lot of Wheeling's sales come from the garbage end of the business"—less-refined products where price and import competition is stiffest—observes a former executive vice president, Thomas D. Moore.

By contrast, Weirton, which itself faces perhaps $1 billion in modernization expenditures over the next decade, is the nation's leading supplier of one major product—tin plate, the steel used principally in food containers—while Wheeling-Pittsburgh holds only meager shares of less lucrative markets.

Another Leg Up

The employee buyout, fashioned during a year and a half of negotiations and exhaustive preparation, gave Weirton another leg up on the competition. The new company started life with a debt load 71% less than Wheeling-Pittsburgh; so low, in fact, that the annual carrying cost on Weirton's debt is less than just two months' payments for Wheeling-Pittsburgh. More significantly, under the terms of the buyout, Weirton workers agreed to accept wages and benefits totaling about $20 an hour, or roughly $1.20 less than the rate paid to Wheeling-Pittsburgh workers, who since 1982 have twice agreed to reduced wages.

At the helms of the companies are two men whose management styles differ greatly. Mr. Carney has ruled Wheeling-Pittsburgh with an iron hand since assuming the top job in 1978 after a 32-year career at U.S. Steel Corp. His management style has often led to conflict while he has been maneuvering the company through a mine field. Mr. Loughhead, on the other hand, is a consensus manager, an executive who firmly believes in employee participation and who eschews confrontation. He is widely credited with transforming what one director says were "God-awful" labor relations at Weirton when the chief executive assumed the job two years ago before the employee buyout was final.

Of course, the situation Mr. Loughhead inherited is conducive to improved labor relations: Since the buyout, top officials at Weirton's

Independent Steelworkers union are intimately involved in key company decisions. The union has three representatives on a 12-man board.

Still, labor-relations problems can arise even at employee-owned companies. For instance labor strife contributed in recent years to troubles at employee-owned Rath Packing Co. of Waterloo, Iowa; the meat-packing concern now has been liquidated.

Besides, Weirton is a company owned but not yet controlled by its employees. Eight outside directors control the board, an important factor in getting banks to finance the buyout. Employees probably won't gain actual voting control until 1989 when the stock, now held in trust, is fully distributed. Thus, workers have little say now in day-to-day operations, a fact that can heighten any frustrations.

Mr. Loughhead, who resigned as president of a rival company, Copperweld Steel Co., to join Weirton, says he did so because "a large employee-owned company was the perfect environment to prove that employee participation could work." He adds, "It's my job to set the tone and the style for participative management. If I simply preach it and don't practice it, it won't go anywhere."

Workers say Mr. Loughhead lives up to his word. A frequent unannounced visitor to the shop floor, the 56-year-old executive welcomes employees' ideas. One recent example: A group of mill workers, frustrated by the frequent breakdowns of two tractors they used, solicited price estimates for a new one. Then, in a presentation to management, they documented how the defective tractors had actually cost the company, in just three years, enough to pay for five new ones. Mr. Loughhead immediately authorized the purchase, over the protests of a few executives who complained that routine budget and purchasing procedures weren't followed.

Yet Weirton's future is by no means certain. When they gain control, workers may refuse to maintain the wage freeze or balk at further productivity-enhancing job cuts—already touchy issues with the rank and file.

While some Weirton workers grumble that there are too many managers around, Mr. Loughhead's involvement seems to help. Employees tell of his memorandum distributed to middle managers early in 1984 encouraging foremen to cooperate with efforts to form employee participation groups—or else. Weirton keeps workers informed with, among other things, candid videotaped messages transmitted weekly over some 60 television sets in the plant and company offices.

Mr. Loughhead's impromptu mill appearances also improve morale. "There's only so much he can do," says steelworker Frank Loggie, "but just the fact that he's there shows you he cares." The mill worker says his crew is "rolling better than ever," trying a little harder for quality. The crew has become more frugal, Mr. Loggie notes, since profitability will translate directly into profit-sharing checks, which workers will begin receiving next year. And productivity is higher. These days it takes Weirton roughly 20% fewer man-hours to produce the same steel product as Wheeling-Pittsburgh.

"You still have guys just going through the motions," says Henry Ciotti, a 42-year mill veteran, "but most of the workers are more conscientious now. They're more concerned about putting in a good day's work."

The contrast with Wheeling-Pittsburgh is striking. Craig A. Smith, a Wheeling-Pittsburgh crane operator, says he gave up making suggestions after a foreman rebuked him for proposing a way to save man-hours. "It's like beating your head against the wall," the steelworker asserts.

Incidents such as these have convinced workers that their foremen are merely following orders to govern mills with a firm hand. Mr. Carney's own, limited direct contacts with workers have reinforced this view, often widening the schism between labor and management. (The 64-year-old executive, who rarely talks to the press, declined to be interviewed for this story.)

Early in 1982, for instance, Mr. Carney paid a surprise visit to the company's new Monessen, Pa., rail mill, where, after summoning about 85 hourly and salaried workers to a private meeting, he launched into what has been described as a tirade, "he practically accused us of conspiring to sabotage his mill," recalls David Kissler, one of the workers who attended the meeting.

Such outbursts—whether on the shop floor or in the corporate suite—are typical of what former employees contend is Mr. Carney's "management by intimidation" style. "Dennis is a forceful guy," says Mr. Kirkwood, the labor consultant. "He's part of a long steel-industry tradition: managers who believe they can get better results using a stick than a carrot."

Since the strike began, however, what was a tenuous relationship with labor has deteriorated into open warfare. Although the unions' drumbeating bears some responsibility for the current crisis, it was Mr. Carney who chose confrontation rather than compromise when he gave the union an ultimatum on July 17. Late that day, a federal bankruptcy judge, Warren W. Bentz, ruled that the company could legally annul its existing labor contract but recommended that the two sides negotiate a compromise.

Nevertheless, within minutes after the ruling, Wheeling-Pittsburgh—already armed with a new contract, printed in anticipation of a favorable verdict—presented its terms to the union in a suite at the Pittsburgh Hilton Hotel. There, United Steelworkers representatives were told they had until 10 the next morning to accept a new contract, one that Wheeling-Pittsburgh said would cut wages and benefits 18% to $17.50 an hour (the union's own subsequent analysis suggests a rate of $15.60).

If the union rejected the company's demand, then another contract would go into effect on July 21, three days later, with the same economic terms but substantially diluted job protection. The meeting lasted only a few minutes; after a heated exchange, the union's representatives left. Only last week, 55 days later, did the two sides meet again, under pressure from federal mediators. No talks have been held since.

Events following the July 17 confrontation have fueled the fire. Financially pinched workers were outraged when the company, unsuccessfully, sought court injunctions to prevent them from receiving unemployment benefits. Tempers also flared when senior management asked the bankruptcy court to approve severance pay for the managers—amounting to as much as $1 million for Mr. Carney alone—in the event their jobs were terminated. (The court hasn't ruled.) Private union polls indicate that pro-strike sentiment among the 8,200 workers is higher now than when it began.

Wheeling-Pittsburgh workers speak of pride when explaining their strike. Weirton workers say it is pride, too, that makes them strive for the success of their company.

Gary Babaryk, a striking Wheeling-Pittsburgh mill operator whose neighbor goes to work each morning at Weirton, paused to consider the contrasting conditions of the two companies one recent night, while delivering the evening meal of stew and cheese sandwiches to pickets. "Throw a dog a bone once in a while and he'll work for you," he said, backing his Horizon hatchback up to a plant gate bedecked with "Carney Must Go" placards. "Weirton gets that and we don't, not for years."

Class Consciousness Raising

Stanley W. Angrist

From 1971 to 1974 Herbert Elish was New York City's Commissioner of Sanitation. The experience taught him how 10,000 well-paid garbage collectors can help bankrupt a great city. Now Elish heads one of the country's largest steel companies and may soon see his workers bankrupt their employer—which is to say, themselves.

In July Elish was named chairman, president and chief executive of Weirton, W.Va.'s Weirton Steel Corp. In 1984 National Steel Corp. sold Weirton to its 7,800 workers on the cheap. The mill, representing an investment of $350 million, brought National Steel less than $200 million—not all of it cash. Thus was created the nation's largest employee stock ownership plan, or ESOP, for an industrial company.

Things have gone pretty well for Weirton since the buyout. In 1984 Weirton earned $60 million on sales of $1 billion. This year sales will probably come in at $1.3 billion, profits at $120 million. There is $90 million in cash in the drawer.

Weirton's worker-owners have happily cut themselves in on this improved performance. Since the buyout, the workers, who now number 8,200, have paid themselves a total of $35 million in profit sharing dividends and allocated to themselves $158 million worth of Weirton stock—about $19,000 of stock per employee. The employee-owners will probably pay themselves another $40 million or more from this year's earnings. (As an ESOP, Weirton's profits are largely sheltered from income taxation by payments into the plan—an enviable subsidy—but workers' profit sharing payments are taxed as ordinary income and, when the company finally issues shares to the workers, the value of those shares will be fully taxed as income.)

Have these goodies made the workers whole for the minor sacrifices they made when they bought Weirton? Depends on how you look at it. Give-backs at that time cut the company's overall labor costs from about $25 an hour to $20 an hour. By contrast, labor costs at Wheeling Pittsburgh Steel Corp., also unionized, are around $18 an hour. But then, Wheeling is in Chapter 11, and is paying nothing into its workers' pension fund.

In any case, if Weirton folks were having their cake and eating it, too, the fun is about to end. Elish says Weirton must spend around $500 million on plant upgrading in the next four or five years to complete the modernization of its hot mill and build a new continuous caster.

Aging plant and equipment aren't Weirton's only problems. Although production has climbed since the workers bought the company, to about 2.6 million tons this year Weirton's product prices are about 3% lower, on the average, than in 1984.

Worse, Weirton's product mix is heavily geared toward tinplate, which winds up largely in food cans. The tinplate market has been shrinking about 2% a year as aluminum and plastic have displaced tin in the beverage can market. Weirton hopes to win back orders with a new convenience-top tinplate can designed to protect against sharp edges. Also under development is a beverage can of tinplate that doesn't require the lid to be pushed into the liquid.

But to produce the new product at reasonable cost, Elish needs that new caster and the other capital improvements. That means borrowing close to $400 million. Finding willing lenders will probably require Weirton's worker-owners to reduce their labor costs and postpone some dividends.

Under the terms of the ESOP, Weirton Steel's employees are to receive one-third of the company's profits if the company's net worth is over $100 million and below $250 million. When net worth reaches $250 million, the contract calls for profit sharing payments to rise to 50% of profits. With net worth likely to exceed the $250 million level next year, Elish fears that banks will be loath to lend Weirton the modernization money it needs to survive.

Elish thinks he can talk the worker-owners into additional givebacks. Says he: "We must increase automation, reduce manning requirements, and increase multicrafting of jobs to make our labor costs more competitive. We are now having conversations leading in that direction."

He will also need to talk with the workers about something else. Each year the company makes a contribution, based on total wages, to the employee stock ownership trust. That contribution determines how many shares of stock will be allocated to the employees. So far, over 3 million shares have been earmarked for that purpose. What can the workers do with their shares? As of now, nothing: The shares are allocated, but not yet issued. But the ESOP agreement has another provision. It states that once Weirton's net worth reaches $250 million, current employees and retirees can demand cash for their stock. If that target is reached next year, and if employees insist on redeeming their shares, Elish's task of finding the money to make the necessary capital improvements will be even tougher.

Will the workers behave like responsible capitalists, ready to postpone money today for money tomorrow? Father Charles J. Schneider, the pastor of Weirton's St. Joseph the Worker Church, notes an encouraging change in Weirton Steel's employees. "When I came to Weirton in 1981," Schneider says, "there was an appalling lack of pride. They felt Weirton Steel owed them a job because their fathers and grandfathers worked for the company. Now that they own the company, that attitude is gone."

Maybe, but listen to Saundra Toma, who works in Weirton's tin mill. "I don't think they should put a megacaster in here," says Toma. "I think we're doing fine like we are. I'm looking forward to my ESOP check next year." Making difficult choices is what running a successful business is all about. The fact is, most people don't like to make such choices. They'd rather leave that to the boss. But at Weirton "most people" are the boss.

Weirton to Seek Cuts in its Work Force

Pamela Gaynor

WEIRTON, W. Va.—To remain competitive, Weirton Steel Corp. must inevitably trim its work force and probably its profit-sharing plan, the company's new chief executive officer said at a news conference yesterday.

Herbert Elish, who was hired to head Weirton in July, declined to say precisely how many jobs might be lost, but estimated at least several hundred.

He added, however, that the company, which employs about 8,000 hourly and salaried workers, hopes to accomplish the reductions through attrition and early retirements.

"We're not going to cut and slash," he told reporters. "There is some time . . . so we can make the reductions in a reasonable and humane way."

The cuts have been widely expected.

Weirton has been profitable in every quarter since it was taken over by its employees more than three years ago.

But the company has been under pressure to reduce its labor costs ever since competitors began gaining wage concessions and new manning agreements from the United Steelworkers union.

Elish said he doesn't foresee any need to "change wage rates" for Weirton's workers, who took a 20 percent pay cut to purchase their company from National Steel Corp.

But he said the company's profit-sharing arrangement "is a subject that needs to be discussed, particularly the 50-percent level."

Weirton currently distributes a third of its net income to workers. But the profit-sharing formula calls for an increase to 50 percent as soon as the company's net worth—currently about $189 million—reaches $250 million.

Without a reduction, Elish said the company might have difficulty financing $500 million worth of planned improvements.

Part III

Change What?

Chapter 6

Change in Form, Forms of Change

If organizational change ever implied just internal managerial projects to fix problems or improve the performance of a business unit or introduce a new reward system, the 1980s changed all that. It became clear that more significant change could be made much faster by buying and selling corporate assets, or deregulating and privatizing whole industries, or creating new alliances among firms, than by struggling patiently to fine-tune operations or motivate employees. Even government bureaucracies such as the British National Health Service found more dramatic change stimulated in corporate culture by a restructuring to decouple the purchasing and delivery of local health services than by all the internal managerial exhortations of years past.

This part of the book deals with the ways in which organizations change their form. We identify three principal methods, connected to each of the three forms of motion. First, organizations can change their *relationship to their environments*—the nature of their ties to their markets and major stakeholders—by restructuring or redefining their identity and boundaries through mergers, acquisitions, divestitures, or alliances and partnerships. Second, they can change the ways in which they operate, the ways people and units relate to each other, corresponding to their organic development over time, through changes in *internal coordination*—their culture and structure. Third, they can change the nature of their *control structures*—the parties involved in the dominant coalition of interests that govern the organization and determine how benefits are distributed among them. Note that only the second form of change is generally considered in the "planned change" literature; yet identity and control change can trigger profound coordination changes in their wake.

Sometimes change in form is triggered by troubles. Therefore it can seem forced or constrained rather than voluntary, since (a) the organization wouldn't do it naturally or evolutionarily; (b) it reflects more than local innovation; and (c) it is imposed from the top or the outside on the rest of the organization. But a shift in form—new partnerships, new relationships, a new governance structure—is also sought by organizations as a way to develop new opportunities in a changing environment.

Organizational Identity and Change at the Boundaries

The most drastic change organizations can make is to alter fundamentally their relationships to their environments—what they supply and what they receive; their ties to other organizations; the expectations external constituencies hold for them; and, therefore, the activities they undertake.

Fundamental *identity change* means that an organization has become something entirely different. But this is an elusive idea. Given all the flux and motion in organizational life—the jockeying for position among competitors, the introduction of new products and phasing out of old ones, the application of new technology and the career passages of people, and so much more—when is an organization ever "the same"?

The answer lies in the nature of the ties that organizations have with their key constituencies or stakeholders, and who these stakeholders are. It is those ties, reflected in the assets the organization manages which provide value for those stakeholders, that give an organization its identity. When those ties are severed or the nature of the transactions is altered, then the organization has changed its identity. Absolute or complete identity change, therefore, involves transformations in every key stakeholder relationship—new in kind, and new in relationship partners: new owners, investors, customers, suppliers, employees, regulators, or source of legal charter.

Organizations are bundles of activity, as we proposed in the introduction to this book. Organizational identity resides in the boundaries placed around sets of activities so that they can be managed and coordinated. Identity change is change of boundaries at the macro level. Internal changes—sweeping reorganizations, major downsizings, or revamping of product lines—do not alter organizational identity unless they impinge upon and redefine relationships with major stakeholders. Consider each of the major forms of restructuring or repositioning as sources of identity change:

- A merger, such as the creation of ABB Asea Brown Boveri in 1987 out of the Swedish Asea and the Swiss Brown Boveri, is a fundamental altering of the boundary between firms, erasing the line and creating a common identity in the eyes of investors, customers, suppliers, and regulators out of what was formerly separate.
- A divestiture, such as the Swedish conglomerate Procordia's sale of its engineering division, creates a new boundary, pushing outside what was formerly inside; some ties may remain between the divested unit and the former parent (such as a financial stake created as part of the terms of the sale), or all ties may be erased.
- An acquisition, such as the acquisition of the British computer manufacturer ICL by the Japanese company Fujitsu in 1990 (while the Canadian Northern Telecom bought ICL's telecommunications operations), alters or erases the identity of the acquired unit. It also changes the identity of the acquirer by enlarging its market scope, bringing new customers, or

requiring relationships with suppliers new to the acquiring company because of the requirements of a different set of products.

- A strategic alliance between firms might result in blurring of the boundaries between them. A close working relationship between a supplier and a customer, such as the computer-maker NCR's product development alliance with chip-maker Intel, blurs the boundary between them and may influence other market relationships of each partner. An alliance between similar companies serving different markets, such as the partnership of SAS, the Scandinavian airline, with Continental in the United States, can cause altered investor relations (equity swaps) as well as joint marketing that alters customer relationships.

In general, when stakeholders are replaced, or when all aspects of relationships with all stakeholders are altered in every respect, then organizational identity has been completely altered, and the organization has become something fundamentally different. Fewer changes in environmental positioning or relationships means more modest identity change. When an organization changes only one stakeholder group, such as being acquired by a new parent corporation, but is left alone in every other respect as a separate entity with its own name and relationship set, then its identity has been altered only slightly in the short term—though longer-term alterations will undoubtedly follow.

It is important to remember that organizations may maintain *multiple identities.* The scope of identity change may be localized in just one of the organization's identities. As we have been stressing throughout this book, the idea of an organization as a single, simple, bounded, coherent entity is simply wrong. Organizations are constructs in the minds of stakeholders, which may be given a common name but in fact may consist of many different activity clusters each with a different legal existence. A small California company with about $100 million in sales is actually eight distinct legal subsidiaries, each of which reports results to legal authorities, though all are also consolidated for reporting purposes of the parent company, which is the majority shareholder of all the subsidiaries. Operationally, however, it consists of four divisions, each with a distinct name that is marketed to customers who think they are dealing with a company by that name—even though it is a smaller part of a larger whole. In one case, it works closely with a partner and, for operating purposes, forms one organization with that partner; that identity, however, is not known to the public. Thus, even in a small company there are differences between its legal identity, operating identity, and public identity.

Characteristics of Identity Changes

Identity changes have several distinctive properties, especially in contrast to internal organizational changes. These characteristics give rise to the major managerial issues in managing the restructuring or redefining of boundaries—the issues that need to be handled well to ensure successful change, that can be too easily fumbled or mismanaged. "Failure" can mean that the deal involved in the identity change is not consummated; e.g., the negotiations for the sale of assets breaks down or the terms of the new customer alliance are not established clearly. But, more often, it means that in the aftermath of the transition, the change in identity does not stick or the desired benefits are not realized.

The first three characteristics of identity changes derive from the institutional environment in which organizations operate.

First, identity changes generally involve formal contracts between stakeholders, and therefore they have significant *legal aspects.* Legal rules may govern the changes, including what is permissible over what time frame, or what additional parties (e.g., government regulators, unions, shareholders, creditors, landlords) must be satisfied before the change can be carried out. Agreements may be subject to the involvement of government officials at the highest levels, around securities laws, antitrust laws, defense considerations (e.g., U.S. rules governing high-technology ventures with Eastern Europe). Even changes in the nature of markets favored and therefore customers served can involve contractual issues. Thus, managerial choices may be highly constrained, guided not by some abstract notion of "best practices" but by institutional rules prevailing in the jurisdictions in which contracts are reviewed. A set of stakeholders involved in the rule-setting process became the targets of managerial action, even though they are generally not part of ongoing organizational operations. Their decisions became more important, for immediate decision purposes, than the actions of more "internal" participants. The internal, however, is often ignored, to the organization's later peril. A common problem in joint ventures and strategic alliances is that top executives pay more attention to the legal aspects of the deal than to forming personal relationships with future partners.

Second, identity changes may be highly *public* while they are in process, not just when the final results are announced to the public. Disclosure rules are only one manifestation of this. Many people and groups that are not direct parties to the transaction may feel an emotional stake. Managerial actions may be scrutinized and second-guessed by the media. A joint venture announcement—e.g., Apple and IBM—is headline news. Sometimes identity changes take on great political importance, as in the controversies in the United States over whether U.S. companies should be sold to foreign investors. The acquisition by the French company St. Gobain of Norton Company, an abrasives manufacturer headquartered in Worcester, Massachusetts, was fought vociferously by members of the community, who felt they were losing their major employer and philanthropist to outsiders who would no longer honor Worcester's interests.

Third, the focus of identity changes is often on *tangible assets:* product flows, buildings, machinery, customer contracts, patent rights, pricing issues, equity stakes, financial payments. Initially, at least, the "change" appears to reside in the transfer of assets, and the attention of those managing the change is on these issues rather than on how the organization will operate later. Managers of this kind of change tend to look for competence in valuing assets and negotiating deals. They surround themselves with professionals from outside (investment bankers, economists, financiers, lawyers) as well as inside (strategic planners) who may be good at assessing value and developing contracts but know little about the softer, less tangible assets or about the operational issues that will have to be managed in the aftermath of the transition.

Major restructuring of key organizational relationships—especially mergers and acquisitions—increases the likelihood of *unilateral managerial action,* which is exercised on everything all at once and further disempowers the rest of the people (Kanter, 1989). Of course, because of all the disruptions, it is more important at times of restructuring than during normal times to make clear that someone is in charge. But some managers interpret this as the need to take drastic steps and make dramatic decisions quickly. They feel that there is no time to explore options or consider ideas from the troops. So people are reminded of their marginal status; signals tell them their positions are vulnerable. Perhaps the press gets announcements and briefings regularly and items run in the media before employees hear about them. Middle managers look dumb and uninformed. Employees feel left out. No one looks or feels good. For example, morale plummeted during one General Foods cutback because insiders heard about the changes from outsiders (consultants or stockbrokers)—sometimes incorrectly (Kanter, 1989). In situations like this, values regarding participation, involvement, or concern for people seem to fly out the window as luxuries of good times. Inevitably, cynicism about the "culture" grows along with distrust of leaders. Relatively minor irritations can turn into genuine and enduring crises for the organization.

Restructuring also increases the likelihood that all organizational contracts will be up for grabs, therefore requiring more management time and attention on boundary-setting matters than operational matters. Any negotiation tends to stimulate others. Since contracts are being revised when organizational identity is changed, other stakeholders who are not participants in the main transaction may want their contracts reviewed—to their benefit—as well. Or the organization undergoing a restructuring may seek to revise other contracts to its benefit in order to pay for the costs of the restructuring, such as renegotiating wage rates in union contracts. Thus, putting one external relationship on the bargaining table tends to lead to others.

Overall, this kind of change appears to be *acute.* It appears to be a matter of decision-making rather than implementation. There is a short time frame for the official transition from one set of contracts to another. The emphasis is on the immediate decision, so as to get through the acute period. But when only those with the skills to make those decisions are involved, it is often difficult to manage the aftermath. With a stroke of the pen, the acquisition deal is consummated, the papers are filed with the appropriate government entity, the press releases are sent, and *voilà!*—another organization identity change has been effected. But now the myriad bits and pieces required to integrate the change into ongoing operations have to be managed.

Banc One (see Chapter 2) often involves people with skills in every aspect of banking in the "due diligence" review process for its new acquisitions so as to ensure an informed transition team that can manage the aftermath as well as the deal. When Southwest Bancshares in Houston merged with Mercantile Texas Corporation in Dallas to form MCorp (which became the eighteenth-largest banking organization in the United States), twenty-one different restructuring task forces were formed a few months after the announcement but well before the merger, each with three to four subtask forces. Participants attributed the absence of conflict and the retention of customers to the cooperation engendered by this activity. But later, even this was not enough in light of the troubled Texas economy; MCorp failed and was bought by Banc One, which soon turned it to profitability through even better management.

Top management typically *overestimates* the degree of cooperation it will get and *underestimates* the integration cost (Kanter, 1989). Numerous studies have shown that acquisitions do not generally improve the financial performance of acquiring firms in the short run. One study, covering 103 active acquirers from 1965 to 1979, showed that, on average, the firms deteriorated in competitive position within their industries, and the extent of deterioration was associated with the number of acquisitions (but not with the degree to which acquisitions were related to the core business). Explanations for the failures of synergy include: resistance by managers of acquired businesses to the consolidation of activities; reduced motivation after the acquisition; expenditure of energy on acquisitions leading to neglect of the preexisting businesses; and too much acquisition activity overloading the management systems. In short, the way the acquisitions process is implemented makes a difference.

Among the many by-products of significant organizational restructuring are *discontinuity, disorder,* and *distraction.* There are gaps between what was once appropriate and what will now be appropriate—until the next change. There is uncertainty about what should be done and the standards to apply. And restructuring produces distractions in the organization; it diverts people's attention from the critical focus. At the same time, leaders may be less available to counter these three dangerous *D*'s. Managers have important immediate tasks to perform and decisions to make. They are called away for meetings, they are engaged in secret deliberations. They are so swamped by urgent *content* priorities (decisions about what to do) that they simply do not have time or attention for *process* matters (observation of how things are going).

For all these reasons, the acute phase of restructurings can result in performance shortfalls, crises of commitment, and competitive vulnerabilities. The competition is likely to exploit weaknesses during the transition, attempting to forge its own relationships with major stakeholders, such as customers and suppliers. If those stakeholders are confused, are ignored, or sense a better deal coming from another relationship, they can be lured away. Soon after a Midwestern medical services company acquired new facilities in one of its regions, the sales force of its major competitor mounted a large-scale campaign, calling on all of the customers of the acquired facilities, warning them of the decline in service they should expect because of the new owner—and won some of them. When Westinghouse Furniture Systems acquired Knoll, a larger furniture company known for design excellence, the competition leaked rumors to the trade press of impending disaster. One particularly formidable competitor even made a mass job offer to twelve of the key managers, with higher compensation promises than they thought Westinghouse would offer.

Abrupt changes, especially those that are externally induced, create managerial difficulties. And the more abrupt and forced, the more likely the identity change is to be accomplished by still more selloffs, closings, liquidations, and reductions in employment. It is easier and faster to manage expenses down than to get revenues up. Even in identity changes designed to create growth, such as acquisitions, managers often must reduce expenses first in order to pay for the cost of the acquisition. This threat to employment creates its own human vulnerabilities.

If mismanaged, restructuring can all too easily make people feel helpless, anxious, startled, embarrassed, dumb, overworked, cynical, hostile, or hurt (Kanter, 1989a). Restructuring thus produces a window of vulnerability, a time when exposure to disease is increased at precisely the same time as the corporate body is temporarily weakened. This threatens not only current productivity, but also the foundation for the future, the organization's credibility, culminating in a *crisis of commitment and a need for people to reaffirm their membership*. Every time the basis of the relationship of employee and company changes, a recommitment is necessary. It is especially ironic that more commitment is needed at the very time when the *basis* for commitment itself is weakened.

The Politics of Identity: What's in a Name?

Not surprisingly, identity changes often involve *image changes,* from logos to slogans, culminating in *name changes*. When U.S. Steel became USX, it was the most visible statement that the company had diversified into other areas and no longer wanted to be known for its steel business. When American Can became Primerica, it signaled a shift out of its traditional packaging business into financial services. Gulf + Western engaged in a particularly dramatic asset restructuring. Once a holding company owning business units in industries as diverse as apparel, mattresses, films, and sugar, it pared down to three core businesses in the early 1980s: publishing (Simon & Schuster), entertainment (primarily Paramount Pictures), and financial services. After selling the financial services unit in the late 1980s and therefore becoming focused on entertainment and communications, Gulf + Western changed its name to Paramount Communications.

Both names and symbols seem the simplest part of identity change, but they are often complex and time-consuming decisions because of the meanings that will be read into them by stakeholders—as well as the desire for names and symbols to endure (Olins, 1990). In the United States, AT&T divested its regional telephone operations by government decree, forcing a major identity change. Today, it competes aggressively in long distance services, telecommunications and computer equipment, and credit cards internationally as well as domestically. It gave up the Bell logo (for the Bell System, as it was formerly known) but kept the name AT&T. AT&T clearly wanted to maintain continuity of public and consumer identity because of the value of the name, even though its operating identity was altered. British Telecom, which underwent identity changes of a milder sort in the 1980s (a shift from government ownership to public stock ownership; the opening of competition; joint ventures; some international expansion), recently decided to be known as BT instead of British Telecom, in order to change expectations about the scope of its operations and to signal a break with the past.

However, the *politics of identity can cause managerial headaches.* Because the name—and other aspects of the new identity—can signify who is ascendant, conflicts can ensue over other boundaries of the new entity. In merger situations, some companies try to avoid difficult conflicts by insisting on strict equality in every respect; e.g., when Connecticut General merged with Insurance Company of North America, the new name, CIGNA, was created to give equal billing to the initials of both companies. But such simple solutions are not always possible. Two newly merged furniture companies were given the name of the one with design excellence, even though that was the acquiree, not the acquirer; some units of the purchasing company refused for many months to use the new name, saying "Who bought whom? We bought them, didn't we?" The result was customer confusion, when telephones were answered several different ways, which the competition further exploited. A Swedish company acquired a successful unit with its own clear market identity, and though the parent company had invested heavily in the overall corporate name and a new logo, the CEO of the parent was reluctant to force any changes on the unit. So the unit not only kept its own name, it issued its own *Annual Report to Shareholders,* which was listed in an airline magazine advertising section alongside the parent company's report. This was clearly a power move on the part of the unit executives, who hoped that they would be able to take the company private or have it spun off as an independent unit.

Some restructurings divide people into conquerors and vanquished. When one group clearly "takes over" another group in a merger or internal restructuring, the conqueror inevitably parades its power in front of the others: "After all, wasn't our ability to buy you a sign of our superiority?" Imagine hearing an executive tell managers from an acquired company: "You are frogs we will teach to be princes." Or imagine watching the acquiring company dismantle the other company's boardroom, taking the best furniture and silver to outfit its own headquarters (Kanter, 1989). Both of these real examples may be extreme, but the same feeling of being "colonized" like a defeated country exists in many groups that are merged with a more dominant entity.

Managing—or mismanaging—multiple stakeholders when organizations restructure played a significant role in one unsuccessful identity change (Jick, 1978). A pending merger between two hospitals aroused much stakeholder opposition and became a public, politicized battle. But that is not all that went wrong. There were problems on nearly every front: incompatible corporate cultures which rendered leaders from one hospital ineffective with the other; a slow process of consolidation of the two systems; and myriad contradictions with respect to what the new identity would be. Even a degree of participation and involvement did not allay the fears of the people involved; employee burnout and tune-out hurt productivity. After months and months of effort, the two hospitals were still functioning as separate institutions. In short, organizations can *claim* an identity change long before their people accept it; the operative identity has not changed at all.

After the "Deal"

The *aftermath leaves many managerial problems to resolve*. First, it may be declared officially that the organization's identity has been changed. On a human level it does not change all that quickly or easily. Honeywell bought General Electric's computer operations well over twenty years ago, eventually forming a joint venture with France's Cie. Bull called Honeywell Bull, and then selling the whole thing to Bull around 1990. After so many years and so many transitions, there are still some managers and professionals in Phoenix who think of themselves as the GE computer group.

Furthermore, major stakeholders like customers may not always accept the identity change. Despite United Airlines' holding company, which bought a hotel chain and a car rental firm, changing its name to Allegis to signify its new unified identity as a complete travel services company, the marketplace refused to treat it that way, preferring to deal with each unit separately. Claimed "synergies" were not present, there was not a good managerial fit among the three, and the conglomerate was eventually broken up and new management brought in.

Managers also have to deal with the fact that vital capabilities may have been lost in the transition. The focus on tangible assets in the deal-making phase of identity changes means that the loss of capabilities is more likely to come in the "intangible" column: know-how or expertise that is in the heads of people who choose to leave because of the change; suppliers that defect; key relationships that have been unraveled. And, of course, the merger might not "take"; the acquisition might fail; the alliance might go sour; the new customer connections might not materialize.

To be successful, identity changes must *not* be managed just as episodes of asset shuffling, without attention to the aftermath. Attention must also be devoted to the ongoing, long-term coordination of organizational action that comes under the heading of internal culture and structure change.

Revolutionary Versus Evolutionary Identity Changes

Because they are dramatic and involve relationships to the environment, identity changes through restructuring, repositioning, and the redefining of boundaries are most likely to arise when the environment shifts abruptly, thus altering the viability of stakeholder ties or creating the potential for new ones. Deregulation and privatization of government holdings in the 1980s, a phenomenon in the United States and Europe, opened the possibility for restructuring and repositioning. The opening of international boundaries creates new market opportunities, which then stimulate mergers, acquisitions, joint ventures, and other forms of alliance. Financial distress experienced by large bureaucratic organizations, especially in industries not only mature but ripe for consolidation because of overcapacity (e.g., chemicals) caused them to consider selling or shuffling assets. The operation of all of these forces for change simultaneously is illustrated by the case of Montedison in Italy, once a state-owned chemical company that privatized and restructured in the wake of worldwide industry changes, changing its identity with respect to many kinds of major stakeholders.

Of course, the public drama associated with this kind of change has led some observers to say that top managers seek them in order to show their courage and effectiveness. Winning the deal seems easier and more controllable than slow improvements in operating businesses. One successful chief executive of a multibillion-dollar U.S. company has commented that some managers consider winning the deal so much a "test of their manhood" (his term) that they will make much higher bids for ventures they wish to acquire than inherent economic or strategic value suggests are justifiable. In this regard, consider the case of Edward Hennessey, long-time CEO of Allied Corporation, held up by the business press as a consummate example of the manager in a mature industry who thought that asset reshuffling alone would save the business. While there were environmental reasons for changing the identity of the business, Hennessey perhaps went beyond what was managerially effective. He turned Allied Chemical into Allied Corporation by restructuring, then thrived on deal-making. He won Bendix by being the "white knight" who saved Bendix from a hostile takeover bid by Martin Marietta. For a time, Allied combined forces with Signal Corporation to become Allied-Signal, but that merger fell apart. Michael Dingman, the former Signal chief executive and a better operating manager than Hennessey, formed the Henley Group with a set of businesses Allied no longer wanted, turning them into a profitable group. Meanwhile, Allied's financial performance continued to be disappointing, and the board finally "encouraged" Hennessey to resign prematurely in 1991. Was it a preference for the quick action and "highs" of deal-making over the slower work of organizational improvement that led to Hennessey's failure?

Restructuring—mergers, acquisitions, divestitures, and liquidations—represents the sharpest and most dramatic identity change, but organizations may also alter their identities more slowly, with much more continuity, as part of a more natural growth and evolution of their constituency or stakeholder relations—for example, by adding new technology that gradually alters product lines and customers for those products, or by forming a limited purpose strategic alliance, which grows into a new venture. Organizations that endure over long stretches of time have changed their identities in the process, but gradually and smoothly, with so much continuity and "naturalness" that they have not had to alter their names. In 1970, when it established its U.S. subsidiary, the Japanese heavy equipment company Komatsu had less than one-third the sales of the world industry leader, Caterpillar, derived primarily from its small bulldozer line, and operated primarily in Japan. In the 1960s it had grown from a small enterprise largely ignored by MITI (the Japanese Ministry of Trade and Industry) through an emphasis on quality and a series of licensing arrangements (with allies and quasicompetitors like Cummins Engine and International Harvester), enabling it to acquire technological capability. In the 1970s the emphasis on new product development grew. By the 1990s Komatsu was a formidable competitor in many product lines, including undersea robotics, with a presence in many countries (Bartlett, 1989; Hamel and Prahalad, 1989).

Even modest boundary changes may cause unanticipated changes that gradually alter an organization's identity. A small investor might raise its stake. A new venture can prove so successful that it becomes more important than the rest of the company. A single unit can serve as the basis for the redefinition of the whole. One new set of relationships can lead to others. New interorganizational relationships can change internal processes.

How Boundary Changes Can Alter Internal Relationships: The Case of Strategic Alliances

In response to rapid technological change and the globalization of markets and competition, companies all over the world are increasingly forming coalitions with other organizations as part of their business strategy (see Porter and Fuller, 1986; Johnston and Lawrence, 1988; Powell, 1987; Harrigan, 1986; Kanter, 1988, 1989). Strategic alliances and partnerships allow organizations to increase their reach without adding fixed capacity—to gain a measure of stability in a turbulent environment by planning jointly with organizations on different points on the value chain, to reduce uncertainty (Thompson, 1967; Aldrich, 1979) or manage power dependencies (Levine and White, 1961; Pfeffer and Salancik, 1978). Besides the direct financial benefits of sharing costs and gaining economies of scale, partnerships lead to improved time to market for new products, especially in Japan (Clark and

Fujimoto, 1989), and more opportunities for innovation (see Kanter and Myers, 1991).

Organizations can open their boundaries in several ways; the kind of alliance selected has implications for the degree of identity change for the partnering organizations.

There are three main types of alliances. *Multi-organization service alliances,* or consortia, are groups of firms that band together to create a new entity to fill a need shared by all of them. They are generally limited in purpose, such as research and development (e.g., ESPRIT and JESSI in Europe), offering the benefits of larger scale with respect to a single issue through resource pooling. Little identity change results. Alliances of the second type are "*opportunistic,*" joint ventures entered to gain some competitive advantage quickly. The allies exploit some opportunity to a greater extent than would have been possible by either firm alone. Each side makes a distinctive contribution, typically either technology or market access. Commitment beyond earning the initial expected return is uncertain and often depends on whether one of the firms has developed internally the capacity for which it originally had sought a partner. These alliances are evolutionary; they may end when one firm acquires the joint venture or even the partner organization.

The third kind of alliance is *complementary,* or stakeholder, partnerships. These are defined by some preexisting interdependency, usually created because each party is on a different position in the value chain (see Porter, 1985; Johnston and Lawrence, 1988). These partnerships are vertical relations among organizations with complementary capacities in which each coordinates activities closely with the others—e.g., supplier–customer ties. Each maintains a separate legal identity, but operationally their identities can be fused, functioning as one production-distribution entity. Examples of the latter abound in retailing. Marks & Spencer, the British retail powerhouse, has such close ties with suppliers and planning and operations so integrated with them that it has been called a "manufacturer without factories," while its suppliers have been called "retailers without shops."

In recent years, there has been an apparent growth in the number of American and European interorganizational alliances and in the scope and strategic significance of these relationships, as well as a recognition of the vital role of alliances and networks in the success of Japanese companies. This recognition has led to studies of the industry conditions favoring coalitions or the choice of organizational form (Bradach and Eccles, 1989), the conditions under which an equity stake is sought (Pisano, 1989), or the reasons alliances dissolve (see Gomes-Casseres, 1987).

In successful alliances, those that endure or fulfill their purpose to the satisfaction of all parties, managers regard the relationships as strategically important (Porter and Fuller, 1986; Kanter, 1989); and therefore provide it with adequate resources, management attention, and sponsorship. The partners share a long-term view of their investment in the relationship, which tends to help equalize benefits to each over time. The interdependence that often leads to the partnerships in the first place helps keep power balanced. Partnership managers work to integrate the two organizations to maintain communication at the appropriate points of contact. This means that both parties knew about the plans and future directions of the other. Finally, successful partnerships became institutionalized, or bolstered by a framework of supporting mechanisms ranging from legal requirements to social ties to shared values (Kanter, 1989).

These success factors imply a significant degree of *intraorganizational* change on the part of both partners in order to accommodate the existence of the partnership and manage it so that it brings benefits to all parties. The new interorganizational arrangements among companies produce shifts in the way the people who work for those firms view their roles and perform their work. Changes in structure, roles, power dynamics, and behavior will occur within the firm when interorganizational relationships go from arm's-length exchanges to closer, more cooperative, and more strategic interactions. The development of explicit alliances with "external" parties should change "internal" organizational dynamics for the firms in such a relationship.

In short, change at the boundaries of the organization "takes" only when it is accompanied by changes in coordination inside the organization. Redefining external relationships, as in the acute phase of restructuring, requires attention to the nature of internal relationships.

Identity change is clearly connected with changes in power—increased ability to mobilize, resources, information, and support (Kanter, 1983). The redefinition of power begins with a rethinking of the company's role vis-à-vis its stakeholders to give them more influence over internal choices in the interest of greater control or influence over the portion of the environment represented by the stakeholder. The greatest amount of internal change, of course, should occur in the wake of relationships with the highest investment and the highest commitment. Consider these propositions about change (Kanter and Myers, 1991):

1. ***As those in closer contact with the organization's partners become more central to the strategic communication flow, their power inside the organization increases.*** The purchasing department in a computer company, for example, is now the conduit for information about new technology which has great value for the resource allocation decisions made by top managers as well as the product design decisions made by other functional departments. But, in order for purchasing staff to be able to flag important data they get from and on suppliers, they must be better informed about the issues and concerns of top management and related professional functions (engineering, manufacturing), and they must have an open channel of communication through which information passes in both directions.

2. *As a partnership develops greater strategic importance, the power of the subunit or department responsible for managing that relationship increases.* The power of the managers in key strategic units increases since their duties are now viewed as more critical to the company's success.
3. *Partnerships decrease the monopoly power of staff gatekeepers on managing external relationships.* An ironic consequence of the increased power for the unit with operating responsibility for the partnership is that that same group loses its monopoly power over its area of expertise.
4. *While enhancing the power of some, partnerships may disempower others (e.g., by displacing them in the communication channel or decreasing their strategic importance).* Partnerships often mean a reduction in power for those not involved. For example, in some cases, partner representatives agreed that it could be difficult or dangerous to report much to others of partnership deliberations.
5. *Partnerships increase the number of functions and the number of people involved in the new external relationships. The staff function changes to include integration and coordination, rather than solely task initiation.* Because they have both strategic and operational significance, complementary or stakeholder partnerships tend to involve linkages, often cross-functional, between several levels of the partnering firms: joint goal setting at the strategic level, joint planning and technical data exchange at the professional level, and direct real-time data links at the operational level. Each of these linkages in and of itself can represent a major departure from previous practice; together they can constitute a new set of structural ties within the firm itself.

The changes in structure and dynamics observed within partnering firms are not wholly (or in some cases even primarily) attributable to their partnership arrangements. Other strategic considerations, such as a desire to reduce costs, to improve technology sourcing to increase innovation, to reduce product development time, or to enter new markets, often drive changes in organization structure and roles, including the very formation of partnerships in the first place. The creation of partnerships is one of a number of new strategic choices made by organizations in response to changing competitive conditions or a changing environment. Cause and effect are difficult to untangle in the study of organizational change. Strategic alliances and partnerships are simultaneously effects and causes of other changes, all in the service of overall strategic choices for the organization.

Thus, there is a natural link between changes in an organization's position with respect to its environment and the internal coordination changes that constitute the second major form of change: change in the way the parts of the organizations (individuals, groups, or organizational units) work together to execute their tasks.

Size, Shape, and Habits: Changing Structure and Culture

To cut costs as well as gain flexibility and responsiveness, organizations are dramatically redesigning their internal forms. Larger, older companies at the mature end of their life cycle are attempting to dismantle the complex and often slow-moving coordination mechanisms they developed as they grew and instead to emulate the looser, less top-heavy style of newer, younger organizations. They are attempting to take on a new shape. For example, as the first step in a successful turnaround in 1990 and 1991, the British retailer BhS cut organizational levels from eleven to five and reduced the number of managers, to put the emphasis where chief executive David Dworkin thought it should be: on support for people on the selling floor. The proportion of BhS employees engaged in selling rose from 60 percent to 80 percent. The number of suppliers was more than halved from a high of about 700, and the remaining external suppliers were given greater responsibility for quality, drastically reducing the size of an in-house quality department. The head of the human resource department cut his own staff from fifty-five to nine people, out-sourcing some activities and delegating others to line managers. Such coordination changes, followed by better merchandising and marketing to attract and retain customers, revitalized the company. Revenues and profits increased, and BhS people at all levels praised the new corporate culture.

Some "shape-up" changes are designed to tackle new opportunities by creating new ways of combining resources and coordinating activities.

- At American Express, the CEO instituted a program called "One Enterprise" to encourage collaboration between different lines of business. One Enterprise led to a range of projects where peers from different divisions worked together on such synergistic ventures as cross-marketing, joint purchasing, and cooperative product and market innovation. Employees' rewards were tied to their One Enterprise efforts. Executives set goals and could earn bonuses for their contributions to results in other divisions.
- At Security Pacific National Bank in California, internal departments became forces in the external marketplace. For example, the bank was involved in a joint venture with local auto dealers to sell fast financing for car purchases. And the MIS department became a profit center selling its services inside and outside the bank.
- At Alcan, the Canadian giant, to aid the search for new uses and applications for its core product, aluminum, managers and professionals from line divisions formed screening teams to consider and refine new-venture proposals. A venture manager, chosen from the screening team, took charge of concepts that passed muster, drawing on Alcan's worldwide resources to build the new business. In one case of global synergy, Alcan created a new product for the Japanese market using Swedish and American technology and Canadian manufacturing capacity.

"Culture" Change Through Structure and Systems Change

In North America and Europe, many companies describe these kinds of changes under the label of "culture change." But what others call "culture," we prefer to call "habits," and we attribute their development to the context—the structure and systems of the organization. Consider one widely praised "culture change," which was really a complete revamping of every significant structure and system. The revitalization that occurred followed the "critical path" outlined by Michael Beer, Russell Eisenstat, and Bertram Spector (1990): change work processes first, then attitude changes will follow.

For Taco Bell, a successful fast-service restaurant chain owned by Pepsico, "culture" change (toward a customer-service-driven organization) was a matter of "coordination" change—redefining the way the parts of the organization worked together toward a single goal. Now growing faster and more profitable than its better-known rival around the world, McDonald's, in a flat and even declining market, Taco Bell managed to cut prices aggressively by redesigning its entire organization model (Schlesinger and Heskett, 1991).

Taco Bell's management examined every aspect of the restaurant operation, then fundamentally altered roles and responsibilities at every level of the corporate hierarchy to support what customers wanted (good food and good service in attractive surroundings) and eliminate wasteful bureaucracy. They:

- reduced the organization structure from seven layers to four
- reduced the span of control from one supervisor for every five-plus stores in 1988 to one for every twenty-plus stores in 1991, and changed supervisors' roles to emphasize coaching and support
- increased training to ensure staffing by talented motivated people, who could operate with less supervision but with more information
- expanded the company's sophisticated information technology (TACO-total automation of company operations) to the store level, freeing restaurant managers from more than fifteen hours of nonproductive paperwork each week while providing real-time performance data on costs, employees, and customer satisfaction
- outsourced much of the preparation work that had been done in the restaurants (like shredding lettuce and chopping tomatoes), shifting its employees' emphasis to customers and their needs, and turning upside down the ratio of front-of-the-house personnel to backroom factory workers
- changed selection practices to identify people who could take responsibility, manage themselves, and respond well to pressure from customers
- required store managers to spend more than half their day (or twice the time they used to) on human resource matters such as developing their unit's employees, after giving *them* training and support in communication, performance management, team building, coaching, and empowerment

- began to change incentive systems by offering stock in the company (through Pepsico's "share power" program); bonuses for store managers, allowing them to earn up to 225 percent of the industry average based on the restaurant's economic and service performance; and wages above the industry average

Our colleagues Leonard Schlesinger and James Heskett (1991) attribute Taco Bell's success to this complex of changes: "It is clear that Taco Bell's success comes from more than lowering its prices. The company has explicitly rejected the prevailing model of service organization in favor of a redesigned system with service at its core.

"While all these changes have been taking place at Taco Bell, McDonald's has focused on more of the same: more advertising and promotion efforts, more new products, more new locations."

Options for Coordination Change

1. *Decentralizing and redeploying* organizations can put more responsibility in the hands of business unit managers and reduce the need for approvals or checkpoints to make it possible to operate without so many layers of hierarchy, and by extension, with fewer people. Andrew Grove of Intel, for example, wanted his company to be an "agile giant"—big enough to win global wars of products, technology, and trade while moving like a small company. To achieve this, he decentralized approval and eliminated middle-management layers. Other companies have cut the number of corporate service personnel while increasing the effectiveness of their activities by breaking up larger central departments, relying instead on business unit staffs to do the work. This eliminates redundancies and tends to replace a watchdog orientation with a service orientation; instead of "controlling" from the top, these staffs are now linked closely to the needs of particular businesses. What remains at the corporate level are minimal staffs carrying out future-oriented tasks such as environmental scanning, professional development, and facilitation of crossbusiness-unit information exchange. In 1992, Asea Brown Boveri (ABB), the electrical engineering giant headquartered in Zurich, had a worldwide human resource staff of four at corporate and a worldwide legal staff of five; the rest was decentralized or eliminated.

An alternative to cutting staff, then, is to redeploy them. Offering new jobs in a more vital sector (along with attractive early retirement options) can, of course, encourage people to leave voluntarily to ply their trades elsewhere. But it also puts those who remain to better use, making them a source of added value. IBM, for example, embarked on an enormous retraining effort after a 1985 business downturn, enabling a whopping twenty thousand or so employees to change jobs—engineers moving into sales, plant workers into systems engineering and, as in other companies rethinking staff, corporate services providers into the field (Quinn, 1988). But IBM in 1992 was still topheavy; in contrast to ABB's four-person worldwide personnel department, IBM was known to have fifty-five staff dealing just with international assignments at their European headquarters alone.

2. *Contracting out.* Of course, companies can decide not to manage certain activities themselves at all, and many are doing so in the name of "focus." For a widget company to be running a cafeteria and a print shop and a law firm, the reasoning goes, is not the best use of widget managers' time. It increases staff, which adds complexity and hierarchy, and anyway, there are specialist firms out there concentrating on running superior cafeterias and print shops and law firms. The company should use their services and concentrate on widgets. The strategy here is to divest all but the solid core. Cut staff to the bone, do without some amenities altogether (Who needs to manage a fleet of jet planes?), and contract out for everything else. Scott McNealy, CEO of Sun Microsystems, terms this a "high leverage" strategy, permitting growth in revenues without growth in the employment base, by utilizing suppliers' capabilities.

The extreme of the contracting-out strategy is represented by companies that are essentially marketing and financial shells working through vast networks of suppliers and dealers. Examples are found in publishing, apparel, and other fashion businesses that have long needed the flexibility to make changes quickly, effected by lean core organizations, using external specialist organizations for particular tasks. For example, Benetton, an Italian apparel producer, owns outright very few of the assets involved in bringing Benetton clothes to consumers; manufacturing is contracted out to numerous small factories, and retail outlets are licensees. Indeed, Benetton is part of a surge of entrepreneurship in Northern Italy based on networks of small firms allying with one another. In 1982, Benetton contracted out work to 220 production units, which employed ten thousand people; many were partially owned by Benetton managers as individuals, but Benetton itself owned only nine facilities as a company (Heskett and Signorelli, 1984). In another sector, Lewis Galoob Toys, maker of "micromachines," board games, and Star Trek toys, contracts out almost everything, including accounts receivable, running a thirty-one-year-old company with almost $70 million in sales with only about one hundred employees.

British consultant Charles Handy (1990) is a principal spokesperson for the view that companies should be organized around a small core of knowhow, relying on a network of other organizations to provide additional functions. This is clearly one strategy small companies can use to grow "big" in market scope and power very quickly. But it is also on the increase for much larger companies, as more flexible strategies take hold. It is not a long leap for companies that consider their manufacturing and sales functions to be "staffs" for business units that are essentially marketing arms to begin to think about whether they should continue to own so many plants and employ so many salespeople when working through contractors would give them more flexibility.

To put it another way, the *corporation-as-department-store,* a gigantic entity with every conceivable aspect of the production chain and every service it uses under its own roof, is being replaced by the *corporation-as-boutique*. *Focus* is the key word.

3. *Turning services into businesses.* In some cases, rather than divesting themselves of staff services, companies are converting them into profit centers, which sell their services on the outside as well as the inside. This is the ultimate post-entrepreneurial, market-oriented response. Let those staff bureaucrats be entrepreneurs, and let the market decide if they add value or not. Among the companies thus deriving revenues from their own corporate services are Control Data, selling personnel services; Xerox logistics and distribution services to customers; General Motors, employee-training programs; and Security Pacific Bank, data-processing and information systems.

Even when corporate staffs are not set loose in the outside market, companies are still starting to treat them as internal vendors who must compete with outside vendors to get their services purchased. Bell Atlantic put on a pay-as-you-use basis the "overhead" charges for corporate staff services, which were formerly assigned uniformly to users and nonusers. As we see in Chapter 8, this market-oriented entrepreneurial approach means that staffs have no budgets unless they sell their services to business unit customers. Corporate staffs must prove to their internal customers' satisfaction that they add value. There are sometimes thorny questions of managing internal transfer payments—whether to set rates at market levels—but the principle is clear: staffs are no longer considered "overhead" but potential sources of value; they are not watchdogs and interveners but suppliers serving customers.

In short, to use the language of prominent economist Oliver Williamson, companies are dismantling the very management layers and service staffs that helped create the corporate hierarchy in the first place and are gradually replacing some of them with marketlike relationships. Many employees are either being replaced with "outside" contractors or becoming contractors themselves.

Thoughtful Reorganizing Versus Mindless Downsizing

There are two principal mistakes some companies make in reorganizing.

First, they exhibit strategic blindness, turning the quest to ensure value added into mindless downsizing and delayering, on the assumption that leanness automatically equals effectiveness. They focus only on the "less" of the "doing more with less" imperative, as if the only good staff were a small staff. They fail to differentiate departments and business units in terms of their future contributions and resource needs; while some can be reduced or stabilized, others might profitably grow. Or their goals are cost-driven instead of effectiveness-driven—get the expenses down instead of the performance up. Or they view employees primarily as costs rather than valuing them as assets, and they fail to see the value (in skills or experience) that walks out the door with terminated staff. Consider the case of Cleveland Twist Drill, a machine tool company featured in a popular Harvard Business School case. A new president from outside was so incensed by high wages in Cleveland that he downsized there, moving the bulk of production to a new plant in the South, only to find productivity lowered because of inexperienced employees. Manufacturing costs were ultimately higher in the South than in the "high-wage plant" where employee experience raised productivity.

Second, some companies assume that if a little cutting is a good thing, a lot must be even better. They starve themselves into a state of organizational anorexia, the disease that occurs when companies become too thin. Cutting people to cut costs, if poorly managed, can actually increase some costs, such as the hidden costs of overload—tasks haven't disappeared, just the people to do them. It would have been better to review the tasks to see what unnecessary or outmoded work could be eliminated, as Exxon U.S.A. did when it conducted its "Hogg law" review (a Texas expression for rules and procedures) to see what red tape could be cut forever.

Furthermore, an organization that is too thin risks numerous implementation failures and dropped balls because of lack of follow-through—from the inability to return phone calls to customers to making plans without communicating them to all the departments that will have to change something as a result. In general, when anorexic companies starve themselves, they also starve innovation. The pressure of activities the company is already committed to drives out the ability to think about preparing for the future; there is insufficient preparation for tomorrow. If an organization gets too thin, it lacks depth in people for backup if a crisis hits, or for development and succession. One company boasted of the money saved by eliminating all but the most experienced middle managers; seasoned people, they reasoned, would save training costs and be able to manage larger groups. But then some of the experienced managers left for better opportunities (after all, they were the most marketable), and the company found itself with no internal successors. Recruitment and training costs shot up. The "leanness" strategy backfired.

Finally, companies that are lean because they substitute outside contracting for internal employment find themselves engaged in another set of difficult management tasks: they must work with other organizations to make sure the work is done to their specifications on their schedule, and they are vulnerable to the whims of other companies on which they rely.

Even managers who push downsizing and delayering as the best assurance of value added are aware that they are walking a tightrope. In a publishing company that had, in an executive's view, "built up fat during the good years," more than a thousand people who "added no discernible value" were cut during a time of profit pressures. Now, he says,

> There is no money for good people who are being asked to do more with less. We need to keep this core. After two years of cutting, we could either boom or fall flat. A move of our headquarters will be the last straw. We are

> running the risk of hitting the bone. First one layoff, then another, then shrinkage, then relocations. All of this equals risk to the division. [Kanter, 1989]

To counter the risk, that executive must increase the effort to create teamwork among the remaining staff—teamwork that will help each contribute to the work of the others.

The challenge, then, is not simply to get lean for the sake of doing so, but to build the kind of cooperation that helps the more focused organization get maximum value from all its remaining resources. *Sustainable* downsizing that will result in a well-functioning organization requires more leadership attention than a one-time cost-saving through layoffs (Tomasko, 1987).

Coordination Changes Without Formal Structure Changes: Building Networks

The need for flexibility suggests that in some cases coordination changes occur informally, without reorganizing the whole company. Networks—floating teams that work across functions, share information, and operate without bureaucracy—are a potent tool. Instead of causing the emotional turmoil of reorganizations or downsizings, companies can enhance teamwork and participation through network-building. Consider the "development network" at the United Kingdom headquarters of Dun & Bradstreet Europe, a group that evaluates and monitors new business-information products, including the customization of existing ones.

> For years, D&B Europe has faced the tensions that afflict so many cross-border and crosscultural organizations. Its computer databases, technical staff, and marketing group are centralized in the United Kingdom—a sensible structure given D&B's position as the only pan-European competitor in its business. But centralization has made it harder and more time-consuming to tailor Europe-wide products to the needs of local customers and to set priorities among competing projects in different countries.
>
> The development network is designed to make these trade-offs more quickly and more skillfully. It is neither a new layer of bureaucracy nor a means to wrest power from the functional organizations. Rather, a core of twelve or so key players meet weekly to monitor the performance of the development process, identify barriers, and devise ways to remove them. One of the network's first steps was to create an investment-management function responsible for identifying which projects get done, in what order, and how quickly—in ways that meet the needs of customers and countries but that also reflect corporate goals and strategies. [Charan, 1991]

Banc One Corporation, discussed in Chapter 2 and portrayed in Chapter 3, provides another network model. Its "Uncommon Partnership" philosophy combines direction and uniform standards from the center with decentralized local bank marketing and pricing activities. But traditional concepts of "centralization" and "decentralization," which stress a "vertical" or hierarchical dimension of organizational life, do not quite capture the essence of how Banc One works. Much of the action is "horizontal," through networks ranging from *ad hoc* task forces to extensive peer communication. Local bank presidents are encouraged to know their counterparts, as are those who head every significant function, and to transfer ideas and innovations through their network. Banc One College and its alumni gatherings are one network-building force. The CEO and corporate staff are another, as they share detailed operational information with every bank to give everyone access to everyone else's numbers, and then continually urge each bank to learn from the best performers. Indeed, travel budgets are kept purposely high at Banc One to facilitate the peer learning process.

Creating many ties between people, and channeling action to networks rather than forcing it through the hierarchy, can be an effective way to change "culture"—the habits that drive daily operations—without the difficulties that full reorganizations entail.

The "New" Organization Model

The management sage Peter Drucker recently used the image of a symphony orchestra to describe the new model of the leaner, flatter corporation (Drucker, 1988). In the orchestra, performers with different skills concentrate on perfecting their professional competence, while a single conductor coordinates the overall performance; performers with similar specialties form self-managed work teams, operating without a bureaucratic hierarchy above them. The image is useful and evocative. But for corporate players to make beautiful music together they must achieve a balance between concentrating on their own areas of skill and responsibility and working together with others. They need to do their own jobs well while keeping one eye on what might be useful for someone else. They need to understand enough about the company's other areas to identify possibilities for joint action and mutual enhancement. They need to focus and collaborate simultaneously. They must function in many roles: as soloists, ensemble players, and members of the orchestra.

Such a model for a "new" organization represents a triumph of process over structure. That is, relationships, communication, and the flexibility to combine resources are more important than the "formal" channels and reporting relationships represented on an organizational chart. In an environment requiring speed and dexterity, what is important is not how responsibilities are divided but how people can pull together to pursue new opportunities.

The ideal is a leaner organization, one that has fewer "extraneous" staff and is thus more focused on doing only those things in which it has competence. In this new form of organization, there are fewer and fewer people or departments that are purely "corporate" or "administrative" in nature; more responsibilities are delegated to those actually producing value for customers, and more services are provided by outside suppliers. Fewer layers of management mean that the hierarchy itself is flatter. Thus, the "vertical" dimension of the corporation is much less important. At the same time, the "horizontal" dimension—the process by which all the divisions and departments and business units communicate and cooperate—is the key to getting the benefits of collaboration.

The third form of change—control change—represents a drastic and revolutionary method for forcing the new organization into being.

The Drama of Control Change: Ownership, Governance, and Stakeholder Voice

Control changes involve the power and politics dimensions of organizational motion—the kinds of change that occur when a new set of players challenge the dominant coalition governing the organization, the group that makes decisions about both the organization's character and the distribution of benefits that flow from its operations. Control changes involve more than simply a replacement of one set of actors with another of the same kind; they imply a shift in the makeup of the dominant coalition—who is represented—and the structure of the organization's mechanism for governance, for adjudicating among interest groups.

Existing stakeholders seek changes in control in order to protect or enhance their interests, to get more of the organization's benefits or more power to shape its future. New players might sense a vulnerability, an opening, and seek a place in the dominant coalition in order to realize a new interest. Both internal micro forces (life cycle pressures, such as maturity and financial trouble) and external macro forces (changing competitive conditions, new relationships between organizations and their organized stakeholders) can make organizations vulnerable to control changes. When stakeholders or interest groups become dissatisfied with organizational performance, or when their role and power change, struggles for control can ensue.

For much of the twentieth century, the major control battles, and therefore control changes in industrialized nations, involved labor relations—the role to be played by unions and other employee associations in governing the organization, and how much of the benefits employees could capture. Depending on the country, other control changes were effected by government as the representative of public interests, through regulating operations, monitoring management, or in some cases outright seizing of assets or ownership of the organization. Industrial developments caused the areas represented by leaders to shift (Fligstein, 1990). There were also battles between financiers or family empires for control of organizations (much like the LVMH case described in "Champagne Shoot-out in France" in Chapter 5).

But these ownership issues were considered aberrations by Western management and organizational theorists—not common experiences that could become the subject of research and theory. For decades after Berle and Means identified the separation of ownership and control as the defining characteristic of the twentieth-century corporation, little attention was paid to ownership and governance as salient issues worth attention.

The 1980s changed all that. Governance controversies involving financial stakeholders took center stage. While the "class struggle" between labor and management was relatively quiescent around the world, the "new class struggle" between aggressive, entrepreneurial corporate raiders and "entrenched" management of established corporations was dominating the news. While management thinkers focused almost entirely on strategies for product markets, the capital markets were playing an even more important role in determining the fate of companies. While organizational theorists continued to focus on the relationships between managers and workers, with some increasing interest in customers and suppliers, economists were recognizing the profound organizational changes occurring as "owners" (holders of equity and debt) took a more active role in determining the form and strategy of the organization. Boards of Directors, once almost invisible actors, took center stage (Lorsch and MacIver, 1989). While sociologists were arguing over whether organizations passively "adapted to" their environments or shaped them, individual corporate raiders were demonstrating just how much activism was possible by dramatically altering the corporate landscape. And in addition to the rise of takeovers and other means by which owners asserted their rights and advanced their interests, governments were also privatizing state-owned organizations, shifting control in massive ways—e.g., the privatization of British Airways and British Telecom and the partial dismantling of the National Health Service in the United Kingdom.

What is at issue in today's control changes, in the United States and Great Britain at least, are financial interests; those with an ownership stake govern the organization. Other stakeholders might try to exercise political power, but in the end Anglo-Saxon corporate governance still revolves around financial stakeholders. Consider the example of a general store in West Tisbury, on Martha's Vineyard island in Massachusetts. The small facility had become a picturesque town landmark. In 1991 the owner of Alley's General Store filed for building permits to expand the structure in order to make it financially viable. The proposal caused a huge public outcry, becoming the subject of numerous town meetings. But unless the townspeople were willing to buy the business or underwrite it financially, they had no legal way to block the expansion. Without special laws, as community members and even customers, they could influence but not control Alley's strategy; only as owners could they exercise control. They would have had to take over the company to change its direction.

Compared with other forms of change, "makeover through takeover"—or through response to the threat of takeover—seemed to some observers to be swifter and more potent, causing greater increases in economic and organizational vitality. One study even found higher productivity growth in industries with higher rates of ownership change (Lichtenberg and Siegel, 1989).

A Favorable Environment and Unfavorable Performance: The Rise of Control Change as a Major Form of Change

An increase in control changes in the 1980s, especially in the United States but secondarily in Europe, then slowing in the 1990s, has been well-documented. Of the hundred largest merger and acquisition transactions in American history, ninety-eight occurred between 1980 and 1989, and the stockholders of more than one-fourth of the Fortune 500 received at least one tender offer to buy their shares, most resisted by management (Davis and Stout, 1991).

This activity was stimulated or made possible by a variety of environmental forces. New financial instruments, such as junk bonds or employee stock ownership plans, made financing available. Information bases and analytic tools permitted investors to assess an array of alternatives or examine the underlying value of an organization's assets. Professional groups such as investment bankers and lawyers developed an interest in finding deals and earning fees from transactions. More active individual investors and more powerful institutional investors watched performance more carefully. Takeovers were wealth-enhancing events for some parties; shares of target firms gained about 30 percent on average upon the announcement of a takeover attempt (Roll, 1988).

Institutional investors—pension funds, mutual funds, insurance companies, etc.—have become more important in both the United States and Europe in recent years. Between 1950 and 1980 institutional investors increased their share of outstanding corporate equity in the United States from 8 percent to 33 percent; by 1990, their share was 45 percent. In Britain, where they played an even larger role, they controlled less than 47 percent in 1975, and 63 percent by 1990 (Taylor, 1990). This concentration of ownership in the hands of pension funds has enmeshed them in controversy over how to exercise their ownership rights. How should they act to encourage economic competitiveness? Should they continue to finance takeovers and LBOs? Should they get involved in management decisions? The California Public Employees Retirement Fund (CALPERS) caused a stir by asking General Motors for information on the selection process for candidates to replace Roger Smith as CEO.

So-called active investors have been even more heavily involved in control changes. These professional investors hold large equity or debt positions, sit on boards of directors, get involved with long-term strategy, monitor management closely, and sometimes even act as managers. They include LBO partnerships such as KKR (Kohlberg Kravis Roberts) and Clayton & Dubilier; entrepreneurs such as Carl Icahn, Sir James Goldsmith, and Warren Buffet; or family funds such as those of the Pritzkers in Chicago and the Bronfmans in Canada (Jensen, 1989).

These new phenomena facilitate the deal-making that precedes control changes. But deals also require vulnerable companies. Agency theory locates the immediate cause of takeovers or control changes in the conflicts between owners and managers. Some recent data (e.g., Davis and Stout, 1991) support agency theory's premises: the market for corporate control involves alternative managerial teams competing for the rights to manage corporate resources (Jensen and Ruback, 1983). The agency problem (of delegation of decision rights by owner-principals to their manager-agents) is solved through management stock ownership or effective management monitoring techniques. But when managers stop protecting the interests of owners by attempting to use for their own purposes funds that would otherwise go to investors, then owners may assert their rights by seeking a shift in control.

For example, in 1988 the 1,000 largest public companies in the United States by sales generated total funds of $1.6 trillion but distributed only $108 billion as dividends and $51 billion more through share repurchases. But according to agency theory, managers resist distributing cash to shareholders because cash reserves (1) increase their autonomy with respect to the capital markets; (2) increase the size of their companies and therefore their compensation (which tends to be related to company size rather than value), their ability to reward middle managers through promotion, and their public prominence and political power (Jensen, 1989).

Clearly, stakeholders seek control changes when they think management strategies will not be beneficial to their interests. Many U.S. companies, including Lockheed and Honeywell, have faced proxy fights in opposition to management strategies or fielding alternative slates for boards of directors. In 1990, 120 proxy resolutions were proposed by institutional investors, up from seventy in 1989 and twenty-eight in 1988. Carl Icahn's unsuccessful proxy contest at USX was not a shadow takeover attempt or a shareholder rights campaign but a disagreement over corporate strategy—would USX function more effectively if its steel-making unit were spun off from its oil and gas operations (Taylor, 1990)?

Hence, troubled companies whose assets are undervalued and whose investors disagree with management over strategic direction or wish to realize more of the asset value through cash distributions are vulnerable to control changes. This is often a life cycle and industry matter. Slow-growth industries, with overcapacity making consolidation or downsizing a productive strategy, may have more companies reshaped through changes in control—e.g., chemicals, brewing, steel, broadcasting, wood and paper products, and tires in the United States. Some industries have already been altered by control changes in the market leaders. For example, in 1984 the leading U.S. tire manufacturers were independent and diversified public companies. In 1985 Uniroyal went private in an LBO and later merged its tire-making operations with those of B. F. Goodrich to form a new private company, Uniroyal

Goodrich. In late 1986 Goodyear defended itself against a hostile takeover threat from Sir James Goldsmith by borrowing $2.6 billion to repurchase nearly half its shares and divesting unrelated operations in oil and gas, aerospace, and resort hotels. In 1988 Firestone was sold to Japan's Bridgestone (Jensen, 1989).

Even when the institutional environment makes it more difficult for individual corporate raiders to take over public companies, industry conditions can make other control changes attractive. Indeed, large corporations may themselves become the "raiders" of the 1990s—as seen in AT&T's hostile takeover of NCR to gain a better position in computers.

The drama, visibility, and controversy surrounding takeovers perhaps gives undue prominence to this variant of revolutionary change. Organizations can also produce their own benign and orderly "revolutions" when they actively seek a shift in governance form as well as ownership stake, in order to increase their effectiveness in response to competitive pressures. Not all control changes are fraught with fierce economic and political battles.

Consider the case of Inmarsat (International Marine Satellite Organization), a mobile telecommunications company headquartered in London and owned by sixty-four telecom companies representing sixty-four countries. Some of Inmarsat's owners and senior managers worried that its original governance system, which resembled the United Nations in its emphasis on country representation, was slow-moving and unwieldly for success in the rapidly growing, highly competitive mobile telecommunications industry (Myers and Kanter, 1992). In addition, lurking behind the scenes were some potential conflicts of interest of a classic political sort about distributions of opportunities and benefits from the partnership. Inmarsat had earlier made an identity change from an organization focused solely on maritime safety applications to an active player in aeronautical and land mobile communications, which created new external stakeholders, including airlines and new sets of manufacturers.

In 1991 Inmarsat undertook a process of self-examination. For one thing, Inmarsat wanted to change before it was forced into it by new satellite telecommunications policies developed by the European Commission. Internal working groups and external consultants generated discussions of alternative ownership arrangements and governance structures, including examination of the structure of Boards of Directors in corporations in major countries.

Governance in Institutional Perspective: The United States, Germany, and Japan

The issue of organizational ownership and control has a strong legal and institutional component. Permissible ownership forms, determined by law, and modes of corporate governance are part of the institutional fabric of a society.

The United States developed the public stock market dominated by individual investors to a greater degree than other countries. Broad public ownership offered managers a reasonably priced source of more or less permanent equity capital that could buffer the company against adversity in a way debt could not. Share ownership allowed individual investors to participate in equity returns and get the benefits of liquidity and diversification (Light, 1989). But with an active market for corporate control and the growth of institutional investors overseeing large pools of capital, a capital structure consisting mostly of equity carried substantial risks of inviting a hostile takeover or other threats to management control. Furthermore, the absence of other stakeholders from the governance structure meant that political battles loomed when control changes were threatened; the public, political arena was the only place where excluded constituencies could voice their interests. The situation was similar in other countries operating under Anglo-Saxon law, such as Britain, Canada, and Australia.

Contrast this with the situation in Germany. Under codetermination, each major company has a board of management; a supervisory board, which includes owner and employee representatives—but none of the members of the board of management; and elected workers' councils at each significant organizational level that must agree on important matters affecting their constituents. Decisions of the management board tend to be collegial, made by consensus. The role of the supervisory board is oversight. It has the sole power to appoint members of the management board, generally for terms of four years or more. It also participates in decisions that significantly affect employment, such as plant closings or foreign facilities. The employee members represent both hourly and salaried employees; some may be chosen by national unions. The owner representatives are elected by shareholders, including the German banks, which are permitted to vote the shares that they hold as custodians, giving German banks a much larger role in corporate governance than banks in the United States can play (Lorsch, 1991).

Volkswagen's management board chairman, Carl Hahn, described his experience this way:

> Codetermination works when persuasive information becomes the basis for agreement. . . . When labor representatives, who are highly accomplished in their own jobs, come on the supervisory boards, they can come to agreement with boards of management over complex and painful business decisions, as long as they know all of the facts. When you consider that our labor people were willing to buy Seat, go into Czechoslovakia, where they know there are low wages, and approve several substantial investments even during the Middle East crisis—well, management can hardly complain. . . . With respect to government, the public authorities, German managers are absolutely free. There is no Japanese- or French-style intervention. [Avishai, 1991]

Variants of co-determination are found in other North European countries, such as the Netherlands and Sweden.

Still another model operates in Japan. Japanese ownership is based on reciprocal shareholdings between companies and their banks, and Japanese companies are tied together in business groups known as *keiretsu*. About 70 percent of Japan's 1,500 public companies are at least 50 percent owned by related companies or financial institutions (Kester, 1990). Owners have multiple relationships, so they can provide help of a number of kinds during times of trouble. For example, large shareholders played a major role in the turnaround of Akai Electric, a manufacturer of VCRs and audio equipment affiliated with the Mitsubishi group. After a major sales loss in 1985 (following twenty-five years of growth), Mitsubishi Bank, owner of 8 percent of Akai's outstanding loans, quadrupled its loans to the company to help it through its financial difficulties and provided three of its officers to serve in senior management positions, including the head of international finance. Mitsubishi Electric, owner of 2.5 percent of Akai's share, tripled its stake and made some direct investments in European operations, and it added several members to the board and sent seven of its top engineers to help Akai develop a line of digital audiotape recorders (Kester, 1990).

Other countries also have mechanisms to help large investors with their governance roles. In the United Kingdom, there are several bodies linking institutional investors, such as the National Association of Pension Funds. They meet on a regular basis, maintain a professional staff of researchers and analysts, and communicate with managers of companies they hold. However, these bodies are not much of a force for change (National Association, 1990).

The Corporate Raider as Master Change Agent?

Drastic control changes such as takeovers force wealth transfers as well as power transfers formerly associated only with revolutionary events such as war (e.g., the breakup of IG Farben after the first World War; Bayer's loss of rights to the name Bayer Aspirin in the United States). Of course, sometimes major transfers of control are sought (such as when owners of growth companies sell their shares to cash in) when natural events such as the death of owners of a family firm precipitate control changes. Both mature, stagnating companies and successful, growing companies may experience control changes. But still, the most dramatic and significant occur when troubled companies are taken over—by raiders, banks, or bankruptcy proceedings.

Some analysts go so far as to argue that control changes are perhaps the primary way—if not the only way—that significant strategic, operational, or cultural change is possible for troubled organizations. Even the *threat* of a control change, which would transform the dominant coalition and threaten current management, stimulates immediate action or corrective moves that would otherwise be deferred. A crisis of control precipitates change. While the threat of going out of business can do the same thing, usually the troubles have deepened to the point where change is more difficult; raiders, at least, look for signs of underlying health, such as assets with marketable value or operations that can be improved.

Would Lucky Stores have restructured and reorganized without the threat posed by Asher Edelman? Could RJR Nabisco have been saved any other way than the KKR leveraged buyout? The evidence is not all in. Certainly large established corporations can make change. But is the external raider a more powerful change agent than all the internal leadership the company can muster?

Control Changes as a Means for Organizational Improvement

Such questions can be answered only by examining what happens in the wake of control changes. While restructuring, reorganizing, and revitalizing can be carried out to some extent at any time by the management of any organization, there are some special properties of control changes.

First, they might permit the *breaking and renegotiating of contracts.* New owners may be able to negotiate more favorable terms with unions or creditors. They may be able to break leases or get out of agreements. Some observers speculated that Continental Airlines, for example, went into bankruptcy primarily as a way to bypass its unions in lowering wages.

Second, when control changes are accompanied by high leverage (to pay for the ownership stake), there might be a form of *discipline through debt.* Some argue that debt serves as a brake stopping management from mistakes, or forcing still more change while there is time to protect value. For example:

> For all the deeply felt anxiety about excessive borrowing, "overleveraging" can be desirable and effective when it makes economic sense to break up a company, sell off parts of the business, and refocus its energies on a few core operations. Companies that assume so much debt they cannot meet the debt service payments out of operating cash flow force themselves to rethink their entire strategy and structure. [Jensen, 1989]

While LBOs do get into financial trouble more frequently than public companies, few ever enter formal bankruptcy, because they are reorganized and management is changed quickly, whereas delays in action would cause even greater losses of value.

Third, control changes often bring *management changes permitting fresh thinking or a fresh start.* A new CEO may find it easier to define and implement a new strategy; the honeymoon afforded a newcomer can bring changes that would not be permitted to an old hand. It is well known that without fresh blood, organizations often revert to familiar habits in times of trouble (Nystrom and Starbuck, 1984; Sutton et al., 1986)—but it is often just those well-learned responses that might have caused the trouble in the first place or, at least, prevented solutions.

The search for appropriate forms of corporate governance has given rise to what Michael Jensen (1989) considers a new organizational form serving as an alternative to the publicly traded company: the leveraged buy out (LBO)

Association. Its centerpiece is an LBO partnership that sponsors going-private transactions, funded by institutional investors and banks, and then counsels and monitors management, which itself owns substantial equity. For example, KKR controls a large and diverse collection of businesses, such as all or part of Duracell, RJR Nabisco, Owens-Illinois, and Stop & Shop. But KKR doesn't act like "corporate headquarters" in a public company; it is much more hands-off and decentralized—e.g., only sixteen professionals and forty-four other employees in 1989 at KKR, the world's largest LBO partnership. Because of managers' equity stake, their pay is tied closely to their performance. And because of their financial structure (a partnership for each business; high debt), LBO Associations have well-defined obligations to their creditors and residual claimants, especially around the distribution of cash. Unlike the situation in public corporations, top managers cannot transfer funds from one business to another. But even Jensen sees potential flaws. LBO partnerships are tending to become deal-driven and to take more of their compensation in front-end fees, thereby increasing their incentives to make any deal and decreasing their incentives to create productive change in the organizations taken over (Jensen, 1989).

Jensen argues that the LBO Association resembles the main banks in Japan's *keiretsu* business groupings. Nissan, for example, was run for years by a former manager from the Industrial Bank of Japan, who became CEO as part of the bank's effort to keep the company from bankruptcy. But now, to the extent that Japan's large companies are coming to resemble U.S. public companies (with limited shareholder power, excess free cash flow, and fewer monitors of management behavior), they could face the growth of bureaucracy and inefficiency, which will trigger control battles—"makeover through takeover"—in Japan (Jensen, 1989).

The Costs of the Battle

Do takeovers enhance economic efficiency by replacing management teams, as Jensen proposes, or do they have corrosive effects on employees and the surrounding community which hurt economic efficiency, as sociologists such as Paul Hirsch (1987) argue?

Some studies have found significant financial improvements following an LBO and no systematic decline in employment, though employment growth slows (Kaplan, 1990; Lichtenberg and Siegel, 1989). Data do not support the idea that takeovers are undertaken in order to promote the downsizing of topheavy firms with highly tenured work forces (Davis and Stout, 1991). But the evidence is mixed, and there is not yet sufficient long-term experience to allow analysis and judgments. In some cases major restructuring akin to what has happened after takeovers has occurred without a change of control and in a gradual, orderly way (Donaldson, 1990).

Clearly, there is turbulence, uncertainty, and anxiety during the control struggle itself. As in any crisis or acute and abrupt change episode, there are many possible threats to retention of the value of ongoing operations during the transition—whatever improvements come later. Customer worries about the ability of the organization to keep delivering its products or servicing them later can cause the deferral of purchases or the search for alternatives, hurting revenues. Supplier concerns about being paid on time can lead to reduced shipments or restrictive terms. Legal or political considerations—for example, the need to get the approval of warring constituencies in a bankruptcy—can make it difficult to raise the capital for improvements that are vital to future organizational health. And employee uncertainty has negative consequences, for example:

- *The costs of confusion.* People can't find things, they don't know their own telephone extensions, and the letterhead hasn't arrived.
- *Misinformation.* Communication is haphazard. Some managers do a better job than others of keeping their people informed. Rumors are created and take on a life of their own, especially when it is not clear who has the "right" information. Some of the rumors are potentially destructive.
- *Emotional leakage.* Managers are so focused on the tasks to be done and decisions to be made that they neglect or ignore the emotional reactions engendered by the change. But the reactions leak out anyway, sometimes in unusual behavior.
- *Loss of energy.* Any change consumes emotional energy—especially if it is perceived negatively. People become preoccupied with the current situation. They feel guilt about the people who are losing something. The mood becomes somber, morale sinks, and it is hard to maintain the usual pace of work.
- *Breakdown of initiative.* Because of the uncertainty and the clear message that top management is redefining its mandates through restructuring, people below become passive and wait to be told what to do. Initiative and spirit are lost. Production of ideas declines, because people say, "Why bother? It's out of our hands. Everything might change again."
- *Weakened faith in leaders' ability to deliver, and the need for scapegoats.* Management can lose credibility because of the shock of a restructuring crisis or the apparent "lurches" in the business strategy. These may represent shortfalls of leadership. The ghosts of false reassurances can come back to haunt leaders. Implicit promises made now seem to be broken (Kanter, 1989).

Furthermore, a control shift can only *permit* or *enable* restructuring, reorganizing, or revitalizing. It does not automatically entail the right moves. A control change is only the facilitator of other changes; it is no guarantee, even with the "discipline of debt" hanging over managers' heads. In the O. M. Scott case, the change via an LBO brought new incentives to managers and was in fact followed by many other organizational changes, but shifts in strategy and structure still need to be determined and then implemented effectively. After assets are sold or control changes effected, managers still have to manage. And a primary ability they need is crisis management skills.

A Note on Crisis Management

Crises present leaders with both a direct and an indirect challenge. The direct challenge is to solve the problem inherent in the crisis itself; the indirect challenge is to prevent the crisis from interfering with other aspects of the company's operations. There is both a problem-solving and a damage control component to crisis management—to surround the acute problem and attack it, and to isolate the crisis so that it does not infect other activities (Lerbinger, 1986; Meyers, 1986; Starbuck et al., 1985).

The Crisis Team—Who Should Lead, Who Should Be Involved

Any time the stakes are high—dangerously high—control insufficient, time short, interest high, and options limited, the CEO's full attention is warranted. In the words of one crisis expert, top management "can't drop everything every time the corporate ship enters hostile waters . . . but if it is headed for a dangerous minefield, the captain should know so and focus his energies on getting through undamaged." It is thus appropriate for the leader to take personal charge, as James Burke of Johnson & Johnson did during the Tylenol crisis. This well-known case involved product tampering by an unknown saboteur who put poison in Tylenol capsules, causing several deaths. Under Burke's direction the company quickly withdrew the product and completely redesigned the package, at great expense. Such personal leadership during crisis is also a way of signaling the company's values—that avoiding harm to the public, for example, is the most important thing the leader can do. Of course, if the leader does take personal charge of the crisis, then he or she must step temporarily out of other activities in order to devote full attention to the crisis and permit decisions to be made in other realms without him or her.

There is a tendency to centralize control during a crisis period, to manage with tighter reins and more power concentrated at the top. The need for fast decisions may preclude participative processes. But this is risky. Centralization may transfer control to inappropriate people; if top managers had the ability to take corrective action, there might have been no crisis in the first place. The role of the Board of Directors is particularly important during a crisis period, because the board has to assess the adequacy of current top management to cope with the crisis.

Facing crises, leaders need help—the resources to do the legwork for crisis problem-solving and decision-making. Effective crisis teams are small enough to work together closely and communicate rapidly and well; and large enough to include (or be able to draw on quickly) all the forms of technical or legal expertise needed to address the crisis adequately. The crisis team needs power, knowledge/experience, creativity, and perspective. Outside help is also appropriate, as there is no time for the organization to learn new material by itself. During one retailer's bankruptcy period, management was supplemented by several law firms, investment bankers, and communication experts.

Communication—What and to Whom

While the crisis team is working, many other stakeholders, both inside and outside the organization, are feeling anxious about events; crises are rarely totally secret. Crises generate uncertainty and anxiety, anger, and fear. Rumors fly. The company must control the messages people receive, perhaps providing a designated spokesperson as a reliable source and maintaining a flow of timely information. Candor about having no answers (and timetables for when answers may be supplied) is often better than silence. Many observers praised Burke of Johnson & Johnson for going on national television early in the Tylenol crisis to reassure the public and to convey J&J's plans. Effective communication addresses both cognitive needs (for facts, data, "hard" information, analysis) and emotional needs (for reassurance, comfort, sympathy, feeling of connection). And it reinforces the values and invokes the symbols that keep the organization together, especially because ongoing operations continue even while the attention of leaders is elsewhere. Motivation of people during a crisis often requires extraordinary efforts, to avoid the paralysis that can set in where there is great uncertainty; setting short-term, achievable goals and using special incentives or recognition programs are helpful ways to motivate performance.

External Relationship Tasks

While control battles or other crises take place, other major constituencies or stakeholders, such as customers or suppliers, might be reevaluating their relationship to the organization. Many have other options and can easily flee. Investors, bankers, suppliers, or customers may have a lower "pain threshold" than management; they may become disturbed earlier; they may be deciding to exit or reduce their stake. Thus, leaders must also decide how to address the concerns of other parties external to the organization. This can require a personal visit from the chief executive or other forms of outreach.

Crises put the spotlight on the company, potentially subjecting it to media or government scrutiny—which sometimes goes beyond the identified crisis itself to uncover problems in other areas. The company and its management are now under a microscope; once in the public eye, other challenges may follow. Being prepared for the extra attention is important. Some crisis experts advise that the company "control" events by behaving proactively—making gestures or taking action before the public or the media make a push.

Monitoring Events

In times of crisis leaders must listen hard, get feedback, and adjust actions accordingly, rather than wall themselves off and shoot the messengers who bring bad news. Crises by definition mean that the organization is not in total control. Feedback is important for another reason—the high degree of uncertainty about the impact of actions to address the crisis. Some crises lead themselves to experimentation, because the "answers" are not known; the results of these experiments must be reviewed before deciding whether to extend the solution elsewhere.

Overall, how well managers assess and deal with a crisis—even one that seems limited to a single aspect of the business—can have major effects on the future success of the company. Crisis often provides a major measure of the strength of a company's management. Companies less able to deal with crisis effectively tend to be characterized by other management and organizational deficiencies. Internal politics interferes with teamwork. There is a lack of communication across functions. Excessive rules and bureaucratic trappings stress procedures over thinking. An atmosphere of fear and insecurity causes people to hide problems and resist change.

Building the Future: Recovery, Reform, Ongoing Operations

As intense and demanding as a crisis period is, it is also important for managers to keep an eye on the future. This means three things.

First, leaders should ensure that the methods of handling the crisis do not so deplete the organization's resources (its capital, people, facilities, stock of energy, know-how and motivation) that it has little left on which to build the future. Such depletion is feared by the critics of takeovers. It is important to weigh *present* actions to solve *present* problems against their consequences for *future* choices. That is, drastic steps taken because of a perceived crisis may come back later to haunt leaders after the crisis has passed—such as cutting too many people with critical skills, making angry attacks, or spending too much money to fight a product liability claim rather than settle it early. One of the "mistakes" new CEO David Dworkin said he made in his rapid restructuring of then-ailing British retailer BhS was firing someone whose capabilities turned out to be essential; he was later rehired and was part of the successful crisis resolution.

Second, leaders should see that investments in tomorrow are still being made even when attention is taken up in handling the acute crisis of today. Ongoing operations must continue, and they must be fed with the investments needed to ensure that they are strong. People must continue to be motivated. Indeed, after a crisis, recovery often requires a new injection of an energized vision so that people who are exhausted by the pressure of the crisis do not slack off. A challenge for Ames Department Stores' CEO Stephen Pistner, as he tried to lead the company out of bankruptcy, was to craft a new strategy and implement it on a prototype basis while fighting numerous fires on numerous fronts: court battles, employee theft, repairs to deteriorating facilities, and bad newspaper publicity. One measure of the success of his new strategy and vision: employee theft declined and those terminated filed no legal protests.

Third, leaders should assess and address the underlying weaknesses or vulnerabilities that contributed to the crisis in the first place. Once the crisis is resolved and life is back to normal, it is easy to forget that the crisis was possible not just because someone out there did something to the company but also because the company had an area of weakness. What is the underlying structural problem that allowed the crisis to develop? How can this problem be solved so that a crisis like that does not recur?

Crises test an organization and its leadership. If unmanaged or mismanaged, they can leave the company in a permanently weakened state. If managed well, however, they have the potential to strengthen the company. For example, organizations can become stronger after a crisis if:

- Change is accelerated. New strategies evolve, especially if the crisis challenges the framework for the business, pushing "frame-breaking change."
- Latent problems are brought to the surface, faced squarely, and handled.
- Heroes and legends emerge, forming the basis for instructive tales illuminating the company's values and showing others how to handle crises responsibly, ethically, and effectively. By the recognition of heroes, feelings or pride in the company and of belonging to a team can also be augmented.
- People are changed—either by turnover or by learning. New managers rise to the fore and old ones are replaced as a result of the "testing ground" provided by the crisis. Some people find themselves rising to the occasion, their skills stretched, the experience adding to their repertoire of abilities.
- Early warning systems are developed; information and communication systems are strengthened. The smart company that has been "burned" ought to be more likely to invest in "smoke detectors" and "firefighting equipment." (Some companies also establish crisis management mechanisms—e.g., teams ready to step in in case of a crisis.)
- Relationships with key constituencies and stakeholders outside the organization are strengthened.

Managerial Implications of Changes in Organizational Form

External relationship realignments, internal relationship and behavior redefinition, and shifts in who has power over organizational decisions—each form of change poses its own particular management requirements, because of the differing content areas that grab managers' attention. But certain shared characteristics of major organizational change must be understood by managers, if the change process itself is to produce the intended results.

First, as we have just seen, changes in form—in the identity, shape, or control of an organization—are often associated with acute episodes of dramatic upheaval—e.g., downsizings, legal battles, or stakeholder agitation. Managers need to perform at least two tasks simultaneously: effective "crisis" management, to prevent events from spinning out of control or losses from mounting at the organization's time of maximum vulnerability; and effective management of the ongoing activities that provide continuity (and cash) while changes are occurring. Organizations stumble when they do not acknowledge both tasks and devote sufficient resources to each.

Furthermore, changes in form are often stimulated by outside pressures and forces, whether it be the movement of customers away from a business or the actions of raiders. As a consequence, "managing change" often means managing the changes *others* are creating for the organization—rather than simply deciding the organization's own direction. Timely acceptance of the reality of these external forces gives managers more time to act—not only to defend their organization but to steer change in desirable directions with minimum disruption.

The success with which organizations change their form depends on the extent to which every aspect of the system—formal structure, information flows, rewards, recruitment, etc.—supports the new definition of what the organization is to be and how it is to operate. Thus, whatever the stimulus for the change in form, and whatever the ostensible problem or opportunity being addressed, the entire character of the organization needs to be reviewed to ensure that major changes stick. Managers can neither mandate nor announce a change in form. Many other stakeholders, relationships, habits, and systems can either support or detract from the new organizational identity or shape.

Because of the volatility experienced by many organizations in today's emerging global economy, the new model of a flexible, lean organization emphasizing networks rather than hierarchies and decentralization rather than top-laden bureaucracy, makes increasing sense. Changing to that kind of organizational form—before "raiders" or stakeholders force it—also makes it easier to encourage and embrace continual innovation without disruptive upheavals in a world of rapid and constant change.

References

Aldrich, Howard E. 1979. *Organizations and Environments*. Englewood Cliffs, NJ: Prentice-Hall.

Avishai, Bernard, 1991. "A European Platform for Global Competition: An Interview with Volkswagen's Carl Hahn." *Harvard Business Review* .Vol. 69 (July–August).

Bartlett, Christopher A. 1989. "Komatsu: Ryoichi Kawai's leadership." Harvard Business School Case. Boston: Harvard Business School Publishing Division.

Beer, M., R. Eisenstat, and B. Spector. 1986. "The Critical Path." Harvard Business School working paper.

Bradach, J. L. and Robert G. Eccles. 1989. "Price, Authority, and Trust: from Ideal Types to Plural Forms." *Annual Review of Sociology*. Vol. 15, pp. 97–115.

Charan, Ram. 1991. "The Power of Organizational Networks." *Harvard Business Review*. Vol. 69 (September–October).

Clark, K. B., and T. Fujimoto. 1989. "Lead Time in Automobile Product Development: Explaining the Japanese Advantage." Harvard Business School Working Paper #89–033.

Davis, Gerald F., and Suzanne K. Stout. 1991. "The Rise and Fall of the Market for Corporate Control: A Dynamic Analysis of the Characteristics of Large Takeover Targets, 1980–1989." Unpublished paper, Northwestern University, Kellogg Graduate School of Management.

Donaldson, Gordon. 1990. "Voluntary restructuring: the case of General Mills." *Journal of Financial Economics*. Vol. 27, pp. 117–41.

Drucker, Peter. 1988. "The Coming of the New Organization." *Harvard Business Review*. Vol. 66 (January–February), pp. 45–53.

Fligstein, Neil. 1990. *The Transformation of Corporate Control*. Cambridge, MA: Harvard University Press.

Gomes-Casseres, B. 1987. "Joint Venture Instability: Is It a Problem?" *Columbia Journal of World Business*. Vol. 22 (Summer), pp. 97–102.

Hamel, Gary, and C. K. Prahalad. 1989. "Strategic Intent. *Harvard Business Review*. May–June, pp. 63–76.

Handy, Charles. 1990. *The Age of Unreason*. Boston: HBS Press.

Harrigan, K. 1986. *Managing for Joint Venture Success*. Lexington, MA: Lexington Books.

Heskett, James L., and Sergio Signorelli. 1984. "Benetton." Harvard Business School Case. Boston: Harvard Business School Publishing Division.

Hirsch, Paul. 1987. *Pack Your Own Parachute: How to Survive Mergers, Takeovers, and Other Corporate Disasters*. Reading, MA: Addison-Wesley.

Jensen, Michael C. 1988. "The Takeover Controversy: Analysis and Evidence." In John C. Coffee, Jr., Louis Lowenstein, and Susan Rose-Ackerman (eds.), *Knights, Raiders and Targets: The Impact of the Hostile Takeover*. New York: Oxford University Press, pp. 314–54.

———. 1989. "Eclipse of the Public Corporation." *Harvard Business Review*. Vol. 67 (September–October), pp. 61–74.

Jensen, Michael C., and Richard S. Ruback. 1983. "The Market for Corporate Control: The Scientific Evidence." *Journal of Financial Economics*. Vol. 11, pp. 5–50.

Jick, Todd. 1987. "Process and Impacts of a Merger: Individual and Organizational Perspectives. Ph.D. dissertation, Cornell University. Ann Arbor: University Microfilms.

Johnston, R., and P. R. Lawrence. 1988. "Beyond Vertical Integration: The Rise of the Value-Adding Partnership." *Harvard Business Review*. Vol. 66 (July–August), pp. 94–104.

Kanter, Rosabeth Moss. 1983. *The Change Masters*. New York: Simon & Schuster.

———. 1988. "The New Alliances: How Strategic Partnerships Are Reshaping American Business." In H. L. Sawyer (ed.), *Business in the Contemporary World*. College Park, MD: University Press of America.

———. 1989. *When Giants Learn to Dance.* New York: Simon & Schuster.

———. 1989a. "The New Managerial Work." *Harvard Business Review.* Vol. 67 (November–December), pp. 85–92.

Kanter, Rosabeth Moss, and Paul S. Myers. 1991. "Inter-Organizational Bonds and Intra-Organizational Behavior: How Alliances and Partnerships Change the Organizations Forming Them." In P. S. Lawrence and A. Etzioni (eds.), *Perspectives in SocioEconomics.* Chicago: M. E. Sharpe.

Kaplan, Steven, 1990. "Sources of Value in Management Buyouts." *Journal of Financial Economics.*

Kester, W. Carl. 1990. *Japanese Takeovers: The Global Contest for Corporate Control.* Boston: Harvard Business School Press.

Lerbinger, Otto. 1986. *Managing Corporate Crisis.* Boston: Barrington Press.

Levine, S., and P. White. 1981. "Exchange as a Conceptual Framework for the Study of Interorganizational Relationships." *Administrative Science Quarterly.* Vol. 5, pp. 583–601.

Lichtenberg, Frank R., and Donald Siegel. 1989. *The Effects of Leveraged Buyouts on Productivity and Related Aspects of the Firm Behavior.* Cambridge, MA: National Bureau of Economic Research.

Light, Jay O. 1989. "The Privatization of Equity." *Harvard Business Review.* Vol. 67 (September–October), pp. 62–63.

Lorsch, Jay W. 1991. "The Workings of Codetermination." *Harvard Business Review.* Vol. 69 (July–August), p. 108.

Lorsch, Jay W., and Elizabeth MacIver. 1989. *Pawns or Potentates: The Reality of America's Corporate Boards.* Boston: Harvard Business School Press.

Meyers, Gerald C., with John Holusa. 1986. *When It Hits the Fan: Managing the Nine Crises of Business.* Boston: Houghton-Mifflin.

Mills, D. Quinn. 1988. *The IBM Lesson.* New York: Times Books.

Myers, Paul S., and Rosabeth Moss Kanter. 1992. "Inmarsat (International Marine Satellite Organization)." Harvard Business School Case. Boston: Harvard Business School Publishing Division.

National Association of Pension Funds. 1990. *Creative Tension? A Collection of Essays on Issues Arising from the Relationships Between the Management of Public Companies and Institutional Investors.* London: National Association of Pension Funds.

Nystrom, Paul C., and William H. Starbuck. 1984. "To Avoid Organizational Crises, Unlearn." *Organizational Dynamics.* Vol. 12, no. 1, pp. 53–65.

Olins, Willy. 1990. *Corporate Identity: Making Business Strategy Visible Through Design.* Boston: Harvard Business School Press.

Pfeffer, J., and G. Salancik. 1978. *The External Control of Organizations: A Resource Dependence Perspective.* New York: Harper & Row.

Pisano, G. 1989. "Using Equity Participation to Support Exchange: Evidence from the Biotechnology Industry." *Journal of Law, Economics, and Organizations.* Vol. 5 (Spring), pp. 109–26.

Porter, M. E. 1985. *Competitive Advantage.* New York: Free Press.

Porter, M. E., and M. B. Fuller. 1986. "Coalitions and Global Strategy." In M. E. Porter (ed.), *Competition in Global Industries.* Boston: Harvard Business School Press, pp. 315–44.

Powell, W. W. 1987. "Hybrid Organizational Arrangements: New Forms of Transitional Developments?" *California Management Review.* Vol. 30, no. 1, pp. 67–87.

Roll, Richard. 1988. "Empirical Evidence on Takeover Activity and Shareholder Wealth." In John C. Coffee, Jr., Louis Lowenstein, and Susan Rose-Ackerman (eds.), *Knights, Raiders and Targets: The Impact of the Hostile Takeover*. New York: Oxford University Press, pp. 241–52.

Schlesinger, Leonard A., and James L. Heskett. 1991. "The Service-Driven Service Company." *Harvard Business Review*. Vol. 69 (September–October).

Starbuck, William H.; Arent Greve; and Bo L. T. Hedberg. 1985. "Responding to Crisis." In Steven J. Andriole (ed.), *Corporate Crisis Management*. Princeton, NJ: Petrocelli Books.

Sutton, Robert I.; K. M. Eisenhardt; and J. V. Jucker. 1986. "Managing Organizational Decline: Lessons from Atari." *Organizational Dynamics*. Vol. 14, no. 2, pp. 17–29.

Taylor, William, 1990. "Can Big Owners Make a Big Difference?" *Harvard Business Review*. Vol. 68 (September–October), pp. 70–82.

Thompson, J. A. 1967. *Organizations in Action*. New York: McGraw-Hill.

Tomasko, Robert. 1987. *Downsizing: Reshaping the Corporation of the Future*. New York: AMACOM.

Chapter 7

Restructuring and Redefining Boundaries: Identity Change

Introductory Notes

This section opens with a trip to Italy, but the issues are global. The experience of Montedison, in "Reinventing an Italian Chemical Company," could fit any large, mature company anywhere that needs transformation.

Montedison underwent dramatic restructuring in a remarkably short time (about five years) under chief executive Schimberni, thoroughly transforming its external identity. Montedison reshaped its business portfolio to get into better businesses in light of worldwide chemical industry overcapacity. In the process its boundaries were redefined with respect to every single existing stakeholder, and new allies further changed its boundaries. Relations were renegotiated with the Italian government (to reduce government ownership), the financial community, the unions (to permit the layoff of 20,000 people), and the other state-owned chemical company (to create facility and business swaps). New relationships were formed with joint venture partners (to enter international markets), consulting firms (to provide expertise) and an international advisory board (to add perspective).

Montedison was soon a totally new company, described as "Italy's first public company"—and better financial results followed. Internal culture change to support the new identity was then implemented through a totally new management team, a new organizational structure, training conferences, and bonus and incentive schemes. But the real change action, the case shows, was the formal restructuring. The culture change was weak, failing to penetrate below the top. It is understandable, of course, that culture change for operations takes much longer than the acute change of restructuring. But the lesson for managers is clear: do not assume that restructuring alone produces coordination change. Do not neglect the issues to be managed in the aftermath of identity and culture change.

The end of the case hints at the restructuring problem that later proved to be Schimberni's tragedy. He continued his emphasis on asset shuffling by initiating a major hostile takeover battle—the first in Italy—paying little attention to the completion of the internal culture change. A few years later he was ousted from Montedison.

Next, we go inside two contrasting mergers to examine the experience of identity change in greater detail. The acquisition of Western Airlines by Delta Airlines, described in "The Human Side of Mergers," was a success in both financial and human terms. Western handled the loss of its identity by paying great attention to the situations of the people involved, and Delta integrated Western smoothly and skillfully.

The sale of one company to another involves much more than the transfer of tangible assets—the airplanes and route structure; it also involves moving people into new roles. Therefore, managing the feelings, fears, and hopes of people takes center stage during the transition. Western managed to transfer an intact, well-functioning organization because of the role its leaders played in modeling responsibility and in allowing people to mourn their losses. Delta, in turn, allayed uncertainties by promising job security and by providing ample information—including information about when key decisions would be made. The merger was a model of effective crisis management.

But full identity change does not necessarily correspond to the official date on which the assets of one organization are transferred. Human and organizational reality may not match legal reality. Full assimilation of Western's people into the Delta organization was a long, slow process, lasting well beyond the official transition period; incompatible corporate cultures and coordination systems meant that clashes and conflicts would linger. Furthermore, a change in one aspect of an organization's identity has repercussions for its other stakeholder relationships; Western's union was "eliminated" in the merger. Would labor relations become an issue for Delta?

Numerous barriers to change can undo even legally mandated restructuring. We shift continents and topics to consider some structural barriers to change in organizational identity: those that reside in the ties between organizations. "The Feudal World of Japanese Manufacturing," by the industrialist Kuniyasu Sakai, is not about how change occurs; instead, it shows how difficult change can be when stakeholder ties are dense and close.

Sakai takes us inside the Japanese system, giving us his point of view as one of thousands of subcontractors to large Japanese companies. Several important insights are particularly relevant to the definition of organizational boundaries. He shows that networks and relationships considered "outside" the boundaries in American and European companies are vital aspects of the operation of large Japanese companies, which allow them to handle fluctuations in the environment without having to change their form in significant ways. That is, a company can easily and quickly tap the advantages of an innovation from a member of the network without having to merge, acquire, or restructure. It can manage downturns in business without divestiture or downsizing by requiring suppliers to cut their prices or to do the layoffs themselves.

In addition, Sakai argues that tight control of the *network of inter-*

organizational relationships prevents change. The whole Japanese social system (including career patterns and social norms) supports the maintenance of the network and the power of the large organizations that preside over it. Therefore, major organizational change would require change in many external relationships, stakeholder expectations, and institutional frameworks. But there are forces for change in the Japanese social system. Smaller and mid-size companies do not like being captive to the keiretsu; they are ready to defect. One lesson for American and European managers who want to do business in Japan: do not try to get the *large* organizations to change but look for cracks in the *network,* at the boundaries of relationships; form relationships with the smaller contractors. An alliance strategy, in which Western organizations redefine their boundaries to work closely with Japanese suppliers, seems to make sense.

The article reminds us of the institutional or social issues involved in organizational change—that we must understand the Japanese system (or the American system or the French system) to see how and whether organizations *can* change. Japanese organizations cannot and will not change their identities by themselves, because they are enmeshed in a network of organizational ties.

One message of this set of portraits is that fundamental organizational change, exemplified by identity change, involves changing relationships to key segments of the environment. But successful transitions involve attention to much more than such "external" negotiations with stakeholders. Leaders must also pay attention to the feelings and responses of the people inside the organization. The human side of change cannot be neglected while leaders are preoccupied with legal and financial negotiations.

Reinventing an Italian Chemical Company

Montedison, 1986

Joseph L. Bower, Neil Monnery,
and William O. Ingle

Reflecting on the years since he became chief executive at Montedison, Mario Schimberni commented on the future he envisioned for his company:

> In 1980 we were 80% a petrochemical company and the other 20% was confusion. Now we are a diversified, interrelated corporation. In five years' time we may have just specialty chemicals and services. But in ten to twenty-five years from now we may well concentrate in businesses interrelating with bioscience—maybe just bioscience and pharmaceuticals, these should certainly be the base. And we would have strong services on the other side.

That these speculations were not fanciful testified to the progress that had been made at Montedison. In 1980, when Schimberni became president, Montedison lost $524 million; it was a company in need of massive restructuring and rationalization. Yet by 1985 net income reached $59 million and the focus of the company had shifted from survival to expansion. This was achieved by changing the company's portfolio of businesses, altering the capital structure, changing the top management and the culture within Montedison and greatly reducing the number of employees. Schimberni noted that

> although 1983 was one of the worst years, I was conscious that management's way of reacting, in terms of their professionalism, had improved. So, in that year I was confident that survival was

assured. From there we could move forward, and our next goal was to achieve adequate earnings for our shareholders on a continuing basis. That is why we spent so much time developing strategies and analyzing the competition. By the second half of 1983 I was conscious that the operating subsidiaries could be run by their respective managements. Consequently I could dedicate my time, and the time of the holding management, to developing the basic structure of the corporation, and thus we entered the growth phase.

By the end of 1985 Schimberni had led Montedison away from its dependence on bulk chemicals to such an extent that there were nine business areas spanning a wide interrelated range of activities. The Petrochemicals and Plastics area encompassed many of the old Montedison businesses, including 50% ownership of the world's leading polypropylene producer as well as plants producing several bulk chemicals and plastics. The Fibers business produced acrylics and polyester. Other traditional business areas were Energy (mostly oil and gas), Fertilizers, Consumer and Fabricated Products (detergents and glassware). Under Schimberni a number of rapid growth areas were developed: the Specialty Chemicals and High Performance Materials; the Health Care business, which had done particularly well in the U.S. market; and the Service Businesses group, through which Schimberni saw a role for Montedison in Italy's rapidly changing retail and financial sectors. . . .

Montedison's Formation

Montedison was formed in 1966 from the merger of Montecatini and Edison. Montecatini had started as a mining company in 1886, and had diversified into the fertilizer, dyes and ammonia businesses early in its history, and then into fibers and pharmaceuticals in the thirties. Edison, although originally a hydroelectric company, had diversified into chemicals and fibers. The merger produced what was to become Italy's largest chemical company.

The initial profits generated by Montedison quickly gave way to losses when the oil crisis struck in 1974–1975, due to the excess capacity in the European chemical industry and an inability to pass on increased costs. Union activism and fears within the banking community further weakened Montedison's position, compelling the government to step in to save the company. Through ENI (National Hydrocarbon Company), I.R.I. (Institute for Industrial Reconstruction), and other agencies, the government bought a 17% share in Montedison in the mid-1970s, making the state the company's largest single shareholder.

The government's influence over Montedison actually exceeded its 17% stake in the company because state-controlled banks also held shares. Effectively under government control, Montedison became increasingly an arm of state social policy, and employment goals seemed to become more important than profits. A reporter for *International Management* (January 1984), commenting on Montedison's troubles, wrote: "The huge, diverse company was little more than a bloated political football, run by political appointees and dedicated more to the furtherance of state social policies than to profitable operations."

With more energy being focused on social concerns, and on anticipating government reaction to management decisions, management attitudes and styles became more political. As Schimberni described it:

> When I became president in 1980, there had been a long period of discontinuity as new top managers kept being appointed by the state. This made managers defensive about their personal power. Everyone looked outside the company, to the state representatives, for support. The style of management was political, not entrepreneurial.

Reevaluating Government Involvement

By the end of the 1970s many state-owned banks, burdened by state participation in ailing industrial enterprises, began to reevaluate this policy. A leader of this movement was Mediobanca, Italy's only investment bank. Even though the government was its largest shareholder, Mediobanca had always been more responsive to market incentives than other state-owned banks, often playing an important role in the stock issues, mergers, and acquisitions of Italy's major industrial companies. Enjoying the confidence of managers in both the private and public sectors, Mediobanca's leaders now began to push for a new industrial policy, including the return to private ownership of some of the state's enterprises.

When Gianni de Michelis became Italy's minister of state participation in May 1980, he recognized that the political climate was changing rapidly and that a fresh approach was needed to deal with the country's industrial crisis. After months of study by a high-level blue ribbon commission, his ministry published a white paper setting forth a new industrial policy. The report paid special attention to the problems of state-owned enterprises and traced their origins directly to the influence of politics on company management. The comprehensive plan he proposed emphasized a more rational and consistent approach to state intervention and called for efforts to: encourage private shareholders to provide risk capital to substitute for state participation; increase the influence of market forces; increase the international scope of Italian businesses, through agreements, joint ventures, and acquisitions; reorient unions and workers toward efficiency and productivity goals; and improve the quality of managers and, especially, replace their current production orientation with a new market orientation.

Mario Schimberni: Gaining Control, Renegotiating Relationships

Mario Schimberni noted that what he needed to succeed at Montedison was "charisma, an iron will, creativity, flexibility, psychological insight and credibility." Judging from his actions and from the opinions of those who worked closely with him, he appeared to bring such qualities with him. Compared to previous Montedison presidents, he lacked one notable attribute. "I am not a political man," he said,

> I made it clear from the beginning that I would manage the company without political goals. In discussions with the government, it was useful that I did not belong to any party; I stood at equal distance from all of them. Although I was born in Rome, as was my father, I do not have extensive family connections to one faction or another.

Schimberni had trained as an economist and worked for SNIA Viscosa before moving to Montefibre in 1975. When he became Montedison's vice president for finance in 1977, he was 53 years old. His influence in Montedison increased when he was put in charge of several key staff departments in 1978. By the time Schimberni became president in 1980, many of the staff units were headed by his appointees and a new management team had begun to form. . . .

Schimberni's first priority was to free Montedison from government interference. He negotiated the sale of the government's 17% stake to a consortium of well-known Italian business families. These powerful industrial families included Agnelli of Fiat, the Pirelli family, and the Bonomi family which owned Bi-Invest. They combined with Mediobanca to form a holding company called Gemina to buy the government's equity. Gemina, with the largest stake in Montedison, thus took over from the government as the leading participant in Montedison's controlling shareholders' consortium. Schimberni was now more easily able to pursue his turnaround strategy with the knowledge that his shareholders were interested in a financial rather than a political or social focus.

In the late 1970s, relations between Montedison and the labor unions had become increasingly tense. After an explosion destroyed a 230,000-ton-per-year cracker (used in the production of ethylene, an intermediate chemical product) at Brindisi in 1977, the unions insisted that the cracker be rebuilt. But the company refused to do so. Unlike Montedison's other major complexes at Porto Marghera and Priolo, the installations at Brindisi were old and relatively inefficient; in addition, they were overstaffed. Giorgio Porta, then director for strategic control and a close advisor of Schimberni's, later said that the negotiations with the unions about rebuilding the cracker "motivated the whole system to change. Montedison began talking to the outside world."

Montedison's frictions with the labor unions intensified when the company announced in January 1981 that it intended to lay off 10,000 workers nationwide. According to Montedison, its turnover per employee ($62 million in 1980) was lower than those of other major chemical groups, such as Hoechst ($71 million), BASF ($106 million), and Dow Chemical ($145 million). The company saw rigorous cuts in staffing levels as the only way to improve profitability at its plants (*European Chemical News,* 1/26/81).

Not surprisingly, the unions disputed these figures, arguing that the company's debt structure and a top-heavy organization made it unprofitable. They called a series of strikes and asked for meetings with government ministers. Urgent negotiations followed, involving four ministers, Montedison's top managers, and several national union leaders.

During these negotiations, Montedison suggested that the government might help remedy the situation by granting the company a special status enabling laid-off workers to be paid 80% of their salary by the *cassa integrazione,* the state-subsidized unemployment insurance system. Montedison would then be responsible for only about 10% of the workers' salaries and would have to agree to rehire them when the situation improved. Within a couple of weeks, this was agreed upon, and, in return, Montedison delayed some of its lay-offs.

Montedison reduced its employees by 20,000 during 1980 and 1981, mostly through lay-offs of both staff and production workers. The reduction continued through the next two years, as capacity swaps with ENI and the closure of fibers plants took place. The reductions were accomplished with relatively little dissent from political and labor factions. According to one competitor, "Montedison has really learned to deal with the state." Cesare Vaciago, who became Montedison's director of labor relations in 1982, gave credit to the unions, saying, "They have decided to help save the chemical industry in Italy. They've been very realistic" (*International Management,* January 1984).

Having secured the necessary flexibility and authority, Schimberni began turning Montedison around by changing not only the strategy of the company but also its structure and many of its senior people.

A New Strategy for Montedison

In 1979, Schimberni hired Giorgio Porta away from Phillips Petroleum and put him in charge of strategic planning. Montedison's planning staff then had about 70 people, most of them econometricians and technical specialists who were not used to doing the kind of business analysis that Porta wanted. He noted:

> They had an overly analytical mentality. They were well-qualified in their fields, but there was always one part missing from their reports . . . the action plan.
>
> Because of the urgency of the situation, I did not have the twelve or fifteen months that it would take to produce a detailed strategic plan. So I simply identified four or five people who knew Montedison's businesses and who could help me understand them. In a month I put out a strategic document.
>
> I functioned like a bull in a china shop. The idea was to challenge people's assumptions. I told them: "Fine, if I'm wrong, prove it to me and tell me why." This caused a lot of reactions and produced a snowball effect. Montedison's people started to think about strategy.

Porta introduced a more detailed planning system in 1981. While this system was not fully implemented that year, his office did issue a planning matrix in which investment strategies to build, maintain or divest a business were recommended for 76 individual businesses, based on the industry's attractiveness and the unit's relative position in its market.

"From 1980, to the middle of 1981," said Porta, "we were dealing with an 'emergency.' Rough ideas were worked out and urgent problems tackled. From mid-1981 to mid-1983, we engaged in 'rationalization,' involving major coordinated efforts to restructure the whole industry." The rationalization of Montedison's portfolio involved a shift in emphasis from basic to fine chemicals, and accompanying organizational changes. These moves were supported and encouraged by new government plans.

Montedison's strategic plan also considered government policies in each business, which had been formulated by Gianni de Michelis. His 1981 Plan for the Chemical Industry called for "polarization" of the industry by creating two national monopolies, one in primary chemicals and another in specialties. Montedison was to be the specialty company, and ENI the commodity producer. Rationalization by swapping or closing plants would follow after that, making each national champion more competitive in Europe. In a third phase, called "internationalization," joint ventures would be set up with strong firms abroad to help the Italians improve their overseas market access and their managerial and technological expertise.

The foundation of this part of the new strategy was a series of facility swaps with ENI's Enichimica, the large state-owned bulk chemicals producer. Schimberni began negotiating with the government in 1980 with the intention of selling the commodity chemicals business to ENI, accepting their specialty business and much-needed cash in return. Though the talks lasted until March 1983, and ENI's leadership changed three times, Montedison's strategy remained constant. According to Schimberni:

> The negotiations required much determination. We knew what we wanted and thus could define the terms of the rationalization. Our job was to convince ENI and the government that our proposal was the best for Italy. We became the national leader in the restructuring effort.
>
> We also made clear what our restructuring timetable was. We said that we would shut down here, lay off people there, on such and such a date. These were the alternative moves if no agreement could be reached on joint actions.

The agreement, finally reached after much negotiation and considerable government pressure on ENI, left Montedison with most of Italy's polypropylene (PP) and polystyrene (PS) capacity and around $300 million in cash. ENI obtained two crackers, some polyethylene (PE) plants, a polyvinyl chloride (PVC) plant and some synthetic rubber plants. These were facilities which Montedison believed would only produce positive cash flows in the longer term and, with the cash shortage resulting from years of losses, were businesses it could not afford to keep. The deal strengthened both companies' positions in the European commodity plastics market.

Internationalization

An important element in Schimberni's plans for Montedison was greater involvement in international markets. The major chemical firms from the United States, Germany, the United Kingdom, and other advanced countries had become global competitors. They not only exported products from their home bases, but also manufactured abroad, raised capital on international capital markets, and entered into joint ventures with other global companies. These companies used their strengths in one country to help them compete in others and could draw on technological and managerial resources from several countries. Schimberni saw the internationalization of Montedison as an absolute requirement for effective competition in this arena.

Montedison's first deals with global companies were in the fibers area. Montefibre, which had long been an independent operating company, went through a restructuring process closely parallel to that of Montedison as a whole. It had lost money every year since 1974 and was put in receivership by the end of the decade. Montedison's holding in Montefibre was then written down and new shares were sold to a consortium of banks and private investors. During the 1970s Montefibre had been active in all the major synthetic fibers, which were mature commodities, and concentrated on acrylic and polyester, which Montedison's planners thought had stronger competitive positions and provided opportunities for differentiation. Montefibre closed all its nylon and cellulosic fibers plants in 1982–1983, putting more than 3,000 workers in the *cassa integrazione.*

Montefibre also followed this strategy internationally. It sold its share in the U.K. joint venture for nylon intermediates to its partner, Monsanto. In return, Monsanto sold Montefibre two acrylic plants, one in the United Kingdom and one in Germany. The prices of the U.K. deals washed out against each other, and Montefibre immediately sold the German plant to Bayer. Without laying out any cash, Montefibre thus acquired an acrylic plant in the United Kingdom. Together with its newly expanded plants in Spain and Italy, this made it the largest acrylic producer in Europe, ahead of Bayer and Courtaulds, with 20% of that market.

Though Montefibre's moves in acrylic were generally seen as in accordance with the EEC's plan for rationalization in fibers, competitors claimed that it was acting contrary to these agreements in polyester. Montefibre had boosted the output of its Italian polyester plant at a time when demand was falling, overcapacity was apparent, and prices were depressed. In replacing an old plant with a large modern one, it reduced its labor force from 27,000 in 1977 to 8,000 in 1983. As a result, Montefibre's polyester operations became competitive with the best German units. With 25% of the market, Montefibre became one of the leaders in European polyesters, in a league with Hoechst and Du Pont.

Montedison had been a leader in the early development of polypropylene (PP) technology. Its technology began to lag behind those of other major competitors when a second generation process was introduced by Solvay and Mitsui in the mid-1970s. In response,

Montedison developed its own second generation process and joined forces with Mitsui to work on a third generation one. In 1982, with 280 research people working on PP, Montedison spent $10 million on R&D for this product alone.

Montedison and Mitsui unveiled a third generation process in 1983 that promised important savings in capital and energy costs. The two companies claimed that their *Spheripol* process using improved catalysts halved the amount of capital needed (compared to a first generation plant), lowered electricity consumption by 30%, and lessened steam use by 90%. The process made plastic resin in a spherical form, removing the need for a final pelletizing step. Also, the process could use the chemical and even refinery grades of propylene, which were cheaper and in greater supply than the high-purity polymer grades required by other processes. As other companies introduced their new PP processes in 1983, Montedison claimed that only its process had been successfully tested on a large scale.

To transform the PP business and continue the move toward higher-margin fine chemicals, Schimberni decided to try to form a joint venture with Hercules International, the dominant PP manufacturer in the United States. Montedison had jointly developed the *Spheripol* process, but with less than 20% of the European PP market, and virtually no share outside of Europe, prospects for its exploitation were limited. To gain share of the market, a joint venture with Hercules seemed attractive. Hercules was the world's largest producer of PP. It could exploit Montedison's process improvements; yet there was little overlap in capacity so there were few antitrust problems. By mid-1983 the negotiations were complete, and a 50–50 joint venture was established between Montedison and Hercules called Himont. Montedison contributed all its PP facilities and around $120 million while Hercules gave most, but not all, of its PP facilities. In addition to the strategic strength in PP, the newly formed Himont gave Montedison substantial experience with the United States market, an attribute that would be increasingly valuable as Schimberni started to build Montedison's international capabilities. . . .

Himont's organization left most of the parents' previous structure intact. Himont Europe was staffed by Montedison's people; and Himont USA by Hercules. This was done to facilitate the transition, but also to avoid complications should the relationship not work out. Schimberni knew the risks inherent in 50–50 joint ventures but was confident about Himont's future:

> In principle, I am against fifty–fifty joint ventures. They are bound to break up if the interests of the parents diverge. But in

> this case, we had a long relationship with Hercules and we knew each other's cultures and management. When there is a long engagement such as this, you can expect that the marriage will be stable.

Approaching Hercules was possible because Montedison already had a joint venture in the pharmaceuticals area with Hercules named Adria Labs. Difficulties had arisen between the two partners because they had differing goals for the company. Montedison viewed Adria as an opportunity for expanding their pharmaceuticals division into the United States, while Hercules saw it as a stand-alone business. The issue was amicably resolved during the Himont negotiations with Hercules swapping their 50% stake in Adria for a 13.5% stake in a new company named Erbamont that combined the Adria assets and all of Montedison's Italian and U.S. health care businesses. Schimberni hoped that Erbamont would grow successfully and become one of the pillars of the new portfolio, counterbalancing the declining, low-margin bulk chemicals business. Through Adria, Montedison could expand its foothold in the United States for Erbamont's products, which would accelerate growth further and ensure it had a presence in the leading market for pharmaceuticals.

Creating the Holding Structure and Reorienting Management

As rationalization negotiations began with ENI in 1980, Schimberni was initiating a massive reorganization of his own company. By year's end, the largest operating divisions were split off to form seven autonomous operating companies, and Montedison S.p.A. became a holding company. . . .

While in most cases the same people continued to head the businesses, their jobs changed markedly. They had previously been loosely responsible for contribution margins, which often did not include working capital costs. After the reorganization, they were responsible for managing working capital, personnel, and other fixed costs, and the results of their operations became much easier to identify. Although they had to plan their own investments, expenses and sales, major financial decisions were still taken at the holding company level. Staff units at the holding company were also responsible for supporting their counterparts in the operating companies, and for designing the overall strategy of the group. . . .

The turnover of top staff made it easier to change Montedison's organizational structure. Between 1981 and 1983, 80% of the managers at the holding company level were replaced. Virtually all of the present management committee members were recruited at this time. Schimberni explained the importance of such changes: "Governments in many countries are declaring that they want to privatize state-owned enterprises. But saying so, or even selling shares, is not enough; it is important to institute management which is profit-oriented and professional, rather than political." [Training conferences every 6 months, monthly strategy briefings, and new bonus systems reinforced this change.]

The wholesale change in top management during restructuring also made modifying the culture at this level possible. Schimberni looked overseas and to Italian managers with international experience for managerial talent capable of bringing a new profit-oriented culture to Montedison. An early arrival was Giorgio Porta from Phillips Petroleum in 1979 to direct the strategic planning that would implement Schimberni's new corporate vision. In 1982 Porta was made managing director of the bulk chemicals division. An American, Jack Sweeney, previously president of a specialty chemicals company in the United States, was hired to head the fine chemicals division. Schimberni hired another American—Howard Harris—to take over strategic planning. Throughout the 1981–1983 period Schimberni appointed American, English, German and other foreigners to executive positions. The American candidates were generally "more profit-oriented than Europeans," noted Schimberni, "and more competitive. They love a challenge." Schimberni managed the cultural mix of company quite consciously, putting "Americans at the holding level or in staff and Germans at the operating levels, because these two cultures did not work well together and Americans worked better with Italians." He also used mostly Italians in negotiations with ENI and the government. . . .

This change of management, with its emphasis on foreign managers, and increased recruiting from Italian business schools, was reinforced by the use of outside consultants. Almost all the major international consulting companies were used at the operating level to help solve specific problems, and to carry out competitor analysis, an area in which Montedison considered itself weak. There was a hope that consultants would leave some expertise and also help change the culture by encouraging greater analysis and profit orientation. . . . In the spring of 1981, Studio Ambrosetti [of Milan, the lead consultants] suggested the creation of an advisory board of outside experts, to advise Schimberni on global strategic issues. As the International Advisory Board, these outsiders proved to be a major influence on corporate culture. . . .

The Aftermath of Restructuring

Schimberni's restructuring had produced significant improvements in performance in 1983, and early in 1984 it was clear that Montedison would turn a profit the following year. Losses were cut in half compared with 1982, financial charges fell from 9.1% of sales to 6.7%, and short-term debt as a share of total debt declined from 43% to 38%.

Between 1982 and 1984 there was a significant improvement in the performance of European chemical companies, as the world economy emerged from the 1980–1981 recession. Operating profits as a percent of sales for the large European chemical companies increased by 50%, and returns on capital rose correspondingly. Thus between 1981 and 1985 for the European chemical companies as a whole, gross operating profits as a percent of sales rose from 11.2% to 13.9% (corresponding figures for Montedison were 7.1% to 10.5%), and gross operating profit as a percentage of net fixed investment plus working capital rose from 17.7% to 26.6% (for Montedison 10.4% to 20.5%).

The most significant contribution to Montedison's balance sheet came from its efforts to raise capital in financial markets. In 1982–1984, Montedison tapped both Italian and foreign capital markets to raise $847 million in stock and convertible bonds and $418 million in medium-term bonds. The last of these issues was a $220 million loan from the largest banking pool ever set up in Italy to finance a private industrial group; Citibank led 57 banks (of which 12 were non-Italian) in this financing arrangement.

But there was concern about the extent to which the turnaround resulted from the improved world economy, and the implications that would have in the next economic downturn, which many considered inevitable. There were also worries about the depth of the changes within Montedison. Rigamonti noted:

> The change in culture has been very concentrated, really it has only affected the top 300 or 400 people. There have been some changes in the companies, for example the structural changes in Montedipe and some use of MBO and bonuses. But generally the culture changed very little below the top.

Schimberni was confident that Montedison had weathered its worst days. Consequently, between 1983 and 1984 he had begun to focus his attention away from survival toward opportunities for growth. In the summer of 1984, Schimberni observed:

> The biggest problems are in the past. Montedison has a new struc-

ture. We have selected our business portfolio; we have clear strategic goals. We know who we are. We are a diversified company, with strengths in primary chemicals, specialty chemicals, energy and services. We know where we want to go. We want to grow in some areas, shrink in others; we want to become more international. Our management is now innovative, flexible, open-minded and accepts the challenge of change. . . .

Schimberni's first move to adjust the Montedison business portfolio proved to be one of the most controversial business issues in Italy. By proceeding with the takeover of Bi-Invest in 1985, Schimberni changed the portfolio in favor of the service sector, and at the same time induced a major shift in the composition of Montedison's shareholders. It was a personal success for Schimberni; he had conducted the whole deal himself, not involving the Management Committee. The implications of the takeover were of considerable importance.

The takeover was a major event not only for Montedison but also for the Italian business community. Bi-Invest, a large diversified company with industrial, financial and real estate interests, was controlled by the Bonomi family. In turn, Bonomi owned 17% of Gemina, Montedison's largest shareholder. Gemina's other shareholders consisted of the most important Italian business families. Agnelli, Orlando, Pirelli and of course Bonomi, and Italy's preeminent merchant bank, Mediobanca.

The purchase of Bi-Invest caused much acrimony in Italian business circles and was closely followed by the press. It started when a group of stock market raiders purchased around 30% of Bi-Invest and then offered their stake to Schimberni. It was bold of them to purchase the shares if this was their only way of disposing of them, for the transaction threatened to upset the modus operandi of the Italian business world. Indeed, no one could remember the last hostile takeover which had occurred on the Italian exchanges, and it could be seen as an attack on the families who had helped Schimberni in Montedison's darkest hour. It even threatened the Italian family business model, by forcing the large family companies to interact publicly, rather than in private as usual, and by endangering the Bonomi family's control of their own company.

Nonetheless Schimberni decided to purchase the raiders' shares, and a heated battle ensued in the courts, on the exchanges, and in the press. Bi-Invest challenged Montedison's right to buy shares which would give it control over a portion of their own stock, and at the same time bought 2% of Montedison's stock as a bargaining tool. Montedison meanwhile purchased further Bi-Invest stock on the market, bringing its stake up to 37% of the company. As these maneuvers occurred, the Italian families, through the press, made clear their disapproval of Schimberni's tactics.

By early September, however, Bi-Invest's attempts to block the takeover were exhausted and Bonomi resigned as chairman of Bi-Invest, with Montedison purchasing the Bonomi family's 32% interest in the company. Those parts of Bi-Invest not sold off were merged with META, Montedison's service company.

After the purchase, META sold Bi-Invest's Gemina stake, largely financing the Bi-Invest purchase, and shortly thereafter the other Gemina shareholders sold their Montedison stock. This brought in a number of new shareholders, most importantly the Varasi family's P.A.F. company which was sympathetic to Schimberni's management and plans. Varasi's 10% holding made it the leader in a new shareholder's syndicate which owned 28% of the company.

Earlier, other changes in ownership had occurred. The commercial banks that had held nearly 50% of Montedison effectively eliminated their holdings in 1984, with much of their stake going to institutional investors abroad. By the end of 1985, 30% of Montedison stock was held outside Italy. Another major piece, around 6% of the company, was taken up by Italian mutual funds. Richard Broyd, a planner who also looked after Investor Relations, pointed to the significance of these moves:

> One of the most important changes since 1984 has been the change in ownership. Montedison's shareholder base is no longer controlled by the old guard of Italian families. Now it's much more a coalition of the new guard—the big insurance companies, the new entrepreneurs like Varasi, and with substantial overseas involvement. These are people who will use their stock to trade not to influence—they vote through the market rather than at shareholders' meetings.

Thus for the first time in two decades Montedison seemed free from the influence of a major shareholder. A diversified group of shareholders meant that management would be free to run the company. In particular the large foreign holdings, in addition to providing a source of funds, meant that a significant portion of the shareholders was not involved in the Italian business or political arena. The press was filled with speculation about how the established families of Italian business would react to this public defeat. But for now, at the expense of straining relations with the old families, Montedison had become "Italy's first public company."

The Human Side of Mergers

The Western–Delta Story

Cynthia A. Ingols and Paul S. Myers

The Context

On September 10, 1986, the front pages of *The Atlanta Constitution* and *The Los Angeles Times* carried the announcement that Delta Air Lines, based in Atlanta, had just purchased Western Air Lines, based in Los Angeles, for almost $900 million. The deal was the result of two weeks of intense discussion, beginning with a telephone call from Delta Chairman David Garrett to Western's CEO Jerry Grinstein and leading soon after to meetings including their respective executive groups, fellow board members, attorneys and accountants. Under terms of the agreement, Western's operations would be merged with Delta's, corporate headquarters would be consolidated in Atlanta, and the merger would be effective April 1, 1987. Although the company's planes would still fly, under the Delta logo, the merger meant an end to Western as an entity.

The Western–Delta deal was not a hostile takeover and did not involve a corporate raider. Indeed, the merger was welcomed by Western. Regarded as the "Rolls Royce" of the airline industry by many, Delta had a strong financial performance record as well as a stable, content work force. Delta's hubs were concentrated in the southern and eastern USA—Atlanta, Dallas, and Cincinnati. With Western's hubs in Salt Lake City and Los Angeles, the two companies were an excellent strategic "fit." Furthermore the companies shared a reputation for excellent quality and service, progressive human resources policies, and strong (though quite different) "family"-type cultures.

With their company on the brink of bankruptcy just three years earlier, Western employees considered the merger a victory, even a reward for their years of sacrifice and effort, turning the company around from $54.5 million losses in 1983 to $67.1 million profit in 1986. Despite the turnaround, CEO Grinstein believed that the success would be short-lived in the highly competitive airline industry. In an age of super-sized carriers, mid-sized Western had three options: acquire another company, be acquired, or grow internally. "But," said Grinstein, "expansion is risky business, especially for a company which has asked for tremendous sacrifices from its workforce." Merger with another major carrier seemed more appropriate for Western. So Grinstein began looking for a suitor. Delta, on its part, had an eye out for its *own* growth opportunities. They found each other.

The Merger: "It's Bittersweet"

The announcement of the Western–Delta merger delighted Western employees. "Everyone was on cloud nine," said veteran pilot Steve Lutz, "people were so excited." Western people expected the merger to yield material benefits. Lutz remarked:

> People were so excited for three reasons. First, everyone expects Delta to be in business tomorrow. Second, Delta offers opportunity, particularly for pilots. If there is no chance to make Captain 3 to 5 years before retirement, then pilots are frustrated. Third, all Western people expect their pay to increase under Delta.

Stability in employment, increase in career opportunities and pay—all in the context of a first-class company—prepared Western employees to hope for the best.

As the April 1st deadline approached, the sadder reality of the disappearance of Western Airlines became clear. Many Western employees had only worked for this one company—a company which "gave us everything," Lutz explained. One long-service secretary poignantly remarked that she felt like she was losing her identity. Surviving the good and bad times together had made the employees a close-knit group. Western was like a family, and there were some people who claimed they knew, by face at least, almost everyone who worked there. It was not unusual for Grinstein or other executives to talk informally with employees throughout the organization. The sense of intimacy and connectedness made Western a special place to work. With feeling, Western employees mourned the death of their airline. Tom Greene, General Counsel and considered by many the "soul" of the company, wrote a "A Final Wish" to eulogize the passing of Western, saying in part:

> . . . And life does go on and this unique company, if it could express a final wish, would want the lives of us who mourn it to go on as well, with joyful memories and a secure knowledge that a fortunate few of us really knew what it meant to be "The only way to fly."

Employees held countless farewell parties. At one gala event all former Board members and CEOs were invited to share their recollections, jokes and stories about their days at Western. Before one secretary who had been with Western for 25 years left the company, a party was held in her honor. A large sheet cake with a picture of a Western plane piloted by a Wally bird (Western's advertising symbol for years) was the centerpiece of the farewell party. Grinstein and the rest of the executive corps attended the event along with about 75 others. In the final days, each department of the company gathered to bid a sad goodbye to some colleagues and speculate about their new life with Delta.

Some earlier mergers in the airline industry (e.g. Republic–Northwest, Continental–Eastern) resulted in notorious labor–management strife, poor service, and customer dissatisfaction. In contrast, *both* Western and Delta worked hard to prepare Western employees for the radical change which they were about to undergo and to make that transition period as smooth as possible. Each firm attended to organizational and individual issues over which it had jurisdiction. And as importantly the two companies consciously worked together closely.

The Prelude

Delta openly welcomed Western employees into its family. The day after the announcement of the merger, Western employees received a letter from Delta's COO Ron Allen and CEO Dave Garrett. In part Allen and Garrett said:

> The most important asset we have at Delta is our people and in this spirit we join hands with you. . . . Delta today is the product of two very successful mergers—Delta/Chicago & Southern, 1953; and Delta/Northeast, 1972. It is our goal to see that the merger of Western into Delta is even more successful than our past mergers and accomplished in a fair and equitable manner for all involved.

Two weeks later Ron Allen (soon after made Delta's CEO) and other Delta executives, accepted Grinstein's invitation to visit the LA headquarters. They toured the entire facility; Allen and Grinstein stopped frequently to talk to Western people along the way.

In early October Delta pilots and flight attendants arrived in Western employee airport lounges with large cakes decorated with the words, "Welcome to Delta." The Delta people mixed with Western folks, answering questions about life in the Delta family. Delta adopted the slogan "The Best Get Better," appealing to the pride in the personnel of both airlines.

Delta did more than offer symbolic gestures and ceremonies to reduce uncertainties for Western personnel. Job security was the paramount concern for Western employees, who knew that the frequent consequence of a merger is layoffs in the acquired company. Delta made it clear that this would not be the case by taking the unprecedented step of guaranteeing a job to every full-time Western employee. Since Delta has not laid off any employees since 1951, job security for Western people was consistent with Delta's treatment of its workforce.

Delta further assured Western employees that they would receive a salary not less than their current earnings. Since Western employees knew that they made considerably less than their counterparts in Delta, many were concerned about when they would receive parity with Delta employees. In a meeting with pilots in Cincinnati, COO Garrett announced that it was not possible to integrate the salary schedules immediately, but that efforts would be made to establish equality within two to three years.

The pledges of jobs and preservation of current salaries allayed the anxieties of Western employees; however, they still faced tremendous uncertainties about changes the future would bring. To answer as many questions as possible, Delta stationed an executive in Los Angeles. This person worked closely with Western personnel. A video produced especially for viewing by Western employees showed scenes of Atlanta, from the high rises of downtown to the gently rolling hills of suburban communities, and described life in "the heart of the New South." At Atlanta's Hartsfield International Airport Delta established a relocation office to assist transplanted Californians to find homes and get settled.

Delta's communication style was one very significant aspect of the merger period. The company's messages were clear, consistent and methodical. A series of memos beginning in January 1987 demonstrate this. The first announced that on February 13, 1986, Delta would provide detailed information on issues ranging from when job offers would be made and what benefit packages would look like, to uniform fittings and reimbursements for relocation expenses. Western employees received their Valentines a day early in the form of a 30-page bulletin providing specific answers to their questions where possible and listing dates by which unresolved matters would be completed.

In the months that followed, Delta kept each commitment it had made. This became a tangible source of credibility for the company, whose reputation for concern about its employees had preceded it. One Western employee commented, "Delta hasn't once had to back up and say 'Hey, that's wrong. We did it wrong.' They're methodical—not fast. But when they give us information it's good, solid." Even when employees had only vague notions about some aspect of the merger, they knew when the specific information would be forthcoming and that it would be reliable.

While Delta figured out the logistics from their perspective, Western executives had their own tasks to manage.

First and foremost, Grinstein and COO Don Lloyd-Jones wanted to turn over to Delta a top-notch company. This meant to Grinstein that "everyone had to stay at their posts to the end." Setting the example for others, neither he nor Lloyd-Jones took vacations during the transition period and they arrived at work promptly each morning at nine and left at five. In a memo to fellow Westerns on September 11, 1986, Grinstein and Lloyd-Jones in part said:

> Although the next 12 to 18 months will be very challenging, we must keep Western running smoothly and with the strong determination that has been our hallmark even in the most difficult times. A vital, successful Western will be beneficial to both companies.

They consistently repeated this message in letters and memos to Western employees over the next 6 months.

The second priority for Grinstein was to signal to Western employees that "the human concerns" were the most important issues to resolve. To emphasize that people were the critical issue in the transition, Grinstein appointed Joe Hilly, the company's employee relations executive, to head the Merger Committee. Under Hilly's leadership, Western reached out to all its employees, just as it had done in other periods of crisis. Western's innovative Health Service Program turned its attention to the stresses caused by the merger. Western's psychologists openly discussed the anxieties and fears caused by a cross-country move—a prospect faced by 1,200 LA employees. Discussion groups, video tapes and individual counseling sessions were provided to deal with employees' emotional wellbeing. A toll-free hotline provided merger updates, and callers could leave questions which in turn would be the subject of subsequent updates.

Most remarkable was Western's attitude toward the 900 or so employees who chose not to join Delta. After a merger announcement it is typical for people in the acquired company surreptitiously to work on their resumés and begin a job search. Secrecy shrouds activities which everyone knows are taking place, but few acknowledge.

This was not the case at Western. Grinstein met with all Western's executives and offered his personal assistance to anyone who was not moving to Atlanta. At times, Grinstein joked, he felt like he was running an executive placement firm. More seriously, he noted that he wanted to eliminate feelings of isolation and panic. Openly helping people in their job search increased their effectiveness in finding positions *and* allowed them to pay more attention to the job which they continued to hold while searching.

Employees at other levels in the organization received help in their search for a job, too. As a way to generate interest in hiring Western's experienced personnel, Joe Hilly sent out a letter to selected Southern California employers which began, "Our loss is your gain—maybe!" Resumés were made available to prospective employers, and Hilly offered his personal assistance in employee selection.

The total impact of the Western and Delta organization working separately and together was a well-informed and remarkably open workforce. Grinstein had created conditions that made it acceptable to discuss feelings, fears and hopes. People spoke of their anxiety about moving to Atlanta or about learning the "Delta way." They talked freely of how they would miss the closeness and intimacy of Western and wondered aloud how they would fit into a culture which was perceived as Southern conservative. But these comments were made in tones of sadness at Western's passing, rather than anger or hostility toward Delta. As Hilly commented: "On April 1, 1987, Grinstein turned over to Delta a remarkably content workforce."

The Results

In September 1987, a year after the initial announcement of the Delta–Western merger, and six months after the actual merger date, the deal was no longer front-page news. Ten thousand former Western employees were interspersed among Delta's original 40,000 workforce throughout the continental USA. Clad in the same blue Delta uniforms, the flight crews of the two airlines appeared indistinguishable.

However, former Western employees were struggling with their diminished organizational power and voice, and with their "subordination" to a large and more powerful entity. There were three main areas where the assimilation was problematic: power, culture and operational style.

Assimilation meant a power distribution different from that to which Western employees had been accustomed. The biggest change was that while Western's workforce was entirely unionized, at Delta only the pilots were organized. Since Delta refused to recognize the unions, their demise had major implications for influence over worklife decisions.

Moreover, though Delta offered employees thorough and credible information on most aspects of the merger, it had remained silent on the all-important matter of seniority. The company said only that the issue would be resolved as soon as possible following the consummation of the merger. This was a critical issue, since in the airline industry seniority lists determine people's pay, work schedules, and, to some degree, status. For flight attendants and pilots, for example, rank on a seniority list might mean the difference between working layover flights to Hawaii and commuter runs to Bozeman, Montana.

Historically the unions at Western had a voice in how and in what areas seniority would govern. Because both Delta and Western pilots belonged to ALPA, Western pilots maintained this power. The two pilot groups began the difficult task of combining their respective lists in January 1987. The negotiations took months and were painstaking and atomistic since both unions were seeking a settlement that most benefited its own rank and file.

Since the other unions would not exist after the merger, this mechanism for employee voice in influencing the negotiation process on seniority lists was not available. As early as February of 1987, Ray Benning, President of the Teamster's local, reported Delta was neither accepting nor returning his calls. Benning believed that Delta had no intention of consulting, let alone sitting with, union officials to work out the seniority system for the mechanics. His prediction proved correct.

The flight attendants faced a similar situation. After April 1 their union disappeared. In May Delta formed a Merger Committee for flight attendants with elected representatives from both Delta and Western. According to former Western employees, Delta gave the Committee the authority to merge the lists as they chose. Nevertheless, six weeks into the process Delta management took over the process, according to former Western flight attendants. The outcome was a system which treated attendants hired before 1971 differently from attendants hired after 1971. This adversely affected long-term former Western attendants, who responded by asking for an arbitrator to adjudicate the fairness of the new system.

Geography also made a big difference, with some ex-Western employees benefiting and others suffering. For example, when Delta purchased Western, it acquired the Salt Lake City (SLC) hub, providing a jumping-off point for Delta planes to the American West and the Orient. To capitalize on this, Delta quickly expanded the SLC base by using former Western managers already living in the city. A former assistant manager of ramp services with Western became an assistant station manager, leading a larger and more diverse Delta team. He spoke with surprise and amusement about the changes in his life: "I get up from the same bed each morning, leave the same house, arrive at the same parking lot, and then find everything different at work, from procedures to policies to dress."

In contrast, a flight control manager originally stationed in Western's LA headquarters transferred to Atlanta. Like many Western middle managers, his transfer to Atlanta involved a demotion. Before the actual move, he said: "Delta needs me as much as they need a rusty beer can," asserting that he expected his new position to be redundant, though Delta was obviously making good on its promise to make people job offers. However, after working as a controller for six months in Atlanta, this man spoke of the "extremely tough culture shock of moving from Southern California to Atlanta," and how difficult it was to have left his parents and married children in the West. His change in rank, combined with Delta's operating style which required him "to check with the supervisor even on the most minor changes," left him feeling undervalued, underutilized and ready to return to California.

Obvious corporate culture differences also presented Western workers with a variety of other assimilation difficulties. For example, the merger coupled an informal, participative Southern Californian workforce with a conservative, Southern company. A few Western pilots used to wear cowboy boots to work; now Delta requires them—as it requires all its pilots—to wear black laced shoes. More fundamental and disturbing to some was an attitude which admitted to "no problems." Accustomed to an organization which concurrently prompted cooperation and allowed open conflict, some Western people were surprised—even discouraged—when Delta provided no structures and little appreciation for alternative viewpoints. One former leader of Western flight attendants saw Delta's hesitation to institute a program similar to the Health Service Program as indicative of Delta's reluctance to deal with employees' personal or work-related problems.

The most notable and frequently cited operational difference was Delta's lack of automation and its reliance, instead, on paperwork. As one pilot joked: "Every time a Delta plane takes off, ten trees fall in Atlanta." A more serious complaint by flight attendants was the length of time it took to make changes in their schedules; under Western, changes used to take only hours, whereas the paperwork at Delta required days. One Western captain saw merit in Delta's approach; he praised the company for its careful record keeping on every facet of the business. But like other former Western folks, he also recognized that Delta needed to move into the age of automation—a task which Delta recognized and was indeed undertaking even then.

The Feudal World of Japanese Manufacturing

Kuniyasu Sakai

. . . In my conversations with Americans and other foreign businesspeople. I am constantly amazed at how little they seem to know about the realities of Japanese industry. At a time when Japan accounts for 15% of the global economy and Japanese executives are busily studying U.S. and European industry, it seems both foolish—and in some ways dangerous—for Western executives to have such a tenuous understanding of their Japanese trading partners.

Over the past four decades, I have built up a group of several dozen small and midsize companies in a wide variety of businesses, most related to electronics manufacturing. I know well the real world of Japanese manufacturing. I also know that foreign executives have no idea how it works.

My businesses produce high-tech products for some of the best-known companies in Japan—all of which are familiar to customers around the world. Yet my companies' names remain unknown, as they should. They exist to support the efforts of the larger companies that can afford to advertise and distribute the products we make. I am happy to leave that business to them. I do not even mind that customers the world over buy products that one of my companies designed and built, all the time praising some famous Japanese company whose logo is on the switch. . . .

The giant Japanese manufacturers have become household names worldwide. Companies like Matsushita, Toshiba, NEC, Hitachi, Sony, and Fujitsu have become strong because they produce what the world wants to buy. Their reputations for advanced R&D, innovative products, low-cost and high-quality manufacturing are legendary. Moreover, they seem to have an uncanny ability not just to invent remarkable new products but also to borrow ideas, rework them, tinker with them, and produce something totally "new" from a product concept that originated elsewhere. . . .

[But] Japan's giant industrial combines are not what they appear to be. They do not develop all of their own product line, nor do they manufacture it. In reality, these huge businesses are more like "trading companies." That is, rather than design and manufacture their own goods, they actually coordinate a complex design and manufacturing process that involves thousands of smaller companies. The goods you buy with a famous maker's name inscribed on the case are seldom the product of that company's factory—and often not even the product of its own research. Someone else designed it, someone else put it together, someone stuck it in a box with the famous maker's name on it and then shipped it to its distributors. . . .

Of course . . . it would make very little sense for an electronics giant like Matsushita to farm out the design, manufacture, and assembly of a refrigerator or microwave oven. These products are ideally suited to mass production in the kind of large, highly automated factories that the giant companies can afford. . . .

But what about products that companies must continually redesign to compete for public acceptance—like headphone stereos, small compact disk players, or personal computers? Redesigning means retooling a production line. It means sourcing new parts and lots of other things. For a typical product, a company might expect to sell 30,000 units in a few months, retool, sell another 50,000 units, redesign some basic components, retool again, see what the competition brings out, retool again, and on and on, throughout the life cycle of the entire product line. Although some of the giant makers are now employing the newest flexible manufacturing systems (FMS) to allow them more freedom in production, this retooling process is something many big companies want to eliminate.

Thus they farm out much of this business to subcontractors—smaller companies they can depend on. These companies in turn, faced with redesigning and producing a product three or four times a year, will subcontract the design or manufacture of a dozen key components to still smaller companies. . . . One electronics company I know has well over 6,000 subcontractors in its industrial group, most of them tiny shops that exist just to fill a few little orders for the companies above them.

How does subcontracting work on a practical level? Consider a product like a personal computer, which requires scores of parts, high-level technology, and critical assembly. Even the most famous, top-selling PCs in Japan are made by subcontractors. How?

The parent company begins with feedback from its retail outlets to provide the basis for internal discussion of what kind of model to build next year. Say it decides it wants to make a 32-bit computer with this kind of drive, that much RAM memory, and so on. It draws up its own plans, its engineers make up blueprints, while other divisions decide on the quantity to be produced, the retail price, and thus the budget for producing it.

Then it gives parts of the blueprints to each of several small subcontractors. The biggest parts, of course, go to its immediate keiretsu partners, who then subcontract the components of those parts to smaller companies, who subcontract even smaller parts to other companies. Essentially, the machine is broken down piece by piece so that many small companies work on it. Almost no small company knows what it's making—just that the shipment is due on this date and for that price.

Even the first test models of the finished computer are made at the subcontractor stage because this is the level at which all the separate components are received from the smallest companies, then assembled and tested. Only at one of the larger subcontractors do the engineers know they're making a 32-bit PC with so much memory, a certain size hard drive, and so on.

One of the interesting by-products of this convoluted manufacturing process is that it is common to make only a handful of test models of a new product. IBM, which controls its production much more closely, can make 100 or 150 test units and run them through every kind of test before manufacturing begins.

An NEC, Fujitsu, or Toshiba might make as few as 5 or 6 trial units because of the involvement of so many subcontractors in the premanufacturing system. Once their engineers are satisfied with the results, they can then set up the kind of mass-production assembly lines they're famous for. But even that will likely take place at one of their primary subcontractors.

Dai Kigyo and Chu-sho Kigyo

When Western executives talk about "Japanese industry," they are almost always referring to the big, famous companies—generally the top 1,000 or so that are listed on the first section of the Tokyo Stock Exchange. To all outward appearances, these businesses are the backbone of Japanese industry, the pillars on which the Japanese economy rests—which is exactly what these large companies would like you to believe. But the reality is quite different. Small to medium-size companies, *chu-sho kigyo,* make up more than 99% of Japanese industry and are the real foundation of the Japanese economy. The large companies, *dai kigyo,* rest at the very top of a huge corporate pyramid.

According to Ministry of Finance statistics, in 1988 there were roughly two million registered joint-stock corporations in Japan (there are many more unregistered family businesses). Among the official Ministry of Finance–registered businesses, more than 600,000, or 30%, were capitalized at less than $14,000. Roughly another 30% were capitalized between $14,000 and $36,000, and another 15% at less than $70,000. In other words, over 75% of all registered Japanese companies are capitalized under $70,000—not what you would call major industry.

In fact, only 1% of all companies in Japan are capitalized over $700,000, and less than half of those qualify as large-scale businesses, according to the Ministry of International Trade and Industry. Yet these are the only Japanese companies you ever hear about. Too many people are attracted by the glamour of the giant companies and miss the other 99% of Japanese industry. But it is a simple fact that Japan's internationally famous companies would not exist without the support of literally millions of unknown small businesses spread across Japan.

Why is this basic truth so little known outside Japan? . . . When I meet Western scholars in Japan, I ask them what kind of factories they have seen. Inevitably, they answer that the big companies have shown them around—which virtually guarantees that they have never seen or even been told of the thousands upon thousands of little shops that keep the giant companies in business. . . .

According to my Japanese dictionary, the word for "subcontractor" is *shitauke*—pronounced sh'ta-ookay. But from talking to Western manufacturers, I'm convinced that something is lacking in the translation. In the West, as I understand it, subcontractors are free agents. Basically, they can work when they want and for whom they want. If they develop a good relationship with one company and want to continue working with it, that's their privilege. If a company treats them badly, they can send an invoice when the contract is finished and say good-bye. They are independent.

Not so in Japan. From the day a subcontractor accepts the first contract—probably from a small subsidiary of one of the giant companies—it has given up its freedom. It is told what to make, when to put it on line, and how much it will get for it on delivery. If the company that placed the order feels a profit squeeze, it can easily order the subcontractor to reduce its final price. If hard times continue, the larger company can demand yet another cut. If it gets to the point that the subcontractor is losing money on each unit it's producing and has cut expenses and streamlined production to the utmost, the "parent" company could demand that it buy some new piece of equipment to increase productivity. And even if the subcontractor neither needs nor wants the equipment, it has no choice: if it refused, the flow of orders from the parent would dry up overnight—and its business would be gone. Of course, the parent would remain unaffected; it can always obtain supplies from any of the scores of other companies in its group.

I know something about the tension between small companies and the big *keiretsu* or industrial groups that swallow them up, as a shark swallows small fish for food. I started my own company 40 years ago. My best friend and I built a small painting factory literally in the ashes of World War II, and we worked there day and night. Gradually the company grew, we hired more staff, orders expanded, and so did our lines of business. By the 1960s, when Japan's electronics revolution was ready to take off, my company was big enough to become a major parts supplier to one of the nation's largest and best-known electronics companies. What I didn't realize was that as soon as I succeeded in becoming such a supplier, I was considered part of its "family." I was expected to be loyal to that company no matter what the sacrifice. For example, I was forbidden to accept orders from any other company, even when times were slow at my main client and my equipment sat idle.

I went to the president of this big company, not to demand my freedom but to profess my sincere desire to support his company's growth and to ask for more work. "Your words are like an expression of affection from an ugly woman," he answered; my willingness to serve his company was of no concern. My loyalty was taken for granted.

I was furious. I tried setting up an independent company to do work for other clients, but my "master" company sent managers around to threaten me: "No more orders, no more money, and a bad reputation throughout the business. Is that what you want, Sakai?" I must have been young and stubborn, for I stood firm against the threats of this big keiretsu, something few Japanese companies could ever contemplate. My old partner (who was by now running our second company) backed me completely, and we decided to keep our businesses independent as far as possible. Needless to say, we saw some hard times after that, but we also grew, and as we grew, I learned the secret of good management that the keiretsu will never understand: the power of smallness.

Many years ago, I explained this simple reality to a visitor from the United States. "How can it be?" he asked. "Why doesn't the subcontractor just refuse to cut its prices and instead sell to another large company?"

This response, unthinkable in Japan but natural for an American, left me speechless. It made me realize how great a gulf lies between our two systems—and how little most people understand about Japan.

Han and Keiretsu

What we call "modern" Japan was born only about 100 years ago. For centuries before that, the nation was divided into small feudal fiefdoms called *han*. Each han was under the control of one man—

the *daimyo*—who lived in a castle town surrounded by the agricultural land that provided his tax base and his power. The daimyo's extended family included people who were related only by marriage and even some who were adopted—but all were entitled to wear the family crest. Below the daimyo's family were his most trusted retainers—samurai of the highest rank who served the daimyo's household—then below them a lower level of samurai and, perhaps, another level.

On the bottom of this social pyramid were the hierarchies of the common people: farmers, artisans, merchants. The commoners, of course, outnumbered the daimyo's inner circle, and it was their work that provided the base on which he could build his castle and rule his fiefdom. Yet the commoners were treated more as property than as human beings. They were expendable resources to support the daimyo and his family.

The same kind of thinking that once dominated the han is at work today. The parent company in a manufacturing group thinks of itself as a daimyo, the supreme power, the apex of a pyramid in which production flows from the bottom upward and rewards from the top downward. The manufacturing daimyo's "family" of dozens of related companies includes some that are large and powerful in their own right—look at the Matsushita subsidiaries, many of which are listed on the stock exchange. Some family members may be related by corporate marriage or adoption.

Beneath the parent company's direct family are the trusted retainers—primary subcontractors—beneath which lies yet another layer of subcontractors. And beneath the subcontractors are layer upon layer of "commoner" companies, which have just a handful of employees whose only function is to produce a small quantity of goods—such as electrical parts—for the company just above them in the pyramid. These companies are tiny; their names and even their existence are unknown to the daimyo at the top. All it wants to see is the steady flow of production.

There were very little interaction among the han of old. Samurai were expected to show unwavering loyalty to their daimyo; they would not have dreamed of deserting their master even if there were work to be found elsewhere. The common people were also bound to their han; most were not even permitted to travel to other fiefs.

The modern corporate han are no different: vertical hierarchy is the hard and fast rule. Smaller companies produce for the next level up. No matter how bad times may get, companies can never leave their industrial group to seek employment elsewhere. And if they tried, no one would hire them—nobody likes deserters, even when they come cheap.

In short, today there is a Toshiba han, an NEC han, a Hitachi han, a Matsushita han, as well as a Toyota han and a Nissan han—a han for every major company in every major industry. . . .

This historical metaphor of the han applies at a larger level as well. Just as groups of daimyo banded together under strong leaders to combine the power of their different han, all the giant manufacturers are members of larger industrial groups designed to further their common competitive goals. Some of these groups are descended from the old zaibatsu, the huge industrial groups that were disbanded after World War II. The names of their member companies are easily recognizable—the Mitsubishi and Sumitomo groups, for example. But outsiders have a harder time identifying other giant groups—the Fuyo Group companies, for instance—because they do not share a common name. In almost every case, keiretsu center around a main bank, which provides financing, information, and organization for the group.

While the old zaibatsu, with their enormously rich and powerful leaders, are dead, the keiretsu influence a wide spectrum of industries. Moreover, each keiretsu has its own distinct personality; to those of us who know them well, each one has certain recognizable features. Some keiretsu are very tight-knit, almost like an exclusive club. Their executives learn to speak a kind of group code, using words in special ways that only other members of the group will understand. If overheard in a restaurant, for instance, their conversation might sound odd or meaningless to keiretsu outsiders.

This group image can be so pervasive that it colors even the most ordinary business transaction. For example, one of my companies in a northern prefecture decided to throw a get-acquainted party in a hotel and invited representatives from dozens of local businesses. It was clear that the party was given to promote better relations with neighboring subcontractors.

We had a fine turnout, and everyone was cheerful—until one of the guests noticed bottles of Asahi beer, and only Asahi beer, on the tables. Most hotels and restaurants in Japan serve only one kind of beer because they buy from one supplier, such as Kirin, Asahi, Sapporo, or Suntory. But even the beer companies are members of giant keiretsu. So the large urban hotels are always careful to serve all four beers at such gatherings to prevent any hint of favoritism. Of course, at a small hotel in the distant provinces, having four separate suppliers just for beer would be a ridiculous extravagance.

Now, Asahi beer just happens to be a member of the Sumitomo group—the president is a former Sumitomo director. The sight of all those bottles of Asahi on the tables sent shivers through some of our guests. The general reaction was, "Why didn't you tell us this was a Sumitomo affair?" The whole mood of the gathering suddenly changed. My people tried to assure our guests that our company had no connection with Sumitomo, but the damage had been done—by the label on a beer bottle.

There are many ways in which the keiretsu affiliation is shown. Beer is just one example. The entire business world in Japan is separated, like lines on a battlefield, to indicate who are friends and who are enemies. If you belong to the Mitsubishi group, for instance, you not only drink Kirin beer to support a member of the group but you also bank with Mitsubishi Bank, buy securities from Nikko and life insurance from Meiji Mutual Life, drive a Mitsubishi car, and insure it through Tokio Marine & Fire.

Sometimes this "keep business within the group mentality becomes ludicrous. For example, Sumitomo Group members are very strongly encouraged to buy their home appliances from group member NEC. If they didn't, NEC (basically a computer and telecom maker) would be hard put to sell any refrigerators or TVs. And this goes right on down through the layers of subcontractors too. I'm sure there are many divisions of big companies that would go out of business if they didn't have thousands of captive customers forced to buy their products.

Keiretsu are the ultimate force in Japanese industry. The manufacturing companies within them are controlled to some extent by the needs and policies of the group—just as each of the manufacturers has its own huge pyramid of subcontractors that functions as a group.

Cracks and Tunnels

All this strength among the industrial combines notwithstanding, strange things have been happening in Japan recently: the walls of the corporate han are still there, but cracks are starting to appear, and even the lines between the keiretsu are no longer inviolable. In large part, this stems from pressures put on the Japanese economy by the sudden doubling of the yen's value between 1985 and 1987. Because most Japanese manufacturers relied on exports for a large part of their income, they saw the sudden yen appreciation as a potentially crippling blow. Profits evaporated as the yen continued to climb. In order to recover their costs, they would have to double their export prices, which in turn would boost retail prices overseas, and ultimately the result would be a plunge in market share.

What did happen? Did retail prices of Japanese exports double?

No.

Did Japanese companies lose market share?

Not significantly.

Did the Japanese trade surplus disappear?

Not by a long shot.

So where did all the money go? What happened to those billions upon billions of dollars—the difference between the Japanese exporters' plummeting sales revenue abroad and their costs at home?

The answer is clear to anyone who ever studied Japanese business seriously. The big companies pretended to tighten their belts. Many put out idiotic press releases about how they were saving scraps of note paper or using pencils down to their stubs to save money. But it was all a sham.

The real savings were achieved the old-fashioned way: the companies ordered their smaller subcontractors to cut prices. As the yen appreciated, they simply ordered more price cuts—and then more again. Yes, a lot of small companies went out of business. But what is that compared to the preservation of the Japanese economy? The large companies are the backbone of industry, or so the large companies insist. They must survive at all costs, they say. And survive they did.

The yen appreciation put a great deal of stress on the Japanese economy and today deregulation in various sectors is keeping that pressure on. The result is an acceleration of the loosening of the keiretsu ties. The keiretsu are not gone by any means—but they no longer have absolute control as they once did. In hundreds of instances, in dozens of ways, the rigid walls between the keiretsu are fracturing, and individuals and companies (and business opportunities) are slipping through.

The biggest cracks in the keiretsu come from changes in workers' attitudes. For decades, Japanese workers have devoted themselves to one employer, working selflessly in the belief that big companies would always return their loyalty. When companies had to lay people off during the oil shocks of the 1970s, it became apparent that this was an illusion. Big companies take care of themselves first and their employees second. Young people today especially realize that big companies and impressive-sounding keiretsu are no longer a guarantee of anything. A majority of young people leaving college 15 or 20 years ago would be proud to join a prestigious group like Mitsui and wear a Mitsui pin in their lapels, regardless of there being better jobs elsewhere.

Today this "I'm a Mitsui man" way of thinking is disappearing fast. The university students who once cherished the "company man" illusion now think it's out of date. Gradually even the allegiance to the corporate group will fade. Already in the finance sector, for example, aggressive companies are beginning to hire talented managers from rival organizations, just as in the West, and some Japanese employees are forsaking company loyalty for a better job across the street.

In fact, the cracks in the keiretsu have been appearing for some time. More than 30 years ago, Matsushita Electric took advantage of the "company castle town" structure common to the factories of many big makers. Matsushita decided to "tunnel under" the walls of a powerful rival, Sumitomo. Matsushita was looking for a way to catch up with NEC—a key member of the Sumitomo Group—in the field of sophisticated communications technology.

Matsushita hit upon a bold and simple plan: it bought some land and built a factory near an NEC plant—producing the exact same kind of products as its established rival next door. It was a clear announcement to NEC's subcontractors that Matsushita was interested in the same kind of work and would welcome them as Matsushita subcontractors. The unwritten rules say that each major manufacturer is responsible for its own subcontractors and that manufacturers will not steal from one another. But Matsushita decided that if it continued to play by the old rules it would fall farther behind in an important technological field. By revising its corporate strategy, Matsushita succeeded brilliantly.

This kind of activity will only increase in the future. The keiretsu walls will never crumble. But more and more cracks will appear. And companies that are quick and aggressive enough to take advantage of the opportunities will grow and prosper. . . .

The way to create change is to get inside. Once inside, it is possible to offer the indentured servants an opportunity to escape, to work as they choose for whomever they choose—and to unleash the pent-up power of Japan's small and medium-size companies. Doing that alone would be a big step toward loosening the grip of the keiretsu.

Chapter 8

Shaping Up, Skinnying Down, and Revitalizing: Coordination and "Culture" Change

Introductory Notes

Identity changes such as restructuring and boundary redefinition involve altering organization–environment relationships and are therefore fundamental to an organization's definition of purpose. To achieve that purpose, a second form of change is required: in coordination and habits—the way that the parts of the organization (individuals and groups) work together.

The first two portraits in this chapter document the connection between external and internal change. Both are cases of change in coordination and organizational culture precipitated by major changes in identity—in effect, the creation of new companies out of existing operations. The interview with Percy Barnevik, CEO of ABB, describes the new organization developed when Sweden's Asea merged with Switzerland's Brown Boveri to form a global company. The interview with Raymond Smith, CEO of Bell Atlantic, deals with the organizational changes that ensued after its formation as a stand-alone corporation (with its own name) out of seven telephone operating companies divested from AT&T. Both interviews provide the CEO's perspective on the development of new forms of coordination—and the steps in the change process required to get there.

ABB designed a complex matrix organization—a "federation of national companies with a global coordination center"—which would ensure both global (through business area organizations) and local responsiveness (through country organizations). The organization was integrated through a lean headquarters and a flexible but powerful internal communications network linking managers across businesses and across the world. ABB tried to take a shape that would have the power of big size but without the bureaucracy; this is a model for the form of change sought by many large organizations today.

Bell Atlantic made several major changes in coordination toward a more flexible, responsive entrepreneurial organization: downsizing to remove unnecessary work; a stress on teamwork and integration across departments; the development of a creative new market-based model for headquarters' staffs (Client Service Groups whose budgets came from their business unit clients); and the Champion Program to identify and nurture new ideas outside the mainstream business units.

These new forms of coordination, however, required a major change in the habits of Bell Atlantic's people—whose millions of daily interactions were the true test of the company's strategy, as Ray Smith saw it. The tools for making this change in "culture" are described in detail in the interview: values statements, requirements for leadership behavior, extensive education for managers, and development of Bell Atlantic symbols, which provided coherence for the efforts (under the label "The Bell Atlantic Way") as well as a common identity for the new corporation. A new culture and vision for the organization also allowed the company to reach beyond its traditional local service areas in developing international strategic alliances—a new set of environmental relationships.

In both ABB and Bell Atlantic, the leaders' role in the change process clearly encompassed more than the vision of the new organizational form. Both CEOs were engaged in constant communication throughout the process, to ensure a common focus and message, to ensure that the whole was knitted together with a common understanding of tasks and efforts. Performance measurements and reward systems changed to support the new kind of coordination. And note that the change in form also entailed a deemphasis of hierarchy and a reliance on informal networks.

ABB and Bell Atlantic sought to shape up because they anticipated new competitive dynamics in Europe and North America. Ford Motor Company's shape-up was occasioned by massive and continuing losses. It was a classic case of a mature bureaucracy in a mature industry needing to change its form in order to survive. "Driving Quality at Ford" takes us on a tour with CEO Donald Petersen through a plant and through Ford's employee involvement activities—the cornerstone of significant changes in coordination, in the ways Ford's people worked together.

Peterson had the vision to pursue new product strategies in the United States modeled after successes in Europe, investing record amounts in product development while record losses were mounting. A set of internal reforms made it possible to develop significant new products with efficiency, speed, and quality: new labor–management relations, in which workers took more responsibility for quality and innovation, and management sought workers' advice; new relationships between functions, coordinated by the new role of "product manager"; goals that were companywide rather than departmental; and leadership training at a new Executive Development Center that also helped build cross-departmental relationships. Ford had to "skinny down," too, in order to shape up.

Is downsizing always the best alternative for stagnant bureaucracies? For a change of pace, test your own views as a shaper of change against a British, a Norwegian, and an American expert through "The Case of the Downsizing Decision." The "case" is actually a set of documents from a British company, given the pseudonym "Universal Products Corporation," because it describes a universal situation. The company faces financial pressures that look as though they could be relieved by a reduction in the size of the staff. But as we have seen throughout this section, downsizing is not the only alternative for helping an organization get in better shape—and even if UPC decides to downsize, it will still face the challenge of revitalization. As David Enfield, managing director of Colgate-Palmolive's United Kingdom subsidiary, said, "Any company considering downsizing as a solution to its strategic concerns should first think through what its strategic concerns are and then fit downsizing into that context."

The very process of making a coordination change—how it is designed and implemented—itself shapes the organization's culture. For this form of change, the *method* is the message.

Two CEOs on Change in Form

The Logic of Global Business

An Interview with ABB's Percy Barnevik

William Taylor

Headquartered in Zurich, ABB is a young company forged through the merger of two venerable European companies. Asea, created in 1890, has been a flagship of Swedish industry for a century. Brown Boveri, which took shape in 1891, holds a comparable industrial status in Switzerland. In August 1987, [Percy] Barnevik [President and CEO] altered the course of both companies when he announced that Asea, where he was managing director, would merge with Brown Boveri to create a potent new force in the European market for electrical systems and equipment.

The creation of ABB became a metaphor for the changing economic map of Europe. Barnevik initiated a wrenching process of consolidation and rationalization—layoffs, plant closings, product exchanges between countries—that observers agreed will one day come to European industries from steel to telecommunications to automobiles. And soon more than a metaphor, Barnevik's bold moves triggered a wholesale restructuring of the Continent's electrical power industry.

The creation of ABB also turned out to be the first step in a trans-Atlantic journey of acquisition, restructuring, and growth. ABB has acquired or taken minority positions in 60 companies representing investments worth $3.6 billion—including two major acquisitions in North America. In 1989, ABB acquired Westinghouse's transmission and distribution operation in a transaction involving 25 factories and businesses with revenues of $1 billion. That same year, it *spent $1.6 billion to acquire Combustion Engineering, the manufacturer of power-generation and process-automation equipment.*

Today ABB generates annual revenues of more than $25 billion and employs 240,000 people around the world. . . . Europe accounts for more than 60% of its total revenues, and its business is split roughly equally between the European Community countries and the non-EC Scandinavian trading bloc. Germany, ABB's largest national market, accounts for 15% of total revenues. The company also generates annual revenues of $7 billion in North America, with 40,000 employees. . . . The company has 10,000 employees in India, 10,000 in South America, and is one of the most active Western investors in Eastern Europe.

In this interview, Percy Barnevik, 49, offers a detailed guide to the theory and practice of building a "multidomestic" enterprise. He explains ABB's matrix system, a structure designed to leverage core technologies and global economies of scale without eroding local market presence and responsiveness. . . .

How do you begin building [a] global organization?

ABB has grown largely through mergers and strategic investments. For most companies in Europe, this is the right way to cross borders. There is such massive overcapacity in so many European industries and so few companies with the critical mass to hold their own against Japanese and U.S. competitors. My former company, Asea, did fine in the 1980s. Revenues in 1987 were 4 times greater than in 1980, profits were 10 times greater, and our market value was 20 times greater. But the handwriting was on the wall. The European electrical industry was crowded with 20 national competitors. There was up to 50% overcapacity, high costs, and little cross-border trade. Half the companies were losing money. The creation of ABB started a painful—but long overdue—process of restructuring.

The same restructuring process will come to other industries: automobiles, telecommunications, steel. But it will come slowly. There have been plenty of articles in the last few years about all the cross-border mergers in Europe. In fact, the more interesting issue is why there have been so *few*. There should be *hundreds* of them, involving *tens of billions* of dollars, in industry after industry. But we're not seeing it. What we're seeing instead are strategic alliances and minority investments. Companies buy 15% of each other's shares. Or two rivals agree to cooperate in third markets but not merge their home-market organizations. I worry that many European alliances are poor substitutes for doing what we try to do—complete mergers and cross-border rationalization.

What are the obstacles to such cross-border restructuring?

One obstacle is political. When we decided on the merger between Asea and Brown Boveri, we had no choice but to do it secretly and to do it quickly, with our eyes open about discovering skeletons in the closet. There were no lawyers, no auditors, no environmental investigations, and no due diligence. Sure, we tried to value assets as best we could. But then we had to make the move, with an extremely thin legal document, because we were absolutely convinced of the strategic merits. In fact, the documents from the premerger negotiations are locked away in a Swiss bank and won't be released for 20 years.

Why the secrecy? Think of Sweden. Its industrial jewel, Asea—a 100-year-old company that had built much of the country's infrastructure—was moving its headquarters out of Sweden. The unions were angry: "Decisions will be made in Zurich, we have no influence in Zurich, there is no codetermination in Switzerland."

I remember when we called the press conference in Stockholm on August 10. The news came as a complete surprise. Some journalists didn't even bother to attend; they figured it was an announcement about a new plant in Norway or something. Then came the shock, the fait accompli. That started a communications war of a few weeks where we had to win over shareholders, the public, governments, and unions. But strict confidentiality was our only choice.

Are there obstacles besides politics?

Absolutely. The more powerful the strategic logic behind a merger—the greater the cross-border synergies—the more powerful the human and organizational obstacles. It's hard to tell a competent country manager in Athens or Amsterdam, "You've done a good job for 15 years, but unfortunately this other manager has done a better job and our only choice is to appoint your colleague to run the operation." If you have two plants in the same country running well but you need only one after the merger, it's tough to explain that to employees in the plant to be closed. Restructuring operations creates lots of pain and heartache, so many companies choose not to begin the process, to avoid the pain.

Germany is a case in point. Brown Boveri had operated in Germany for almost 90 years. Its German operation was so big—it had more than 35,000 employees—that there were rivalries with the Swiss parent. BBC Germany was a technology-driven, low-profit organization—a real underperformer. The formation of ABB created the opportunity to tackle problems that had festered for decades.

So what did you do?

We sent in Eberhard von Koerber to lead the effort. He made no secret of our plans. We had to reduce the workforce by 10%, or 4,000 employees. We had to break up the headquarters, which had grown so big because of all the tensions with Switzerland. We had to rationalize the production overlaps, especially between Switzerland and Germany. We needed lots of new managers, eager people who wanted to be leaders and grow in the business.

The reaction was intense. Von Koerber faced strikes, demonstrations, barricades—real confrontation with the unions. He would turn on the television set and see protesters chanting, "Von Koerber out! Von Koerber out!" After a while, once the unions understood the game plan, the loud protests disappeared and our relationship became very constructive. The silent resistance from managers was more formidable. In fact, much of the union resistance was fed by management. Once the unions got on board, they became allies in our effort to reform management and rationalize operations.

Three years later, the results are in. ABB Germany is a well-structured, dynamic, market-oriented company. Profits are increasing steeply, in line with ABB targets. In 1987, BBC Germany generated revenues of $4 billion. ABB Germany will generate twice that by the end of next year. Three years ago, the management structure in Mannheim was centralized and functional, with few clear responsibilities or accountability. Today there are 30 German companies, each with its own president, manufacturing director, and so on. We can see who the outstanding performers are and apply their talents elsewhere. If we need someone to sort out a problem with circuit breakers in Spain, we know who from Germany can help.

What lessons can other companies learn from the German experience?

To make real change in cross-border mergers, you have to be factual, quick, and neutral. And you have to move boldly. You must avoid the "investigation trap"—you can't postpone tough decisions by studying them to death. You can't permit a "honeymoon" of small changes over a year or two. A long series of small changes just prolongs the pain. Finally, you have to accept a fair share of mistakes. I tell my people that if we make 100 decisions and 70 turn out to be right, that's good enough. I'd rather be roughly right and fast than exactly right and slow. We apply these principles everywhere we go, including in Eastern Europe, where we now have several change programs under way.

Why emphasize speed at the expense of precision? Because the costs of delay are vastly greater than the costs of an occasional mistake. I won't deny that it was absolutely crazy around here for the first few months after the merger. We *had* to get the matrix in place—we couldn't debate it—and we *had* to figure out which plants would close and which would stay open. We took ten of our best people, the superstars, and gave them six weeks to design the restructuring. We called it the Manhattan Project. I personally interviewed 400 people, virtually day and night, to help select and motivate the people to run our local companies. . . .

What form is your organization taking now?

We are in the process of building [a] federation of national companies, a multidomestic organization, as I prefer to call it. That does not mean all of our businesses are global. We do a very good business in electrical installation and service in many countries. That business is superlocal. The geographic scope of our installation business in, say, Stuttgart does not extend beyond a ten-mile radius of downtown Stuttgart.

We also have businesses that are superglobal. There are not more than 15 combined-cycle power plants or more than 3 or 4 high-voltage DC stations sold in any one year around the world. Our competitors fight for nearly every contract—they battle us on technology, price, financing—and national borders are virtually meaningless. Every project requires our best people and best technology from around the world.

The vast majority of our businesses—and of most businesses—fall somewhere between the superlocal and the superglobal. These are the businesses in which building a multidomestic organization offers powerful advantages. You want to be able to optimize a business globally—to specialize in the production of components, to drive economies of scale as far as you can, to rotate managers and technologists around the world to share expertise and solve problems. But you also want to have deep local roots everywhere you operate—building products in the countries where you sell them, recruiting the best local talent from the universities, working with the local government to increase exports. If you build such an organization, you create a business advantage that's damn difficult to copy. . . .

There are advantages to a multidomestic presence. India needs locomotives—thousands of locomotives—and the government expects its suppliers to manufacture most of them inside India. But the Indians also need soft credit to pay for what is imported. Who has more soft credit than the Germans and the Italians? So we have to be a German and an Italian company, we have to be able to build locomotive components there as well as in Switzerland, Sweden, and Austria, since our presence may persuade Bonn and Rome to assist with financing.

We test the borderlines all the time: How far can we push cross-border specialization and scale economies? How effectively can we translate our multidomestic presence into competitive advantages in third markets?

Is there such a thing as a global manager?

. . . Global managers are made, not born. This is not a natural process. We are herd animals. We like people who are like us. But there are many things you can do. Obviously, you rotate people around the world. There is no substitute for line experience in three or four countries to create a global perspective. You also encourage people to work in mixed-nationality teams. You *force* them to create personal alliances across borders, which means that sometimes you interfere in hiring decisions.

This is why we put so much emphasis on teams in the business areas. If you have 50 business areas and five managers on each BA team, that's 250 people from different parts of the world—people who meet regularly in different places, bring their national perspectives to bear on tough problems, and begin to understand how things are done elsewhere. I experience this every three weeks in our executive committee. When we sit together as Germans, Swiss, Americans, and Swedes, with many of us living, working, and traveling in different places, the insights can be remarkable. But you have to force people into these situations. Mixing nationalities doesn't just happen.

You also have to acknowledge cultural differences without becoming paralyzed by them. We've done some surveys, as have lots of other companies, and we find interesting differences in perception. For example, a Swede may think a Swiss is not completely frank and open, that he doesn't know exactly where he stands. That is a cultural phenomenon. Swiss culture shuns disagreement. A Swiss might say, "Let's come back to that point later, let me review it with my colleagues." A Swede would prefer to confront the issue directly. How do we undo hundreds of years of upbringing and education? We don't, and we shouldn't try to. But we do need to broaden understanding.

Is your goal to develop an "ABB way" of managing that cuts across cultural differences?

Yes and no. Naturally, as CEO, I set the tone for the company's management style. With my Anglo-Saxon education and Swedish upbringing, I have a certain way of doing things. Someone recently asked if my ultimate goal is to create 5,000 little Percy Barneviks, one for each of our profit centers. I laughed for a moment when I thought of the horror of sitting on top of such an organization, then I realized it wasn't a silly question. And the answer is no. We can't have managers who are "un-French" managing in France because

95% of them are dealing every day with French customers, French colleagues, French suppliers. That's why global managers also need humility. A global manager respects a formal German manager—Herr Doktor and all that—because that manager may be an outstanding performer in the German context.

Let's talk about the structures of global business. How do you organize a multidomestic enterprise?

ABB is an organization with three internal contradictions. We want to be global and local, big and small, radically decentralized with centralized reporting and control. If we resolve those contradictions, we create real organizational advantage.

That's where the matrix comes in. The matrix is the framework through which we organize our activities. It allows us to optimize our businesses globally *and* maximize performance in every country in which we operate. Some people resist it. They say the matrix is too rigid, too simplistic. But what choice do you have? To say you don't like a matrix is like saying you don't like factories or you don't like breathing. It's a fact of life. If you deny the formal matrix, you wind up with an informal one—and that's much harder to reckon with. As we learn to master the matrix, we get a truly multidomestic organization.

Can you walk us through how the matrix works?

Look at it first from the point of view of one business area, say, power transformers. The BA manager for power transformers happens to sit in Mannheim, Germany. His charter, however, is worldwide. He runs a business with 25 factories in 16 countries and global revenues of more than $1 billion. He has a small team around him of mixed nationalities—we don't expect superheroes to run our 50 BAs. Together with his colleagues, the BA manager establishes and monitors the trajectory of the business.

The BA leader is a business strategist and global optimizer. He decides which factories are going to make what products, what export markets each factory will serve, how the factories should pool their expertise and research funds for the benefit of the business worldwide. He also tracks talent—the 60 or 70 real standouts around the world. Say we need a plant manager for a a new company in Thailand. The BA head should know of three or four people—maybe there's one at our plant in Muncie, Indiana, maybe there's one in Finland—who could help in Thailand.

There are three forums for coordination:

- The BA's management board resembles the executive committee of an independent company. Karlsson chairs the group, and its members include the presidents of the largest power transformer companies—people from the United States, Canada, Sweden, Norway, Germany, and Brazil. The board meets four to six times a year and shapes the BA's global strategy, monitors performance, and resolves big problems.

- Karlsson's BA staff in Mannheim is not "staff" in the traditional sense—young professionals rotating through headquarters on their way to a line job. Rather, it is made up of five veteran managers each with worldwide responsibility for activities in critical areas such as purchasing and R&D. They travel constantly, meet with the presidents and top managers of the local companies, and drive the coordination agenda forward.
- Functional coordination teams meet once or twice a year to exchange information on the details of implementation in production, quality, marketing, and other areas. The teams include managers with functional responsibilities in all the local companies, so they come from around the world. These formal gatherings are important, . . . but the real value comes in creating informal exchange throughout the year. The system works when the quality manager in Sweden feels compelled to telephone or fax the quality manager in Brazil with a problem or an idea.

It is possible to leave the organization right there, to optimize every business area without regard for ABB's broad collection of activities in specific countries. But think about what we lose. We have a power transformer company in Norway that employs 400 people. It builds transformers for the Norwegian market and exports to markets allocated by the BA. But ABB Norway has more than 10,000 other employees in the country. There are tremendous benefits if power transformers coordinates its Norwegian operation with our operations in power generation, switchgear, and process automation: recruiting top people from the universities, building an efficient distribution and service network across product lines, circulating good people among the local companies, maintaining productive relations with top government officials.

So we have a Norwegian company, ABB Norway, with a Norwegian CEO and a headquarters in Oslo, to make these connections. The CEO has the same responsibilities as the CEO of a local Norwegian company for labor negotiations, bank relationships, and high-level contacts with customers. This is no label or gimmick. We *must* be a Norwegian company to work effectively in many businesses. Norway's oil operations in the North Sea are a matter of great national importance and intense national pride. The government wouldn't—and shouldn't—trust some faraway foreign company as a key supplier to those operations.

The opportunities for synergy are clear. So is the potential for tension between the business area structure and the country structure. Can't the matrix pull itself apart?

BA managers, country managers, and presidents of the local companies have very different jobs. They must understand their roles and appreciate that they are *complementing* each other, not competing.

The BA managers are crucial people. They need a strong hand in crafting strategy, evaluating performance around the world, and working with teams made up of different nationalities. We've had to replace some of them—people who lacked vision or cultural sensitivity or the ability to lead without being dictators. You see, BA managers don't own the people working in any business area around the world. They can't order the president of a local company to fire someone or to use a particular strategy in union negotiations. On the other hand, BA managers can't let their role degrade into a statistical coordinator or scorekeeper. There's a natural tendency for this to happen. BA managers don't have a constituency of thousands of direct reports in the same way that country managers do. So it's a difficult balancing act.

Country managers play a different role. They are regional line managers, the equivalent of the CEO of a local company. But country managers must also respect ABB's global objectives. The president of, say, ABB Portugal can't tell the BA manager for low-voltage switchgear or drives to stay out of his hair. He has to cooperate with the BA managers to evaluate and improve what's happening in Portugal in those businesses. He should be able to tell a BA manager, "You may think the plant in Portugal is up to standards, but you're being too loose. Turnover and absenteeism is twice the Portuguese average. There are problems with the union, and it's the managers' fault."

Now, the presidents of our local companies—ABB Transformers in Denmark, say, or ABB Drives in Greece—need a different set of skills. They must be excellent profit center managers. But they must also be able to answer to two bosses effectively. After all, they have two sets of responsibilities. They have a global boss, the BA manager, who creates the rules of the game by which they run their businesses. They also have their country boss, to whom they report in the local setting. I don't want to make too much of this. In all of Germany, where we have 36,000 people, only 50 or so managers have two bosses. But these managers have to handle that ambiguity. They must have the self-confidence not to become paralyzed if they receive conflicting signals and the integrity not to play one boss off against the other.

Isn't all this much easier said than done?

It does require a huge mental change, especially for country managers. Remember, we've built ABB through acquisitions and restructurings. Thirty of the companies we've bought had been around for more than 100 years. Many of them were industry leaders in their countries, national monuments. Now they've got BA managers playing a big role in the direction of their operations. We have to convince country managers that they benefit by being part of this federation, that they gain more than they lose when they give up some autonomy. . . .

How can an organization with 240,000 people all over the world be simple and local?

ABB *is* a huge enterprise. But the work of most of our people is organized in small units with P&L responsibility and meaningful autonomy. Our operations are divided into nearly 1,200 companies with an average of 200 employees. These companies are divided into 4,500 profit centers with an average of 50 employees.

We are fervent believers in decentralization. When we structure local operations, we always push to create separate legal entities. Separate companies allow you to create *real* balance sheets with *real* responsibility for cash flow and dividends. With real balance sheets, managers inherit results from year to year through changes in equity. Separate companies also create more effective tools to recruit and motivate managers. People can aspire to meaningful career ladders in companies small enough to understand and be committed to.

What does that mean for the role of headquarters?

We operate as lean as humanly possible. It's no accident that there are only 100 people at ABB headquarters in Zurich. The closer we get to top management, the tougher we have to be with head count. I believe you can go into any traditionally centralized corporation and cut its headquarters staff by 90% in one year. You spin off 30% of the staff into free-standing service centers that perform real work—treasury functions, legal services—and charge for it. You decentralize 30% of the staff—human resources, for example—by pushing them into the line organization. Then 30% disappears through head count reductions.

These are not hypothetical calculations. We bought Combustion Engineering in late 1989. I told the Americans that they had to go from 600 people to 100 in their Stamford, Connecticut, headquarters. They didn't believe it was possible. So I told them to go to Finland and take a look. When we bought Strömberg, there were 880 people in headquarters. Today there are 25. I told them to go to

Mannheim and take a look at the German operation. In 1988, right after the creation of ABB, there were 1,600 people in headquarters. Today there are 100.

Doesn't such radical decentralization threaten the very advantages that ABB's size creates?

Those are the contradictions again—being simultaneously big and small, decentralized and centralized. To do that, you need a structure at the top that facilitates quick decision-making and carefully monitors developments around the world. That's the role of our executive committee. The 13 members of the executive committee are collectively responsible for ABB. But each of us also has responsibility for a business segment, a region, some administrative functions, or more than one of these. Eberhard von Koerber, who is a member of the executive committee located in Mannheim, is responsible for Germany, Austria, Italy, and Eastern Europe. He is also responsible for a worldwide business area, installation materials, and some corporate staff functions. Gerhard Schulmeyer sits in the United States and is responsible for North America. He is also responsible for our global "industry" segment.

Naturally, these 13 executives are busy, stretched people. But think about what happens when we meet every three weeks, which we do for a full day. Sitting in one room are the senior managers collectively responsible for ABB's global strategy and performance. These same managers individually monitor business segments, countries, and staff functions. So when we make a decision—snap, it's covered. The members of the executive committee communicate to their direct reports, the BA managers and the country managers, and the implementation process is under way.

We also have the glue of transparent, centralized reporting through a management information system called Abacus. Every month, Abacus collects performance data on our 4,500 profit centers and compares performance with budgets and forecasts. The data are collected in local currencies but translated into U.S. dollars to allow for analysis across borders. The system also allows you to work with the data. You can aggregate and disaggregate results by business segments, countries, and companies within countries. . . .

Once you've put the global pieces together and have the matrix concept working, what other problems do you have to wrestle with?

Communications. I have no illusions about how hard it is to communicate clearly and quickly to tens of thousands of people around the world. ABB has about 15,000 middle managers prowling around markets all over the world. If we in the executive committee could connect with all of them or even half of them and get them moving in roughly the same direction, we would be unstoppable.

But it's enormously difficult. Last year, for example, we made a big push to squeeze our accounts receivable and free up working capital. We called it the Cash Race. There are 2,000 people around the world with some role in accounts receivable, so we had to mobilize them to make the program work. Three or four months after the program started—and we made it very visible when it started—I visited an accounts receivable office where 20 people were working. These people hadn't even *heard* of the program, and it should have been their top priority. When you come face-to-face with this lack of communication, this massive inertia, you can get horrified, depressed, almost desperate. Or you can concede that this is the way things are, this is how the world works, and commit to doing something about it.

So what do you do?

You don't inform, you *overinform*. That means breaking taboos. There is a strong tendency among European managers to be selective about sharing information.

We faced a huge communications challenge right after the merger. In January 1988, just days after the birth of ABB, we had a management meeting in Cannes with the top 300 people in the company. At that meeting, we presented our policy bible, a 21-page book that communicates the essential principles by which we run the company. It's no glossy brochure. It's got tough, direct language on the role of BA managers, the role of country managers, the approach to change we just discussed, our commitment to decentralization and strict accountability. I told this group of 300 that they had to reach 30,000 ABB people around the world within 60 days—and that didn't mean just sending out the document. It meant translating it into the local languages, sitting with people for a full day and hashing it out.

Cannes and its aftermath was a small step. Real communication takes time, and top managers must be willing to make the investment. We are the "overhead company." I personally have 2,000 overhead slides and interact with 5,000 people a year in big and small groups. This afternoon, I'll fly up to Lake Constance in Germany, where we have collected 35 managers from around the world. They've been there for three days, and I'll spend three hours with them to end their session. Half the executive committee has already been up there. These are active, working sessions. We talk about how we work in the matrix, how we develop people, about our programs around the world to cut cycle times and raise quality.

I'll give a talk at Lake Constance, but then we'll focus on problems. The manager running high-voltage switchgear in some country may be unhappy about the BA's research priorities. Someone may think we're paying too much attention to Poland. There are lots of tough questions, and my job is to answer on the spot. We'll have 14 such sessions during the course of the year—one every three weeks. That means 400 top managers from all over the world living in close quarters, really communicating about the business and their problems, and meeting with the CEO in an open, honest dialogue. . . .

Championing Change

An Interview with Bell Atlantic's Raymond Smith

Rosabeth Moss Kanter

Competing in the telecommunications industry is increasingly a world game. Rapid scientific advances are increasing communications speed and blurring the distinction between information technologies and communication technologies—computer companies are in the communications business, and telephone companies are selling systems integration. The old-fashioned Phone Company—once a monopoly in the United States and a government ministry elsewhere—is now subject to forces of competition, through changing regulation or privatization.

Few industries as old have been transformed so dramatically in such a short time, and further transformations are on the horizon. The U.S. edge in the telecommunications sector may well depend on the skill with which change—human, organizational, and technological—is managed.

Bell Atlantic Corporation was formed in 1983, in preparation for the breakup of the Bell System telephone monopoly on January 1, 1984. It is one of seven U.S. regional telecommunications holding companies (sometimes called "baby Bells") created when AT&T was required by judicial decree to divest its local telephone operations, ushering in the era of greater competition.

Bell Atlantic began with a charter to provide local telephone service in six mid-Atlantic states and the District of Columbia. By 1990, Bell Atlantic was introducing new products and services at a rapid clip, starting ventures and forming alliances throughout the *world, and pursuing leadership in the information technology industry of the future. The corporation reported 1989 earnings of over $1 billion on revenues of $11.4 billion, with 76% of its revenues from its regulated local telephone business.*

Bell Atlantic's vision centers around the creation of the "Intelligent Network," a computer-driven network capable of transmitting audio, video, and data signals through speedy fiber-optic lines. Calling itself the world's most efficient telephone company, Bell Atlantic today has the lowest costs among the regional firms. It provides telephone service over 17 million access lines—more lines than any other baby Bell.

Raymond Smith, 53, became Bell Atlantic's CEO in January 1989, adding the responsibilities of chairman of the board in July 1989. . . . He worked closely with his predecessor Thomas Bolger to shape the business concept and to eliminate vestiges of the traditionally complacent, monopolistic mind-set known as having "Bell-shaped heads."

How did you view the state of your business when you became Bell Atlantic's chief executive?

I saw that the way we had been managing all of these years was going to have to change. The problem was clear. The intrinsic growth of the core business would not sustain the company in the competitive global economy of the twenty-first century.

The difficulty of addressing our basic business problem was complicated by competition on one side and regulation on the other. Even our 3% projected growth rate was subject to considerable, well-financed competition in the most profitable lines. As a regulated company, we owed a subsidy to the local telephone rate-payers, so we were limited in what we could earn in the core business. And the legislation and judicial decree that broke up the Bell System restricted the kinds of businesses we could enter. For example, the Cable Act of 1984 kept Bell Atlantic from competing in the cable television business in our region.

How did you think the company could increase its rate of growth in revenues and earnings?

We identified five initial strategies. Four of them would sound familiar to many businesses: improved efficiency; substantially improved marketing to protect market share; new products and services; and entirely new businesses operating outside of our territory and outside of the United States.

The fifth strategy was one we had to work on right away. It involved regulatory reform that we called "incentive regulation" to allow us to benefit from our own initiatives while protecting the telephone rate-payers. We worked intensively with regulators and crafted social contracts with consumer groups and those most affected by telephone rates, such as senior citizens and people with disabilities.

With incentive regulation accomplished, we could concentrate on the business growth strategies. But none of our strategies could be achieved with the company culture in place after the breakup. So I had to focus on the culture first.

What was wrong with the culture?

The company had grown out of a long-standing monopoly, with the centralized organizational structure and culture of a monopoly. In the old Bell System culture, no operating company could introduce a product of its own. The way a small work center in a small town in Pennsylvania would operate was mandated by the central staff. There was no strategic planning, no product development, no long-range planning in the operating companies. It was all centralized at AT&T.

What was the consequence of that?

The operating companies had an implementation mentality. They did not understand the initiative, innovation, risks, and accountability necessary to meet our business goals. Managers were held accountable for implementation of a process or practice exactly as it was written, not for the end result. Managers simply could not imagine rewriting a process even if they knew a better one. They were maintenance managers, not business mangers.

When I told those same managers that we wanted improved marketing, new products, and new business, it was a mental shock. We had no experience to draw on. And the ways we were accustomed to operating impeded our ability to achieve our goals.

How so?

Cross-departmental competition raised costs and prevented new initiatives. This problem was a consequence of our heritage.

The old Bell System was like a great football team with the best athletes and the best equipment. Every Saturday morning, we'd run up and down the football field and win 100 to 0 because there was no one on the other side of the line of scrimmage; we were a monopoly. Being human, the football players found their competition inside the team. This sometimes resulted in lowest common denominator solutions and substantial inefficiency. Despite dedication and hard work, it often took more resources to get things done than were ever really needed.

The conventions of behavior grew out of cross-departmental

competition and were very parochial. There was no true unifying concept to rally around. I represented my department, you represented your department, and we behaved as if we were opposing lawyers or political opponents.

When did you begin to see that this kind of behavior had to change?

In the early 1980s, when we began to see real competition. Tom Bolger, my predecessor as CEO, and I agreed that we needed a new culture to support our business strategies.

Where did you start?

We started by articulating the values of the corporation. I was personally involved, with another officer, in the design of seminars in which 1,400 managers spent half a week to think through our values and state them clearly. At the seminars, a draft was handed out for discussion. These managers were actively engaged in editing the document word by word. New categories were suggested; eventually, "teamwork" became "respect and trust." I attended virtually every seminar and met with the participants for five or six hours a week.

Ultimately, we agreed on five values: integrity, respect and trust, excellence, individual fulfillment, and profitable growth, with a paragraph of description explaining each.

What happened when the sessions were completed and the statement of values was published?

Not enough! It became very apparent to me and to the managers involved that we needed to move from general statements of values to concrete behaviors and work practices, or what we called the "conventions" of day-to-day business life. So when I became CEO, I announced a ten-year transition to a new way of working together.

Every corporation today is full of rhetoric like "it's time to change" or "we need a new way" or "we want to get rid of bureaucracy." What did you do to show people that you meant it?

One of the first steps I took was to engage the senior officers in a serious examination of our obligations to the corporation. I personally prepared a list of 12 specific guidelines. In a series of day-long meetings, I suggested to each of the top 50 people in Bell Atlantic that they had broad corporate obligations that went beyond their departmental responsibilities. There were arguments and debates about the obligations, but in the end they stood. It took a year to get the required understanding and commitment.

We made quality a corporate imperative in our 1989 strategic plan, designing a Quality Improvement Process using the Baldrige Award criteria and starting our own Quality Institute. We developed an organized program of internal communications for all employees outlining our obligations to each other, the opportunities ahead, and the need and reasons for change. We called this the Bell Atlantic Way.

What is the Bell Atlantic Way, and why did you think you needed it?

Simply stated, the Bell Atlantic Way is an organized, participative method of working together that allows us to get the most out of our own efforts and maximize our contribution to team goals. The Bell Atlantic Way includes the conventions of daily behavior subscribed to by all of us.

In a large business, the most important determinant of success is the effectiveness of millions of day-to-day interactions between human beings. If those contacts are contentious, turf-oriented, and parochial, the company will flounder, bureaucracies will grow, and internal competition will be rampant. But when employees behave in accountable, team-oriented and collegial ways, it dramatically improves group effectiveness.

The Bell Atlantic Way isn't limited to a list of dos and don'ts, but it does seem to boil down to a few specific behaviors. For example, the plaque on my desk says, "Be Here Now." That just means that it's important that I listen and be totally involved in any discussion we may have. I'm not looking over my shoulder. I'm not taking phone calls. I'm not doodling or having side conversations while you are making a presentation.

In such a large corporation, how do you get people to operate by these codes of behavior?

With the help of consultants, we designed forums to introduce the Bell Atlantic Way to 20,000 managers. The officer group, roughly 50 people, attended first. Then the officers acted as executives-in-residence at forums for the rest of the managers and supervisors. Most of us have been through the sessions two or three times.

We teach the conventions, we don't just talk about them. Each one is impressed on forum participants in experimental exercises that help us examine ourselves and remind us of our obligations to each other. And our responsibilities don't stop at the end of the forum. I'm spending a great deal of my own time in the field meeting with employees and talking about the Bell Atlantic Way. Each of the officers has developed departmental programs of reinforcement and support back on the job.

Why is it important for you and the other officers to spend scarce executive time on this, involving yourselves in a personal way?

We must ourselves model what we are asking others to do. We call this "the shadow of the leader." We are asking people to change their behavior, to accept a new set of conventions for working together. And I try to provide reinforcement in every way I can. For example, I always wear my Quality button to impress colleagues with my rabid dedication. It serves to remind us that we have a very special obligation to support those who are supporting the corporation.

It took about a year for top management to internalize the concepts of this change, to recognize it, and to begin to support it fully. Now changes have started to accelerate. We're seeing as much change every three months as we used to see in three years.

What are some tangible signs of change?

The language is changing. The decision process is changing. People are becoming more accountable, more team-oriented, and more effective. For example, our budget process is no longer bitter and contentious. It's still painful and always difficult, but it's much less of a hassle and never personal.

There has been remarkable improvement among the top 400 people of the company who decide on budgets, projects, priorities, and resource allocation. As corny as it may seem, managers will now open sessions saying, "We've got to break the squares today," referring to one of the Bell Atlantic Way games—meaning we've got to compromise here, break out of thinking about only our own territories. We may know that the corporation has to reduce budgets; so we all must give something up for the good of the whole company.

In the old culture, if I contributed resources for the good of the corporation, I'd lose the support of my own group. Now it is no longer acceptable for someone to say, "I've done my bit. I've met my goal. I'll sit back until you meet yours." It's not acceptable to complain to third parties about the boss or the company or some other department. Someone who does that is likely to be asked, "What did they say when you told them?" One manager said that bitch sessions used to be the social event of the week, but now they're no fun. We expect people to accept accountability for results.

How do you get accountability?

We had to make sure that our reward system encouraged people to focus on results consistent with larger business goals. The first step was to base compensation on corporate and team results as well as individual results. Today the corporate performance award is a much higher percentage of compensation than it was in the past. It used to be zero—or such a tiny percentage that it never meant anything. Now the award has a long-term as well as a short-term component for a growing percentage of managers, and it is worth more than a few bucks. It's also flexible; the definition of team can include local groups as well as the whole corporation.

A significant factor in an individual's performance evaluation is whether they have also contributed to the overall team goals. Our team goals include customer service. We look at the customers' attitudes through telephone surveys—whether or not they feel we are conforming to their requirements 100% of the time. We must reach a minimum level of performance on customer service measures before there are any corporate incentive awards.

Our reward and appraisal system is not perfect, but at least it is getting better. However, even the best evaluation system will not produce the desired behavior unless people understand our business problem and our strategies.

Do your employees get this basic business information?

Now they do, but that was not always the case. As I traveled throughout our company before becoming CEO, I found that very few people really knew what we were trying to do as a company. Sometimes they understood the departmental objectives, and certainly they knew their own objectives, but most people had no idea how to put their day-to-day work life into a corporate context. Actions of the corporation such as the purchase of a new business or the consolidation of an operations center were often a mystery.

How did you clear up the mystery?

My senior officers and I wrote out what we thought was the basic business problem we were trying to solve. We added the specific strategies to solve it, the departmental goals, and finally the individual objectives that were the employees' contributions to the goals. Then we shared it with everyone.

This was somewhat new. The notion of intellectually engaging all of our employees in the solution of the basic business problem was so different from the past that we had to communicate clearly and personally. So we asked the 400 top people in the company, the key managers and communicators, to understand the overall strategy totally and fully, internalize it, and go forth and share it with others. There was a brief hiccup in the company while this idea was absorbed, but then it took off.

You were also giving top managers a big kick in the pants. You were arousing them to action. Shouldn't they have known the strategy and been communicating it all along?

I don't think of it that way. From my first day on the job, I should have made sure that we were all on the same wavelength. I didn't realize that everyone wasn't behaving like a CEO and thinking about the basic corporate problem all day long. When 99% of someone's efforts are engaged in getting a departmental job done, the broad goals of the corporation begin to fade if they are not constantly reinforced. As the head coach and teacher, I hadn't really taught the game plan or the course well enough. So I went on the stump, enlisted the aid of a number of others, and spread the word.

Now the top 400 certainly know our business problem. They know our purpose, vision, and strategies, and how they fit together. Because the top 400 talk about this, thousands of other Bell Atlantic employees know it too. They can translate their personal and departmental objectives to those of the company. This makes it easier to deal with the tough realities we face.

What are the tough realities?

We had to eliminate jobs to get our costs on line and reduce wasteful bureaucracy. This is one of the biggest culture shocks we faced. People used to join a Bell System company with the expectation that they'd be taken care of from cradle to grave.

We've tried to do two things to cushion the blow. The first is to level with people. We tell them about the problems in the United States—the troubled companies and the layoffs, plant closings, and ruined careers that come from complacency. We explain that this is the way life is in a competitive world. Wishful thinking won't bring back the old world of no change and total security.

In U.S. business today, the understanding of the real world is vital to survival. In our industry, for example, we have a choice of having a larger number of low-paid employees who will be subject to layoffs, or we can have a smaller group of well-paid, efficient employees with security obtained through hard work and providing customers with more value than they can get elsewhere.

The second thing we do is to try to make stressful changes like downsizing in a participative manner. We eliminated one whole level of management, and we did it by involving the employees in the decision. We had no overall template for the organization, the way the Bell System did in the past. We allowed each organization to eliminate the level it wanted the way it felt was appropriate. After all, almost any organization will succeed if the people feel empowered, are recognized for what they do, and understand the purpose of their jobs.

The idea for this initiative came from New Jersey Bell. The officers thought they could run the business more efficiently if they eliminated a management level, but they wanted to leave the choice of which level to the departments. The departments examined the situation and made the right decision. It worked so well, we made this a Bell Atlantic–wide effort. People in jobs that were about to be eliminated participated in the discussions. Naturally, they were not enthusiastic about cutting their own jobs, so in practice the decision was left to the boss. Still, the "soft" aspects of the organizational change—appreciation, recognition, sharing—were given as much importance as the hard side of reducing the head count.

Was work eliminated along with the level? The criticism of downsizing in many companies is that the people are gone, but the work remains.

Unfortunately, that's true. We saw no way to eliminate all the work first. We reluctantly concluded that we had to reduce the force and then empower the people to eliminate the rest of the work.

On the first day of the new organization, some groups had only eight people to do the workload of ten. But the individual departments were empowered to create the organization they thought would be most efficient. They worked hard to eliminate those activities that were least important. That sort of prioritizing can't be done by some superstaff.

What made you believe that people who had been accustomed to following central mandates would be effective at setting priorities?

People were able to do this because of what they learned from the Bell Atlantic Way. An important part of change is moving from a culture in which people are handed procedures to follow mindlessly to one that helps them make tough choices. This is a difficult process and we're still involved in it. It requires guts and a lot of honest communication.

In the seminars, we play a game with poker chips. The blue chips are valuable; the white chips are practically worthless. Participants learn that it is vital to understand priorities and know what those priorities are based on, such as the goals of the corporation and not just the goals of the subgroup. The blue chips mean First Things First—priorities. I carry one in my wallet as a reminder.

How do people feel about being involved in a tough restructuring process?

In our regular employee survey, workers cited our downsizing as one reason for improved morale. They told us that although resources are very tight, Bell Atlantic is now a much better place to work. They said since some of the disaffected, cynical people have left, there is much less time for bureaucracy.

What else are you doing to reduce bureaucracy?

We are determined to revolutionize staff support, to convert a bureaucratic roadblock into an entrepreneurial force.

Large staffs that are not subject to bottom-line pressure tend to grow and produce services that may be neither wanted nor required, and their allegiances generally lean toward their professional positions rather than toward their clients. We had to do something to change this.

Three years ago, when I was vice chairman and the staffs reported to me, I decided to place the control of discretionary staff and support expenditures in the hands of those people who were paying for them, that is, the profit centers, the bottom-line groups. We also had to eliminate duplicate staff groups at corporate headquarters and in the operating companies.

Our approach was to create small profit centers within the staff groups, called client service groups or CSGs. For example, the training department became the Training and Educational Services CSG. The accounting department formed the Accounting Operations CSG.

How do the client service groups work?

They sell their services both to the corporate headquarters and to the operating companies. Each year, CSGs develop a budget and an array of products or services based on what Bell Atlantic clients have committed to fund, plus approved amounts for ad hoc or unanticipated business. They have to meet market tests, providing the same value as any outside organization. The CSGs' total annual expenses must equal anticipated revenues (billing credits) from customers. The goal is to break even.

CSGs market their services continuously through items in internal publications, CSG newsletters and brochures, 800-number hotlines, and exhibits at trade shows. The Training and Educational Services CSG publishes a 370-page catalog of offerings. The Information Systems Professional Services CSG heralds new software, programming possibilities, and applications in a regular newsletter.

CSG account managers stay in touch with customers to learn about their needs, answer their questions, facilitate provision of services, and forecast demand. Monthly bills from the CSGs to customers itemize specific services and costs in detail, helping clients to understand and control these costs.

The profit-center customers have to follow a few simple rules. They must give the client service group an opportunity to bid on a project, formally or informally. If the internal organization wins the bid, they use the internal organization. If an outside company wins, they can use the outside firm. But they cannot create their own media group or their own business research group. We want no internal competition.

What happened when you introduced this major structural change?

First of all, it was believed that the client service groups wouldn't work. In some quarters it was considered a dingbat idea that would go away. Still, the first year got off to a pretty good start.

The second year brought a budget crunch and nearly destroyed the process. The budgets of the client service groups were cut by the central financial staffs without the clients' agreement. This is absolutely counter to the rules we devised. It wasn't done surreptitiously, just out of misunderstanding, but it happened. The new groups called foul, and we did some damage control to restore their budgets. There were also cases in which individual departments tried to form their own support groups under different labels, under different names.

In the third year, there is no question that the client service groups are working.

What results are you getting?

Market pressures are keeping the client service groups at a reasonable level. Expenditures for discretionary staff services are generally flat, while other corporate expenses have gone up. Because of pent-up demand, some CSGs have seen their budgets increase; for example, internal clients wanted more operations support programming. But the Business Research CSG encountered a substantial decline.

The most important fact is that spending for discretionary staff support activities is now controlled by the clients. That's changed the whole nature of staff groups. Not everyone is totally comfortable with this yet; it is much more fun to set a budget based on your professional opinion and let other people pay for it than to compete for resources. The idea is so different that it is very tender and will require careful cultivation.

I see great progress in attitudes and behavior. We put on one of the largest technical expositions in the United States to let our vendors like AT&T, IBM, and Siemens show us their stuff. Last year as I was walking through it, I was astonished to see the Medical CSG selling its services. I turned the corner, and there was another client service group hawking its wares. Both were selling back to their own company as vigorously as any vendor.

Because they have to do the work of selling their services to their clients and all the additional accounting, the groups are learning to be business managers. They are slowly becoming more entrepreneurial.

Are other people at Bell Atlantic acquiring entrepreneurial skills?

We are committed to identifying potential corporate entrepreneurs, training them, and developing their ideas into new businesses. We do this primarily through our Champion program.

The Champion program arose from one of our companies, Chesapeake & Potomac Telephone, and we spread it across the whole corporation in 1989. The program provides seed money, guidance, and training to potential entrepreneurs who propose new products and services. People at any level can make proposals. If projects are accepted, their proposers can run them. And they can invest a portion of their wages in the project, in exchange for the prospect of a piece of the action when their product has been marketed.

Are you getting results?

In the first year, 36 Champions were accepted into the program. In 1989, 39 were added. By late 1990, there were about 33 products and services in the pipeline, several of them near the commercialization stage. Projects include *Creative Connections,* a line of designer phone jacks; *Emerg-Alert,* prerecorded emergency messages targeted to latchkey children and the elderly; *CommGuard,* a package of backup phone services in case of a system breakdown; local usage information services for all lines in a Centrex system; and a do-not-disturb service.

Champion's most noteworthy success is *Thinx,* new software so innovative that its creator, Jack Coppley was one of five finalists for *Discover* magazine's award honoring engineers and scientists making technological breakthroughs. *Thinx* is an intelligent graphics program integrating data with images to help users explore relationships visually and apply data or calculations automatically.

Jack learned about Champion when he attended a meeting introducing it in 1988. At that time, he was a budget manager for the network services staff, but he was intrigued by the opportunity Champion represented. Some of Jack's initial ideas were rejected, but his software idea was warmly received.

After going through the steps to test the idea and develop the business plan, Jack became head of a 20-member team that worked out software glitches, chose the *Thinx* name, and designed packaging. The product was unveiled at Comdex, a large trade show, in November 1989. Jack came home with triple the number of customer leads he had anticipated. In September 1990, *Thinx* hit the market and received rave reviews.

Champion has now become an actual revenue source in our strategic planning process. That's the ultimate testimony of importance in a corporation—a business plan with dollars of investment and targeted returns. In five years, we expect annual revenues of over $100 million from Champion projects. My question when I first saw the

1995 projection was, "Is this hope or smoke?" I was told that the figure was conservatively stated!

There are potentially thousands of great, innovative ideas in a company our size. The Champion program encourages people to take responsibility for acting on them.

How do the internal cultural and operational changes you've described translate into advantage in the marketplace?

We were always an efficient company, but our new approaches are breaking new ground. Our management process provides another major differentiation factor in world markets. When you match our track record of efficiency and quality service with a state-of-the-art understanding of how to manage large, technologically complex organizations, you've got a terrific package.

The most efficient communications networks in the world don't come from just modern switching machines but from computer operating systems and skilled technicians that operate them—all working in an empowered, accountable organization.

This forms an excellent launching pad for new businesses. Our systems-integration business, for example, is a natural evolution of that theme. It began as a computer-maintenance business with relatively low margins. But it has evolved into the largest independent field-service business in the country, adding products and services and moving up the value chain to application software, disaster recovery, system operation, consulting, and so on.

You have a very strong vision for what the information system linking the world will be in the future.

It's probably the most important vision in our corporation. I think it is the major contribution that Bell Atlantic will make to the United States. We see the Intelligent Network changing not just our company but changing civilization.

The Intelligent Network means virtually unlimited memory and logic, instantaneous transport to anywhere in the world, providing intellectual linkages between human beings. These links are equivalent, in my mind, to the revolution of the printing press or perhaps even writing or speech. In the near future, a telephone conversation could start in English at one end and be heard in French or Japanese at the other. Information will eventually go to wherever a person is—at home, at work, in a car, or strolling in the park.

What steps are you taking to realize this vision?

We are building the Intelligent Network for the service area in the Bell Atlantic regulated territory. We have introduced 30 new technology-based services, more than any other regional company. We are leading in deploying the nervous system of the Intelligent Network, Signaling System 7. We've added massive computer capacity and will have a million miles of fiber-optics transport throughout the territory in the next few years. The computers hold extensive database information about customer needs and wants. Fiber optics allow a signal to travel 10,000 times faster than copper wire.

By being focused in the transport and use of information, we realized the capabilities of the Intelligent Network. Our densely populated territory allowed us to visualize and build these kinds of links easily. We concluded, perhaps before others, that this network architecture was a revolutionary way to provide intelligence. We coined the term "Intelligent Network" and began to sell it to our counterparts. The Intelligent Network is a new notion that came out of our search for distinction, our search for a future. The whole world has now accepted it.

How is Bell Atlantic gaining the resources and capability to realize the Intelligent Network vision worldwide?

We recognized very early on that we needed strategic alliances. We've formed partnerships with Siemens, IBM, NTI, and others, including big companies, small companies, and government ministries.

Partnering is a very serious business in Bell Atlantic. Some companies seek strategic alliances because it seems like a good idea in theory or it looks good to be associated with prestigious partners. But often the overall goal of the alliance is lost in the process. Substantial investments are made by large corporations, but little top management attention is given thereafter. Predictably, the local bureaucracy sets up prickly barriers and mousetraps to prove that the new joint venture partner doesn't really understand the business and is an enemy, not a friend.

We can't afford to make that mistake because alliances are too vital for our growth plans, especially outside of the United States. The international field almost always calls for the formation of consortia because of the scale of investment or the preference of governments for local participation. We had to have partners in every one of our investments.

To make sure we are working with our partners effectively and building on their capabilities, we have had to develop a culture of tolerance, listening, and intellectual curiosity, not intellectual arrogance. . . .

Driving Quality at Ford

Gregg Easterbrook

On a very dark day in 1980, Donald Petersen, newly chosen president of Ford Motors, visited the company design studios. Ford was in the process of losing $2.2 billion, the largest single-year corporate loss in U.S. history. The future seemed equally bleak. Most Fords could charitably be described as iron thunder lizards. There was no minimum to the number of them Petersen could sell.

Petersen had come to review proposals for a new Thunderbird—the model that had been Ford's flagship but through the 1970s had grown about as exciting as a tuna trawler. He was shown the customary sketches of big, boring boxes. Ford designers, truth be told, hated their own designs. Often they had tried to propose interesting cars like the Europeans and Japanese were building. Top management always shot them down. There was only one kind of car headquarters wanted to hear about: A Car Just Like Last Year's.

After examining some sketches, Petersen looked up at the designers and asked, "Are you proud of these?" There was a pause. In big corporations people are handsomely paid not to say what they think.

"No. I'm embarrassed by them," Jack Telnack, Ford's chief of design, answered. Then the designers wheeled out clay models of a different type of Thunderbird—aerodynamically smooth, European-influenced. There was even a sporty version configured for the BMW crowd with a small high-tech engine, a five-speed transmission, and no chrome. When was the last time anyone saw a *stick* in a *Thunderbird?* Maybe 1956.

This Thunderbird design represented everything cars are supposed to be and Detroit products never are. Functionality. Taking the driver seriously. Appealing to the customer's better judgment, rather than the market research department's lowest common denominator. Headquarters was bound to hate it.

Petersen said go ahead.

It was the day the scales finally fell from Detroit's eyes. . . .

"People complain that Petersen is too quiet," said Joseph Kordick, a Ford general manager. "That's because he's listening. They don't know how to deal with a CEO who actually listens to the people beneath him."

One day in April, Petersen and I toured a stamping plant in Monroe, Michigan. The plant is only one hour from Ford world headquarters, yet no Ford CEO had ever seen it.

Petersen travels in a Taurus family sedan. Not a limo, not even a Lincoln. There's a phone up front and an adjustable reading light rigged into the backseat headliner. Without these extras, you can have the car the CEO of a $39 billion corporation rides in for about $12,000.

His reception at the plant is a triumph of minimalism. A guard stands in the street to point toward the parking lot; that's it. Some plant officials show Petersen to a small, stuffy conference room—Monroe is a manufacturing facility, as opposed to an assembly plant, which means the inside is noisy and grimy. There is no evidence of any special cleanup or fuss in anticipation of the boss.

Supervisors and UAW members crowd into the conference room for a short speechmaking session during which Petersen seems uncomfortable being the center of attention.

Stan Cronenwett, the plant manager, gives Petersen a blue barracuda jacket like the ones plant supervisors wear. He puts it on. Then Les Burnett, Building Chairman of Local 723, hands Petersen one of the sharp black-and-gold softball jackets of the local, with "honorary member" stitched beneath his name. In big-industry labor relations, this just doesn't happen; most major industrial unions would be more likely to give the CEO a cement overcoat. Petersen seems genuinely pleased. He is also perplexed as to which of the jackets he should wear onto the plant floor. "We outnumber you," Burnett notes. Petersen goes with the union label.

Petersen has invested nearly all his moral capital in a labor relations reform program called employee involvement. "At first we thought the employee involvement program was a lot of B.S.," Burnett tells me as we walk along the factory floor, "but now we think it's for real." He points to a wheel-making line. "See that? The hourly people control that whole line. There's no supervisor. I never would have believed I would live to see anything like that or to be saying nice things about the company."

A few years ago Monroe was on the verge of closing. Now, though total staff is down from 3,000 to 1,750, its future appears secure. Over the opposition of UAW national leadership, the local made concessions on job classifications, which in "mature" industries are often a greater problem than wages, as they tend to force companies to retain outdated, unproductive methods. Thirty-three robots have been added to Monroe since 1982, when there was no automation. Much of the plant's new equipment comes from Japan. Watching a gigantic, $5 million, imported transfer press spit out parts, I felt a sudden delight to think that I might be witnessing Japanese capitalism selling us the rope that would be used to hang *them*—equipment we would use to catch back up.

Petersen spends considerable time poking around the plant, questioning workers. Then he heads to another conference room to meet with the employee involvement committee. There are 19 UAW members here, and each recites an idea his subunit has found to save money. Petersen respectfully questions each in turn, then delivers compliments. It's a slow, ritualistic session in which any Japanese manager would feel at home. Petersen shows no impatience, though this room, at the center of the production area, is even hotter and stuffier.

Some tales the workers tell confirm your worst suspicions about old Detroit. Frank Giarmo notes his department had trouble with steel provided by a particular supplier. The steel was hard to machine and had been for years. Finally Giormo's employee involvement group called up the supplier to ask what the problem was—and discovered that no one had ever told the supplier how his product was being used. The supplier quickly changed chemical formulas to make the steel more malleable.

During the session, another worker, Charles Johnson, actually tells Petersen, "I'm proud to be a member of the Ford family." Afterwards Pat McCarty, a member of the local bargaining committee, notes, "Five years ago nobody would have dreamed of saying that. Or if they had, they would have been booed down."

Of course, even five years of enlightenment is insufficient to drive out decades of bad feelings. "It used to be that we practiced strictly two-by-four management; if anybody got out of line, we hit them with a two-by-four," said Bob Gindorf, a Ford plant supervisor. Such attitudes die hard, and though Ford factories are becoming better places to work, some still offer the traditional mix or physical stress, mental strain, and management arrogance that is a recipe for alienation.

Seeds of change were planted in the 1960s, when Ford began to rotate more executives to its European division. One purpose was a kind of initiation ritual: pledges were supposed to return to headquarters, a place employees bewilderingly refer to as "the Ford division of Ford," grateful to be back in the company's prestige center. Instead many, Petersen among them, returned disenchanted with Ford products. "Every year we had a higher percentage of managers who had spent time in Europe and, when they came back, didn't have such built-in prejudices against functionality," he said.

In fact, exposure to Europe helped turn Petersen into a discriminating enthusiast. He became, in the words of former Ford executive John Steward, "a plain and simple car nut, a guy who loves to look at cars, to talk about them and bomb around in them." Petersen is a graduate of Bondurant—the California school where amateurs are taught to drive like professional race car jockeys—and has made the course a rite of passage for other current Ford executives.

Though Petersen was able to sell his fellow managers on the virtues of small cars like the downsized Mustang, he met resistance to his plan to shift the company as a whole toward European-style cars. "In 1980 the continuing majority view within the industry was that cars such as the Thunderbird Turbo were simply going too far," he explained. "They said a driver-oriented [American] car could simply never sell. It was tremendously frustrating."

What finally changed attitudes? The withering losses of the early 1980s. "I'd like to think we could have reformed the company without that shock. But realistically, I doubt it very much," Petersen said.

Louis Lataif, a Ford vice president, put it this way: "A large organization will keep right on doing whatever it's doing as long as the profits hold out. Individual buyers [in the 1970s] were telling us they didn't like the products, but as an organization we didn't hear them until the message was written in big, big numbers." Like billions.

Petersen decided to go for broke. He decided Taurus/Mercury Sable would be the first Detroit attempt at a crossover car—targeted at the typical family buyer, yet imbued with European handling characteristics and functionality.

Taurus, Petersen decreed, would be European in every detail: tight handling, no mushy ride; exterior styling dictated by aerodynamics; interior styling dictated by ergonomics. Ford engineers dissected an Audi 5000, which they considered to have the world's easiest-operating trunk, and designed the Taurus trunk mechanism accordingly. They laboriously analyzed the Toyota Camry hood balancing mechanism to determine why it worked better than Ford's, and patterned the results into Taurus. The "detent" of dashboard switches—the clunks and clicks made—was redone until the switches felt solid, not like they would come off in your hand. Even the configuration of the engine compartment was designed, to ease maintenance.

Anyone with more than a casual interest in cars values such subtleties: they are the essence of the German approach to auto engineering. But could Ford, a mass manufacturer garnished with Madison Avenue hype, sell these touches to suburbia? When Taurus plans leaked, even the automotive "buff books" said Petersen was going in over his head—making a car too refined for the average American to appreciate.

Petersen says his years in product development had convinced him that it wasn't hype that sold cars: cars sold cars. And he wanted a car the company could sell on its merits. "I can remember long conversations with the creative people at our ad agencies," he said. "I'd go through their ads and circle hyperbole, underline excessives, cross out the obviously touched-up photographs. I'd say, what's the matter, aren't our cars good enough as it is? Eventually I decided that if they had to exaggerate what the cars were about to sell them, it was our [management's] fault, not theirs."

Through the auto recession years of the early 1980s Petersen sank more than $3 billion into Taurus development. That means that during the same period Ford was sustaining record losses, it was making record product investments, something industrial policy deep-thinkers say American corporations never do. Ford's losses correspond almost exactly with Taurus development costs; in a sense the company's troubles were the price of forcing itself to make a quality car.

The gamble paid off. Taurus and Sable, released after Christmas in 1985, were the auto world's hits of the year. Both sold with a three-month back order, with their assembly plants running double shifts. Ads for the cars talked strictly about features and function, not baseball games. Detroit finally made a buck by not underestimating the intelligence of the American public.

In pursuit of quality, G.M., Ford, and Chrysler each have initiated various internal reforms. Ford's are the most striking.

Labor reform came first. "The adversarial relationship with labor had reached the point of dysfunction," Stewart said. "People were really ready for something different." In the early 1980s Ford hired a gifted labor relations manager named Peter Pestillo at about the same time Donald Ephlin, the brightest light of the UAW, took charge of the union's Ford division. The program of employee involvement, roughly what the Theory Z proponents called quality circles, was initiated. Assembly-line workers actually started talking to the "salary side"—their supervisors.

In a key test of employee involvement, early Taurus mock-ups were taken to a Ford assembly plant in Atlanta and handed over to the workers for their analysis. This may sound like an obvious, commonsense step—production people are bound to see things engineers miss—but in the long-running saga of mutual throat-cutting that is modern labor relations, the thought of *management* going to *workers* for advice is radical.

Production workers examining Taurus suggested numerous changes, noting for example that interior assembly required several screws of only marginally differing sizes; they were replaced with a standard screw.

In another case, workers gave Ford marketing advice. A compact called the EXP, similar to the Escort, was scheduled to expire with the 1986 model year. Layoffs were in the cards for the Wayne, Michigan, plant where Escorts and EXPs are made.

Rather than bewail the situation, UAW members at Wayne expropriated a few surplus EXPs and tinkered with them until they had assembled an alternative—a new model having more sheetmetal in common with Escort, which cut overhead and made the car more attractive. Management was persuaded to keep the workers' concept in production as the "Escort EXP." Now selling briskly, the Escort EXP has performed a demographic miracle of sorts for a domestic industry plagued with aging customers—its buyers' median age is 24.8, lowest of any car sold in the U.S.

As worker relations improved, a system called Statistical Process Controls—which sounds like the product of a bad MBA thesis but is said to separate meaningful information from eye-glazing data—was instituted at Ford with the aid of a management guru named Dr. Edwards Deming. . . .

What the UAW now calls "enthusiastic cooperation" at the factory level is, Ford comptroller David McCammon says, a primary reason the company judges its car quality to have improved 51 percent since 1980.

Yet while relations with hourly workers were being brought into the future, Petersen seemed hesitant to extend the same level of progress to the salaried side. Here the shadow of Henry Ford II, who remained on the board and in control of nearly 40 percent of the company's stock, continued to fall across Dearborn. It was painful enough, from the Deuce's ego standpoint, that Petersen was fundamentally changing the Ford product line. How could he restructure headquarters without repudiating the founder's son altogether?

"When Henry II was here we all lived in constant fear," said one Ford veteran. "It was death to disagree with him." The Deuce seemed privately to enjoy setting off internal rivalries.

Of near-legendary status were disputes between the design bureau and body engineering, which had to translate style into metal. Though their buildings are adjacent on the Ford "campus," officials of the two departments often communicated by memo, refusing to meet face to face. "We talked about quality all the time, but I was not personally convinced upper management was behind it," Manoogian said.

Before becoming president, a serendipitous thing happened to Petersen—temporary exile to Truck Operations. Trucks represent big money for the auto industry. Despite their business value, however, trucks, like European operations, were traditionally low-status to Ford top management. Headquarters directed its rigidity and paranoia inward. Petersen, freed, would have a revelation.

"As I worked at Ford through the years I just couldn't stand the infighting that was going on, the pointless jockeying for position," he said. "Then I went to Truck Operations, which had a positive sense of self, lots of stability, and worked together as a group.

"After a while it struck me. *These guys are having fun.* They enjoy what they're doing. There is little petty bickering. And they are doing their job perfectly well, thank you, without a whole lot of complicated orders from a large superstructure. It was clear they knew something I didn't know."

In the fall of 1984, as Ford's fortunes were rebounding, Petersen assembled his plan for "participatory management"—employee involvement at a white-collar level. . . .

The company sent representatives to . . . "excellent" companies . . . such as Procter & Gamble and Xerox, seeking advice. One result was putting a product manager—someone with overall authority for a finished product, not just its parts—in charge of each new project. Quarterly departmental goals were replaced with general companywide goals. A statement of company guiding principles was printed up for employees to carry in their shirt pockets. (General Motors would later make a similar declaration and print it on similar cards—a difference being that while the Ford card is decorated simply with a Ford logo, the GM card sports the image of Chairman Smith.) Compensation for the company's top managers was altered to focus on five-year gains, instead of short-term Wall Street ticks.

Petersen further decided that managers should hold nonstructured, no-agenda meetings—*nonstructured* being as welcome a term in the normal corporate lexicon as, say, *bra-less* or *tax increase.* Richard Hartshorn, another Ford executive trainer, told me, "Caldwell wanted everything very crisp, controlled, written down in books. You'd bring these loose-leaf binders into a meeting and read from them aloud for hours. There'd be a layer of nervous executives in front, followed by the 'amen row' behind them, aides furiously flipping through the binders and nodding no matter what was said. It was incredibly stifling."

All 3,000-plus top Ford managers went through a week of deprogramming at the newly opened Ford Executive Development Center (FEDC), located on the 38th floor of a tower in the Renaissance Center in downtown Detroit. Originally Ford's elite management tier was to move there. Petersen said no, not wanting the top handful of executives physically removed from everybody else in suburban Dearborn. He gave suites over to the new development center.

Darkness of Motown's Edge

Because quotas on Japanese imports continue to shelter U.S. automakers from "basic economics," many commentators contend that the recovery of Detroit is an illusion. . . . A key fact often overlooked, however, is that new automaker profits have less to do with prices than with costs. Detroit has been cutting costs—mainly personnel costs—with a vengeance.

Total Ford employment declined 28 percent from 1978 to 1985, a reduction of nearly 143,000 people, although the company built nearly as many cars in 1985 as when attrition started. The axe has fallen about equally on management and labor. Comptroller McCammon speaks pridefully of "our 27th consecutive quarter with a reduced corporate headcount." Ford recently announced that 10,000 more white-collar workers would be let go by 1990.

Decreased labor costs lead directly to increased profits per car. In 1978 Ford earned $2.8 billion pretax on 6.6 million vehicles, or about $421 per sale. Last year the company made $3.6 billion on 5.6 million, or $643 per vehicle sold. (Improved profits from non-auto services such as financing cloud this comparison. Car prices themselves are not the explanation, as they have risen somewhat more slowly than the Consumer Price Index.)

McCammon acknowledges the cuts show Ford was featherbedded on the factory floor and in the management suite alike. . . .

While Ford shrank staff because of economic necessity, managers did not take long to discover that, as with so many big hierarchies, the place runs better with fewer people around. The quality of Ford engineering, for example, has improved during a period when nearly a quarter of the engineers have been let go. "There is no question that we are happier and more effective because we are smaller," [design chief] Telnack said.

The Case of the Downsizing Decision

Barry A. Stein

Andrew Jordan sat at his desk, absentmindedly watching a barge chug slowly upstream on the Thames. The dinner meeting he had scheduled with a select group of senior managers at Universal Products Company, Ltd. would begin in an hour. For three years, it had seemed enough to focus on the business problems of UPC's Connectors Division, and Jordan, the division's general manager, had made it the most profitable unit in the company. His success had brought him tremendous respect at UPC. Now problems not of his own making threatened to undermine all those years of hard work.

Should he support Charles Rampart's downsizing plan or fight it? And how?

Jordan sighed and looked again at the file on his desk. It contained, as he knew all too well, just four short items: (1) a prestigious merchant bank's "Advisory Bulletin" on UPC's current situation; (2) a confidential memo from his boss, Charles Rampart; (3) a memo from Sam Godwyn, Jordan's own VP for Marketing and Sales, to which was attached a copy of an anonymous e-mail message; and (4) a memo from Mary Wyatt, his finance VP. For the last time—he hoped—Jordan opened the file.

GRENVILLE
MERCHANT
BANKERS

EQUITIES
GROUP

March 25, 1991

Important Advisory Bulletin on Universal Products Company, Limited.

GMB Equities Group is downgrading its rating on Universal Products Company, Ltd. common stock from "hold" to "sell." Although analysts believe the 32-year-old electrical products company has underlying strengths, the inability of senior management to capitalize on those strengths means that, for the time being, UPC is not a sound investment.

The surprise announcement late last Friday that UPC Chairman and CEO Sir Randolph Charteris, CBE, is retiring is only the most recent in a long line of shocks at the company. Since the prominent London solicitor became chairman in 1975, the company has been plagued by slower and slower growth. Falling stock prices, defections of critical staff, and the loss of several major accounts over the past three years have made it obvious that something is seriously wrong. To make matters worse, construction costs for UPC's new global headquarters came in significantly over budget – causing much lower than expected 1990 earnings.

Sir Randolph's resignation and his immediate replacement by Mr. Charles Rampart, formerly corporate vice president for technology, constitute the clearest possible demonstration that the board of directors finally lost confidence in the company's leadership. However, Rampart is little known outside the company, and it remains unclear whether his appointment reflects a temporary accommodation that enables the board to continue with some semblance of order or whether he is genuinely seen as a leader who can resolve UPC's growing troubles.

UPC at a Glance

UPC's global operations and 38,350 employees are organised in five largely autonomous divisions – Switchgear, Connectors, Wire & Cable, Diversified Products, and ElectroTek. The first three represent the company's traditional businesses, while the latter two reflect new markets and proprietary technology. Both Connectors and Switchgear have been able to maintain strong market position and profitability – with the recent performance of Connectors Division an especially bright spot. By contrast, Wire & Cable has been the least satisfactory of the five business units. Performance at Diversified Products has been extremely erratic – at present, it is showing surprising strength – and results at ElectroTek have been unequivocally disappointing.

Management's Challenge

The investment community is waiting to see serious action from the new management on two fronts. First, the company must get control of its costs, which have mushroomed in recent years. The minor redundancies announced by the company last August have had almost no impact on this situation. It is understood that a far deeper cutback is under consideration, a step that could do much to restore confidence in the company.

Second, management have to develop a strategy for maintaining the company's significant and profitable participation in electrical connectors and switching equipment while actually creating the new sources of revenue that they promised would come from ElectroTek and Diversified Products. As for Wire & Cable, UPC must either fix it (not an easy task, given its market and competition) or eliminate it (not necessarily easier since it embodies a considerable and aging fraction of the company's fixed assets).

At Friday's close, UPC common was quoted at 63⅜, continuing a fairly steady decline from its modern high of 91½ at the end of 1988. Note that the present P/E ratio is still quite high, reflecting investors' recognition of the company's potential competitive strength. But without evidence that management are able to turn those strengths to good advantage, the stock's decline is likely to continue. In our view, UPC is at a crossroads, and much will depend on Mr. Rampart's actions.

GRENVILLE HOUSE 28 HIGH TIMBER STREET LONDON EC4V 3SB

Universal Products Company, Ltd.
Docklands, London E7A 6F8

COMPANY CONFIDENTIAL

MEMORANDUM

To: Andrew Jordan, SVP and GM, Connectors Division
From: Charles Rampart, Chairman and CEO
Date: April 3, 1991
Subject: Downsizing Program

Dear Andrew,

I promised you and your colleagues that I would think over our discussion at the Executive Operations Committee meeting this morning. Having done so, I want to confirm my decision to carry out a deep across-the-board reduction of UPC's staff.

Obviously, a decision like this is hard for everyone, and I appreciated the candor at this morning's meeting. Although there's no point in rehashing my thinking yet again, I do at least hope that we all understand – if not wholeheartedly accept – the logic of spreading this heavy burden across the entire company.

I have set as our overall objective a figure of about 11%, with fully half of that to come from the managerial and professional ranks. We therefore need to reduce the present complement at Connectors Division from 6,720 to not more than 6,000. I trust that we can begin to show specific action within two weeks and that the entire effort will be very largely concluded by June 3, two months from today. Please let me know by the end of the week how you propose to accomplish this.

Andrew, let me close on a more personal note. I understand completely how difficult this is. As you know, I've been in similar situations before, and it is a manager's worst task. But I feel we have very little choice, and the board of directors agree fully. What's more, across-the-board cuts are the only way to accomplish this necessary downsizing quickly and fairly. This is a case of "the sooner, the better." Dragging it out is in no one's interest.

In the final analysis, we owe it not only to our shareholders but also to our employees and other stakeholders as well. I am determined that those of us investing our time and our careers in UPC will have stable and satisfying employment and a fair return on our various investments.

I know I can count on your support in this difficult but critical task. I'll certainly need it.

Universal Products Company, Ltd.
Connectors Division
Docklands, London E7A 6F8

To: Andrew Jordan, SVP and GM
From: Samuel Godwyn, VP for Marketing and Sales
Date: April 5, 1991
Subject: Downsizing

You asked me to set out as starkly as possible the argument I was making at yesterday's staff meeting. Put simply, I think Charles's decision to go for across-the-board cuts is a disaster. It's a disaster for Connectors Division, certainly, but it is also a disaster for UPC as a whole. In fact, it will hobble our ability to look after the long-term, strategic growth of the company.

1) Across-the-board cuts are panic masquerading as a plan. It defies business sense to ask for equivalent cuts from our division, which under your leadership has been the most profitable of the company, and from Wire & Cable, which we all know is a basket case. Granted, some kind of downsizing is necessary. But to cut across the board is to take a blunt axe to the company when a surgeon's scalpel is called for. Not all divisions and corporate functions are created equal. Some units deserve additional investment, not retrenchment. Others probably deserve to be terminated altogether. The company needs to figure out where its going, then cut accordingly.

2) Across-the-board cuts will seriously harm our division's ability to compete. We have worked damn hard to become as lean as possible. Indeed, if the entire company controlled costs the way Connectors has done, UPC wouldn't be in this mess. Why should we be punished for our own good management? Any more cuts will hinder our capacity to build sales and improve service, which, of course, is precisely what Connectors needs to do to contribute to the revitalization that Charles says he wants to bring about. We will lose good people, have to delay product-development projects already in the pipeline, and most likely alienate our customers as well.

3) Across-the-board cuts will destroy already-poor morale. I assume you saw the rogue e-mail message that has been making the rounds (I've attached a hard copy, just in case you haven't). I know Charles got a first in maths, but damn it, this company isn't a machine. Does anyone disagree that last August's redundancies were handled poorly? If we come back to people seven months later with arbitrary across-the-board cuts, they are going to go through the roof.

There comes a time in every manager's career when he has to fight a bad decision made by his boss. Andrew, I believe you must be prepared to do that now. First, we should put together the best alternative plan we can and persuade Charles to bring it to the board. Second, you should coordinate with those senior managers you know will share this general perspective – like Tom Lewellyn in corporate strategy. Finally, we should be prepared to fight this all the way – even if that means a well-orchestrated leak or two in the financial press.

Date: 1APR91
To: sgodwyn
CC: Global division distribution list, via ConnectNet
Subject: April Fools, of course

Fool me once, shame on you. Fool me twice, shame on me! Last August, when
hundreds of undeserving folks left UPC, our very own Sir Randy said,
"I'm going to make sure this never happens again." Well guess what chaps:
Sir Randy's good intentions have paved the usual path to the usual
destination. Now we're all going to pay for it. Rampart is one of the
faceless men from corporate. Unless our Jordie's stuffed with more than
straw, we'll all be April Fools.

Universal Products Company, Ltd.
Connectors Division
Docklands, London E7A 6F8

To: Andrew Jordan, SVP and GM
From: Mary Wyatt, VP for Finance
Date: April 5, 1991
Subject: Company Downsizing

Re: your request for a memo outlining my position on the downsizing, I'm quite clear as to the path we should take in this ghastly business, and I hope you agree. There is no doubt that cuts of 11% will hurt Connectors Division badly in the short term. But it would be a terrible mistake for us to focus only on the narrow needs of the division when the future of the whole company is at stake. That is the real issue at hand.

We have to think strategically and take into account the political dimensions of this decision. Charles is a wonderful choice for chairman, although not everyone knows it yet. He's thoughtful, well-informed, completely trustworthy and honourable, and damn smart. As head of technology, he has shown that he knows how to help – and not just Connectors but everyone. UPC's problem has been a lack of systematic action and investment; Charles will give us that – once he has the board's confidence and support.

Our job is to help him get that support. It would be quite humiliating for Charles if we opposed his first decision of consequence. Granted, across-the-board cuts may not be the best way to downsize, but under the circumstances we don't have the luxury of figuring out the very best way. There is already great skepticism about UPC's future, both inside and outside the company. Charles has got to act and act fast.

As I said at the staff meeting yesterday, I'm all for fighting bad decisions. But I also believe it's important to pick your fights intelligently. Mounting some kind of internal rebellion right now is a notoriously bad bet. It's likely to lead us into a morass of interdivisional and interfunctional rivalries that will take years to sort out. After all, other division heads can argue that they've been controlling costs too and making significant investments that just haven't paid off yet. Who's to say that cuts in their shops would be better for the business than cuts in ours?

I'd much rather support Charles on this decision, however painful that may prove to be, in order to buy the political goodwill to win other struggles further down the road. Surely, you can read his intentions between the lines. If you back Charles strongly now, we'll be at the top of the list when it comes time for UPC to make internal investments in the future. We'll have a good chance to be a new focus for growth. Indeed, we might even end up gaining staff.

This may sound harsh, but it's the only realistic way to think of the situation: we're not laying off 11% of our staff. We are investing in the future credibility and effectiveness of our new chairman.

Three experts who have dealt with corporate restructuring address these questions.

1. DAVID ENFIELD, *chairman and managing director of Colgate-Palmolive Limited, U.K.*:

Andrew Jordan's decision is not whether to support the cuts but *how* to make them. The key issue here is UPC's need to restore itself to financial health and to create a business strategy for its future. Any company considering downsizing as a solution to its strategic concerns should first think through what its strategic concerns are and then fit downsizing into that context.

Downsizing is a much needed first step for UPC on the road to preserving its independent status and getting back to financial health. The company is in imminent danger of losing its independence. The stock has already declined by one third in the past year. Unless the price is stabilized quickly and performance reversed, UPC will be targeted for acquisition. The consequences of inaction would be far more draconian than an 11% cut in staff. However, Jordan must make the moves in a manner that drives home to all employees the logic behind them—that without these moves UPC will cease to be an independent entity.

As a manager, Jordan has three immediate tasks. He must quickly make it clear that he supports the new chairman's decision and that the real issue is the survival of UPC. Second, he must develop a specific plan to reduce his staff by 11% and formulate a revised business strategy to maintain the health of his division. Finally, he must devise a way to minimize the impact on the morale of those remaining as well as those being let go.

Jordan's easiest step will be justifying his support for Rampart's decision. By explaining how the investment community perceives UPC and sensitizing his division to the threat posed to the company, Jordan will provide a backdrop for the immediate moves. He need not apologize that the successful Connectors Division has to suffer, since this is an external threat to the company at large with little regard to individual units.

The next step—identifying specific redundancies—is more difficult. As the memos from Godwyn and Wyatt indicate, his managers have strongly divergent views. Jordan will first need to gain their individual support for what is to happen and then be prepared to start the cuts at this level if his direct reports are not prepared to match his degree of commitment. Jordan and his team will then need to review his division's business priorities, focusing on the trends in business practice among his customers and major competition. They should challenge the very nature of the division's manner of doing business, with a view to creative change. Finally, recommendations for change, both internally and those that affect the division's relationship with corporate headquarters, should be communicated to Rampart.

However, Jordan should not automatically demand an equal 11% cut in each of his departments. Rampart may have had his political reasons for this evenhandedness, but from a business point of view, the move is a mistake. After all, Rampart is no stranger to UPC and probably could have better tailored an overall 11% cut to the strengths and weaknesses of the company. Jordan would be better advised to be more selective if he is to remain true to the needs of his own division.

The third step—the redundancy strategy—is both easy and difficult. A combination of reasonably generous redundancy payments, counseling, and outplacement services should ease the pain of those being let go. It is more difficult to retain the loyalty and morale of those remaining and to successfully install the changes in working practice and responsibilities that will inevitably be required. Jordan's biggest challenge will be to rally his remaining people together, focus them on the business, and provide them with a sense that UPC and Connectors Division is getting through its problems and remains a productive and stimulating place to work.

Jordan also needs to work on the broader issue of UPC's return to health. He could start by raising several important questions at the dinner meeting with the select group of senior UPC managers. First of all, Jordan should probe just how much autonomy continues to be affordable for each of the five divisions. Considerable duplication probably exists in traditionally overstaffed areas such as administrative and support functions. These resources could even be shared and rationalized. Obviously this will be a highly sensitive subject involving past history, turf, and culture, but Jordan is as well placed as any to broach the issue and if necessary to pursue it with Rampart. Truthfully examining every aspect of the company for waste could lead to savings of more than 11%.

Yet staff costs are only one element of expense. UPC needs to look critically at controlling projected expenses in all its divisions. Jordan must also take a lead in addressing cost—as a start, by pointing out the need for clear control illustrated by the overbudget construction of the new headquarters.

Finally, of course, Rampart and his senior management need to develop and agree on UPC's future overall business strategy. This clearly cannot be done overnight. Jordan, as a member of senior management, has a right to ask Rampart what his plans are, and to enlist the dinner group as an initial forum to commence the development of ideas and suggestions to help Rampart in this critical task. Downsizing alone is not the answer to UPC's problem but only the first step in a bigger process.

2. Emmanuel Kampouris, *president and CEO of American Standard Inc., a leading supplier of air-conditioning, heating, and plumbing equipment to the construction industry:*

Andrew Jordan has his work cut out for him. He must convince Rampart to develop a broader vision of his company and not just make generic cuts in the workforce. Jordan should agree to personnel reductions only under the condition that Rampart present these moves as a prelude to a new direction at UPC, one where the company has a clearly defined mission and an organizational structure consistent with its new philosophy.

Across-the-board layoffs are the worst way to reduce costs. Cutting by percentage is a crude and ineffective short-term solution to a deep-rooted problem. It's instant gratification that does nothing to fundamentally remedy the situation. After a downsizing action, temporary employees are often brought in to work in positions left vacant by the laid-off personnel. Jordan will find that in no time he will be fighting the issue of excess personnel once again if these replacements become permanent. The only course at UPC is to find a way to eliminate excess staff permanently.

The real solution here is to rationalize the work, not the workers, and to do so in a manner that prevents the problem from creeping back. Successful companies reduce costs by reducing useless layers of work rather than blindly cutting people.

This process is not easy. Management must begin by stripping away everything in the company that is not adding value. They must, in a sense, go right to ground zero by scrutinizing the work load and reducing it to the essentials. Rampart must eliminate all middle managers that exist only as power brokers and impediments to communication. He should find where the power structure of the organization prevents workers at every level from taking responsibility. Throughout the company, Rampart must undo bureaucracy.

Once UPC has eliminated the nonessential work load, it can rebuild the organization using only those people necessary. In the long run, this could result in *more* than an 11% reduction in staff. If UPC reduces the work load intelligently, the smaller workforce will be asked to do less—not more.

By making these moves, Rampart will create something far more useful than a smaller company: a more responsive and efficient company. In fact, the corporation will be free of the communication roadblocks endemic to overstaffing and middle management.

Rampart should also devise a costs goal—not a personnel target. Consistent with a philosophy of distributing responsibility lower and lower in the organization, Rampart should let everyone reduce costs the way they see fit. As part of his broader strategy, however, Rampart may set the timetable for these moves.

Creating a leaner, more responsive organization is just one step of an overall philosophy. Once Rampart creates a delayered, responsive company with open lines of communication and no middle management, the new organizational mind-set will turn its concern from how it is structured to what is important to its customers.

3. ROALD NOMME, *senior vice president for organization development at Norsk Data Group, a Norwegian computer company based in Oslo:*

To decide that downsizing is necessary is the easy part. Far more difficult is knowing how to implement a downsizing so that it really accomplishes the objective of revitalizing the company. Depending on how it is carried out, downsizing can strengthen employee morale or destroy it. It can be a solution to a company's problems or a serious new problem in its own right.

Unfortunately, UPC's Charles Rampart is going about it in the worst possible way. Granted, UPC has serious problems, and the impatience in the financial community is an important danger sign. But it is no reason to rush through across-the-board cuts that are completely disconnected from any long-term strategic vision. In this respect, Connectors Division marketing vice president Samuel Godwyn is right: across-the-board cuts are "panic masquerading as a plan."

Rampart's overall approach to change is also faulty. His strategy is simply to order people to change. He decides on cuts across-the-board, presents his decision at a morning meeting, then sends his direct reports a rather cursory memo confirming his decision and asking their support. What Rampart fails to grasp is that gaining his top managers' agreement to the downsizing plan is not enough. He must also secure their "alignment"—their active conviction that the proposed changes not only are necessary but will prove effective. Such a haphazard and cavalier approach to change is likely to lead to disaster. Loyal managers like Jordan may go along grudgingly with Rampart's decision but without the internal commitment necessary to make the downsizing work.

Andrew Jordan has to persuade Rampart to rethink his downsizing decision. First, he should tell Rampart that this is not the type of decision that can be presented at a half-day meeting and then discussed in memos. Instead of spending two to three months figuring out how to cut 11% of the work force across-the-board, UPC managers should take that time to struggle with the difficult strategic issues facing the company.

To begin this process, Rampart and his entire top-management team have to get together, face-to-face, over one or even a number of days to thrash out a common view of the company's strategic situation and options. What are the long-term prospects of the company's various businesses? What should the company do about Wire & Cable? How should UPC target the burden of cost reductions? And how should the company handle the all-important communications issues in order to convince employees of the necessity of the decisions made? The end result of this exercise should be a new strategic direction that includes not only cuts but also new investments.

Jordan should also explain to Rampart that the best way to bring about change is to let the employees actively participate in it. That way, they develop insight into the reasons why change is necessary. Therefore, once corporate management crafts a new strategic vision, Rampart should invite UPC employees to take part in developing the methods for its implementation. Such an approach may be more time-consuming, but it leads to far more effective and long-lasting changes—not the least because participation tends to strengthen employee morale.

Once this strategic vision and participatory change process is in place, the organizational context will exist for Jordan to take a fresh look at his own division. It may well be that his business can prosper and become considerably more profitable, even in the short run, if he plans for immediate cost reductions. After all, most organizations still have considerable slack, no matter how lean and efficient they think they are. What's more, the fact that the whole UPC group is introducing stronger measures may result in improved productivity for Connectors.

Finally, Jordan has to work with his own management team to get them to understand the need for hard measures. Once again, the key is face-to-face interaction that will allow managers to confront and resolve the negative feelings and the conflicts inevitable in downsizing situations. In this way, Jordan's direct reports can also develop a shared picture of the current situation and the company's future potential.

Chapter 9

Makeover Through Takeover: Control Change

Introductory Notes

Who would have imagined that esoteric questions of corporate finance would become front-page news in many parts of North America and Europe? Change in control—in ownership, governance mechanism, and/or financial covenants that were once the stuff of internal power and politics but are of little interest to the outside world—has emerged in recent years as one of the potentially most powerful and controversial forms of change.

The interest in this form of change derives not from the mere replacement of one set of owners with another, or from the substitution of one form of financing with another. The potency comes from the occasion control change presents for quickly and urgently rethinking every aspect of the organization, including its identity and coordination—its strategy, structure, and culture. The drama comes from the clash between two kinds of actors: aggressive, analytic entrepreneurs with no sentimental attachment to organizational traditions, valuing the organization only as a package of assets, and unafraid to make sweeping transformations, and established (some would say "entrenched") managers and employees who want the organization to continue, for whom survival of the entity they have known and from which they derive their livelihood is the preeminent goal.

The events recounted in "Lucky Stores: Restructuring to Survive the Takeover Threat" are indeed dramatic. The Lucky case illustrates the type of organizational change that became commonplace in the 1980s as the pace of heated merger and acquisition activity increased within the financial community. Troubled companies were vulnerable to raiders, although not all of them succumbed. Lucky Stores erected a successful defense against the raider Asher Edelman, transforming itself in the process. This sort of revolutionary change is:

1. Drastic and of enormous magnitude
2. Executed quickly, with little room for miscalculation
3. A response to a clearly identifiable and imminent threat to the organization's very existence

These three characteristics significantly influenced the decisions that contributed to Lucky's defense strategy, the execution of that strategy, and its impact on the organization and its members.

Several change management issues arise in acute form during a control battle that are always part of the political agenda for leaders: how to mobilize resources (and stakeholders) to win the battle for support; how to carry out sufficient restructuring to ensure a better position and market value for the company in order to have benefits to distribute to stakeholders; how to preserve ongoing operations while dealing with a crisis. Crisis management requires extraordinary actions, and it provokes extraordinary reactions. We see the complex interplay of emotions and events that characterize matters of power and politics—the actions of CEO Lillie and raider Edelman, the interests of each lead actor, as they struggle for constituency support. Each said they were operating for the larger good, but each had his or her own personal stake in the outcome. For Lillie, the prize was keeping his job, with all of the privileges and status associated with that. For Edelman, the goal was financial gain. In microcosm Lillie versus Edelman mirrored employee versus shareholder constituencies.

The Lucky portrait raises important questions about the organizational "makeover" that takeovers and their threats engender. Was Lucky "lucky" to be alive? Was Edelman a help or a hindrance? Did he wreak more havoc than good? Would Lillie have acted as quickly without Edelman? As effectively? More effectively? Can leaders make appropriate long-term decisions while under the gun of a crisis? Or, as Edelman argued, did management "destroy the company" just to keep him out? Two years after the events described in this article, Lucky was successfully taken over by American Stores.

Are corporate raiders indeed consummate agents for change for corporations? Or are they a costly distraction forcing changes to be made too hastily, with only a short-term financial orientation?

"Lessons from a Middle Market LBO: The Case of O.M. Scott" provides a different example of the impact on an organization of changes in control. In 1986, the managers of O.M. Scott, then a division of the conglomerate ITT, bought out the company with the help of a leading leveraged buyout (LBO) firm, Clayton & Dubilier. This radical change in financial structure and concentration of equity ownership resulted in a dramatic improvement in Scott's operating performance.

The authors attribute this improvement to new incentives for Scott's manager-owners as well as the disciplinary force of debt. They show the relationship between form of ownership and internal decisions about products and production. In addition, a new governance structure ensured that management was more closely monitored, in some respects, yet at the same time freer from bureaucratic interference (and the overhead costs entailed) than it was under ITT parentage. The relationship of the LBO firm, C&D, to Scott was one of clear goal-setting and help when needed; Scott's management was then left alone to make operating decisions. This new structure—in a smaller company owned by its managers—appears to have enabled them to make different and better decisions than under ITT rule.

The O.M. Scott portrait offers an unusually detailed look from inside at the incentive system and governance mechanism put in place after an LBO—indeed, the authors would say, an almost inevitable result of the change in control. But, of course, managers still have to manage well despite the formal ownership of the company. Control changes by themselves do not create appropriate and effective product-market strategies or forms of coordination; they merely readjust the incentives.

Lucky Stores

Restructuring to Survive the Takeover Threat

Lisa Richardson and Alistair Williamson

In the fall of 1986, Lucky Stores, one of America's largest retailers with 1985 sales of $9.3 billion, fell prey to a hostile takeover attempt by New York corporate raider Asher Edelman. Eight months later, after a hurried, massive restructuring and a protracted legal battle, the company negotiated a standstill agreement with Edelman. By paying $2.8 million to cover legal expenses incurred in the takeover attempt, Edelman agreed not to attempt a future takeover of Lucky for at least three years. The challenge posed by the New York arbitraguer changed the perspective of Lucky Stores' top executives about how its business should be run.

Even though Lucky Stores ended up selling four of its five operating units to fend off Edelman, shrinking dramatically from its high of $2.3 billion in assets and operating 582 stores in May 1987 as compared to 1,460 stores in May 1986, the company regained its footing quickly enough to emerge as a stronger force in the marketplace. Having turned in three consecutive quarters of record operating performance, Lucky management agreed that its decision to concentrate on the food retailing business had strengthened the company, substantially increased shareholder value, and moved from being a disappointment to many Wall Street investors to a company at which they were taking a fresh look.

With the organization's survival at stake, Lucky's management examined how the company got into such a vulnerable position, and concentrated on developing strategies to ensure that it would not

happen again. In this process, the board, top management, and outside professionals hired by the organization to assist in the restructuring redesigned Lucky's portfolio and focused its attention solely on the retail food business. Within six months of Edelman's takeover attempt, the company was in only one of the many businesses in which it had formerly engaged.

History: 1930 to 1984

Since 1930, Lucky Stores, Inc., had successfully grown through expansion and acquisition. Charles L. Crouch, the founder, began by buying six California Piggly Wiggly grocery stores on the San Mateo peninsula and converting them into "Lucky Stores." Soon after, Crouch acquired the bankrupt Peninsula Stores Company and initiated an expansion program that brought financial success to the 16-store chain by 1947.

Crouch's departure in 1947 temporarily stunted the pace of Lucky's expansion. However, the 1955 appointment of Fred A. Ferraggiaro, retired chairman of the Bank of America, heralded a new era of growth based upon an active acquisition strategy. Stores in Sacramento, Los Angeles, and San Diego became part of the Lucky network, making the company a statewide chain by 1956.

Acquisition of the San Diego–based Food Basket stores brought the next leader committed to helping Lucky expand. Food Basket founder Gerald A. Awes's 11-year administration adroitly moved Lucky Stores into the modern era of national supermarket chains and ushered in an era of diversification.

Awes's first major acquisition was the two-store Gemco chain in 1962, which he changed from a jewelry company, Gem Co., to a large chain of membership general merchandise stores. Customers paid $1 for a lifetime membership, which gave them access to low-price general merchandise goods and groceries. By 1986, Gemco consisted of 80 department stores located mainly in California, with a few stores in Nevada and Arizona.

Lucky successfully differentiated itself from its competitors by pricing all products almost 3% below others', rather than just selecting a handful of products for weekly promotion. The reduced margin enabled Lucky to reduce its advertising and promotion budgets significantly, simultaneously increasing centralization, including a manual of procedures that ensured that individual store managers had little input into product pricing decisions.

In 1972, S. Donley Ritchie became CEO and immediately initiated an acquisition spree into nonfood retailing. Lucky bought restaurants, drugstores, family department stores, fabric stores, automotive supply stores, and women's apparel stores; it opened its own specialty sporting goods and discount department stores. By 1980, Lucky was the 8th largest retailer in the United States, operating over 1,500 stores in a broad range of retail trades, as the chart below demonstrates.

Food Stores:	Lucky, Eagle, Food Basket, Kash N Karry
Department Stores:	Gemco, Memco (in DC/ MD/ VA)
Specialty Stores:	Pic-A-Dilly, It's-A-Dilly, L&G, Yellow Front
Fabric Stores:	Hancock, Fabric Warehouse
Automotive Stores:	Kragan, Dorman's, Checker
Restaurant Chains:	Sirloin Stockade, Fred Gang's, Cinders

Although Lucky's management touted the virtues of its diversification to shareholders, saying in the 1981 Annual Report, "Geographic and store-type diversification have substantially reduced the Company's vulnerability to difficult economic or competitive conditions in a specific region of the country or retail business segment," there were also signs of strain. In 1982, after four years of deteriorating performance, Ritchie announced, "We realized we just can't do everything well." At the peak in 1979, Lucky earned $98 million on $5.8 billion in sales; in 1982 it earned only $92.2 million on $8 billion in sales.

After a period of indiscriminate acquisition, top executives at Lucky were well aware of the difficulties involved in managing an overly diverse portfolio of stores, recognizing the need to simplify the company and limit diversification. If the business did not fit (restaurant, apparel), was too small (drugstores, sporting goods, Florida service stations), or was too geographically diverse to support warehousing and distribution operations, Lucky sold it.

Nevertheless, Lucky management believe diversification could be a successful strategy as long as it was monitored well and the companies conformed to the distribution system that made the grocery segment, the foundation of the company, so successful. For example, in 1982, specialty retailing contributed 27% of Lucky Stores' total profits on only 8.5% of sales. A 1983 reformulation of corporate strategy resulted in the decision to retain the specialty retailing division and other high-margin stores.

Lucky management continued its housecleaning through 1984. Because the bulk of specialty retailing profits came from the automotive segment and from the fabric segment, not from apparel, management unloaded the women's apparel businesses It's-A-Dilly and Pic-A-Dilly in August. Despite all these efforts to revitalize the company through divestiture, Lucky's 1984 stock prices of $1.84 a share fell 10% below 1983. Moreover, California disrupted the fourth-quarter performance of over half of Lucky's

Gemco stores, causing consternation to company executives who were counting on strong holiday sales, and investment in merchandising systems at Gemco burdened its operations and compounded its financial difficulties.

John Lillie's Arrival

New leadership, in the person of John Lillie, arrived in 1985, becoming CEO soon afterward. Lillie promptly sold 17 Chicago-area Eagle supermarkets and 77 retail auto parts stores (a surprise to many considering the company had just built 76 auto parts stores two years earlier). Nevertheless, Lucky Stores' economic troubles increased as an eight-week fourth-quarter supermarket strike paralyzed Gemco once again; Gemco's pretax earnings continued to fall even as sales grew. The outlook did not look good for Lucky Stores. A Dun & Bradstreet credit report attributed decreased profits in 1985 to the strike and to larger expenditures for store improvements, which were part of a campaign to reposition the company's business.

By November of 1985, Lucky management was well aware of the company's vulnerability to a takeover attempt. After poor financial performance in the first two quarters of 1986 in which earnings decreased by 25% from 1985, the investment community exerted considerable pressure on Lucky management. Many claimed Lucky Stores was a prime candidate for an LBO, a hostile takeover, or a corporate restructuring because of its undervalued real estate holdings and long-term leases. The Wall Street firm of Wood Gundy issued a report in September 1986 which further fueled public speculation about an imminent takeover. The firm asserted that although "fundamentals point to a stock price of $18 to $20 . . . our breakup value for Lucky is $37 to $40 per share." Consensus had it that if Lucky sold its specialty stores, it would emerge as "a cleaner company with a lot less negatives."

Following a takeover attempt in the summer of 1986 by the Haft family's Dart Group on rival Safeway stores, Lucky's board heeded the advice of its banker, Goldman Sachs, and thoroughly investigated a "shareholders' rights" plan (that is, a takeover defense plan). At an August 7 board meeting, five independent directors formed a special takeover committee to review the suggested plan. On August 24, 1986, the board approved the adoption of the shareholders' rights plan. One of the provisions of this plan limited the voting rights of holders whose stake exceeded 10%. Rather than having one vote for every share owned, each stakeholders' share in excess of 10% would have $\frac{1}{100}$ of a vote. Other provisions also made a hostile takeover more difficult. They included staggered terms for directors, elimination of cumulative voting for directors, and requiring an 80% vote rather than a 50% majority in order to change the company bylaws. These and other moves were not enough to deter Asher Edelman.

The Raider's Entrance

On September 17, Edelman informed Goldman Sachs that he held 3% of Lucky Stores' common shares and would very likely purchase more. Shortly after, Edelman almost doubled his Lucky Stores holdings and formulated several well-defined objectives for the undervalued retail chain. He hoped to realize value from the acquisition by accomplishing three goals:

1. Increasing ROA by selling off Gemco, a money loser that had most of its value in its real estate and leasehold interests
2. Increasing the company's low margins by raising the level of products sold in the supermarket division or adding some specialty products
3. Increasing Lucky's P/E ratio by making it a regional supermarket business. This required unloading all underpriced specialty businesses.

Although Edelman did not issue a firm tender offer, he claimed later that he was serious about acquiring Lucky Stores and would have done so had Lucky management not worked out such a formidable defense.

After recovering from the initial shock of Edelman's proposal, John Lillie and the board determined how they would defend the company from the takeover threat. The board was well aware that one of the best defenses would be stellar financial performance, so company leadership tried to keep "business as usual" despite Edelman's threatening common share offer. Only three executives left their regular posts in order to respond to the takeover issue. While chairman John Lillie, chief financial officer Edward Grubb, and secretary and counsel Chris McLain focused exclusive attention on Edelman's bid, president Larry Del Santo assumed full responsibility for running the business. Aside from these three individuals, no one else from Lucky's top management involved themselves in the defense process.

In the week that followed, the executive management team worked with the special board committee to evaluate alternative strategies. In September, Lucky's top management announced that the most desirable alternative for the company was a restructuring which would sell or spin off all nonfood operations and would result in an immediate distribution of the proceeds to shareholders.

Events moved quickly thereafter.

Oct 2	Board authorized sales of Gemco chain
Oct 5	Board deemed Edelman's offer of $35 per share inadequate
Oct 9	Board finalized Gemco sale and arranged $450 million stock repurchase plan
Oct 14	Edelman proposed new price of $37 per share
Oct 17	Board and Edelman debated over magnitude of repurchase
Oct 22	Board rejected $37 proposal and considered $700 million repurchase plan
Oct 23	Board challenged Edelman over repurchase size and Edelman withdrew proposal
Oct 30	Board discussed restructuring issues with Edelman which included tax law changes and the need to accomplish restructuring in 1986
Nov 6	Board approved comprehensive restructuring plan which included reincorporation in Delaware and $575 million repurchase plan
Nov 7	Board announced restructuring terms.

Here is what that meant to the major affected units.

The Dayton Hudson Corporation, a Minneapolis-based diversified retail conglomerate, identified itself early as an interested buyer of Lucky's Gemco stores. Dayton Hudson owned Target Stores, a chain in direct competition with Gemco stores, and wanted to acquire Gemco's real estate holdings and store locations. It took a little time to disassemble Gemco after Lucky agreed to sell 76 of the 80 stores. Within 12 days, Lucky sold off all of Gemco inventory, closed the doors of 56 food departments to make retail space available for general merchandise liquidators, and initiated an intensive campaign geared to attract Gemco shoppers to Lucky food stores.

In December, Lucky sold the profitable Checker and Kragen auto part chains for $155 million in cash to Northern Pacific Corporation, a privately held real estate development and retailing company that included Schucks, another auto parts chain.

Despite the fact that the sale of Yellow Front Stores was the smallest transaction and had been approved by the board well before the appearance of Asher Edelman, it proved the most difficult deal of all to complete. Not until April 22, 1987, did Lucky sell Yellow Front to Kenmore, a private company controlled by Daniel J. Sullivan. Proceeds of the sale totaled $50 million, for a net gain of about $15 million.

Lucky Stores spun off the Hancock Textile division to shareholders in mid-1987 by distributing all Hancock stock on a one-for-three basis to Lucky shareholders as a special one-time dividend. For complex reasons, this required the company to reincorporate in Delaware, where corporate law permitted large distributions of capital to shareholders and made it harder to file lawsuits against directors. This was done, and the Hancock shares were distributed and traded separately on the New York Stock Exchange.

Asher Edelman, who by that time controlled over 6% of Lucky shares, was outraged over the tactics management used to fend him off, and he accused Lucky's board of "destroying the company to keep me out." Edelman viewed the Gemco sale glumly, believing Lillie sold it too cheaply and at too high a human cost. He also maintained that he would have completed the sale on a tax-free basis, which would have saved between $100 and $200 million, and would have ensured the reemployment of at least 80% of the 14,000 Gemco workers. (Edelman's claim that he would have negotiated a job-saving sale was inconsistent with his past behavior. He had never done so in the past. For example, when he bought Data Point in 1985, he put more than 3,000 people—nearly half of the workforce—out of work.)

When Schuck's bought Checker and Kragen Auto Parts, Lucky's executive vice president responsible for the chain became the senior vice president of finance for the *new* chain, Checker Schuck's Kragen (CSK). Reflecting upon the merger, he mentioned that while Schuck's had only 90 stores to Checker's and Kragen's combined 385, the companies had a good management fit. The strategic goals Checker and Kragen already had in place continued; CSK adopted a program that called for up to 100 new stores per year over the next five years, as well as a plan to retrofit 80% of the existing stores. The companies also fitted well in terms of store placement; only a handful of markets were served by both companies. Profits were up 60% for the first half of 1987.

Since Hancock Textile Company's stock was spun off to the shareholders as an independently managed and publicly traded company in April of 1987, its fortunes have grown. An apocryphal tale is circulating that in the corporate offices there hang portraits of two highly praised and revered men: Mr. Hancock, the founder of the chain, and Asher Edelman, the man responsible for the chain's autonomy and recent sound financial success.

Asher Edelman was not quite as well thought of by former employees of Gemco. Gemco's union raised money during the preclosing days by selling baseball caps with an insignia on the front showing a wood screw followed by the word "Edelman." Nevertheless, not all employees kept their hostility aimed at Edelman. Reported a former Gemco assistant manager:

> I have only been in a Lucky's one time since the closing. It so happens that the closest grocery store to my house is a Lucky's and I was going out of my way to go anywhere but Lucky. A friend that I was talking to felt the same way. Kind of like you see a Lucky's truck go by and you groan. They're everywhere. There is a feeling that management should have saved us. It was just a matter of time until we would have been very profitable.

The rapid-fire unfolding of events represented only the surface aspect of Lucky's restructuring program. Management, well aware of employees' concern and anger, was preparing them for the consequences of closing Gemco. One Gemco union official said, "We're not just going to lay down and be destroyed. The workers have a right to expect that when they've given . . . their blood and their sweat to the company, they should continue to have employment." Nevertheless, many employees did lose their jobs. Controversy and tension between management and workers and among employees further divided the already splintered organization. For instance:

- All Gemco food service employees were Lucky employees and could expect employment within Lucky, but all nonfood employees were laid off. In fact, within less than a year after Gemco's closing, nearly every interested ex-Gemco employee was working in Lucky's.
- Most Gemco employees were part of either the Northern or the Southern Food division; yet, whereas the Northern Food Division's labor contract protected employees with seniority, the Southern Food Division's labor contract provided little protection.
- In the Northern Food Division, seniority provisions meant that 24 Gemco food managers had to be absorbed into Lucky. When the combined list of Lucky and Gemco food managers was ranked according to seniority and qualifications, the weakest managers ended up being Lucky Stores employees; 24 Lucky managers had to step back and become assistant managers.

The operating differences between the Northern and the Southern food divisions negatively affected employee morale during the Gemco shutdown phase. As employees became aware that one division was taking steps while the other was not, doubts arose and tensions multiplied. Despite Lillie's regular press releases and publicly posted employee memos, the seemingly inconsistent information confused and frightened people. Many felt betrayed and stopped paying attention to what the company was telling them.

While the confused food employees anxiously wondered about the length and number of layoffs, they at least had the consoling prospect of a job within Lucky. The general merchandise employees had no such assurance and recognized that even if they were rehired by Target, the Dayton Hudson chain taking over former Gemco sites, they would take a considerable pay cut. Sam Parker, former Gemco CEO, noted:

> The rate for a person working as a retail clerk was far beyond the marketplace for general merchandise clerks. Consequently, it was damned near impossible for them to go out and replace their earnings by taking a job at the same skill level. They were used to a compensation that was like a supermarket's and not a general merchandiser's.

During the fall of 1986, gaps widened between Northern and Southern food division employees, between Gemco food and nonfood personnel, and between Gemco and Lucky workers. To Gemco employees, the store had always seemed to be two stores under one roof. A former Gemco food manager who was placed in a Lucky store reported:

> At Gemco it was the grocery department and "the other side." We never went out of the grocery department. The variety side was the one losing all the money. It was taking our store away. The two sides were run with different sets of policies and each side reported to a different set of management. We had the same union, but different contracts. It was like there was a line: they didn't cross it and we didn't cross it.

Gemco food employees complained that the Gemco variety side had been milking Lucky for years and blamed Lucky's top management for allowing that to happen and for putting their jobs in jeopardy.

Despite these tensions, executives reported that "managers were working 80 hour weeks and people down in the ranks of the organization were working their tails off." Although bonuses based on a percentage of the money brought in during liquidation provided some incentive for managers to liquidate their own careers (one assistant manager received a $14,000 bonus on top of her severance package), many employees were deeply committed to Gemco—their only place of employment for 20 years. A long-time employee expressed common feelings about the Gemco closing this way:

> On the very last day we shut down before going into liquidation, my store manager and two assistants went to lock the door. It was some kind of ceremonial thing and the store manager started to cry. Then the other manager started to cry too. I didn't want to go near them because both of them were bawling—grown men hanging onto each other.

CEO Parker even noted cases in which customers were as saddened by the closing as employees were. He stated, "Every time I went into a store I was overwhelmed with the dedication of people, and very surprised at the customers—actually crying in the store, hugging the management people."

Overall, though top management can say, "The company survived and is strong and therefore we succeeded," they failed to preserve Lucky Stores' empire and its reputation as an admired employer. For those at the operating levels who were laid off, it was a humiliating experience; one man said, "For me it was really degrading . . . it makes you question your manhood, not being able to provide for your family." Even for those who weren't laid off, the restructuring did not bring welcome change. A warehouse worker said, "We were forced into jobs we didn't want to do. There's been a lot of tension and real aggressive attitudes. Everyone's being pushed around by management and they take it out on each other."

John Lillie himself was proud of the results of restructuring and believed this pride was shared by every Lucky employee. He noted, "People are proud of what happened in our restructuring. They feel they won—and because we did the right things—and did them well. It was an effort of 60,000, not 30 or 40." Regarding the layoffs, he commented, "We made an enormous effort to supply outplacement services for our people. We showed great sensitivity, which is consistent with our values—we value people highly."

For example, Northern Food Division President Dick Goodspeed said, "Although one of the toughest days of my life was when I had to tell 1,100 people they were out of work, when the nonfood people went away, management focused on running our core business—food. Lucky's a much stronger company, much more clearly focused than ever before." Northern Food Division District Manager Steve Fitzpatrick also evaluated the restructuring positively, commenting, "The sale of Gemco was a success and Lucky Stores picked up more than 40% of their business. We didn't erode; we didn't have to lay off. When something happens you have to act swiftly. There were scares but you couldn't help that."

Sam Parker noted that in recent years many Gemco employees had been unhappy and frustrated over management's abortive attempts to revive the troubled chain. As he pointed out,

> They needed someone to blame for the problem . . . when everyone is essentially caught up in the process it's amazing how people respond to it; the general picture was that we're all in the same boat together. Everybody felt to some extent like a victim of circumstance—they were able to depersonalize and say "we're just a victim of another of these Wall Street maneuvers." Asher gave Lucky a rationale for doing what they might have done anyway, and allowed people to focus their negatives on something outside

> the business. It therefore meant that they worked hard at the liquidation rather than saying "screw it, why should I do anything?"

Nevertheless, Parker noted that while many people in the stores worked hard during the liquidation period, there was "a group of people who immediately began to focus on their next career—mentally and physically resigning from the business, still on the payroll, but focusing on other things." This group of dissatisfied employees included "well over half of the officers of the business."

Lucky executives argued that Edelman merely forced their hand and served as a catalyst for responsive action to already acknowledged problems. In late September, the *New York Times* commented, "Restructuring is not just a novel idea at Lucky Stores, where food stores are opened and closed with great regularity. Over the last few years the company has disposed of 550 stores while opening 520 others. And during this period it withdrew altogether from the restaurant business." Evidently, before Edelman challenged Lucky management, other types of restructuring had been successfully executed. What Edelman did do, according to CFO Edward Grubb, was "bring us into the full realization that it had to be now rather than later." Further, Lillie's appointment in the early 1980s may have been part of a long-range plan for corporate restructuring; he was the first president who had no prior history with the company and who was experienced with takeover attempts, a credential which made him well suited to manage a drastic corporate restructuring.

Edelman's takeover threat can be perceived as facilitating the company's restructuring and accelerating the speed with which it could implement its plans. By challenging top executives to improve the company's financial performance or lose control of the company, Edelman became a scapegoat for unpopular board decisions. One executive at Lucky Stores said, "The press hit us hard on laying off 14,000 people, but heck, it was going to happen anyway—it made it easier for us to do it." Note the following "Letter to the Editor":

> As you know, many articles have been written and published in your newspaper regarding the buyout threat at Lucky Stores and the closing of Gemco. We, the employees of Lucky Stores, would like to express our opinion on how we will be affected by this.
>
> True, legally, Asher B. Edelman is within his rights to attempt a buyout, but morally, he is beyond comprehension.
>
> What he is attempting to do eventually will affect the livelihood of close to 68,000 people, and place many in the unemployment lines. This comes at a time when unemployment is already too high, and with the holiday season upon us, many families will not have much to be thankful for if he is allowed to continue.

It is not right that one man can destroy the financial security of so many people.

We feel the public may not know, and has the right to know, that Lucky Stores and Gemco personnel are not the only people who will eventually feel great financial losses at the hands of Edelman. Others include our suppliers; the small independents that we do business with (and their families); the other businesses within the shopping centers where a Gemco store once brought in the customers, and the customer who shops at Lucky's.

Thousands of people will suffer if this takeover is completed. Edelman has stated that he intends to liquidate the southern region of Lucky/Gemco (he has already forced closure of Gemco), merely for the purpose of profit, with no remorse for what happens to the families involved. We are not talking about a piece of paper showing ownership—we are talking financial disaster for thousands.

We feel like a member of our family has just been told they are terminally ill—Lucky Stores, in our opinion, is not terminally ill. We can, and will, survive if the stockholders question Edelman's motives. We all have to work to survive.

Signed by Maggie Weber and 250
other Lucky and Gemco employees

On the other hand, here is one response to that letter:

In an October 26 letter by Maggie Weber and 250 disgruntled employees of Gemco, financier Asher B. Edelman was faulted for threatening to make a tender offer for the purchase of Lucky Stores, Gemco's parent corporation.

Weber and others fail to find any blame with the current management of Lucky for allowing the company to fall into such disrepair that it has become worth more dead than as a surviving entity.

They also fail to realize that current Lucky officers, in order to preserve their own jobs, ordered the liquidation of Gemco stores rather than allow the company to be taken over by Edelman.

But most of all, they do not see that the ultimate reason for the closure of Gemco is that the employees, along with the union representing them, have insisted on wages far beyond what discount stores can sustain.

If Edelman had not made an offer for Lucky, inevitably it would have died a natural death, suffering from the same symptoms that have caused the demise of W.T. Grant, The Akron, White Front, FedMart, and Zoyds all within the past decade.

Terry R. Reiter
Chief Executive
California Digital Inc.

Lessons from a Middle Market LBO

The Case of O.M. Scott

George P. Baker and Karen H. Wruck

In 1986 The O.M. Scott & Sons Company, the largest producer of lawn care products in the U.S., was sold by the ITT Corporation in a divisional leveraged buyout. The company was founded in Marysville, Ohio, in 1870 by Orlando McLean Scott to sell farm crop seed. In 1900, the company began to sell weed-free lawn seed through the mail. In the 1920s, the company introduced the first home lawn fertilizer, the first lawn spreader, and the first patented bluegrass seed. Today, Scott is the acknowledged leader in the "do-it-yourself" lawn care market, with sales of over $300 million and over 1,500 employees.

Scott remained closely held until 1971, when it was purchased by ITT. The company then became a part of the consumer products division of the huge conglomerate, and operated as a wholly owned subsidiary for 14 years. In 1984, prompted by a decline in financial performance and rumors of takeover and liquidation, ITT began a series of divestitures. Over the next two years, total divestitures exceeded $2 billion and, after years of substandard performance, ITT's stock price significantly outperformed the market.

On November 26, 1986, in the midst of this divestiture activity, ITT announced that the managers of Scott, along with Clayton & Dubilier (C&D) a private firm specializing in leveraged buyouts, had agreed to purchase the stock of Scott and another ITT subsidiary, the W. Atlee Burpee Company. The deal closed on December 30.

Clayton & Dubilier raised roughly $211 million to finance the purchase of the two companies. Of that $211 million, almost $191 million, or 91% of the total was debt: bank loans, subordinated notes, and subordinated debentures. The $20 million of new equity was distributed as follows: roughly 62% of the shares were held by a C&D partnership, 21% by Scott's new subordinated debtholders, and 17.5% by Scott management and employees.

After this radical change in financial structure and concentration of equity ownership, Scott's operating performance improved dramatically. Between the end of December 1986 and the end of September 1988, sales were up 25% and earnings before interest and taxes (EBIT) increased by 56%. This increase in operating earnings was not achieved by cutting back on marketing and distribution or R&D. In fact, spending on marketing and distribution increased by 21% and R&D spending went up by 7%. Capital spending also increased by 23%.

In terms of its capital structure, managerial equity ownership, and improvement in operating performance, Scott is a highly representative LBO. Three major academic studies of LBOs have collectively concluded that following an LBO:

- The average debt-to-capital ratio is roughly 90%
- Managerial equity ownership stakes are typically around 17–20%
- Operating income increases by about 40%, on average, over a period ranging from two to four years after a buyout

Such findings raise major questions about the effects of changes in organizational and financial structure on management decision-making. For example, does the combination of significant equity ownership and high debt provide management with stronger incentives to maximize value than those facing managers of public companies with broadly dispersed stockholders? Are the decentralized management systems with pay-for-performance plans that typically accompany LBOs likely to produce greater operating efficiencies than centralized structures relying largely on financial controls? Are LBO boards, characterized by controlling equity ownership, an improvement over the standard governance of public companies where directors have "fiduciary duty," but little or no equity ownership?

Although the broad evidence cited above suggests that the answer to all these questions is yes, little academic research to date has examined the changes in organizational structure and managerial decision-making that actually take place after LBOs. In 1989, we were given the opportunity to examine confidential data on the Scott buyout and to conduct extensive interviews with C&D partners and managers at all levels of the Scott organization. We found that both organizational structure and the management decision-making process changed fundamentally as a consequence of the buyout.

In the pages that follow, we attempt to explain the role of high leverage, concentrated equity ownership, and strong governance by an active board in bringing about specific operating changes within Scott. Critics of LBOs will doubtless continue to object that highly leveraged capital structures lead to an unhealthy emphasis on "short-term" results. But the changes we witnessed at Scott lend no support to this view. These changes ranged from sharply increased attention to working capital management, vendor relations, and an innovative approach to production to a much greater willingness to entertain long-range opportunities presented by new markets and strategic acquisitions. Especially in light of Scott's post-LBO performance and spending patterns, it would be difficult to argue that any of these initiatives sacrificed long-term value for short-run cash flow.

Changes in Incentives and Compensation

Management Equity Ownership

The final distribution of equity in the postbuyout Scott organization was the product of negotiations between C&D and Scott's management—negotiations in which ITT took no part. ITT sold its entire interest in Scott through a sealed bid auction. Eight firms bid for Scott; although bidding was open to all types of buyers, seven bidders were buyout firms. ITT was interested primarily in obtaining the highest price for the division.

Scott managers did not participate in the buyout negotiations and thus had no opportunity to extract promises or make deals with potential purchasers prior to the sale. Scott managers had approached ITT several years earlier to discuss the possibility of a management buyout at $125 million; but at that time ITT had a no-buyout policy. The stated reason for this policy was that a management buyout posed a conflict of interest.

Each of the bidders spent about one day in Marysville and received information about the performance of the unit directly from ITT. Prior to Martin Dubilier's visit, Scott managers felt that they preferred C&D to the other potential buyers because of its reputation for working well with operating managers. The day did not go well, however, and C&D fell to the bottom of the managers' list. According to Tadd Seitz, president of Scott:

> To be candid, they weren't our first choice. It wasn't a question of their acumen, we just didn't think we had the chemistry. But as

we went through the controlled bid process, it was C&D that saw the greatest value in Scott.

There is no evidence that ITT deviated from its objective of obtaining the highest value for the division, or that it negotiated in any way on behalf of Scott managers during the buyout process. C&D put in the highest bid. ITT did not consider management's preferences and accepted this bid even though managers were left to work with one of their less favored buyers. Nor did ITT concern itself with the distribution of common stock after the sale.

Immediately following the closing, C&D controlled 79.4% of Scott's common stock. The remaining shares were packaged and sold with the subordinated debt. C&D was under no obligation to offer managers equity participation in Scott, and the deal clearly could be funded without any contribution by managers. But, on the basis of their experience, the C&D partners viewed management equity ownership as a way to provide managers with strong incentives to maximize firm value. Therefore, after C&D purchased Scott, it began to negotiate with managers over the amount of equity they would be given the opportunity to purchase. C&D did not sell shares to managers reluctantly; in fact, it insisted that managers buy equity and that they do so with their own, not the company's, money.

The ownership structure that resulted from the negotiations between C&D and Scott management [involved] 24,250,000 shares outstanding, each of which was purchased for $1.00. As the general partner of the private limited partnership that invested $14.9 million in the Scott buyout, C&D controlled 61.4% of the common stock. The individual C&D partners responsible for overseeing Scott operations carried an ownership interest through their substantial investment in the C&D limited partnership. Subordinated debtholders owned 20.6%.

The remaining 17.5% of the equity was distributed among Scott's employees. Eight of the firm's top managers contributed a total of $2,812,500 to the buyout and so hold as many shares, representing 12% of the shares outstanding. Tadd Seitz, president of Scott, held the largest number of these shares (1,062,500, or 4.4% of the shares outstanding). Seven other managers purchased 250,000 shares apiece (1% each of the shares outstanding). As a group managers borrowed $2,531,250 to finance the purchase of shares. Though the money was not borrowed from Scott, these loans were guaranteed by the company.

The purchase of equity by Scott managers represented a substantial increase in their personal risk. For example, Bob Stern, vice president of Associate Relations, recalled that his spouse sold her interest in a small catering business at the time of the buyout; they felt that the leverage associated with the purchase of Scott shares was all the risk they could afford.

Top management had some discretion over how their allotment of common shares was further distributed. Without encouragement from C&D, they chose to issue a portion of their own shares to Scott's employee profit-sharing plan and other employees of the firm. Although they allowed managers to distribute the stock more widely, C&D partners felt that the shares would have stronger incentive effects if they were held only by top managers. Craig Walley, general counsel for Scott, described the thinking behind management's decision to extend equity to additional managers and employees as follows:

> We [the managers] used to get together on Saturdays during this period when we were thinking about the buyout to talk about why we wanted to do this. What was the purpose? What did we want to make Scott? One of our aims was to try to keep it independent. Another was to try to spread the ownership widely. One of the things we did was to take 3% of the common stock out of our allocation and put it into the profit-sharing plan. That took some doing and we had some legal complications, but we did it. There are now 56 people in the company who own some stock, and that number is increasing. Compared to most LBOs that is really a lot, and Dubilier has not encouraged us in this.

A group of 11 lower-level managers bought an additional 687,500 shares (2.8% of the total), and the profit-sharing plan bought 750,000 shares (3.1%). These managers were selected not by their rank in the organization, but because they were employees who would be making decisions considered crucial to the success of the company.

The substantial equity holdings of the top management team, along with their personal liability for the debts incurred to finance their equity stakes, led them to focus on two distinct aspects of running Scott: (1) preserving their fractional equity stake by avoiding default (including technical default) on the firm's debt; and (2) increasing the value of that stake by making decisions that increased the long-run value of the firm.

If the company failed to make a payment of interest or principal, or if it violated a debt covenant, it would be "in default" and lenders would have the option to renegotiate the terms of the debt contract. If no agreement could be reached, the company could be forced to seek protection from creditors under Chapter 11. Because both private reorganizations and Chapter 11 generally involve the replacement of debt with equity claims, one likely consequence of default is a substantial dilution of the existing equity; and to the extent managers are also equityholders, such dilution reduces their wealth. But managers face other costs of default that are potentially large: they may end up surrendering control of the company to a bankruptcy court, and they could even lose their jobs. In this sense, equity ownership bonds managers against taking actions that lead to a violation of the covenants.

We examined Scott's debt covenants in detail to determine what managerial actions lenders encouraged and prohibited. . . . The overall effect of these covenants is to restrict both the source of funds for scheduled interest and principal repayments and the use of funds in excess of this amount. Cash to pay debt obligations must come primarily from operations or the issuance of common stock. It cannot come from asset liquidation, stock acquisition of another firm with substantial cash, or the issuance of additional debt of any kind. Excess funds can be used for capital expenditures only within prescribed limits, and cannot be used to finance acquisitions or be paid out as dividends to shareholders. Thus, once the capital expenditure limit has been reached, excess cash must be either held, spent in the course of normal operations, or used to pay down debt ahead of schedule.

A second important effect of equity ownership was to encourage managers to make decisions that increased the long-run value of the company. Because managers owned a capital value claim on the firm, they had strong incentives to meet debt obligations and avoid default in a way that increased the long-term value of the company. That is, managers had strong incentives to resist cutbacks in brand-name advertising and plant maintenance that would increase short-run cash flow at the expense of long-run value.

As mentioned earlier, there were no cutbacks in productive capital spending at Scott. In fact . . . capital spending, R&D, and marketing and promotion expenditures all increased significantly over the first two years after the buyout. Thus, in Scott's case, high leverage combined with equity ownership provided managers with the incentive to generate the cash required to meet the debt payments without bleeding the company.

The increase in capital expenditures following Scott's LBO is one way in which Scott differs from the average LBO. The large-sample studies cited earlier find that capital spending falls on average following an LBO. Whether this average reduction in capital expenditures creates or destroys value is difficult to determine, because not all corporate spending cutbacks are short-sighted. To make that determination, one has to know whether LBO companies were spending too much or too little on capital expenditure prior to their LBOs. The large stockholder gains from the leveraged restructuring movement of the 1980s suggest that much prior corporate "long-term" investment was little more than a waste of stockholder funds in the name of preserving growth.

High leverage combined with leveraged equity ownership provides strong incentives for managers to evaluate long-term investments more critically, to undertake only value-increasing projects, and to return any "free cash flow"—that is, cash in excess of that required to fund all positive-NPV investments—to investors. Leverage will cause managers to cut back on productive expenditures only if such cutbacks are the only way to avoid default *and* the cost to managers of default is greater than the loss in equity value from myopic decisions.

The LBO sponsor—in this case C&D—also plays an important role in guiding such investment decisions and preventing short-sighted cutbacks. Indeed, the experience and competence of the sponsor in valuing the company, evaluating the strengths of operating management, and arranging the financial structure is critical to an LBO's success.

CHANGES IN INCENTIVE COMPENSATION

Among the first things C&D did after the buyout was to increase salaries selectively and begin to develop a new management compensation plan. A number of managers who were not participants in the ITT bonus plan became participants under the C&D plan. The new plan substantially changed the way managers were evaluated and increased the fraction of salary that a manager could earn as an annual bonus. While some of these data are confidential, we are able to describe many of the features of C&D's incentive compensation plan and compare it with the ITT compensation system.

Salaries. Almost immediately after the close of the sale, the base salaries of some top managers were increased. The president's salary increased by 42%, and the salaries of other top managers increased as well. Henry Timnick, a C&D partner who works closely with Scott, explains the decision to raise salaries as follows:

> We increased management salaries because divisional vice presidents are not compensated at a level comparable to the CEO of a free-standing company with the same characteristics. Divisional VPs don't have all the responsibilities. In addition, the pay raise is a shot-in-the-arm psychologically for the managers. It makes them feel they will be dealt with fairly and encourages them to deal fairly with their people.

In conversations with managers and C&D partners, it became clear that C&D set higher standards for management performance than ITT. Increasing the minimum level of acceptable performance forces managers to work harder after the buyout or risk losing their jobs. Indeed, there was general agreement that the management team was putting in longer hours at the office. Several managers used the term "more focused" to describe how their work habits had changed after the buyout.

The increase in compensation also served as the reward for bearing greater risk. As stated earlier, Scott managers undertook substantial borrowings to purchase the equity. Requiring managers to borrow to buy equity and adopting an aggressive incentive compensation plan greatly increases managers' exposure to Scott's fortunes. Because managers cannot diversify away this "firm-specific" risk in the same way passive investors can, they require an increase in the expected level of their pay to remain equally well off.

Finally, C&D may have increased salaries because Scott managers are more valuable to C&D than they were to ITT. Consistent with this argument, managers at Scott felt ITT depended on them much less than did C&D. One Scott manager reported: "When ITT comes in and buys a company, the entire management team could quit and they wouldn't blink." As we will discuss later, ITT created a control system that allowed headquarters to manage a vast number of businesses, but did not give divisional managers the flexibility or incentives to use their specialized knowledge of the business to maximize its value.

Because C&D relied much more heavily on managers' operating knowledge, it was presumably willing to pay them more to reduce the risk of the managers quitting. At the same time, C&D was not completely dependent on incumbent managers to run Scott. Several C&D partners had extensive experience as operating managers. These partners had on several occasions stepped in to run C&D buyout firms, and they were available to run Scott if necessary. But, they clearly lacked specific knowledge of the Scott organization and were thus willing to provide financial incentives to incumbent managers to secure their participation.

Bonus. Scott's bonus plan was completely redesigned after its buyout. The number of managers who participated in the plan increased, and the factors that determined the level of bonus were changed to reflect the postbuyout objectives of the firm. In addition, both the maximum bonus allowed by the plan and the actual realizations of bonus as a percentage of salary increased by a factor of two to three.

After the buyout 21 managers were covered by the bonus plan. Only ten were eligible for bonuses under ITT. The maximum payoff under the new plan ranged from 33.5% to 100% of base salary, increasing with the manager's rank in the company. For each manager, the amount of the payoff was based on the achievement of corporate, divisional, and individual performance goals. The weights applied to corporate, divisional, and individual performance in calculating the bonus varied across managers. For division managers, bonus payoff was based 35% on overall company performance, 40% on divisional performance, and 25% on individual performance. Bonuses for corporate managers weighted corporate performance 50% and personal goals 50%.

At the beginning of each fiscal year performance targets (or goals) were set, and differences between actual and targeted performance entered directly into the computation of the bonus plan payoffs. All corporate and divisional performance measures were quantitative measures of cash generation and utilization and were scaled from 80 to 125, with 100 representing the attainment of target. For example, corporate performance was evaluated by dividing actual EBIT by budgeted EBIT, and dividing actual average working capital (AWC) by budgeted AWC; the EBIT ratio was weighted more heavily, at 75% as compared to a 25% weight assigned the AWC ratio. The resulting number, expressed as a percentage attainment of budget, was used as a part of the bonus calculation for all managers in the bonus plan.

Thus, the bonus plan was designed such that the payoff was highly sensitive to changes in performance. This represented a significant change from the ITT bonus plan. As Bob Stern, vice president of Associate Relations, commented:

> I worked in human resources with ITT for a number of years. When I was manager of staffing of ITT Europe we evaluated the ITT bonus plan. Our conclusion was that the ITT bonus plan was viewed as nothing more than a deferred compensation arrangement: all it did was defer income from one year to the next. Bonuses varied very, very little. If you had an average year, you might get a bonus of $10,000. If you had a terrible year you might get a bonus of $8,000, and if you had a terrific year you might go all the way to $12,500. On a base salary of $70,000, that's not a lot of variation.

• • •

The new bonus plan gives larger payouts and appears to generate significantly more variation in bonuses than occurred under ITT. Average bonuses as a percent of salary for the top ten managers increased from 10% and 17% in the two years before the buyout to 66% and 39% in the two years after, a period during which operating income increased by 42%. There also appears to be much greater variation in bonus payout across managers within a given year. In the two years prior to the buyout, bonus payout ranged from 5% to 27% of base salary, whereas over the two years following the buyout, it ranged from 16% to 94% of base salary.

In addition to measures that evaluated management performance against quantitative targets, each manager had a set of personal objectives that were tied into the bonus plan. These objectives were set by the manager and his or her superior, and their achievement was monitored by the superior. Personal objectives were generally measurable and verifiable. For instance, one objective for a personnel manager was to integrate the benefits package of a newly acquired company with that of Scott within a given period. An objective for the president of the company was to spend a fixed amount of time outside of Marysville talking to retailers and salespeople. At the end of the year, the superior evaluated whether the manager had achieved these objectives and quantified the achievement along the same 80–125 point range. This rating was then combined with the quantitative measures to come up with a total performance measure.

The weighted average of corporate, divisional, and personal target achievements was then used to determine total bonus payoffs. . . . [P]ayoffs were varied with rank and performance. If a manager achieved an 80% weighted average attainment of target goals, the payoff varied from about 30% of salary for the CEO to about 10% for lower-level managers. At 125% attainment, bonuses varied from about 100% to about 30%. Between 80% and 125%, bonus payouts as a percentage of salary varied linearly with target attainment. Below 80%, payments were at the discretion of the president and the board.

The combination of equity ownership by eight top managers with a more "highly leveraged" bonus plan for thirteen others substantially changed the incentives of the managers at Scott. For those managers who held equity, the bonus plan, with its emphasis on EBIT and working capital management, served to reinforce the importance of cash generation. Those managers who were not offered equity were nevertheless provided financial incentives to make the generation of cash a primary concern.

The Monitoring of Top Managers

. . . At the close of the buyout Scott's board had five members. Only one, Tadd Seitz, was a manager of the firm. Of the remaining four, three were C&D partners: Martin Dubilier was the chairman of the board and voted the stock of the limited partnership; Henry Timnick was the C&D partner who worked most closely with Scott management; and Alberto Cribiore was a financing specialist. The outside director was Joe Flannery, then CEO of Uniroyal, which had been taken private by C&D in 1985. Later, Flannery left Uniroyal and became a C&D partner. He stayed on the Scott board, becoming an inside, rather than outside, director.

Over the next few years three new directors were added. One was an academic, one was a consumer products expert, and one, Don Sherman, was the president of Hyponex, a company acquired by Scott after its buyout. The academic, Jim Beard, was one of the country's leading turf researchers. Henry Timnick described the process of putting him on the board as follows:

> Our objective was to find the best turf specialist and researcher in the country. We wanted someone to keep us up with the latest developments and to scrutinize the technical aspects of our product line. We found Jim Beard at Texas A&M. It took Jim a while to be enthusiastic about being on the board, and it took Tadd a while to figure out how to get the most out of Jim. After Jim was appointed to the board, we encouraged Tadd to have Jim out on a consulting basis for a couple of days. Now Tadd is making good use of Jim.

Seitz and Timnick wanted an individual with extensive experience in consumer products businesses to be the second outside director. They chose Jack Chamberlain, who had run GE's Consumer Electronics Division as well as Lenox China and Avon Products. All board members were stockholders; upon joining the board they were each given the opportunity to purchase 50,000 shares at adjusted book value. All the directors chose to own stock.

This board structure was typical for a C&D buyout. Martin Dubilier explains:

> We have tried a number of board compositions and we found this to be the most effective. If you have too many insiders the board becomes an operating committee. Outsiders fortify the growth opportunities of the firm.

The board of directors met quarterly. A subset of the board, the executive committee, met monthly. The executive committee was made up of Martin Dubilier, Tadd Seitz, and Henry Timnick. In their meetings they determined policy, discussed personnel matters, and tested Seitz's thinking on major issues facing the firm. The board meetings were more formal, usually consisting of presentations by members of the management team other than Seitz.

The Operating Partner

In each of C&D's buyouts, a partner with extensive operating experience serves as "liaison" between the firm's managers and C&D.

The operating partner functions as an advisor and consultant to the CEO, not a decision-maker. Henry Timnick was Scott's liaison partner. He had been CEO of a division of Mead that was purchased through a leveraged buyout, and had since worked with several of C&D's other buyout firms. Timnick spent several weeks in Marysville after the buyout closed. Following that period, he was in touch with Seitz daily by telephone and continued to visit regularly.

Timnick would advise Seitz, but felt it was important that Seitz make the decisions. When he and Seitz disagreed, Timnick told him, "If you don't believe me, go hire a consultant, then make your own decision." Initially, Seitz continued to check with Timnick, looking for an authorization for his decisions. Henry Timnick explains:

> Tadd kept asking me "Can I do this? Can I do that?" I told him, "You can do whatever you want so long as it is consistent with Scott's over-all-strategy."

This consultative approach to working with Scott managers was quite different from ITT's approach. Martin Dubilier explains:

> ITT challenges managers not to rock the boat, to make budget. We challenge managers to improve the business. Every company takes on the personality of its CEO. Our main contribution is to improve his performance. All the rest is secondary.

• • •

Organizational Changes and Changes in Decision-making

The changes in organizational structure and decision-making that took place at Scott after the buyout fall broadly into two categories: improved working capital management and a new approach to product markets. These changes were not forced on managers by C&D. The buyout firm made some suggestions, but the specific plans and their implementation were the responsibility of Scott managers. Few of the changes represent keenly innovative or fundamentally new insights into management problems. As one observer noted, "It ain't rocket science." These changes, however, led to dramatic improvements in Scott's operating performance.

Management's ability and talents did not change after the buyout, nor did the market or the assets they were managing. The only changes were those in the incentive structure described earlier and in the management control system. According to Scott managers, the biggest difference between working at Scott before and after the buyout was an increase in the extent to which they could make and implement decisions without approval from superiors.

ITT, by contrast, maintained control over its divisions through an inflexible formal planning and reporting structure. Changing a plan required approval at a number of levels from ITT headquarters, and a request for a change was likely to be denied. In addition, because ITT was shedding its consumer businesses, Scott managers found their requests for capital funds routinely denied. After the buyout, Seitz could pick up the phone and propose changes in the operating plan to Timnick. This, of course, improved the company's ability to respond quickly to changes in the marketplace.

The Working Capital Task Force

Shortly after the buyout, a task force was established to coordinate the management of working capital throughout the company. The members of the task force were drawn from every functional area. The group was charged with reducing working capital requirements by 42%, or $25 million dollars, in two years. They exceeded this goal, reducing average working capital by $37 million. The task force helped Scott managers learn to manage cash balances, production, inventories, receivables, payables, and employment levels more effectively.

Cash Management. . . . When Scott was a division of ITT, cash coming into Scott bore little relation to the cash Scott was allowed to spend. After the LBO, all of Scott's cash was available to managers. They needed to establish a system to control cash so that operations were properly funded, and to meet debt service requirements. Walley describes the process as follows:

> In the first six months after the LBO we had to bring in a state-of-the-art cash management system for a business of this size. We shopped a lot of treasury management systems and had almost given up on finding a system that would simply let us manage our cash. We didn't need a system that would keep track of our investment portfolios because we had $200 million borrowed. Finally, we found a product we could use. Under the LBO cash forecasting has become critical. I mean cash forecasting in the intermediate and long range. I don't mean forecasting what is going to hit the banks in the next two or three days. We could always do that, but now we track our cash flows on a weekly basis and we do modeling on balance sheets, which allows us to do cash forecasting a year out.

Production and Inventories. Between 1986 and 1988, the efforts of the task force increased the frequency with which Scott turned over its inventory from 2.08 to 3.20 times per year, or by 54%. During this period both sales and production increased. Because Scott's business is highly seasonal, inventory control had always been a management problem. Large inventories were required to meet the spring rush of orders; however, financing these inventories was a cash drain. Scott's production strategy under ITT exacerbated the inventory problem. Before the buyout, Scott produced each product once a year. Slow-moving products were produced during the slow season so that long runs of fast-moving products could be produced during the busy season. Before the spring buying began, almost an entire year's worth of sales were in inventory.

The old production strategy took advantage of the cost savings of long production runs. But, under ITT, managers did not consider the tradeoff between these cost savings and the opportunity cost of funds tied up in inventory. The cash requirements of servicing a large debt burden, the working capital–based restrictions in the debt agreements, and the inclusion of working capital objectives in the compensation system gave managers a strong incentive to consider this opportunity cost. As Walley explained,

> What the plant managers had to do was to figure out how they could move the production of the slow-moving items six months forward. That way the products we used to make in May or early June would be made in November or December. Now [instead of producing long runs of a few products] production managers have to deal with setups and changeovers during the high-production period. It requires a lot more of their attention.

Managing inventories more effectively required that products be produced closer to the time of shipment. Because more setups and changeovers were necessary, the production manager's job became more complicated. Instead of producing a year's supply of one product, inventorying it, and then producing another product, managers had to produce smaller amounts of a variety of products repeatedly throughout the year.

Inventories were also reduced by changing purchasing practices and inventory management. Raw material suppliers agreed to deliver small quantities more often, reducing the levels of raw materials and finished goods inventories. By closely tracking inventory, Scott managed to reduce these levels without increasing the frequency of stock-outs of either raw materials or finished goods.

Receivables and Payables. Receivables were an important competitive factor and retailers expected generous payment terms from Scott. After the buyout, however, the timing of rebate and selling programs was carefully planned, allowing Scott to conserve working capital. Scott also negotiated with suppliers to obtain more favorable terms on prices, payment schedules, and delivery. Lorel Au, manager of Contract Operations, stated,

> Within two months of the LBO, the director of manufacturing and I went out to every one of our contract suppliers and went through what a leveraged buyout is, and what that means. We explained how we were going to have to manage our business. We explained our new goals and objectives. We talked about things like just-in-time inventory, talked terms, talked about scheduling. Some suppliers were more ready to work with us than others. Some said, 'OK, what can we do to help?' In some cases, a vendor said, 'I can't help you on price, I can't help you on terms, I can't help you on scheduling.' We said: 'Fine. Good-bye.' We were very serious about it. In some cases we didn't have options, but usually we did.

The company succeeded in getting suppliers to agree to extended terms of payment, and was also able to negotiate some substantial price cuts from major suppliers in return for giving the supplier a larger fraction of Scott's business.

Scott managers felt that the buyout put them in a stronger bargaining position vis-à-vis their suppliers. Walley states:

> One reason we were able to convince our suppliers to give us concessions is that we no longer had the cornucopia of ITT behind us. We no longer had unlimited cash.

The suppliers understood that if they did not capitulate on terms, Scott would have to take its business elsewhere or face default.

Employment. Scott had a tradition of being very paternalistic toward its employees and was a major employer and corporate citizen in the town of Marysville. Some have argued that an important source of cash and increasing equity value in buyouts is the severing of such relationships. There is no evidence of this at Scott. Scott's traditional employee relations policies were maintained, and neither wages nor benefits were cut after the buyout. Scott continues to maintain a large park with swimming pool, tennis courts, playground, and other recreational facilities for the enjoyment of employees and their families. The company also continues to make its auditorium, the largest in Marysville, available for community use at no charge.

Scott did begin a program of hiring part-time employees during the busy season rather than bringing on full-time employees. This allowed the company to maintain a core of full-time, year-round employees who enjoyed the complete benefits plan of the company, while still having enough people to staff the factory during busy season. As a consequence, average annual full-time employment has dropped by about 9%, entirely through attrition, over the first two years after the buyout.

New Approaches to the Product Markets

Scott is the major brand name in the do-it-yourself lawn care market and has a reputation for high-quality products. Ed Wandtke, a lawn industry analyst, says of the company:

> O.M. Scott is ultra high price, ultra high quality. They absolutely are the market leader. They have been for some time. No one else has the retail market recognition. Through its promotions, Scott has gotten its name so entrenched that the name and everything associated with it—quality, consistency, reliability—supersede the expensive price of the product.

In 1987, Scott had a 34% share of the $350 million do-it-yourself market. Industry experts report, however, that the market had been undergoing major changes since the early 1980s. Indeed, Scott's revenue fell by 23% between 1981 (the historical high at that time) and 1985. The buyout allowed Scott managers the flexibility to adapt to the changing marketplace, assuring a future for the company.

The do-it-yourself market was shrinking because an increasing number of consumers were contracting with firms to have their lawns chemically treated. Seitz had proposed that Scott enter this segment of the professional lawn-care market for years, but ITT continually vetoed this initiative. Among the first actions taken after the buyout was the creation of a group within the professional division whose focus was to sell to the commercial turf maintenance market. Within two years, the segment comprised 10% of the sales of the professional division and was growing at a rate of almost 40% per year.

In response to major changes in Scott's product markets, the company also made a major acquisition less than two years after the buyout. At the time, Scott's position in the do-it-yourself market was being challenged by the growth of private label brands sold at lower prices, and by a shift in volume away from Scott's traditional retailers—hardware and specialty stores—to mass merchandisers. Under ITT Scott managers did not try to develop new channels of distribution. Timnick described it as too "risky" an experiment for ITT. The acquisition of Hyponex gave Scott access to the private label market. Says Wandtke,

> With Hyponex, Scott will capture a greater percentage of the home

> consumer market. Hyponex is a much lower priced product line. It gives them [Scott] access to private labeling, where they can produce product under another label for a lesser price. . . . This will improve their hold on the retail market.

Hyponex was a company virtually the same size as Scott, with $125 million in sales and 700 employees, yet the acquisition was financed completely with bank debt. The successful renegotiation of virtually all of Scott's existing debt agreements was required to consummate the transaction. Because the new debt was senior to the existing notes and debentures, a consent payment of $887,500 was required to persuade bondholders to waive restrictive covenants. That such a large acquisition was possible so soon after the buyout demonstrates the potential flexibility of the LBO organizational form. It also demonstrates the ability of contracting parties to respond to a valuable investment opportunity in the face of restrictions that appear to forbid such action. . . .

We attribute the improvements in operating performance after Scott's leveraged buyout to changes in the incentive, monitoring, and governance structure of the firm. . . .

Part IV

Change How?

Chapter 10

The Challenges of Execution: Roles and Tasks in the Change Process

Our company is in need of a profound transformation. We've read all the books. We know all the concepts and theories: transition management, frame-breaking, paradigms, empowerment, culture change, and so on. But we don't know how to* implement *the transformation. We don't even know how to make the theories operational.

—Manager in a leading *Fortune 100* company

Implementing change. The phrase sounds reasonable enough, and yet "managing" change is probably one of the most troubling and challenging tasks facing organizations today. Implementing a major and lasting change requires managers to develop skills akin to a juggler's. Instead of balls, however, managers must juggle tasks, striking a delicate balance between individual and collective actions, paying attention to the content as well as the process of change, and pursuing both short-term and long-term goals.

Considering the complexity of the task, it is no wonder that many managers feel overwhelmed—unable to keep all the balls of change in the air at the same time. The vice president is too busy to add "change" related tasks to her already crowded schedule of "normal" activities; the production manager nods his head during the meeting on managing change, but forgets the message as soon as he's back on the factory floor; or the company launches a change effort with great fanfare and enthusiasm, but then loses momentum one year into the program and calls it quits. Consider the results of a 1990 *Wall Street Journal* survey of 164 chief executive officers. Although the CEOs recognized that personal communication helps create more employee commitment to change, 86 percent said other demands prevented them from devoting more time to communicating.

Another study examined the large gap between declared participatory management styles and what is actually practiced. A survey of 485 upper-level managers from 59 firms found unequivocal support for the concept of participatory management and a willingness and desire to support such a change. Nevertheless, managers generally did not install such systems, blaming an absence of opportunities to discuss the implementation process and a lack of leadership (Collins, Ross, and Ross, 1989).

To help address such problems, change experts have devised tactics over the years to help managers do a better job on everything from crafting a vision to rewarding employees for productive behavior. Most managers at medium- to large-size U.S. companies have been exposed to these tenets. Yet the track record overall is disappointing. As many of the portraits in this book illustrate, there continues to be a great deal of disquiet in the workplace over the effectiveness of change efforts. Despite volumes of literature on planned change, legions of consultants, and the best efforts of corporate leaders, organizational change still appears to be a chaotic process. It is frequently mismanaged, beset by unexpected developments, and often largely unfulfilled.

This chapter examines why seemingly sensible advice on implementing change is solicited, accepted, and then often ignored. It then also offers suggestions on key steps that can improve the implementation process. We present two broad themes: (1) Change is extraordinarily difficult, and the fact that it occurs successfully at all is something of a miracle. (2) Change is furthered, however, if and when an organization can strike a delicate balance among the key players in the process. No one person or group can make change "happen" alone—not the top of the organization mandating change, not the middle implementing what the top has ordained, and not the bottom "receiving" the efforts.

We stress the difficulty of change efforts to dispel well-intentioned attempts to portray "change" as a discrete process, which when followed "correctly" leads more or less inevitably to the new desired state. Implicit in this notion is the idea that the benefits of change, while perhaps not immediately perceived, will eventually be realized, and the whole organization will go forward thriving on the chaos that the process drags in its wake. Anyone who has been even marginally connected with a change effort knows this isn't so.

Our second theme—that no one makes change happen alone—sounds a more positive note. Successful change builds on constructive interactions among multiple groups within an organization. Three basic groups must be coordinated if change is to be effectively implemented: ***change strategists, change "implementors,"*** and ***change recipients***. As we shall show, each group carries its own assumptions, agendas, and reactions. Unless these are considered both at the outset and during the unfolding of the change process, the most well-meaning efforts will be thwarted.

A brief illustration makes this point. A consultant describes an experience he had teaching managers in a large company about engineering change:

> When I went to this company, it seemed all their efforts to change were stricken with paralysis. I started off by talking to the middle managers. The group seemed very receptive, but afterwards, someone came up to

me and said, "That was a very well-done workshop with interesting ideas, but you had the wrong group here. It's not middle managers who make change happen. It's our bosses."

So I offered the same workshop to the senior managers. Again, the crowd responded eagerly, but a manager broke in near the end and declared, "That was a fascinating workshop, and we know there are many changes we have to manage. But you really ought to be talking to the vice presidents and the president. They are the ones who can make change happen."

Finally, assuming that the company's leaders would readily accept responsibility for implementing change, I presented my ideas one more time to the top of the organization. "That's all very well," responded the president. "But there's a limit to how much we can do. Most of the time, it's the middle managers who actually determine whether change gets implemented or not."

While each level acknowledged its dependence on the others, there was clearly no process for working through change issues together. As a result, change in this company seemed destined to fail. In more successful change efforts, the key players have developed a process that enables them to work together.

The Messy Terrain of Change

> ***How are you supposed to change the tires on a car when it's going 60 miles per hour?***
>
> **—Epitaph of a change agent**

Real-life stories of corporate change rarely measure up to the tidy experiences related in books. The echo of the consultant's enthusiasm fades as the hard work of change begins. No matter how much effort companies invest in preparation and workshops—not to mention pep rallies, banners, and pins—organizations are invariably insufficiently prepared for the difficulties of implementing change. The responsibility for this situation lies in several areas.

Both the popular press and the academic literature tend to consider organizational change as a step-by-step process leading to success. Recent writings have grown more sophisticated—taking into account the often divergent methods called for in different change scenarios (Dunphy and Stace, 1989; Nadler and Tushman, 1989; Allaire and Firsirotu, 1985; Goodman *et al*, 1982); acknowledging that corporate transformation should be a continuous, ongoing process rather than a short-term fix (Kilmann and Covin, 1988); and recognizing change as a reciprocal learning process between the top of the organization and the bottom (Beer, 1988). But all too often many treatises on organizational change fail to concede that difficulties lie along the way.

This unrealistic portrayal of the change process can be dangerous. Already organizations are inclined to push faster, spend less, and stop earlier than the process requires. Such inclinations are further strengthened by an illusion of control that in fact does not exist. Managers are sometimes misled by consultants or authors who make change seem like a bounded, defined, discrete process with guidelines for success. They feel deceived; instead of a controllable process, they discover chaos.

In the real world, organizations cannot plot one change to be rationally and tenaciously pursued. Most corporations must stake out multiple changes at once, and the change goals themselves must be continually reexamined, altered, added to, or even abandoned. Instead of one vision to guide an organization's overall direction, many companies find they must pursue separate and sometimes even competing visions, such as a quality vision, a customer vision, and a human resources vision. Instead of one powerful, centralized, and charismatic change leader, many companies now rely on teams of collaborating individuals who hammer out the emerging details of the change process through bargaining, compromise, and negotiation.

The larger and more complex the change, the more likely it is that this kind of overlap and complexity will occur. The organizational analysts David Nadler and Michael Tushman (1989) have identified one set of characteristics that can bedevil the change process. Any large-scale change, they claim, entails at least some of the following four traits:

- *Multiple transitions.* Rather than being confined to one transition, complex changes often involve many different transitions. Some may be explicitly related; others are not.
- *Incomplete transitions.* Many of the transitions that are initiated do not get completed. Events overtake them, or subsequent changes subsume them.
- *Uncertain future states.* It is difficult to predict or define exactly what a future state will be; there are many unknowns that limit the ability to describe it. Even when a future state can be described, there is a high probability that events will change the nature of that state before it is achieved.
- *Transitions over long periods of time.* Many large-scale organizational changes take a long time to implement—in some cases, as much as three to seven years. The dynamics of managing change over this period are different from those of managing a quick change with a discrete beginning and end.

What is the experience of implementing change really like? Here is how the chief executive officer of a major U.S. airline describes managing multiple changes during the tempestuous period of the late 1980s:

> It beat any Indiana Jones movie! It started out with a real nice beginning. Then suddenly we got one disaster after another. The boulder just missed

us, and we got the snake in the cockpit of the airplane—that's what it's all about! You've got to be down in the mud and the blood and the beer.

This vivid description captures a sense of the drama involved in wrestling with complex, real-time issues day after day in a changing environment. Today's companies are composed of and affected by so many different individuals and constituencies—each with their own hopes, dreams, and fears. For these companies, operating in a global environment—with all the regulations, competition, and complexity that implies—managing organizational change does indeed require a juggler's skills.

Unfortunately, the unsettling nature of this process is often neglected in change "success" stories, leading those who "make" change to judge their own performance too harshly. Instead of the crisp, logical, and forward-moving process they have seen described, their own best efforts may feel like just "muddling along"—poking their fingers in the dike as a flood of demands and forced modifications threatens to pour down over them. One manager implementing multiple changes at a large Midwestern manufacturing company described her sensations this way: "I feel like I need to be smarter. There's just no way I can do it. Then I realize it's not related to my inexperience at all, it's just the situation.

This kind of frustration is part of the terrain of change. In fact, while the literature often portrays an organization's quest for change like a brisk march along a well-marked path, those in the middle of change are more likely to describe their journey as a laborious crawl toward an elusive, flickering goal, with many wrong turns and missed opportunities along the way. Only rarely does a company know exactly where it's going, or how it should get there. Indeed, "Everything looks like a failure in the middle. In nearly every change project, doubt is cast on the original vision because problems are mounting and the end is nowhere in sight" (Kanter, 1991).

Change is often messy, chaotic, and painful, no matter what leaders do to smooth the process. Take the case of the manager of a venerable control systems company trying to face up to the reality of shrinking orders and dwindling market share. After a careful analysis of market needs and corporate capabilities, the manager decides to shift the company's focus from producing a large range of systems to manufacturing a smaller stable of more advanced, value-added products. To accomplish this, she must lay off almost one-fourth of the company's most senior employees. Although she does her best to make the layoffs humane—offering generous retirement packages, as well as counseling services—both the employees who leave and those who remain respond with anger, bitterness, and distrust. Did the manager bungle this change effort?

Probably not. In fact, there is no way to make laying off employees pleasant, and yet it can be an important and necessary step in restructuring an organization and returning it to competitive form. Change agents generally make unpopular decisions. An organization is made up of many different constituencies, and each group is likely to be affected by—and to react to—any given change differently. The portraits in this book on General Motors illustrate dramatically the pressures and second-guessing change agents can expect from critics both inside and outside an organization.

A manager need not do anything as drastic as laying off workers to trigger intense reactions within an organization. Realigning a company's chain of command, shifting resources from one part of an organization to another, or even introducing new computer systems can result in temporary chaos. The well-known change expert Chris Argyris (1985) argued that almost any action that disturbs the organizational status quo or represents a threat to an individual's habitual way of doing things is likely to provoke defensive, and often counterproductive, behaviors—behaviors learned early in life. "Defensive routines are probably the most important cause of failure in the implementation of sound strategy . . . ," Argyris wrote. "[W]e are dealing with how we are taught from a very early age to cope with threat."

Those who make change must also grapple with unexpected forces both inside and outside the organization, as discussed in the earlier chapters in this book. No matter how carefully the leaders prepare for change, and no matter how realistic and committed they are, there will always be factors outside of their control that may have a profound impact on the success of the change process. Those external, uncontrollable, and powerful forces are not to be underestimated, and they are one reason why some researchers have questioned the manageability of change at all.

Take the case of Northwest Airlines. In 1985 the carrier launched a carefully plotted cultural overhaul aimed at improving communication and increasing worker participation. As the program was beginning to take hold in 1986, Northwest acquired its Minneapolis rival Republic Airlines—the largest airline merger by that point. The aftermath was far more turbulent than the successful merger of Western and Delta described in Chapter 7.

Within hours of the acquisition's completion, the effort to merge the systems of the two Minneapolis-based carriers exploded. Union leaders, enraged by what they insisted was inept handling of the merger, encouraged workers to protest—leading to strikes and eventually sabotage. One year later, in the midst of continuing turmoil, Northwest Flight 255 crashed after takeoff from Detroit, killing 156 people in the nation's second worst aviation accident to date. Finally, in 1989, Northwest became the unwilling object of a hostile takeover attempt. A few months after a friendly buyer stepped in, most of Northwest's management team resigned. So much for planned changes.

While this may be an extreme example of the forces that buffet a change process, any number of events outside a company's control can render the best change plan obsolete. Shifts in government regulations, union activism, competitive assaults, product delays, mergers and acquisitions, and political and international crises are all realities of corporate life today, and leaders cannot expect to implement their plans free of such interruptions. All forms of motion are in play simultaneously. The world does not stand still while leaders manage a change.

This, then, is at least part of the terrain of change and the resultant challenge of implementation. Change is usually more complex than expected. Change agents may feel overwhelmed with frustration, or "lost" in the middle of the process. In order to realize their goals, managers may have to make decisions that are unpopular with at least part—if not all—of the organization. And throughout the process, the rest of the world continues to grow, change, and make demands. As experts note, "Change management is not a neat, sequential process" (Beckhard and Harris, 1987). Unfortunately, it is a process that defeats many who strive for substantive change.

Given that change is far more complex than the literature—and consultants—often suggests, is there anything useful to be drawn from such advice? Should managers simply fold up their tents and forgo any attempt to implement change systematically? Of course not. Moreover, there are many examples of successful change that have been built on reasonable advice. Our point is that rational suggestions for implementing change are most useful when they are addressed to the entire range of people involved in the change process. In the next section we shall meet the players whom we believe to be the real implementors of change and explore their differing roles in the process. Subsequently we shall look at the typical advice given to these "changemakers" and see how that squares with our cast.

The Changemakers: Strategists, Implementors, Recipients

Organizational change is typically modeled as a three-part process that takes the flawed organization, moves it through an arduous transition stage, and deposits it at the end in the enriched, desired state (see Figure 10–1). Whether the three phases are called Unfreezing, Changing, and Refreezing (Lewin, 1947), a Three-Act Drama (Tichy and Devanna, 1986), or a transition from current state to future state (Beckhard and Harris, 1987), the same major themes emerge:

- The company must be awakened to a new reality and must disengage from the past, recognizing that the old way of doing things is no longer acceptable.
- Next, the organization creates and embraces a new vision of the future, uniting behind the steps necessary to achieve that vision.
- Finally, as new attitudes, practices, and policies are put in place to change the corporation, these must be "refrozen" (as Lewin put it) or solidified.

This model is a prescription for creating a *temporary stability* so that things will work (i.e., can change) for some period of time. Further, a specific category of people—namely, change "agents"—are meant to fulfill this pre-

FIGURE 10–1

Models for the Change Process

MODEL	PROCESS		
Lewin (1947)	Unfreezing	Changing	Refreezing
Beckhard and Harris (1977)	Present State	Transition State	Future State
Beer (1980)	Dissatisfaction ×	Process ×	Model
Kanter (1983)	Departures from Tradition and Crises	Strategic Decisions and Prime Movers	Action Vehicles and Institutionalization
Tichy and Devanna (1986)	Act I Awakening	Act II Mobilizing	Act III (Epilogue) Reinforcing
Nadler and Tushman (1989)	Energizing	Envisioning	Enabling

scription. Indeed, some argue that the planned change literature is largely aimed at the "experts" in the change process, namely external consultants! (Covin and Kilmann, 1989).

But recall, however, how many forces "conspire" to frustrate change and to destabilize the process. Moreover, change is effected by a combination of actors, a much more varied group than the literature often suggests. Because there are multiple parties (and stakeholders) involved in making change happen, and because their assumptions, perspectives, and even agendas may not always converge, there is in fact a natural *instability* built into the change process. Thus, both external and internal dynamics are at work to rock the change boat. But whereas many of the external forces we mentioned are truly uncontrollable, or at a minimum unpredictable, organizations can control the way the various actors in the change drama interact. And if these actors share an understanding of what change is needed, of how that can be effected, and of the "price" to be paid, then the change process has a far better chance of succeeding.

Who, then, is really involved in implementing change? We would argue that change is successful only when the entire organization participates in the effort. But the organization isn't a monolith; it can be divided into three broad change categories: change strategists, change implementors, and change recipients.

Strategists lay the foundation for change and craft the "vision." They oversee the links between the organization and its environment—its marketplace, its stakeholders—that give the organization its identity; they specialize in managing the first of our three kinds of motion.

Implementors develop and enact the steps necessary to enact the vision; they manage the coordination among parts and the relationships among people that give the organization its internal shape and culture, specializing in our second kind of motion, the internal development of the organization.

Recipients, finally, adopt—or fail to adopt—the change plan. Their response to the promised distribution of tasks and rewards determines whether interest groups mobilize to support or oppose the change effort, either "refreezing" the organization in new habits or resulting in political turmoil—corresponding to our third kind of motion. Recipients, in fact, give the desired change its ultimate shape and sustainability. Strategists and implementors who fail to take that fact into account do so at their peril.

Breaking all the players in a company into three distinct groups is, of course, an oversimplification. The roles often overlap, and any given person in an organization is likely to assume each of these roles at some point during the different phases of the change process. Nevertheless, these dramatis personae roughly correlate to the phases of the ideal change process; each group also more or less embodies the tasks that accompany the effort. And there are concrete numbers involved: for a given change, the strategists are few; the implementors constitute a larger group, and the recipients are the most broadly represented. Let us examine these roles—and their assumptions—more closely, and see how they interact.

Change Strategists

Change strategists are responsible for identifying the need for change, creating a vision of the desired outcome, deciding what change is feasible, and choosing who should sponsor and defend it. They tune into the external and internal environment, assessing the forces for change. CEOs, top management, and consultants typically, but not exclusively, are change strategists. They involve themselves in broad design issues related to the resources their change ideas will absorb; they do the big-picture work, reading the external signs and the perceived pressures for change. With their overview of the organization, they attempt to master the possibilities.

As initiators and conceptualizers, strategists inherently experience more *control:* since they originate the need, the "plan," and the impetus for change, the idea is lodged within them. Positively, this means they feel compelled to influence others to pay attention to their issues and to develop or modify the change agenda. Negatively, their "vision" can congeal. Having fixed on the solution to the problem they have delimited, they can "lead" their organizations into ill-fated efforts.

A growing literature is devoted to providing guidelines for what is often called the "leadership" role (e.g., Allaire and Firsirotu, 1985; Tichy and Devanna, 1986; Nadler and Tushman, 1989, 1990; Hambrick and Cannella,

1989; Beer and Walton, 1990). Theoretically, while the role may be performed by a group, it tends to be described in terms of a single person. David Nadler and Michael Tushman (1989) see this individual as having a special "feel" or "magic," and thus use the term "magic leader": someone who helps articulate the change and capture and mobilize the hearts and minds of the organization.

Embedded in this leadership role are several tasks: determining the ultimate extent of the change needed and its degree of urgency; assessing whether the change is short- or long-term; deciding if the change is cultural, structural, etc. These interwoven tasks, in turn, become represented in distinctive behaviors—envisioning, energizing, and enabling (Nadler and Tushman, 1989). The leaders are typically portrayed as the critical ingredient in instituting change; if they are missing, the change is not likely to occur (Collins, Ross, and Ross, 1989).

Implicit in these leader-centered descriptions, however, are indications that while the role is necessary it is hardly sufficient. Implementation must be part of a change's earliest formulation—one reason why we prefer change strategist to change leader to describe this role. And strategists must pay attention to all the constituencies that must be "sold" on change, not just to *what* should be changed (Hambrick and Cannella, 1989). The need thus goes beyond envisioning, energizing, and enabling to encompass crafting the implementors' task. It includes recognizing that a change strategy is as much a matter of selling as it is of substance. That is, many constituencies will have to live with the change, and their support is critical to its diffusion, as well as its success.

In sum, while change strategists can fairly easily impact organizational structures and resource allocation, it is more difficult for them to influence cultures and individuals (Allaire and Firsirotu, 1985). These are more directly shaped by change implementors and change recipients.

Change Implementors

Change implementors "make it happen," managing the day-to-day process of change. They are concerned with the motion inside the organization, with coordination and habits. They are often assigned their role and given a mandate to institute the change on behalf of the change strategists. Depending on the extent of the "vision" they are given, they can either develop the implementation plan or shepherd through programs handed down to them. Simultaneously, they must respond to demands from above while attempting to win the cooperation of those below.

Thus, implementors are "sold" on the change in some fashion, whether personally believing in its merits or doing it because the boss said so. In addition, they are monitored and rewarded (or punished) according to the perceived effectiveness of the change's implementation.

Most organizational development literature has been directed at these change implementors, although more recently the perceived audience has been broadened to include managers at large (see Beer and Walton, 1987, for example). This voluminous literature tends to address step-by-step practical advice (e.g., Lippitt, Langseth, and Mossop, 1985; Kirkpatrick, 1986; Beckhard and Harris, 1987; Woodward and Buchholz, 1987). And it has an overwhelmingly positive premise. Change is beneficial. There tends to be little advice on how to arrest change or how to resist becoming an "adopter" (Fitzgerald, 1988).

Thus, the focus is on the major issues facing implementors: intervention tactics for overcoming resistance; communication tools; how to develop transition structures; training and development; reward systems; and the like. Advice may be directed at technical, cultural, or political dimensions (Tichy, 1983), and may focus on individuals, groups, or the entire organization.

The more complex and large-scale the change, the more important it becomes that interventions be well thought out and consistent with each other (Mohrman, Mohrman, and Ledford, 1989). A series of choices among tactical options is thereby needed (Lawler, 1989). This includes whether to use a pilot test or to go pan-organization; whether to be as participative throughout the process as the goals might warrant; whether to change certain systems sequentially or simultaneously; whether to reject the old or accentuate the new; whether to use a "programmatic approach" or to have each unit develop its own interpretation; and whether to drive change bottom-up or top-down. (We address some of these tactical choices in Chapter 14.)

Change strategists may often—but not always—play a secondary role in making these choices. For their part, change recipients are more focused on the outcomes and consequences of the choices. Partly as a result of this, implementors often gripe about being caught in the middle. As the list of decisions they must make demonstrates, implementors face a daunting task. They often feel that they have insufficient authority to make change happen entirely on their own, and that they fail to receive the support from above to move forward. And the more the "recipients" balk at the decisions implementors make, the more frustrating the task becomes.

Change Recipients

Change recipients represent the largest group of people that must adopt, and adapt to, change. Thus, their response and reaction to change can fundamentally reshape that change. These are the institutionalizers: their behavior determines whether a change will stick. The concept of "organizational readiness to change" that is frequently assessed in the early phases of a change effort is an indication of how important the "users" actually are. Another indication of change recipients' influence on the course and nature of a change process is the high failure rate of change. One study, for example, found that dissatisfied leaders who attempted to impose change on organizational members who were not "ready" usually failed (Spector, 1989). Therefore, it is important for leaders to spread *dissatisfaction* if lasting change is to occur.

Recipients appear in the organization change literature primarily as sources of resistance. However, what is vital to a successful change effort is understanding how recipients *perceive* the change and how they *experience* it. This point of view is all too often underplayed by leaders, managers, and experts alike. Indeed, if the majority of the organization that "uses" a change is considered only in terms of potential resistance, a self-fulfilling prophecy can result—treated as likely resistors, they fight the change.

Consider an example that tracks recipients' response to a change over time. One case study of a "highly effective" turnaround of an ailing assembly plant described the "euphoria" expressed almost universally by the management team. By all indications, workers (i.e., recipients) shared this enthusiasm: absenteeism, turnover, and grievances were all down. Despite these positive signs, however, line workers interviewed following the three-year turnaround were largely unimpressed with the improvements and claimed that their jobs remained fundamentally the same (Guest, Hersey, and Blanchard, 1977). Perhaps the recipients were less a part of the "turnaround" than others assumed.

Recipients are often too distant from the source of the change. One observer put it this way: "Visionary light, like any other, diminishes in proportion to the square of the distance, so it may not shine very brightly out on the shipping dock or in the union hall down the street" (Fitzgerald, 1988).

Resistance to change is not an inevitable by-product of change efforts, nor is it purely emotional. Recipients resist change for reasonable and predictable reasons; for example (Kanter, 1985):

- *Loss of control.* Too much is done *to* people, and too little done *by* them.
- *Too much uncertainty.* Information about the next steps and likely future actions is not available.
- *Surprise, surprise!* Decisions are sprung full-blown without preparation or background.
- *The costs of confusion.* There are too many things changing simultaneously, interrupting routines and making it hard to know the proper way to get things done.
- *Loss of face.* The declaration of a need for change makes people feel they look stupid for their past actions, especially in front of peers.
- *Concerns about competence.* People wonder about their ability to be effective after the change; will they be able to do what is required?
- *More work.* Change requires more energy, more time, more meetings, and more learning.
- *Ripple effects.* One change disrupts other, unrelated plans.
- *Past resentments.* A legacy of distrust based on unkept promises or unaddressed grievances makes it hard to be positive about the change effort.
- *Real threats.* The change brings genuine pain or loss.

Unless carefully conceived, therefore, even change programs aimed specifically at eliciting more employee participation can backfire. For example, workers will not participate in decision-making when an organization's *real* decisions are made outside those forums; when their jobs do not benefit from participative decision-making; when seniority continues to "count" more than competence; or when other such mixed messages exist (Neumann, 1989). Sometimes "participation [can be] something the top orders the middle to do for the bottom (Kanter, 1983)." In fact, being ordered to participate does not feel much different from being ordered to do anything else. And when the rhetoric of participation does not match the actual ways people are included, cynicism follows.

Ships Passing in the Day: How Views of Change Differ

As this brief tour of changemaker roles demonstrates, the understanding and impact of a change effort can vary considerably from one group to another (see Figure 10–2). Implementors, for example, are fighting the near daily fires, interruptions, and impediments attendant to working through the

FIGURE 10–2

Three Key Changemakers

	Role and Mind-set	Orientation to Change (Kind of Motion)	Action Focus	Typical Organizational Level	Dominant Stage of Involvement
Change Strategist	Visionary Instigator Corporate view	External environment	Ends Corporate values and business results	Top	Unfreezing
Change Implementor	"Project image" Translator Division or department	Internal coordination	Means Overcoming resistance "Project image"	Middle	Changing
Change Recipient	User and adapter Institution-alizer Personal view Operational	Distribution of power and proceeds	Means–end congruence Personal benefits	Bottom	Refreezing

change effort, while often doing their "real" jobs at the same time. Meanwhile, the strategists anxiously await and test for positive results, striving to harmonize the effort and seeking to emphasize collective dedication and agreement. Recipients, for their part, are being confronted by often conflicting signals about what is important. They tend, as a result, to be far more testy about both the need for change and its ability to be implemented than either of the other two groups. That these three groups—strategists, implementors, and recipients—usually represent hierarchical realities confounds the problem further. Thus, the varying experiences, tasks, priorities—and ongoing work—of these three change groups lead to very different assumptions about a change effort.

The following description is at once extreme and typical, but it demonstrates our point. Imagine an effort at a quality transformation, originated and motivated by senior management strategists. After a couple of years, the strategists are more likely to judge the change a success than either the implementors or the recipients. They want to declare victory and go forward. Implementors, having lived with frustration and disappointment that the change has not moved fast enough or deep enough, are more critical of the results. The Indiana Jones scenario mentioned earlier is all too apparent to them. Finally, recipients, the "beneficiaries" of conflicting signals emanating from the other two groups, often think "this too shall pass."

In addition to the different frame of reference each group brings is the fact that each enters the change process at a different point. As often happens, the change strategist is impatient for action and exhorts the implementor to minimize time-consuming involvement steps. Even when participation is seemingly attempted, recipients will often report that they were insufficiently heard, involved, or informed. And when things break down, the implementor regretfully reflects, "I thought they understood and supported the change!"

Strategists are notorious for initiating major organization alterations by issuing a decree to the recipients, directly bypassing implementors (Connor, 1983). Implementors frequently decide to modify the direction of a change without gaining the strategists' endorsement. And most often, the impact of the change on the recipients is ignored or underestimated by both strategists and implementors. As one expert said, "[U]nderneath liberal enthusiasm for a more democratic climate of employee participation was impatience and intolerance that discredited those who stood in the way of progress" (Fitzgerald, 1988). Recipients had once again been bypassed and deceived.

Ten Commandments for Executing Change

Now that we have met the changemakers—all three action roles—we must examine the "script" they are to use. At the outset of this section we introduced the basic model for change. Accompanying this three-step process are a number of tactics that have become standard operating procedures for any organization attempting to achieve significant organizational change. These constitute a kind of "ten commandments" for implementing change (Figure 10–3). While this grouping is our own, the concepts are familiar and have been drawn from a wide range of sources.

1. *Analyze the organization and its need for change.* Managers should understand an organization's operations, how it functions in its environment, what its strengths and weaknesses are, and how it will be affected by proposed changes in order to craft an effective implementation plan (Nadler and Tushman, 1989).

2. *Create a shared vision and common direction.* One of the first steps in engineering change is to unite an organization behind a central vision. The ideal vision is not merely a statement of mission, a philosophy, or a strategic objective. Rather, it is an attempt to articulate what a desired future for a company would be. It can be likened to "an organizational dream—it stretches the imagination and motivates people to rethink what is possible" (Belgard, Fisher, and Rayner, 1988).

3. *Separate from the past.* Disengaging from the past—or pattern breaking (Barczak, Smith, and Wilemon, 1987)—is critical to the "unfreezing" process which Kurt Lewin described back in 1947. It is difficult for an organization to embrace a new vision of the future until it has isolated the structures and routines that no longer work and has vowed to move beyond them.

4. *Create a sense of urgency.* Convincing an organization that change is necessary isn't that difficult when a company is teetering on the edge of bankruptcy or floundering in the marketplace. But when the need for action is not generally understood, a change leader should generate a sense of urgency without appearing to be fabricating an emergency, or "crying wolf." Whether calling this motivating reaction "dissatisfaction" (Beer, 1980; Beer and Walton, 1990) or a "felt need for change" (Tichy and Devanna, 1986), a sense of urgency is critical to rallying an organization behind change.

FIGURE 10–3

The Ten Commandments

1. Analyze the organization and its need for change.
2. Create a shared vision and common direction.
3. Separate from the past.
4. Create a sense of urgency.
5. Support a strong leader role.
6. Line up political sponsorship.
7. Craft an implementation plan.
8. Develop enabling structures.
9. Communicate, involve people, and be honest.
10. Reinforce and institutionalize change.

5. *Support a strong leader role.* An organization should not undertake something as challenging as large-scale change without a leader to guide, drive, and inspire it. These change advocates, or "magic leaders" (Nadler and Tushman, 1989, 1990) play a critical role in creating a company vision, motivating company employees to embrace that vision, and crafting an organizational structure that consistently rewards those who strive toward the realization of the vision.

6. *Line up political sponsorship.* Leadership alone cannot bring about large-scale change. Success depends on a broader base of support built with other individuals who act first as followers, second as helpers, and finally as co-owners of the change (Nadler and Tushman, 1989). This "coalition-building" should include both power sources—"the holders of important supplies necessary to make the change work"—and stakeholders—those who stand to gain or lose from the change" (Kanter, 1983).

7. *Craft an implementation plan.* While a vision may guide and inspire during the change process, an organization also needs more nuts-and-bolts advice on what to do, and when and how to do it. This change plan is a "road map" for the change effort (Beckhard and Harris, 1987), specifying everything from where the first meetings should be held to the date by which the company hopes to achieve its change goal.

8. *Develop enabling structures.* Altering the status quo and creating new mechanisms for implementing change can be a critical precursor to any organizational transformation. These mechanisms may be part of the existing corporate structure or may be established as a full-fledged parallel organization (Stein and Kanter, 1980). Enabling structures designed to facilitate and spotlight change range from the practical—such as setting up pilot tests, off-site workshops, training programs, and new reward systems—to the symbolic—such as changing the organization's name or physically rearranging space (Lawler, 1989).

9. *Communicate, involve people, and be honest.* When possible, change leaders should communicate openly and seek out the involvement and trust of people throughout their organizations. Full involvement, communication, and disclosure are not called for in every change situation, but these approaches can be potent tools for overcoming resistance and giving employees a personal stake in the outcome of a transformation (Beer, 1980).

10. *Reinforce and institutionalize the change.* Throughout the pursuit of change, managers and leaders should make it a top priority to prove their commitment to the transformation process, reward risk-taking, and incorporate new behaviors into the day-to-day operations of the organization. In their Three-Act model for change, Noel Tichy and Mary Anne Devanna (1986) describe Act III, or the phase for institutionalizing change, as "shaping and reinforcing a new culture that fits with the revitalized organization."

These ten commandments are not the only tactics the planned change literature advocates, but they capture the essence of the advice typically offered. Further, each of the three changemaker groups we've introduced would surely agree that these are sensible and valuable guidelines. But just as surely, they would differ over how these are practiced and interpreted.

For example, let's take Commandment 1—analyzing the organization and its need for change—and imagine how the three groups might comment on this effort.

STRATEGISTS: The competition is at our heels, our product development is lagging, and customers are unsatisfied. We must reorient the troops to meet this challenge—or else.

IMPLEMENTORS: Hey, we're still doing the quality push you guys said was how we'd meet "the challenge"; it's not half implemented.

Do we need to "do" customers just yet?

RECIPIENTS: We haven't mastered statistical process control; already we're pulling apart the line to accommodate that and everyone's confused. We cannot absorb "customers" yet.

This is a highly realistic scenario in light of the fact that most organizations "do" multiple changes. And, if we revisit the point made earlier, that strategists often believe (and want) change to happen more quickly than is perhaps feasible, we realize that they assume that the previous change is in fact "done." To strategists, it *is* time to introduce another change. Thus, for Commandment 2—create a shared vision and a common direction—strategists may be crafting that vision and direction unaware of the reality facing the two other changemaker groups.

The cascade of potential collisions continues with Commandment 3—separate from the past. Depending on the flurry of change the organization has recently experienced, the immediate "past" may have existed for a short time period indeed. In fact, if multiple changes are in effect, it is unclear what is to be disengaged from. Do we stop working on quality improvements to focus on customers, for example? Separating from the past can generate chaos if the pace of change is too quick.

For the strategists, departing from the past can make a great deal of sense. "Let's start from square one," they say. If, however, implementors are still "doing" the previous change, as implied above, they may not be able to find "square one." Recipients may greet what they perceive to be unnecessary upheaval in their efforts with a yawn, with cynicism, or with outright resistance.

One more commandment shows how different changemaker roles can differ in interpretation and assumptions: Commandment 4—create a sense of urgency. From the strategists' vantage point, urgency originates with need for change in the first place. They might see very real threats that require deep and rapid action. Implementors might believe that the need is not so drastic or that instead of deep change, perhaps more modest alterations will work. Alternatively, implementors might see that the situation is even worse than the strategists have described; hence, they might double the pressure on recipients. Not only are the strategists pushing, the implementors are, too.

Creating a sense of urgency for change recipients needs careful consideration. Is this a threat—do this or the pink slip? Is this crying wolf? Is the organization setting up unnecessary antagonism, or adversarial conditions, where they need not be?

Charting a Course for Change

Some of the collisions described above can be a matter of blatant incompetence, mismanagement, or even ignorance; commandments, after all, can be disregarded or broken. More often, however, such disconnections result from the divergent roles in the change process. Inherent instability and conflict are brought on by these roles as a result of their interdependence. The basic interests, mind-sets, experiences, and goals of each group differ fundamentally (Kotter, 1984). Thus, it is not surprising that breakdowns occur and that the ten commandments—as sensible as they may seem—are not "obeyed."

But there are some effective ways to harness and steer an organization's motion even in the midst of instability. By simply being aware of potential disruptions and pitfalls in the change process, organizations will be in a better position to manage change. The chapters that follow illustrate that strategists, implementors, and recipients, while occupying different worlds do not have to be separated by large chasms. Change is indeed possible, but it needs to be charted carefully.

Four "rules of the road" are essential in charting a change effort that will end up where it was intended to go. (1) Appreciate the differences inherent in other "changemakers'" viewpoints. (2) Respect—but challenge—the ten commandments and their applicability within your own organization. (3) Ensure that the dialogue and communication among the various constituencies has meaning and purpose. And (4) respond flexibly, even opportunistically, not only to what occurs outside of the organization, but also to how the change process is faring within the organization.

There is nothing remarkable in such advice. Like the ten commandments themselves, it reeks of common sense. However, applied within the understanding of the three broad changemaker roles, these four "rules" *facilitate* any change effort. They are not guarantees, simply enablers.

1. Appreciating Other Changemakers' Differences

Clearly, an appreciation of the differences among changemakers begins with the acknowledgment that change will not occur unless those who are involved are in harmony. Implementation is more than a mandate given to the "middle" to involve the "bottom" in the bidding of the "top." Once again, this seems like deceptively obvious advice.

But unless a change is predicated on the assumption that "we" are all making the change, it has a slim chance of success. That is, a glance at the three broad implementation roles shows that they, in fact, encompass the entire organization; everyone ipso facto *is* an implementor. This by no means implies that everyone does the same thing or has the same responsibilities. But the differences among the roles cannot be appreciated unless all roles are acknowledged to be a part of the change "play."

The consultant Barry Oshry (1991) examined the dynamics that occur in interactions among "tops," "middles," and "bottoms"—dynamics he considers "predictable." Tops and bottoms have different priorities, he argues, and want different things from one another. When a middle assumes that she or he must resolve these differences, failure is inevitable. He claimed that the experience of being a middle typically leads to "gradual disempowerment in which reasonably healthy, confident, and competent people become transformed into anxious, tense, ineffective, and self-doubting wrecks." This is a familiar description of the experience of change implementors; they not only feel caught in the middle of others' agendas and wishes, they feel obligated—or are told—to resolve those differences. As a result, they internalize the conflicts.

Oshry suggested a series of tactics for minimizing this sense of frustration and disempowerment: be top when you can, and take the responsibility of so doing; be bottom when you should; be coach; facilitate; and integrate with other middles. Thus, to break out of conflict and paralysis, the "middle," our implementor, should take on the viewpoint of the strategist at times and the recipient at other times. This can be called "appreciating" the differences.

Appreciating the differences among the implementation roles is a prerequisite to applying the subsequent "rules of the road" we recommend. The commandments cannot be evaluated, dialogue and communication cannot be meaningful and reactions cannot be flexible unless the effects derived from these "rules" are brought into harmony with the different change roles. That harmony will not be possible unless the roles themselves are understood.

2. Evaluating the Ten Commandments

Former American President Ronald Reagan and Soviet Premier Mikhail Gorbachev used to refer to an old Russian joke whose punchline was "trust but verify." A similar spirit should be invoked for the ten commandments. Trust the common sense they espouse, but ensure that they are truly applicable to the particular organization and changemaker categories within it. Effective changemakers use the advice embedded in the commandments as a blueprint; while the rough outlines are there, the individual company must fill in the details that bring the drawing to life.

Considering that the ten commandments arose from an earlier era, it is not at all surprising that they appear to fall short in some respects. Most of the planned change efforts of the 1960s and 1970s involved an outside consultant coming in to an isolated plant or division to work on a discrete change program, such as fostering better communication between workers. But most companies in the 1990s find themselves facing large, systemwide changes. These organizations must first put a strong personal imprint on the process. They may follow the commandments, but they also find ways to honor their own specific needs, cultures, and styles. A study of innovation in the Norwegian shipping industry found that "[i]nnovative change efforts . . . that incorporated the spirit and techniques of inquiry, discovery, and invention, produced more significant and lasting innovations and greater understanding of why they do or do not work" (Walton and Gaffney, 1989).

Tailoring the commandments to give them meaning within an organization requires a process similar to the one in which each commandment was considered from each changemaker's perspective. Debate can be triggered through a series of questions, including: Are we addressing the real needs of the company, or following the path of least resistance? How shared is the vision? How do we preserve anchors to the past while moving to the future? Does everyone need to feel the same sense of urgency? Can change recipients, far down in the hierarchy, have an impact? How do we handle those who oppose the change? When should progress be visible? How do we integrate special projects to mainstream operations? When is it wise or best to share bad news? Now that we have gotten this far, is this the direction we still want to go? How much change can the organization absorb?

Posing questions like these helps keep an organization focused and flexible (see below). Moreover, by challenging the particular commandments, managers are reminded that implementing change is an ongoing process of discovery.

3. Ensuring Meaningful Communication

Experts on organizational development have touted the importance of communication for decades; indeed, the ninth commandment itself advocates open communication. But communication as we use it here goes beyond keeping people informed of change efforts.

Too often, "communication" translates into a unilateral directive. Real communication requires a dialogue among the different changemakers—a give-and-take that allows these different "voices" to express themselves and to be listened to (Ashkenas and Jick, 1990). Consider the list of questions that can challenge the applicability of the ten commandments. Forums should be devised so that the various change constituencies can pose those types of questions—contributing ideas, reactions, and complaints; confronting each other's underlying reasoning and assumptions; and overcoming "defensive routines" (Argyris, 1990). By listing and responding to concerns, resistance, and feedback from all levels, changemakers gain a broader understanding of what the change means to different parts of the organization and how it will affect them.

As with most management techniques, encouraging this kind of give-and-take requires both time and effort, but the results can be all-important. The chairman of Motorola, Bob Galvin, was able to foresee the need for critical changes precisely because he was so well connected with managers farther down in his organization. As recounted in the Motorola case in Chapter 11, Galvin created such meaningful dialogues largely by setting the model with his own behavior. In addition to installing participative management programs, he sent out a clear message about his own accessibility by "walking the halls" and sharing lunch with employees from all levels of the corporation. Moreover, he created an opportunity for multiple levels of managers and employees to shape a new direction for the corporation collaboratively. The labor-intensive dialogue at Motorola helped not only to uncover the need for change but also to attack its implementation.

Jack Welch of General Electric is another change leader who has been uncommonly successful at encouraging dialogue between different layers of his company. GE's Work-Out Program, described in one of the portraits, has as one of its key goals the regular exposure of corporate leaders to the candid opinion of the workers they oversee. "Real communication takes countless hours of eyeball to eyeball, back and forth," Welch has declared. "It means more listening than talking. . . . It is human beings coming to see and accept things through a constant interactive process aimed at consensus."

4. Reacting Flexibly and Opportunistically

Advice embedded in the ten commandments places a premium on action—on taking charge. But this focus on action assumes a level of control that simply doesn't exist when large-scale change is being implemented. Those who want to embrace change must be as adept at *reacting* as they are at acting, and they must be flexible in the way they pursue their goals and implement their strategies.

This flexibility should start with considering the commandments themselves. In addition to challenging their applicability for the particular organization, and examining the advice from the various changemakers' perspectives, the commandments themselves need contemplation. They may have an unintended underside. Seemingly constructive change behaviors such as pattern breaking, experimenting, and visioning each carry their own risks (Barczak, Smith, and Wilemon, 1987). Experimenting, for instance, can cause a company to lose its focus or can paralyze decision-makers who are faced with too many options. And visioning can be inappropriate when it leads to an inflexible adherence to a single goal or points a company in the wrong direction.

Moreover, the commandments could be accused of having a built-in paradox. They are largely designed to help strategists and implementors implement change with fewer risks and more control. And yet change by its very nature requires risk taking and letting go. Thus, while the commandments may serve to minimize failure, maximize control and predictability, and define the end state, a transformation may actually require maximizing experimentation and risk taking, tolerating unknowable consequences, and evolving toward—rather than targeting—an end state.

Thus flexibility, as used here, transcends exploration of tactics; it should challenge, or be prepared for the consequences of, basic strategy. In many cases, this involves wrestling with paradox. Take, for example, the third commandment—separating from the past. As already mentioned, the perception of "the past" can be very different according to the perspectives of strategists, implementors, and recipients. But there is a deeper issue here: while it is unquestionably important to make a break from the past in order to change, it is also important to hang on to and reinforce those aspects of the organization that bring value to the new "vision." That is, some sort of stability—heritage, tradition, or anchor—is needed to provide continuity amid change. As the changes multiply, arguably this past-within-the-future becomes even more essential.

The fifth commandment urges a strong leader role, and yet many organizations of the 1990s do not have just one leader at the helm of their change effort. And the model presented here posits various changemaker roles. Thus, whereas a change effort may seem to demand a leadership role, the fact that there are three implementation roles, all of whose input is vital to success, requires some flexible wrestling with how change is to be managed, and by whom.

Finally, even the apparently elementary advice of the seventh commandment—craft an implementation plan—must be accompanied by an important caveat: Too much planning can lead to paralysis, indecision, and collapse. Organizations that are locked in a rigid change "schedule" of planned goals and events may find themselves following something that no longer meets their evolving needs, much less those of the world around them. Indeed, preprogrammed models may be unrealistic (Beer and Walton, 1987); instead, companies should remain true to the goals of the change, but be flexible about the means. (Of course, there is a paradox embedded in this suggestion as well. Profound change may have to tolerate unknowable consequences, as indicated earlier, which may necessitate evolving goals!)

A way out of these paradoxes within paradoxes (i.e., a way of developing the flexibility to deal with the ramifications of a change effort), is to learn to take (or make) change one step at a time, gauging the effectiveness of each move before going on. For some, this may be a disconcerting approach. As alluded to earlier, change implementors have a common sensation of just "muddling along" without making clear progress.

But in fact, properly managed, "muddling along" can be a most effective way of handling multiple changes and complex situations. The theorist James Brian Quinn (1980) has dubbed this piecemeal approach to strategic planning "logical incrementalism"; he suggests this may be the most common way in which well-managed organizations change their strategy. A member of a team trying to introduce design changes at the plant level of an organization observed, "It's stupid to flounder around, but maybe floundering is a necessary period of adjustment" (Hirschhorn, 1988).

According to Quinn, "The most effective strategies of major enterprises tend to emerge step-by-step from an iterative process in which the organization probes the future, experiments, and learns from a series of partial (incremental) commitments rather than through global formulations of total strategies." Others point similarly to a "process of iterative planning, where plans are revised as frequently as new events and opportunities present themselves, bounded only by the intent of the change and how much energy is available" (Nadler and Tushman, 1989).

Responding to Situational Requirements

> ***[P]eople assume the end, and consider how they can get it, by what means. Where it seems that the end can be produced by several means, they consider which means does it most easily and best. Where the end is produced by one single means, they examine how that comes about, and what will produce it, until eventually they arrive at the first cause, which in fact is the last in the process of discovery.***
>
> **—Aristotle, Ethics III.3**

The appropriate way of thinking about change implementation has less to do with obeying "commandments" and more to do with responding to the "voices" within the organization, to the requirements of a particular situation, and to the reality that change may never be a discrete phenomenon or a closed book. Managing change today is actually managing a cascade of change; most people are bleary-eyed with their "change agendas."

The new and almost unimaginably complex world facing most organizations today calls for new and, ideally, imaginably—tolerably—complex approaches to managing change. Yet the more we have studied change, and the more we brush up against its effects, the more humble we have become about dictating the "best" way to do it. Behavioral scientists themselves disagree on a number of fundamental implementation issues. A recent book attempting to pull together the best in practice (Mohrman et al., 1989) recognized discord among its own contributors on such basic questions as whether there is a logical sequence to the change process; whether change "agents" can lead an organization through a process that cannot be explained ahead of time; even whether change can be planned at all.

Thus, the ideas presented here have been aimed less at endorsing a particular methodology than at helping people "do" change effectively while in the middle of the change process. At a minimum, there is no such thing as "a change" any longer. There is a sequence of multiple, overlapping changes reflecting constant motion in an activated environment, with each change triggering others. No longer can a single change theme—e.g., quality—presuppose upheavals in the organization. Thus, the basic tenets of implementation can be challenged, but they should not be overturned. Rather, there is a need for more "software" to improve their utility in light of greater complexity.

A more organic approach to change seems the only appropriate way to deal with the reality of most change processes. Institutionalizing change is not the real goal; institutionalizing the journey may be, however. Being able to challenge, react, yes, even act on occasions—that is how we think the flux is "managed." This may be a disheartening conclusion for those who would like change to be engineered as precisely as is a piece of machinery.

In the end, however, this conclusion may cheer the growing number of internal and external changemakers who find dictates from on high insufficient for the real challenges they face. Such leaders are already recognizing the importance of acknowledging the diversity of implementors, the need for challenging and tailoring "commandments," the quintessential value of dialogue, and the need for constant flexibility. Although managing change will never be easy, with the right attitude and approach, it can be a most gratifying adventure.

References

Allaire, Y., and M. Firsirotu. 1985. "How to implement radical strategies in large organizations." *Sloan Management Review*. Winter, pp. 19–34.

Argyris, Chris. 1985. *Strategy, Change, and Defensive Routines*. Cambridge, MA: Ballinger.

———. 1990. *Overcoming Organizational Defenses*. Boston: Allyn & Bacon.

Ashkenas, Ronald, and Todd Jick. 1990. "Organizational Dialogue." Working paper.

Barczak, Gloria; Charles Smith; and David Wilemon. 1987. "Managing large-scale organizational change." *Organizational Dynamics*. Autumn, pp. 232–35.

Beckhard, Richard, and R. Harris. 1987. *Organizational Transitions*. Second Edition. Reading, MA: Addison Wesley.

Beer, Michael. 1980. *Organization Change and Development: A Systems View*. Dallas: Scott Foresman.

Beer, Michael. 1988. "The critical path for change: Keys to success and failure in six companies." In R. Kilmann and T. J. Covin (eds.), *Corporate Transformation*. San Francisco: Jossey-Bass, pp. 17–45.

Beer, Michael, and Elise Walton. 1987. "Organizational change and development." In M. Rosenzweig and L. Porter (eds.), *Annual Review of Psychology*. Palo Alto, CA: Annual Reviews, pp. 339–68.

———. 1990. "Developing the competitive organization: Interventions and strategies." *American Psychologist*. Vol. 45, no. 2, pp. 154–61.

Belgard, William; K. Kim Fisher; and Steven Rayner. 1988. "Vision, opportunity, and tenacity: Three informal processes that influence formal transformation." In R. Kilmann and T. J. Covin (eds.), *Corporate Transformation*. San Francisco: Jossey-Bass.

Collins, Denis; Ruth Ann Ross; and Timothy Ross. 1989. "Who wants participative Management? The managerial perspective." *Group and Organization Studies.* Vol. 14, no. 4 (December), pp. 422–45.

Conner, Daryl. 1983. "Determinants of Successful Organizational Change." O.D. Resources, Inc., Atlanta.

Covin, Teresa, and Ralph Kilmann. 1989. "Critical issues in large-scale change." *Journal of Organizational Change Management.* Vol. 1, no. 2, pp. 59–72.

Dunphy, Dexter C., and Douglas Stace. 1989. "Evolution or transformation? Incremental versus transformational ideologies for organizational change." *Australian Graduate School of Management* (University of New South Wales).

Fitzgerald, Thomas. 1988. "Can change in organizational culture really be managed?" *Organizational Dynamics.* Autumn, pp. 5–15.

Goodman, Paul S., and associates. 1982. *Change in Organizations.* San Francisco: Jossey-Bass.

Guest, Robert H.; Paul Hersey; and Kenneth H. Blanchard. 1977. *Organizational Change Through Effective Leadership.* Englewood Cliffs, NJ: Prentice-Hall.

Hambrick, Donald, and Albert Cannella. 1989. "Strategy implementation as substance and selling." *Academy of Management Executives.* Vol. 3, no. 4, pp. 278–85.

Hirschhorn, Larry. 1988. *The Workplace Within.* Cambridge, MA: MIT Press.

Kanter, Rosabeth Moss. 1983. *The Change Masters.* New York: Simon & Schuster.

———. 1985. "Managing the Human Side of Change." *Management Review* (April): 5–56. On videotape as *Managing Change, the Human Dimension.* Cambridge, Mass.: Goodmeasure Inc., One Memorial Drive.

———. 1991. "Improving the acceptance and use of new technology: Organizational and inter-organizational challenges." In National Academy of Engineering (ed.), *People and Technology in the Workplace.* Washington: National Academy Press, pp. 15–56.

Kilmann, Ralph, and Teresa Covin (eds.). 1988. *Corporate Transformation.* San Francisco: Jossey-Bass.

Kirkpatrick, Donald. 1986. *How to Manage Change Effectively.* San Francisco: Jossey-Bass.

Kotter, John. 1984. *Power and Influence.* New York: Free Press.

Lawler, Edward. 1989. "Strategic choices for changing organizations." In A. Mohrmann, S. Mohrmann, G. Ledford, T. Cummings, and E. Lawler (eds.), *Large-Scale Organizational Change.* San Francisco: Jossey-Bass, pp. 255–71.

Lewin, Kurt. 1947. "Frontiers in group dynamics." *Human Relations.* Vol. 1, pp. 5–41.

Lippitt, Gordon; Peter Langseth; and Jack Mossop. 1985. *Implementing Organizational Change.* San Francisco: Jossey-Bass.

Mohrman, Susan; Allan Mohrman; and Gerald Ledford. 1989. "Interventions that change organizations." In A. Mohrman, S. Mohrman, G. Ledford, T. Cummings, and E. Lawler (eds.), *Large-Scale Organizational Change.* San Francisco: Jossey-Bass, pp. 145–53.

Mohrman, Susan; A. S. Mohrman; G. Ledford; T. Cummings; and E. Lawler (eds.), 1989. *Large-Scale Organizational Change.* San Francisco: Jossey-Bass.

Nadler, David, and Michael Tushman. 1989. "Organizational framebending: Principles for managing reorientation." *Academy of Management Executive.* Vol. 3, pp. 194–202.

———. 1990. "Beyond the charismatic leader: Leadership and organizational change." *California Management Review.* Winter, pp. 77–97.

Neumann, Jean. 1989. "Why people don't participate in organizational change." In Richard Woodman and William Passmore (eds.), *Research in Organizational Change and Development.* Greenwich, CT: JAI Press, pp. 181–212.

Oshry, Barry. 1991. "Converting middle powerlessness to middle power: A systems approach." *National Productivity Review.*

Quinn, J. B. 1980. "Managing strategic change." *Sloan Management Review.* Vol. 21, Summer, pp. 3–20.

Spector, Bert. 1989. "From bogged down to fired up: Inspired organizational change." *Sloan Management Review.* Summer, pp. 29–34.

Stein, Barry, and Rosabeth Kanter. 1980. "Building the parallel organization: creating mechanisms for permanent quality of work life." *Journal of Applied Behavioral Science,* pp. 194–210.

Tichy, Noel. 1983. *Managing Strategic Change: Technical, Political, and Cultural Dynamics.* New York: John Wiley.

Tichy, Noel, and Maryanne Devanna. 1986. *The Transformational Leader.* New York: John Wiley & Sons.

Walton, Richard, and Michael Gaffney. 1989. "Research, action, and participation: The merchant shipping case." *American Behavioral Scientist,* Vol. 32 (May–June), pp. 582–611.

Woodward, Harry, and Steve Buchholz. 1987. *After-Shock: Helping People Through Corporate Change.* New York: John Wiley & Sons.

Chapter 11

Sensing the Environment, Creating Visions: Change Strategists

Introductory Notes

The portraits in this chapter provide a glimpse of both the excitement and the confusion involved in envisioning change. They highlight the typical challenges and difficulties associated with designing the overall focus and game plan for major change. Steve Rothmeier, former chairman of Northwest Airlines (described in "Northwest Airlines Confronts Change"), likens change to the adventures of the film hero Indiana Jones, fraught with unpredictable threats and landmines. The conventional change-management idea that change is a "program" directed at following a "plan" to an "end-state" is irrelevant, if not dangerous, under such circumstances.

The task of the change strategist, then, is to create a vision and a pathway to realizing it out of all the uncertainty and chaos, in concert with key constituencies. The change strategist is responsible for the organization's direction and identity—its relationship to its environment, the promises it makes to its stakeholders; he or she must determine when and how to reshape that identity and mobilize the rest of the organization behind the new vision.

The Northwest Airlines portrait takes place in a pressured industry facing major environmental change in the 1980s. At Northwest "turbulence" was experienced not only in the air while flying but also in the offices of top management. When Steve Rothmeier became CEO, he inherited a company with strong financials and employee loyalty, but also a history of union acrimony and inadequate capabilities in both people and technology, compared with its competitors. His early challenges as a change strategist were relatively straightforward and commonplace: how to develop a message that would inspire people, and how to communicate it more effectively than the underground messages coming through the rumor mill.

Then events swamped any orderly change plan. In rapid succession Northwest faced a merger, systems breakdowns, union fights, media scrutiny, and a crisis—a plane crash—of unprecedented proportions in the industry. Rothmeier was a victim of events rather than a shaper of them; he even received death threats. As in any crisis (see the end of Chapter 6), grand ideas about visions and culture changes had to be put aside while immediate logistical problems were solved. So much for strategy.

Even though the ultimate crisis confronting Northwest seemed to derail the efforts to reposition the company for external competitiveness and change its internal operating style, it had a positive effect. The crisis provided an occasion for Rothmeier to talk with his people in new ways; his people, in turn, were brought closer together as they faced the seriousness of Northwest's situation. A bigger and better change effort, Operation Breakthrough, grew out of the crisis, and it had more commitment from Northwest's people. The lesson for change strategists: problems are not distractions getting in the way of change programs; they represent prime opportunities for rallying people behind a common cause.

Rothmeier learned in still another way that even as CEO he did not control events. Despite leading the airline to record profits, he lost his job in a takeover.

Just how much a chief executive should do personally to lead change is the theme of the set of vignettes about leadership at General Motors, one of the most visible organizations in the United States and known worldwide as an industry giant. "Behind the Steering Wheel at General Motors" offers contrasting views of what GM's change strategy should be. Chairman Roger Smith's dream of innovation and change for GM in the 1980s (in "The Innovator") is nowhere near as radical as dissident director Ross Perot's advice to the company (in "How I Would Turn Around GM"). Smith presents the traditional, conservative, orderly model of a change strategy: the leader sees a need after discussion with a few aides; he or she commissions a study to diagnose the present state; the study recommends a reorganization. So far, so conventional. Top-down, mechanical, and bloodless—a change strategy style matching an executive who denied there was anything wrong with how the corporation used to operate, thereby undercutting his own change message.

Ross Perot, swashbuckling founder of Electronic Data Systems (EDS), who sold his company to General Motors in 1984 and gained a seat on the GM Board of Directors, crafts the polar opposite change strategy: talk toughly, bluntly, and concretely, and go for dramatic action right away. Instead of commissioning studies, bring the new model of a lean, flexible, innovative, and responsive organization into being right away. In short, "How I Would Turn Around GM" is not only bold, it is detailed. It is a call to revolution. It asks the CEO and senior managers to get involved in an immediate and compelling way—going into the field, living with the troops, learning from stakeholders (customers, dealers, stockholders, mechanics). Perot's strategy is highly participative in that it calls for massive mobilization and involvement of many members of the organization; yet it also offers strong guidance and direction, especially in its call for absolute excellence.

Compare the Perot style with Smith's view of his task in "The Painful Reeducation of a Company Man: An Interview with Roger Smith." And further compare it with the advice given by experts to Smith's successor in "Advice for G.M.'s Bob Stempel." Malcolm Salter's call for a reexamination of GM's capacity in light of industry changes would seem to necessitate Perot-type boldness. The vision created by a change strategist does not have to be a soft, squishy statement of hopes and wishes; it can be a concrete call to action.

Motorola faced a different situation in the 1980s from the industry downturn GM experienced. "Bob Galvin and Motorola, Inc." portrays an attempt by Motorola's chairman to stimulate his senior managers to create their own vision of a new Motorola, at a time when the "old" Motorola was going just fine. Motorola in 1983 was an enlightened, progressive, and successful company. But in keeping with his role as manager of the link to the external environment, CEO Bob Galvin saw the need for repositioning Motorola in a changing external environment. Furthermore, rapid expansion, one of the life cycle challenges described in Chapter 2, had created structural and managerial problems, including unwieldy complexity.

In Galvin's view, leadership meant engaging and empowering other people, a philosophy reflected in shared leadership at the top. He was a good listener who walked the halls and listened to the feedback. It was unlikely that he could take the bold stance of a Ross Perot, nor did Motorola require such a shakeup. Therefore, Galvin invited top managers to join him in crafting a vision and change plan to close the gap in understanding and perspective among different levels in the company. He wanted to develop leadership opportunities for talented people throughout the organization who would, in time, instigate change.

People are often not prepared for the Galvin style of change strategy. Note the reactions at Motorola, even after years of experience with a Participative Management Program. Those hearing Galvin's invitation could not quite believe it. They wondered what he meant and whether he was serious.

Thus, the portraits offer contrasting types of change strategists, each appropriate to the particular company's situation and the particular leader's personal preference. But they also offer a common set of lessons about the task. Change strategists are engaged in a search for the appropriate vision and focus, the best way to communicate the message and its rationale, even while recognizing the complexity, confusion, and chaos that come with constant organizational motion. They must develop a motivational message that transcends the chaos and encourages other people to begin the hard work of making the vision a reality.

Northwest Airlines Confronts Change

Susan Rosegrant and Todd D. Jick

I thought it would beat any Indiana Jones movie. The change effort starts out with a real nice beginning, and then suddenly you get one disaster after another: The boulder just misses you, and you get the snake in the cockpit of the airplane. That's what it's all about. You've got to be down in the blood and the mud and the beer.

—Steve Rothmeier, former CEO of Northwest Airlines

When Steve Rothmeier took over as CEO of Northwest Airlines in January 1985, [he] set to work in an environment which seemed under continual fire—both from within and from without.

Since Congress's deregulation of the airline industry in 1978, there had been a steady stream of almost yearly challenges which had forced carriers to react as nimbly as possible in order to stay aloft. In 1979, a growing fuel shortage, and the temporary grounding of the popular DC10 aircraft because of safety concerns, played havoc with airlines' schedules and routes. The 1981 air traffic controllers' strike significantly reduced available air space, forcing another round of route and schedule negotiations. In addition, People Express and a slew of other low-cost airlines that started up in the early 1980s added a new competitive twist—forcing cross-industry fare cuts and stirring up union–management acrimony, as established carriers looked to recoup lost passenger dollars by lowering wages and revising work rules.

This onslaught of changing conditions and increased competition took a heavy toll. Although 20 new carriers had taken wing from the time of deregulation up to the end of 1984, a full dozen jet airlines had filed for bankruptcy protection during the same period.

Northwest Airlines was by no means immune to the pressures which accompanied deregulation. First under the tutelage of Donald W. Nyrop, chief executive from 1954 until 1979, and then under M. Joseph Lapensky, from 1979 to 1985, the Minneapolis/ St. Paul–based carrier had become known both for its conservative financial controls and for its hard-line labor relations policies. Although the airline's financial savvy had given it a strong balance sheet, the antagonistic stance taken toward labor had saddled the airline with a track record of union dissent. Just during the decade of the 1970s, Northwest endured four separate strikes.

Perhaps the greatest challenge that Rothmeier faced as he took over in 1985, however, was to transform Northwest into a more responsive, customer-driven service organization capable of competing in the new era. For, despite the fact that six years had passed since deregulation, Northwest still displayed neither the technological capabilities—such as sophisticated travel agent computer reservation systems—nor the people skills that were being honed at such major competitors as American Airlines, United, and Delta.

Rothmeier was intimately familiar with Northwest's strengths and weaknesses: Except for a brief stint in marketing at General Mills, the Minneapolis-based food products company, Rothmeier had spent his entire professional career at the airline. Armed with a marketing degree from Notre Dame and an MBA from the University of Chicago, Rothmeier joined Northwest in 1973 as a financial analyst and soon became Nyrop's protégé. Ten years later he was named president and chief operating officer, and in 1985, at the age of 38, he became the youngest chief executive officer of any major U.S. airline.

Reshaping Northwest

When Rothmeier took over at Northwest, he saw the faithfulness and pride of its employees as one of the airline's greatest assets. "There is a tremendous loyalty here," he declared. "We went through a 93-day pilots' strike in 1972, and a 103-day pilots' strike in 1978. Everybody came back to work. Nobody left Northwest. They could complain and moan about it, but everybody came back to work, and there was a deep-seated pride that was really remarkable."

But if loyalty was the airline's greatest asset, in Rothmeier's estimation, the unions were its greatest liability, and were at the heart of many of the problems he was trying to change. With 95% of its employees belonging to a union, the carrier was the most highly unionized airline in the world, Rothmeier declared. "We had to drive a wedge between union leadership and union membership," he asserted. "Instead of creating an environment where union employees went to a shop steward to solve a problem, I wanted them to come to their managers to solve that problem. I wanted them to be part of the team."

Specifically, Rothmeier believed that it would be next to impossible for employees to embrace the importance of such concepts as emphasizing customer service and participating in management decisions as long as they were wedded first to the union cause. Moreover, while the airline might have been able to prosper against a backdrop of labor–management hostility in the past, Rothmeier was convinced that such acrimony could prove fatal in the new era of deregulation.

"The world has changed," he recalled saying. "I used to go tell the union members, 'Every carrier's expanding at double digit numbers. Everybody's growing at enormous rates, but guess what? The pie isn't really that big. The appetites are growing larger than the pie is. And that means that you can take all this fraternal stuff and stick it right up your nose, because if United Airlines does it better than we do, that union guy over there is going to get your job.'"

Northwest, in many respects, was in a reasonably strong position when Rothmeier took over: The airline was the dominant U.S. carrier in the Pacific, and it had a particularly strong domestic presence in its Twin Cities hub. As a result, Rothmeier . . . had to carefully craft a change rationale that would acknowledge the airline's strengths, yet still push for substantial improvements. "You've got to slant the message to something that will grab people," Rothmeier explained.

To accomplish this, Rothmeier said, he focused less on issues of survival, and instead tried to stress the difficulties Northwest would face in hanging on to its "championship" status. "We all know that it's tougher to repeat as national champion than it is to get there the first time," he asserted. "We'd tell them, 'We're in a knock-down, drag-em-out fight, and there is nothing un-American about going home every night with perspiration on your brow. There's nothing un-American about getting paid eight hours of pay for eight hours of work each day.' That's what you need to defend the national championship." . . .

But reaching all the participants of Northwest's geographically diverse and mobile organization proved extremely difficult. "The most frustrating thing was the amount of time it took to change a large organization," he recalled. "In the airline business, pilots and flight attendants are away all the time. You can't get them in one room. You can't get them in ten rooms! So you have an incredible communications problem, because the rumor mill works better than anything else." He added: "Rumors travel instantly. But facts weren't so easy to relay."

To help reach all the airline's employees, Rothmeier filmed a series of videotapes explaining Northwest's mission and how the organization was trying to change. But this medium, also, was limited in its usefulness. "You've got a 30-minute video, the pilots and flight attendants watch it, and then they're off to catch a flight, and the whole rumor mill starts all over again," he complained. "'The boss said this.' Well, the boss didn't say that, but that's what they thought they heard the boss say. That was the biggest frustration. The communications process was so unwieldy."

The Republic Merger

. . . Rothmeier was also facing the troubling question of how Northwest could survive against the growing dominance of such "megacarriers" as American and United. In January 1986, one year after he became CEO, Rothmeier announced that Northwest would acquire long-time archrival and fellow Minneapolis/ St. Paul–based carrier, Republic Airlines.

For the next nine months, until the acquisition became effective in October, Rothmeier's energies were largely focused on the merger. . . . On October 1, 1986, Northwest Airlines completed its $884 million buyout of Republic Airlines—the largest merger in the airline industry to date. The merger, which nearly doubled the carrier's size to almost 33,500 employees, made Northwest the fifth largest airline company. Most industry observers applauded the move, claiming that it positioned Northwest strongly to compete through the second half of the 1980s and beyond. Within hours of the merger, Northwest's Twin Cities operations had come to a virtual standstill.

When Northwest's systems balked following the merger, Rothmeier wasn't altogether surprised. Because of Department of Transportation antitrust regulations, Northwest and Republic were prohibited from engaging in detailed scheduling, pricing, and marketing discussions prior to the merger's final approval, he said. Moreover, after giving the acquisition careful thought, he concluded that most of the integration glitches would have to be worked out after the two airlines' systems had already been combined. "From my understanding of the airline business, if you didn't put all the departments and their divisions together at once, you would be solving problems that would just create more problems," he explained. "You had to find out how these two computer systems really interfaced. You had to find out how the crew scheduling worked. It's a very, very complex business."

What did surprise Rothmeier, though, was the speed of the collapse. "When we did it, I said, 'In 48 hours, we'll know every problem we have in the system, and then we'll have to work our way out of it,'" he recalled. "It didn't take 48 hours. It took about two hours. And we had every problem and 400 more that we never dreamed of."

In the early days following the acquisition, most of the difficulties Northwest experienced were simply the result of trying to merge two highly disparate operations. Flight delays, double-booking of passengers, and lost luggage were all too frequent occurrences. But even worse, Rothmeier recalled, was the unexpected intensity of the union discord which followed the merger.

Because the unions representing Republic were, for the most part, different from those representing Northwest, there was a tremendous uproar as the rival unions fought to win employee backing for the right to represent the combined organization. At one point, Rothmeier said, he was dealing with almost 20 different negotiating units. Moreover, union leaders made the most of the fact that some Republic employees were paid less than their counterparts at Northwest, having accepted wage cuts a few years earlier in an attempt to salvage their struggling airline. "We knew we were going to be in bad shape for 18 months or so after the merger," Rothmeier recounted. "What we didn't count on was that we'd get the opposition from the unions. We really believed that they had more sense of what was necessary for long-term survival."

Rothmeier found it particularly difficult to deal with the former Republic union leaders, who were making the most of the differences between the two carriers' cultures. "What better way for them to fight for representation than to paint the big competitor across the street that took strikes in 1962, 1964, 1970, 1972, 1975, 1978, and 1982 as this great big ogre who had no respect for its people, and who kicked the crap out of them all the time," he fumed. "They came to negotiate with management with a list of demands that would have bankrupted the carrier, and they knew it, but they also knew that they could go back then and just stir up the operation. They had a planned program to try and destroy the service levels of the airline and bring the company to its knees."

As he struggled to repair and improve the airline's beleaguered post-merger operations, as well as to counter escalating union demands, Rothmeier said, he still hadn't lost sight of . . . efforts to encourage a new, more participative culture at Northwest. But, by necessity, the change effort had taken a backseat to the logistical problem of resolving the daily confrontations which now typified his job. "At that point it was just like combat," Rothmeier explained.

"You're in the fight now, and guess what? There are more tanks on the other side than you thought, they've got heavier artillery, and you're up to your butt in alligators." He added: "Your plan is still there to try to change the culture, but one of the things you find out is that the company you just acquired probably isn't going to buy into the program. You're planning to give them a new chance in life, and they don't believe that."

To make matters worse, as one of Minneapolis's largest employers, Rothmeier's every move was being scrutinized by the press, who often characterized him as cold or ruthless. Yet, Rothmeier insisted that throughout the ordeal, his relationship with workers overall was excellent. "The union always came back through the media and portrayed me as a guy who sat in the office and never talked to the troops," he exclaimed. "They knew that was absolute bullshit. That was all part of the propaganda by the union leadership to try to portray me differently than I was, to try and drive that wedge between management and the employees."

Although he had a "very capable" team of executive vice presidents who helped him chart a course through those difficult times, Rothmeier often felt alone in the spotlight. "There isn't anybody that's going to help you at that point," he reflected. "I did talk to a lot of other CEOs who had been through similar processes, but it was never magnified by the media. To get away, I went down to my exercise room and lifted weights."

Looking back on the strife which followed the merger, Rothmeier claimed that if he had to do it over again, he would follow his instincts and impose more controls on the whole process. "I think we were way too participative in the early stages," he said. "We spent too much time trying to satisfy the newcomers and trying to educate them, instead of saying, 'You've got a choice. This was an acquisition, fellows, either do it our way or go do something else.'"

Moreover, although he believed there was value in eventually working toward a more participative culture, Rothmeier contended that there would always be a limit to how much freedom employees should be allowed in an airline environment. People Express's failure, he asserted, was indicative of what could happen if management gave up too much control. "In order to have a safe airline, you've got to have procedures, you've got to have discipline, and you've got to have structure," he explained. "You can't manage by seance."

In the months following the acquisition, Northwest rapidly put in new systems and practices to accommodate the combined operation. But although many of the technical snafus were solved, the relationship between labor and management just grew uglier. By the summer of 1987, Rothmeier said, mechanics and baggage handlers were conducting an unofficial slowdown; the carrier had topped the government's list of passenger complaints; there had been a few instances of antiunion employees being beaten up; and Rothmeier himself had received death threats.

But Rothmeier didn't have much time to worry about the threats: his attention was soon pulled elsewhere. As he lifted weights in his suburban home one hot August night, he got a phone call telling him that a Northwest flight had crashed on takeoff from Detroit.

The Crash

On August 16, 1987, Northwest Flight 255 crashed after takeoff from Detroit, killing 156 people. The accident was later attributed to pilot error. It was the second worst disaster in American aviation history, and the worst disaster by far in Northwest's 61 years.

Rothmeier didn't go to Detroit immediately after the crash, in part because he feared the media would exploit the situation and use it for its own purposes. But within two weeks, Rothmeier held sessions at the Detroit, Memphis, and Twin Cities airports to meet with every one of the employees involved in the accident. "I explained, first of all, how much we appreciated what they did and how difficult it was," he recounted. "I had spent one year in Vietnam picking up Killed-in-Actions and shipping them home, so I knew what the hell was going on in Detroit." He added: "I talked with them and told them what my experiences were and shared some of this. We did more with our employees after the crash than any airline had ever done in history."

As he worked to piece things back together in the weeks after the accident, Rothmeier was struck by how the disaster affected people. For the flying public, he said, it seemed to serve as a lightning rod for complaints and criticism. "You have to recall that service in general in the airline industry was bad at that point, and we stunk," he explained, "but the reaction by the public was absolutely unbelievable. We had complaints about incidents that never even happened, and about flights that were nonexistent. That's when we spiked the 47 complaints per 100,000 passengers, the worst in the industry at that time."

But if the traveling public was vitriolic, within Northwest itself the crash had an oddly cathartic effect. According to Rothmeier, the combination of union intimidation, passenger antagonism, and, finally, the crash forced many employees to realize that things had to change. "The cards and the letters and the phone calls I got said, 'Boss, you've got to do something about this now,'" he recalled. "Why do we have people sabotaging the operation? Why do we have people tearing off baggage tags and making customers mad, who then come back and vent it at me?' Everybody focused on the fact that we've got to live differently, or we're going to go right down the dumper."

A few months after the crash, Rothmeier approved a more far-reaching change effort than the airline had ever attempted before. Dubbed Operation Breakthrough, the program included a range of initiatives, from "Town Hall Meetings"—employee forums chaired by Rothmeier which were designed to encourage two-way dialogue—to Station Action Teams—groups based at outlying stations, made up of union, employee, and management representatives, which were given the autonomy to handle a range of issues without corporate involvement. "We basically quadrupled the size of the change program we had at Northwest, made it for the whole airline, and were far more explicit," Rothmeier stated. "We stood up and said, 'What don't you like? Tell us right now.' They could get up and pour hot tea on us if they wanted to." . . .

With Operation Breakthrough in place, 1988 proved to be a banner year for Northwest, according to Rothmeier. The efforts to efficiently combine Northwest's and Republic's operations were finally bearing fruit in record profits. One by one, Rothmeier was reaching contract agreements with the same unions he had been fighting one year before. And by early 1989, Northwest had achieved the second best on-time record of the major airlines and had reduced passenger complaints to the point where its service was rivaling industry leaders.

But even as Rothmeier seemed poised to enjoy a stretch of relative peace and prosperity at the airline, his calm was shattered once again. In March 1989, outside investors—including Pan Am Corp. and billionaire Marvin Davis—began a bidding war for Northwest, which culminated in the friendly buyout of the airline in August by Wings Holdings, Inc., a Los Angeles–based investor group headed by Alfred Checchi. At the end of September, Rothmeier and four other top executives, including John Horn, abruptly announced their resignations from the airline.

"We told the union back when they were doing all those disruptive things that they were risking their own jobs," Rothmeier asserted. "Had we not had a disruption of the magnitude we had in 1987, we would have produced higher earnings a half year earlier, and with a normal airline price/earnings multiple on our stock, we'd never have been taken over."

Even with all the turmoil, however, Rothmeier left Northwest satisfied that he had accomplished what he set out to achieve. "We took care of the customer, we took care of the employees, we took care of management, and we took care of the shareholder like the shareholder had never been taken care of before," he declared. "We won this one, and we got paid off to do it, too."

Behind the Steering Wheel at General Motors, 1985–90

The Innovator

Cary Reich

As great a breakthrough as the Toyota joint venture was, Smith came to understand that real change at G.M. wouldn't simply be the product of dialogues with a close aide or dinner conversations with other corporate chieftains. Now, in the words of Bill Hoglund, head of the Saturn program, he had to "get the organization to respond to his creative drive." And that would require a fundamental transformation of the corporate anatomy.

As it happened, the lever he needed was already to hand. During his first months in office, president Jim McDonald had become convinced that some kind of organizational overhaul was needed to improve the manufacture of vehicles produced in North America. A task force was assembled under John Debbink, a 33-year company veteran who headed the Delco Moraine division.

Not long after the task force began meeting, Debbink says, Smith weighed in: "Roger saw that it had broader ramifications than just North American vehicle operations. It took on his personal sponsorship." The consulting firm McKinsey & Company was called in, and suddenly the project was transformed into a two-year-long soul-searching examination of the entire corporation. More than 500 executives were asked some fundamental questions: What are we doing wrong? What can we do better?

"We got a lot of candid playback," says Debbink, "playback that was in some sense shocking to the executive committee. They'd say, 'How could any officer of this corporation say *that?*' "

Catharsis may be good for the soul, but Smith recognized that within the delicate internal mechanism of a corporation, catharsis can be unsettling—raising expectations to unrealistic levels for some, breeding fear and insecurity in others. "He tried to avoid a feeling of panic in the organization," Debbink recalls. Says Smith: "We said that all we were going to find out was whether we needed to change anything or not. And I think that helped build the acceptability, that this wasn't just something that those crazy guys on the 14th floor were ginning up because they didn't have anything to do."

The conclusions the study group reached were sobering. The corporation had become risk-averse. In Debbink's words: "It didn't pay to take too many chances in the General Motors culture, because the penalties for failure were rather severe." What's more, the decision-making process was incredibly time consuming and cumbersome. In essence, G.M. management had become a vast white-collar assembly line; even minor questions had to travel from one end to the other, through layer after layer of supervisors, before a decision could be reached. In the end, nobody was fully responsible for anything, and buck-passing was rampant.

The solution the task force proposed—and the corporation ultimately adopted in January 1964—was radical. G.M.'s five car divisions and its Canadian car operations were reorganized into two groups, each of which would take on total responsibility for the cars it produced. The assembly division and the Fisher body division were disbanded, their functions taken over by the two new groups, Oldsmobile-Buick-Cadillac and Chevrolet-Pontiac-G.M. of Canada.

The guiding principle behind it all was to increase the decision-making power of staff at every level of the company and to loosen the chain of command. In a broad sense, this was accomplished by giving the two divisions total control of the cars they produced. On a more down-to-earth level, subordinates were given more direct access to their bosses. "I have 15 people reporting to me now," says Lloyd E. Reuss, head of the Chevrolet-Pontiac-G.M. Canada group. "In the past, it would have been eight or nine."

The new approach meant that top management could more clearly determine who deserved the credit or blame for a particular decision—reward the successful managers and root out the unsuccessful. And it had another key advantage. "Participative management," as the program was labeled, gave workers the chance to make more decisions, to play a larger role in reaching decisions. It can be, as Reuss points out, "an important motivator in bringing out new ideas in people." . . .

For all his eagerness for innovation, Roger Smith is wary of totally repudiating the system that spawned him. He goes out of his way to praise his predecessors; almost in the same breath in which he calls for sweeping change, he says that there was nothing wrong with the way the company used to operate. The chairman has also maintained many of the old corporate rituals including "meeting week," the once-a-month marathon of policy committee sessions that is the bane of action-oriented executives' existence.

In part, all this may reflect that old conservative streak. But it may also stem from Smith's determination to maintain corporate cohesion at a time of upheaval. Internal rumblings about his innovations can still be heard. Hundreds of white-collar computer workers, for example, have talked about forming a union because of their unwillingness to be swallowed up by E.D.S.

Smith has no illusions about the pace of change. "It's coming slow," he admitted to a group of his managers. "The easy thing is moving the boxes around on the organization chart. The hard part is changing the system."

How I Would Turn Around GM

Ross Perot

When GM acquired Electronic Data Systems in 1984, it also acquired a singular executive as a board member. Too singular, as it turned out, for Ross Perot's unbridled energy and zeal were more than the company could stomach. GM bought his stake and sent him packing, but Perot has forgotten neither what he saw nor what he hoped to change.

This is what I would recommend. Many of these ideas have been considered at GM, and many are incorporated into the GM–Saturn personnel philosophies. But talking about them won't produce results. The key ingredient is to put these ideas into practice throughout GM—execute, execute, execute!

1. Call together the top officials of the company and announce:

• GM has more talent, more money, more research capability, and more manufacturing facilities than any other carmaker. Logically it should be first and best in building the finest cars in the world. It is not. GM has failed to tap the full potential of its resources, especially its people. This must be changed.

• Starting today, GM is going to become the finest car manufacturer in the world.

• Every GMer must understand that there are too many car plants in the world. GM is playing all day every day in an economic super bowl. It is a harsh game—the losers lose their jobs and their companies. GM doesn't have to lose to the Japanese, Germans, Ford, or

Chrysler. GM can win and keep its people at work only by being the best—by building the best cars in the world.

• From this point forward, GMers will fight in the marketplace—not with one another. GMers will no longer waste energy on divisive internal struggles for power and turf. This energy must be focused, like a laser, to make the finest cars in the world.

• Starting today, the historic power struggles between the financial staff and car builders will not be tolerated. Financial people will be responsible for maintaining accounting information. People who know how to build cars and serve customers will make the product decisions. Accountants will not sap the productivity of car builders with guerrilla warfare—a GM trademark that has gone on for decades and seriously damaged GM's effectiveness.

• Starting today, GM's relationship with the United Auto Workers will be a team relationship, not an adversarial one. GM and the UAW must recognize that they can build the finest cars in the world only by working closely together. With 800,000 jobs at stake, GM must win. GM's suppliers, with millions of jobs at stake, depend on GM to win. The U.S. economy is counting on GM to win.

• Starting today, in order to build the finest cars in the world, GM will listen to its customers, listen to its dealers who sell the cars to customers, listen to the men and women who assemble its cars in the factories, and listen to the engineers who design its cars. The watchword will be: "Listen, listen, listen" to the customers and the people who are actually doing the work. Their ideas, fresh from the marketplace, will make GM the best in the world.

• Starting today, any commitment made to GM people and customers will be kept. GM can earn their trust and respect only by honoring commitments and standing squarely behind its products.

• Starting today, customer problems with GM cars will not be looked upon as legal problems but as service problems that must be solved *immediately*. From now on, ***the customer is king!***

• Eliminate all waste, starting at the top and working through every level of the company. This includes items such as chauffeured limousines, heated garages, multitiered layers of executive dining rooms, and a vast array of other relics from the past that have nothing to do with building the best cars in the world. The 25th floor of the GM Building in New York, used one day a month by the board of directors, will be closed and leased to another company. Huge staffs, now in place, act as buffers shielding the people running the company from reality. These staffs will be abolished, opening up lines of communication. After eliminating all waste at the top, GM will start working its way down to get rid of waste wherever it is found.

• Replace all current outside members of the board of directors. . . .

• Starting today, words like "management," "labor," "bonus-eligible," "salaried," and "hourly" will no longer be used.

• From this day forward, everyone is a GMer. Everyone will be a full member of a tightly knit, unified GM team.

• Starting today, every person on the GM team will be dealt with as an individual, not a commodity. Every person will be treated with dignity and respect. Every person is equal and will be treated as an equal.

• As of today, all people who manage in an authoritarian way will be fired. GM cannot tap the full potential of the people with a manager whose philosophy is "I had to eat dirt for 30 years, so now it is my turn to make the other guys eat dirt."

• All bonuses and financial incentives will be determined by a single set of rules. All GMers will win or lose together. Never again will the GMers who do the work be told one day, "It was a bad year and profit sharing will not be paid," and on the next day see the senior officials, whose bad decisions caused the problem, receive millions in bonuses. In military terms, the new philosophy will be: "First feed the troops, then the officers."

• From this point forward, the primary financial incentive offered will be GM stock. There is only one way to make the stock go up: Be the best. Build the finest cars in the world and sell these cars profitably at competitive prices. This focuses every GMer on the same goal.

• Starting today, as GM goes through the transition to build the finest cars in the world, all sacrifices will start at the top. In the future the people who work in the factories will be the last, not the first, to be affected. The people who make the decisions determine whether GM wins or loses. They, not the people who do the work, will be the first to pay for mistakes.

• Starting today, the word "management" will no longer be used at GM. Leadership will be required to build the finest cars in the world, not management. Inventories can be managed—people will be led.

• Starting today, most committees will be scrapped. The old system gets so many people involved that nobody can be blamed for failure, and nobody makes a decision. That system must be junked.

• No longer can a person rise to the top of GM by simply keeping his nose clean, or "not doing anything wrong." Starting today, the future of GM belongs to people who are willing to step out in front, make decisions, accomplish great things, take risks, make mistakes, and accept responsibility for their failures. The days of having lower-level GMers take the blame for mistakes of senior people are over.

2. After explaining this to the top 500 people in the organization, the CEO of GM would break them into groups of fewer than 50 and meet with each group for several hours to listen to their ideas and recommendations. He would then:

- Fine-tune the plan based on their responses.
- Take this plan to the leadership of the UAW. After explaining the plan, he would listen to their ideas and suggestions and fine-tune it again.
- Put together about ten groups representing a cross-section of the entire organization, from senior executives to newly hired trainees in the factory; then present this plan to each of these groups and fine-tune the plan further according to their responses.
- Immediately organize a leadership training program for every leader in GM and the UAW and work out the logistics for training thousands of people quickly. During this training program, GM must leave absolutely no doubt that any GM leader who does not deal with others according to the spirit of this plan will not be a leader on the new GM team.

The CEO will personally lead all of the activities listed in Item 2. GM's leadership will then:

3. Take this plan to every person in GM so that each will understand the new rules for success, understand that GM is going to become the best in the world, and understand the vital importance of making these changes *now*.

4. Immediately send several hundred senior leaders to the field for several weeks to visit the factories (these visits must be in depth—not superficial plant tours), visit with and *listen* to the people, learn their reactions, and communicate to them that these changes are real—not just more public relations talk. While at the factories, GM's senior people would spend evenings visiting with second- and third-shift workers.

5. Ask the dealer network to put together a cross-section of GM customers. The top leaders will attend meetings around the world and listen to the customers who own GM cars.

6. Ask GM dealers to meet with them in small groups, and spend a great deal of time listening to the dealers' ideas about how to improve GM cars.

7. Visit with mechanics who repair GM cars and listen to their ideas.

8. Organize a series of meetings with GM stockholders to listen to the company's owners.

9. In all of these meetings the leaders of the corporation will be joined by leaders from product design and engineering, leaders from the UAW, and others who actually build the cars. The end result of this firsthand exposure will be to give every member of the GM team great sensitivity about what must be done to build the finest cars in the world.

10. GM's leadership will keep these new communication lines wide open as it builds the new GM. Timely, demand field knowledge will become GM's road map for success.

11. At all times during this transition the leadership of GM should be in the field, living with the troops, sharing victories and defeats, and solving the problems as quickly as they occur. Above all, the GM leaders must be out front. They must learn by direct experience and lead by example.

12. The leadership must reward excellence while those who won are still sweating from the effort. Celebrate victories. Learn from defeats. And then get back in the ring and win!

13. Finally, the leadership must work night and day to make GM such an exciting, rewarding place that GMers look forward to coming to work. They will relish taking on all competitors and beating them fairly.

The Painful Reeducation of a Company Man

An Interview with Roger Smith

Business Monthly

Q: How do you deal with those people who don't recognize the need for change?

A: You've got to either convince them, work around them, or get rid of them. That's the hard fact of life. Who are the people who don't want to do that? The guys that have a year and a half to go, the guy that's worried about his job and doesn't feel comfortable dealing with people.

Q: How would you describe your own role in managing change at GM?

A: Primarily allocation of resources and people—make sure we get the proper team, get the focus, put it up before the team, and see that we head off in the right direction.

Q: Since you have the advantage of a lot of experience, what would you tell managers who are contemplating major changes in their companies?

A: First of all, you've got to have a vision of where you want to go, what you want to be. You ought to have goals. Then you need objectives. Then you need strategies. Then you need execution. And in the execution phase, I guess I'd have to tell them, communication is important, and so is a good system of measurement so you know where you are.

Q: Some people see an example of mixed messages coming from top management when you say that regaining market share is critical to GM's success, and yet, as market share falls, executives still get significant bonuses.

A: Let me give you one of Roger's Rules, okay? That is, mixed messages come with multiple goals. If you have more than one goal, you're going to have mixed messages going out. You want higher market share, you want higher profits, you want faster to market, you want lower costs. You're going to get mixed messages.

Q: Those are competing goals.

A: That's exactly right. We have to balance those things. What we try to do on market share is change our attitude to say we want to profitably increase our market share. So we say, "Let's get our profit margins up there, and let's go after that market share from a good profit position rather than go after profit from a market-share position."

Advice for G.M.'s Bob Stempel

Paul C. Judge

August 5, 1990. The General Motors Corporation got a new chairman last week: Robert C. Stempel, 57 years old, who joined G.M. in 1958 and rose through the ranks as an engineer. Gone is Roger B. Smith, 65, who retired after a turbulent decade marked by record profitability as well as a steady decline in market share. . . .

Mr. Stempel inherits a company whose domestic market share of 35 percent has been growing slightly since January, ending a slide of 10 points under Mr. Smith. G.M. is well positioned in the lucrative European market, and some analysts have recommended the company's stock to investors, saying G.M. holds greater potential for earnings growth than either the Ford Motor Company or the Chrysler Corporation.

But the problems that hurt G.M. in the 1980's are far from solved, chief among them the fact that the company has more plants than it needs in North America. Moreover, the company's labor relations are generally regarded as fractious. Industry observers are watching to see how Mr. Stempel's G.M. will address its burdensome overcapacity problem during the contract talks now under way with the United Automobile Workers.

. . . Industry experts were asked what they thought Mr. Stempel should be doing. He needs to roll out a very straightforward, simple agenda with some key points.

Symbols are extraordinarily important. Anything Mr. Stempel does is going to be symbolic to somebody, so it is crucial for him to manage those symbolic actions effectively. G.M. has its own constituents—hourly workers, union leaders, suppliers, midlevel managers, top executives, customers, dealers, the news media, Federal and state governments—and Mr. Stempel needs to establish himself as a symbol of leadership with every group.

A symbol of his leadership with labor, for instance, would be shutting down the 14th floor of the G.M. building, where the top executive offices are located, and have management spend a week in the plants. The idea would be to come down to the level of ordinary workers, to build a bridge.

Mr. Stempel would benefit if he spent some time improving G.M.'s relations with the media. There is a general feeling among executives at G.M., and other auto companies, that spending time with the media is time spent not doing your job. But the real job is communicating, and the most effective way to do that is through the media. General Motors tries to manage access to its top people more rigidly than it should. . . .

Mr. Stempel has to figure out how to have a lot fewer workers, and he must do it without dramatically fracturing relations with the U.A.W. The company probably will have to buy a lot of workers out of jobs. But one of the big issues facing Mr. Stempel is the absolute need to reduce excess manufacturing capacity, and to do it very quickly.

Maryann Keller

Automotive analyst and vice president of Furman Selz Mager Dietz & Birney, a New York securities firm. Her 1989 book, Rude Awakening: The Rise, Fall and Struggle for Recovery at G.M., *is a critical account of the Smith years.*

Underlying General Motors' problems is a corporate culture that is pretty unyielding and unwilling to recognize that the auto world doesn't really revolve around G.M. any more.

Mr. Stempel has to create a corporate culture that turns catchy phrases like "listening to the voice of the customer" into reality, and that channels everybody's energy in the direction of identifying and solving problems.

But part of General Motors' handicap is that it cannot even identify the problems it faces, let alone solve them.

The auto industry faces challenges in the 1990's that will make the 80's pale in comparison. General Motors has to know that old solutions like throwing money at a problem won't work and will be more dangerous during a time of intense global competition.

Mr. Stempel will have to turn G.M. into a company that confronts the reality of Japanese multinational auto makers of immense strength. At least three Japanese multinationals—Toyota, Honda and Nissan—have the power to take on G.M. in all of its markets. If Mr. Stempel recognizes that, some solutions may flow from it, like don't throw money at problems, pick markets carefully, pick products carefully. . . .

I don't think Mr. Stempel has to lay out a 5-year plan. But what he does and what he says will be interpreted carefully by employees at G.M., who are wondering whether it will be business as usual or making the "voice of the customer" into reality.

That sense of expectation can quickly turn into disappointment, or it can help Mr. Stempel to get things done.

Harold J. Leavitt

Walter Kenneth Kilpatrick Professor of Organizational Behavior and Psychology, emeritus, at the Stanford University Graduate School of Business.

I feel hesitant about giving advice when it isn't solicited. The first thing I'd tell Mr. Stempel, however, is that he needs a new top management team.

Everyone at the company should read *The Reckoning* [David Halberstam's book about the auto industry] to understand the rigidity of their own culture and how much it needs to be changed. This isn't something you do incrementally. You take some serious steps. However, I don't think a single individual can do much.

In my opinion, the organization needs more innovativeness and imagination. Mr. Stempel ought to flatten out the layers of management and reward people for their initiative.

Malcolm S. Salter

Chairman of the Advanced Management Program at the Harvard Business School.

Robert Stempel and General Motors need our encouragement more than our advice—encouragement to continue a revolution at the company that is unprecedented in the history of American business. The task of consolidating this revolution in product quality, cost structure, management organization and process, labor relations and vendor relations should not be underestimated.

Nowhere is the task more complex than in resizing the corporation's manufacturing base—that is, closing redundant and inefficient plants.

If, under a reasonably optimistic scenario, United States passenger car sales in 1992 rebound to 10.5 million units from 9.9 million in 1989 *and* imports hover around 3 million cars *and* North American Japanese transplants increase their sales to 1.6 million cars from last year's 1.1 million, then capacity utilization in the Big Three's plants will be below 75 percent—even after factoring in announced plant closings. And if G.M.'s share of Big Three factory sales increases from its current 52.3 percent to, let's say, 55 percent in 1992, then G.M. will be operating at only 73 percent of capacity.

From a long-term profit point of view, this is an unacceptable state of affairs. Unless General Motors miraculously recaptures its lost share in a market that now includes some 30 auto makers selling 600 different models to American consumers, more plants must be closed.

But how to do this when the current contract talks with the U.A.W. are centering on job security? And how does G.M. maintain employee morale and commitment when the number of available jobs will be shrinking and layoffs increasing? And how can G.M. meet its continuing responsibilities to its investors and its many local communities as this restructuring continues?

These are not problems for amateurs. Come to think of it, Mr. Stempel needs not only our encouragement to complete the revolution at G.M., but also our sympathy. Complicated times are ahead.

Bob Galvin and Motorola, Inc.

Todd Jick and Mary Gentile

On April 24, 1983, the biennial meeting of Motorola, Inc.'s top 153 officers was drawing to a close, and Bob Galvin, chairman and chief executive officer of the $4 billion company, was about to offer his concluding comments. The theme of the two-day session had been "Managing Change," an appropriate topic, since the 55-year-old producer of electronics equipment had experienced a year of 15% growth—or half a billion dollars between 1982 and 1983. Galvin knew that the message he had in mind was surprising in light of the company's apparent success.

Increasingly as he "walked the halls" of the corporation, Galvin had heard more and more complaints. Managers were upset by longer product development cycles, by too many layers in the management structure, and by ponderous, inflexible decision approval processes. Galvin interpreted these frequently heard complaints in the context of a rapidly changing competitive environment. He recognized the growing threat from Japanese manufacturers to key Motorola products, such as cellular telephones and semiconductors. And much to the annoyance of his senior managers, he often asserted "we haven't even begun to compete internationally yet."

Galvin believed that the firm's current inability to respond quickly and flexibly to the changing needs of the customer could prove fatal in the coming global competitive crisis. Still, he kept asking himself if he, as chief executive officer, could make the kinds of changes Motorola needed. If he did nothing else in his last years before retirement, he wanted to reposition Motorola on the path toward renewed competitiveness. He knew this would be all the more difficult because many of his managers did not recognize the problems he saw. As he approached the speaker's podium, Galvin reflected that "I suppose I've been preparing for this speech for the last 45 years."

Motorola, Inc.

Galvin Manufacturing Company was founded by Paul V. Galvin, Bob Galvin's father, in 1928. The Chicago-based firm's earliest products were alternating electrical current converters and automobile radios. Paul Galvin dubbed the car radio he developed the "Motorola"—from motor and victrola—and in 1947 this became the company's name as well.

From their firm's modest beginning with less than $1,500 in working capital and equipment, Paul Galvin and his brother, Joe, tried to create a humane and democratic work environment for their employees; everyone, from Paul Galvin himself to the newest production line employee, was addressed on a first-name basis; the Galvins had replaced the typical time clock in the plant with an employee honor system; and by 1947, Paul Galvin established a profit-sharing program for the 2,000 workers the firm then employed. As a result of such efforts, Motorola remained union free.

Over the years, Motorola extended its product base to include home radios, phonographs, televisions, and transistors and semiconductor components. By 1983, however, under Bob Galvin's leadership, the firm had sold many of its consumer electronic businesses and developed other markets based on new technology. By then, the firm was composed of five geographically dispersed sectors or groups:

1. *The Semiconductor Products Sector,* with 1982 net sales of $1.3 billion, produced such products as microprocessors, memory chips, and integrated circuits.
2. *The Communications Sector,* with 1982 net sales of $1.5 billion, produced products such as: two-way radios, paging devices, and cellular telephones.
3. *The Information Systems Group (ISG),* with 1982 net sales of $485 million, produced an integrated line of data transmission and distributed data processing systems.

4 & 5. *The Automotive and Industrial Electronics Group (AIEG)* and *The Government Electronics Group (GEG)* had combined 1982 net sales of $564 million. AIEG produced such

> products as fuel-injection systems, electronic engine controls and instrumentation, and electronic appliance controls. GEG conducted research in satellite communications technology.

This product-focused organizational structure grew out of Paul and Bob Galvin's emphasis on the customers' interests and their concern that a large, centralized organization might not be responsive enough to those interests. Over the years, Motorola had gradually decentralized. In the 1950s Paul Galvin formed divisions; in the early 1960s Bob Galvin established product lines with product managers who managed specific marketing and engineering areas, but who purchased the centralized manufacturing and sales functions. By the 1980s, the groups and sectors structure was in place, along with a multilayered matrix system of management. At the close of 1982 Motorola had approximately 75,000 employees, with operations in 15 foreign countries as well as the United States.

Bob Galvin

Bob Galvin joined the firm as a stock clerk in 1944, without completing his college degree. He worked in a variety of positions until 1948, when he became executive vice president. He became president in 1956, and chairman/chief executive officer in 1964.

Galvin was an equitable and accessible manager. His leadership style was rooted in humility and an abiding respect for his father's values. He often quoted Paul Galvin when explaining a decision he had made, and in assessing his own influence at Motorola, he pointed to the "privilege" of his long service with the firm, as well as to the "mantle" he had received from his father: "I am fortunate to carry some of his reputation, in addition to what I've earned myself." He was a serious and thoughtful man who defined his role as "leading the institution: I try to be a good listener, to look for the unattended, the void, the exception that my associates are too busy to see."

Over the years he had championed not only various reorganizational efforts and product/market shifts but a variety of participatory management, executive education, and strategic planning programs. For example, in the late 1960s, Motorola developed a technology innovation planning process—the Technology Roadmap— which involved the periodic projection of future technological developments and the subsequent planning and reviewing of the firm's progress against that projection.

In the 1970s, Motorola developed the Participative Management Program (PMP) as a means to enhance productivity and employee involvement in the firm. PMP divided employees into small groups that met to discuss problems and potential improvements in their area of responsibility. Each group sent one member to report its ideas to the group one level up, which thereby enhanced communication in all directions. PMP efforts were also tied to a bonus incentive program.

Galvin's style and the Motorola culture were clearly people-oriented. High value was placed on senior service, and in fact, no employee with more than ten years' service could be fired without approval from Galvin himself. John Mitchell, Motorola's president, commented: "Bob *is* the culture here."

Some Motorola managers, however, criticized Motorola's "low demand environment," a tone set by Galvin himself. He devoted significant attention to the development of a strong managerial succession at Motorola and consequently was quite confident in Motorola's senior managers—his "family," as he called them. He felt convinced that if he but pointed out a problem to his officers, they would certainly be motivated and capable of resolving it appropriately. From time to time he gave a speech on leadership as he perceived it including the following excerpt:

> Again we see the paradox of the leader—a finite person with an apparent infinite influence.
>
> A leader is decisive, is called on to make many critical choices, and can thrive on the power and the attention of that decision-making role. Yet the leader of leaders moves progressively away from that role.
>
> Yes, he or she can be decisive and command as required. Yet that leader's prime responsibility is not to decide or direct but to create and maintain an evocative situation, stimulating an atmosphere of objective participation, keeping the goal in sight, recognizing valid consensus, inviting unequivocal recommendation, and finally vesting increasingly in others the privilege to learn through their own decisions.

Galvin hoped to encourage this "privilege" through the variety of innovative programs that Motorola adopted.

Motorola in 1983

Galvin believed, in that spring of 1983, that Motorola was poised on the edge of a new competitive era. The company had just come through a recession in the semiconductor industry which had caused an 8% downturn in earnings between 1980 and 1982. Difficult as that period had been, however, Motorola's losses had been far less severe than those of competitors like Texas Instruments and Intel. "Motorola did see their profits slip by 6% during the worst year of the recession. But their arch-rivals, TI and Intel, experienced a 49% and 72% drop, respectively."[1] And Galvin wanted to build on Motorola's strengths at a time when performance was beginning to look strong again. Although the first quarter was a bit slow, sales seemed to be on the upswing as Motorola faced the summer of 1983, and Galvin saw the national economy and his firm gearing up for rapid growth in the next few years. He recognized this growth as a blessing and a threat.

Increases in sales and earnings were welcome, of course, as was the accompanying confidence within the firm. However, rapid expansion brought new structural and managerial challenges and exacerbated existing deficiencies. In addition, confidence could engender a dangerous complacency that made change all the more difficult. And finally, Galvin was all too cognizant of the cyclical nature of the semiconductor and computer industries and the growing threat of Japanese competition in both the communications and the semiconductor sectors of the business.

Galvin was also looking internally. One of Galvin's favored management techniques was walking the halls of the organization, listening to the ideas and the complaints of Motorola's employees, especially the middle managers. Galvin believed these managers were in touch with "real world" implementation issues that higher-level managers might miss because of their need to oversee so many different functions and systems. Galvin was a strong believer in open communications, and he encouraged employees at all levels to sit down with him in the company cafeteria at lunch or to catch him in the halls of the firm to share their ideas and their criticisms.

Structural Issues

The issues he heard about in spring 1983 were disturbingly consistent with concerns that had been building throughout the 1970s. Galvin identified them as "structural concerns." Employees complained of the problems engendered by the sheer size and complexity of Motorola's matrix organization. Objective and methodology conflicts routinely developed between Motorola's customer-oriented functional managers (in sales or distribution, for example) and their product line managers. Although traditionally Galvin had always stressed the importance of staying close to the customer and the customer's needs, the complexity of the firm's products often

[1] James O'Toole, "Second Annual NM Vanguard Award," *New Management*, Vol. 3, no. 2 (Fall 1985), p. 5.

caused product line managers to be more technology-driven than market-driven in their planning and managing processes.

No single manager was clearly responsible for a particular project through all its cycles, from its origin in customer discussions through design, development, testing, production and into sales. Consequently, project deadlines set by engineers carried little weight with the production staff, and the needs of the sales and distribution managers were poorly integrated into the realities of the manufacturing area. Galvin was alarmed by the ever lengthening product development cycles.

Motorola's lines of authority were as often dotted as solid and spans of control were narrow. As the company grew and its products multiplied, management layers increased as well. One company study, completed in 1983, reported nine to twelve layers between first-line managers and the executive level, with an average span of control over five people or fewer. Thirty percent managed three or fewer people. Individuals were struggling to preserve their turf and budget and maintain internal performance standards. Long-term competitive strategy and customer needs were obscured by short-term incentives, and employees felt both overmanaged and underdirected.

Top management's efforts to energize the firm and to enhance creative cooperation translated into programs like the periodic technology review and PMP, with their step-by-step procedures and committee-based processes. Such programs involved employees at all levels and kept critical issues before them, but some managers worried that their format was too mechanistic and that they enabled employees to comply with the letter rather than the spirit of the programs.

Finally Motorola's chief executive office was structured as a triumvirate with Bob Galvin as chairman, William Weisz as vice chairman, and John Mitchell as president. Galvin defined their respective responsibilities as follows: "John Mitchell is running the business; Bill Weisz is managing the company; and my job is to lead the institution. And in a way, they are all the same thing." Mitchell elaborated: "Bill Weisz and I share the COO position. I handle the Communications Sector, the Automotive and Industrial Electronic Group, and Japan; Bill handles the Semiconductor Products Sector, the Information Systems Group, and the Government Electronics Group." Galvin saw the chief executive office as a model of democratic practice and open communications for the firm.

However, this tripartite structure was one of the other complaints that circulated among Motorola's managers. Mitchell explained: "They call us the three bears and they ask 'why can't you be single in voice, style, and direction?' "

Galvin reviewed the concerns he gathered from Motorola's managers; from his son, Chris, who worked in the Communications Sector; and from his own observations. Taken alone, he believed they were cause for concern. When he also considered the rapid growth Motorola appeared to face as the economy emerged from the last two years of recession and the growing competitive threat from Japan, Galvin became convinced that it was time for action.

Japanese Competition

Motorola was one of the world's leading producers of two-way radios, cellular telephone systems, semiconductors, and microprocessor chips, and Japan was competing in and threatening each of these markets. The firm faced Japanese market practices such as "dumping" (selling product at less than "fair value" as a way to increase market share quickly) and "targeting" (the cooperative efforts of a group of Japanese firms, supported by Japanese law, to break into and capture a particular international market, such as computer memory chips). In response to these challenges, Galvin worked with federal foreign relations and trade committees, attempting to fight "unfair" trade practices and protectionism:

> Testifying before the Senate Foreign Relations Committee last September [1982], he said U.S. policy on trade in high-technology products should make it clear that this country "will not accept a situation where foreign national industrial policies, based on non-market mechanisms and unreasonable trade practices, enable any country to disrupt U.S. markets, prevent reasonable access to its home markets or give unjustified advantage to its firms in pursuing Third World markets."[2]

Galvin also knew, however, that he had to make changes closer to home, within Motorola. His success in obtaining an order from Nippon Telegraph & Telephone Public Corporation for paging devices in early 1982 was a result both of pressure from the United States government and Motorola's efforts to produce 100% defect-free product. And even during the difficult recession years of 1981–1982, Motorola continued to invest in research and development, in order to position itself competitively for the market growth it believed would follow. Galvin thought that effective competition with the Japanese meant not only modifications in federal trade regulations but Motorola's investment in R&D, enhanced productivity, and

[2]Grover Herman, "Competing with the Japanese," *Nation's Business,* November 1982, p. 48.

quality control. And he believed the means to this end were through the company's employees. This was consistent with the kind of thinking behind PMP, ten years earlier.

As Galvin considered his company's current condition and challenges, he felt a great sense of personal urgency. He was 61 years old, nearing retirement, and he wanted to leave a strong and healthy company to his family of managers. And although he wasn't certain how to implement a process of "renewal" at Motorola, he was quite confident of the need. He remembered his father's advice to "just get in motion" when action was required, confident that he would find his way.

Motorola Biennial Officers' Meeting: April 1983

Galvin came to the Officers' Meeting with his mind full of a recent trip to Japan. He had been impressed by the commitment of the industry employees he saw there and with the cutting-edge production technology the Japanese firms utilized. On the long plane ride back to the United States, Galvin had been reading the current management best seller *In Search of Excellence.* Its authors, Peters and Waterman, advocated simpler organizational structures with direct ties to the consumer.

With all these observations, conclusions, and influences in his mind, Galvin felt an uncanny, undeniable immediacy in his senior officers' discussion of their efforts to manage change. Every time an individual complained of too many layers of command, Galvin winced, "There it is again." Each time an officer mentioned the absence of realistic and convincing deadlines that made sense across departments, Galvin sighed, "There it is again." He knew he needed no more evidence. He was sure of his message and of its significance.

As the meeting drew to a close, his staff expected Galvin's usual clear, concise concluding summary. Instead he stood up and issued a challenge. He called upon his senior managers to take a fresh look at their organizations and to consider structural changes—smaller, more focused business units. He wanted to decrease the many layers of management and to bring management closer to the product and the market. Galvin spoke with ease and conviction: "My message was spontaneous in tone and mood, but it had been building out of years of experience. I had been hearing this message from my middle managers and I'm a good listener."

In his speech, Galvin stressed Motorola's

> . . . constant thrust for renewal. Renewal is the most driving word in this corporation for me, the continual search for ways to get things done better.
>
> As I walk the halls, I keep my ears open and I keep picking up

> signals. A middle manager might tell me that he can't understand how the business did because we keep aggregating our results into one big number. Or another might tell me he thinks he has a good idea but he can't get the authority to get it done.
>
> I see a welling up of the evidence of need and today I think the window is open. So I decided to express my concern and my conviction to you, confident that you share my insights and that together we will find our way to an organized effort of change. When we come together in two years, we will report and share the changes made and the lessons learned.

Galvin had not discussed this presentation with Weisz or Mitchell beforehand. Nor had he explicitly addressed with his Human Resources staff the issue of structural reorganization as the key method of a change at Motorola. He was confident that he knew his audience, his "constituency," and that they would welcome his challenge.

As Galvin concluded, however, and managers stood and began to move out of the room, the buzzing conversations were colored by surprise and confusion more than eagerness. Suddenly the firm's rising sales were a problem. Was this just another PMP pep talk? Was Galvin serious about restructuring the organization? Who would be responsible for this? Even Galvin's wife, Mary, turned to him later that evening and asked: "What exactly did you have in mind, Bob?"

That was Friday evening. On Monday morning, the calls started coming in to Galvin's office, to Joe Miraglia, corporate vice president and director of Human Resources, and passed back and forth between the various senior managers. Rumors were spreading: people wanted to know what had Galvin been reading, and with whom had he been talking? One senior manager jested that perhaps Galvin was miffed that Motorola had not been mentioned enough by the authors of *In Search of Excellence.* But everyone wanted to know: what did Galvin mean and was he serious?

Chapter 12

Action Tools and Execution Dilemmas: Change Implementors

Introductory Notes

This set of portraits points to the rocky terrain of implementing change. It is difficult to create an orderly, logical plan for significant organizational change as if this were just another "project." The visibility, the stakes, the conflicts, the pain, the constraints, and the fatigue all seem to come with the territory. Looking back on the experiences of change implementors is simultaneously sobering—because the task is so much harder than they imagined—and motivating, because it is also possible to accomplish so much.

None of the cases shows finite completion or a single formula for success. They reflect ongoing processes of trying to reach broad transformational goals through step-at-a-time projects—continuous improvement that never ends, but with an accumulating series of accomplishments as the process continues. As we proposed in Chapter 1, small-c changes gradually multiply to create big-C Change. But despite the differences in the issues facing each company's change implementors, there are common experiences with the complexity, the struggle, and the craft associated with implementing change effectively.

Changing a bank culture at Security Pacific ("The Dilemmas of a Changemaker") or introducing a more global market orientation at a division of Honeywell ("Three in the Middle: The Experience of Making Change at Micro Switch") were thorny, difficult long-term endeavors. But the change implementors who personally played significant leadership roles in these efforts, and who discuss the changes in their own words, reflect a combination of skills that helped them through the process: *flexibility* in adjusting activities to fit the conditions they encountered as they took each step; *opportunism* in taking advantage of unexpected events to move the change process forward in new ways; *thoughtful reflection* and *self-awareness* in considering the feedback from their actions and taking others' views into account; and *perseverance* as they kept on going through the predictable ups and downs, the emotional highs and lows, of the change marathon. Though disheartened at times, they bounced back continually, carrying on despite resistance. Bouncing back is a universal secret of success.

Change agents such as Bill Shea at Security Pacific or Deb Massof at Micro Switch are not just in the middle of an organization; they are also in the middle of a long-drawn-out change process. Both of these situations create special challenges for them.

Leading long-term change as a middle manager requires maintaining support outside one's own territory—the support of the key change strategist, higher-level "bosses," or peers in other departments—while concentrating on the reactions of the change recipients inside it. Bill Shea had to worry about whether senior executive ranks continued to back his endeavors when his own department was grumbling about his changes. In retrospect, he wished he had spent more time publicizing the early small-scale successes to the rest of the organization. Similarly, at Micro Switch the change managers were in danger of losing contact with both the top and the bottom of the organization. They faced ongoing issues of how much control top managers would let them have. At the same time, they had to be careful not to get too far ahead of those below, to not push them farther and faster than they were ready to go.

There is often euphoria at the beginning of a change process from the excitement of being handed a change mandate, coupled with the "high" of early easy successes by making the obvious changes that people long desired. This brief euphoria gives way to disillusionment and even despair when change implementors and their teams realize that the change is going to take really hard work. At both Security Pacific and Micro Switch, the change process was accompanied by feelings of overwork and overload. The extra work associated with change had to be acknowledged and handled. Furthermore, early enthusiasm can sometimes lead change implementors to tackle too much too soon. Resistance sets in when people simply are not ready for the change, even with incentives. At Security Pacific, resistance even took the form of jokes told behind the boss's back.

The implementation of change requires many, many people throughout the organization to change many, many daily work habits. All significant changes, no matter how triggered or how aimed, ultimately rest on coordination and culture changes. Therefore, even the diverse changes in these portraits seem to rest on a foundation of participation and involvement. The GE experience, in "Toward a Boundary-less Firm at General Electric," and the British Air experience, in "British Air's Profitable Private Life," magnify the Security Pacific and Micro Switch change efforts literally a thousandfold, in the numbers of people involved in implementing change.

Jack Welch and his managers at GE emphasized a vision of a "liberated" and "empowered" organization. The GE portrait describes the innovative change process known as Workout. Workout involved cross-functional and cross-level dialogue in a series of three-day town meetings designed to scrutinize, and improve on, every aspect of GE operations. Thousands of people looked for changes they could make to reduce bureaucracy and create a faster-moving, more flexible organization.

Often Workout began with solving simple problems—the "rattlers" that could be shot, i.e., solved on the spot. But they also took on more difficult problems with more complicated solutions, which they called "pythons" because they took longer to unravel. Even customers and suppliers were included in Workout sessions; for example, twenty Sears buyers meeting with twenty GE sales/service people. Despite enthusiasm for Workout, however, there were still areas of understandable resistance to overcome, such as legitimate worries that eliminating wasteful activities might also mean eliminating one's own job. Change implementors have to make sure that the rewards of being engaged in change outweigh the losses.

British Air was privatized in 1987 and quickly became one of the world's most profitable airlines. The early part of its turnaround followed a familiar pattern, one similar to the examples of restructuring and skinnying down in Chapters 6, 7, and 8. The workforce was cut, and a new management team was brought on board, representing a break with the past and a fresh start. Change strategists did their work of creating a strategy and a vision, soon embedded in such symbols as slogan, uniforms, and insignia. But change implementation involved everybody. British Air's Customer First aspiration was made real through its People First program of employee workshops and employee teams that generated innovative ideas for improvements. One team, for example, decided to add footrests to business class seats after spending the night sleeping in rooms with only BA airline seats. A variety of rewards provided incentives for the changes; the fact that many employees were also stockholders undoubtedly helped them care even more about the company's marketplace performance.

All of the change efforts portrayed here took place over a period of years. Unlike the radical turnarounds and time pressure of crisis management discussed at the end of Chapter 6 and in Chapter 9, these changes had the luxury of time. And time was indeed necessary to reeducate people in the new habits required for participation and involvement. In each case, it took a long time for "empowerment" to be anything more than empty rhetoric. Bill Shea's early attempts at involvement were met with passivity. Deb Massof's invitation to get involved in shaping their own destiny at Micro Switch was greeted with blank stares. At first, people wanted managers to tell them what to do; they resisted thinking for themselves. Thus, an important task of change implementors is to help people gain confidence by educating them in business facts and figures as well as change techniques. To believe they are truly "empowered," people need knowledge and information.

Change implementors, these portraits show, must have the courage to provide an occasional "kick in the pants," jolting people out of complacency as Bill Shea did with his innovation audit data. They must also have the wisdom to provide a frequent "shot in the arm" as well—the boost to the human spirit that comes when people are appreciated for their small successes and thanked for a job well done.

The Dilemmas of a Changemaker

William Shea

In the past few years, the once peaceful, predictable, and profitable world of banking has become volatile. Now that aggressive nonbank competitors like brokerage houses and retail stores have entered the arena, every aspect of the banking business has come under fire. So in 1979, when I left my career in marketing and manufacturing to become director of personnel at one of the nation's largest banks, I was entering an electric environment, charged with change, laden with opportunities: new services to offer, new products to design, new competitors to confront, new risks to weigh, new promises to keep.

The changes in the industry meant that banks in general—and my bank in particular—would have to rethink their business. The crux of our new mission was to transcend our role as a bank, comfortable but no longer competitive, and evolve into a company that offered a menu of profitable financial services. To do this, we needed to develop a new agility among our staff. They had to become more adaptive, quicker in their responses to change and opportunities than they had been in the past.

My charge was to effect the necessary changes in the personnel department so that they, in turn, could keep pace with the changes throughout the company. Or better yet, so that personnel could be among the pacesetters.

By banking industry standards, our personnel department was better than most. It provided the staple services—job training, employee relations, placement, benefits, and compensation. But some of these services, while adequate or even exemplary in the old banking environment, fell short in the newly competitive financial services industry.

When I took over the department, I discovered that about two-thirds of the staff were very good under existing standards; the others weren't. Job security was the norm, and pink slips the rare exception. Complicating this tradition was the fact that the bank, like most other businesses, applauded line functions, and did not consider the personnel department a highly desirable stop in the career paths of "barn-burner" performers. . . .

Banks (and ours was no exception) had developed a culture that closely resembled the atmosphere in a gentlemen's club. All behavior was tempered with a veneer of gentility: Everyone was civil and courteous, everyone was agreeable and tactful, everyone honored social boundaries. Public outbursts, tantrums—even honest, open arguments—were "unfortunate incidents." . . .

The gentlemen's club caused problems in communicating the need for change. Since our bank was doing quite well in comparison with other banks, the employees credited themselves with superior work; from my perspective, there was still plenty of room for improvement. I wanted dramatic change; they preferred the status quo. These differences fostered mutual suspicion. They were leery of my ideas and my methods, and, frankly, I didn't have much confidence in their traditions. All told, it was a tense, and somewhat precarious, relationship. . . .

I tried to avoid the standard pitfalls of the newcomer who arrives with a headful of preconceptions and a fistful of memos. So, for the first few months, I declared a moratorium on change. I wanted to give myself time to fully understand the workings of the department, to unravel the politics, and to scout the staff for leadership talent. I believe that the value of this reconnaissance justified the delay—besides, it's easier to promote change when you understand history.

Once I had a clear sense of where we were headed, I discussed my plans with the staff. I posed critical questions about the future. I probed for responses, I broke the meetings into smaller groups to discuss the implications of the plans. I wanted reactions—positive or negative—and I wanted confirmation: Did they understand the ideas? Did they recognize the juggernaut rolling toward our department? Did they spot the opportunities on the horizon?

Unfortunately, instead of ideas, I got the rote response, "Hey, you're the boss, just tell us what to do." When the meetings failed, I set up committees to work on different aspects of decentralization. I was careful to assign only short-term, "doable" tasks to each group, because I didn't want to trigger a wave of frustration and excuses.

I really don't know how well these early committees worked. In retrospect, I suspect that I was moving too fast and bristling against the traditional thinking in the department. Also, as I discovered later, the staff hadn't yet developed the insights and the skills to work productively as a team.

My next step was even less popular, if nevertheless inevitable: I had to clean out the deadwood. My first carefully considered—and probably long-overdue—dismissals sent a shockwave through the entire department. Despite my assurances to the remaining staff, there was a general air of distress and resentment.

When a manager gets rid of the worst performers, the next tier—the weak but not the worst—will usually take the hint. I tried to encourage voluntary departure by promoting the idea that the bank was not the proverbial "last stop," that there were, in fact, other employers in the area who would welcome fresh talent. Apparently that was a radical notion, and it was not well received. . . .

I tried to involve the division managers of the department in my staff-building, staff-toning efforts by assigning them the task of cleaning out their own areas. Their instructions were to encourage the promising, dismiss the weak, realign the misfits, recruit new talent, and generally strengthen the labor pool. I encouraged them to work with their subordinates to plan individual development programs and to confirm those plans in formal development contracts. As bargaining chits, I offered funding, training, time off, and whatever it took to support the individual growth of employees.

Once again, the results didn't match my expectations. Instead of the positive, energetic mood I envisioned, the closed door conferences between division managers and staff churned new waves of anxiety. In hindsight, I can see that I was asking too much, too soon. The division managers lacked the leadership skills to conduct this kind of program. Besides, I was asking them to implement a program that they didn't quite understand and hadn't yet accepted—asking them to enlighten their staffs when they themselves were still fumbling clumsily in the dark.

My Socratic Soapbox

My staff-building campaign wasn't limited to realigning and replacing. I also wanted to revitalize the staff through an ambitious training program. To me, it seemed only fair that if I planned to ask more of my staff, I had to empower them to meet the demands. Also, I hoped that by encouraging them to venture outside the bank for formal training, they'd be exposed to a fresh, nonbank frame of reference. They'd see and hear—firsthand, not through me—that things were done differently in other industries.

So I tried to promote process courses. For example, one that might focus on conference leadership: how to stimulate discussion and gather information at the meeting table. Others might examine constructive conflict resolution, listening skills, or (perhaps most appropriate of all) how to manage organizational change.

PROJECT: DECENTRALIZATION

All of my efforts to develop the staff—to instill new perspectives and remedy old habits—were, in a sense, the cultural groundwork for my core mission: to decentralize the department. The most promising design seemed to be a client-based model, not unlike that of an advertising agency. A designated group within the department would serve the needs of one client. This group would operate as a full-service team, just as in an ad agency a team of writers, artists, marketers, and media buyers collaborate to service an account. In our situation, the group would include a compensation specialist, a benefits coordinator, a staff development expert, and whoever else was needed to deliver complete personnel services. Rather than McDonald's or Procter & Gamble, our clients would be the operating divisions within the bank.

In addition to these client-based groups, I felt that we needed a corporate personnel staff to handle matters that involved two or more groups and who would work on strictly corporate matters. With all of the daily operating chores decentralized to the groups, this corporate staff could focus on broader, more far-reaching programs.

I tried to involve the staff in their own reassignment decisions because I wanted to establish a participatory style for department management. I met with them to discuss their own interests, ambitions, and judgments about themselves. Then, when it came time to select the corporate staff, I shifted the thinkers, researchers, and program developers into that group. Those who wanted their jobs to be finite, who wanted to arrive at work with a checklist, spend eight hours ticking off items, and leave feeling that the job was finished, I assigned to the decentralized operating groups.

For the operating staff in each of the newly formed service groups, the transition was fairly smooth. Expectations hadn't changed drastically, and some of the old behaviors were still appropriate. The content of their jobs was familiar; only the context and the clientele had changed.

The transition was much harder for the managers who headed up these service groups. For them, expectations had changed dramatically and, in fact, were still evolving; there were no traditions, no frame of reference. Under the new structure, each new group personnel officer managed one of the service groups in the personnel department, but reported directly to the head of an operating group. This was a major shift in reporting. Obviously, I was surrendering direct control over these managers, but I was willing to accept that loss in the true spirit of decentralization. . . .

Most of the line managers went along with the plan, because I was transferring only about five people each from my payroll to theirs and because the reduced administrative charges would offset the increase. In meetings with the line managers, I explained each item on the budget—each service they were receiving—and encouraged them to weigh the benefits of the service. My general stance was that the personnel department was no longer going to presume to know what each of the major bank groups needed. These decisions should come from the operating management. I was instantly one of the good guys, white hat and all.

But popularity wasn't my mission. My agenda was to build a relationship of trust and confidence, to encourage the managers to see the value of having one of the new group personnel officers on the management council of their operating group. And, to some extent, the strategy worked, although a true partnership was slow to develop.

The Resistance Movement

By the end of my second year, I could see progress. The old single-minded, isolationist culture was beginning to diffuse, and I detected a growing commitment to new ideas and methods. Unfortunately, though, the results were short of my expectations.

Something in my approach was amiss; the change wasn't complete, and the progress was sputtering. Some of the staff members were enthusiastic, strongly committed to a shared vision of a dynamic, proactive department. But too many of their colleagues were recalcitrant. There was a movement afoot, undeclared and informal, to resist my efforts and undermine my programs. The most resistant staff formed antagonistic cliques that would retreat and snicker behind my back. Others muffled their complaints, concentrated on familiar tasks, and reverted to a "business as usual" workstyle. Another form of resistance was to plead overload. Staff members would say things like, "The work's so backed up now that I couldn't possibly take on another project." My response was to give the beleaguered staff more resources, then watch the results. In time, they got the message.

Our weekly staff meetings became another occasion for resistance, sometimes expressed through complaints about the workload, sometimes through silence, sometimes through body language, sometimes through jokes intended to divert discussion. Basically, these antics at the conference table signaled a lack of confidence in each other—and, of course, in me.

The problems stemmed, too, from skepticism about my standards. Many of the staff still didn't believe my claims that there were better ways than the bank's ways. So, in their minds, I was asking the impossible. My ideas were utopian, my standards unrealistic.

Catalyst for Change: The Goodmeasure Innovation Audit

During my second year, as these reactionary forces gained momentum, I realized that we needed to renew our commitment to change. In fact, what we needed was a system to cope with changes—to identify, sustain, project, and reinforce them. Rather than rely on our staff to create the system, I looked for a consulting team outside the bank.

With high hopes and great expectations, I launched the Goodmeasure Innovation Audit. I admit that my motives were not solely to provide the staff with a scorecard that would measure our progress. I wanted the Audit to shock the department out of its complacency. . . .

The results of the Audit were invaluable. The action agenda we developed for the coming months included these specific recommendations:

- Creation of a steering committee to oversee all change activities
- Development of a strategic plan for the department that included a system for management of change
- Creation of an overall advisory task force, with additional task forces to address such issues as internal communication, staff development, and research

The results of those recommendations have been remarkable. It's important to remember that collaboration and teamwork were not the norm in the department. But through the task forces, the staff got their first real taste of teamwork. To their great surprise, they liked it. And the impressive work of these task forces helped to erode the prevailing myth that committees were no damn good and that only individuals could succeed.

Over time, the task force system developed its own vitality and its own regenerative powers. New issues emerged and spawned the next generation of task forces, one to explore our relationships with users, another to design programs for organization and management development. Each newly christened task force confirmed the power of collaboration, and each helped to break down the barriers—personal, organizational, and perceptual—that had handicapped the department.

My role in the change process has varied from day to day, month to month. I was, at times, a prophet, an ogre, a critic, a taskmaster, an evasive boss, and a tireless supporter. But I was consistent in my commitment to change and to my mission as a change agent.

In hindsight, I can spot flaws in my behavior and costly errors in judgment. I can see, for example, that I should have been more alert to the staff's feelings of conflict between the immediate demands of their jobs and the additional demands imposed by change management. For many, I'm sure that overload was a genuine issue and an honest plea (although for others, it was an alibi). If I had more quickly realized the legitimacy of the issue, I might have been able to work with the staff to plot individual coping strategies—clearer priorities, extra help.

Another mistake I made was to tolerate the grumblings of the resisters—the pessimists, the cynics, and the saboteurs—for far too long. On several occasions, I allowed individuals to disrupt meetings and berate new programs. More broadly, I allowed them to pollute the atmosphere in the department. I can see now that I should have taken immediate action, that there was no gain in allowing these open, prolonged expressions of doubt.

I also think that I should have found ways to dramatize—and publicize in bank media—the success of our change management program. Not only would these endorsements have provided rewards for the staff, they would also have attracted the attention of bank management. My hesitancy to "go public" stemmed in part from reluctance to claim success for a job half-done. I didn't want the kudos to be premature. In retrospect, I can see that a careful publicity effort would have bolstered the campaign for change and possibly inspired other departments in the bank to mimic our efforts.

Finally, if I could project myself backward in time, I would devise ways to test bank management's commitment to change. Then, I would have been able to recognize the true supporters and take steps to co-opt the skeptics. The management of the bank had agreed to the need for change. But when it came time for action, their commitment was inconsistent and sometimes contradictory. Fortunately, I had the freedom and the resources—financial and staff—to propel the project.

I wish I could report that the changes I envisioned are complete, that the department is now a model, that my once raw canvas is now a masterpiece. But I'm like a painter who can never set down his brush. He sketches the outline, paints the scene, then after stepping back to view his work, returns to the easel. He wants to dab a little more yellow across the horizon, smooth out the rough textures, blend new shades, and dot new highlights. It's hard to quit. It's hard to step back and say, "That's it. My work is done."

Three in the Middle

The Experience of Making Change at Micro Switch

Susan Rosegrant and Todd Jick

As a change agent, some days you're going to be a star, and some days you're going to be a turkey, but if you're true to what you think is right, you'll end up OK And, hell, if they fire you for doing the right thing, then you didn't want to work for that company anyway.

—Rick Rowe
Director, Matériel

People are struggling so much because they're trying to understand what this desired state is. I have been told I'm supposed to do this, this, this, and this—well, which one do I tackle first, and with what kind of focus, and what's the time frame?

—Deb Massof
Director, Aerospace, Ordnance, and Marine Marketing

Now is the time for determination and just grunting it out. And that's where we're going to start seeing some folks say, "Ah, baloney, I'm not cut out for this amount of frustration. I'm tired of trying to balance all this." It's not for the faint-hearted right now.

—Ellis Stewart
Director, Fabricating Operations

Prologue

It was midsummer 1990, and Micro Switch was changing. In fact, the manufacturer of switches and sensors, a division of Honeywell, Inc., was embroiled in change. For the last three years, the Freeport-based company, in the rural northwest corner of Illinois, had been striving to transform itself from a mature provincial business into a more dynamic, customer-driven, global operation capable of surviving into the 21st century. Indeed, most of the division's managers believed that without profound changes, Micro Switch's days would be numbered.

Recently, the responsibility for shepherding this change effort had begun to fall more and more on the shoulders of the company's directors—a group of 19 middle managers who reported directly to the vice presidents under the division's general manager. In order to form a more cohesive and skilled "change agent team," both the vice presidents and the directors had begun attending a series of formal off-site team-building and training sessions beginning in November 1989. Rick Rowe, Deb Massof, and Ellis Stewart all had been active participants in these "Eagle Ridge" sessions, named for the meeting site.

After the second of the Eagle Ridge sessions in March 1990, Rowe, Massof, and Stewart each had tried to describe in their own words how it felt to be a change agent in the middle of the process—detailing both the pleasures and pains of making change. Four months later, each of the three directors had sat down and revisited many of the same subjects again. The second time, however, their comments were colored by changing circumstances. It was becoming clearer by the day that most of the "easy" changes had already been accomplished, they claimed. Moreover, a stubborn business slump facing both Honeywell and Micro Switch, as well as many other U.S. manufacturers, threatened to sap both the energy and the resources necessary to keep the change effort moving.

Rowe, Massof, and Stewart all had declared their dedication to change, no matter how rocky that road might prove to be. Yet after they each finished talking, a final unspoken question seemed to be on all of their minds: Had something gone wrong, or was this the way a successful change process was supposed to feel?

Change at Micro Switch: 1987–1990

Founded in 1937 and acquired by Honeywell in 1950, Micro Switch in its early years had established a solid reputation as an industry leader in switches, sensors, and manual controls, making thousands of products ranging from simple lawnmower switches to sophisticated controls for NASA's first manned orbit around the earth in 1962. The company had also established itself as a reliable source of profits for Honeywell. But as aggressive and international competitors attacked Micro Switch's traditional markets with less expensive products in the late 1970s and early 1980s, and as switching technology began shifting from electromechanical to electronic and solid-state, the division's performance began to suffer. Honeywell, the Minneapolis-based company offering products and services in information processing, automation, and controls, did not release figures for its divisions. But Micro Switch's operating profits began a downward tumble in 1985 which put its corporate overseers on red alert.

To make certain Micro Switch regained its competitive spirit, Honeywell recruited Ramon Alvarez, a 49-year-old company veteran who had already helped turn around two other divisions. Arriving in September 1987, with the corporate charge to do what was necessary to revitalize Micro Switch, Alvarez set in motion a wide-ranging mix of change actions. First, Alvarez and his staff crafted a three-year plan for the company, put together a mission statement, and created a new vision for Micro Switch—"Growth through quality solutions to customer needs." Next, Alvarez initiated a rigorous annual strategic planning process, to make the company more competitive, responsive, and financially savvy. And, finally, Alvarez instituted a broad communication, recognition, and quality program known as APEX—an acronym for Achieve Performance Excellence.

In its first year, APEX was designed to convince Micro Switch's more than 4,000-member workforce that change was necessary and to give each employee specific ways to help strive for excellence. The program included an employee suggestion system and awards for meeting performance objectives.

By its third year, APEX had become more sophisticated. At the heart of the 1990 program was a network of committees and councils, dubbed Building Block Councils, to encourage divisionwide involvement in six key strategic areas: a customer satisfaction council, to set standards for products and customer relationships, and create practices to meet those standards; a quality council, to establish and help achieve overall quality standards for satisfying customers; a goals council, to find appropriate ways to measure progress in reaching division goals; an awareness council, to promote awareness of quality issues throughout the division; a training council, to ensure employees get the training they need to improve quality and customer satisfaction; and a recognition council, to develop and oversee an effective recognition policy. Rowe, Massof, and Stewart each chaired one of the councils.

In addition, Alvarez had put a number of key "platforms"—or change-building steps—in place, ranging from such efficiency-boosting improvements as installing a network of personal computers, to such process-oriented programs as Barrier Removals, in which each group within the division identified specific barriers to quality which they could attack and remove. As these platforms began to yield improvements, they reinforced the value of the more difficult organizational and attitudinal changes which still lay ahead.

With these efforts in place, Alvarez had activated a final critical component in his plan to revitalize Micro Switch—the systematic training of a change agent team. Beginning with the first Eagle Ridge session in November 1989, Alvarez had begun to focus more and more on Rowe, Massof, Stewart, and the rest of the division's directors. "We have spent the past two years putting this team into position, conditioning it, and preparing it for the 1990s," Alvarez had declared in his opening speech at the first Eagle Ridge session. "While we all have a fear of the unknown, I think we have with us tonight a team that has made enormous changes over the past two years, and welcomes the opportunity to anticipate the future and manage it." With the conclusion of the second Eagle Ridge, the time had come for the team of young change agents to assume a larger role.

Rick Rowe

It was late March 1990. Rick Rowe had returned to the office from the second Eagle Ridge session a few days earlier, and just like after the first session, Rowe was charged up and ready to go. He had already run a one-day "mini Eagle Ridge" for about 30 of his extended staff. Now the 40-year-old Rowe was still pondering many of the issues raised at Eagle Ridge—such as empowering the workforce and changing established behaviors—and wondering how to bring them alive for the lower ranks of the organization. "We've gotten where we got to on the backs of the people," he declared, "and now what we have to do is transform them. How do we take the people of Micro Switch to a different place."

A few months before, Alvarez had named Rowe to chair the Building Block Council on Recognition. Rowe's initial charter was to ferret out the best ways to recognize, motivate, and reward employees in an effort to reinforce the beliefs and behaviors—emphasizing quality and customer satisfaction—that Micro Switch now sought from its workforce. In addition, the council was to see that these forms of recognition—whether an award or a simple "thank you"—became consistently practiced throughout the division.

Rowe seemed a natural choice for the job. Except for a two-year hiatus, he had been at Micro Switch since 1977, first as an engineer, now as the director of matériel, responsible for procurement under the vice president of operations. As a self-proclaimed "local boy" with "real, simple values," Rowe seemed to have a strong affinity for Micro Switch's employees, as well as a desire for them to share his own enthusiasm. In particular, he wanted to prove to the work force that the division—under Alvarez—was now responsive to input from all levels of the company. "We're trying to institutionalize that we care, we show it, we go out and talk to people," he explained. "I'm really convinced that all of our employees should feel like I do: greatly empowered, very focused, basically happy, challenged, recognized in some form, and enjoying the work they have." He added: "People go out and self-actualize on bowling. Why can't we self-actualize more at work?"

As newly appointed head of the recognition council, Rowe had been interviewing 300 randomly selected Micro Switch employees to elicit their ideas about rewards and recognition. The consensus on how to make people feel more appreciated turned out to be more simple than he expected: most important was to just say thank you. But Rowe uncovered other issues in the course of talking with co-workers which he found more troubling and less easily solved. Among these was the issue of empowerment itself. "I think people absolutely have bought hook, line, and sinker that we have to change to survive," he mused. "Where we're getting hung up in the process right now is our people then have said, 'OK, we buy it. Boy, we're in trouble. You guys in management, you tell us what to do now.' And our response back has been, 'Wait a minute, we want to empower you. And we want you to tell us what we should do.'" He added: "You essentially are empowered to do anything you want to do, but what hangs people up is you have to have the courage to use this power."

Not only were employees confused about how to suddenly take power into their own hands, Rowe said, the multiple changes taking place at Micro Switch had left many people at all levels of the company grasping for something to hang onto—something familiar or some point of safety. "When you're confronted with change and the unknown, for most people, it's very scary and they need an anchor," Rowe explained. "So I'm asking my people, 'What's the anchor for our factory? What's the anchor for our salaried people?' We would like to believe that management is the anchor for our employees."

Rowe was also concerned about how to keep Alvarez, the rest of the change agents, and himself from getting worn down by the process. Even the apparently indefatigable Alvarez, he said, occasionally claimed he was tired. And with a possible five to eight additional years necessary to institute a major change at Micro Switch, there could be plenty of opportunity to become fatigued and frustrated. "There's a danger for change agents that you get so far ahead in understanding where the company needs to go, and then you look back and say, 'Where the hell is everybody?' " Rowe noted. "That's scary. On a personal basis you're at risk because you're out there sticking your neck way out and you look back and no one's there. You get tired when you're too far out in front."

Although Rowe might have been operating the same way he always did, the positive reinforcement he was feeling, and the excitement of working with others in the organization toward a common goal was clearly a new and motivating sensation. "I wasn't ostracized before, but I felt I wasn't progressing at the rate I should," he remarked. "The real difference is it wasn't as much fun. This is like a playground! Right now, for someone like me, this environment we've created is like I've died and gone to heaven. I don't ever want this to end."

Four months later, it had become more apparent than ever that the business slump was not going away, and that Micro Switch's management team had to face the fact that Honeywell probably wouldn't provide funding for any of the more ambitious revitalization programs waiting in the wings. In fact, even some of the basic programs already in place were undergoing careful scrutiny. "I can see how far we've come in three years," Rowe insisted. "But the downside is that very few companies which have attempted to change succeed in the long run, principally because the owners can't endure the 7-to-10-year total transition period. In a lot of companies, the business doesn't quite measure up to standards, and someone who is holding the checkbook gets impatient."

The slump's timing was particularly hard for Micro Switch, Rowe contended, coinciding as it did with a natural slowdown in the change process itself. The easy changes had already been made. Now the company had to tackle deeply ingrained behaviors and processes which were holding the division back from reaching its goals. And while the first Eagle Ridge session had left most of the participants almost euphoric, the second session had felt more like plain work, and that sense had lingered. "We're at this lull where a lot of the excitement has worn off, and now we're into hard work," Rowe acknowledged. "Change takes so goddamn long. You get real frustrated by it and run the risk of losing people's attention."

One of the key messages that stuck with Rowe after Eagle Ridge was that behaviors reflect beliefs: If you want to change someone's behavior, you must first change their underlying beliefs. But in addition to changing people's beliefs and rewarding the behaviors it wanted, something Micro Switch had done fairly successfully, Rowe maintained that it was also time for the division to get tougher about discouraging the behaviors it didn't want. "We haven't stressed enough of the attitude we're looking for in people," Rowe declared. "For a long time, we've said that as long as people do an adequate job, that's OK. But if you think about anything else we do in life, we don't let people who have bad attitudes play on our teams, we get rid of them—we tell them that they can't play, or we trade them, or we let them go. Who says we have to employ people who don't want to be a part of our team?"

Reassigning or firing a large number of workers wouldn't be an easy move to make, Rowe admitted, particularly in Freeport, where Micro Switch was the main game in town. "It's real hard to look at people and to say, 'We didn't make you a manager for life,'" he confessed. But according to Rowe, the time might have come for Micro Switch to make these hard choices in the interest of survival. "We're running out of time," he asserted. "My big concern is that in every case I've seen, it takes 7 to 10 years to make the change. I don't know that we've got 7 to 10 years."

Deb Massof

A few days had passed since the second Eagle Ridge session and, like Rowe, Deb Massof was still struggling to digest all of the change-related topics presented there. "What's intriguing about Micro Switch right now is that there are so many changes going on at one time," she declared. "I think people do want to change. They do want to do good. But they're real frustrated at not knowing what to change."

When Deb Massof joined Alvarez's management team early in 1988, she was immediately pegged as an outsider. For starters, at 32 years old, she was considerably younger than most of the managers. Massof had her own misgivings about coming to Micro Switch. It wasn't just the move from Minneapolis, a thriving cosmopolitan center, to Freeport, a town of about 27,000 surrounded by farmland. It was also leaving behind the fast-paced environment of Honeywell for a division which appeared resistant to change. "I used to think this place was stuck in a time warp," confessed Massof, who first visited Micro Switch a decade earlier. "Not many things have changed since 1980. That was probably the scariest thing for me. It's such a deep culture."

Massof's goals during her first 18 months with the AOM unit in many ways paralleled what Alvarez was trying to accomplish with the division overall: to make people aware of the need for change; to compensate for years of neglect; and to start drawing people into both the revitalization process and daily operations in ways they had never been involved before.

According to Massof, this was easier said than done. In her area, there was no time at first to think about "fine-tuning" the change process. Instead, she was faced with getting much greater involvement in using management tools like market research and strategic planning in order to get the business moving again. "We were working very hard on just understanding this market we were in," she explained. "We thought we understood our customers, but I was shocked at how much we didn't know about the people we got all this money from."

Even in the process of implementing these steps, Massof was introducing her staff and employees to what for them was a radical new way of doing things. After just a few months on the job, for example, Massof called a general meeting to begin brainstorming for the unit's strategic plan, which Massof was determined to turn into a vital "living document"—a plan with daily significance for the entire unit. Because strategic planning at Micro Switch formerly had been the sole province of top management, employees at lower levels had never had a say in such issues before. She recalled the strategic planning kickoff meeting: "I got so many blank stares, as though to say, 'What on earth are you asking us to do?' All I heard was griping for weeks, and I thought, 'This is the biggest mistake I've ever made.' "

Massof didn't back down, however. She pressed her subordinates to continue meeting a couple of times a week, and as the division-wide strategic review process neared, the meetings increased to almost daily. The hardest part, Massof recounted, was to encourage independent thinking from employees who had never been expected to contribute before. Now, looking back on the process from a year's distance, Massof deemed it one of her group's greatest successes. When the time came for AOM to present its plan to the division, it was not Massof or her boss who introduced the strategy, but the cross-functional business teams which had invested so much time, energy—and complaints—in crafting it. "To get them together in a room to do strategic management was real weird for them," she laughed. "But I think they're feeling better about it now, and better about themselves."

Four months later, Massof seemed more at ease with the unsettling sensation of being in the midst of change. Moreover, now in the middle of July 1990, she finally could point to a few examples of successful organizational change. Her group had recently completed its second strategic planning process, and this year—despite her initial forebodings—the participants had taken up the plan without complaining, and had brought a new level of skill and detail to the task. "We spent very little time bemoaning the time it would take—we actually had buy-in!" she exclaimed. "We established a benchmark on change by doing something right in 12 months." She added: "These people two years ago would not have had the confidence to get up in front of the general manager, and talk about their business, and tell the general manager what he should do."

Massof was still confronting many of the same obstacles which had discouraged her in March—in particular, the sheer number of changes waiting to be implemented. "My major frustration is that there are too many things that you know *need* to be changed," she stated. But at the same time, Massof appeared less troubled by the sense of always having too much to do. "We're all trying to be Super People—we're all trying to do everything at the same time, so we're spread a little thin," she mused. "It's a natural part of the process, but as part of that process, you can also step back and say we need to focus."

Ellis Stewart

The second Eagle Ridge session had ended just a few days before, but Ellis Stewart was already sifting through the materials he had brought back with him, trying to figure out how to incorporate the best of the new concepts into one of the many internal business manuals he had designed. Alvarez had named the 44-year-old Stewart to head the Building Block Council on Training just a few months before, but for Stewart, absorbing and repackaging change management techniques was a labor of love—one he had been doing on his own for years. "I do it because it's fun to do and it helps the cause," he claimed, and then gestured at a shelf piled high with management books. "There's no excuse for a business manager today not to know what is going on and not to have some ideas."

Stewart had logged almost 20 years at Micro Switch when Alvarez took over, and had risen to the position of director of fabricating operations, responsible for producing precision engineered parts for Micro Switch and other Honeywell divisions. Stewart's roots went deep and revealed a loyalty which the last decade of management practices had not shaken. "When I came here, the place literally could do no wrong," he asserted. "In many markets we were the only game in town, so we named our price and got it. From the standpoint of a middle manager, this place has been a fantastic place to work."

The Eagle Ridge sessions, on top of the intensive strategic planning process which Alvarez had instituted, had begun to drive home a concept of cooperation and teamwork that was foreign to many of Micro Switch's managers. "We've got big egos, and teamwork becomes the biggest challenge," Stewart conceded. "We have some folks who think that if they don't control everything that they need, then they can't succeed. The ego thing tends to cloud objectivity—mine and everybody else's." He added: "It hasn't been until the last 18 months that we have tended to look around to see who's got something that's really good that we can copy. Up until then, it was, 'Well, Rick did something, but now I'll go do my own thing.'"

In addition to teamwork, Stewart also saw a number of other issues needing attention. "What is it going to take to get the rest of our management team to articulate the visions for their own areas as well as Ray can do it for the division, and as well as I and a number of other folks can do it for our parts of the division?" he asked. "That's a tall order. We have to learn a lot of things, we have to change the way we act a little, and we have to be a little less stuffy—get excited from time to time."

Stewart seemed deeply committed to the changes taking place in the last two and a half years. "We have a general manager who has boundless energy and who sets the example," he declared. "Not that he doesn't sometimes make us feel bad if he blows up at us, because that can happen. He's a very intense person. But his creative energy has changed the work environment." He added: "We tried to remind our folks, we're optional. We've got to be the best there is in this kind of business, or eventually we won't be around—that's the law of nature."

Four months later, Stewart's nervous energy seemed somewhat tempered. Like Rowe and Massof, Stewart worried that the business slump had hit at a particularly inopportune time—knocking the wind out of the change effort just when it needed a boost. "We have lots of projects under way, lots of new product development work, tons of energy being expended, long workdays, people working on weekends and taking their work home, but there's just no growth," he lamented. "What we need is some growth to take advantage of all the work we've done."

Even Alvarez, whose energy and optimism had often sustained Micro Switch in the past, was showing signs of strain, Stewart said, "Ray and a number of us are concerned that the organization is doing a lot of things, but doesn't appear to be changing rapidly enough to take advantage of the investments that we've made," he explained. "We are not on this upward rocket that we'd expected to be on by now, and that is weighing extremely heavily."

The company also had a schism between those who were committed to change and those who were not. On one hand were the change leaders like Rowe, Massof, and Stewart himself, who were in danger of taking on more change than they could handle. And on the other hand was a group straddling all levels of the organization which still appeared unconvinced of the need for change.

Both of these groups needed attention, Stewart maintained. Those who had thrown themselves wholeheartedly behind change were in danger of burning out, or becoming paralyzed by the sheer magnitude of the tasks they had taken on, he warned. "A friend of mine used to talk about the stool of life," Stewart mused. "There are four legs on that stool—your work, your hobbies, your family, and your religion—and as long as you keep those four legs the same length, it's a stable situation. But if you get one a lot shorter or longer than the others, it's unstable and the stool will fall over." He added: "I keep cautioning people in our career development workshops about that. At some point in time you have to live with a lopsided stool, but you can't live with it for long."

But in almost the same breath, Stewart admitted that there were times when he grew discouraged, and brooded about some questions that simply couldn't be answered. "I think this is the right process, but I'm not so sure whether the timing was right," he reflected. "Is this the year—is this the decade—that we should have done this with Micro Switch? Could the business have continued to thrive and grow under the old way of working, and perhaps even done better during this same period of time? I don't know. I'm always going to wonder about that."

Toward a Boundary-less Firm at General Electric

Mark Potts

Just inside the entrance to the main building at General Electric Co.'s sprawling management development center here is an amphitheater-like classroom known affectionately—and officially—as The Pit. A couple of times a month, GE Chairman John F. Welch Jr. comes to stand at the foot of The Pit and take tough questions from GE managers taking classes at the center.

Protected by the anonymity of numbers, the several dozen participants at the sessions pitch gripes and opinions at the chairman.

Welch, who gives as good as he gets, long has relished these sessions as a way to take the pulse of his huge company. And two years ago, he hit upon a way to put the format to a constructive use in rethinking GE.

Traveling back to GE's headquarters in Fairfield, Conn., aboard a company helicopter, Welch and James Baughman, GE's manager of corporate management development, were marveling over the particularly pitched nature of that day's session with 150 GE managers in The Pit. "These people were pretty outspoken about, 'Why can't we get the money to fix this?'" Welch recalled. "They were quite specific about their business—'Why aren't we doing this in our business?'"

Said Baughman: "We seemed to have found a way to open them up and get them talking about the things that had been bugging them over the years, particularly about the slowness of the pace of our ability to move."

Over the noisy swirl of the helicopter rotors on the short trip, Welch and Baughman wondered "if we could only find a mechanism where [employees] could get in front of their leadership and not have retribution," Welch recalled. By the time the copter had touched down, the two men had dreamed up a unique program called "Workout."

The name was taken from the company's then-current program to install physical fitness centers in many of its facilities. And the intent is similar. Welch envisions Workout as a way to trim the fat in GE's bureaucracy, to reduce what he calls "administrivia" and then to attack even larger questions about GE.

Welch is challenging GE's 300,000 employees to use Workout to fundamentally question the way the company conducts its business. Through a series of town-meeting-like Workout sessions throughout the company, GE employees are examining all sorts of company practices, with promises of no retribution and immediate feedback—and action—by management.

The three-day Workout sessions have taken on subjects as trivial as the number of manager approvals needed to obtain work gloves and as important as the way some businesses draw up their annual budgets.

Many Workout sessions break problems into two categories—"rattlers" and "pythons." Rattlers are simple problems that can be "shot"—solved—on the spot. Pythons, more complicated to unravel, take a little longer.

Less than two years after the first Workout session, they have become a pervasive part of GE's corporate culture—nearly 1,000 Workouts, involving 50 or so employees each, have taken place since the process was started. Despite some initial skepticism that the company would use the process to identify and eliminate unneeded jobs, even leaders of some of GE's toughest union locals are becoming Workout advocates.

Still, Workout is not a miracle cure, and some bugs remain. Some GE employees, mindful of the more than 100,000 jobs eliminated by Welch in the 1980s, worry that the process will be used to have them unwittingly identify additional jobs that can be cut—something Welch adamantly denies.

There also have been problems getting some GE managers to go along with the sessions. It often takes a change in management style to get an executive to listen to—much less act quickly and effectively upon—the tough suggestions that come out of Workout sessions, particularly those that touch on management turf issues such as approval systems, meetings and planning.

Every Employee Involved

Over the next decade, GE will hold at least 700 of the sessions a year and Welch expects every GE employee to be involved in at least one

Workout. "If you think about getting the idea from those closest to the work and letting them keep pouring them out, you just keep getting better practices and better practices." Welch said. "Productivity grows."

In the process, Welch also wants to break down boundaries between managers and employees and even those between the company and its suppliers and customers, who also are being invited to Workout sessions to air their gripes.

Workout is part of a broader effort by Welch to create what he calls a "boundary-less" company, in which ideas, customer contracts, technology and management practices flow smoothly throughout GE's dozens of disparate businesses, which range from light bulbs to jet engines to railroad locomotives to NBC-TV's "Late Night With David Letterman."

His aim is to achieve what he calls an "integrated diversity" that will keep GE's annual growth in double digits. Aspects of what he's describing sound more like the management talk around a small Silicon Valley startup than that of a behemoth with $54.6 billion in annual revenue.

In his 10 years as GE's chairman, Welch, 54, already has made major structural changes, eliminating those 100,000 jobs, selling businesses that aren't ranked first or second in their fields and acquiring RCA Corp. in 1985 in one of the biggest corporate takeovers in history.

But because it strikes right at the heart of GE's corporate culture and represents a significant rethinking in the way companies are managed, Workout is perhaps the most unusual of Welch's efforts to remake GE—and it is being closely watched by the rest of corporate America.

GE long has been a leader in corporate organizational theory—the same decades-old bureaucratic management system that Welch is trying to dismantle was the model for the planning systems for many of the rest of the nation's large corporations—and his latest strategy, if successful, is likely to be adopted by countless other companies. GE is being deluged with inquiries from firms looking for information on Workout and the "boundary-less" concept.

"He's perceived as a nut, [but] Jack Welch is the Gorbachev of American industry, with one fundamental difference—unlike Gorbachev, who talks about change, Jack Welch does it," said W. Walker Lewis, chairman of Strategic Planning Associates Inc., a Washington management consulting firm that does work for GE.

A Rich Process

By almost all accounts, Workout is a rich process.

"The idea is to challenge every single piece of conventional wisdom, every book, every rule,'' Baughman said. ''We're sort of saying, 'For the duration, let's turn everything on its head.' And, 'Everything is guilty until proven innocent.' ''

''We just basically took out pens and paper and started crossing out things. . . . We removed the work that was meaningless,'' said one Workout participant, Ralph Strosin, a manufacturing manager at GE's magnetic resonance imaging (MRI) division in Milwaukee. Strosin's Workout group focused on reducing the amount of time it takes to identify and fix problems in the manufacturing of MRI devices used for medical diagnostics, and it cut between two weeks and two months off the process—a 50 percent savings.

Although each of GE's businesses is allowed to run Workout its own way, the basic format is the same: A three-day session, involving employees from all levels of the business, shop floor to front office, meeting to discuss ways to improve the way the company is run.

Top management of each business appears at the beginning of the three-day session and at the end; in between, the sessions are run by outside facilitators—usually business school professors—who can draw out employees' opinions dispassionately. The facilitators are the only outsiders involved in the program and they eventually will be phased out in favor of session leaders from inside the company.

Top Managers on Deck

On the third day, the Workout group presents recommendations to management, which must respond instantly to the specific requests. Some are approved on the spot; others are rejected, with explanations. More complex issues are taken under consideration with a response promised. Any issue not properly dealt with becomes fair game for the company's next Workout session, which usually is just a few weeks later, with a different set of players.

Participants say Workout sessions, especially those involving first-time participants, often start out timidly. But with prodding from the facilitators—and with top divisional management outside the room to remove any intimidation—suggestions on how to improve the business and reduce bureaucracy begin flying fast and furious.

Many of the suggestions—at least at first—can seem trivial. At one Workout session, the editor of a plant newspaper complained that she had to get approval from several different managers to get the paper to press every month; the process was ordered simplified. Many Workout gripes, not surprisingly, center on similar complicated approval processes for routine matters, as well as on the frequency and length of meetings and the nuisance of redundant business forms.

Such "administrivia," as any worker knows, can be the source of much aggravation and wasted time. And as such annoyances get chipped away, larger issues emerge, as does a process for dealing with them.

At a Workout session at a GE silicone plastics plant in Waterford, N.Y., for example, participants brought up the plant's centralized quality control system, set up when the facility was built 40 years ago and never reorganized as the plant expanded over the years. The antiquated system forced workers to use a jerry-built system of pneumatic tubes and motorized carts to move product samples from factory floor to the distant lab—rather than testing them on the spot.

"It was almost like out of the Dark Ages," Welch said. "So right there we agreed to break up this lab and move it out."

"You start out with things like filing systems and 'Hey, why do we have all these reports?' " said Jeff Bunten, an operations manager at GE's electrical equipment supply division in St. Louis who has been through two Workouts. "The next step in the process is to focus on the customer—use the tools we developed in removing those impediments to focus on the customer."

Some divisions have adapted Workout to the budgeting process, calling in workers from all levels to make suggestions about where to spend and save money. Some are using it to address specific problems—a session held by NBC Sports knocked nearly $1 million out of the cost of televising professional football games. And others are inviting customers and suppliers to join the process, reasoning that inefficient, frustrating interactions with those critical constituencies can be as damaging to a business as internal problems.

"It allows us to bring a group of buyers from Sears to spend three days with us on what are we doing wrong serving Sears, how can we serve them better," Welch said of the Workouts with customers. "Forty Sears buyers, 40 GE sales-service people for three days together—that's a better relationship."

GE's management says it believes Workout helps labor relations by increasing dialogues between workers and management, and even leaders of the company's toughest union locals are being won over.

"I'm sold on it, and I'm probably one of the bigger radicals," said Norm Mitchell, president of Local 761 of the Electronic, Electrical Salaried Machine and Furniture Workers union, which represents 11,000 workers at one of GE's largest plants, its appliance-making complex in Louisville.

"It's empowering people," Mitchell said. "It brings people together. It gives people the feeling that they've got a part of the business. . . . You can go into a room and feel you have as much power as the guy sitting beside you."

Mitchell said he hopes a Workout-like system can be used to raise issues to be tackled in the next round of contract negotiations.

In a reversal of GE's traditional engineer-precise corporate culture, in which virtually everything the company does is measured in some form, GE's top management says it is deliberately not keeping score of the results of individual Workouts. While some internal employee publications carry box scores tracking the progress being made on "rattlers" and "pythons" in individual businesses, even that rankles the company's executives a bit.

"It's nonmeasurable," Welch argued. "I'm going to measure it in market share, increased productivity and all those things over a decade. . . .

"In the first year, we got a lot of GE people [asking], 'How do we know we're doing well?' I said, 'Take it on faith.' . . . Every measurement of a macro sense we look at" shows it.

British Air's Profitable Private Life

Steve Lohr

LONDON—in the early 1980's, state-owned British Airways P.L.C. was known for its service—infamously so. One well-worn joke was that B.A. stood for "bloody awful."

At London's Heathrow Airport, British Airways supervisors were known for "balcony management." They strolled out from their offices onto the balcony overlooking the check-in counters, then scurried back to their desks, rather than go down and risk meeting passengers face to face. Passengers found that service ran from slipshod to surly.

As one frequent British Airways flyer, Sir John Egan, chairman of Jaguar P.L.C.,recalled, "The attitude was that the customer was an irritating part of the process."

Today, the contrast could scarcely be greater. Privatized in 1987, British Airways has transformed its image, its service and its financial results. It has become one of the world's most profitable major airlines. Most analysts expect it to announce pretax profits of some $435 million on revenues of $7.14 billion for the year ended March 31. The stock, traded on the New York Stock Exchange through American depository receipts, is within points of its high for the year of $36.50 a share.

Once a Money Loser

That is a far cry from the early 1980's. Inefficient and overstaffed, the airline was losing about $200 million a year. After Margaret Thatcher's Conservative Government announced in 1982 that it intended eventually to sell British Airways to private investors, The Financial Times sniffed that it might lure some investors, but only because "every market sports a few masochists."

Indeed, British Airways provides a textbook case of how new management methods and attitudes can revive a major company in a service industry. The airline, which serves 166 cities in 80 countries, already carries more passengers internationally than any other airline, including its larger American rivals, and it is Europe's biggest carrier.

It is at the forefront of the industry's globalization. The 12-nation European Community, partly forced by America's lead in deregulation and partly because of its own commitment to abolish internal trade barriers by 1992, is moving toward a freer market in air travel—which should offer great opportunities to efficient carriers like British Airways.

The industry trend today is toward global airlines, or at least toward global groupings of carriers, typically linked by shared computer reservation systems. Dan Kasper, an aviation specialist at Harbridge House, a Boston-based management consultancy, expects the industry to be dominated by 20 or fewer of these global groups by the turn of the century.

"British Airways is extremely well positioned to be a global airline," said Mr. Kasper, formerly director of international aviation at the Civil Aeronautics Board. "It is far ahead of most of its European competitors."

In late 1987, British Airways and United Airlines initiated a joint marketing program to integrate their route networks and flight schedules. The pact is regarded as a prototype of the global alliances to come.

British Airways' extraordinary comeback can be traced to 1981, when Mrs. Thatcher installed John King, a veteran British industrialist, as chairman of the national carrier. A blunt-spoken Conservative Party loyalist, who was later awarded a peerage, he shared Mrs. Thatcher's belief that British industry drastically needed reforming.

So, Lord King, who was (and still is) chairman of Babcock International Ltd., which makes power generators, slashed the British Airways workforce to 36,000 from 59,000. The airline's losses, including extraordinary losses for settlements paid to those pared, surged to more than $920 million in the fiscal year ended in March 1982. The cutbacks were wrenching, but most analysts agree that they were long overdue. Previous managers had shied away from taking tough action.

Lord King wanted to send the message throughout the airline, which was created in 1972 by the merger of British European Airways and the British Overseas Airways Corporation, that he was making a clean break with the past. He jettisoned some longtime suppliers and hired a new advertising agency, the up-and-coming Saatchi & Saatchi P.L.C. Its campaign, with the slogan "The World's Favorite Airline," was hailed in the advertising community as slick, innovative and a ground-breaking example of global marketing.

Still, British Airways needed a lot more than image-burnishing and cost-reduction. So, in 1983, Lord King and the board brought in a new chief executive: Colin Marshall, a seasoned marketing professional who had worked at Avis Inc. and Sears Holdings, a big British retailing concern that is not related to the American retailer. For his work at British Airways, he was knighted in 1987.

Sir Colin, now 55 years old, recalled that when he came aboard, his experience with airlines was "a lot from the other side of the fence—as a frequent traveler." During early meetings with senior British Airways executives, he had a rude awakening. "There was very little understanding of what the passengers wanted and what the marketplace was all about," Sir Colin said. "And 'marketing' was a word that did not exist in the company. They had a commercial director, but no marketing director."

During Sir Colin's first year at British Airways, more than 100 senior managers were eased out. But he also found a "solid core" of promising managers, he said. He quickly put together a six-person team, including himself, to "get started hauling this airline back up the hill."

With all the layoffs, staff morale plunged. To get it back up and to signal a change in direction to customers, British Airways' planes were repainted, workers' uniforms were redesigned, and the company was given a new insignia and a new motto, "To Fly, to Serve."

In 1984, the carrier introduced its "Putting People First" program developed by Time Manager Inc., a Danish company. Employees attend two-day workshops intended to instill the ethos of service.

Employee Workshops

Virtually all British Airways employees—from managers to baggage handlers—have attended the seminars by now, often more than once. The programs involve a clear statement of corporate objectives, morale boosting, team activities and role-playing to pinpoint customer desires. The point is: British Airways' survival and the employees' livelihood depend on constantly upgrading service to remain competitive.

"It's a package of programs to cement the corporate culture," said

Justin Pannell, manager of the Customer First Program, the airline's overall campaign. "And what it is all about is getting everyone involved in the process of problem solving."

Undoubtedly, two other forces serve to encourage a more team-like attitude today at British Airways: 94 percent of the employees bought shares when the company was privatized in 1987, and nearly all the workers are on some form of profit-sharing program.

The Personal Touch

The worker teams have been instrumental in upgrading service. For example, a year ago, British Airways focused on improving its business-class service, a high-profit-margin market for airlines. One team suggested that when serving meals on intercontinental flights, appetizers, main courses and coffee could be served on separate trays, increasing the number of "customer contacts." On a London–New York flight, the business-class passenger now receives 16 personalized contacts, or "touches," from a stewardess.

Also, seats in business class on intercontinental flights offer a footrest when reclined. The seat design was chosen after employees, including senior executives, slept in rooms furnished only with airline seats.

The service upgrading is aimed at increasing British Airways' share in key markets during deregulation. The pattern common to most deregulated industries is that the large, efficient operators get bigger; small, specialized concerns thrive by focusing on "niche" markets, and the middle-size concerns are forced to merge or go out of business.

British Airways executives express no doubts about where they intend to fit in. "Our strategy is for growth, and we will look for opportunities wherever they may be," Lord King said.

"We decided it is not possible for one airline by itself to be a truly global airline," Sir Colin said. "So we set out in search of other associations to give us and our customers the equivalent of a global airline."

Despite uncertainties about Europe's move to open skies, British Airways stands as good a chance as any rival in Europe. "British Airways has the favored position," said Christopher Will, an analyst for Shearson Lehman Hutton Inc. in London. "It has led the way in Europe in making the shift to operating as a market-driven airline instead of as a government bureaucracy."

Chapter 13

Angered or Energized?: Change Recipients

Introductory Notes

For change to be not only implemented but institutionalized, the third "voice" in the process must also be heard—that is, those who are directly affected by all the proposed change, who must enact it and then live with its consequences. Change recipients might be employees, customers, managers, suppliers, stockholders, creditors, unions, regulators, the public at large, or any other key stakeholder.

All too often, such constituencies are ignored and underregarded, especially when change is viewed as a mechanistic matter of defining an "end state" and then announcing a series of steps to bring it into being. But ignoring or underestimating any of them can be dangerous, a fact that is apparent in numerous change cases throughout this book. Although being on the receiving end of change is traditionally associated with lower-level employees without much power over organizational outcomes, more powerful stakeholders are also change recipients. Anyone who was not included in the original decision to make the change is bound to react to the fact of change. Indeed, people can react even to the possibility of change. And the first reaction is likely to be a self-protective one: What is in it for us?

Popular book titles to the contrary, few people seem to thrive on chaos. Responses to change are often, to varying degrees, negative. All change involves some loss, even positive change. And many changes that are heralded by strategists and implementors as positive can be greeted, at first, with skepticism and cynicism. Overcoming such reactions and getting people to embrace change depends almost entirely on how the change is managed. The IBM portrait ("IBM's Blue Mood Employees") and the Sealy portrait ("Takeover: A Tale of Loss, Change, and Growth") underscore how these reactions are fraught with emotion and follow predictable patterns, starting with shock and escalating into anger before fading into acceptance. If there is "disconnection" between the change strategists' aims and the impact on recipients, the harm that results can hurt the people involved as well as weaken the chances for an effectively managed change.

The first portrait summarizes the unedited reactions of IBM employees and managers, expressed via IBM'S electronic mail network, to recent changes. People expressed heartfelt concerns, frustrations, and anger with the direction IBM was taking. Senior managers denied the validity of the information, since those who spoke out over the network were not a representative sample, and IBM has long been noted for its frequent scientific employee surveys. Yet those who speak out are often those who are willing to act on their feelings and, in turn, influence others. Managers need to listen to those who feel distanced from the change process and adversely affected by the consequences. One striking reaction that is true of change recipients in many situations: some IBM'ers expected the chief executive to *do* more, not just to complain about the company's inaction. Often change recipients get tired of talk. They think that it is those above them who resist change. Even more than the change itself, they fear that *nothing* will happen—that they have had to undergo all the anxiety or extra effort of change with no clear improvements in their own situation or the company's prospects.

In "Takeover," the experience of receiving change is eloquently described by Dwight Harshbarger, a former vice president of human resources at Sealy. He makes clear that the magnitude of the emotional reactions engendered in him—as well as in others—by the turbulence of a takeover stems from the fact that work is such an important part of people's self-identity. (Change strategists who treat job loss as a simple economic transaction fail to recognize the emotional meaning of work.)

Traumatic change can be paralyzing, or can result in ritualistic behavior in which the appearance of normality is created without any real work being accomplished, as identified in our discussion of restructuring in Chapter 6. But, Harshbarger indicates, this is also not a permanent state. Recipients have choices about how they treat adverse circumstances—whether they become permanent failures or growth experiences. Harshbarger eventually accepted the change and even used it as an opportunity for reflection and learning.

People at IBM and Sealy shared a common experience. They felt they were excluded, adversely affected, or disfranchised by the changes in their organizations. It is just those kinds of situations that give rise to overt as well as covert resistance to change, that can lead political factions to form, that can lead interest groups to coalesce in opposition to the change. In Harshbarger's case he faced his trauma alone, finding that he could not easily talk to his peers. But some change recipients find strength in solidarity with others, fighting the changes. And all the talk about emotional attachments in these articles should not blind us to the other benefits people extract from their participation in organizations that also trigger power struggles: paychecks, control over resources, prestige, and other forms of access to financial and social wealth. When recipients feel damaged in *those* interests, political forces are set in motion that can impede the success of the change itself or produce unintended and costly side effects.

However, some companies are more successful at crafting a process that provides a workable direction, a flexible implementation approach, and a more positive experience for those affected by the change. "GE Keeps Those Ideas Coming" returns to General Electric's Workout process, the subject of a portrait in Chapter 12, to illustrate the beginnings of a very different way of treating recipients. Change recipients are not simply accepting the proposed changes but actively contributing to their shaping. They thus become change implementors themselves, advancing the process and, in turn, encouraging still other recipients to become implementors too.

The view from inside GE's Workout is exciting. In heated sessions, people produce a striking array of useful ideas, ideas that were long bottled up. A contagious enthusiasm comes from having been "told to shut up for twenty years, and then someone tells you to speak up," as one worker put it. Once the genie is let out of the bottle, it is impossible to stop. People who taste the fruits of empowerment want more.

The GE portrait also shows some of the elements in making changes stick. In addition to the forum for ideas provided by Workout, and the mandate for bosses to stay out of the way except to act on their people's ideas, GE provided an array of tools to make it possible for recipients to be active participants. There were concrete action vehicles, from best practice workshops to company visits, as well as analytic tools that everyone learned to use, such as process maps, resulting in a common vocabulary and methodology for improvement. Embedding the new processes and roles in performance reviews was another way to institutionalize the change. And giving hourly workers control over the process by training them as facilitators was a way to increase their skills while ensuring their involvement.

Jack Welch's aspiration for GE to be a "boundary-less corporation," as defined in Chapter 12, was thus also reflected in Workout's blurring of the boundaries between change recipients and change implementors. A more personal version of this blending of implementor and recipient perspectives is portrayed in "Downsizing: One Manager's Personal Story." Amy Levy describes her transfer of experience from having once been a devastated change recipient to becoming a manager whose painful implementation mandate was to downsize her organization. As an implementor, she sought ways to minimize the devastation for her own recipients. She "broke every rule" so that the recipients could exercise more choice and control over their fate. Her new rule of thumb was very simple: How would I want to be treated in the same situation? Perhaps other Amy Levys with negative experiences as recipients will attempt to implement change with a more sympathetic and involving approach.

This chapter highlights both the perils and the promise for recipients of change. When there are gaps separating strategists, implementors, and recipients in the change process, it is far more difficult to control what are indeed the more controllable aspects of the process. But the gaps can be bridged. In the final analysis, perhaps effective change should really be defined as the state of affairs in which there are no change recipients *per se* and no separate change strategists either, but only change implementors.

IBM's Blue Mood Employees

Paul B. Carroll

A wistful fantasy making the rounds at International Business Machines Corp. involves altering the company's ubiquitous "Think" signs by adding the words: "Or Thwim."

Such a defacement would never actually happen at IBM, where spontaneous outbreaks of candid expression are scarcer than nose rings. The company is so inscrutable that it gives managers job titles like "59," so authoritarian that it audits employees' phone-mail greetings to check them for inappropriate language, and so woodenly bureaucratic that it refers to firing as Management Initiated Attrition.

But these are bad times at IBM, and angry employees are, for once, speaking their minds. "People would stand and watch without comment as an IBM manager tossed thousand-dollar bills off the nearest bridge, [fearing that a challenge] could be 'a career-limiting move,'" one employee complains. "At this rate, IBM will soon go the way of the railroads, [which] also had stodgy managements and employees who prided themselves on being 'company men,'" another glumly predicts.

Strained Loyalty

Those remarks were among thousands recorded on an electronic computer bulletin board that two low-level managers, acting on their own, set up in late May of 1991 to give everyone at IBM a chance to sound off. After about a week the managers decided that this Democracy Wall had gone far enough and closed it down, erasing the file from the central computer. But several employees have helped piece together a nearly complete copy, providing a rare unfiltered glimpse at some of this uneasy behemoth's internal discourse.

What emerges suggests a company deeply at odds with itself. IBM employees find themselves under unprecedented pressure, and many resent it. But the patrician company has been good to them over the decades, so few know how to deal with the disloyal thoughts they keep having.

IBM executives say they have sorted through a backup copy of the messages (some signed, some unsigned, and all traceable to their senders) to find any helpful suggestions, but they dismiss the idea that the complaints show the mood of the IBM workforce. Mary Lee Turner, an IBM vice president, angrily insists that the comments on the bulletin board are chit-chat "totally unrepresentative of what's going on at IBM."

Specific criticisms recorded on the bulletin board were cordial but telling. "I personally believe that every employee above the ?? level should be furnished a personal computer for use at home" to become more familiar with the technology, one contributor wrote. "But even with the employee discount it is less expensive to buy a competitor's machine. Sorry, but that's how it is."

Where the Buck Stops

Evaluations of IBM's chairman, John Akers, ranged from appreciative to bitter. One participant in the forum complained about the 35% raise Mr. Akers received this year, at a time when IBM's stock price has plunged, its market share has shriveled and many of its employees have gone without raises for a year or more. The rank and file, he wrote, "will pull together long after John Akers has retired (and hired an accountant to figure out what to do with all the stock he owns)." "If [Mr. Akers] won't take the responsibility for the empty politics and do-nothing performance of middle management, then who should?" asked another, evidently referring to Mr. Akers's much-publicized recent complaint that his employees spend too much time around the water cooler and too little worrying about their jobs.

But one employee said: "I think John Akers is a capable human being who has been part of the set of causes for a problem and now has the opportunity to be part of the set of solutions for that problem. I believe he's capable of making that transition from cause to solution. Are we?"

Most of the suggestions for getting the company out of its present hole recommended doing in the middle manager. "We have a vast hierarchy of management whose singular talent is that of career advancement," one employee wrote. Another used a parable: "The U.S. Secretary of State was a guest at Moscow's May Day parade. Wave after wave of machines of destruction rolled by: missiles, tanks and artillery. Then came the Red Army in precision formation. . . . Finally, there was a large group of what appeared to be civilians trudging behind the army in some disarray. The Secretary turned to his host . . . and asked, who were these civilians? 'Those are the middle managers of the Soviet economy. You have *no idea* of the damage they can cause!' "

The irony of IBM employees attempting spontaneous bulletin-board group therapy wasn't lost on the participants. As one of them observed, IBM is a bureaucracy trying to tear down a bureaucracy. Participants were told they couldn't cite a widely circulated memorandum about Mr. Akers's frustrations and expostulations because the details were confidential—even though the memo had been reprinted in scores of newspapers around the world. The forum's managers, having started this exercise in self-criticism, at one point forbade griping. (The managers couldn't be reached for comment.)

Still, this was a lot more *glasnost* than people at IBM are used to; bulletin boards are used extensively at the company, but almost exclusively to exchange technical information. One contributor to the forum wrote that all the people in his area, himself included, had vowed to speak their minds if they ever came across a senior executive—then, en masse, "painted the walls nice and shiny" and clammed up when Senior Vice President Carl Conti came to visit. He added: "By the way, Mr. Conti looks very young in person!!!"

That kind of inhibition underlies any number of IBM's problems, according to forum participants, who used the phrase "big gray cloud," or BGC, to denote aloof senior managers. "I've heard a lot of talk about process . . . but I haven't seen anything to suggest that our planning cycle is close to a process—unless repeatable chaos counts as one," an employee wrote. "It seems to me to be based on wishful thinking and task forces—someone in the BGC decides we need product X at time T and commissions a task force to design it. Six months later it gets killed and the same 'process' gets repeated—only now we're six months further behind the competition." The writer, a programmer, said her last four projects had been killed.

Many complained that the pressure on IBM has caused it to break faith with its original canon. "IBM has always been a special place. When it abandons its Basic Beliefs, it will become just another GM, AT&T or Exxon," one employee wrote.

These people tended to welcome the furor over the Akers memo and other recent events because they might lead to change. "My worst fear is that [this] . . . will become little more than a brief, wholly ignored little episode and we will all . . . march back to another meeting where we're told that the floggings will continue until morale improves," one said.

In spite of all this, senior vice president Walt Burdick says IBM's official morale survey shows that spirits are high. And what of the complaint that the people in Armonk are so out of touch that they're just a big gray cloud? Mr. Burdick looks out the window of his office, where a summer evening's fog is threatening to obscure the orchard below, and says with a chuckle: "How can I refute that?"

Takeover

A Tale of Loss, Change, and Growth

Dwight Harshbarger

The more familiar a story becomes—no matter how dramatic or tragic to begin with—it eventually begins to lose some of its interest and become commonplace. Ivan Boesky is yesterday's news. T. Boone Pickens's or Carl Icahn's plans to launch corporate takeovers are as often found on page 11 as page 1 of *The Wall Street Journal.* So, when I thought about recounting my experience in living through a corporate takeover, I wondered what interest there could be in my topic. I remembered a story about the late Jack Warner, head of Warner Brothers Studios, when he reviewed the script for the 1939 Bette Davis film, *Dark Victory,* which was about a woman losing her eyesight as a result of a brain tumor. (Ms. Davis would receive an Academy Award nomination for her performance.) After reading the script, Warner commented, "Who wants to see a dame go blind?"

As I thought about my topic, I asked myself, "Who wants to hear a story about an executive losing his job in a takeover?" But, as in *Dark Victory,* perhaps it's all in how the story is told. . . .

The Sealy Takeover

From 1981 through early 1987 I was vice president of human resources for Sealy, Inc., the leading brand name in bedding in the United States. I reported to the president of the company and was one of six executives who were members of the operating committee, the company's senior management group. After the takeover, some of which I will describe, I left Sealy. I later returned to consult with the new company on management development issues.

In 1986 Sealy had its second consecutive most profitable year in history on sales of $500 million worldwide, with nearly $200 million of that coming from plants directly owned and operated by Sealy, Inc., and the remainder from licensed or franchised manufacturers. Then, on Friday, June 13, 1986, Sealy lost an antitrust case in federal district court. The case stemmed from restraints that were placed on two licensees, Ohio Sealy and Sealy of Michigan, in the 1970s. The damages were $41 million, automatically trebled under antitrust statutes to $123 million. For purposes of comparison, the latter amount was nearly as large as the net worth of the company and roughly equivalent to the funding President Reagan was asking Congress to authorize in aid to the Nicaraguan contras.

Sealy was a privately held company, with majority ownership of the stock resting with three families. By mid-autumn, one of the three families decided that enough was enough and they wanted out. The company was for sale: There would be a change in ownership. The future became uncertain, and stress levels, already high as a result of the antitrust suit, began to rise.

In November my colleagues and I were nearing the completion of a leveraged buyout of the company. We were trying to grab the brass ring that may come only once during an executive's ride on the merry-go-round of corporate life. Then, for no apparent reason, the company's principal shareholders were suddenly incommunicado. They had been under considerable stress and I remarked—to use an old Chicago underworld term—that they had taken to the mattress.

On the Tuesday before Thanksgiving, we were shocked to learn that Sealy, Inc., had just been sold to the Ohio Mattress Company, the parent company of Ohio Sealy and one of our adversaries in the litigation. The brass ring had suddenly and unexpectedly been grabbed by a competitor. Happy Thanksgiving. By the end of December, the company had undergone a takeover. Merry Christmas. My senior colleagues and I greeted the New Year with foreboding, and with good reason: by mid-March, most of us were unemployed.

Perspective on Stress in a Takeover

The intense emotional impact of a takeover grows out of the very personal and powerful nature of work and the culture surrounding it. Work gives structure and meaning to our lives. It is a stable arrangement of an environment that demands competent responses from us and serves as a major source of rewards, frustrations, and learning experiences. In exchange for our efforts and contributions we receive compensation and personal satisfaction.

We commit ourselves to furthering the growth and development of our employer's business and the culture in which we spend a third of our lives because we care. In time, our work and our work culture become important parts of our identities. In answer to the question, "What do you do?" we reply with such answers as, "I'm an electrical engineer—one of the Commonwealth Edison people." In answering that question we do two things: We imbed ourselves in the parent culture and, most important, we define ourselves. An activity—what we *do*—becomes a state of being—what we *are.*

Most people are serious about their work. Some work harder than others, and competence may vary along many dimensions, but people want to exert at least enough control over their work life to hold a job and make some contributions to their organization. Many employees set high standards and work energetically to attain career and business success. Barring major downturns in business performance, most jobs can be securely held by exhibiting behaviors that are valued in our culture—hard work, thrift, achievement, dependability, innovation, and loyalty. However, the possibility of job loss is always there, for there is no such thing as tenure in the business world.

With virtually no warning, all this is suddenly at risk in a takeover. The assumptions on which the rules of daily work life are based become uncertain. It's similar to finding yourself suddenly playing Chinese baseball. The game is similar to American baseball, except for one thing: Whenever the ball is in the air, the defensive team can move the bases. You don't know where to run.

The initial shock and reactions of employees on the receiving end of a takeover have a parallel in psychological literature, principally in theory and research on dealing with death and other forms of major personal loss. Shock, disbelief, anger, bargaining, and finally acceptance . . . characterize the experience. The announcement of a takeover triggers the initial reaction, but thereafter everybody seems on a different timetable as they progress through the stages of reactions to loss.

In the daily life of the company, people find it increasingly difficult to locate a common ground for their old relationships. One person may be "in shock" for weeks while another may be at the stage of experiencing anger toward those responsible for the whole mess. Meanwhile, the guy down the hall is coolly planning his survival strategy. They find they cannot talk about their experiences or work together. They have big problems. In a 100-person office there are thousands of one-on-one relationships. Suddenly, these work relationships and the participants themselves are both stressed and shaky. . . .

All this is intensified by the intimate connections between work and the rest of our lives and identities. As each of these connections is threatened we anticipate the loss to come and the personal and financial trauma just around the corner. We are scared. Both real and anticipated losses and their associated stresses become burdensome. Some people are able to cope and adapt; others aren't. But we all change.

My division—the human resources division—was the one people turned to for help during those troubled times. I had to look beyond my own problems, because there was much work to be done. Under these conditions thinking clearly—never very easy—became a major task. The combination of cognitive strain and emotional stress from June 1986 through March 1987 was unlike anything I had ever known. It was both brain and bone wearying!

Stages of Change

Takeovers go through predictable stages. . . . I will simply describe some of my experiences as a psychologist, executive, and participant observer in a takeover.

Stage 1: The Bomb Drops

The announcement of a takeover brings life in a corporate office to a halt. There is shock, disbelief, tears, and long faces and slumped shoulders. A psychological time bomb has been dropped. As in the aftermath of the explosion of a neutron bomb, physical property remains intact, but most life, or in this case work, ceases.

Once the paralysis wears off, usually in a matter of a few days, a semblance of normality returns. People come to work, write memos, continue projects, and hold meetings. But nothing much happens. Important decisions take longer and longer to make and, eventually, aren't made at all. Who knows what the new owners will want?

For the sake of analogy, imagine that it is France, 1940. Paris has just fallen. The occupying forces are coming and the radio daily reports their troop movements. The end of a way of life is near. We can only wait.

And imagine seeing some of our colleagues trying to anticipate the whims of the occupying force and scheming to ingratiate themselves with them. It is Vichy France psychologically revisited.

Stage 2: Occupation

It all happens very quickly. A new CEO comes on board; a few key responsibilities are shifted. Some names are added to the organizational chart, and lines of authority are broken and re-formed. Work life again has a structure and rules, but they aren't well known yet and some of them aren't well thought out by the new power elite. For some people the game becomes one of figuring out and testing the new rules; for others it is anticipating the new culture that will result and what life will be like, should they survive.

This stage of the takeover is also infused with a kind of morality. "We must be right," the victors say, "or we wouldn't have won the battle. Now we'll show those guys how to really run a company." On the other side the losers wonder when and how they sinned and angered the gods. What both sides will later learn is that they share many strengths and weaknesses. Once this occurs it is easier to build a lasting peace.

Stage 3: Purges

Being at or near the top of the pyramid of power in any organization requires substantial emotional investment. It carries with it many, many rewards, but it also carries considerable risk. You are an instrument of that culture, a part of the establishment that makes things happen. If the organization ever changes in ways counter to your interests, you're not likely to fit in any longer. And as control of the culture slips from your grasp, you may find that you don't *want* to fit in any longer. . . .

Stage 4: The Merger

For those who remain in the acquired company a new reality begins to intrude into everyday life: that the source of power, from which all decisions flow, is no longer *here*. Rather, it is *there,* in a place called the "home office." Slowly, the survivors begin to travel to this new land, returning to tell of the customs of that land and its people. Those who hear these tales nod approvingly and say, "We, too, shall do those things." When the survivors unexpectedly meet in the halls of the new company, their joy and expressions of kinship are moving. They have survived a war. It's great to be alive—and have a job!

Stage 5: Merging and Emerging

Companies are not acquired because they are sick and dying. They are acquired because they have something of value—good products, competent people, or effective systems. Acquiring companies don't make acquisitions for fun or because they are on a power trip. They do it because it's good for business. Assets may be undervalued; economies of scale and imaginative synergies may be possible. Boards of directors and top management believe that these two companies, merged, can be better and more profitable than if they remained two distinct and separate entities.

As the acquiring and the acquired companies interact and learn each other's strengths, a different company emerges. There are subtle shifts in values, new ways of doing business, a new benefits package, and improved manufacturing methods, among others. Then, slowly, the language begins to change. The present is distinguished from the past by such phrases as "the old company," in reference to both the acquiring and the acquired organization. As power is restructured, new experiences lead to new benchmarks in the work life of the culture. Something new and different is being created.

It is this "something new" that shareholders and management are betting on. It will make money for them, provide jobs and opportunities for employees, and give better products to consumers—that is, they hope it will. Remember the statistics on post-merger financial performance: It drops in more than half the cases. And, at least in publicly held companies, when this happens the newly merged companies themselves may become targets for a takeover. The hunter becomes the hunted.

A Postscript

And what of Sealy? Eight months have passed; a new company is emerging. The people, products, and systems of Sealy, Inc., Ohio Sealy, and six independently owned licensee organizations have merged within the parent company. Financial performance is strong, stock values have increased, and sales are up. The culture has been strengthened by a combination of selective retention and enlightened severance policies.

There are no guarantees of success or survival in this life. But I'm betting that the new Sealy will do well.

And what of me? Eight months is enough time to assess some of the personal learning that has grown out of this experience, including:

- *A realization of my limitations and strengths.* For me power has always been a fascinating force—one to be seized, managed, and channeled. As the takeover gained momentum, it became as big and as controllable as a tidal wave. In its face I became acutely aware of my limitations. But I also learned to adapt, survive, and find energy when I wondered if that were possible.
- *Care in awarding trust.* During the attempted leveraged buyout and in the waning days of the old company, promises were made, then broken, by people I trusted. Self-interest outweighed

loyalties. I learned to fight back, not only harder but smarter, and to test the personal realities of business loyalty more carefully.

- *A renewed faith in people.* In the midst of lingering feeling caused by the takeover battle, former adversaries extended olive branches and led efforts to build a new culture and a lasting peace. In the process they spoke of the importance of human values in business. As people were severed from the organization the new management acted in ways consistent with those values. They did it when they didn't have to and when, at least in the short term, a lot of money could have been saved if they had acted otherwise.
- *Wanted: an opportunity to do it right.* Acquisitions, mergers, and takeovers will continue to be part of American business life. As I lived through this experience I hoped I would never encounter anything like it again. However, I've changed my mind. I would like to experience another one—but this time with an opportunity to act on what I learned and more positively shape what will inevitably be a wrenching experience for people and profit-threatening issue for the business. There are ways to do it right, and I'd like to give it a try.

GE Keeps Those Ideas Coming

Thomas A. Stewart

Calling General Electric just a company is like calling California just a state. GE has 298,000 employees, more people than live in Tampa, St. Paul, or Newark, New Jersey. Last year they were paid $13 billion, a sum greater than the personal income of all the residents of Alaska, Montana, North Dakota, South Dakota, Vermont, or Wyoming. GE grossed $58.4 billion; its sales *growth*—$3.8 billion—exceeded the *total* sales of all but 126 Fortune 500 industrial companies.

Few corporations are bigger; none is as complex. GE makes 65-cent light bulbs, 400,000-pound locomotives, and billion-dollar power plants. It manages more credit cards than American Express and owns more commercial aircraft than American Airlines. Of the seven billion pounds of hamburger Americans tote home each year, 36% keeps fresh in GE refrigerators, and after dinner, one out of five couch potatoes tunes in GE's network, NBC.

This is the outfit that Chairman John F. Welch Jr., 55, wants to run like a small business. In the Nineties, Welch believes, a corporate Gulliver is doomed without the Lilliputian virtues he calls "speed, simplicity, and self-confidence." To get them, the scrappy CEO has mounted a radical assault on the canons of modern management—which GE largely wrote.

"We've got to take out the boss element," Welch says. By his lights, 21st-century managers will forgo their old powers—to plan, organize, implement, and measure—for new duties: counseling groups, providing resources for them, helping them think for themselves. "We're going to win on our ideas," he says, "not by whips and chains."

A brave notion, even radical, verging on the touchy-feely. But at GE? Don't get us wrong. Welch is not about to sacrifice profit on the altar of lofty sentiments. As Stephen Joyce, a vice president at GE Capital, puts it, "Hey, this *is* GE." But Welch maintains there is no contradiction between his hard-nosed reputation for demanding superior performance and soft concepts like employee involvement. Explaining the point of the exercise, he says, "The only ideas that count are the *A* ideas. There is no second place. That means we have to get everybody in the organization involved. If you do that right, the best ideas will rise to the top."

To get those ideas percolating, GE is dismantling executive power and handing pieces of it over to "process champions," who might be veeps in TV programming or janitors on a cleaning crew. Says Harvard business school professor Len Schlesinger, one of about two dozen academics and consultants GE has hired to coach employees through the change: "This is one of the biggest planned efforts to alter people's behavior since the Cultural Revolution."

Welch and his lieutenants have selected three weapons, management techniques called Work-Out, Best Practices, and Process Mapping. The first jimmies the locks that keep employees out of the decision-making process; the second seeks to smash the "not invented here" syndrome and to spread good ideas quickly from one part of GE to another; the third is the tool the others most depend on. All foster lots of employee involvement. Combined, they are designed to sustain the rapid growth in productivity that, Welch says, is the key to *any* corporation's survival in the competitive environment of the Nineties.

That strategy has risks. No big old U.S. company has ever proved that "soft techniques" can deliver the goods over the long haul. But Welch is willing to bet his sterling reputation on the new initiatives. Rather than try them in pilot programs, he has, in effect, hurled them at the entire organization and yelled, "Catch!" With the game well under way, *Fortune* has become the first outsider allowed to range widely through the company to see how it is being played. . . .

GE was a different company from the one Welch had taken over in 1981. By 1989 he had squeezed 350 product lines and business units into 13 big businesses, each first or second in its industry. He had shed $9 billion of assets and spent $18 billion on acquisitions. He collapsed GE's management structure, a wedding cake that had towered up to nine layers high, and scraped off its ornate frosting of corporate staff; 29 pay levels became five broad bands. Victims dubbed Welch "Neutron Jack" after the neutron bomb, a Pentagon idea for a weapon that would kill people but leave buildings standing. That was a misnomer: Welch eliminated 100,000 jobs and flattened buildings too. Those tough actions beefed up GE's total stock market value from $12 billion in 1980 (11th among U.S. corporations) to $65 billion today (second only to Exxon).

"The hardware was basically in place by mid-1988," Welch says. "We liked our businesses." But colleagues remember his frustration. Every time he visited the Pit, he told people, "I hope you're as brave when you're back home as you are here." They weren't. Former vice chairman Lawrence Bossidy (now CEO of Allied-Signal) recalls, "People were telling us, 'You say you want openness and candor, but that's not happening at our place.'" Further structural change wasn't the answer. Welch was asking for something much harder: cultural change. . . .

[James] Baughman [director of management development] had a plan. In January 1989, Welch announced it to 500 top operating managers at their annual confab in Boca Raton, Florida. They heard that Fairfield had a new program, that corporate was hiring top-flight consultants and B-school professors to facilitate it, and that it wasn't optional. It was called Work-Out.

Work-Out is, essentially, a place. It's a forum where three things can happen: Participants can get a mental workout; they can take unnecessary work out of their jobs; they can work out problems together. Work-Outs started in March 1989. Like kernels of corn in a hot pan, they began popping one at a time—in GE Plastics' silicones unit in Waterford, New York; at NBC; in the lighting business—then in a great, noisy rush. No one keeps count, but Baughman guesses that 40,000 employees—better than one in eight—will take part in at least one Work-Out in 1991.

Initially, all followed the same format, which Welch likens to a New England town meeting. A group of 40 to 100 people, picked by management from all ranks and several functions, goes to a conference center or hotel. It's a gaffe to wear a tie. The three-day sessions begin with a talk by the boss, who roughs out an agenda—typically, to eliminate unnecessary meetings, forms, approvals, and other scutwork. Then the boss leaves. Aided by the outside facilitator, the group breaks into five or six teams, each to tackle part of the agenda. For a day and a half they go at it, listing complaints, debating solutions, and preparing presentations for the final day.

It's the third day that gives Work-Out its special power. The boss, ignorant of what has been going on, comes back and takes a place at the front of the room. Often senior executives come to watch. One by one, team spokesmen rise to make their proposals. By the rules of the game, the boss can make only three responses: He can agree on the spot; he can say no; or he can ask for more information—in which case he must charter a team to get it by an agreed-upon date.

"I was wringing wet within half an hour," says Armand Lauzon, the burly, blunt-spoken head of plant services at the GE Aircraft Engines factory in Lynn, Massachusetts. His employees had set up the room so that Lauzon had his back to his boss. "They had 108 proposals, I had about a minute to say yes or no to each one, and I couldn't make eye contact with my boss without turning around, which would show everyone in the room that I was chickenshit." Ideas ranged from designing a plant-services insignia as a morale booster to building a new tinsmith shop, and Lauzon said yes to all but eight.

Electrician Vic Slepoy makes no apology for the ordeal Lauzon suffered: "When you've been told to shut up for 20 years, and someone tells you to speak up—you're going to let them have it." Lauzon is not complaining. Work-Out proposals will save plant services more than $200,000 in 1991. The biggest hit: a yes to letting Lynn's tin knockers bid against an outside vendor to build new protective shields for grinding machines, based on a design an hourly worker sketched on a brown paper bag. They brought in the job for $16,000 vs. the vendor's quoted $96,000.

That was an ideal Work-Out result: It not only saved GE money but it also brought work to a labor force that had plenty of reason to mistrust the company. Lynn employs 8,000 people, down from 14,000 in 1986. The angry local of the International Union of Electronic Workers had voted down the previous two national contracts. Welch, who grew up in nearby Salem, asked a gathering of union members last year, "Why do you guys poke your finger in my eye every three years?" Simple, explains Slepoy, his Massachusetts accent a lot like Welch's: "We had the feeling they were trying to phase us out. Now at least we have an avenue to make a pitch for our jobs."

They're more courtly in Louisville, Kentucky, where GE makes appliances, but no less theatrical. At a Work-Out held at the Ramada Inn in nearby Bardstown one team's job was to find ways to improve the environment in Building One, which makes clothes washers and dryers. The place got so steamy in summer you'd think the machines on the assembly line were already hooked up and running. The fixes were simple: Open some vents that had been shut years ago for no remembered reason, and buy a few fans and blowers. To make their point, the team led boss Jeff Svoboda out to the parking lot. The temperature was in the 90s and team members took their sweet time setting up an easel and flip charts while Svoboda stood in the sun. They got one of the quicker okays in the annals of Work-Out.

Artificial? You bet. Steve Kerr, a USC business professor and Work-Out facilitator, says Work-Outs start as "unnatural acts in unnatural places." The stagecraft gives workers a safe way to taste empowerment. The same goes for the boss: Even if *his* boss is in the room, he is forced to make his own decisions. His boss can't overrule him later without jeopardizing the whole process. Kerr says Welch has made it plain that it's "a career-limiting move" to obstruct the efforts of a Work-Out team.

By using early Work-Outs to go after irksome minor issues like excess paperwork—"low-hanging fruit" in company parlance—GE gets quick victories on the board. The easy pickings often have big benefits. At NBC, Michael Sherlock's operations and technical services department used Work-Outs to scotch forms that totaled more than two million pieces of paper a year. . . .

Technician Al Thomas led one such team at GE Plastics' Burkville, Alabama, plant, which makes Lexan, a polycarbonate used in auto bumpers and milk bottles. Its mission: to increase the "first-pass yield"—the percentage of resin that ends up as salable pellets without having to be melted and run again through the factory's extruders. "There were no home runs," Thomas says, but the team hit 26 singles. They installed a computer terminal on the extrusion floor to give workers early warning of problems upstream where resins are made. They realigned pipes that pour pellets into cartons to reduce spillage. They vetted the procedures manual; a Post-it note on one page reads, "This procedure is totally unnecessary and useless." Hourly workers, not engineers, are writing a new version. The team met daily for three months and spent about $10,000. When they were done, 37% of the waste was gone. And, says Thomas, it was fun: "We learned a lot without bosses looking over our shoulders." . . .

As Work-Out began to spread through GE, headquarters was laying in ammo for another assault on business-as-usual. Again the impetus was Welch's pursuit of ideas to increase productivity. It was Welch himself who first voiced what later seemed obvious. Other companies get higher productivity growth than GE. Why not kick their tires? . . .

The project, which GE called Best Practices, took more than a year. There's a crucial difference between Best Practices and the benchmarking lots of companies do. Benchmarkers usually study nonpareils in particular functions—"What can our shipping department learn from L.L. Bean's?" GE was looking less for nuts and bolts than for attitudes and management practices. Basically, says Baughman, GE's question was, "What's the secret of your success?" . . .

Crotonville turned the Best Practices findings into a course, which it gives to a dozen people a month from each of GE's ten manufacturing businesses. The service businesses, which need to pay special attention to issues like managing information technology, have their own course, based on research at nonmanufacturing companies like American Express.

The class teaches three essential lessons. The first is that other companies have much to teach GE—something easy to forget in a century-old giant that hasn't had a down quarter in a decade. Second is the value of continuously improving processes, even in small ways, rather than taking big jumps. . . .

The third lesson is that processes need owners—people whose responsibility and authority reach through the walls between departments. That's how Best Practices folds back into Work-Out and explains why, more and more, the people who go to Crotonville for the course are not senior management but Work-Out teams that are wrestling with, say, a supplier-relations issue. . . .

"Demand for change creates demand for tools," says Baughman. GE meets it with Process Mapping, an old technique that the company has put on the dais along with Work-Out and Best Practices. A process map is a flow chart showing every step, no matter how small, that goes into making or doing something. Elaborate process maps use diamonds, circles, and squares to distinguish work that adds value from work that doesn't, like inspection. These are furbelows, not really necessary. What's essential is that every step be mapped, from the order clerk picking up the phone to the deliveryman getting a signed receipt.

Process mapping sounds simple, but it's not. To do it right, managers, employees, suppliers, and customers must work on the map together to make sure that what the company thinks happens really does. When a team from GE's Evendale, Ohio, plant mapped the process of making turbine shafts for jet engines, the job took more than a month, and the map went all around a conference room.

When a process is mapped, GE has—often for the first time—the ability to manage an operation in a coherent way from start to finish. Before, says John Chesson, general manager of component manufacturing at Evendale, "we strove for worker efficiency and machine efficiency. Now what drives us is the efficiency of total asset management." For example, in pursuit of 100% machine utilization, all rotating parts used to go to a central steam-cleaning facility between operations; now the shaftmakers have their own cleaning booths because the process map revealed that the time saved more than paid for the additional equipment. The map also helped the shaft team pinpoint sources of imperfect parts and rearrange equipment to achieve a more continuous flow through the factory. The result was a 50% time saving in 1991, a $4 million drop in inventory, and a good shot at getting seven inventory turns a year vs. 2.6 before.

Nowhere have GE's new management techniques come together more impressively than in the appliance business. A year ago senior vice president Gary Rogers toured the Montreal plant of GE Appliances' Canadian subsidiary, Camco, to see how it had adapted the ideas of a small New Zealand appliance maker, Fisher & Paykel. Camco's manufacturing head, Serge Huot, had found a way to transfer Fisher & Paykel's job-shop techniques to the high-volume Canadian factory, dramatically speeding operations. The change hadn't been trouble-free—Camco had problems making all models available at all times—but the normally taciturn Rogers was excited.

What happened next shows how GE's new management techniques work. Rogers called a town-meeting Work-Out to introduce the ideas and the vision—which amounts to a build-to-order manufacturing style. For example, building a dishwasher takes just hours, but it takes about 16 weeks for a change in the pattern of consumer demand to affect the product mix at the end of the assembly line in Louisville. The goal: reduce the cycle by 90% while actually increasing availability—the odds that a given model is on hand when a customer orders it. Finance manager David Cote assembled a cross-functional team to install Camco's system, now called Quick Response. Work-Out teams began sticking process maps on the walls—more than 500 in all. One result among many: Workers in the distribution center now get production schedules in a new way that allows them to tell truckers well in advance when their loads will be ready—a simple change that will save almost a day's time and will cut $3 million in inventory.

More than 200 Louisville managers and employees toured the Montreal operation. Others took a GE jet to Crotonville to take the Best Practices course, including a group with two shop stewards from the refrigerator plant. The trip was meant to show union and management leaders the potential payoff from process-oriented, nonhierarchical cooperation and to help soften a relationship that had become a rigid that's-not-my-job-description faceoff. Another purpose was to study companies, one of them a textile manufacturer, that had mastered high-volume build-to-order manufacturing. . . .

Since implementing Quick Response in January, GE Appliances has cut its 16-week cycle by more than half while increasing product availability 6%. Inventory costs have plunged more than 20%—a major reason the group has weathered the recession with steady profits despite a 5% decrease in volume. The program has cost less than $3 million, Rogers says, and has already returned a hundred times that. . . .

The revolution at General Electric is still fragile, and middle management is one of the weaker points. David Genever-Watling, senior vice president of industrial and power systems, says, "You need unselfish, open-minded executives to run the process," and they are still a rare breed at GE or anywhere else. Many managers may have the courage of Welch's convictions: It's hard to know whether they fully understand their changed role or are simply responding to the fact that support for Work-Out has become one of the criteria in their annual review.

The same goes for workers. In Schenectady, New York, union business agent Lou Valenti says, "I'm behind the process 200%," and was reelected without opposition last year; at Lynn, workers who went through Work-Out were told by colleagues that it's a ploy to win votes for the new contract—but in July the Lynn local approved a three-year national pact for the first time since 1982. At NBC, excited network and affiliated station executives have decided to hold a Work-Out at the 1992 affiliates meeting—usually a gathering more memorable for sizzle than for steak. But Steve O'Donnell, head writer for the David Letterman show, says, "I've seen more boneheaded cost cutting than innovative management."

Change is catching on fast, however. So many Work-Outs are happening at GE that outside facilitators like Schlesinger and Kerr are training GE employees to take their place. Some are hourly workers. It's a tough job: Sessions can get frighteningly heated, and facilitators need to know when to step in, when to keep out, and how to get help from engineers and other experts if teams need it. Bob Huff, a machinist at Evendale, finds the job draws on his experience leading church groups and riding Brahma bulls in rodeos, as well as his study of consultant Marvin Weisbord's six-point model of organizational development.

Occasionally now, Work-Out teams form themselves, springing up in response to a problem or opportunity rather than to a formal charter. Gary Rogers says he and his managers sometimes don't hear about a Work-Out till someone shows up to present its findings or ask for technical help.

And Welch can point to results where they will always matter most at GE, in the numbers. Productivity—which GE measures by dividing real revenues (with price increases factored out) by real costs (after discounting for inflation)—will rise 5% in 1991, according to Welch, "with almost no layoffs and, due to the recession, no increase in volume." GE expects to get five dollars in sales for every dollar of working capital invested—16.3% more than in 1988, the year before Work-Out and Best Practices began.

Welch admits that it will take a decade before GE's new culture becomes as hard to change as the one it is supplanting. By then, he says, GE's hierarchies could actually wither away: "Even in a horizontal structure you'll still have product managers, still need accountability," he says, "but the lines will blur. The functions will go away, if you will. There will be core technologies at the center of each business. Aircraft engines will always need real experts in combustion. They'll reside in the core. But teams will move together from left to right, from product idea to product delivery, reaching into the core as they need to in order to get the job done."

Ten years from now Welch will be 65. It is conceivable that he will have run GE for 20 years, longer than anyone since Charles Coffin, who retired in 1922 after 33 years at the helm. Looking ahead, he hopes to leave behind "a company that's able to change at least as fast as the world is changing, and people whose real income is secure because they're winning and whose psychic income is rising because every person is participating."

And managers? "They will be people who are comfortable facilitating, greasing, finding ways to make it all seamless, not controllers and directors. Work-Out is the fundamental underpinning of the training of the next generation of managers." In some evolved form, Work-Outs will be natural acts in natural places: No longer a means to change GE's culture, they will *be* the culture. Unrealistic? Perhaps. But, says Rodger Bricknell, who leads the effort in power systems, based in GE's ancient Schenectady works, there comes a point where employee involvement is impossible to turn off. As he says, "If you teach a bear to dance, you'd better be prepared to keep dancing till the bear wants to stop."

Downsizing

One Manager's Personal Story

Amy Levy

I remember vividly how devastated I was when I was fired from a job I dearly treasured. Working for a congressman and giving it my all, I really felt I was making a difference. But the world fell out from under me when I was called into my boss's office (a new top aide the congressman had hired) and told that I was to leave the office immediately—and in two weeks my paycheck would stop coming.

During those two weeks I was in a motorcycle accident, one that resulted in back and leg injuries requiring a four-month convalescence.

But, to this day, some 20 years later, I still contend that the emotional injuries to my pride and self-worth as a result of being fired were much more serious than the physical injuries I sustained as a result of the accident.

A New Perspective

What I learned from that experience has changed the way I manage employees. It has helped me to be a better manager.

When an employee's performance doesn't match expectations, and I have to sever his or her relationship with the company, I try to go the extra mile for that person. He or she is not totally at fault. The management of my organization is at least as much to blame—for hiring the wrong person for a job, or for failing to spell out expectations clearly enough, or for not managing the individual employee effectively enough. In addition, when an employee must leave his or her job, we at least attempt to give him or her a financial safety net while seeking other employment.

And I must say I felt pretty good about my approach to the whole issue—until recently.

For some unknown reason—call it arrogance or stupidity—as I read about cutbacks and layoffs throughout virtually every industry in this country, it had not occurred to me that my department would be affected in any significant way. And while the company for which I work is not anticipating significant layoffs, my department has been targeted for cutbacks in expenses over a three-year time frame that we are most certainly going to feel.

I have read about and experienced firsthand what a staffer goes through when his or her job has been eliminated. But I was totally unprepared for the management side of this emotional issue.

Working in different corporations, I had learned that numbers mean power; namely, how many employees work for me and how large I can grow my organization. There was always more work to be done. There was always a way to justify adding staff. And as I learned how to manage, I always found a way to motivate employees and make them very productive.

In doing so, I was taken unawares in one area. Many managers would call it a mistake. That is, I grew personally close to the people who worked for me. By committing myself to supporting them, training them, standing by them when they got into trouble, I grew work groups that were more like families than departments in an organization whose reason for being, ultimately, resides at the bottom line. My efforts wound up creating a department of very high performers that was also very oversized. The issue of cutting jobs and the attendant emotional baggage were not things I had bargained for.

I was personally torn apart by the thought of leaving people without jobs and incomes. Like everyone, a large part of my identity is bound up with the job I have. My job becomes part of the way I see myself. It becomes a measure of my own self-worth. Now, the idea of forcing others into a situation where their feelings of self-worth would be called into question was emotionally draining. My anxiety index soared.

Dealing with a Downsizing

I read everything I could find on how to deal with a downsizing. And I decided to break every rule. Give employees a little bit of notice, the experts say. I told them months in advance that their jobs might be eliminated. "Make sure you have a clear picture of what you are going to do" is another homily offered to managers compelled to downsize. I informed employees of what might happen, describing several possible scenarios. In general, my rule of thumb for the actions I took involved one acid test: How would I want to be treated in the same situation? I prided myself on having a participative management style, always asking the people who worked for me for their input and showing respect for their ideas. When it came to downsizing, I wouldn't see why this issue was any different from others we had faced. In fact, I told myself, it was *more* personal and *more* important to them than *any* of the others. Why shouldn't they be given all the possibilities so that they'd be able to make the best decisions for themselves?

Part V

Action

Chapter 14

Where to Begin

Fine-tuning is no longer enough.

Company survival today depends on courage and imagination—the courage to challenge prevailing business models, and the imagination to invent new services, new products, and new markets. Competitive success in the 1990s will belong to companies that escape the tyranny of their served markets to create new ones, a process that requires sweeping challenges to obsolete assumptions. Increasingly, neither business leaders nor rank-and-file employees question *whether* to change but *how.*

The challenge of change is not simply a large-scale conceptual and philosophical issue. It is every bit as much an immediate practical issue: choosing first steps and concrete actions. This final chapter addresses questions of practice, suggesting specific guidelines for those who want to steer change. Leaders of change need to answer such questions as:

- What is this change supposed to do? What should be different when it is successfully "finished?"
- What actions might specifically help get there? Because change, by definition, involves territory that we have not yet experienced, how will we know what works?
- Which is the best way to get started? Even the uninformed and unprepared can see a large number of practical possibilities, out of the many things they have the capacity to do. Which of the alternatives makes the most sense?

The "what" being changed—the aspects of business performance or organizational life being adjusted—is not an end in itself. Rather, it is largely a means to bring about some new state of the organization at a later time, a "new state" that usually cannot be "done" by a direct step. Instead, what is required is a sequence of actions, more or less local, and generally long and complex. These local actions should solve problems and be useful in themselves, providing immediate benefits and results—an important and often overlooked tactical consideration. The sailor at sea in a storm cannot change the boat's rigging design, though that might be precisely the right "new state" for future storms. She has first to get the boat to shore safe and sound.

The best way to select initial actions with any likelihood of success is first to understand two things.

1. *The sources of organizational success.* Whatever the specific changes sought, they are intended to promote success in some definable sense. That means knowing how organizations succeed, and what things help them do it more reliably, because those are the things that should be introduced or reinforced.
2. *The success factors in organizational change.* As we have tried to show throughout this book, many problems and failures associated with organizational change initiatives arise from naïve, inaccurate, or misleading prescriptions. These need to be replaced with more robust and accurate working models.

Why Organizations Succeed: Assessing Change Strategy

Deliberate attempts to change organizations, whatever the specific form they take, are ultimately driven by someone's belief that the organization would, should, or must perform better. Therefore, all models of organizational change, whether explicit and formal or implicit in the practices or methods used, inevitably make assumptions about the sources and requirements of business success, and about what it takes for at least that unit to succeed. For example, if more and enhanced teamwork is one element at the core of a company's change program, as it is at Corning Glass, General Motors' Saturn Division, or Procter & Gamble's technician plants, their key executives must be convinced either that one cause of past disappointments has been insufficient or incompetent teamwork, or that one source of evident success has been widespread or effective teams.

These convictions may be made explicit or simply assumed as given; they may be backed up with empirical data and thoughtful analysis or simply casual seat-of-the-pants opinions; they may be based on deeply held and long-standing philosophical positions or instead on pragmatic judgments about this particular situation; they may reflect the organization's own experience or they may reflect someone else's; and, of course, they may be essentially right or deeply wrong. Whatever the case, they will determine the shape of the change program just as firmly. In the end, the perceived value of these primary initiating assumptions will be calculated from the overall success of the organization. And, if the program does succeed, experts and journalists will praise it and popularize that idea as the new key to success.

The more accurate the model, the likelier it is in general that the change program will succeed in its intentions. However, even if the model is extremely appropriate, there is no guarantee whatever that a program based on it will succeed nor, for that matter, that a change program based on an inaccurate model will necessarily fail. Success models, whether accurate or not, will have conditions to which they apply, and any particular situation may not meet those conditions. Furthermore, the actual implementation may be appropriate or not, and well carried out or not, and will in any case create independent effects of its own. Finally, the total change will almost certainly involve many other elements and considerations, some of which may be more critical than those singled out, or may produce results by some other, unrecognized process. Nevertheless, without a plausibly accurate success model, or at least a process for developing one, the ability to mount reliable change campaigns will remain low.

These issues are especially relevant under three conditions: (1) when the change is intended to affect the organization in the long term rather than the short; (2) when it attempts to deal with capital-C "Change" (transformation) and not simply small-c "change" (fine-tuning); and (3) in terms of the Big Three model introduced in Chapter 1, when the change is nearer type 1—movement of the organization in its environment—than type 3—internal adjustments and political realignments. Where these conditions are more nearly met, the change strategist's understanding of the roots of both organizational success and effective change needs to be accurate. This implies a grasp of appropriate general models of success. But it also needs diagnostic skills of a high order, providing an ability to assess accurately what is going on in the specific organization now.

The Sources of Success

Organizational success can have two very different interpretations, both of which are relevant. It can mean, first, success of the organization in its market, a matter of its relationship with customers and other stakeholders; and it can mean, second, the activities and actions required to bring about those results. What happened to get there, and what was done to stay there? These are preeminently the concerns of the change strategist. A look at each of these will provide a foundation for the discussion of organizational change to follow.

External success goals suggest environmental interventions, which aim to modify the organization's relation to its supply or demand markets and, therefore, to change the organization's identity. This includes new products or services, sales or distribution channels, alliances and ventures, mergers and acquisitions, recapitalizations or LBO/ MBOs, the organization's relationship or positioning to competitors, and its access to new or greater resources.

Internal success goals suggest operational intervention, which aim to modify the organization's internal structures, processes, and systems, and its use of available resources and opportunities, and, therefore, to change the organization's coordination or culture. This includes programs aimed at quality and productivity, workforce surveys, motivation and commitment, training and education, career paths and development, organizational design and development, information systems and facilities redesign or "re-engineering," reward and recognition systems, and restructuring in general.

Virtually all of what is usually subsumed under the label "organizational change" is contained in the second category. Interventions in the first category are rarely thought of as aspects of "organizational change" at all; rather, they are simply "normal" ongoing business decisions and activities. (Control changes, our third form of change, involve political and economic realignments that then can trigger *either* external or internal changes.)

Furthermore, *how* these initiatives are undertaken varies greatly, and it is here that the concerns and actions of the change strategist become the core of the issue of change implementation.

Successful Change: Bold Strokes and Long Marches

Leaders engage in two types of actions that help promote and sustain organizational success, which can be called "bold strokes" and "long marches."

Bold strokes are big strategic decisions or major economic initiatives, such as buying another company, closing some plants, or allocating critical resources to the development of a new product or technology. Long marches are more operational initiatives, such as combining several divisions, transforming quality or customer relationships, or enhancing organizational effectiveness.

These two action streams are very different in practice. Bold strokes can be mandated largely by the executive actions of one or a few people. Organizations are often forever changed when a CEO decides to buy this, sell that, discontinue product lines, or enter the European market. On the other hand, long marches, as the name suggests, require the personal support of many people and *cannot* be mandated in practice. Chief executives can attempt to

FIGURE 14-1

Leader Actions: Comparing Bold Strokes and Long Marches

	Bold Strokes	*Long Marches*
Time frame	Fast	Slow
Locus of action	Decisions at top	Initiatives throughout
Leader control	High can command results	Low can initiate but not command
Initial results	Clear acts, impact	Unclear acts, impact
Later results	Erratic	Dependable
Culture impact	Habits unchanged	Habits can change

order costs cut, cycle time reduced, management competence enhanced, or products developed faster, but these are only paper decisions. Improving quality, the integration of acquired units, or customer relationships are classic long marches. They simply cannot be done by fiat.

Consider the case of Ford, in "Driving Quality at Ford," in Chapter 8. Under Donald Petersen's leadership Ford executed a conspicuously successful turnabout in the early 1980s. The reasons articulated by Petersen himself, and by many who use Ford as an example, tend to focus on the operational change programs, including Petersen's personal leadership, quality ("Quality is Job 1"), participative management, reduced cycle time (at Ford mainly focused on parallel engineering), and continuous improvement.

These would not by themselves have produced visible results without several bold interventions. Very early in his tenure as CEO, Petersen shut several assembly plants and other facilities, cutting the payroll in the process, to the point where the company could be profitable on much smaller production runs.

He also fundamentally redirected the styling of Ford cars in a dramatic shift from tradition. Ford thus became the first American automaker to produce "European looking" vehicles as embodied in the Ford Taurus and the Mercury Sable. These cars won wide acclaim, from critics and consumers alike. And new relationships with suppliers were undertaken.

It was following these moves that Ford embarked on the more widely noted internal initiatives associated with quality and organizational adjustments. Although these had very beneficial effects, the company, according to insiders, is still highly bureaucratic, and many of these initiatives have been either sharply reduced or stopped altogether. Even at their peak, such things as participative management and QWL (quality of work life) methods were never really routinized across the whole company. Perhaps Ford's early success was driven more by Petersen's strategy than by his operational actions.

Petersen's change strategy thus began with some bold strokes, followed by a long march. Typically, however, long marches, precisely because they involve many or most of an organization's members and require unusual commitment sustained over a long time, are much more difficult. And Ford's ability to sustain it evidently dropped over time. Since then, Ford has visibly lost some of its momentum, a change that culminated in a very large loss in 1991.

Consider another example, General Electric (portrayed in Chapters 12 and 13). As at Ford, the CEO, Jack Welch, began his tenure with a series of even more striking bold strokes. They included divestitures and sales of several major operating units, subsidiaries, and divisions that didn't meet his stated objectives for the company, namely, to stay only in businesses likely to stay number one or number two in their markets. Besides what occurred as a consequence of the divestitures, Welch was also responsible for a substantial additional reduction of GE's workforce, which earned him the nickname of "Neutron Jack."

After completing those tasks, Welch executed what looked like a remarkable about-face, launching the "Workout" program described in the portraits in this book and culminating in a letter to stockholders in the 1991 Annual

Report, which announced that GE would no longer welcome or reward managers who "only" made their numerical targets. Welch announced that it would now *also* be necessary to make them the right way, specifically by being supportive and helpful to other people, and encouraging their development. A too-aggressive and tough management style—the very thing people had thought Welch himself stood for—would end people's careers. This, as at Ford, represents a bold stroke followed by a long march. Whether it will succeed is not yet clear; it will certainly be interesting to watch and see.

But this is not to conclude that only bold strokes will work. Xerox, discussed in Chapter 2, rather dramatically turned itself around after a steep drop in market share in a market it created and once owned. Its strategy was much more of a long march than a bold stroke. The Xerox turnaround demonstrates how much visible commitment and top management attention is required to complete a long march successfully. General Motors, on the other hand, as reflected in portraits in Chapter 11, appeared unwilling to make the necessary bold strokes, but was evidently equally unwilling to invest adequately in a long march. Indeed, the argument between Ross Perot and Roger Smith is illuminating; Perot urged bold strokes, which Smith rejected in favor of what he called a long march—but what turned out to be inadequate movement. Often it takes bold strokes to galvanize an organization into starting a march.

The change strategies complement each other. Both are needed, both can work, and both can fail. Bold strokes are easier to launch and execute; long marches are fundamentally more difficult. Often both are necessary, supporting each other. Xerox did not have an appropriate bold stroke option. General Motors did, and does; it announced at the end of 1991 that it was planning to close a large number of manufacturing plants and reduce its total workforce by about 15 percent, all over a period of eighteen months. Still, as at Ford and GE, even if GM's bold stroke is successful in the short run, it will need to be followed by a long march. Control changes, as discussed in Chapters 6 and 9, are certainly bold strokes, but they do not result in organizational revitalization without long marches.

In theory, every organization needs both kinds of action. But in practice, because of characteristics of the firm, its industry, its leaders, and its relationship to the environment, some narrower orientation will be visible. Some companies, for example, will be more likely to launch bold strokes, while others will be engaged in a series of long marches. Organizations develop dispositions toward dealing with problems in a certain way. This is not merely a matter of management style; rather, it is driven by some realities of the organization, its economic and competitive environment, and its resource portfolio.

In general, it is clear that virtually all organizations succeed some of the time; the reasons are as variable as the situations. Therefore, it is *much* more interesting, as well as much more important, to look at firms that are successful over *extended* periods, particularly when those periods exhibit some turbulence and include a variety of contingencies. What counts is not the occasional or "one-off" success, but the capacity to succeed regularly and reliably. And here, in the task of routinizing success, the key ingredient is what might be called good organizational habits.

"Habits" are created and then supported by the organization's character, the mechanisms, standards, and procedures that assume and enable that particular style. In excellent organizations, habits will "work" for a relatively long time. Inevitably, however, there comes a time when a very different approach is required. At that point, the organization is likely to falter. This becomes a critical juncture; some firms make the transition and go on to continuing success, many do not.

This is one of the reasons organizational diagnosis and understanding are critical. Organizations succeed in part because they are competent to recognize and to understand exactly what factors and features encourage their people's patterned behavior, in both appropriate and inappropriate ways. From this point of view, both problems and successes represent important opportunities to reevaluate the organization's habits and the sort of behavior it systematically encourages in its people. To understand these things is to recognize how and where management can effectively intervene.

Every large and complex organization has many thousands of people who have each day the opportunity, or are literally required, to take action on something. We think of these as "choice points." For an organization to succeed, in any long-run sense, these millions of choices must be more or less appropriate and constructive, day in and day out. But this is an immensely difficult problem, because it requires the ultimate in decentralization—literally to the individual level—along with centralization in the sense that those individual choices must be coordinated and coherent.

As we have pointed out, the importance of coordinating and guiding those millions of individual choices varies to some degree with the organization's situation. Some strategic actions of the organization's leaders—long marches—require more continuing support from people within the organization than do others—such as bold strokes. Still, in setting a strategic focus on improving performance or competitive position, leaders are also, whether aware of it or not, inevitably launching a program of deliberate organizational change. The critical task of change implementors, our second change role, is to ensure congruent effort along both those objectives, the strategic management and the change management.

When Organizational Change Works: Building the Future Through Understanding the Past

Overall, as the preceding chapters demonstrate, the history of the development and application of methods of deliberate organizational change present us with curious results. Efforts to plan and manage change effectively to help organizations, whether by solving vexing problems, seizing tempting opportunities, or simply improving operational effectiveness, are *not* reproducibly or reliably linked to organizational success.

Some planned change programs have evidently been very successful, as seen by their architects or managers and by external observers and evaluators. Many point, for example, to GE, Ford, ABB, Bell Atlantic, or British Air (as seen in portraits in this book). But there are also many cases of failure. Generally the reasons for failure are relatively clear; one can see in retrospect what should have been done, and how to reduce those problems and traps in the future. But there are also many intermediate cases in which the right things seem to have been done reasonably well, but without producing the right results. In those instances, people understood and followed the best available methods, the organizations provided the necessary resources, and the efforts were supported by committed management.

The problem is, therefore, that planned organizational change efforts work erratically—not that they never work. But the factors differentiating what works from what does not are elusive. There is an apparent unrelatedness between the best practice and desirable results.

Part of the resolution of this apparent inconsistency follows from a closer look at the relationship between the circumstances surrounding an organization (its environment) and the action alternatives available to its stakeholders and managers. Under some circumstances, an organization's success or failure is not mainly influenced by its own actions. If these circumstances are conducive to success, success there will be, even if the organization's own capacity to manage is feeble. If, on the other hand, circumstances favor failure, even superheroes at the helm would not prevent it. At either of these times, managers' options may not be limited, but their influence surely is.

There are numerous examples. IBM, after a period of remarkable growth, profitability, and market dominance, is struggling with a string of losses and problems. A senior executive recently said, "We thought that we were doing everything right, that we knew exactly how to run this company. Now we're learning that it had nothing to do with us. We were just lucky."

Even from an admittedly overly simplistic view, the proportion of either good or poor results attributable to "luck" varies widely. However, except in the very worst of circumstances, which fortunately are also the most rare, leaders can still make a significant difference, sometimes even to the point of reversing what would otherwise seem an inevitable outcome. As Chapter 1 argued, organizations are not coherent and "single-minded" entities, all elements of which are pushing in the same direction. On the contrary, they are extremely complex and varied, and contain within themselves the seeds of many different directions and opportunities. Change leaders must appreciate these alternative forces, ideas, and experiences, and must know the means by which they may be used to ameliorate or overcome unhelpful external forces. Careful analysis of organizations after significant change makes it clear that the *real* change process, as opposed to the *stated* one, took advantage of just this potential.

Most organizations, managers, or consultants begin recording events at the moment they become conscious of their own strategic actions and neglect or overlook the groundwork that has already been laid. Popular models of planned change, like the strategic planning frameworks from which they derive, are assumed to start when leaders make an explicit decision to seek a well-constructed new course of action. Such models reflect a bias toward official history and suggest that only top management or formal actions count. Generally, however, by the time high-level organizational odometers are set at zero to record a change process, many less perfect and less public events that set the stage for the official decision process have already occurred, such as the grassroots innovations that usefully depart from organization tradition (Kanter, 1983). Lack of awareness of the "prehistory" of change makes many conclusions about how a particular organization managed a change suspect, and perhaps impossible to replicate, even by those same organizations.

Predictably, retrospective accounts of change processes often distort the real story. Early events and people recede in importance as later events and people take center stage. Conflict disappears into consensus. Equally plausible alternatives disappear into obvious choices. Accidents, uncertainties, and confusions disappear into clearsighted strategies. Multiple activities disappear into single thematic events. The fragility of change disappears into a public image of solidity and full actualization.

Organizations seeking total transformation cannot avoid this messy, mistake-ridden, muddling stage. This is when people get comfortable with change, tailor it to their circumstances, and take charge of the process. And the full direction of change becomes clear only after action is under way. Companies embracing a Total Transformation Master Plan without laying the groundwork are merely postponing confrontation with messy reality. But, as shown elsewhere in this book, some organizations actually succeed at both little-c and big-C change. How do they do it?

How Change Really Comes About

Productive organizational changes, changes that increase a company's capacity to meet new challenges, tend to come about through a combination of five major building blocks. As identified in *The Change Masters* (Kanter, 1983), these patterns are often observed more after the fact than as a part of a formal planning process. However, whether recognized or not, it is these characteristics that enable change efforts to succeed. Thoughtful change managers, then, will benefit from looking for them and supporting their potential value.

Event 1. Grassroots Innovations. Because of the constant motion in and around organizations, there are always activities that deviate from organizational expectations or formal intentions. Some might be random or chance events reflecting coordination problems or "loose couplings" in the system; i.e., no one does everything entirely according to plan even if he or she intends to, and slight local variations on procedures may result in new ideas. Some might be the result of "accidents"; i.e., events for which there is no contingency plan, or the organization's traditional sources are exhausted, so the company innovates by default, turning to a new idea or a new person just to fill a gap. Others might be deliberate innovations designed to solve a problem—the kind of constant experimentation found in Japanese consumer electronics companies or in GE's Workout. Or a "hole" in the system may open up because another change is taking place: a changeover of bosses leaving a temporary gap, a new system being installed that does not yet work perfectly.

All these constitute "unplanned opportunities" for experiments or innovations that pave the way for further change. The ideas or experiences resulting from these unusual or new events then constitute "solutions looking for problems"—models that can be applied elsewhere.

Departures from tradition provide the organization with a portfolio of grassroots innovations—a *foundation in experience* that can be used to solve new problems as they arise or to replace existing methods with more productive ones. This foundation in experience also suggests the possibility of a new strategy, one that could not be developed as easily without the existence of those experiences. At the same time, they condition the direction of any new strategies. In effect, it is hard to see where you want to go until you have a few options, but those options do not limit later choices.

One lesson is straightforward: an organization that wants change should

FIGURE 14–2

Major Events in Change Histories: The Change Funnel

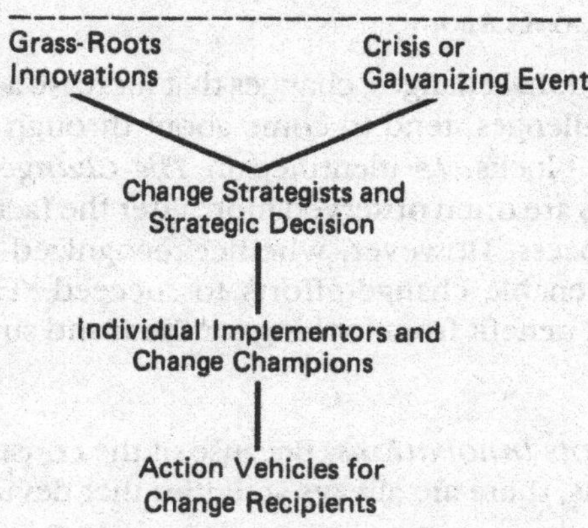

promote local experiments and variations on any plan. Those variations—sometimes more than the plan itself—may be the keys to future successes. And there need to be enough of these experiments to give organizational policy-makers choices when they start reformulating strategies. This constitutes the internal equivalent of a "diversified portfolio" for turbulent times.

Successful experiments or small-scale innovations have another important value for the change process: they demonstrate the organization's capacity to take productive action. An unfortunate number of change efforts seem to begin with the negative rather than the positive: a catalog of problems, a litany of woes. But identification of potential opportunities or descriptions of strengths seems to be a better and faster way to begin. In our own experience helping corporations develop new modes of operating, we have found it valuable to look for the already existing innovations that signal an ability to make the shift, and then to use these as the organization's own foundation for solving its problems and designing a better system. Exemplars—positive innovations—are better to highlight than trouble spots when one is trying to move a whole system. At Xerox, for example, these "exemplars" were known as "proof sources"—unambiguous proof of possibility.

But unusual events do not by themselves produce major change. Large systems are capable of containing many contradictions and many departures from tradition that do not necessarily affect the organization's central tendency. What is more, innovations can easily disappear. Thus, "deviant" events result in overall change only under certain circumstances. Chief among them is a crisis or galvanizing event.

Event 2. Crisis or Galvanizing Event. The second cluster of forces causes the organization to pay attention to the need for change. Some crises are clearly external, such as a lawsuit, an abrupt market downturn, a critical raw material shortage, or a competitor's new-product introduction. Others occur within an organization's borders but outside current operating frameworks—e.g., a new demand from a higher-level official, an alternative technology, or a growing staff turnover problem.

The event or crisis seems to require—even demand—a response. If the crisis is defined as insoluble by traditional means, if traditional solutions quickly exhaust their value, or if stakeholders indicate that they will not be satisfied by the same old response, then a nontraditional solution may be pushed forward. One of the grassroots experiments or local innovations may be grabbed, if only in desperation. In effect, variations from tradition create potential, but until the system has enough of a "crack" in its shell, they are not able to penetrate. Cultural differences play a role here. For example, some Japanese organizations are prone to identify crises with what seems to the Western observer to be almost hysterical rapidity, using them to startle people into innovation.

At the same time, effective response to a crisis may depend on the tradition-departure factor. That is, if the organization already has in hand the possibility of a response with which it has experience, it can move much faster to make the changes the crisis seems to demand. Random departures from tradition that had occurred in a hit-or-miss fashion, it seemed, helped Procter & Gamble develop a new team-based work system in its factories that later became a full-blown model for the company.

But neither small-scale innovation nor crisis alone guarantees changes without two other conditions: explicit strategic decisions in favor of change, and individuals with enough power to act as "prime movers" for its implementation.

Event 3: Change Strategists and Strategic Decisions. Only now do we get to the point in the process identified in most of the "change management" or "strategic planning" literature as the beginning. Here strategies are developed that use the potential shown in Event 1 to solve the problems inherent in Event 2. A new definition of the situation is formulated, along with a new set of plans that lifts the local innovations from the periphery to center stage and reconceptualizes them *as* the emergent tradition rather than as departures from it. While "strategic" is clearly an overused word, it does stress the deliberate and conscious articulation of a direction, saving the organization from change via "drift." Absent that kind of strategy formulation to build on a set of innovations, the innovations will drift away, or so many innovations will pass by that none will gain the momentum to take hold. But the organization's readiness to engage in this formulation is the experience it has already had.

Not surprisingly, more flexible and innovative organizations have an advantage here. More people participating in the search for ideas, as in the General Electric, British Air, and Bell Atlantic portraits in this book, create pressure to do something with them. More overlap, communication channels, and team mechanisms keep more ideas circulating. And the existence of teams and teamwork at the top, drawing together many areas and exchanging ideas among them, increase the likelihood of tying together external circumstances and grassroots experience.

These new strategies build new methods, products, and structures into official plans, which in turn serve many purposes other than the obvious, as the organizational theorist Karl Weick (1979) has pointed out:

> Plans are important in organizations, but not for the reasons people think. . . . Plans are symbols, advertisements, games, and excuses for interactions. They are *symbols* in the sense that when an organization does not know how it is doing or knows that it is failing, it can signal a different message to observers. . . . Plans are *advertisements* in the sense that they are often used to attract investors to the firm. . . . Plans are *games* because they often are used to test how serious people are about the programs they advocate. . . . Finally, plans become *excuses* for *interaction* in the sense that they induce conversations among diverse populations about projects that may have been low priority items.

In short, strategic decisions help set into motion the next two major clusters of events in "change."

Event 4. Individual Implementors and Change Champions. Any new strategy, no matter how brilliant or responsive, no matter how much agreed upon and admired, will probably fail without someone with power pushing it. We have all had the experience of going to a meeting where, although many excellent ideas are developed and everyone agrees to a plan, nothing happens because no one takes any responsibility for doing anything about it. Even assigning accountabilities does not always guarantee implementation without a powerful figure pushing the accountable party to live up to it. Hence the importance of the corporate entrepreneur who remains steadfast in his or her vision and keeps up the momentum of the action team even when its effort wanes, or of a powerful sponsor or "idea champion" for innovations that require help beyond the actions of the innovating team. Empowering champions is one way managers solidify commitment to a new strategy.

Leaders push change in part by repetition, by mentioning the new idea or the new practice on every possible occasion, in every speech, at every meeting. There may be catch phrases that become "slogans" for the new efforts; Raymond Smith, the CEO of Bell Atlantic, portrayed in Chapter 8, developed and popularized the "Bell Atlantic Way." A major recent program at IBM was called "Just Say Yes" (to customers).

What is important about such communications is certainly not the pat phrases but that they remind people about the firm commitment of leaders and implementors to the changes. It is all too easy for people in a company to make fun of slogans if they are unrelated to specific actions or are not taken seriously by the managers themselves. Champions pushing a new strategy have to make absolutely clear that they *believe* in it and that it is oriented toward getting something that they want, because it is good for the organization. They might, for example—and should—visit local units, ask questions about implementation, and praise efforts consistent with the thrust. The personal tour by a top executive is an important tool of prime movers.

This is especially important for changes that begin with pressures in the environment and were not sought by the organization—changes in response to regulatory pressures or shifts to counter a competitor's strategy—because the drive for change must become internalized, especially if it originated externally. Otherwise, implementors cannot push with conviction, and the people around them will avoid wholehearted implementation.

People in organizations are constantly trying to figure out what their managers *really* want—which statements or plans can be easily ignored and which have command value—because there are too many things, suggesting too many courses of action, for people to act on. Leaders have to communicate strategic decisions forcefully enough, and often enough, to make their intentions clear. Otherwise, nothing happens.

A chief executive of a major entertainment company—a man with a reputation for "toughness" and a knack for making people fall all over themselves to please him—was astonished to realize that his division managers had not acted on a certain business development request he had made. He badgered them to explain. Sheepishly, one manager confessed: "We didn't believe you meant it at first. You throw so many requests at us we can't possibly do all of them. We wait to see which ones you're committed to—the ones you remember to ask about next time."

Worse yet, overzealous subordinates, trying to interpret vague statements from the top, take strong action in the *wrong* direction. We call this the "*Murder in the Cathedral* problem," after T. S. Eliot's play. The drama, set in 1170, describes the events that followed when King Henry II of England said in frustration that he wished someone would get rid of that "troublesome priest" (the archbishop of Canterbury). His aides thereupon slaughtered Thomas à Becket in Canterbury Cathedral, and Henry spent the rest of his life doing penance. Many other unintended or even wrongful acts occur in organizations because leaders are often unclear about what they really wanted or don't want.

A few clear signals, consistently supported, can help steer an organization in a new direction: they are signposts in a morass of organizational messages. The job of prime movers is not only to "talk up" the new strategy but also to manipulate those symbols which indicate commitment to it. The devices that can be used to redirect that organizational attention range from the mundane (reports required, meeting agendas) to the spectacular.

At Raychem, then a small, rapidly growing high-tech company, the CEO, Paul Cook, shook his executives out of their customary thought patterns by staging an elaborate hoax. The annual executive conference began at the usual place with a rather long-winded recital of standard facts and figures by the CEO himself. His soporific speech was interrupted after an hour by the arrival of a fleet of helicopters, which flew the whole group to another, more remote place where the "real" meeting began—steadily punctuated by surprises like elephants on the beach—all stressing creativity, change, and stretch. A few such events can have importance far beyond their local effect.

Leaders can also demonstrate their belief in the new thrust the same way leaders do in the military—by being the first over the top. They are among the first to try it out, to demonstrate, to go to the training program for it, or to model it in their own behavior. One senior vice president of a leading West Coast bank wanted to show his people that he really meant it when he exhorted them to take risks in selling the bank's lending services. He rode into the bank one morning on a horse, dressed as the "Loan Arranger," shooting water pistols at his staff and shouting: "Meet your lending goals or else!" Doing something this outrageous in a dignity-conscious bank was a clear signal that he would support risk-taking in others.

Thus, leaders push, but for implementors to complete the process they need ways to embody the change in action.

Event 5. Action Vehicles. The last critical cluster of events in productive change involves adding mechanisms that allow the new action possibilities to be realized in practice. The actions implied by a change remain ideas and abstractions until concretized in actual procedures, structures, or processes. Change recipients need to know what the change means for *their* activities.

Too many ideas are only partially implemented by organizations in the form of policy or mission statements while people scratch their heads wondering what this means they should actually *do*. Quality programs encouraging "customer focus" often suffer from this syndrome: lots of official endorsement and leaders pushing, but no new vehicles to support action. Sophisticated proponents of quality often decry the reduction of the concept to its manifestations in particular programs ("Quality is more than just a quality circle, it is a process. What counts is the journey.") But without some specific vehicles it may well be impossible to realize the principle.

This is a matter of balance. Organizations always have to steer a course between the need to express change in concrete actions, and the danger of falling into faddism and action for its own sake—and too great emphasis on "the big picture—with the danger that it becomes just another campaign that will pass in time. It helps to keep in mind that journeys are not simply *to* somewhere; they are also *from* somewhere—almost by definition, somewhere unsatisfactory.

Change from What? The Unsatisfactory Present

Change implementors must be concerned not only about changing *to* what: they must also be concerned with changing *from* what. The path of progress is not determined simply by the destination, a fact often overlooked by those who too glibly accept "benchmarking" results as a fixed road map for change. And even though every organization has its own uniqueness, some general principles can be discerned from observations of many organizations seeking change.

Most organizations, as it turns out, are riddled with problems, dysfunctional practices, and counterproductive arrangements. Though externally they may appear to be sophisticated and deliberate instruments of collective purpose, operationally they are often technologically bulls in society's china shop, with people lurching from one point to another, often seemingly out of control, and steered more by their sheer momentum and by chance encounters than by design.

James Boswell, the biographer of the eighteenth-century scholar Samuel Johnson, once accompanied the ever curious Dr. Johnson to the performance of a celebrated dog that walked on its hind legs. Boswell was disappointed; the dog, he said, didn't walk very well and did not always respond appropriately to its master's instructions. Johnson demurred, *"It's not how well the thing is done,"* he said, *"It's that the thing is done at all."* Just so with most large organizations.

Larger corporations, more or less universally, are often not very effective.

And the larger a company gets, the greater its potential for problems, as the discussion of "liabilities of age and size" in Chapter 2 argued. Even the best—the so-called excellent organizations—are only moderately effective *when judged by their capacity to use their resources well, especially their people.* This standard, the utilization of organizational capacity, is just as important as the widely used measure of the utilization of manufacturing capacity, although the latter is much easier to measure. By this broader standard, large organizations, especially, are a rather poor lot.

In large organizations, people and systems operate much more effectively some of the time than they do most of the time. Therefore there must exist a large reservoir of potential effectiveness that only occasionally gets tapped. This is such an elementary phenomenon of organizational life that it goes largely unremarked, and very few people ever ask the critical question: Can we operate in general the way we operate on occasion?

What accounts for the difference in levels of performance in the first place? Can it be people? Is it the quality of managers? Do some organizations have an extra allotment of bad apples in their barrel? No. We suggest that the quality of people is not the major issue at all. There are plenty of differences among organizations, and surely some have more incompetent or misguided people than others. But, in fact, the productivity of most people—as against organizations—is actually quite phenomenal, once we take into account the extraordinary effort and ingenuity with which they manage to do their work despite the apparently endless roadblocks, sources of resistance, and interference that are characteristic of large organizations. Daily, people are forced to violate formal policies, disobey instructions, and put themselves at risk to solve the problems they confront. Productivity is often measured as if people performed on a flat racetrack; in reality, it is an obstacle course.

The source of the problem is that some organizations *in action* are based on fundamentally inaccurate premises that produce inherently flawed structures and processes. Of course, these premises continue because they are so embodied in some national cultures and conventional practice that they are hardly ever questioned, never mind seriously confronted. This diagnosis is also confirmed by the fact that better organizational answers that are more accurate and powerful are well known but rarely used in practice.

> Wrong Premise One: All organizational outcomes can be traced to the specific contributions of individuals; rewards can and should be allocated accordingly.

American, British, and some European companies remain devoted to the proposition that only individuals make a difference (Hofstede, 1991). Psychology thus becomes the quintessential American social science. This leads to the blaming of genuine victims, the canonization of accidental heroes, and a general incapacity to design more powerful social and organizational structures.

Wrong Premise Two: People cannot be trusted; they work only as necessary, are interested mainly in money, and come equipped with fixed capacities, limits, and inclinations.

Since the publication of *The Human Side of Enterprise* in 1960, Douglas McGregor's terms Theory X and Theory Y have been part of the linguistic armament of every manager. Yet, it takes only the most cursory look to see that many present organizational arrangements are based largely on Theory X (although nearly everyone claims a commitment to Theory Y). For example, reward systems, especially in these "individualistic" countries, are based in practice on a managerial "cream rises to the top" theory. If people "have it," they'll show it, and the best way to help is to let them fight it out. The unfortunate consequences include a staggering underutilization of people's potential and capacity, and a focus on selection and matching of people with jobs (both treated as fixed entities) rather than on development, growth, and change.

Wrong Premise Three: Executives are largely responsible for their organizations' successes (and failures). *"If we're doing well (poorly), I must be making the right (wrong) decisions."*

In the French writer Antoine de St. Exupery's classic fable, the Little Prince visits a small planet inhabited by the King of the Universe. The King tells his visitor that he makes everything happen. The Little Prince, duly impressed, asks him to make the sun go backward. *"You don't understand,"* says the King. *"The secret to being King of the Universe is to know what to ask for."* Most executives are reluctant to accept this lesson.

Real managers, they think, make many orders. Frustrated CEOs then wonder why their explicit instructions often fail to be carried out. *"Am I in charge here or not?"* they ask. The answer, to a generally underrecognized degree, is *"No, you're not."* In an important sense, no one is really in charge of an organization. As pointed out earlier, some things can be done by mandate, by bold strokes—for example, buying another company or closing a plant—in part because the tasks are simple to define, and in part because one person in the right position can technically or legally bring it about. But such tasks as developing a high-productivity organization, responding fully to customers, or changing "culture" cannot be ordered. They require a long march. It is a matter, at root, of the limits of authority.

We are not arguing that these premises are the only important ones or that they are without validity. Clearly, people do count as individuals; they *do* have limits, and they differ in critical respects; and managers *do* need to make decisions, many of them authoritative. We are merely arguing that, in the long run, and often in the short, replacing these wrong assumptions with three others will produce significantly better results. It is interesting to note that these "better premises" are often associated with Japanese culture and that of the rapidly growing "Little Tigers" in Southeast Asia (Hofstede, 1991).

Better Premise One: Organizations are collective instruments whose outcomes mainly reflect joint effort.

Individuals do make special contributions, to a great degree because the organization encourages and enables it. To borrow a line from the great scientist Sir Isaac Newton, if some people see farther than others, it may be because they stand on the shoulders of a giant (organization). Correspondingly, when people fail, it may be because they are not allowed access to the organizational shoulders.

Better Premise Two: People are interested in and capable of doing better rather than worse, being more rather than less effective, and increasing their skills, competence, and knowledge.

Far from being fixed instruments, people share a remarkable facility for growth and development through their whole lives. Organizations have much to do with whether or not that potential is recognized, engaged, or realized. More effective businesses, and the more effective units in all organizations, are usually that way because they empower people broadly, maintain consistent standards, offer them rich and varied opportunities, provide appropriate rewards, and systematically coordinate their actions.

Better Premise Three: The key task for managers, particularly senior ones, is to create a system that enables and helps others to act consistently in organizationally appropriate ways.

This "enabling" function recognizes that executives ought to be primarily concerned *not* with solving specific operational problems but with increasing their organization's capacity to act appropriately, to respond to emerging contingencies, and to make good use—present and future—of potential resources. People throughout the organization need enough power—access to tools—to solve their own problems and contribute to larger objectives. In the short run, and close at hand, someone else can "do it" for them. But in the long run, and over time, no one can. This might be called the "Hook-and-Ladder Principle": The driver who controls the rear wheels of a fire engine is sooner or later going to be critically important; it can't all be done from up front.

This is true for several fundamental reasons. The greater the organizational distance and the more levels between "where the rubber meets the road" and those making decisions, the greater the distortion and the slower the response. In such a case, results tend to be too late or inadequate. Second, psychological ownership and commitment are lacking. People who watch others "do it" are part of the audience, not the show. Finally, it takes practice and opportunity to develop the necessary skills and to sharpen them over time. These improved premises are as critical to managing change as they are to other managerial tasks.

Implementing Change: A New Managerial Mindset

Getting ready for change implementation thus requires that managers think about organizations in some new ways. The first element of a change-friendly mindset is simple to state, difficult to do: *understand and accept reality*. There is great reluctance to recognize just how fundamentally flawed many organizations are. This is a splendid example of what sociologists call "pluralistic ignorance." Everyone is aware of the same thing, but because people think it true only for themselves, all pretend otherwise. Refusal to face the deep flaws at the core of organizations deflects attention from the real problems to the symptoms.

The second element of a change-friendly mindset requires senior managers to *accept a different orientation about their role and responsibility* and to shift from simply blaming individuals (including themselves) for problems, or rewarding them for successes. Instead, they must recognize that results, both for better and for worse, are often largely reflections of particular organizational structures and characteristics. Only with that perspective can executives address organizational problems as an exercise of leadership rather than an admission of personal failure.

The third element is an *understanding that most of an organization's major problems are probably not unique errors or mistakes*. Most problems recur. As managers know only too well, they "solve" problems only to have them pop up again and again. Problems mainly reflect existing underlying organizational patterns, reflecting the organization's character. Implementors can create the new patterns they want, but only by recognizing and facing up to one central fact: recurring problems are as much "products" of the organization as are the products the company markets. Both are predictable and logical consequences of the organization's design.

The fourth element is *evidence and examples that demonstrate convincingly the shortfall between the organization's present reality and its future possibilities*. One primary source of evidence is the high level of unusual internal performance we referred to earlier. If an organization did it once, it ought to be able to do it again and again. Another is benchmarking results, examples of internal and external "best practices" or role models that can serve as both inspiration and demonstration.

The fifth and final element is a *change execution plan that meets at least four criteria:*

- It involves and empowers people throughout the organization.
- It reflects a valid conceptual framework.
- It is driven by and tied operationally to the organization's critical goals and objectives.
- It is based on a thorough understanding of the actual situation. Accurate diagnosis based on valid data is essential.

Given that understanding, how can the need for planning be balanced against the need to ensure continual adjustment? What does *helpful* planning look like, and what are its elements?

Making It Happen and Making It Stick

Effective implementation of change builds on the Ten Commandments outlined in Chapter 10 to include eight important steps.

1. Coalition Building: Assembling Backers and Supporters

A critical first step is to involve those whose involvement really matters in getting the implementation process off the ground *before* proceeding with other actions, and before going public with the change program. Share it first with potential allies and discuss it with key people. Feedback from these discussions (what one company calls a "sanity check") often improves the original idea. Specifically, seek support from two general groups: (1) power sources and (2) stakeholders.

Power sources are the holders of important supplies necessary to make the change work: information (expertise or data), resources (money or materials), and support (legitimacy, political backing). Getting them behind the change—willing to invest their "power tools" in it—can be critical. Just as entrepreneurs need investors, so do leaders of change. Backers might also include key inside executives (or experts, opinion leaders respected by the

FIGURE 14–3

Eight Elements in the Planning of Change

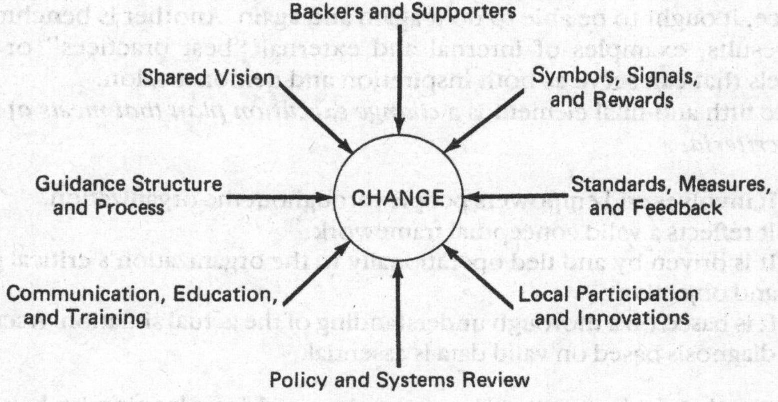

staff, or an important board member), or useful outsiders such as consultants, financial backers, and government officials.

Stakeholders include everyone who stands to gain or lose from the change. It is especially important to canvass the potential losers early in the process, if they are remaining in the picture, and to determine whether they can be given a piece of the action and converted into allies or else must be removed or neutralized before significant action begins. When stakeholders are organized (e.g., in unions), it is even more critical to consult with their leadership early or to define a strategy for dealing with them.

2. Articulating a Shared Vision

Once key supporters and investors have been assembled, it is important to articulate and spread the vision, the mission, goals, and desired results of the change.

A vision is a picture of a destination aspired to, an end state to be achieved via the change. It reflects the larger goal people need to keep in mind while concentrating on concrete daily activities. A vision is not necessarily a detailed and full-blown strategy; sometimes it is better seen as a general statement of purpose. One old lesson about organizations is that if goals are easily translated into actions, the actions become ends in themselves. Furthermore, without an articulated vision, changes launched by a manager can seem arbitrary or whimsical, and are therefore mistrusted or resisted. A vision shows that change efforts are guided by larger goals others can endorse, particularly if they've helped shape them.

What matters about a vision of the destination is both understanding and agreement. The *details* can (and often should) be worked out in the implementation process, but the general *goals* should be clear and reasonably stable from the start. First, sharing the vision ensures that the reason for making certain specific changes is understood, so that people do not confuse means with ends. For example, an effort to reposition the company for greater competitiveness that begins with cost-cutting can be confused with "just another cost drive" if the vision does not show why it is more than that. Otherwise, there is a risk that support will be lost and proactive contributions not made. Second, sharing the vision is critical in getting others to buy into it and make it theirs.

An inspiring vision can be highly motivating, helping overcome the reluctance to embrace change that comes from anxiety over uncertainty. All changes involve some risk and some discomfort; an exciting goal or a significant mission can make the risk worthwhile and the discomfort endurable.

3. Defining the Guidance Structure and Process

A major issue in effective implementation is to sort out and assign accountability and responsibility. It is important to identify "who's in charge" overall as well as who is responsible for carrying out discrete tasks. Even though this may seem obvious, even highly sophisticated companies have been known to launch a whole series of actions and programs to refocus the business without giving much thought to either their coordination or the allocations of responsibilities and accountabilities for each activity. The same people who are managing ongoing operations may also be expected to implement change at the same time; moreover, there may be little guidance or oversight from anyone.

Clarity about who is guiding the change and where various activities "report" can help build commitment and avoid confusion and chaos. Possibilities for the "change manager" include:

- The manager himself or herself (But this may be too time-consuming, given other responsibilities.)
- Another line manager (same problem)
- A temporary "transition manager" reporting to the unit manager (This provides a dedicated resource who can keep overall management involved and also work with a steering committee.) or
- A "steering committee" composed of the unit manager and key others with a stake in the process (This has the advantage of tapping multiple sources of knowledge and ensuring ownership of the change.)

In general, the more significant, complex, and time-consuming the change, the more important it is that time and people be dedicated to the change effort itself.

Similarly, depending on the nature of the activities involved in making the change, tasks may be identified in separate chunks and assigned to task forces or transition teams with either full-time or part-time responsibility. Task forces operating alongside the regular line organization for ongoing activities can be an effective way of generating widespread involvement in the change and widespread enthusiasm for it.

Regardless of the structure and reporting/oversight process chosen, it is important that they be clear to all participants. If new groups like task forces are formed, it is also important to clarify when they disband, how they are linked to the rest of the organization, and how their performance will be measured. Task forces have a tendency to take on a life of their own; they need to be reminded to communicate to the wider organization and reviewed periodically to ensure that they are on track. A schedule of meetings with the change manager or steering committee is also helpful.

4. Ensuring Communication, Education, and Training

Implementation of a change means that many people have to reorient, redirect, or engage in new activities—and they need the motivation, information, and skill to do so. Thus, managers need to plan for communication and education: when, how, and to whom information will be disseminated;

when and how participants will be exposed to the new knowledge or skills necessary for carrying out their piece of the change process. Significant capital investments in major change efforts can fail to meet their targets because of a failure to invest in human capabilities, to use the system, to manage in new ways, or to understand fully the implications of the change.

Change managers also need to communicate with the whole organization either all at once or in steps; they can go out to various sites or bring key players to one location, communicate face to face or establish more impersonal media, do it once at the launch or on a continuing basis. Whatever strategy is chosen, two-way, face-to-face, continuing communication for the organization as a whole is especially important for changes that are:

- Of great strategic importance
- Of large scope
- With implications for many parts of the organization, or
- Involving many behavioral changes in day-to-day operations.

For this reason, managers leading a major "cultural" change should devote a significant part of their time to travel to major facilities for discussion sessions and to appearances at management education seminars. They may even launch changes with a "road show" in major locations. Executive conferences to introduce a change with fanfare and flair can create excitement, and the process can cascade down as participating managers get information and materials to carry back to their own units or to run their own communication sessions.

Similarly, the desirable formality of the education and training component depends on assessment of the new skills or procedures to be mastered. Big changes involving many new skills and a change in behavior patterns and work environment benefit from formal training programs to build skills, and also from peer networks that can help support the change. It is unfortunate that many companies misdiagnose this, neglecting to invest sufficient time or resources in upgrading people's skills when changes are implemented. This omission can undercut or even destroy programs.

5. Undertaking Policy and Systems Review

In successful businesses, strategy, resource allocation, organization structure, daily operations and systems, the work environment, and people are all adequately aligned. In general, there should be a reasonable fit between policies and systems, which reinforces the organization's ability to carry out its strategic task. Changes in one major element may thus necessitate compensating or complementing changes in another.

Those implementing a major new course of action need to ensure that a continuous reassessment and readjustment process exists. Clearly, for example, changing organization structure without considering resource allocation, compensation policies, or communication systems might undermine or shift the goals of the change.

There are a number of ways to ensure this review. For example, a general manager can charge functional or product/market managers reporting to him or her to review their specific departments in light of the desired change. For changes that have implications for relationships across areas, cross-functional teams may be established to review existing policies or systems and to develop new ones as needed. Or, for policies with broad organizational relevance, such as "information systems" or "reward systems," special task forces might be convened, reporting to the overall manager or to the change management team.

6. Enabling Local Participation and Innovation

Even though this is labeled step 6 in order of logic, it should be step 1 in the thinking of management. It is impossible to plan every step or every detail of an implementation effort from the top. Even if a leader could overcome the commitment problem, he or she would still be faced with the crystal ball problem—limited ability to anticipate every contingency surrounding a change or implementation effort. Even if this were possible, it would be extremely costly and thus wasteful. Furthermore, every change—no matter how well thought through in advance—is also a kind of experiment in which there is a chance to learn from the experience of doing it and thus even to improve on the initial plan.

The implementation process will benefit, then, from leaving some local options or local control over the details of the change. The extent to which different areas or different units can do it their own way depends on the kind of change. Of course, some may require more uniformity than others. (Note, however, that those at the top often tend to think more uniformity is necessary than those below.) Formal approaches for doing this range from explicit pilot tests, using different models, to greater local autonomy or options. In any case, it is important to build two things into the implementation plan:

1. Clarity about what is fixed or given versus what is open for local variation and positive encouragement of local innovation where it is allowable (We suggest more of the latter except where it might compromise overall coherence.)
2. A communication and coordination process to get information about the variations, to spread useful ideas across areas, and to resolve any conflicts that might occur as a result of any differences (Possibilities include: reporting on local projects at quarterly conferences; charging a task force with monitoring and documenting projects; or using a corporate education program or video series to disseminate information.)

Periodically, the change guidance team or steering committee should review implementation projects and consider their implications: Where do we need to redirect our efforts? How is the change being implemented differently in different places, and what can we learn from that? What can be done to take greater advantage of opportunities?

7. Ensuring Standards, Measures, and Feedback Mechanisms

How do we know the change has happened? How do we know it has been successful? Along the way, how do we know it's on track and that events are likely to lead to the desired change? How can we get information to monitor the impact of the process of the change on the people carrying it out?

While planning for implementation, it is thus equally important to plan for measurement and evaluation. Two kinds of measures are helpful:

1. *Results measures*—how we will know that we're "there" and that we have "done it."
2. *Process measures*—how we will know we are doing the things all along that will get us to "it," or whether readjustments are in order.

Routine data collection—either impersonal measures such as surveys or quantitative data, through managers checking in personally with people and operation, or via consultant interviews or focus groups—can allow the change management team to monitor progress and make midcourse adjustments. Process measures are particularly important. Often these can be developed by teams or special assignments, and of course can themselves be improved over time.

8. Providing Symbols, Signals, and Rewards

Sometimes managers announce a new emphasis or strategic direction, but skeptical employees and other managers (who may have been through this before or who may think this is just another impulse of their impulsive boss) withhold commitment or drag their feet on implementation actions. After all, even tangible actions (starting a new division, consolidating operations, or increasing financial investment in new products) take on meaning or importance only as part of a larger strategic thrust, and they can be more or less successful and more or less reversible, depending on the fervor with which they are pursued.

Organization members often wait for the signals that say "we mean it." (Or "we don't really mean it." For example, a decentralization campaign and a new formal organization chart doesn't help much if the general manager still insists on personally reviewing small decisions.) The leadership actions described earlier at Raychem (elephants on the beach) or Security Pacific (the manager as "Loan Arranger") provided important symbols and, despite the frivolity involved, important signs that the boss was serious about change.

New or special rewards are also an effective way to signal management's commitment to the change—finding new heroes, recognizing new achievements, offering special incentives. Rewards—or just sheer fun—are also important in motivating people to engage in the extra hard work that change requires. Conversely, maintaining a reward system that encourages business as usual does *not* help. It is particularly important to provide rewards for action on the change program itself, such as participation in a task force or time spent training others.

Tactical Choices

Often, change programs or methods associated with them are presented as if they were recipes; only this specific series of actions, carried out in exactly this way, will produce the results desired. Organizations that have been successful are only too quick to draw that conclusion and to market their recipe. Nothing could be farther from the truth.

In fact, every change program or implementation plan, like every attempt to execute any decision, whether of purely local relevance or fundamental to the success of a giant organization, is full of opportunities for alternative courses of action. Not only is there not "one best way"; there are usually many paths for implementation of a given direction, change, or innovation, each of which might be useful and appropriate in some set of circumstances.

The issue, therefore, is for the change manager to consider the relationship between a set of options and the particular character of the situation within which those choices must be made. The determination is not precise, of course, but indicative. The more important some factors are, the more plausible or appropriate a certain choice may be. For example, here are some of the most critical choices facing the change manager, along with the central factors to be kept in mind.

Everywhere vs. pilot sites? Should the change be introduced across the organization (rolled out) or step by step?

General factors to take into account:

- Degree of support for the change
- Extent to which change and its implications are well understood
- Sheer amount of change involved; change complexity
- Organization's experience with managing change
- Urgency of change, and
- Competitive environment and anticipated competitor response

Benefits of pilots/tests:

- Examine alternative models
- Use extra time, plus pilot results, to sway opinion and build support
- Learn from experience, modify model, or
- Develop implementation expertise to make full implementation more efficient and effective

Risks of pilots/tests:

- Mobilize resistance
- Permit skepticism about leaders' commitment to the change (e.g., withhold support because "this too will pass")
- Impede transfer due to NIH syndrome (others reject because "not invented here")

- Prolong uncertainty, anxiety
- Cost of running two systems, or
- Can't mount all the programs/projects needed to support the change (e.g., because too costly just for a pilot site)

How best to use pilots/tests:

- Keep overall strategy clear (and role of pilot in the strategy)
- More than one site helpful—one sure to succeed, one problematic (if load for success, results can be written off as not applicable to "my" area)
- Build knowledge and involvement of rest of organization
- Document and learn; make experience transferable

Fast vs. slow? How useful is it to attempt to move very quickly, for example, by devoting greater resources?

General factors to take into account:

- Cost: resource needs and availability
- Skills available; how much new capability required
- Urgency
- Competitive environment (how fast competition will exploit vulnerabilities or copy strategy)
- Degree of support for the change
- Complexity of the change
- Degree to which steps or areas are intertwined and interdependent, so that work can't be done on one without immediately affecting or being affected by the others.

Is it better to ***work through existing structures and roles***, or to ***create new roles,*** or groupings, or structures?

General factors to take into account:

- Skills available; whether current people in current roles can manage the new state
- Amount of time required for change and transition management tasks *per se*
- Degree to which ongoing operations need to run at peak efficiency while the change is being implemented

Should the change be ***mandatory*** or ***voluntary?***

General factors to take into account:

- Power of leaders to compel compliance
- Degree of support
- Organizational norms and culture; degree to which autonomy valued
- Motivational issues: volunteers tend to "believe," persuade others
- Urgency of the situation
- Risks of slippage or inefficiencies if not everyone complies

Should this be viewed as a *break with the past* or as continuity with tradition?

If possible, should we start over or refurbish existing structures? This is one of the trickiest choice points in major change: balancing the revolutionary potential of a fresh start, as in a "greenfield" new site startup in a new location with new people (e.g., General Motors' Saturn Project), against the need for continuity, because organizations are, after all, managing ongoing operations that include valuable experiences as well as sunk costs. Financial cost is, of course, not the only consideration in deciding whether to break with the past; there is also a question about the signal sent to all the people currently in the organization. If all investment, energy, and excitement go to a startup, it is highly demotivating to those responsible for current revenues, and can lead to deterioration of current operations from lack of investment. One solution is to couple startups or greenfields with added opportunity to invest in changes and improvements in current operations.

Getting Started

Before we address where a company begins, let's see where a company emphatically should *not* begin.

- Not with a Master Plan and a Total Program
- Not by trying to start at the *end* of the change process, when the shape of the new markets or the details of the new practices are well understood, can be readily communicated and institutionalized, and are able to be routinized
- Not by simply copying the current practices of companies that successfully transformed their businesses and ignoring all the false starts, messy mistakes, and controversial experiments that got them there

It is important to remember that change looks revolutionary only in retrospect. The connotation of "change" as an abrupt dysfunction, then a clean break, does not always match its reality.

Because early actions have consequences for one's ability to act later, they should be chosen with particular care. Later actions can be left more general and open-ended, since they will necessarily be shaped by the results of early actions. But early actions can carry particular weight. They should:

- Address an immediate, acute, potentially costly business problem (e.g., a key executive threatening to leave, a critical customer defecting, a major machinery breakdown)
- Shape or reinforce a vision or strategy used to guide all future actions—that is, reinforce a direction or principle
- Send a strong signal of commitment to the change, and
- Demonstrate the nature of the effort required

Launching deliberate change is a matter of respecting three critical criteria that embody the lessons about organizational motion and organizational potential considered throughout this book.

1. *Begin with use-directed, action-oriented information from all stakeholders.* Improve the quality of information about the realities of customers' and employees' situations. Discover what people actually do and assess how the organization's processes actually work. Diagnosis is essential—particularly from the point of view of the stakeholders. The best part of the Malcolm Baldrige National Quality Award in the United States, for example, may be that it gives companies a checklist of items to use for self-assessment; the worst part is that it encourages some companies to mount a Total Program to Fix Problems before they have even discovered a direction for change. Similarly, a real transformation does not begin with a glamorous new product or a program that capitalizes on a current bandwagon, such as quality or environmental concern (though that may be critical eventually), but simply by the provision of better information, such as how the business actually works today.

In addition to collecting concrete information about today's realities, consider unmet needs. Explore both customers' and employees' hopes and dreams. Examine the organization from the perspective of its owners; is "shareholder value" being realized? Take into account the views of other stakeholders, from suppliers to regulators. Then come back to customers. At the heart of market shifts in any industry is the changing nature of value as defined by customers. There are no products any more, in the narrow sense; there are only services. Even manufacturing companies should be thinking about the services their products offer and what they permit people to do, not the products themselves. How customers can *use* what a company produces is what creates a market for it.

2. *Build on platforms already in place.* Begin by stepping back to define strengths and potentialities in existing resources, experiences, and bases. For example, Volkswagen may or may not be correct in some ultimate planning-analytic sense in its belief that a strong European base is an excellent vehicle for global success, but that's what Volkswagen has, and it might as well make the most of it. VW cannot will itself into being another kind of company overnight; it must make changes out of its existing capabilities.

Every company, regardless of its difficulties, has some positive innovations to build on; some seeds of the future already blossoming. Even in troubled industries, some companies do well; for example, Dillard Department Stores in U.S. retailing. Even in troubled companies, some departments do well, providing a platform for growth, for example, the crafts department in another, more distressed retail chain.

Moreover, it is important not to insult people by assuming that the organization has no experience with the new phenomenon, as some companies do when they launch Total Quality Programs with the implicit message that no one has focused on quality until then.

3. *Encourage problem-solving and incremental experimentation that departs from tradition without destroying it.* Many companies begin Major Change Programs with training when they should really begin with *doing*. Experimentation produces options, opportunities, and learning; training can then be provided to the innovating teams. A proliferation of such modest experiments adds to the organization's own experience with elements of many different business models. These elements also help micro- and macro-changes to be joined, with major change often constructed out of the micro-actions of numerous entrepreneurs and innovators, as well as the larger actions of decision-makers.

So-called breakthrough changes are actually related to the interplay of a number of smaller changes that together provide the building blocks for constructing the new organization. Even when attributed to a single dramatic event or a single sharp decision, major changes in large organizations are more likely in fact to represent the accumulation of accomplishments and tendencies built up slowly over time and implemented cautiously. "Logical incrementalism," to use James Brian Quinn's term, may be a better way to describe how major corporations change their strategy:

> The most effective strategies of major enterprises tend to emerge step-by-step from an interactive process in which the organization probes the future, experiments, and learns from a series of partial (incremental) commitments rather than through global formulations of total strategies. Good managers are aware of this process, and they consciously intervene in it. They use it to improve the information available for decisions and to build the psychological identification essential to successful strategies. Such logical incrementalism is not "muddling," as most understand that word. [It] honors and utilizes the global analyses inherent in formal strategy formulation models [and] embraces the central tenets of the political or power-behavioral approaches to such decision making. [Quinn, 1980]

The right kinds of integrative mechanisms, including communication between areas, can ensure coordination among the local strategies or substrategies and micro-innovations that ultimately result in a company's strategic posture. In short, effective organizations benefit from integrative structures and cultures that promote innovation below the top and learn from them.

Seen in this light, there is a link between micro-level and macro-level change and innovation: the actions of numerous managerial entrepreneurs and problem-solving teams, on one hand, and the overall shift of a company's direction the better to meet current challenges on the other. The buildup of experiences from successful small-scale innovations or even the breakthrough idea that an innovator's work may eventually produce, in the case of new products or new technological processes, can then be embraced by those guiding the organization as part of an important new strategy.

In short, consider problem-solving action first, formal programs later. Get experience first; make a "strategy" out of it second. In many cases new structural possibilities from experiments by change implementors, and even recipients, make possible the formulation of a new strategy to meet a sudden external challenge of which even the implementors might have been unaware. The new strategy, in effect, elevates local experiments and experience to the level of policy. This is the ultimate form of change mastery for the new ideal of the flexible organization—change as an ongoing quest.

Major change built on a rapid succession of experiments from an existing platform resolves an important dilemma surrounding the very idea of corporate transformation. A company cannot neglect existing businesses while leaping into new ones. It cannot shut down one day and reopen as something totally different the next. Experimentation both requires and builds confidence. It permits a company to write its own case studies of successful change and to learn from its own experience. Large numbers of small experiments reduce risks while providing alternatives. The best can then be chosen for dissemination throughout the organization.

Where to begin the change process is clearly a complex determination, requiring organizational self-scrutiny. But *when* to begin is simple:

Now!

References

Hofstede, Geert. 1991. *Cultures and Organizations: Software of the Mind.* London: McGraw-Hill Book Company (UK) Limited.

Kanter, Rosabeth Moss. 1983. *The Change Masters: Innovation for Productivity in the American Corporation.* New York: Simon & Schuster.

McGregor, Douglas M. 1960. *The Human Side of Enterprise.* New York: McGraw-Hill Book Co.

Quinn, James Brian. 1980. *Strategies for Change: Logical Incrementalism.* Homewood, IL: Richard D. Darwin.

Weick, Karl. 1979. *The Social Psychology of Organization.* Second edition. Reading, MA: Addison Wesley.

Index